Foundations of
Mixed Methods Research

Foundations of
Mixed Methods Research

Integrating Quantitative and Qualitative
Approaches in the Social and Behavioral Sciences

Charles Teddlie

Louisiana State University, Baton Rouge

Abbas Tashakkori

Florida International University

Los Angeles • London • New Delhi • Singapore • Washington DC

For information:

SAGE Publications, Inc.
2455 Teller Road
Thousand Oaks,
  California 91320
E-mail: order@sagepub.com

SAGE Publications Ltd.
1 Oliver's Yard
55 City Road
London EC1Y 1SP
United Kingdom

SAGE Publications India Pvt. Ltd.
B 1/I 1 Mohan Cooperative
  Industrial Area
Mathura Road, New Delhi 110 044
India

SAGE Publications Asia-Pacific Pte. Ltd.
33 Pekin Street #02-01
Far East Square
Singapore 048763

Printed in the United States of America

Library of Congress Cataloging-in-Publication Data

Teddlie, Charles.
Foundations of mixed methods research: Integrating quantitative and qualitative approaches in the social and behavioral sciences/Charles Teddlie, Abbas Tashakkori.
    p. cm.
Includes bibliographical references and index.
ISBN 978-0-7619-3011-2 (cloth)
ISBN 978-0-7619-3012-9 (pbk.)
  1. Social sciences—Research—Methodology. I. Tashakkori, Abbas. II. Title.

H62.T294 2009
001.42—dc22   2008011833

Printed on acid-free paper

13   10 9 8 7 6 5

Acquiring Editor:	Vicki Knight
Associate Editor:	Sean Connelly
Editorial Assistant:	Lauren Habib
Production Editor:	Sarah K. Quesenberry
Copy Editor:	Cheryl Duksta
Typesetter:	C&M Digitals (P) Ltd.
Proofreader:	Jenifer Kooiman
Indexer:	Michael Ferreira
Marketing Manager:	Stephanie Adams
Cover Designer:	Candice Harman

Contents

Preface

This is our third book on mixed methods in the social and behavioral sciences, following up on *Mixed Methodology: Combining the Qualitative and Quantitative Approaches* (1998) and *Handbook of Mixed Methods in Social and Behavioral Research* (2003). This book is noticeably different from the other two books in many ways, and yet it is undeniably similar in others.

Mixed Methodology: Combining the Qualitative and Quantitative Approaches was one of a handful of books that appeared in the late 1980s and 1990s, heralding mixed methods as a third methodological approach in the human sciences. *Handbook of Mixed Methods,* written by a talented group of authors who were already practicing mixed methods in their own diverse fields, was a declaration of the independence of mixed methods from qualitative and quantitative approaches. Probably more than any other source at this point in time, the *Handbook* has demonstrated the diversity and richness of ideas in or about mixed methods both within and across disciplines.

This book, *Foundations of Mixed Methods Research: Integrating Quantitative and Qualitative Approaches in the Social and Behavioral Sciences*, is different from the other books in that it chronicles a number of interesting and exciting changes that have occurred over the past 5–10 years as mixed methods research has matured and is intended to serve as a textbook as well as a sourcebook. *Foundations* is similar to the other two books in that it features several familiar topics of continued importance to the mixed methods community.

The two purposes of *Foundations* (as a sourcebook and textbook) are linked by commonality of material and separated by complexity of presentation. We can only hope that we have not made the book too simple for professional scholars and researchers or too complex for students just learning about mixed methods.

The structure of *Foundations* includes two sections and an epilogue. The two sections are "Mixed Methods: The Third Methodological Movement" (Chapters 1–5) and "Methods and Strategies of Mixed Methods Research" (Chapters 6–12). The first section focuses on definitions, history, utility, and paradigm issues, whereas the second section takes the reader through the mixed methods process—from asking research questions to drawing inferences from results.

This book covers six issues previously discussed in the *Handbook* plus six additional topics. The six issues from the *Handbook* are discussed in the following chapters of this text:

1. The nomenclature and basic definitions used in mixed methods research: Chapters 1 and 2

2. The utility of mixed methods (why we do it): Chapters 1 and 2

3. The paradigmatic foundations for mixed methods research: Chapter 5

4. Design issues in mixed methods research: Chapter 7

5. Issues in drawing inferences in mixed methods research: Chapter 12

6. The logistics of conducting mixed methods research: Chapters 6 through 12

Six additional areas are addressed in *Foundations*:

1. The history of mixed methods research—from antiquity through the 21st century: Chapters 3 and 4

2. Mixed methods research questions: Chapter 6

3. Sampling issues in mixed methods research: Chapter 8

4. Data collection issues in mixed methods research: Chapters 9 (pre-data-collection considerations) and 10 (data collection)

5. The analysis of mixed methods data: Chapter 11

6. Identification and presentation of mixed methods examples and exemplars of mixed methods research: found throughout, especially in Chapters 6 through 12

We revisit several of these issues in the epilogue, which is concerned with unresolved and future issues. We share with the reader some of our own reflections and concerns about the current state of methodology in the social, behavioral, health, and educational research fields. These issues include political concerns, guidelines for conducting and publishing mixed research, and pedagogical topics.

Because this book serves as a textbook, we have included several pedagogical tools, such as content summaries and objectives at the beginning of each chapter, chapter summaries and previews at the end of each chapter, key terms and a glossary, and review questions and exercises. We have also included three exemplary studies in appendices to the text, which can be found at our companion Web site (www .sagepub.com/foundations). Several review questions are linked to these appendices.

Readers should note that words in **bold** indicate that they are key terms for the chapter where they are located. Words in *italic* indicate (1) a key term that has already appeared but is also important in the current chapter, (2) an important term new to the current chapter but not designated as a key term, (3) words or phrases highlighted for emphasis, or (4) words referred to as terms (e.g., the term *multimethods* on p. 20).

The glossary presents almost 300 terms associated with mixed methods, including essential qualitative and quantitative terms. Some of the definitions in this glossary were taken from the glossary of the *Handbook*, others came from authors currently writing about mixed methods, and still others are original to our design, analysis, and inference typologies and frameworks.

We had multiple editors while producing *Foundations*, starting with C. Deborah Laughton, who helped us conceptualize the book, and ending with Vicki Knight, who greatly facilitated our completing it. Our Sage team included Sean Connelly and Lauren Habib, and we thank them for all of their contributions. We also thank two sets of anonymous reviewers (2004, 2007), whose comments strengthened the book.

We want to acknowledge Burke Johnson as coauthor of Chapters 3 and 4, which outline the history of mixed methods research. Through his collaboration and contribution, Burke has enhanced our understanding of many philosophical and historical issues related to mixed methods research.

Many of our current and previous students have enriched this book (and our own learning) through the years. We would like to thank Tiffany Vastardis for her assistance in preparing the sections on ethics and Dr. Fen Yu for her assistance in organizing the glossary. Our special thanks also go to Mary Anne Ullery and Drs. Maria G. Lopez and Tarek Chebbi for their assistance in locating some of the examples.

We want to especially thank the members of the mixed methods community, who have provided us with so many of the concepts that enliven *Foundations*. These scholars are recognized throughout, particularly in Chapter 4, where we delineate three distinct subgroups: those from the United States; those from Europe, where there has been a healthy mixed methods scene for some time; and those from the World Bank, who have contributed a number of important, international mixed methods studies over the past few years. Two special colleagues among them, Vijayendra Rao and Michael Woolcock, were more than kind in sharing their work and their ideas with us.

One final note—we apologize for using the terms *qualitative* and *quantitative* so many times in this book, especially because we advocate that there is no dichotomy but rather a continuum between the terms. We use these terms in many discussions in this book, as proxies for a variety of diverse and complex concepts, constructs, techniques, political/personal ideologies and lenses, and even marketing tools. Although we use the terms as an artificial dichotomy at times, we try to demonstrate that they represent positions along multiple dimensions, each consisting of a continuum. These terms are perhaps necessary now for pedagogical reasons, but *mixed methods research will have taken a quantum leap forward when they no longer permeate our writings.*

Publisher's Acknowledgments

SAGE gratefully acknowledges the contributions of both anonymous and the following reviewers

Joseph J. Gallo
University of Pennsylvania

Nataliya Ivankova
University of Alabama at Birmingham

SECTION I

Mixed Methods

The Third Methodological Movement

CHAPTER 1

Mixed Methods as the Third Research Community

Objectives

Upon finishing this chapter, you should be able to:

- Explain what Kuhn meant by the term *paradigm* and the concept of a community of researchers

- Distinguish among the three communities of researchers in the social and behavioral sciences: qualitatively oriented methodologists, quantitatively oriented methodologists, and mixed methodologists
- Explain the differences in how researchers from the three methodological communities approach a research problem

- Describe the paradigms debate, using the concepts of the incompatibility and compatibility theses
- Discuss the issue of coexistence among the three research communities

Mixed methods research has been called the third path (Gorard & Taylor, 2004), the third research paradigm (Johnson & Onwuegbuzie, 2004), and the third methodological movement (Teddlie & Tashakkori, 2003) by various individuals writing in the field. We refer to it as the *third research community* in this chapter because we are focusing on the relationships that exist within and among the three major groups that are currently doing research in the social and behavioral sciences.

Mixed methods (MM) research has emerged as an alternative to the dichotomy of qualitative (QUAL) and quantitative (QUAN) traditions during the past 20 years. Though this book focuses on MM, its relatively recent emergence must be examined within the context of its two older cousins. We believe that MM research is still in its adolescence, and this volume seeks to more firmly establish the foundations for this approach.

This chapter has three purposes: (1) to briefly introduce the three communities of researchers in the social and behavioral sciences, (2) to demonstrate how the three research orientations differentially address the same research problem, and (3) to briefly discuss issues related to conflict and concord among the three communities.

Several terms are briefly introduced in Chapter 1 and then presented in greater detail later in the book. Because paradigms are referred to throughout Chapter 1, we define the term here. A **paradigm** (e.g., positivism, constructivism, pragmatism) may be defined as a "worldview, complete with the assumptions that are associated with that view" (Mertens, 2003, p. 139). Each of the three communities of researchers in the social and behavioral sciences has been associated with one or more paradigms.

The Three Communities of Researchers in the Social and Behavioral Sciences

Basic Descriptions of the Three Methodological Movements

In general, researchers in the social and behavioral sciences can be categorized into three groups:

- Quantitatively oriented social and behavioral scientists (**QUANs**) primarily working within the postpositivist/positivist paradigm and principally interested in numerical data and analyses
- Qualitatively oriented social and behavioral scientists (**QUALs**) primarily working within the constructivist paradigm and principally interested in narrative data and analyses
- **Mixed methodologists** working primarily within the pragmatist paradigm and interested in both narrative and numeric data and their analyses

These three methodological movements are like communities in that members of each group share similar backgrounds, methodological orientations, and research ideas and practices. There appear to be basic "cultural" differences between these researchers in terms of the manner in which they are trained, the types of research programs they pursue, and the types of professional organizations and special interest groups to which they belong. These cultural differences contribute to a distinct sense of community for each group.

Thomas Kuhn (1970) described such scientific communities as follows:

Scientists work from models acquired through education and through subsequent exposure to the literature often without quite knowing or needing to know what characteristics have given these models the status of *community* paradigms. (p. 46)

These three methodological communities are evident throughout the social and behavioral sciences and continue to evolve in interesting and sometimes unpredictable ways.

The Quantitative Tradition: Basic Terminology and Two Prototypes

The dominant and relatively unquestioned methodological orientation in the social and behavioral sciences for much of the 20th century was QUAN and its associated postpositivist/positivist paradigm. **Quantitative (QUAN) methods** may be most simply and parsimoniously defined as the techniques associated with the gathering, analysis, interpretation, and presentation of numerical information.

QUAN researchers originally subscribed to the tenets of **positivism**—the view that "social research should adopt scientific method, that this method is exemplified in the work of modern physicists, and that it consists of the rigorous testing of hypotheses by means of data that take the form of quantitative measurements" (Atkinson & Hammersley, 1994, p. 251). **Postpositivism** is a revised form of positivism that addresses several of the more widely known criticisms of the QUAN orientation, yet maintains an emphasis on QUAN methods.[1]

For instance, the original position of the positivists was that their research was conducted in an "objective," value-free environment; that is, their values did not affect how they conducted their research and interpreted their findings. Postpositivists, on the other hand, acknowledge that their value systems play an important role in how they conduct their research and interpret their data (e.g., Reichardt & Rallis, 1994).

Research questions guide investigations and are concerned with unknown aspects of a phenomenon of interest. Answers to quantitative research questions are presented in *numerical* form. A **research hypothesis** is a specialized QUAN research question in which investigators make predictions—based on theory, previous research, or some other rationale—about the relationships among social phenomena before conducting a research study. **Quantitative (statistical) data analysis** is the analysis of numerical data using techniques that include (1) simply describing the phenomenon of interest or (2) looking for significant differences between groups or among variables.

A variety of classic texts guides the QUAN community, including a trilogy of works by Donald T. Campbell and associates that constitute the core logic for the tradition (e.g., Campbell & Stanley, 1963; Cook & Campbell, 1979). The third in this series of books, *Experimental and Quasi-Experimental Designs for Generalized Causal Inference* (Shadish, Cook, & Campbell, 2002), was published in the 21st century and effectively updates the QUAN tradition. Berkenkotter (1989) described these books as charter texts for the postpositivist/QUAN orientation.

Boxes 1.1 and 1.2 contain descriptions of two prototypical researchers, named Professor Experimentalista and Professor Numerico, who are members of the QUAN researcher community.[2]

Box 1.1

Prototypical QUAN Researcher #1: Professor Experimentalista

Professor Experimentalista is employed by the psychology department at Flagship University. She conducts her research in the laboratories of Thorndike Hall, and her subjects are

(Continued)

(Continued)

freshman and sophomore students. Professor Experimentalista works in an area known as attribution theory, and she reads the latest journals to determine the current state of knowledge in that area. She uses the hypothetico-deductive model (described in Chapters 2 and 4) and generates a priori hypotheses based on Smith's XYZ theory (as opposed to Jones's ABC theory). Professor Experimentalista hypothesizes that her experimental group of subjects will respond differently than the control subjects to closed-ended items on a questionnaire devised to measure the dependent variables of interest. With her colleague, Dr. Deductivo, who is known for his ability to ferret out significant results, Dr. Experimentalista tests the hypotheses using statistical analyses.

Box 1.2
Prototypical QUAN Researcher #2: Professor Numerico

Professor Numerico is a medical sociologist at Flagship University. He typically uses questionnaires and telephone interviews to collect his research data. Participants in his studies are adolescents and young adults. Professor Numerico's research focuses on predicting risky behaviors that might lead to contracting AIDS. One of his research interests is to test the adequacy of three theories of behavior prediction: the theory of reasoned action, the theory of planned behavior, and the health belief model. Professor Numerico hypothesizes that the health belief model predicts the risky behaviors of young adults more accurately than the other two theories. He uses complex statistical procedures to predict participants' behaviors based on a number of potentially important factors.

The Qualitative Tradition: Basic Terminology and a Prototype

Qualitatively oriented researchers and theorists wrote several popular books during the last quarter of the 20th century. The authors of these texts were highly critical of the positivist orientation and proposed a wide variety of alternative QUAL methods. Their critiques of positivism, which they pejoratively labeled the received tradition, helped establish QUAL research as a viable alternative to QUAN research.

Qualitative (QUAL) methods may be most simply and parsimoniously defined as the techniques associated with the gathering, analysis, interpretation, and presentation of *narrative* information.

Many qualitatively oriented researchers subscribe to a worldview known as **constructivism** and its variants (e.g., Howe, 1988; Lincoln & Guba, 1985; Maxcy, 2003). Constructivists believe that researchers individually and collectively construct the meaning of the phenomena under investigation.[3]

Answers to qualitative research questions are narrative in form. **Qualitative (thematic) data analysis** is the analysis of narrative data using a variety of different inductive[4] and iterative techniques, including categorical strategies and contextualizing (holistic) strategies. Because these strategies typically result in themes, QUAL data analysis is also referred to as thematic analysis.

The QUAL community also has a variety of classic texts, including Glaser and Strauss (1967), Lincoln and Guba (1985), Miles and Huberman (1984, 1994), Patton (1990, 2002), Stake (1995), and Wolcott (1994). Three editions of the *Handbook of Qualitative Research* (Denzin & Lincoln, 1994, 2000a, 2005a) have enjoyed great popularity and may be considered charter texts for the constructivist/QUAL orientation. Box 1.3 contains a description of the prototypical QUAL researcher, named Professor Holistico, who is a member of the QUAL research community.

The Mixed Methods Tradition: Basic Terminology and a Prototype

The MM research tradition is less well known than the QUAN or QUAL traditions because it has emerged as a separate orientation during only the past 20 years. Mixed methodologists present an alternative to the QUAN and QUAL traditions by advocating the use of whatever methodological tools are required to answer the research questions under study. In fact, throughout the 20th century, social and behavioral scientists frequently employed MM in their studies, and they continue to do so in the 21st century, as described in several sources (e.g., Brewer & Hunter, 1989, 2006;

Greene, Caracelli, & Graham, 1989; Maxwell & Loomis, 2003; Tashakkori & Teddlie, 2003a).

Mixed methods (MM) has been defined as "a type of research design in which QUAL and QUAN approaches are used in types of questions, research methods, data collection and analysis procedures, and/or inferences" (Tashakkori & Teddlie, 2003a, p. 711). Another definition appeared in the first issue of the *Journal of Mixed Methods Research*, in which MM research was defined as "research in which the investigator collects and analyzes data, integrates the findings, and draws inferences using both qualitative and quantitative approaches or methods in a single study or program of inquiry" (Tashakkori & Creswell, 2007b, p. 4).

The philosophical orientation most often associated with MM is pragmatism (e.g., Biesta & Burbules, 2003; Bryman, 2006b; Howe, 1988; Johnson & Onwuegbuzie, 2004; Maxcy, 2003; Morgan, 2007; Tashakkori & Teddlie, 1998, 2003a), although some mixed methodologists are more philosophically oriented to the *transformative perspective* (e.g., Mertens, 2003). We defined **pragmatism** elsewhere as

a deconstructive paradigm that debunks concepts such as "truth" and "reality" and focuses instead on "what works" as the truth

---

Box 1.3
Prototypical QUAL Researcher: Professor Holistico

Professor Holistico is employed by the anthropology department at Flagship University. He conducts his research regarding female gang members in urban high schools around the state. Professor Holistico is developing a theory to explain the behaviors of these individuals, some of whom he has gotten to know very well in his 2 years of ethnographic data gathering. It took some time for him to develop trusting relationships with the young women, and he has to be careful to maintain their confidence. He has gathered large quantities of narrative data, which he is now reading repeatedly to ascertain emerging themes. He discusses his experiences with his colleague, Professor Inductiva, who is known for her keen analytical abilities and use of catchy metaphors. To check the trustworthiness of his results, Professor Holistico will present them to members of the gangs in a process known as member checking.

regarding the research questions under investigation. Pragmatism rejects the either/or choices associated with the paradigm wars, advocates for the use of mixed methods in research, and acknowledges that the values of the researcher play a large role in interpretation of results. (Tashakkori & Teddlie, 2003a, p. 713)

MM research questions guide MM investigations and are answered with information that is presented in *both narrative and numerical* forms. Several authors writing in the MM tradition refer specifically to the centrality of the research questions to that orientation (e.g., Bryman, 2006b; Erzberger & Kelle, 2003; Tashakkori & Teddlie, 1998).

Mixed methods data analysis involves the integration of statistical and thematic data analytic techniques, plus other strategies unique to MM (e.g., data conversion or transformation), which are discussed later in this text. In properly conducted MM research, investigators go back and forth seamlessly between statistical and thematic analysis (e.g., Onwuegbuzie & Teddlie, 2003).

Mixed methodologists are well versed in the classic texts from both the QUAN and QUAL traditions as well as a growing number of well-known works within the MM field (e.g.,

Creswell, 1994, 2003; Creswell & Plano Clark, 2007; Greene, 2007; Greene & Caracelli, 1997a; Johnson & Onwuegbuzie, 2004; Morgan, 1998; Morse, 1991; Newman & Benz, 1998; Reichardt & Rallis, 1994; Tashakkori & Teddlie, 1998, 2003a). Box 1.4 contains a description of a prototypical MM researcher named Professor Eclectica, who is a member of the MM community.

An Example of How the Three Communities Approach a Research Problem

Introduction to an Evaluation Study (Trend, 1979)

An often-referenced article from the MM literature is a study conducted by Maurice Trend (1979) involving the evaluation of a federal housing subsidy program involving both QUAN and QUAL methods. Others have used this article to demonstrate several aspects of MM research, such as the difficulty of conducting studies using researchers from both the QUAL and QUAN orientations (e.g., Reichardt & Cook, 1979); how MM research can be informed by the separate components of QUAL and QUAN research

---

Box 1.4
Prototypical Mixed Methodologist: Professor Eclectica

Professor Eclectica is employed in the School of Public Health at Flagship University. She is interested in children's health issues, especially the prevention of diabetes in middle-school children. Her research program involves both hypotheses related to weight loss and research questions related to why certain interventions work. Professor Eclectica was trained as a sociologist and has expertise in QUAN data analysis that began with her dissertation. She has also gained skills in QUAL data gathering and analysis while working on an interdisciplinary research team. Her research involves interventions with different types of cafeteria offerings and differing types of physical education regimens. She spends time in the field (up to 2 weeks per site) interviewing and observing students to determine why certain interventions work while others do not. Her analyses consist of a mixture of QUAL and QUAN procedures. She describes her research as *confirmatory* (the research hypothesis regarding weight) and *exploratory* (the research questions regarding why different interventions succeed or fail). She tries to integrate her QUAL and QUAN results in dynamic ways to further her research program.

(Maxwell & Loomis, 2003); the value and credibility of QUAL and QUAN data when discrepancies occur (Patton, 2002); and the balance in results that can be achieved when differences between the QUAL and QUAN components are properly reconciled (e.g., Tashakkori & Teddlie, 2003c).

In this chapter, we use the Trend (1979) study in a different way: as a vehicle for demonstrating how the three research communities address the same research problem. Although the study became mixed as it evolved, it started out with two separate components: one QUAN and one QUAL. It became mixed when the evaluators had to write reports that synthesized the results from the two separate components. Trend (1979) described the components of the study as follows:[5]

> Three types of reports were envisioned by HUD and Abt Associates. The first consisted of comparative, cross-site function reports. They were to be based mostly on quantitative analysis and would evaluate program *outcomes*. Eight site case studies were planned as a second kind of product. These were designed as narrative, qualitatively based pieces that would enrich the function reports by providing a holistic picture of program *process* at the administrative agencies. A final report would then digest the findings of all the analyses and convert these into policy recommendations. (p. 70, italics in original)

Trend's (1979) opinion was that "different analyses, each based upon a different form of information, should be kept separate until late in the analytic game" (p. 68). Because the QUAL and QUAN components were conducted separately from start to finish, followed by Trend's MM meta-analysis using both sources, this study provides a unique example of how the three communities approach the same research scenario.

The overall project consisted of eight sites located in different areas of the United States. At each site an administrative agency was selected to implement a federal housing subsidy program, whose goal was to provide better housing for low-income families. Each site was to serve up to 900 families. Trend's (1979) article focused on the results from one site (Site B), which had three distinct geographical areas: two rural areas with satellite offices and one urban area with the site's central office.

The Quantitative Approach to the Evaluation Study

The QUAN component of this study is a good example of an *outcomes-based evaluation,* where the emphasis is on whether a program has met its overall goals, typically measured quantitatively.[6] The QUAN component was set up to determine if the use of direct-cash housing allowance payments would help low-income families obtain better housing on the open market. The QUAN research questions in this study, which were established before the evaluation began, included the following:

- Did the sites meet their stated goals in terms of enrolling families in the program (i.e., up to 900 families per site)?
- Was the minority population (African American) represented proportionally in the number of families served by the program?
- Did participants actually move to better housing units as a result of the program?
- Were potential participants processed "efficiently"?
- Did the sites exert proper financial management?

Teams of survey researchers, site financial accountants, and data processors/analysts at the Abt Associates headquarters conducted the QUAN component of the study. Numeric survey data were gathered on housing quality, demographic characteristics of participants, agency activities, expenses, and other relevant variables. A common set of six forms was employed to follow the progress of participating families. Teams of survey researchers interviewed samples of participants at scheduled times during the process using structured interview protocols. Accountants kept track of all expenditures, and this information became part of the database. Trend (1979) noted that "eventually, the quantitative data base would comprise more than 55 million *characters*" (p. 70, italics in original).

In summary, this component of the evaluation exhibited several prototypical characteristics of QUAN research, including the establishment of well-articulated research questions before the study started, the development and use of numeric scales to measure outcome variables of interest, the employment of professional data gatherers (e.g., survey researchers, accountants) to collect information, and the statistical analysis of the data using computers at a central location. Significant efforts were put into generating an "objective" assessment of the success of the federal housing subsidy program using QUAN techniques.

The computer-generated QUAN outcome data indicated that Site B had done quite well compared to the other sites. Site B completed its quota of enrolling 900 households in the program, and participants experienced an improvement in housing quality that ranked second among the eight sites. Trend (1979) stated additional results of the study: "The cost model indicated that the Site B program had been cheap to run. Revised calculations of site demography showed that minorities were properly represented in the recipient population" (p. 76). Figure 1.1 illustrates the conclusions from the QUAN component of this study.

The Qualitative Approach to the Evaluation Study

The QUAL component of this study is a good example of a *process-based evaluation*, where the focus is on how the program is implemented and how it is currently operating or functioning,

Figure 1.1   QUAN Researcher's Point of View

typically measured qualitatively.[7] The QUAL component of this evaluation involved the generation of eight case studies by observers using field observations, interviews, and documents (e.g., field notes and logs, program planning documents, intraoffice communications). The purpose of the case studies was to provide a holistic description of what actually occurred at each of the program sites.

Unlike the QUAN component, the QUAL research questions were generic in nature, involving the description of what actually happened in the field when the programs were initiated and how the programs evolved during the first year of operation. As the observations and interviews were conducted, several issues emerged at each program site, and the observers used those problems or concerns to continually refocus their research questions.

Each site had one observer (typically an anthropologist), who was assigned to that site for the first year of the program. Observers were assigned office space by the administrative agency at each site and allowed to collect data daily. They regularly collected field notes and logs and mailed them to the evaluation headquarters. These data "eventually totaled more than 25,000 pages" (Trend, 1979, p. 70).

Unlike the conclusions from the QUAN component, the QUAL data indicated that there were serious problems with the manner in which the program was implemented and operating at Site B. The Site B observer reported that there had been problems from the beginning: There was a delay in opening the local offices (one main urban office, two rural ones), and potential families' initial response to the program was slow to develop.

As a result of these problems, Site B administrators were forced to increase their efforts to enroll the site's 900 families. Progress in recruiting families was the slowest at the urban center; the two rural offices met program recruitment requirements more easily.

Recruitment quotas were established by the administrative agency to increase enrollment at the urban center, and conflict emerged between the staff at the urban office and the administrator who had set the quotas. Difficulties escalated at the urban office when staff began to complain about overwork, and personality conflicts emerged. Conditions were different at the rural offices, where the staff members also worked hard but found time to make home visits and inspect all recipient housing units.

Another problem at the urban office concerned the recruitment of minorities. Because African Americans oversubscribed at the urban site (unlike the rural sites), the administrative agency ordered the urban office to curtail their enrollment. Some staff members were angry with this recruiting policy (which they considered racist), and several employees resigned at the end of the enrollment period with months still left on their contracts.

The discrepancies between the QUAN and QUAL results became an issue when the Site B observer wrote an essence paper detailing themes that had emerged from the QUAL analyses, including office strife, personality conflicts, managerial incompetence, and so forth. Trend (1979) was the overall manager of the case studies and had requested the essence papers from each of the observers as a prelude to the final case study.

This component of the evaluation demonstrated several classical characteristics of QUAL research, including the use of emerging (not predetermined) questions to guide the research; the use of unstructured and semistructured observations, interviews, logs, and documents as data sources; an emphasis on providing a holistic description of the social scene as it emerged from the QUAL data sources; and a close and empathic relationship between the observer and the program participants. The observer at Site B was comfortable with the "subjective" orientation of the essence paper because QUAL research is constructivist in nature, and the paper reflected an informed understanding or reconstruction of the social reality of the program as implemented at Site B. Figure 1.2 illustrates the conclusions from the QUAL component of this study.

Figure 1.2   QUAL Researcher's Point of View

The Mixed Methods Approach to the Evaluation Study

The specific MM study described by Trend (1979) emerged as a result of the unexpected discrepant results between the QUAN and QUAL components at Site B.[8] As noted in the previous section, the conclusions from the observer at Site B contradicted the results from the QUAN analysis of program effects at that site. The QUAN data indicated that the program was working, whereas the QUAL data pointed out serious problems with program implementation. The MM approach was used to explain such apparent discrepancies between the QUAN and QUAL results.

The evaluation study as presented in the Trend (1979) article is an example of what has been called a *parallel mixed design*,[9] in which the QUAN and QUAL components are conducted separately (and in a parallel manner), followed by a *meta-inference process*, which integrates the results. (See Chapter 7 for more details regarding this design.)

The research questions for an MM study are a combination of those from the separate QUAL and QUAN components, plus any questions that might emerge as inferences are made. This study asked the following additional questions: Why were the results of the QUAN and QUAL components discrepant? What explanation can be derived from the combined data that would reconcile the differences?

Trend (1979) rationalized these new questions as follows:

> We had to answer the question of how a program could produce such admirable results in so many of its aspects, when all of the observational data indicated that the program would be a failure. What had happened, and how? (p. 78)

Although Trend (1979) was not the observer at Site B, he became involved in writing a revised essence paper after the evaluation company asked the observer to rewrite the report in a manner more consistent with the QUAN results. Trend and the observer then began reanalyzing the data, looking for information that might help them reconcile the differences. One major breakthrough came when they split the data into three parts based on office location (two rural, one urban). They found that very different processes were at work at the rural and urban sites:

- More in-depth investigation led to the discovery of inconsistent patterns of results across the sites, which were more important than the overall average pattern of results in understanding program impact.

- The rural context produced many advantages for the program. Potential recipients there were more likely to be White and to have smaller families and higher incomes, which led to lower-than-average housing subsidies. These lower subsidies reduced the average subsidy paid across all program recipients, thereby contributing to the overall positive QUAN results. Also, families were easier to recruit in the rural areas, and this increased the total number of recipients.

- The urban context had numerous disadvantages. The initial oversubscription of African American families in the urban area led to a quota system that fueled some staff members' negative feelings, which resulted in their alienation from the program. Ironically, this led to some positive QUAN effects because workers left their jobs early, thereby resulting in lower

program costs when they were not replaced. The quota system and small staff size led to a mass-production process in the urban office that increased the number of recipients in a supposedly "efficient" manner.

A number of other factors related to the urban/rural context differences made the overall discrepancies between the QUAN and QUAL results more understandable. Trend (1979) concluded that "by treating Site B as a single piece the quantitative analysts had missed almost all of what we were now discovering" (p. 80).

Six versions of the essence paper were written before it was finally accepted. Though the reconciliation of the discrepancies in the MM data was obviously necessary to truly understand the contextually distinct aspects of the program, the meta-analysis of the QUAN and QUAL data took Trend and the observer 10 weeks to complete. MM research is often more expensive than QUAL or QUAN research alone due to increased data gathering, analysis, and interpretation costs.

If only the QUAN data had been analyzed, then an inaccurate (too positive) picture of the federal housing-subsidy program would have resulted. Similarly, if only the case study had occurred, then an inaccurate (too negative) picture of the program would have emerged. When the data were mixed, a more accurate overall picture emerged. In this evaluation, MM first allowed the opportunity for divergent views to be voiced and then served as the catalyst for a more balanced evaluation.

In summary, the evaluation study conducted by Trend and his colleagues exhibited several classical characteristics of MM research, even though it was not planned to be an integrated study: the use of both predetermined and emerging research questions to guide the study, the use of both QUAL and QUAN data sources, the use of both QUAL and QUAN data analyses, and the innovative use of MM techniques to integrate the QUAN and QUAL findings in a manner that made sense. Figure 1.3 illustrates the context-bound conclusions from the MM component of this study.

Figure 1.3   MM Researcher's Point of View

The Three Methodological Communities: Continuing Debates or Peaceful Coexistence?

The three methodological communities have experienced periods of both philosophical conflict and peaceful coexistence over the past four decades. During this time, the QUAL community first emerged to challenge the traditional QUAN orientation and then the MM community visibly surfaced. This section briefly describes the *paradigms debate* or *paradigm wars* (e.g., Gage, 1989) that occurred as the QUAL community's

positions gained acceptance, challenging the preeminence of the QUAN community.

Thomas Kuhn (1962, 1970, 1996) popularized the notion of competing paradigms and paradigm shifts in his book *The Structure of Scientific Revolutions*. The paradigms debate in the social and behavioral sciences (circa 1975–1995), which was particularly widespread in educational and evaluation research, is a good example of proponents of competing paradigms disagreeing about the relative merits of their theoretical positions. (See Chapter 5, Box 5.1, for more details regarding Kuhn's positions on paradigms.)

These disagreements were largely a product of the QUAL community's intense criticisms of issues associated with what they called the received tradition of the positivist paradigm. In place of the positivist paradigm, many QUALs posited constructivism as a better theoretical perspective for conducting research. The simplest definition of the **paradigms debate** is the conflict between the competing scientific worldviews of positivism (and variants, such as postpositivism) and constructivism (and variants, such as interpretivism) on philosophical and methodological issues (e.g., Gage, 1989; Guba & Lincoln, 1994; Howe, 1988; Reichardt & Rallis, 1994; Tashakkori & Teddlie, 1998).

As constructivism emerged, some authors (e.g., Guba & Lincoln, 1994; Lincoln & Guba, 1985) set up **paradigm contrast tables** summarizing the differences between positivists and constructivists on philosophical issues such as *ontology, epistemology, axiology,* the possibility of generalizations, the possibility of causal linkages, and so forth.[10] These contrast tables presented fundamental differences (i.e., dichotomies) between paradigms, thereby indicating that the paradigms were not compatible with one another.

A major component of the paradigms debate was the **incompatibility thesis**, which stated that it is inappropriate to mix QUAL and QUAN methods due to fundamental differences in the paradigms underlying those methods (e.g., Guba, 1987; Sale, Lohfeld, & Brazil, 2002; Smith, 1983; Smith & Heshusius, 1986). The incompatibility thesis is associated with the supposed link between paradigms and research methods. According to this thesis, research paradigms are associated with research methods in a kind of one-to-one correspondence. Therefore, if the underlying premises of different paradigms conflict with one another, the methods associated with those paradigms cannot be combined.

Mixed methodologists countered this position with the compatibility thesis, exemplified in the following quote:

> However, the pragmatism of employing multiple research methods to study the same general problem by posing different

specific questions has some pragmatic implications for social theory. Rather than being wedded to a particular theoretical style . . . and its most compatible method, one might instead combine methods that would encourage or even require integration of different theoretical perspectives to interpret the data. (Brewer & Hunter, 2006, p. 55)

On a philosophical level, mixed methodologists countered the incompatibility thesis by positing a different paradigm: pragmatism (e.g., Howe, 1988; Maxcy 2003; Morgan, 2007; Tashakkori & Teddlie, 1998). A major tenet of Howe's (1988) concept of pragmatism was that QUAL and QUAN methods *are compatible* (the **compatibility thesis**), thereby rejecting the either-or choices presented by the incompatibility thesis. Pragmatism offers a third alternative (combine both QUAL and QUAN methods) to the either-or choices (use either QUAL methods or QUAN methods) of the incompatibility thesis. Howe (1988) described the thesis as follows: "The compatibility thesis supports the view, beginning to dominate practice, that combining quantitative and qualitative methods is a good thing and denies that such a wedding is epistemologically incoherent" (p. 10).

The paradigms debate waned considerably in the mid- and late 1990s (e.g., Patton, 2002), largely because "most researchers had become bored with philosophical discussions and were more interested in getting on with the task of doing their research" (Smith, 1996, pp. 162–163). Mixed methodologists were actively interested in reconciliation of the communities, and MM provided a justification for and a place to combine QUAN and QUAL methods.

Therefore, the paradigms debate has been resolved for many researchers (especially mixed methodologists) currently working in the social and behavioral sciences.[11] Nevertheless, there is a vestige of the debate that particularly affects graduate students and less experienced researchers: the tendency to remain QUANs or QUALs based on initial research orientation. Gorard and Taylor

(2004) described this unfortunate phenomenon as follows:

> The most unhelpful of the supposed paradigms in social sciences are the methodological ones of "qualitative" and "quantitative" approaches. Unfortunately, novice research students can quickly become imprisoned within one of these purported "paradigms." They learn, because they are taught, that if they use any numbers in their research then they must be positivist or realist in philosophy, and they must be hypothetico-deductive or traditional in style. . . . If, on the other hand, students disavow the use of numbers in research then they must be interpretivist, holistic and alternative, believing in multiple perspectives rather than the truth, and so on. (p. 149)

Boyatzis (1998, p. viii) employed the respective terms **quantiphobe** and **qualiphobe** for researchers who have a fear or dislike of either QUAN or QUAL methods. We might add *mixiphobes* as another type of researcher, one who subscribes to a purely QUAL or QUAN orientation and has a fear or dislike of MM. Interestingly, MM is still controversial in some quarters (e.g., Denzin & Lincoln, 2005b; Howe, 2004; Sale, Lohfeld, & Brazil, 2002), and potential researchers should be aware of this point of view (discussed more in Chapter 5).

Though distinct, these communities can coexist peacefully, so long as no group proclaims its superiority and tries to dictate the methods of the other groups. Our position is for greater dialogue among the three communities, each of which contributes greatly to an understanding of many complex social phenomena. This understanding will be accelerated when researchers realize that some research questions can only be answered using QUAN methods, whereas others can only be answered using QUAL methods, and still others require MM.

Of course, our advocacy for integration is not a new stance: Many eminent QUAL and QUAN scholars have expressed similar thoughts during the past 50 years. For instance, Barney Glaser and Anselm Strauss (1967), the originators of the QUAL method known as grounded theory, made the following statement some 40 years ago:

> Our position in this book is as follows: there is no fundamental clash between the purposes and capacities of qualitative and quantitative methods or data. What clash there is concerns the primacy of emphasis on verification or generation of theory—to which heated discussions on qualitative *versus* quantitative data have been linked historically. We believe that *each form of data is useful for both verification and generation of theory. . . . In many instances, both forms of data are necessary* . . . both used as supplements, as mutual verification and, most important for us, as different forms of data on the same subject, which, when compared, will each generate theory. (pp. 17–18, italics in original)

Reichardt and Cook (1979) stated the same sentiment from the postpositivist perspective:

> It is time to stop building walls between the methods and start building bridges. Perhaps it is even time to go beyond the dialectic language of qualitative and quantitative methods. The real challenge is to fit the research methods to the evaluation problem without parochialism. This may well call for a combination of qualitative and quantitative methods. To distinguish between the two by using separate labels may serve only to polarize them unnecessarily. (p. 27)

Summary

The three research communities were introduced and prototypical researchers within each were presented: Professor Experimentalista and Professor Numerico (the QUAN community), Professor Holistico (the QUAL community), and Professor Eclectica (the MM community). Basic differences among the three groups were delineated in several areas.

We argue throughout the text that these three communities are culturally distinct, each with its own educational and social backgrounds, research traditions, and perceptions of how research should be conducted. Despite this, we also argue that the three communities can coexist peacefully.

An evaluation study was described, and then accounts were given showing how researchers from each of the three communities approached the study. Discrepancies between the QUAN and QUAL results from this study were reconciled using the MM approach.

Finally, there was a brief discussion of the paradigms debate and of issues related to conflict and concord among the three communities. We and many other mixed methodologists advocate peaceful coexistence based on the compatibility thesis and the idea that each community is more suited to answering certain types of research questions.

Chapter 2 continues our presentation of various contrasts among the three methodological communities. The chapter includes a summary of an MM article, which is located in Appendix A located at www.sagepub.com/foundations. A continuum is then introduced to describe the interrelationships among the three communities. This continuum is used throughout the text as one of its major unifying themes. Finally, issues of nomenclature and utility in MM research are discussed.

Review Questions and Exercises

1. What are (a) postpositivism, (b) quantitative methods, and (c) statistical analysis?

2. What are (a) constructivism, (b) qualitative methods, and (c) content analysis?

3. What are (a) pragmatism, (b) mixed methods, and (c) mixed methods data analysis?

4. Find a journal article that employs QUAN methods only. Summarize it in one page.

5. Find a journal article that employs QUAL methods only. Summarize it in one page.

6. Find a journal article that employs MM. Summarize it in one page.

7. Compare your MM journal article to the QUAN and QUAL articles. Discuss major differences among the three articles.

8. Describe how Trend (1979) and his colleagues used MM to reconcile discrepant QUAN and QUAL results.

9. What was the paradigms debate and how did the incompatibility thesis contribute to that debate? What is the compatibility thesis and how did it help to reconcile the paradigms debate?

Key Terms

Compatibility thesis

Constructivism

Incompatibility thesis

Mixed methodologists

Mixed methods (MM)

Mixed methods data analysis

Paradigm

Paradigm contrast tables

Paradigms debate

Positivism

Postpositivism

Pragmatism

Qualiphobe

Qualitative (QUAL) methods

Qualitative (thematic) data analysis

QUALs

QUANs

Quantiphobe

Quantitative (QUAN) methods

Quantitative (statistical) data analysis

Research hypothesis

Research questions

Notes

1. Very few researchers in the social and behavioral sciences would refer to themselves as positivists at this point in time due to the discrediting of many of the original philosophical positions of that paradigm. Many QUAN researchers, however, consider themselves to be postpositivists today.

2. We present two prototypes of QUANs because there are major differences between experimentalists (Professor Experimentalista) and individuals who work primarily with surveys and other descriptive QUAN designs (Professor Numerico). We did not want to give the impression that all QUANs are experimentalists.

3. There are many perspectives or traditions (e.g., critical theory) associated with QUAL research in addition to constructivism and its variants, as noted by Creswell (1998), Denzin and Lincoln (2005b), and others. Glesne (2006) summarized the relative importance of constructivism as follows: "Most qualitative researchers adhere to social constructivism or a *constructivist* paradigm" (p. 7, italics in original).

4. *Inductive logic* involves arguing from the particular to the general, which is how inductive analyses occur: The researcher uses a variety of facts to construct a theory. More information on inductive and deductive logic is presented in Chapters 2, 3, and 5.

5. HUD refers to the U.S. Department of Housing and Urban Development, which was the agency funding the study. Abt Associates is the evaluation firm that undertook the evaluation.

6. QUAL data may also be used in outcomes-based evaluations, but these were not emphasized in the Trend (1979) study.

7. QUAN data may also be used in process-based evaluations, but these were not emphasized in the Trend (1979) study.

8. Though the evaluation plan originally called for a final MM report based on a "digest of [the] findings of all the analyses" (Trend, 1979, p. 70), that report was not discussed in the Trend article or in this summary of it. It appears that the original digest would have been heavily weighted toward the QUAN component.

9. We refer to the Trend (1979) study as an example of a parallel MM design, but it is important to remember that the author of the study did not use this term. Our designation of this study as a particular type of MM design is based on an *ex post facto analysis* of its design characteristics.

10. Philosophical terms associated with the paradigms debate are defined in Chapter 5. The contents of the original Lincoln and Guba (1985) paradigm contrast table are presented in Table 5.1.

11. Despite this overall trend toward coexistence, the gap between QUALs and QUANs increased in the educational research field in the United States during the tenure of the G. W. Bush administration with a small-scale reenactment of the paradigms debate due to the establishment of a distinctly postpositivist QUAN orientation in the U.S. Department of Education. More details are presented in Chapters 4 and 5.

CHAPTER 2

The Fundamentals of Mixed Methods Research

Objectives

Upon finishing this chapter, you should be able to:

- Distinguish between methodologies, methods, and paradigms
- Name and define terms associated with quantitative (QUAN) research on several basic research dimensions
- Name and define terms associated with qualitative (QUAL) research on several basic research dimensions
- Name and define terms associated with mixed methods (MM) research on several basic research dimensions
- Read a mixed methods research article and identify its important quantitative, qualitative, and mixed methods components

- Describe the QUAL-MM-QUAN continuum
- Compare and contrast various definitions and conceptualizations of mixed methods
- Describe the major advantages of mixed methods

Chapter 2 is broken into five sections. In these sections, we identify differences among methodologies, methods, and paradigms; provide more details about the three methodological movements; provide an extended description and analysis of an MM study; discuss issues related to MM definitions; and explain the use of MM research.

In the first section, we explain three important conceptual terms: *methodology, methods,* and *paradigm,* which are often used interchangeably and confusingly. It is important that researchers have a common understanding of what these terms mean and how they are distinct from one another to avoid confusion in describing MM research.

In this chapter, we also present more than 30 terms and definitions that further delineate comparisons among the three methodological communities. A table summarizes those distinctions.

We go on to present a summary of an MM article, which is contained in its entirety in Appendix A, located at www.sagepub.com/foundations. We make numerous comments on the article, especially with regard to how MM designs are used and how the QUAN and QUAL approaches are integrated in a research project.

The QUAL-MM-QUAN continuum is then introduced as an alternative way of perceiving the interrelationships among the three methodological communities. We and other colleagues (e.g., Johnson & Onwuegbuzie, 2004; Newman & Benz, 1998; Niglas, 2004) believe that the QUAN and QUAL approaches are not dichotomous and distinct. They have been presented as dichotomies in this text thus far for pedagogical reasons (i.e., to help the reader understand the differences among the research orientations in their pure form); however, we think it is more accurate to perceive each component of a research study as representing a point along a continuum. We present this continuum and some of its characteristics. (The QUAL-MM-QUAN continuum is discussed further in Chapter 5.)

Two issues related to MM terms and definitions are briefly discussed: the need for a distinct MM language and the choice of using either a "bilingual" or a common language in MM research. The chapter ends with a discussion of the major advantages of MM in answering research questions.

Differences Among Methodologies, Methods, and Paradigms

Much of Chapters 1 and 2 involve definitions of basic terms used in QUAL, QUAN, and MM research. The first topic discussed in this chapter concerns the differences among three basic concepts: paradigms, methodologies, and methods. This is a special concern for MM research because the field has had a history of confusing, or contradictory, definitions of basic vocabulary, such as *multimethods,* a term that is rarely used today (e.g., Brewer & Hunter, 2006). Lois-ellin Datta (1994) referred to these conceptual issues several years ago when she described "mixed-up models" that derived from the "lack of a worldview, paradigm, or theory for mixed-model studies," concluding that "such a theory has yet to be fully articulated" (p. 59).

In Chapter 1, we used Mertens's (2003) definition of *paradigm* as a "worldview, complete with the assumptions that are associated with that view" (p. 139) because that description seems to echo the viewpoints of several others (e.g., Creswell & Plano Clark, 2007; Lincoln, 1990; Rallis & Rossman, 2003; Van Manen, 1990). Morgan (2007) recently referred to *paradigms* "as systems of beliefs and practices that influence how researchers select both the questions they study and methods that they use to study them" (p. 49).

Jennifer Greene (2006) defined a *methodology* of social inquiry as having four domains:

1. Philosophical assumptions and stances, including issues in the philosophy of science (e.g., the nature of reality) and theoretical justification (e.g., core constructs of particular disciplines)

2. Inquiry logics, which involves "what is commonly called '*methodology*' in social science" (p. 93, italics added) and includes inquiry questions and purposes, broad inquiry designs and strategies, sampling logic, criteria of quality, and so forth

3. Guidelines for practice, which involves the specific *methods* for conducting inquiries, "the 'how to' of social science inquiry" (p. 94), and includes specific sampling strategies, analysis techniques, and so forth

4. Sociopolitical commitments in science, which are concerned primarily with issues of values (axiology) and answer questions like "Whose interests should be served by this particular approach to social inquiry, and why?" (p. 94)

Many of the topics that Greene (2006) discussed under Domains 1 and 4 were considered paradigm issues (e.g., the nature of reality, the role of values in research) during the *paradigms debate* introduced in Chapter 1 and discussed in more detail in Chapters 4 and 5. On the other hand, the topics discussed by Greene under Domains 2 and 3 are directly related to considerations of research methodology and research methods.

Clert, Gacitua-Mario, and Wodon (2001) provided a clear-cut distinction between methodology and method: "A methodological approach involves a theory on how a research question should be analyzed. A research method is a procedure for collecting, organizing and analyzing data" (p. 7). Combining the descriptions from Clert et al. and Domains 2 and 3 from Greene (2006), we developed the following definitions:

- A research **methodology** is a broad approach to scientific inquiry specifying how research questions should be asked and answered. This includes worldview considerations, general preferences for designs, sampling logic, data collection and analytical strategies, guidelines for making inferences, and the criteria for assessing and improving quality.

- Research **methods** include specific strategies and procedures for implementing research design, including sampling, data collection, data analysis, and interpretation of the findings.
- Specific *research methods* are determined by the *overall methodological orientation* of the researchers.

To summarize, a paradigm is a worldview including philosophical and sociopolitical issues, whereas a research methodology is a general approach to scientific inquiry involving preferences for broad components of the research process. Research methods are specific strategies for conducting research.

Why did we choose the title *The Foundations of Mixed Methods Research* for this text, rather than *The Foundations of Mixed Methodology*? Although the first five chapters and the epilogue of this book address both paradigm and general methodological issues, the greater part of the book (Chapters 6–12) discusses specific MM research techniques. Until we get a *greater consensus within the MM community* concerning what constitutes *mixed methodology* in broad terms (i.e., in terms of an overall design typology), then the term *mixed methods* is more appropriately used.

Finally, the reader should beware of writings about MM that blur the distinctions between paradigms, methodologies, and methods. For example, "mixed methods research paradigm" (or "qualitative paradigm" or "quantitative paradigm") is conceptually unclear language that should be avoided (Gorard & Taylor, 2004). Mixing these levels leads to continued conceptual fuzziness.

More Details Regarding the Methodological Communities

Chapter 1 presented some basic terminology related to the three methodological communities. This chapter introduces several more important QUAL, QUAN, and MM terms together with definitions. These terms are briefly introduced in these two chapters and then expanded on throughout the text.

Almost all of the concepts introduced in Chapters 1 and 2 can be compared across several important dimensions. For example, constructivism, pragmatism, and postpositivism are terms related to QUAL, MM, and QUAN methods, respectively, and they can be compared with one another across a dimension labeled "paradigms."

Table 2.1 summarizes the dimensions of contrast[1] among the three methodological communities

that are discussed in Chapters 1 and 2. The rows in Table 2.1 represent the dimensions of contrast, whereas the columns represent the three methodological communities.

Figure 2.1 presents the three research communities and their separate points of view. The following sections of this chapter present the distinctions among the three communities in more detail.

Table 2.1   Dimensions of Contrast Among the Three Methodological Communities Discussed in Chapters 1 and 2

Dimension of Contrast	Qualitative Position	Mixed Methods Position	Quantitative Position
Methods	Qualitative methods	Mixed methods	Quantitative methods
Researchers	QUALs	Mixed methodologists	QUANs
Paradigms	Constructivism (and variants)	Pragmatism; transformative perspective	Postpositivism Positivism
Research questions	QUAL research questions	MM research questions (QUAN plus QUAL)	QUAN research questions; research hypotheses
Form of data	Typically narrative	Narrative plus numeric	Typically numeric
Purpose of research	(Often) exploratory plus confirmatory	Confirmatory plus exploratory	(Often) confirmatory plus exploratory
Role of theory; logic	Grounded theory; inductive logic	Both inductive and deductive logic; inductive-deductive research cycle	Rooted in conceptual framework or theory; hypothetico-deductive model
Typical studies or designs	Ethnographic research designs and others (case study)	MM designs, such as parallel and sequential	Correlational; survey; experimental; quasi-experimental
Sampling	Mostly purposive	Probability, purposive, and mixed	Mostly probability
Data analysis	Thematic strategies: categorical and contextualizing	Integration of thematic and statistical; data conversion	Statistical analyses: descriptive and inferential
Validity/trustworthiness issues	Trustworthiness; credibility; transferability	Inference quality; inference transferability	Internal validity; external validity

Figure 2.1   The Three Research Communities and Their Points of View

More Details Regarding the Quantitative Tradition

This section presents and defines additional terms associated with the QUAN tradition. Most of these terms are located in the right-hand column of Table 2.1.

QUAN research is often confirmatory in nature and driven by theory and the current state of knowledge about the phenomenon under study. A **theory** "is generally understood to refer to a unified, systematic explanation of a diverse range of social phenomena" (Schwandt, 1997, p. 154). Theories are often (but not always) used in QUAN research to generate propositions or hypotheses that can then be tested using statistical techniques. **Confirmatory research** involves conducting investigations to test propositions that are based on a specific theory or a *conceptual framework*.[2] Theory in QUAN research is usually

a priori in nature; that is, the theory precedes the gathering of data. **Descriptive research**, on the other hand, is conducted with the goal of exploring the attributes of a phenomenon or the possible relationships between variables (for examples in MM, see Christ, 2007).

QUAN researchers typically employ **deductive logic or reasoning**, which involves arguing from the general (e.g., theory, conceptual framework) to the particular (e.g., data points). The **hypothetico-deductive model** (H-DM) is a model employed by QUANs involving the a priori deduction of hypotheses from a theory or conceptual framework and the testing of those hypotheses using numerical data and statistical analyses. (See the definition of the H-DM in Chapter 4, Box 4.1.)

QUAN researchers use a variety of well-defined research designs, including correlational, survey, experimental, and quasi-experimental.

Correlational research looks at the strength of the relationships between variables. For instance, we could pose a QUAN research question that would examine the relationship between the average annual temperature of water in the Gulf of Mexico and the annual number of named hurricanes. If the correlation were positive and strong, we would conclude that as the average temperature of water in the gulf increases, so does the number of hurricanes.

QUAN **survey research** is a systematic method for data collection, with the goal of predicting population attributes or behaviors (e.g. voting, consumer behavior). In usual survey research, predetermined questions are presented in a pre-arranged order to a sample that is usually representative of the population of interest. **Probability sampling** is typically associated with QUAN research and involves selecting a large number of units from a population in a random manner in which the probability of inclusion of any member of the population can be determined. (See Chapter 8 for a more complete definition of probability samples.)

Experimental research is a type of research design in which the investigator manipulates or controls one or more independent variables (treatments) to ascertain their effects on one or more dependent variables. An **independent variable** is a variable that is presumed to influence or affect a dependent variable, whereas a **dependent variable** is a variable that is presumed to be affected or influenced by an independent variable. Experimental changes in the characteristics of an independent variable (e.g., stress) are hypothesized to cause changes in the characteristics of a dependent variable (e.g., heart disease). Human participants are randomly assigned to treatments in experimental research.

Quasi-experimental research (e.g., Cook & Campbell, 1979) includes research designs that are similar to experimental research in terms of having treatments, outcome measures, and experimental units. Quasi-experimental research does not, however, use random assignment to treatment conditions, usually because doing so is not feasible (e.g., students in a school cannot be randomly assigned to a new reading program because of practical and ethical constraints).

Statistical analysis is the analysis of numeric data using descriptive and inferential techniques. **Descriptive statistical analysis** is the analysis of numeric data for the purpose of obtaining summary indicators that can efficiently describe a group and the relationships among the variables within that group.

Inferential statistical analysis may be defined generically as "that part of statistical procedures that deal with making inferences from samples to populations" (Wiersma & Jurs, 2005, p. 489). In Chapter 11, we define inferential statistics as the analysis of numeric data involving (1) the testing of the differences between group means or the relationship between variables or (2) the determination of whether or not these differences or relationships are truly different from zero. Inferential statistical analysis often involves an estimation of the degree (probability) of error in making those inferences.

Internal validity is defined by Shadish, Cook, and Campbell (2002) as "the validity of inferences about whether the relationship between two variables is causal" (p. 508). The internal validity of a hypothesized cause in an experiment is enhanced to the degree that plausible alternative explanations for the obtained results can be eliminated. The same logic holds for nonexperimental QUAN research.

External validity is defined by Shadish et al. (2002) as "the validity of inferences about whether the causal relationship holds over variations in persons, settings, treatment variables, and measurement variables" (p. 507). External validity may be defined more succinctly as the generalizability of the QUAN results to other persons, settings, or times. (These validity issues are discussed in more detail in Chapter 12.)

More Details Regarding the Qualitative Tradition

QUAL research has gained widespread acceptance in the past 20 to 30 years, as described by Denzin and Lincoln (1994):

Over the past two decades, a quiet method-ological revolution has been taking place in the social sciences. . . . the extent to which the "qualitative revolution" has over-taken the social sciences and related profes-sional fields has been nothing short of amazing. (p. ix)

The terms in this section are additional terms associated with the QUAL tradition and are dis-cussed in more detail throughout the text. Most of these terms are located in the second column of Table 2.1. Their presentation here highlights the differences between the QUAL and QUAN traditions presented in the previous section.

QUAL researchers typically employ **inductive logic or reasoning,**[3] which involves arguing from the particular (e.g., data) to the general (e.g., theory). **Grounded theory**, for example, is a methodology for theory development that is grounded in narrative data that are systemati-cally gathered and inductively analyzed (e.g., Strauss & Corbin, 1998). Patton (2002) noted these distinctions as follows:

Inductive analysis involves *discovering* pat-terns, themes, and categories in one's data, in contrast to *deductive analysis* where the data are analyzed according to an existing framework. (p. 453, italics in original)

QUAL research is often, but not always, exploratory in nature (Creswell, 2003). **Explor-atory research**[4] generates information about unknown aspects of a phenomenon. Although exploratory research fits well with the inductive nature of QUAL research, it is also common in QUAN research.

There are several traditions associated with QUAL research (e.g., Creswell, 1998; Patton, 2002), including grounded theory, critical theory, phenomenology, biography, and case study. Probably the tradition that is the most readily identified with QUAL research is ethnography, which originated in cultural anthropology and sociology during the late 1800s and early 1900s. **Ethnography** involves describing and interpreting human cultures using data collection techniques such as participant-observation, interviews, and artifact collection (e.g., Chambers, 2000; Fetterman, 1998; Hammersley & Atkinson, 1995; Tedlock, 2000; Wolcott, 1999). An ethnographic research design is a QUAL research design in which data are gathered through well-established techniques with the goal of gaining an in-depth understand-ing of a distinct culture.

It is beyond the scope of this chapter to review all of the traditions associated with QUAL research, but the critical theory and case study traditions are briefly introduced due to their popularity among QUAL researchers. **Critical theory** involves studying human phenomena through an ideological perspective (e.g., femi-nism) and seeking social justice for oppressed groups (e.g., Capper, 1998; Kincheloe & McLaren, 2005). This orientation is discussed in detail in Chapter 5 under the term *transformative perspective.*

Case study research (e.g., Stake, 1995, 2005; Yin, 2003) involves developing an in-depth analysis of a single case or of multiple cases. Case study research emerged from several fields, such as political science, evaluation research, business, law, and so forth. Data collection for case study research typically involves a variety of sources that may include QUAN data relevant to the case or cases. Many MM studies employ case studies as the QUAL component of the overall design.

Purposive sampling is typically associated with QUAL research and may be defined as selecting a relatively small number of units because they can provide particularly valuable information related to the research questions under examination. Chapter 8 provides more details on 15 specific types of purposive sampling techniques.

Almost all QUAL data analysis can be divided into two types: categorical strategies or contextu-alizing strategies. **Categorical strategies** break down narrative data into smaller units and then rearrange those units to produce categories that facilitate a better understanding of the research question. **Contextualizing (holistic) strategies** interpret narrative data in the context of a coher-ent whole "text" that includes interconnections among the narrative elements.

Researchers working in different QUAL traditions have a tendency to prefer either categorical or contextualizing strategies. For instance, researchers working in the grounded theory tradition often employ categorical strategies because the first phase of analysis in many grounded theory studies involves breaking down data into units and then developing emerging categories of meaning from those units.

Trustworthiness is a global term used by some QUALs as a substitute for QUAN validity issues. It was defined by Lincoln and Guba (1985) as the extent to which an inquirer can persuade audiences that the findings are "worth paying attention to"[5] (p. 300). **Credibility**, a QUAL analogue to internal validity, may be defined as whether or not a research report is "credible" to the participants whom the researchers studied. Credibility techniques include prolonged engagement, persistent observation, and triangulation. **Transferability**, a QUAL analogue to external validity, includes the transferability of inferences from a particular *sending* context (the research setting) to a particular *receiving* context (other similar settings). (Trustworthiness issues are discussed in Chapter 12, Table 12.2.)

More Details Regarding the Mixed Methods Tradition

This section contains additional terms associated with the MM tradition in the social and behavioral sciences. Most of these terms are located in the third column of Table 2.1. On some of the dimensions in Table 2.1, the column describing the MM tradition contains a combination of the techniques found in both the QUAL and QUAN traditions. For instance, the form of data used in MM studies can be both narrative (QUAL) and numeric (QUAN). Similarly, MM research can simultaneously address a range of both confirmatory and exploratory questions, a point that is discussed in a later section of this chapter entitled "The Utility of Mixed Methods Research."

MM research also uses both deductive and inductive logic in a distinctive sequence described as the inductive-deductive research cycle, the chain of reasoning (Krathwohl, 2004), the cycle of scientific methodology (Tashakkori & Teddlie, 1998), and the research wheel (Johnson & Christensen, 2004). This **inductive-deductive research cycle** may be seen as moving from grounded results (observations, facts) through inductive inference to general inferences, then from those general inferences (or theory, conceptual framework, model) through deductive inference to predictions to the particular (a priori hypotheses). Research on any given question at any point in time occurs somewhere within this cycle, which is displayed in Figure 2.2.

Figure 2.2 represents the complete cycle of scientific methodology and illustrates the MM response to the inductive-deductive dichotomy. It is clear that this cycle involves both inductive and deductive reasoning processes. It is also clear that induction could come first, or deduction could come first, depending on where one is in terms of studying the phenomenon of interest.[6]

Investigators working in the MM tradition have created typologies of distinct MM research designs, and we provide details of them in Chapter 7. We list two of the more well-known MM research designs in Table 2.1, parallel and sequential mixed designs, which are defined as follows:

1. In **parallel mixed designs** (also called concurrent or simultaneous designs), the QUAN and QUAL strands of the study occur in a parallel manner, either simultaneously (starting and ending at approximately the same time) or with some time lapse (i.e., data collection for one strand starts or ends later than the other). The QUAL and QUAN phases are planned and implemented to answer related aspects of the same basic research question(s).

2. In **sequential mixed designs**, the QUAN and QUAL strands of the study occur in chronological order. Questions or procedures (e.g., the sample or data collection techniques) of one strand emerge from or are dependent on the

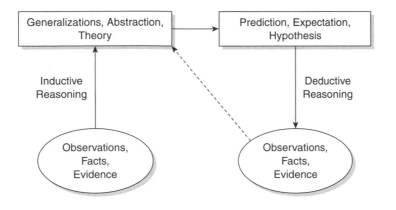

Figure 2.2   The Inductive-Deductive Research Cycle (cycle of scientific methodology)

previous strand. The research questions for the QUAL and QUAN phases are related to one another and may evolve as the study unfolds.

Sampling is an area where MM studies can employ both probability (primarily QUAN) and purposive (primarily QUAL) procedures, plus a number of other techniques unique to MM studies. These techniques are described in Chapter 8.

MM data analysis involves the integration of the statistical and thematic techniques described earlier in this chapter, plus a number of other unique strategies, such as triangulation and data conversion. **Triangulation** refers to the combinations and comparisons of multiple data sources, data collection and analysis procedures, research methods, investigators, and inferences that occur at the end of a study.[7] **Methodological triangulation** was discussed by Denzin (1978) and refers to "the use of multiple methods to study a single problem" (Patton, 2002, p. 247). This type of triangulation has been used to refer to the application of both QUAL and QUAN methods in an MM study. For instance, data obtained through survey (QUAN) and case study (QUAL) methods regarding the effect of a new reading curriculum could be triangulated to provide a more comprehensive understanding of that curriculum. Triangulation

techniques are used both in analyzing MM data and determining the quality of that data.

Data conversion (transformation) occurs when collected QUAN data are converted into narratives or when QUAL data are converted into numbers. **Quantitizing** data (e.g., Miles & Huberman, 1994) is the process of converting QUAL data into numbers that can be statistically analyzed. **Qualitizing** data (e.g., Tashakkori & Teddlie, 1998) refers to the process whereby QUAN data are transformed into narrative data that can be analyzed qualitatively.

Inference quality is a term that has been proposed to incorporate the terms *internal validity* and *trustworthiness* (Tashakkori & Teddlie, 2003c, 2008). **Inference quality** refers to the standard for evaluating the quality of conclusions that are made on the basis of both the QUAN and QUAL findings. Inference transferability is an umbrella term that has been proposed to incorporate the terms *external validity* (QUAN) and *transferability* (QUAL) (Tashakkori & Teddlie, 2003c; Teddlie & Tashakkori, 2006). **Inference transferability** is the degree to which the conclusions from an MM study may be applied to other settings, people, time periods, contexts, and so on. (Further details regarding inference quality and inference transferability are located in Chapter 12.)

The QUAL-MM-QUAN Continuum

Thus far, we have described the methodological communities in terms of their having three separate or distinct sets of characteristics. A more accurate and productive way of looking at the relationships among these communities is to imagine them as three overlapping circles with a two-pointed arrow running through them from the left (QUAL orientation) through the middle (MM orientation) to the right (QUAN orientation) or vice versa (right to left). Figure 2.3 illustrates this.

The left circle represents the "purist" (e.g., Rossman & Wilson, 1985; Smith, 1994) QUAL tradition with its constructivist roots, greater emphasis on exploratory research questions, emphasis on narrative data, inductive logic, ethnographic methods, variants of QUAL data analysis, and so forth. The right circle represents the "purist" QUAN tradition with its postpositivist roots, greater emphasis on confirmatory research questions, focus on numeric data, deductive logic, experimental methods, statistical analyses, and so forth. The middle circle represents the MM tradition, which is a combination of the other two traditions. The two-pointed arrow represents the *QUAL-MM-QUAN continuum*.

Newman, Ridenour, Newman, and DeMarco (2003) discussed a model similar to the QUAL-MM-QUAN continuum, which they called the *qualitative-quantitative interactive continuum*:

> Qualitative and quantitative research makes up a false dichotomy. . . . Debating their comparative worth is pointless because multiple research perspectives enable social science researchers to approach questions of interest within a wide variety of ways of knowing. There are many right ways to approach research, not only one right way. One's purpose provides a way to determine the optimal path to studying the research question. Along the continuum are entry points through which a researcher can locate himself or herself and the study. (pp. 169–170)

A research team's initial entry point onto the exploratory-confirmatory continuum is based on whether they are primarily interested in testing theory (confirmatory phase of a study), generating theory (exploratory phase of a study), or both (simultaneously testing and generating theory) *at that point in time*. Either of these scenarios may be employed by a QUAN-oriented or a

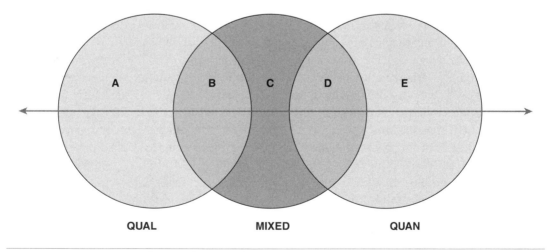

Figure 2.3 The QUAL-MM-QUAN Continuum

Note: Zone A consists of totally QUAL research, while Zone E consists of totally QUAN research. Zone B represents primarily QUAL research, with some QUAN components. Zone D represents primarily QUAN research, with some QUAL components. Zone C represents totally integrated MM research. The arrow represents the QUAL-MM-QUAN continuum. Movement toward the middle of the continuum indicates a greater integration of research methods and sampling. Movement away from the center (and toward either end) indicates that research methods are more separated or distinct.

QUAL-oriented researcher. They move across the continuum in the optimal way to further answer the initial and evolving research questions. MM research involves moving across the continuum seamlessly (and without impediment from the false dichotomies of the incompatibility thesis) to pursue answers to research questions.

We discuss the QUAL-MM-QUAN continuum in more detail in Chapter 5. Table 5.3 in that chapter applies that continuum to several methodological dimensions.

An Example of a Mixed Methods Study

Appendix A (www.sagepub.com/foundations) contains an example of an entire MM study. We present this example at this point in the text so that readers can see how the QUAN and QUAL components of an MM study were integrated at different points in the research study. Comprehending this integration process is necessary to truly understand MM research.

This study described in this article by Ivankova, Creswell, and Stick (2006) is a good example of MM because it illustrates how a particular MM design was implemented throughout a research study. We inserted more than 50 comments throughout Appendix A (www.sagepub.com/foundations), highlighting important aspects of the implementation of this study. The remainder of this section provides a brief overview of the article and the comments. The reader is encouraged to read the article in its entirety because it illustrates many of the issues related to the actual planning and conducting of an MM study.

The abstract of the study (Appendix A, pp. 1–2) provides a general explanation about the use of MM design in this research project. This abstract describes the type of MM design employed (i.e., sequential explanatory), explicitly states that both QUAL and QUAN data are collected and analyzed in the project, and notes that both types of data are integrated in the results section.

On page 2 of Appendix A (www.sagepub .com/foundations), the authors provide an explicit rationale for using MM designs in settings where neither QUAL nor QUAN methods "are sufficient, by themselves, to capture the trends and details of a situation." In other words, MM designs are required in situations where neither QUAN nor QUAL methods alone would be sufficient to answer the research questions.

The overall purpose of this illustrative research study is presented on page 5: to understand students' persistence in an academic program (i.e., a doctoral program in educational leadership). The QUAN component of the study was aimed at identifying factors that significantly predict students' persistence, whereas the QUAL component focused on explaining the processes whereby this occurred. The QUAN component of the research study occurred first, followed by the QUAL component.

The QUAN and QUAL research questions are summarized on pages 5 and 6 of Appendix A (www.sagepub.com/foundations). These research questions are complementary in nature, with the answers to the QUAN research questions leading to a more precise formulation of the QUAL research questions.

Details regarding the study's MM design are featured throughout the article because the authors are using this "illustrative" research study to demonstrate how a sequential MM design is conducted "from theory to practice" (Appendix A, p. 1, note article's title). We inserted several comments related to the design: It is defined on pages 2 and 4, problems in its implementation are noted on page 3, its advantages and limitations are presented on page 5, and so forth.

The sample for the QUAN component of the study (see Appendix A, p. 7) included more than 200 participants who had been enrolled in the academic program during a 10-year period. These individuals were further subdivided into four groups (or strata) based on their characteristics (beginning group, matriculated group, graduated group, withdrawn/inactive group). The sample for the QUAL component of the study (see Appendix A, pp. 9, 15–16) was a much smaller subsample of the QUAN sample: One "typical" participant was purposively selected from each of the groups in the QUAN sample for a total sample size of 4 individuals in the QUAL sample. Purposive sampling techniques used in this study included typical case sampling and maximum variation sampling. (Chapter 8 provides more details on these sampling techniques.)

The data source for the QUAN component was the 207 completed questionnaires. The core items on the questionnaire represented 10 composite variables, which are described in Appendix A (p. 6). These composite independent variables for the QUAN component of the survey were derived primarily from three theoretical models of student persistence. The data sources for the QUAL case studies were more diverse and complex, including seven distinct types of information (e.g., telephone interviews, researchers' notes, transcripts and academic files, photos, responses to open-ended items on questionnaires, information on selected online classes), which are described on page 9.

The QUAN data were analyzed using both descriptive and inferential statistics. The profile of the typical program participant, which was generated through information from frequency distributions and mean scores, is presented on page 8 of Appendix A (www.sagepub.com/foundations). Discriminant function analysis (i.e., a type of inferential statistic) was used to answer the QUAN research questions regarding which of the 10 independent variables were significantly related to students' persistence. As noted in the article, only 5 of the 10 independent variables significantly "contributed to the discriminating function as related to the participants' persistence" (p. 8).

The five factors that were statistically significant predictors in the QUAN analysis were then represented by five open-ended questions on the QUAL interview protocol, thereby producing a point of integration between the two components of the study, as described on pages 16–17 of the article. Four themes emerged from the subsequent QUAL analysis of the complex case study data (i.e., quality of academic experiences, online learning environment, support and assistance, student self-motivation), as described on page 10. Experiences in each of those four areas were important in explaining the students' decisions to continue in (or withdraw from) the program.

Concerns related to the quality of the QUAN data were addressed in this study through the determination of the reliability and validity of the questionnaire items (see Appendix A, pp. 6–7). Several techniques were used to establish the trustworthiness of the QUAL data, as enumerated on page 9: triangulation of different data sources, member checking, thick descriptions, confirming and disconfirming of evidence, and audits. The authors also briefly discussed the inference quality of the combined QUAN and QUAL data on page 21.

Methods for integrating the components of the study included the following: selecting the participants for the QUAL phase from those who had participated in the QUAN phase, developing the QUAL data collection protocols based on results from the QUAN statistical analyses, and integrating the QUAN and QUAL results in the discussion of outcomes. The reader can find more details on integration techniques used in this study in Appendix A (www.sagepub.com/foundations), pages 2, 13–15, and 21.

The following list includes other interesting facets of the study presented in Appendix A:

- An example of quantitizing data on page 10
- An example of qualitizing data on page 16
- Good examples of the use of visual models in MM research on pages 18 and 19, in Table 4 (p. 33), and in Figure 1 (p. 34)

Issues Related to Mixed Methods Terms and Definitions

The Need for a Distinct Mixed Methods Language

An interesting distinction exists between the QUAN and QUAL traditions with regard to the issue of common terms and definitions. Traditional QUAN definitions of basic constructs and designs have long been established in classic texts (e.g., Campbell & Stanley,1963; Cook & Campbell, 1979; Shadish et al., 2002) and in the annals of statistics and measurement journals. Though there is slow evolution in the QUAN methodological research field, no one expects large changes in the basic paradigm of postpositivism or the constructs and research designs associated with this worldview.

Common definitions of QUAL constructs and designs, on the other hand, have been slow to develop, with the occasional exception, such as Thomas Schwandt's (1997) excellent *Qualitative Inquiry: A Dictionary of Terms*, which we refer to throughout this text. Many of the leading figures in QUAL research do not believe that such codification of terms is either possible or even desirable.

A reasonable question for mixed methodologists at this point in time is, do we want a common nomenclature, with an established set of terms and definitions? We believe that most mixed methodologists would answer with a resounding "yes" because the lack of an overall system of terms and definitions has created confusion and imprecision in past MM writing and research.

Several authors have consistently defined some terms uniquely associated with MM, such as *data conversion,* with its two subprocesses *quantitizing* and *qualitizing.* These terms have been defined specifically enough to be applied consistently across a number of sources (e.g., Bazeley, 2003; Boyatzis, 1998; Johnson & Turner, 2003). For instance, Sandelowski (2003) described her use of quantitizing techniques in a study in which she transformed narrative interview data into numeric data that were then analyzed using Fisher's exact probability test (Sandelowski, Harris, & Holditch-Davis, 1991). In her qualitizing example, she discussed taking quantitatively derived clusters of numeric data and transforming those into distinct qualitatively described "profiles" using grounded theory.

Other terms with widely accepted meanings include the basic MM designs, such as *sequential designs, parallel designs,* and *conversion designs.* These designs and their characteristics are discussed in detail in Chapter 7.

On the other hand, as MM research has evolved, certain terms have been defined in an inconsistent manner. Past literature shows that the terms *multimethod design* and *mixed design* have been confused with one another. There seems to be a particular issue with the term *multimethod design,* which has been defined quite differently by different authors:

- The use of two QUAN methods (Campbell & Fiske [1959] employed the term *multi-trait-multimethod matrix* to connote the use of more than one QUAN method to measure a personality trait)
- The use of QUAL and QUAN methods as two distinctly separate parts of one research program (Morse, 2003)
- The use of both QUAN and QUAL methods or the use of two different types of either QUAL or QUAN methods (QUAL/QUAL or QUAN/QUAN) as described by Hunter and Brewer (2003)[8]

Throughout this text, we are more interested in the consistent use of the term *mixed methods* and the research designs associated with it. To further this definition, we proposed a typology of research designs that consistently incorporates both mixed and multimethod designs (Teddlie & Tashakkori, 2006). This typology is presented in Chapter 7.

Johnson, Onwuegbuzie, and Turner (2007) addressed the issue of the definition of MM research. They presented 19 different definitions of MM research from experts in the field, noting that there were both similarities and differences among them. Five common themes emerged from an analysis of the definitions, including *what* is mixed (QUAN and QUAL research), *when* the mixing is carried out, the *breadth of the mixing,* and *why* the mixing is carried out.

Based on this analysis, Burke Johnson and his colleagues (2007) presented the following rather broad definition of MM research:

Mixed methods research is the type of research in which a researcher or team of researchers combines elements of qualitative and quantitative research approaches (e.g., use of qualitative and quantitative viewpoints, data collection, analysis, inference techniques) for the purpose of breadth of understanding or corroboration. (p. 123)

The Choice of "Bilingual" or Common Terminology for MM Research

The major decisions that mixed methodologists have to make concerning terms and definitions is whether to:

- Use a bilingual nomenclature that employs both the QUAL and the QUAN terms for important methodological issues, such as validity or sampling
- Create a new language for mixed methodology that gives a common name for the existing sets of QUAL and QUAN terms
- Combine the first two options by presenting new MM terms that are integrated with well-known QUAL/QUAN terms

We believe that it is essential for social and behavioral scientists today to be methodologically bilingual: Scholars should have at least a minimum degree of fluency in both the QUAL and QUAN languages and be able to translate back and forth between the two. It is especially important that researchers be able to recognize, in both languages, terms that describe the same basic concepts, such as *external validity* and *transferability*.

We also believe that mixed methodologists should develop a new nomenclature that transcends the separate QUAL and QUAN terminologies under certain circumstances. Three conditions should be met before mixed methodologists develop new terms:

- The described QUAN and QUAL processes should be highly similar.
- The existing QUAL and QUAN terms must be overly used or misused.
- Appropriate alternative terminology must exist.

For instance, the term *validity* has more than 35 different meanings within the QUAL and QUAN traditions. When a term has so many different meanings, it becomes meaningless. This is a case where mixed methodologists can develop their own terminology to replace the confusion of the multiply defined QUAL and QUAN terms because the processes across the two orientations are very similar and there appears to be an appropriate alternative terminology. Chapter 12 presents an extended demonstration of how the terms *inference quality* and *inference transferability* can be used to encompass the currently used QUAN and QUAL terms.[9]

Another example from MM involves the overuse of the term *triangulation* in several disciplines, such as nursing. Sandelowski (2003) addressed this issue as follows:

> When any kind of research combination is designated as triangulation, there is no inquiry that is not triangulated. Having too much meaning, the word *triangulation* has no meaning at all. . . . Triangulation appears as a "near-talismanic method" (Miles & Huberman, 1994, p. 266) for democratizing inquiry and resolving conflicts between qualitative and quantitative inquiry. (p. 328, italics in original)

Triangulation is a veritable "magical" word in many disciplines using MM research, having been developed through a series of insightful works (e.g., Campbell & Fiske, 1959; Denzin, 1978; Jick, 1979; Patton, 2002). Triangulation is a word that most researchers, regardless of their own methodological orientation, associate with MM. We would not want to discard a word with "near-talismanic" meaning, so what do we do when it appears to be overused to the point where it means nothing? Can the term be rehabilitated, or does it carry too much baggage?

Earlier in this chapter, we defined *triangulation* as the combinations and comparisons of multiple data sources, data collection and analysis procedures, research methods, and inferences that occur at the end of a study. This definition was made quite broad to cover the most important aspects of research that have been associated with triangulation (both as a process and as an outcome). Data sources, data collection methods, and research methods have all been tied to triangulation techniques in seminal articles and chapters on the topic (e.g., Denzin, 1978; Patton, 2002). Creswell and Plano Clark (2007) use the triangulation design as one of their four major types of MM designs. Although we have broadened the definition *triangulation* to make it more consistent with the literature, it is unclear whether the term is still useful.

The Utility of Mixed Methods Research

The utility of MM concerns *why* we employ them in our research projects. With the plethora of research methods associated with the QUAL and QUAN traditions, why would we bother combining them, or generating new techniques, to conduct MM research?

The ultimate goal of any research project is to answer the questions set forth in the beginning of the study. There appear to be three areas where MM research is superior to the single approach designs:

- MM research can simultaneously address a range of confirmatory and exploratory questions with both the qualitative and the quantitative approaches.
- MM research provides better (stronger) inferences.
- MM research provides the opportunity for a greater assortment of divergent views.

Addressing Confirmatory and Exploratory Questions Simultaneously

One of the dimensions on which QUAN and QUAL research is said to vary is the type of

question answered by each approach. Some authors have suggested that QUAL research questions are exploratory (i.e., they are concerned with generating information about unknown aspects of a phenomenon), whereas QUAN research questions are confirmatory (i.e., they are aimed at testing theoretical propositions).

Others disagree with this dichotomization of research questions (e.g., Erzberger & Prein, 1997; Tashakkori & Teddlie, 1998, 2003a). For example, Punch (1998) provided this argument against the dichotomization:

> Quantitative research has typically been more directed at theory verification, while qualitative research has typically been more concerned with theory generation. While that correlation is historically valid, it is by no means perfect, and there is no necessary connection between purpose and approach. That is, quantitative research can be used for theory generation (as well as verification) and qualitative research can be used for theory verification (as well as generation). (pp. 16–17)

We agree with this statement regarding the generation and verification of theory. What happens when you want to do both in the same study? *A major advantage of mixed methods research is that it enables the researcher to simultaneously ask confirmatory and exploratory questions and therefore verify and generate theory in the same study.*

Many of the research projects that we supervise are doctoral dissertations where the student wants to accomplish two goals in the same study:

- Demonstrate that a particular variable will have a predicted effect on (or predicted relationship with) another variable
- Answer exploratory questions about how and why that predicted (or some other related) relationship actually happens

An example of this two-faceted questioning procedure is an educational research dissertation by Stevens (2001). In this study, Stevens wanted to examine and describe the changes in a set of middle schools that resulted from the introduction of an external change agent (Distinguished Educator) associated with a statewide school accountability program. It was hypothesized that teachers in schools with a Distinguished Educator would perform better on measures of teacher effectiveness than teachers in schools without a Distinguished Educator.

A QUAN quasi-experimental design confirmed this hypothesis: Teachers in schools with a Distinguished Educator had significantly higher rates of effective teaching than teachers in schools without a Distinguished Educator. Though this result was important, Stevens (2002) also wanted to know how this result occurred. Simultaneously with gathering the QUAN data, she conducted case studies in each of the schools using QUAL techniques such as observations, interviews, and document analysis. Results from the QUAL analyses indicated that the Distinguished Educators were perceived as having a positive influence on (1) teacher collaboration and sharing, (2) the expectations of both teachers and students for student learning, and (3) the quality of instruction. These Distinguished Educator activities were directly or indirectly related to the higher rates of effective teaching.

This MM study could not have been conducted exclusively within either the QUAN or the QUAL traditions. The mixed methods design allowed the doctoral student to simultaneously test a quantitatively derived hypothesis and explore in greater depth the processes whereby the relationship occurred.

The GAIN evaluation (Riccio, 1997; Riccio & Orenstein, 1996) is another example of an MM research study that answered confirmatory and exploratory questions simultaneously. GAIN, a welfare-to-work program created by the California legislature, provided welfare recipients with job search assistance, basic education, vocational training, and so on. GAIN's goals were to increase employment and reduce reliance on welfare. Three of the goals of the evaluation

(Rallis & Rossman, 2003) can be stated as either research hypotheses or questions:

1. What are GAIN's effects on employment and on the number of individuals on welfare? This can be restated as the following hypothesis: Individuals in the GAIN program will have higher employment rates and will be less likely to remain on welfare than individuals not in the GAIN program.

2. What can we learn about the California counties' experiences in implementing GAIN and the recipients' participation and experiences?

3. How did different program strategies influence the results?

The first evaluation question is confirmatory in nature: The evaluators (or at least their funding agency) expected GAIN to have a positive effect on employment and welfare-roll figures. This question was restated in the preceding list as a research hypothesis that was tested by statistical analysis of QUAN data generated by a large-scale experimental study, in which welfare recipients were randomly assigned to GAIN or a control group.

The second and third questions were exploratory in nature and were aimed at describing the counties' experiences in implementing GAIN, the recipients' experiences, and how various strategies influenced results. A variety of data sources were used to answer these questions: field research, case files data, surveys of both staff and program recipients, and so on. These exploratory questions were vital to the evaluation because without them the evaluators would not know how the program's effect occurred.

Providing Stronger Inferences

Several authors have postulated that using MM can offset the disadvantages that certain methods have by themselves (e.g., Brewer & Hunter, 1989; Creswell, Plano Clark, Gutmann, &

Hanson, 2003; Greene & Caracelli, 1997b). For example, Johnson and Turner (2003) referred to the *fundamental principle of mixed methods research:* "Methods should be mixed in a way that has complementary strengths and nonoverlapping weaknesses" (p. 299). Two of the functions of MM research described by Greene et al. (1989) concerned the strengthening of inferences: triangulation and complementarity.

A classic MM combination involves using in-depth interviews in conjunction with mailed questionnaires. One type of data gives greater depth, whereas the other gives greater breadth; together it is hoped that they yield results from which one can make better (more accurate) inferences.

Erzberger and Kelle (2003) presented a good example of a study (Krüger, 2001) whose inferences were stronger because they resulted from both QUAN and QUAL data. This occupational life study, conducted in West Germany, had two major data sources:

1. Standardized questionnaire data on the occupational life courses of a sample of men (birth cohort of 1930), including starting and end points of employment, starting and end points of periods of unemployment, illnesses, and so on

2. Open-ended interviews where the men discussed their interpretations and perceptions of their occupational and domestic lives

The researchers expected great stability in the occupational life courses of the cohort because the men had worked during West Germany's postwar period (i.e., the 1950s, 1960s). This "era of the economic miracle" was characterized by traditional orientations and norms, including gender-role patterns with regard to the tasks, obligations, and rights of men and women.

The QUAN data indicated that the great majority of the men in the cohort had been fully employed almost all of their lives, except for short periods of joblessness or sickness. There were few interruptions in their highly stable careers.

The QUAL data agreed with and extended the results from the analysis of the QUAN data. The in-depth interviews included questions about the men's interpretations of their work biographies, their perceptions of their role as a breadwinner, and their participation in household and family work. Paid labor had a high importance for the men in the study, who perceived it as their fair share of the total work effort for the family. They considered breadwinning as their central moral obligation and as fulfillment of their family work duties.

The consistency between the experiences of the respondents related to their occupational life course (quantitatively described through the standardized questionnaires) and their subjective interpretations of these experiences (qualitatively determined through their responses to the open-ended questions) made the inferences from the study much stronger. Having both sources of data also made the reporting of the results much more interesting.

Providing the Opportunity for a Greater Assortment of Divergent Views

What happens if the QUAN and the QUAL components lead to two totally different (or contradictory) conclusions? (See more details on this issue in Chapter 12.) According to Erzberger and Prein (1977), divergent findings are valuable in that they lead to a reexamination of the conceptual frameworks and the assumptions underlying each of the two components. Divergent findings may lead to three outcomes: (1) the possible transformation of data types (quantitizing, qualitizing), (2) inference quality audits (Tashakkori & Teddlie, 1998), and (3) the design of a new study or phase for further investigation (e.g., Rossman & Wilson, 1985).

Deacon, Bryman, and Fenton (1998) summarized the advantages of this reexamination:

Whatever short-term inconvenience this may cause, in many cases the reappraisal and re-analysis required can reap long term analytical rewards: alerting the researcher to the possibility that issues are more multifaceted than they may have initially supposed, and offering the opportunity to develop more convincing and robust explanations of the social processes being investigated. (p. 61)

The different inferences from MM research often reflect different voices and perspectives. Such diversity of opinion is welcome in MM research.

Trend's (1979) evaluation study, presented in detail in Chapter 1, is a good example of how MM research allows for the presentation of divergent viewpoints. The QUAN data in Trend's study initially indicated that the federal housing-subsidy program was working, but divergent information from the QUAL data indicated some serious implementation problems. The results were painstakingly reconciled by a two-evaluator team, who used a context-specific explanation to clarify the discrepant results.

The utility of the MM approach has been recognized in a wide variety of disciplines. For instance, seven separate chapters on MM research from different fields were contained in the *Handbook of Mixed Methods in Social and Behavioral Research* (Tashakkori & Teddlie, 2003a): psychology, sociology, education, evaluation research, management and organizational research, the health sciences, and nursing. Box 2.1 summarizes the advantages that MM research brought to evaluation research associated with school reform in Nicaragua from the point of view of the evaluators.

Summary

This chapter continued the introduction of the three distinct research communities in the social and behavioral sciences. The descriptions of these communities and of other concepts associated with MM resulted in the definition of some 60 basic terms in Chapters 1 and 2. While we make distinctions across these three traditions, we

Box 2.1
Utility of the Mixed Methods Approach in an Evaluation of School Reform

The Nicaraguan government in 1993 undertook a decentralization initiative in education by granting management/budgetary autonomy to certain schools. Major goals of the project were to successfully implement the reform and to enhance student learning. The evaluation was mixed in nature: QUAN methods were used to assess learning outcomes, and QUAL methods were used to assess whether or not the reforms actually took place in the schools.

Rawlings (2000, p. 95) concluded that the use of the MM approach demonstrated the utility of the approach in a number of ways. First, it increased evaluation capacity in the Ministry of Education due to the intuitive nature of the QUAL approach and the robustness and generalizability of the QUAN work. Second, the MM approach strengthened the inferences from the research results through triangulation of both QUAL and QUAN sources.

Third, the QUAL work provided the policy makers with a better understanding of the school contexts, which would have been more difficult to convey with QUAN data alone. Fourth, the research provided insight into the marginalization of teachers and the absence of certain expected outcomes of the reforms, particularly outcomes related to pedagogy. Finally, the MM data highlighted how context affects reform implementation, especially in poor schools with splintered social psychological environments.

also argue that "real" research in the social and behavioral sciences occurs at some point on the QUAL-MM-QUAN continuum. This continuum is discussed throughout the text and serves as a foundation for understanding MM research.

A section in Chapter 2 analyzed the MM study in Appendix A (www.sagepub.com/foundations), focusing on the employed MM research design and the integration of QUAL and QUAN components throughout the study. Comments were made in the article, reinforcing the description in the text and providing further detail. After reading this chapter, students are expected to be able to identify the QUAL, QUAN, and MM components of published articles and to discuss how integration across the methods occurs.

We discussed issues related to MM terms and definitions, including the criteria for creating new terms to replace the traditional ones. Some of these new MM terms were introduced. We also discussed the utility of MM research, including three basic reasons why one might use MM rather than one of the traditional approaches.

Chapter 3 is the first of two chapters devoted to the history and philosophy of the social and behavioral sciences. *Philosophy* in this context is defined as the conceptual roots that underlie the quest for knowledge within the human sciences. A basic understanding of that philosophy (and history) is required to understand the emergence of MM over the past two decades. Chapter 3 covers events and issues before the 20th century; Chapter 4 focuses on the 20th century and beyond. Some readers may wish to skip one or both of these chapters, and directions for doing so are presented in the first part of Chapter 3.

Review Questions and Exercises

1. Define paradigm, methodology, and methods. Give an example of each.

2. Distinguish the QUAL, MM, and QUAN positions on the purpose of research.

3. Distinguish the QUAL, MM, and QUAN positions on the role of theory and the use of different types of logic.

4. What is the QUAL-MM-QUAN continuum? Describe the overlapping methodological circles. Explain the continuum in terms of the inductive-deductive dimension or inductive-deductive research cycle.

5. Under what circumstances might it be better to define a new MM term rather than employ already existing "bilingual" terms from the QUAL and QUAN research traditions?

6. What should mixed methodologists do if their QUAL and QUAN results diverge or lead to different interpretations of the phenomenon under study?

7. Describe six key differences among the three communities of social and behavioral scientists.

8. Describe a hypothetical research study that requires MM. Describe how you would integrate the collection of QUAN and QUAL data in that study.

9. Reexamine the MM research study in Appendix A located at www.sagepub.com/foundations (Ivankova et al., 2006). In your own words, answer the following questions:

   a. What was the overall purpose of this study?
   b. What are the quantitative research questions?
   c. What are the qualitative research questions?
   d. How are the quantitative and qualitative questions linked?
   e. What is the sample for the quantitative component of the study? How was it selected?
   f. What is the sample for the qualitative component of the study? How was it selected?
   g. What is the quantitative data source?
   h. What are the qualitative data sources?
   i. Summarize the quantitative analyses and how they addressed the quantitative research questions.

j. Summarize the qualitative analyses and how they addressed the qualitative research questions.

k. How were concerns about the quality of the quantitative data addressed?

l. How were concerns about the quality of the qualitative data addressed?

m. What methods were used to integrate the qualitative and quantitative components of the study?

n. This study has an example of quantitizing data. Describe it.

o. This study has an example of qualitizing data. Describe it.

Key Terms

Case study research

Categorical strategies

Conceptual framework

Confirmatory research

Contextualizing (holistic) strategies

Correlational research

Credibility

Critical theory

Data conversion (transformation)

Deductive logic or reasoning

Dependent variable

Descriptive research

Descriptive statistical analysis

Ethnography

Experimental research

Exploratory research

External validity

Grounded theory

Hypothetico-deductive model (H-DM)

Independent variable

Inductive-deductive research cycle

Inductive logic or reasoning

Inference quality

Inference transferability

Inferential statistical analysis

Internal validity

Methodological triangulation

Methodology (research)

Methods (research)

Parallel mixed designs

Probability sampling

Purposive sampling

Qualitizing

Quantitizing

Quasi-experimental research

Sequential mixed designs

Survey research

Theory

Transferability

Triangulation

Trustworthiness

Notes

1. Researchers working in the QUAN tradition tend to hold similar positions with regard to the Table 2.1 dimensions, whereas there are several viewpoints among QUAL researchers. For instance, under the role of theory many QUAN researchers adhere to some a priori theory (conceptual framework) that leads to

hypotheses or predictions. On the other hand, there are at least four different positions that QUAL researchers take toward theory (Creswell, 2003). (See Chapter 6 for more details.)

2. A **conceptual framework** (Tashakkori & Teddlie, 2003a) is a "consistent and comprehensive theoretical framework emerging from an inductive integration of previous literature, theories, and other pertinent information. A conceptual framework is usually the basis for reframing the research questions and for formulating hypotheses or making informal tentative predictions" (p. 704).

3. See Table 3.1 in Chapter 3 for a more detailed distinction between inductive and deductive logic/ reasoning.

4. We recognize that QUAL research can also be used in confirmatory studies. For example, Yin (2003) discussed several case studies that explored causal relations, such as Allison and Zelikow's (1999) *Essence of Decision: Explaining the Cuban Missile Crisis.*

5. Guba and Lincoln (1989) later proposed other criteria for assessing the quality of QUAL research, such as fairness, ontological authenticity, educative authenticity, catalytic authenticity, and tactical authenticity.

6. As mixed methodologists, we believe that the *inductive-deductive research cycle* depicted in Figure 2.2 is a closer depiction of what social scientists do in the course of their research than the *hypothetico-deductive model* described in Box 4.1.

7. Denzin (1978) delineated the terms *data triangulation, theory triangulation, investigator triangulation,* and *methodological triangulation,* which are defined in Chapter 4.

8. Brewer and Hunter (2006) recently presented a thorough examination of what they called multimethod research, which is distinct from mixed methods research as used in this text and other standard references. Bergman (2007), in a review of the Brewer and Hunter (2006) text, concluded that the "book fails to address contemporary issues in qualitative and mixed methods research. It is not a book about mixing methods" (p. 102).

9. Bryman (2006b) discussed a process whereby researchers "devise new criteria specifically for mixed-methods research" (p. 122). He called these new terms *bespoken criteria,* a term which describes the process whereby *inference quality* and *inference transferability* were derived.

CHAPTER 3

Methodological Thought Before the 20th Century

Charles Teddlie and R. Burke Johnson

Objectives

Upon finishing this chapter, you should be able to:

- Discuss Stages 1–4 in the history and philosophy of the human sciences
- Compare and contrast inductive and deductive research logics

- Delineate relativism and absolutism and trace their historical tension
- Delineate idealism and materialism and trace their historical tension
- Explain why distinctions such as induction/deduction, relativism/absolutism, and idealism/materialism hold historical importance in the human sciences
- Describe the inductive-deductive research cycle
- Compare and contrast the Sophists', Plato's, Herodotus's, and Aristotle's philosophical orientations
- Discuss the contributions of Bacon, Descartes, Galileo, and Newton to the scientific revolution and the philosophy of science
- Explain Hume's and Mill's methods for establishing causality
- Distinguish between rationalism and empiricism in the human sciences

The Three Methodological Communities and the Inductive-Deductive Research Cycle

The three communities of scientists described in Chapters 1 and 2 did not spontaneously appear over the past two centuries as the social and behavioral sciences[1] emerged. All three groups have historical origins stretching back centuries.

The purpose of this chapter and Chapter 4 is to describe the evolution of research methods in the social and behavioral sciences, thereby situating mixed methods (MM) within that context. Chapter 3 describes the history and philosophy before the 20th century; Chapter 4 does the same for the 20th century and beyond.

The material in this chapter is necessarily brief, serving only as an introduction to several complex issues. Some readers may prefer to skip both Chapters 3 and 4 and move on to contemporary paradigm considerations described in Chapter 5.[2] Other readers may prefer to skip Chapter 3 but then read Chapter 4 because it

discusses events of more recent significance. Although Chapters 3 and 4 provide background for the paradigm issues discussed in Chapter 5, it is not necessary to read these chapters to understand Chapter 5. We recommend that readers skipping Chapter 3 or 4 examine the key terms for both chapters in the glossary.

The following history focuses on several major points of comparison among the three groups of researchers. In Chapter 2, we introduced what we labeled the *inductive-deductive research cycle*. In this chapter, we introduce additional tensions between the quantitative (QUAN) and qualitative (QUAL) viewpoints that are relevant to the research cycle. A change in philosophical and methodological emphasis within a field of study (e.g., from one part of the inductive-deductive research cycle shown in Figure 2.2 to another) can result in what Kuhn (1962, 1970, 1996) called a *paradigm shift*.

We provide, in Table 3.1, definitions of several pairs of related concepts that have emerged in the history of thought, with many originating in ancient Greece. We elaborate on these concepts in this text, but, for now, take a moment and read the definitions, which are important in understanding many of the issues presented in Chapters 3–5.

Now, we briefly characterize the general orientations of the three methodological communities on several conceptual dimensions:

1. QUANs—Professors Experimentalista and Numerico (Boxes 1.1 and 1.2 in Chapter 1) emphasize *deductive logic* in their research; that is, their formal research starts from a general theory or conceptual framework and may involve hypotheses from which their observable consequences are deduced (i.e., which must logically be observed if the hypotheses are true). After deducing what, logically, must be seen in the world *if the hypotheses are true*, our QUAN researchers gather empirical data and test their hypotheses. Professor Numerico is not always as strict as Professor Experimentalista about having formal hypotheses. He is, instead, interested in finding

Table 3.1   Philosophical Concept Pairs That Are Especially Useful for Characterizing Differences Among Quantitative, Qualitative, and Mixed Methods Research Communities (Johnson, 2008)

Materialism Versus Idealism

Materialism is the doctrine, held by many natural scientists, that the world and reality is most essentially and fundamentally composed of matter. The competing doctrine, which is called **idealism**, holds that ideas and "the mental" (including the social and cultural) are most fundamentally real.

Empiricism Versus Rationalism

Empiricism is the doctrine that knowledge comes from experience. The competing doctrine is **rationalism** according to which knowledge is viewed as coming from reasoning and thought.

Deduction Versus Induction

According to one longstanding viewpoint, *deduction* refers to reasoning from "the general to the particular," and *induction* refers to reasoning from "the particular to the general." According to many current writers in philosophy, these terms are defined as follows: *Deductive reasoning* is the process of drawing a conclusion that is necessarily true if the premises are true, and *inductive reasoning* is the process of drawing a conclusion that is probably true.

Absolutism Versus Relativism

Absolutism is the doctrine that there are many natural laws and unchanging truths concerning the world. The competing doctrine, called **relativism**, rejects making broad generalizations and holds that true or warranted knowledge can vary by person or group, place, and time.

Nomothetic Versus Ideographic

Nomothetic methods are concerned with identifying laws and that which is predictable and general. In contrast, **ideographic methods** are concerned with individual, specific, particular, and oftentimes unique facts. The natural sciences are nomothetic (although they might study single cases in search of general laws), and the humanities tend to be more ideographic in approach and focus.

Naturalism Versus Humanism

Naturalism is the doctrine that the focus of science should be on the natural/material world and that researchers should search for physical causes of phenomena. **Humanism** is the doctrine that researchers should focus on the more human characteristics of people, including free will and autonomy, creativity, emotionality, rationality, morality, love for beauty, and uniqueness.

---

relationships among variables and predicting future behaviors (e.g., using statistical models to predict risky sexual behaviors). Both professors' research logic is predominantly *deductive*, arguing from the general (theory, conceptual framework, hypotheses) to the particular (data points). We trace the development of the *hypothetico-deductive model* throughout Chapters 3 and 4.[3] Using the concepts from Table 3.1, the QUAN researcher prefers the positions of materialism, empiricism, rationalism (in the form of logic/mathematics), deduction, absolutism, nomothetic methods, and the doctrine of naturalism.

2. QUALs—Professor Holistico (Box 1.3) emphasizes *inductive research logic* in his research; that is, his research starts with data that he has collected, from which he then generates theory. The research logic is inductive, placing an emphasis on particular/local data as well as arguing from the particular (data points) to the general (theory). We discuss inductive logic throughout Chapters 3 and 4, beginning with Aristotle's contributions.

LeCompte and Preissle (1993) differentiated between QUALs and QUANs as follows:

> The inductive-deductive dimension refers to the place of theory in a research study. . . . Purely deductive research begins with a theoretical system, develops operational definitions of the propositions and concepts of the theory, and matches them empirically to some body of data. . . . deductive researchers hope to find data to match a theory; inductive researchers hope to find a theory that matches their data. Purely inductive research begins with collection of data—empirical observations or measurements of some kind—and builds theoretical categories and propositions from relationships discovered among the data. (p. 42)

Using the concepts from Table 3.1, the QUAL researcher prefers the positions of idealism, empiricism, rationalism (in the form of construction of knowledge), induction, relativism, ideographic methods, and the doctrine of humanism.

3. MM researchers—Professor Eclectica (Box 1.4) explicitly uses both inductive and deductive logic, depending on the phase of the research cycle in which she is working. In the Chapter 1 example, she used deductive reasoning to predict that participants experiencing interventions will lose more weight than will participants in the control group. She then used inductive reasoning to piece together all of the QUAL information regarding why the interventions succeeded. The MM researcher has respect for all of the positions shown in Table 3.1, often in a balanced manner (where soft versions of both positions are used)[4] or in a dialectical manner (where the strong versions of the position are used alternately to inform researchers' thinking).

Why Study the History and Philosophy of the Social and Behavioral Sciences?

A basic understanding of the history and philosophy of the human sciences is necessary to understand the significance of the emergence of MM over the past two decades. The *philosophy of the social and behavioral sciences* is defined here as the conceptual and philosophical roots and presuppositions that underlie the quest for knowledge within the human sciences (e.g., Hollis, 2002; Ponterotto, 2005).

If you use MM in your research, you may encounter criticism from QUALs or QUANs (or both), who are certain of the correctness of their respective positions. It is valuable to have a basic understanding of how methodological viewpoints evolved, so you can justify using MM.

To provide this background, we must go back to antiquity, where the distinction between inductive and deductive reasoning and many other important conceptual distinctions originated. Other authors have also presented insightful historical analyses concerning the evolution of the research traditions in the social and behavioral sciences (e.g., Denzin & Lincoln, 2005b; Johnson, Onwuegbuzie, & Turner, 2007; Lincoln & Guba, 1985; Onwuegbuzie & Leech, 2005; Vidich & Lyman, 2000).

In Chapter 3, we describe four stages in the evolution of research methods and methodological communities in the human sciences before the 20th century:

1. Antiquity, starting with the Greek philosophers

2. The Middle Ages, starting with the fall of the Western Roman Empire and ending in the 15th century

3. The scientific revolution and the Enlightenment during the 16th, 17th, and 18th centuries

4. The 19th century, with a focus on the emergence of the social and behavioral sciences

We describe four other stages (Stages 5–8) from the 20th century and beyond in Chapter 4.

Two general points regarding this historical analysis are important. First, this is a history emphasizing the growth of scientific ideas and developments in Western civilization. Second, the overall review in Chapters 3 and 4 is especially concerned with what has happened since 1900. Nevertheless, it is important to describe the first 20–25 centuries of science in Western civilization because the major issues, concepts, and debates arose during this time. It is important to remember that researchers "stand on the shoulders of those who came before" them, and they should carefully listen to others before making syntheses and claiming that an idea is fully their own.[5]

Table 3.2 serves as an advance organizer for Chapters 3 and 4, indicating that one or the other type of reasoning has dominated during most epochs. The following narrative also demonstrates that, since antiquity, philosophers/scientists

have been combining inductive and deductive reasoning.

We developed our historical sketch from a number of sources. We describe one of those sources, an essay by Sergey Belozerov (2002) titled "Inductive and Deductive Methods in Cognition," in Box 3.1.

Stage 1: Antiquity

Observation is, of course, the oldest methodological technique in the human sciences. Early Greek philosophers employed observational techniques more than 25 centuries ago, and many other ancient peoples (e.g., Babylonians, Egyptians, Hebrews, Persians) predated the Greeks' use of

Table 3.2   Changes in Deductive/Inductive Orientation Over Time, Focusing on Dominant Disciplines or Disciplines of Interest in This Analysis ·

Time Period	Dominant Disciplines or Disciplines of Interest in This Analysis; Events	Dominant Deductive/Inductive Orientation
Stage 1: Antiquity (Greek states, Roman Empire)	Philosophy; early sciences	Exclusively deductive at first (Aristotle's prior analytics), followed by the introduction of the inductive orientation (Aristotle's posterior analytics)
Stage 2: Middle Ages	Medieval philosophy (church dominated); decline in sciences	Deductive (Scholasticism)
Stage 3: 16th through 18th centuries	Emergence of modern physical and biological sciences	Increasingly inductive, with empiricism in ascendance; some rationalism (deductive orientation)
Stage 4: 19th century	Focus on early social and behavioral sciences	Primarily inductive, with positivism (empiricism) dominating; idealism emerges in social sciences; hypothetico-deductive model foreshadowed
Stages 5–8: 20th century and beyond	Social and behavioral sciences	Primarily inductive with variants of positivism dominating first half of century; refined hypothetico-deductive model introduced; challenge of constructivism (inductive); second half and beyond a combination of deductive, inductive, and mixed orientations

Box 3.1

Sergey Belozerov's "Inductive and Deductive Methods in Cognition"

Sergey Belozerov (2002) made a similar analysis to that in Table 3.2, comparing seven historical eras in the physical and biological sciences based on trends in the use of inductive and deductive logics.

Belozerov's analysis of eras in the "hard" sciences included antiquity (inductive methods prevalent), the Dark Ages (dominance of scholastic-deductive methods), the Renaissance (prevalence of inductive methods), the 18th century (dominance of inductive methods), the 19th century (balance between methods), the first half of the 20th century (dominance of deductive methods), and the second half of the 20th century (severe dominance of deductive methods). Interestingly, he described the hard sciences in the second half of the 20th century as suffering from a serious imbalance with deductive logic dominating inductive logic.

Our analysis of the "human sciences," found in Table 3.2, concludes that there was a mixture of inductive and deductive logic operating at the end of the 20th century and the beginning of the 21st century.

these techniques. It is with the Greeks, however, that we start our description of the evolution of the methodological communities.

This first lengthy time period extends from around the 5th century B.C.E to the fall of the Western Roman Empire in the late 5th century C.E.[6] The physical and biological sciences (physics, astronomy, chemistry, earth sciences, biology) as well as history and early forms of political science and psychology trace their origins to antiquity.[7]

A renowned trio of Greek philosophers included Socrates, who was the mentor of Plato, who was the mentor of Aristotle. Socrates (470–399 B.C.E) is known for the Socratic method, which consisted of asking a series of focused questions aimed at demonstrating to responders that they were not in possession of the essential "Truth" or the requirements for true knowledge. To varying degrees, these three philosophers claimed that people can discover Truth through careful a priori reasoning and thought but that the vast majority of individuals (including Socrates) had not reached this level of understanding. The Socratic approach to knowledge added a critical and reflective component to

thinking that remains an important part of Western civilization.

Plato (429–347 B.C.E.) established "The Academy" to continue and further develop Socrates' ideas. Still today, the word "Academy" refers to a place of academic and intellectual activity, and his Academy can be viewed as the first university. Plato was a proto-rationalist and a proto-idealist.[8]

Plato posited that true knowledge is of only the ideal *forms*, which are perfect, unchanging, and eternal. These forms contrast with beliefs based on the *physical world* of material particulars, which are changeable, fluctuating, temporary, and, therefore, misleading. Plato was a proto-idealist because he considered the forms to be the most real entities. He believed that the forms are the source of true knowledge. Plato was also a proto-rationalist due to his emphasis on contemplation and rational thought as the route to Truth. An example of this approach is based on triangles. There are many imperfect manifestations of triangles, but one can come upon a true understanding of an ideal and perfect triangle through a priori reasoning (i.e., reasoning to knowledge based on thought instead of observation). Plato believed that understanding the idea of the form of a triangle provides greater insight into what a triangle is than do the details about any particular triangle. Truth was in the forms, not in the observed particulars.

Plato can be viewed as a strong advocate for deductive methods and the certainty he believed they could provide. Plato emphasized the existence and importance of unchanging, absolute truth, and he disdained inductive or other experiential methods that he saw as providing the basis for mere belief rather than fact. Plato's quest for Truth continues to be the guiding goal of some present-day QUAN researchers who search for universal laws, especially in the highly mathematical physical sciences. Plato argued for certain Truth (i.e., knowledge rather than belief) not just in the domains examined by mathematics and physical sciences but also in more human domains that today academicians call ethics, political science, and education. For example, Plato suggested (in the dialogues) the possibility of Truth regarding value-laden social concepts, such as justice, virtue, and the best form of government.

A counterargument for Plato's claim of certain Truth is located in the work of the Sophists, especially Protagoras of Abdera (490–420 B.C.E.). Protagoras famously claimed "man is the measure of all things," which concisely expressed his argument for relativism. Protagoras's well-known statement also foreshadows a measurement claim often made in contemporary QUAL research: "The researcher is the instrument of data collection." For Protagoras, universal truth and knowledge do not exist; they depend on the person and vary in relation to place and time. Protagoras shifted the debate about truth and knowledge from logic and science to the social and psychological worlds of people.

Protagoras believed that some arguments and positions are better than others. Protagoras's skepticism concerned singular, essential, and universal truth. He emphasized debate and oratory, stressed the importance of convention, and

acknowledged the importance of cultural differences. Because of this, Protagoras was an early humanist. In short, Protagoras searched for his answers in the human world of experiences, and he is an example of a proto-QUAL researcher because of his emphasis on relativism and humanism.

Another important early humanist is the "father of history," Herodotus (484–425 B.C.E.). His famous history of the Greco-Persian wars blended facts and interpretation, making use of oral history and storytelling. He also included the study of groups and individuals, as well as personal and cultural contexts. He used a combination of these methods to construct the meaning of events for humanity. Rather than using natural-science methods, Herodotus studied people and events from a more subjective and cultural-historical perspective. To this day, history tends to rely more on humanistic and ideographic approaches than on traditional scientific approaches (e.g., Johnson & Christensen, 2008). Ideographic approaches focus more on understanding particular events, people, and groups, in contrast to nomothetic approaches, which focus on documenting scientific or causal laws.

The next philosopher of interest, Aristotle (384–322 B.C.E.), had wide-ranging interests, including metaphysics, psychology, ethics, politics, logic, mathematics, biology, and physics. In contrast to Plato, Aristotle was interested in observing, describing, and explaining entities in the physical world in which people and other things exist. Because of his interest in the knowledge obtained through the senses or experience, Aristotle can be viewed as a proto-empiricist.[9]

One of Aristotle's greatest accomplishments was in biology, where he used inductive logic by observing and making general classifications of genera and species, some of which still stand today. Unlike Plato, Aristotle placed some faith in *endoxa* ("reputable opinions") held by many or most people in a community (especially the older, wiser members). Aristotle liked this sort of opinion because it likely had survived the "tests" of multiple arguments and time.

Unlike Plato, for Aristotle the forms and matter are not separate but exist together in the same objects. The forms also are seen in the second of Aristotle's four explanatory causes of change: material, formal, efficient, and final. Examples of Aristotle's four causes are located in Box 3.2. Although modern sciences generally consider efficient causes to be the proper subject of investigation because this type of cause is closely related to the idea of force and activity (i.e., if you do A, then B results), the other causes are still viewed as important by some scientists. For example, structuralists/functionalists in sociology and in cognitive science use the idea of final or teleological cause, and cognitive scientists sometimes refer to what might be viewed as material causes.

Aristotle and the other scientists of antiquity used the method of passive observation, which involves detailed scrutiny of objects but little direct experimentation. Their data consisted of QUAL descriptions of the similarities and differences among fish species, for example. Even though the Greeks did not have many tools for scientific measurement, Aristotle also made QUAN assertions such as the following: Heavier objects fall faster than lighter ones, with the speed being proportional to their weight. Although Galileo proved him wrong some 19 centuries later, Aristotle's curiosity about a law of acceleration of falling objects and his attempt to quantify it demonstrates his interest in QUAN research and measurement.

Aristotle articulated two philosophies: one that uses pure deductive reasoning aimed at understanding the "innate forms" (described in *Prior Analytics*) and one that involves detailed empirical investigations of nature employing inductive reasoning (described in *Posterior Analytics*). He thus laid the groundwork for scientific thought, which relies on both inductive and deductive methods. Although Aristotle is more often remembered for his deductive or syllogistic reasoning, perhaps his definition of inductive reasoning and his use of observation and classification were greater contributions. According to Aristotle, inductive reasoning involves observing as many examples of a phenomenon as possible and then looking for the general underlying principles that explain that phenomenon.[10]

In some ways, Aristotle might be viewed as a proto-mixed methodologist. First, he articulated the importance of a combination of inductive and deductive approaches to knowledge. Second, he noted that probabilistic (i.e., inductive) reasoning is perhaps the best we can do when studying human thinking and action (i.e., psychology).

Box 3.2
An Example of Aristotle's Four Causes

An automobile may serve as an example of Aristotle's causes. The *material cause* of an automobile is the metal, plastic, and other materials used to construct it. The *formal cause* is the mental image or blueprint held in the minds of the automobile company's engineers as the automobile is constructed. The *efficient cause* is the agent: who or what actually constructed the automobile together with their tools. In this case, that would be the automobile company and its employees. The *final cause* (the "that for the sake of which") is the function or purpose for the automobile that led to its construction. In this case, the final cause is to provide locomotion across roads (e.g., Dancy, 2001). Much of current science focuses on the efficient cause because of interest in learning how to bring about change in the world.

Third, he emphasized the importance of balancing extreme ideas in his principle of the golden mean.

Stage 2: The Middle Ages

The Middle Ages extended from the fall of the Western Roman Empire in the 5th century until the end of the 15th century. We discuss this lengthy era in only a few paragraphs because there was a marked deemphasis on scientific knowledge in Western civilization during this time.[11]

There are a number of reasons for this decline, but the one most relevant to our analysis is the ascendance of Church orthodoxy[12] in education and authority. The Church essentially became the state religion and source of stability during this time of the emergence of Western Christendom. Religious authorities, such as priests and monks, were among the individuals most often educated during the Middle Ages.

During this time, there was a movement away from the inductive generation of knowledge toward a model in which knowledge was deduced from scriptures and writings of particular ancient philosophers, such as Plato and Aristotle; however, the Church selectively used their writings. Some "scientific" ideas continued from Aristotle and others who put the Earth at the center of the universe. The Church sanctioned this belief and claimed it must be true because of the biblical account of the day when the Sun and Moon stood still (Josh. 10:12–13).

Scholasticism, the philosophical system dominant in Western thought during the Middle Ages, was based on the authority of the Church and selected philosophical writings (e.g., Aristotle's works on natural philosophy and syllogistic logic). Scholasticism was the leading philosophy of the great universities of the Middle Ages (e.g., Bologna, Cambridge, Oxford, Paris). The Middle Ages is summarized well by the idea of "the great chain of being," according to which everything has its natural place in a divinely planned universe. At the top of the great hierarchical chain is God and at the bottom is matter, such as earth and rocks (Lovejoy, 1936/1976).

Advances did occur in science and philosophy during the Middle Ages. Roger Bacon (1214–1294) advocated the teaching of science in universities, documented past scientific advances, and advocated for the use of experiments. In philosophy, a debate took place concerning the existence of universals. On one side of the debate, the realists claimed that universals exist prior to and independent of particular objects (e.g., conceptual abstractions, such as "house," are real); the other side, the nominalists, claimed that reality only exists in particulars. Peter Abelard (1079–1142) took a moderate or mixed position (the conceptualist position), claiming that universals exist in the mind and that particulars exist in particular objects in the world. Abelard's method was similar to some contemporary mixed methodologists' attempts to find logical and workable solutions to seemingly intractable issues.

Stage 3: The Scientific Revolution and Its Aftermath

The third stage encompasses much of the 16th–18th centuries. The scientific "revolution" and several philosophical/intellectual reactions to it (e.g., empiricism, rationalism, materialism, idealism) occurred during this time. Events during this period influenced how the human sciences emerged in Stage 4.

The Scientific Revolution

The scientific revolution occurred in Europe from roughly 1500–1700. The scientific revolution brought about a paradigm shift (Kuhn, 1962, 1970, 1996). It overthrew the medieval worldview (the great chain of being), the philosophy of Scholasticism, and earlier conceptions of science. New scientific formulations came in the works of Copernicus, Descartes, Galileo, Bacon, Kepler, Newton, and others. Empiricist philosophers, such as Locke and Hume, and rationalist philosophers, such as Descartes and Leibnitz, founded early modern philosophy as they attempted to provide a philosophical foundation for scientific knowledge. Although we now separate philosophy and science, scientists during this period were called natural philosophers. It would not be until the first half of the 19th century when William Whewell would coin the English word *scientist* that is used today.

Francis Bacon (1561–1626) was among the first to argue against Scholasticism and deductivism. Bacon advocated an inductive method, which posited that the foundation of knowledge comes through experience rather than through a priori thought or deductive reasoning. In his methods book, Bacon outlined his inductive, observational, experimental approach to science. Bacon named his book *The New Organon* to emphasize that his thinking had moved beyond the collection of Aristotle's works, titled *The Organon*. The Greek word *organon* meant "instrument or tool." Bacon emphasized a shift from the old instrument of logic (especially deductive or syllogistic logic), as seen in much of Aristotle's work (and in Scholasticism), to the new instruments of experience and data that are systematically obtained through observation and experimentation.

According to Bacon's method, researchers were to follow certain prescribed steps while removing themselves (i.e., their values, biases) from the research process. Bacon emphasized the *empirical method* as the way to gain knowledge. Scientists should steadfastly follow the method of induction, which would result in the progressive accumulation of knowledge.

To keep researchers' personal beliefs out of the process, Bacon explained that they must avoid the following actions:

- *Idols of the tribe*, which were errors inherent in the human mind and ways of perception
- *Idols of the cave*, which resulted from researchers' unique or particular idiosyncratic biases resulting from their backgrounds
- *Idols of the marketplace*, which resulted from ambiguities and equivocation in language use

- *Idols of the theatre*, which resulted from prior theories and philosophies taught to researchers by authorities

Bacon was a proto-empiricist. Schwandt (1997) defined contemporary **empiricism** as follows:

> . . . the name for a family of theories of epistemology that generally accept the premise that knowledge begins with sense experience. . . . A strict empiricist account of knowledge (or strict empiricism) in the social sciences holds that claims about social reality or human action are verifiable with reference to brute data. A brute datum is a piece of evidence expressed as an observation statement that is free of any taint of subjective interpretations. (p. 37)

In sum, Bacon's new inductive science relied on active observational strategies, including experiments and personal experiences, and it deemphasized rationalism and metaphysics. Starting with Bacon, Aristotle's efficient cause (who or what produced the thing under study) became modern science's central concern.

The new cosmology of the scientific revolution is seen in Copernicus's (1473–1543) assertion of an approximately heliocentric (Sun-centered) solar system and a rejection of the Ptolemaic (Earth-centered) system.[13] Later, Galileo (1564–1642) advanced the heliocentric viewpoint based on observational data gathered by focusing the telescope toward the moons, planets, and stars. The Church censured Galileo for his cosmological claims. The Church would not change its long-held doctrine (which viewed the Earth as the center of universe), especially because Europe was engaged in a century-long series of religious wars between Protestants/Calvinists and Catholics.

Galileo also conducted physics experiments, some of which were empirical and some of which were mental "thought experiments." Galileo clearly viewed both experimental research data and mathematics as important for the conduct of science. Based on intuition and his empirical study of falling objects, Galileo rejected the

Aristotelian theory that heavier objects fall faster than lighter objects. The discovery of universal laws would require a more active observational system than Aristotle had possessed.[14]

At this point in history, one can discern a marked shift from an Aristotelian, passive observational system to a Baconian/Galilean, active observational system, which uses more sophisticated measurement instruments and active experimentation. Intervention in natural settings (via experiments) became a cornerstone of the new science.

Isaac Newton (1642–1727) also made extensive use of experimental and observational techniques. Newton is best known for his theory of universal gravitation and his three laws of mechanics, which help explain what holds the universe together. The law of gravitation states that any two bodies attract each other with a force that is directly proportional to the product of their masses and inversely proportional to the square of the distance between them. Newton based his universal theory on a synthesis of his and others' work (e.g., Kepler, Galileo).

Although Newton called his method inductive, it is clear that he also relied heavily on deduction (especially in the form of mathematical axioms).[15] It is important to understand that the term induction has *not* been consistently used throughout history. Furthermore, most researchers in practice have used a combination of inductive and deductive logic, despite claims to the contrary.

Newton also stressed the importance of analysis (i.e., separating entities to understand their components) and synthesis (i.e., putting entities back together into their wholes). This is seen in Newton's use of prisms to separate light into its seven constituent colors and recomposing the separate rays into white light.[16]

Although Table 3.2 indicates that empiricism and inductive logic dominated much of the scientific revolution, it also indicates that some individuals, such as Descartes, emphasized deductive logic during this period. Rene Descartes (1596–1650), a mathematician and rationalist philosopher, invented the Cartesian coordinates and analytic geometry and famously stated,

"I think therefore I am." Descartes argued that basic axioms or starting hypotheses for science (e.g., one's idea that one exists, geometric axioms) are clear and distinct ideas that must be true; from these foundational ideas he hoped to deductively demonstrate other ideas.

Descartes was confident in his ideas because "God would not deceive him." Descartes belonged to the philosophical movement known as **rationalism**, which says reasoning (including a priori or pure reasoning) is the primary source of knowledge. In short, empiricism and rationalism offer different foundational logics or epistemologies, with empiricism emphasizing induction (i.e., observation, experience, experimentation) and rationalism emphasizing deduction (i.e., formal deductive logic, mathematics).

Contributions of British Empiricists and Continental Rationalists

The generally inductive orientation of 16th and 17th century scientists was supported philosophically by the British empiricists (Locke, Berkeley, Hume, Mill). Their philosophical empiricism would later have a strong influence on classical and logical positivism during the 19th and 20th centuries.[17]

According to empiricism, all knowledge ultimately comes from experience. The founder of British empiricism, John Locke (1632–1704), famously introduced the concept of *tabula rasa* to describe the human mind as a "blank tablet" at birth. Empiricism continues to be an important theory of how knowledge comes about. Empiricism supported liberal ideas about the improvability of all individuals' knowledge and lives: Individuals simply had to modify their environments.

David Hume (1711–1766) built on John Locke's empiricism. Hume's formulation of cause-effect relationships is especially relevant for understanding scientific methodology. Prominent 20th century QUAN methodologists Thomas Cook and Donald Campbell (1979) contended that Hume's writings include "probably the most famous positivist analysis of cause" (p. 10). Prominent 20th century QUAL methodologists Yvonna Lincoln and Egon Guba (1985) stated that "virtually all modern formulations [of causation] can be viewed as extensions or rejections of Hume's proposition" (p. 133). Although Hume proposed many rules to consider when making claims about cause and effect relations, three conditions for causal inferences are most prominent:

- *Physical contiguity* between the presumed cause and effect
- *Temporal precedence* (the cause has to precede the effect in time)
- **Constant conjunction** such that the cause has to be present when the effect is obtained

For example, when a cue ball strikes a pool ball, you can see physical contiguity (nearness) of the cause (cue ball) and the effect (pool ball), temporal precedence (the cue ball moves first, and the pool ball moves second), and constant conjunction (you observe this many times). Some writers draw from the Humean legacy the need for research studies to be replicated so that the presumed causal connection is demonstrated many times (Maxwell, 2004).

Many philosophers view Hume as a skeptic about causation because he claimed that causality is merely an idea. Hume said causation is not deductively provable, and scientists' ideas about causation rest on mere convention, which philosophers of science do *not* endorse as a secure foundation for knowledge. To make causal statements, Hume says researchers must go beyond their experience and make claims about what they cannot see. Hume's well-known skepticism about causation was a major blow for philosophers/scientists who thought that research provides certain knowledge. Hume's skepticism became a key part of the philosophy of empiricism and positivism, which became more interested in *description* (e.g., of universal laws of nature) and rejected the use of "metaphysical" concepts such as *causation.*

Hume's criterion of constant conjunction has led some scientists to rely on high statistical correlations as evidence for causal relationships. Other scientists have criticized this perspective, noting the dictum that a strong association between variable X and variable Y does not necessarily imply that changes in X cause changes in Y. The relation between variables X and Y might be due to a third variable, Z, and once one controls for that confounding variable, the original relationship is no longer observed.

John Stuart Mill (1806–1873) was a 19th century British empiricist, who is known for his extensive work on inductive causal analysis.[18] Mill developed the following methods or rules for determining causation:

- Method of agreement—When examining a set of heterogeneous cases that have the outcome of interest, the cause is the one factor that all of the cases have in common.
- Method of difference—When comparing two groups that are similar on all characteristics except for one factor, the cause is the one factor that the cases experiencing the outcome have but the cases not experiencing the outcome do not have.
- Method of concomitant variation—When the outcome varies along with variations in a factor, that factor might be the cause.
- Method of residues—When you know that part of a phenomenon is due to a certain cause, you can infer that the rest of the phenomenon is due to other causes.

Cook and Campbell (1979) contended that Mill added to Hume's analysis this additional criterion for causation: Rival or alternative explanations for a presumed cause-effect relationship must be ruled out before a relationship between two variables can be accepted as causal. This criterion (called here the rule-out-all-rival-hypotheses criterion) is met by using all of Mill's methods for determining causation, rather than relying on mere correlation. That is, rather than relying on covariation alone, Mill demonstrated that researchers must think about multiple issues (addressed by his methods) to make strong claims of causation.

Thus, Hume's concept of constant conjunction led to future generations of researchers who valued high correlations in causal studies, and Mill's methods led others to focus on conducting experimental/quasi-experimental esearch with its emphasis on the elimination of rival explanations. Both correlational and experimental research are discussed in more detail in Chapters 11 and 12 (the analysis and inference processes in MM research). Ultimately, all causal research today needs to show a relationship between the causal and outcome variables (thanks to Hume) and build on the criterion of systematically ruling out all rival explanations for any presumed causal relationship (thanks to Mill).

The philosopher Immanuel Kant (1724–1804) famously took as his project the reconciliation of empiricism (the senses are the foundation for knowledge) and rationalism (rational thought is the foundation for knowledge). He asserted that humans have a priori forms of intuition (e.g., only being able to interpret the world as occurring in absolute time and space) and that human minds impose a common or universal set of categories on all experience (e.g., quantity, quality, modality, relation). Kant claimed that the mind *constructs* experience, albeit in a universal way. For Kant, the content of knowledge comes from experience (similar to the empiricists), but the form of knowledge is constructed using a universal set of categories or concepts.

Kant thought he had saved the classical and rationalist idea of knowledge as truth (which had been "knocked off its pedestal" by Hume) while also respecting experience as a source for truth. His solution was that humans have universal and certain knowledge about *phenomena* (i.e., things knowable by the senses), but they cannot have knowledge about *noumena* (i.e., things as they are in themselves; the world as it really is). Kant showed that experience (empiricism) and deductive rational thought (rationalism) can be combined, but the cost of integration is that researchers will only obtain knowledge of what they experience.

Kant's solution led to idealism. There are many varieties of idealism, but most claim that reality is fundamentally mental, which contrasts with materialism and its claim that reality is fundamentally material. Idealism has an important place in the history of the social sciences because it provides a place for the reality of nonmaterial concepts and *culture*. Kant's form of idealism is called transcendental idealism. Although Kant claimed individuals construct their worlds, he believed they construct it using the same categories. The transcendental part of Kant's philosophy emphasized that everyone's experience has common components. Subsequently, other idealists would eliminate the transcendental part of Kant's idealism, thereby allowing the idea of different cultural constructions.

Because this is a book on MM research, it is important to note that according to Kant quantity *and* quality are essential concepts for all humans' experiences of phenomena. Kant was, therefore, a proto-mixed methodological thinker in that he reconciled different viewpoints and emphasized quantity and quality.

The Enlightenment Project

The Enlightenment was an 18th century European social/philosophical movement that brought the ideas of the scientific revolution to nonscientists and turned the rational eye of science onto society, promising similar successes in the realms of politics, psychology, sociology, and history (Gay, 1969). The Enlightenment idea of spreading knowledge to everyone is exemplified by the 35-volume encyclopedia project led by editor/philosopher Denis Diderot (1713–1784). Other notable *philosophes* from the Enlightenment include Voltaire (1694–1778) and Montesquieu (1689–1755).

The **Enlightenment Project** emphasized the following ideas:

- Reason as a universal characteristic of humans
- Epistemologies concerned with experience and the quest for foundations and certainty (e.g., rationalism, empiricism, positivism)
- Social and moral progress
- Humanitarian political goals (e.g., Hollis, 2002; Schwandt, 1997)

The words *enlightenment* and *modernism* are often used as synonyms. Hollis (2002) characterized *modernism* as follows:

> The whole grand attempt to discover all nature's secrets, including those of humanity, has become known as "the Enlightenment Project." The schoolroom door opens with the progress of Reason in discovering and exploring the modern physical world. Then it adds the growth of the social sciences in the eighteenth century, as the light is turning on the enquiring mind itself and the nature of society. (p. 5)

The ideas of the Enlightenment are still an important part of the fabric of contemporary society, but many scholars have criticized those ideas, especially postmodernists. Johnson and Christensen (2008) explained *modernism* (as contrasted with *postmodernism*) as "a term used by postmodernists to refer to an earlier and outdated period in the history of science that viewed the world as a static (i.e., unchanging) machine where everyone follows the same laws of behavior" (p. 393).

Humanist and postmodern scholars contend that the Enlightenment emphasized rationality *at the expense of* other considerations, such as humans' nonrational and emotional sides, variations in thinking and valuing across cultures, and individual freedom of choice. The 19th century movement of romanticism also reacted negatively to the Enlightenment emphasis on rationality. Nineteenth century idealism and romanticism were especially important historical movements that influenced the development of QUAL research.

Stage 4: The Formal Emergence of the Social and Behavioral Sciences in the 19th and Early 20th Centuries

Although the *natural sciences* first developed in antiquity and blossomed during the scientific revolution, the *social and behavioral sciences* did not formally emerge until the 19th century. The human sciences took longer to emerge partly because humans have had more difficulty focusing on and understanding their own behaviors and characteristics (e.g., their consciousness) than humans have had understanding nature (the material world). Another reason is that natural sciences and their supporting technological innovations were given priority in governmental funding. Many developers of the human sciences wanted to apply the "scientific" model provided by the natural sciences, which led to QUAN social and behavioral research. Other developers viewed the human sciences as radically different from the natural sciences, which led to QUAL social and behavioral research (Harrington, 2000; Prasad, 2002).

The invention of instruments such as telescopes and microscopes greatly accelerated the study of natural phenomena because they could be investigated in unprecedented ways. Comparable technological advances in the human sciences have not occurred, although recent developments in neuroscience methodology are promising. (See Box 3.3 for a discussion of the use of MM in neuroscience research.) In QUAL research, the investigator is often said to be the instrument of data collection, which harkens back to Protagoras; this kind of measurement has strengths and weaknesses.

Box 3.3
Brain Imaging and MM

Recent technological developments in neuroscience may provide the human sciences with the type of technological breakthroughs that allowed the physical and biological sciences to advance rapidly. Positron emission tomography (PET) and functional magnetic resonance imaging (fMRI) are promising technologies for assessing brain functioning. These noninvasive brain imaging techniques allow neuroscientists to understand the relationship between specific areas of the brain and the functions that they serve. They allow researchers to watch the brain in action.

Moghaddam, Walker, and Harré (2003) argued that cultural biases toward these more "objective" technologies have necessitated the inclusion of QUAL methods for assessing subjective perceptions in the research. Using examples concerning dyslexia and other cognitive disorders, Moghaddam et al. developed an argument for the use of MM (both QUAL and QUAN techniques) in the investigation of these maladies: "The identification of relevant brain states and processes depends on the ability of participants to identify their subjectively presented mental states and processes efficiently and adequately" (p. 132).

By the late 19th century, all the pieces were in place for the emergence of the social and behavioral sciences, to which we now turn.

The Delineation of Disciplines in the Social and Behavioral Sciences

Sociology started its development as a separate discipline during the 1840s thanks to August Comte (1798–1857), who coined the term *sociology* to mean the scientific study of society. In addition to Comte, the classical sociological theorists are Karl Marx (1818–1883), Max Weber (1864–1920), and Emile Durkheim (1858–1917). Marx constructed a theory of class conflict and movement of societies toward socialism. Durkheim emphasized social order, the functional value of institutions, and the influence and reality of social structures. Weber linked macro social structures (status, power, religion) with micro phenomena (individuals' thought processes and perspectives) in his sociology.

Wilhem Wundt (1832–1920) is oftentimes designated the founder of experimental psychology because he established the first psychological laboratory. He also started the first psychology journal and sometimes is called the father of psychology. Psychology in the 20th century and through today has given the highest methodological status to the *experimental method* of research. The scientific method, with experimentation at its core, came to define the discipline of psychology. Sigmund Freud (1856–1939) emphasized the importance of the unconscious and was the originator of psychoanalysis. Psychoanalysis became the first large-scale, formalized clinical therapy in psychology.

A schism in psychology, between clinical/practice (that is more QUAL in approach) and experimental/research (which is more QUAN in approach), has been evident throughout its history. The QUAN tradition has generally dominated psychology as an academic discipline, especially through behaviorism, which dominated much of 20th century psychology (e.g., Hothersall, 1995). Because of the preeminence of QUAN research in academic psychology, the associated QUAN methods (experimentation, statistical analysis) have dominated the methodology of the discipline.

Anthropology also emerged in the last half of the 19th century. The two largest branches of anthropology are physical (i.e., archaeology) and cultural anthropology.[19] Archaeology focuses on studying ancient cultures through material remains and artifacts. *Cultural anthropology* studies human cultures (i.e., shared values, rituals, language) and their social structures. Several pioneering anthropologists worked in the 1800s, including Edward Tylor (1832–1917) in England and Lewis Henry Morgan (1818–1881) in the United States.

One can argue that the German immigrant scholar Franz Boas (1858–1942) founded American anthropology. Boas was a **cultural relativist**; that is, he argued that each cultural group must be studied and accepted as having its own way of doing things. Two of Boas's famous students were Ruth Benedict (1887–1948) and Margaret Mead (1901–1978). Acceptance of cultural uniqueness has not been popular with the more QUAN-oriented anthropologists, who have emphasized methods for determining universal laws.

By the mid-20th century, a more nomological or scientific branch of anthropology gained prominence in the work of Leslie White and Julian Steward in what came to be known as ecological anthropology. The scientific side of anthropology also is seen in the work of the structuralists, such as Claude Levi-Strauss and Marvin Harris. During the 1970s, the humanistic approach in anthropology gained status again, and postmodernists and poststructuralists increasingly gained voice.

The academic discipline of education formally emerged in the late 19th century. State-supported normal schools for teacher education first appeared in the United States in the late 1830s. By the 1870s, several state universities had created normal departments or pedagogical schools. Lagemann (2000) described how educational research developed:

> The result by 1920 was a fairly clear consensus concerning the problematics of education research. . . . between roughly 1890 and

1920, education research emerged as an empirical, professional science, built primarily around behaviorist psychology and the techniques and ideology of quantitative measurements. (p. 16)

Educational theory has been interdisciplinary, although it has most closely followed psychological theory (especially learning theory). Educational research was, and still is, divided between the "soft" humanist practitioners and the "hard" scientific researchers. The QUAN versus QUAL debate has found, perhaps, its most supportive home in education.

The Emergence of Positivism and Idealism

August Comte claimed that societies and thought evolved through three stages: the theological stage, the metaphysical stage, and the *positive* stage. The third and last stage was the time of scientific thought or *positivism*. Comte coined the word *positivism* in the 1820s, and he is the founder of classical positivism. *Positivism* is a science of facts and laws and certainty, and Comte's meaning suggested a *scientism* in which *only* science provides useful knowledge. Since the time of Comte, positivism has had many supporters and many opponents.

Interestingly, even though Comte aimed for researchers to discover facts and laws, he did not like the concept of *causation* because he considered it too metaphysical (Laudan, 1971). According to Comte, causation falls outside the realm of real science and is to be avoided. The scientist makes and tests predictions and constructs explanations describing the objective world (e.g., its laws). Comte claimed his method was "inductive," but Lauden disagreed:

> It is a qualified inductivism at best, and certainly one far removed from the Baconian variety. Comte's most significant departure from traditional approaches to induction

was his refusal to require that acceptable theories must be "generated" by some inductive logic of discovery. Where more orthodox inductivists . . . had insisted that scientific theories must be inductively arrived at, Comte argues that the *origin* of a theory is irrelevant and that what counts is its confirmation. (p. 41)

Comte's positivism competed with 19th century idealism for dominance in the emerging social sciences. Idealism (along with romanticism and humanism) was important for the emergence of QUAL research, and positivism was important for QUAN research.

Kant's transcendental idealism helped make *constructivism* a serious philosophical concept; however, other forms of idealism emerged in the 19th century. Continental philosophy accepted relativism and favored QUAL research. Examples of more culture-friendly versions of idealism were provided by Johann Herder (1744–1803), who claimed that nations have their own, unique *volksgeist* or spirit, and Gottlieb Fichte (1762–1814), who claimed that reality and knowledge are constructed by the mind and what humans believe to be objective is actually quite subjective. Another early constructivist and proto–mixed methods researcher was Giambattista Vico (1668–1744), who argued for use of *both* the hard sciences and the softer humanistic sciences when constructing explanations of human thought and behavior.

In this 19th century setting of the positivists versus the humanists, romanticists, and idealists, the proto–mixed methods thinkers Wilhem Dilthey (1833–1911) and Max Weber advocated that the human sciences study the feeling, experiencing, subjective side of humans in combination with the harder scientific, rationalist, objective approach. Dilthey and Weber proposed the method of **Verstehen**, which is a German term meaning empathetic understanding. The natural sciences have no analogous counterpoint (e.g., Bakker, 1999; Teo, 2001) because of their focus on physical phenomena.

Dilthey posited a scientific dualism between the natural and human sciences (or *naturwissenschaften* vs. *geisteswissenschaften*). According to Dilthey, the natural sciences provide causal *explanations* of natural phenomena from an outsider perspective; the human sciences provide *understanding* of human behavior from the human actor's internal point of view (e.g., Harrington, 2000; Ponterotto, 2005; Schwandt, 1997; Teo, 2001). Dilthey believed that the social scientist "must engage in a psychological reenactment . . . or imaginative reconstruction of the experiences of human actors to understand human social life and history" (Schwandt, 1997, p. 171).

Dilthey founded descriptive psychology, which "holistically characterizes the experience of human beings; it appreciates all aspects of a human being's thoughts, feelings, and desires and includes relevant sociohistorical contexts" (Welty, 2001, p. 224). Dilthey further made the following claims:

- Researcher values enter into decisions about the phenomenon to be studied and how it is studied (i.e., the value-ladeness of facts).
- It is impossible to separate the researcher and the phenomenon under study because the subject of the research is a product of the researcher's mind.
- The researcher is both a subject and object of the research being conducted, having a subject-subject relationship with the objects under study (not an observer-object relationship).
- The meaning of human experiences is context bound (e.g., Berkenkotter, 1989; Greene, 2007; Smith & Heshusius, 1986).

These positions are similar to those currently held by constructivists and are an important part of MM research because of the focus in MM on dialectical understanding of both the QUAN *and* the QUAL perspectives (e.g., Greene, 2007; Greene & Caracelli, 1997b; Johnson & Onwuegbuzie, 2004). In short, MM researchers want both scientific explanation and human understanding.

By the late 1800s, the lines were roughly drawn between the communities of scholars/researchers—the QUALs and the QUANs. Tesch (1990) put it well:

> From the beginning tension arose between those scholars within each field who were believers in the admirably "objective" results achieved in the much older natural sciences, and those who felt that the "human" sciences needed a different approach because of their complexity and the existence of a phenomenon unknown in the mechanical world: consciousness. . . . The debate is still with us. (p. 9)

Referring to Table 3.1, QUANs generally have emphasized materialism, absolutism, naturalism, and nomothetic methods for the production of nomothetic or law-like knowledge, and QUALs generally have emphasized idealism, relativism, humanism, and ideographic methods for the production of ideographic or individual or particular knowledge.

The Foreshadowing of the Hypothetico-Deductive Model and the Emergence of Experimentation in Psychology

We defined the hypothetico-deductive model (H-DM) in Chapter 2 as a QUAN model that involves the following elements:

1. The statement of a hypothesis based on a theory or past experience and the deduction of the observable consequences that must occur if the hypothesis is true

2. The testing of the hypothesis by collecting new data and using statistical analyses to check for statistical significance of the finding

More practically, the method involves coming up with ideas and testing them. The H-DM is frequently attributed to 20th century philosophers of science, such as Karl Popper and Carl Hempel (e.g., Achinstein, 2004; Medawar, 1990), but it was foreshadowed by several 19th century methodologists, including William Whewell (1794–1866), John Stuart Mill, William Jevons (1835–1882), and Charles Sanders Peirce (1839–1914).[20]

William Whewell distinguished between what later would be called the **context or logic of discovery** (i.e., the formulation of theories and hypotheses) and the **context or logic of justification** (i.e., the testing of theories and hypotheses). Before Whewell (e.g., Newton, Bacon), these two components of scientific method were blurred, and both were assumed to be components of what was called the inductive method of science. Whewell emphasized the logic of justification or empirical testing of hypotheses as the key part of the scientific method, but he also pointed out that the context of discovery involved creative insight, which leads to genuinely new hypotheses and potentially new knowledge. The logic of discovery played an important role in discussions regarding the H-DM in the 20th century. (See Box 4.2 in the next chapter for more detail.)

Wundt established the first experimental psychology laboratory at the University of Leipzig in 1879. In an experiment, it is key that the researcher give one group a treatment condition, withhold the treatment from the control group, and then check to determine the outcome of the treatment. By the turn of the 20th century, many writers in the United States were calling for psychology to become laboratory based and experimental. During the 20th century, experimental research using the H-DM proliferated, especially in psychology and the health sciences. Sir Ronald Fisher's (1890–1962) statistical method of null hypothesis testing also became popular.[21]

The experiment became the epistemological foundation for psychology. Psychology and other social and behavioral sciences literally defined their disciplines by adherence to the scientific method, which included experimentation. For example, psychology was the scientific study of the mind and behavior, sociology was the scientific study of society, and government changed its name to political science and became the scientific study of government/politics.

The Development of Basic Statistical and Anthropological Methods

As the human sciences emerged, a parallel development occurred in the statistical techniques used to support QUAN research. In the 19th century, many basic statistical concepts and techniques (e.g., the bell curve, standard deviation, correlation, *t* test) were developed. These techniques were used extensively in the next century, along with the experimental method and the H-DM. Three notable statistical pioneers in the 19th century were Quetelet, Gosset, and Pearson, who set the stage for further work by Fisher and others in the 20th century (see Box 3.4 for details).

On the QUAL side, methods were emerging in anthropology at the end of the 19th century. The British Association for the Advancement of Science (BAAS) publication titled *Notes and Queries on Anthropology*, which was largely written by Edward Tylor in the early 1870s (Stocking, 1992), emphasized the development of open-ended narrative lists of the contents and "traits" of cultures. Fieldwork became the standard QUAL method during this time as anthropologists attempted to document different cultures. Archaeologists focused on "dirt methods" of uncovering artifacts left behind by past cultures. Understanding the language of each culture was of key importance in gaining access to people's ways of thought and behavior.

Summary

This chapter traced the early history of scientific thought through four distinct stages:

- Antiquity—the early scientific work of the Greeks in metaphysics and the physical and biological sciences

---

Box 3.4
A Quartet of Influential Statisticians

Adolphe Quetelet (1796–1874) was a Belgian mathematician who described the "average man" in terms of characteristics (e.g., height, weight). He described the properties of the normal distribution, including its bell shape. William Gosset (1876–1937) worked in the Guinness brewery and invented the student's *t* test while studying small samples of beer for quality control.

Karl Pearson (1857–1936) applied statistics to issues related to evolution and heredity. Pearson coined the term *standard deviation* and made contributions to the development of the correlation coefficient and regression analysis.

These statisticians, and others, set the stage for Sir Ronald Fisher to redefine statistics in the 1920s in terms of data reduction and hypothesis testing. He invented the analysis of variance (ANOVA), which became the major statistical tool for testing experimental hypotheses in the human sciences in the 20th century. He and Pearson also had a well-known debate about the relative value of large sample sizes and correlational analyses as opposed to smaller sample sizes and the use of precise distributions for hypothesis testing. (For more information, see Stigler, 2002.)

- The Middle Ages—Church-dominated medieval philosophy characterized by a decline in science
- The scientific revolution—the beginning of modern physical and biological sciences
- The 19th century and early 20th century—emergence of human sciences, including sociology, psychology, anthropology, and education

We organized the material in this chapter around the inductive-deductive research cycle, with each scientific period characterized as dominated by inductive reasoning, deductive reasoning, or a combination of the two. We also used several additional dichotomies or continua, as shown in Table 3.1, to demonstrate that the differences between QUANs and QUALs are multidimensional. We recommend that readers examine the table periodically and consider their own position on the dimensions shown in the table.

Chapter 4 continues our description of the evolution of research methods in the human sciences with Stages 5–8 (the 20th century and beyond). The pace of changes in the social and behavioral sciences increased considerably during this period and included the explicit emergence of the QUAL and MM orientations as distinct research communities. Though we divided the history of the sciences into two chapters, many of the themes introduced in Chapter 3 are continued in Chapter 4.

Review Questions and Exercises

1. What were the major events in the development of the QUAL and QUAN methodologies during the four historical stages described in this chapter? Summarize these events in terms of the inductive-deductive dimension and any other relevant dimensions from Table 3.1.

2. Why might Aristotle be called the first mixed methodologist?

3. What are the differences between empiricism and rationalism?

4. Write a short essay describing the Enlightenment Project.

5. Hume's concept of causation is associated with correlational research, whereas Mill's methods for determining causation are associated with experimental research. Explain the difference.

6. Describe Dilthey's distinction between the natural sciences and the human sciences, including his concept of *Verstehen*. Explain how he was a proto-mixed thinker.

7. What were the origins of sociology, psychology, anthropology, and educational research?

8. Search the Internet to learn more about the philosophers/scientists introduced in this chapter. Select three or four of these individuals who were born within a span of years not to exceed 100 (e.g., Descartes, Locke, Newton). Discuss the similarities and differences among these individuals.

9. Select a philosopher/scientist discussed in this chapter who is of particular interest to you. Write a short essay describing how the individual changed the human sciences.

Key Terms

Absolutism

Constant conjunction

Context or logic of discovery

Context or logic of justification

Cultural relativist

Empiricism

Enlightenment Project

Humanism

Idealism

Ideographic methods

Materialism

Naturalism

Nomothetic methods

Rationalism

Relativism

Scholasticism

Tabula rasa

Verstehen

Notes

1. The terms "social and behavioral sciences" and "human sciences" are used interchangeably throughout this text.

2. Conversely, some readers may desire more detailed historical or philosophical information, and we recommend these sources: Achinstein (2004), Bunnin and Tsui-James (2003), Cottingham (1988), Gower (1997), Kuhn (1962, 1970, 1996), Losee (2001), Sherratt (2006), Viney and King (1998), and Willis (2007), plus others cited in Chapters 3–4.

3. We argue later that QUANs have historically used (and sometimes currently use) inductive logic in their research, but we will retain the arbitrary dichotomy between the emphases of QUALs/QUANs for now, with QUALs emphasizing particulars and QUANs emphasizing the general.

4. In philosophical arguments, "soft versions" of positions are weaker, less dogmatic, and more open to interpretation and compromise than are "strong versions."

5. We used a modified version of Newton's famous statement "If I have seen further . . . it is by standing upon the shoulders of giants." Newton apparently stood on others' shoulders in generating his pithy claim. John of Salisbury wrote in 1159 that "Bernard of Chartres used to say that we are like dwarfs on the shoulders of giants, so that we can see more than they, and things at a greater distance, not by virtue of any sharpness of sight on our part, or any physical distinction, but because we are carried high and raised up by their giant size." (Quote from Bragg, 1998.)

6. B.C.E is an abbreviation for "Before Common Era" that replaces the previously used B.C. C.E. is an abbreviation for "Common Era" that replaces the previously used A.D.

7. We derived information related to the Greek philosophers from Arrington (2001), Brumbaugh (1981), and others.

8. We use the prefix *proto-* to mean an early but not yet fully developed or labeled version of an intellectual movement.

9. The well-known Raphael painting "The School of Athens" contrasts Plato and Aristotle by depicting Plato as pointing up to the other world of the forms, and Aristotle pointing out to the immediate, empirical, or particular world in which we all live.

10. We derived information related to Aristotle from Alioto (1992), Dancy (2001), Thompson (1975), and others.

11. We derived information related to science during the Middle Ages from Gracia (2003), Kovach (1987), and others.

12. The "Church" is the Roman Catholic Church in the historical western part and the Orthodox Church in the historical eastern part of the Roman Empire.

13. Copernicus argued for a heliostatic system with a *stationary* sun; he also was wrong on many details which would be corrected later (e.g., he thought that orbits around the sun were circular rather than elliptical).

14. We derived information related to Galileo from Morphet (1977), Geymonat (1965), and others.

15. To read Newton's original explanation of the rules in his "inductive" scientific method, see Achinstein (2004).

16. We derived information related to Newton from Gjertsen (1986), Gleick (2003), and others.

17. We derived information related to the British Empiricists from Collins (1967), Woolhouse (1988), and others.

18. Much of Mill's writing on causation is available online at www.la.utexas.edu/research/poltheory/mill/sol.

19. Two additional branches of anthropology are biological anthropology (focusing on how humans adapt to their environments over long time periods) and linguistic anthropology (focusing on human language both at a single point in time and across time).

20. For the history of QUAN scientific methods, see Achinstein (2004).

21. Refer to Box 11.2 in Chapter 11 for a discussion of the null hypothesis, alternative hypothesis, and statistical significance.

CHAPTER 4

Methodological Thought Since the 20th Century

Charles Teddlie and R. Burke Johnson

Objectives

Upon finishing this chapter, you should be able to:

- Discuss the last four stages (Stages 5–8) in the history and philosophy of the human sciences
- Describe the history and ideas of classical positivism (see Chapter 3) and logical positivism
- Discuss problems with positivism
- Describe the hypothetico-deductive model
- Describe some of the beliefs of the post-positivists (e.g., theory-ladenness of facts)
- Explain why the discovery of grounded theory was so important to the qualitative community
- Discuss the emergence of mixed methods research in the 20th century
- Discuss the causal model of explanation
- Contrast the incompatibility and compatibility theses
- Describe and contrast the Enlightenment Project and postmodernism
- Explain why the logic of the social and behavioral sciences is inherently mixed

History and Philosophy of the Human Sciences in the 20th Century and Beyond

In Chapter 4, we follow our discussion of Stages 1–4 in the evolution of human sciences research methods with a description of the four stages (Stages 5–8) that occurred in the 20th century and beyond:

5. 1900 to World War II, the traditional period in the social and behavioral sciences, with positivism generally dominating

6. End of World War II to 1970, the post-positivist era in the social and behavioral sciences

7. 1970–1990, a period of diversification and advancement in all methodological communities in the human sciences

8. 1990 to the present, characterized by institutionalization of mixed methods (MM) as a distinct methodological orientation

The separate visions of human research held by the experimentalists and ethnographers at the end of the 20th century are still present today, though the overall methodological landscape has changed considerably. The domination of the "received tradition" (logical positivism) characterized the first half of the 20th century, and the various challenges to that tradition dominated the second half. These trends resulted in the more methodologically diverse community of scholars of today, including an expanding MM community.

Stage 5: The Traditional Period (1900 to World War II)

Research Methodology During the Traditional Period

By the early 20th century, researchers and philosophers of science were emphasizing the *context of justification* and the testing of hypotheses at the expense of the more creative phase of science (i.e., *the context of discovery*). Karl Popper (1902–1994) boldly stated that science has no need for induction:

> There is no induction: we never argue from facts to theories, unless by way of refutation or "falsification." This view of science may be described as selective, as Darwinian. By contrast, theories of method which assert that we proceed by induction or which stress verification (rather than falsification) are typically Lamarckian: they stress instruction by the environment rather than selection by the environment. (Popper, 1974, p. 68)

Popper (1974) and others felt that the context of discovery was "mere" psychology, not science. Finding the proper balance between the discovery and the testing (i.e., justificatory) aspects of science was widely debated throughout the 20th century and continues today.

Denzin and Lincoln (2000b, 2005b) defined a number of "moments" in qualitative (QUAL) research. The first is labeled the "traditional period," extending from the early 1900s through World War II. We agree with these writers that positivism, and its variants, were generally dominant during this period.[1]

The debate between proponents of positivism and idealism continued, but the positivists prevailed, especially in psychology and education. Lagemann (2000) described what she called the defeat of John Dewey (1859–1952) and the triumph of Edward Thorndike (1874–1949):

> Thorndike's psychology was narrowly behaviorist. Eliminating all considerations of consciousness, it reduced human actions to little more than responses to stimuli. . . . Dewey had formulated a conception of behavior that, contra Thorndike, was both holistic and purposive. (p. 62)

Dewey, the philosopher most often associated with classical *pragmatism* and MM research, presented a social, contextualized, interdisciplinary view of human science that was out of step with the dominant, mechanistic scientism of this period.

The *Vienna Circle,* a group of philosophers/scientists who were active from the 1920s until World War II, started the philosophy known as **logical positivism**. Logical positivism marked the beginning of the philosophy of science as a distinct field of study, and it initially dominated that field. Logical positivism was a hybrid that descended from the empiricism of John Locke and David Hume, Auguste Comte's classical positivism, and several other perspectives.[2] Phillips (1987) defined logical positivism as follows:

> Name of a position developed in the 1920s by members of the Vienna Circle; its most notorious tenet was the **verifiability principle of meaning (verification principle)**, which stated that something is meaningful only if it is verifiable empirically (directly, or indirectly, via sense experience), or if it is a truth of logic or mathematics. (p. 204, bold added)

The logical positivists argued against any kind of *metaphysics,* which meant any speculation that could not be verified by empirical methods, such as "philosophical claims about reality, truth, being, and so on" (Schwandt, 1997, p. 91). They considered Freud's classification of mental activity (id, ego, supergo) to be metaphysical because it was not empirically verifiable.

The behaviorist orientation[3] in psychology, exemplified in the work of B. F. Skinner (1904–1990), Edward Thorndike, John Watson, and others, was closely related to positivism. *Behaviorism* may be defined as follows:

> Behaviorism considers psychology the study of behavior because behavior is observable and usually measurable. Behaviorists tend to have faith in experimental research, animal studies, and situations that allow for the direct demonstration of relationships between manipulations of the environment and changes in behavior. (Gilgen, 1982, p. 8)

Behaviorists and positivists agreed that only what could be measured and experienced could enter into the domain of "science," which led to difficulties even in the natural sciences (e.g., sub-atomic particles, galaxies beyond the reach of telescopes). Human values fell outside of science, a place seen as a fully objective and rational enterprise.

Many technical advances were made in quantitative (QUAN) methodology during this period (e.g., statistics, measurement). Clark Hull (1884–1952) advocated for a hypothetico-deductive model (H-DM), in which psychologists generate experiments used to statistically test hypotheses derived from formal postulates (e.g., Gilgen, 1982; Hothersall, 1995). The majority of researchers viewed QUAN research as good research and were optimistic about its potential.

Problems With Logical Positivism

Logical positivism produced some serious problems with no simple solutions. Objections to positivism, especially in the human sciences, increased throughout the 20th century.

Two issues were of particular importance: induction and verification.[4] The **problem of induction** may be defined as follows: no matter how many times one observes that Y follows X, one can never be sure that the *next* observation of X will be followed by Y. In short, researchers can never prove universal theories or laws using inductive logic alone because one cannot observe all cases (e.g., Hollis, 2002; Phillips, 1987).

Logical positivists originally argued that research could identify which theories were true. However, this brought with it the **problem of verification**, which states that a wide range of observations can confirm more than one theory and that many competing theories seemed to have abundant confirming observations (e.g., Phillips, 1987). In other words, complete verification of scientific theories and laws is rarely, if ever, possible. Popper (1968) was especially aware of this problem and argued that empirical (or inductive) support for theories is plentiful but provides little evidence for truth.

Popper (1968) noticed that his acquaintances who subscribed to a particular theoretical viewpoint

(e.g., Freud, Skinner) found verification of their theories everywhere: "Whatever happened always confirmed it" (p. 35). Popper said that, because of this problem of confirming "evidence," researchers should propose "bold conjectures" that are more easily falsified through empirical tests. This practice would continually eliminate bad hypotheses and theories from the scientific literature.

Another problem for positivism was its over-reliance on *operationalism* (i.e., "all scientific entities and their properties are definable in terms of the operations by which they are measured") (Phillips, 1987, p. 205). Operationalism is useful for reminding researchers to carefully describe how they measure theoretical constructs.[5] A problem emerges, however, when a researcher argues that "reality" is completely defined by particular operations of measurement (e.g., Campbell, 1988; Cronbach, 1991). The MM response to this problem is to posit multiple measures of the same phenomenon and recognize that constructs might be more than what is currently measured.

Continued Development of Qualitative Research Methods

Franz Boas (1858–1942), Bronislaw Malinowski (1884–1942), and others improved anthropological fieldwork methods in the early 20th century. The British Association for the Advancement of Science's *Notes and Queries on Anthropology* (4th ed.) was published in 1912 and emphasized the importance of *native terms* (Stocking, 1992). Malinowski (1922) systematically described fieldwork procedures, especially those involving participant observation.[6] Boas's work, such as the *Handbook of American Indian Language* (1911), emphasized a linguistic orientation and the collection and analysis of documents (Stocking, 1992).

Although the study of culture has also been a central concept in sociology, sociologists have focused on the study of cultures and subcultures in technologically advanced societies. Anthropological/sociological field-study techniques were well established by the middle of the 20th century, resulting in classic works such as *The Polish Peasant in Europe and America* (Thomas & Znaniecki, 1920), *A Black Civilization: A Social Study of an Australian Tribe* (Warner, 1937), and *Street Corner Society* (Whyte, 1943/1955).

Mixed Methods Research During the Traditional Period

This period witnessed important MM research with relatively little controversy. Margaret Mead provided an early example with *Coming of Age in Samoa* (1928) in which she combined psychological tests with ethnographic procedures (Stocking, 1992, p. 312). Maxwell and Loomis (2003) concluded that "a case could be made that mixed methods was more *common* in earlier times, when methods were less specialized and compartmentalized and the paradigm wars were less heated" (p. 242, italics in original).

Several authors (e.g., Brewer & Hunter, 2006; Erzberger & Kelle, 2003; Hunter & Brewer, 2003) identified classic MM studies from the traditional period. Brewer and Hunter (2006) presented three such examples:

- The Hawthorne studies, which began in 1924 and continued for several years (Roethlisberger & Dickson, 1939)
- The studies of "Yankee City" (Newburyport, Massachusetts) as an example of community life in the United States (Warner & Lunt, 1941)
- The Marienthal study, conducted during the 1930s economic depression in Austria but not published in the United States until 40 years later (Jahoda, Lazersfeld, & Zeisel, 1971)

In the Hawthorne studies (Roethlisberger & Dickson, 1939), the researchers used interviews and observations as they tried to understand what became known as the Hawthorne effect. For example, a part of the overall study known as the bank wiring observation room study involved extensive observations of social relations among workers. In a narrow sense, the Hawthorne effect refers to increased worker productivity due to their being studied. In a broad sense, the Hawthorne effect is an example of reactivity (i.e., research participants oftentimes react to being studied; hence the need for unobtrusive methods, which are discussed in Chapter 10). The Hawthorne studies, conducted by multiple researchers and lasting several years, emphasized experiments *and* extensive interviewing, observation, and life-history data.

Stage 6: The Postpositivist Era (End of World II to 1970)

Further Work on the Hypothetico-Deductive Model

During this period, scientists/philosophers began to speak of the H-DM as a general statement of the scientific method. The idealized five-step version of the H-DM is shown in Box 4.1.

The H-DM may be seen as an attempt to address the problems of induction and verification by substituting the H-DM for inductive reasoning and substituting the falsification principle for the verification principle (e.g., Hollis, 2002; Notturno, 2001; Willig, 2001).

Box 4.1
The Hypothetico-Deductive Model

Schwandt (1997) provided the following description of the H-DM:

The steps in the ideal version of the method are the following: (1) Theory provides the definitions, assumptions, and hypotheses about human behavior from which (2) predictions about behavior are logically deduced. (3) These predictions are then tested through a process of empirical observation. (4) From the results of observations, the inquirer concludes either that the theory appears consistent with the facts (i.e., it explains the behavior) or the theory is inconsistent with the facts. (5) If it is consistent, no further work is needed. If it is inconsistent, then the theory must either be discarded in favor of a better theory or modified to accommodate the newly acquired facts. (p. 66)

The problem of induction concerns the fact that researchers cannot prove a theory using inductive logic alone because they cannot observe all cases. The H-DM, as actually used by practicing researchers, uses both deductive and inductive logic, and, as in all empirical research, the researcher does not obtain deductive proof; the researcher only obtains probabilistic (i.e., inductive) evidence for his or her conclusions.

The H-DM emphasizes the logical deduction of outcomes that must occur if a hypothesis is true and the researcher's subsequent data-driven tests of the hypothesis. If the hypothesis *is* supported, one has inductive support (i.e., one doesn't have deductive proof but one does have some supporting evidence for the truth of the hypothesis). If the hypothesis *is not* supported, Popper (1934/1959) dictates the use of deductive logic and he optimistically concludes that the hypothesis (that makes a general claim of a principle or a law) has been falsified.[7]

Popper's (1934/1959) **falsification principle** asserts that a hypothesis must be falsifiable: According to this principle, it must be possible to determine a priori the pattern of empirical data that prove the hypothesis is false. For Popper, the problem with verification (see Box 4.2) was addressed because observations were no longer used to confirm (verify) a hypothesis but only to disconfirm (falsify) it. Popper thought the purpose of science was to focus on critically eliminating false theories/hypotheses. (At the same time, as noted earlier, most researchers claim support for their hypotheses when the data support them, even though Popper rejected this kind of inductive support.)

Philosophers of science have found many problems with the H-DM, including those summarized in Box 4.2. In the next section of this chapter (Stage 7), we note that the H-DM or covering law model of explanation has been replaced in the human sciences with the **causal model of explanation**. (See Box 4.3 for details regarding the causal model of explanation.)

From the perspective of our historical analysis, the important point here is that the H-DM was frequently discussed and commonly used for several decades, even though philosophers never

---

Box 4.2

Issues Regarding the H-DM

Several issues have been discussed concerning the H-DM. First, one must have a theory in order to test the theory, but where does the theory come from and is there logic for theory discovery and construction? The H-DM seemed to neglect the logic or context of discovery. Second, if the observed facts are consistent with the hypothesis, what should one claim? Debate took place over whether the theory is *verified, confirmed, proven, corroborated,* or just *not falsified*. Third, if the observed facts are inconsistent with the hypothesis, should

(Continued)

(Continued)

the theory be viewed as wrong and discarded, or should a background assumption be viewed as what is wrong (e.g., perhaps the lack of support for the hypothesis was due to poor measurement)?

Logical positivists assumed that when the data were consistent with the hypothesis they could claim the theory had been verified. But philosophers of science noted that this reasoning was based on a logical fallacy known as affirming the consequent (i.e., if p then q; q; therefore p). One is not logically justified in concluding that p is true just because q is found. The logical positivists realized this problem and changed their goal from *verification* to *confirmation*, which amounted to a weaker claim of support. Probability theory (if a hypothesis is supported, then the theory is *probably* true) was increasingly developed by some positivists. Some were not satisfied with this solution because they wanted proof, not just evidence.

Popper's "solution" was to rely on a deductively valid argument form known as *modus tollens* (i.e., if p then q; not q; therefore not p). His solution was to rely on falsification; he claimed that researchers could falsify theories. The problem with this solution is that researchers want to claim that their theory is true or supported strongly, whereas Popper's *modus tollens* solution only allows theories to be falsified.

Carl Hempel's (1905–1997) solution was for researchers to shift the topic from the truth of a theory to the quality of an explanation. Hempel and Oppenheim (1948) called their version of the H-DM the covering law model of scientific explanation (also known as the deductive-nomological model). (This is the version of the H-DM in Box 4.1.) Hempel's idea was that a general law explained the outcomes. A problem with this solution is that it is rare to find general laws in the human sciences. One way out is to predict that laws would be forthcoming in the future. In the philosophy of science, these issues still have not been fully resolved.

fully agreed on how much one could claim based on his or her research findings. We believe that most practicing researchers agree with the general statement about the H-DM made earlier: that positive evidence is taken as tentative support for theories, but our test must be in principle falsifiable and rigorously conducted.[8]

Some QUAN researchers like to think of their method as thoroughly deductive, although it appears impossible to eliminate all inductive traces from it. The H-DM approach emphasizes deduction, and it clearly emphasizes the *testing* of hypotheses rather than the inductive discovery or *generation* of hypotheses. *Eventually, this orientation in the QUAN community toward emphasizing deductive logic (along with other important factors)* *led many in the QUAL community to choose inductive logic as part of their basic orientation.*

The Prevalence of the Postpositivist Position

Dissatisfaction with positivism became increasingly widespread throughout the human sciences during the 1950s and 1960s, thereby increasing the appeal of *postpositivism.* Landmark postpositivistic works (e.g., Campbell & Stanley, 1963; Hanson, 1958; Hempel, 1965; Kuhn, 1962, 1970, 1996; Popper, 1934/1959; Toulmin, 1960) appeared, gaining widespread credibility throughout the social scientific community (e.g., Phillips, 1987).

There are many definitions of *postpositivism,* which generically refers to any paradigm posited as a replacement for positivism (Schwandt, 1997). We use a narrow interpretation, focusing on postpositivism as the intellectual heir to positivism. Postpositivism, from our point of view, is a replacement that is still bound to the quantitatively oriented vision of science (cf. Reichardt & Rallis, 1994). Postpositivism is currently the predominant philosophy for QUAN research in the human sciences.

Reichardt and Rallis (1994) argued that some of the most influential QUAN methodologists of the 1950–1970 period (e.g., Campbell & Stanley, 1963) were "unabashedly postpositivist," holding the following beliefs:

- **Theory-ladenness of facts**—Research is influenced by the theory or framework that an investigator uses (e.g., Hanson, 1958; Phillips, 1990).
- Fallibility of knowledge—This position addresses the verification issue in that one can never prove a theory or causal proposition (e.g., Cook & Campbell, 1979; Popper, 1934/1959).
- **Underdetermination of theory by fact**—"a number of theories . . . can equally (but perhaps differently) account for the same finite body of evidence" (Phillips, 1987, p. 206).
- **Value-ladenness of facts**—Research is influenced by the values of investigators. For example, the **experimenter effect** refers to the idea that how the experimenter looks or acts may affect the results of a study (e.g., Rosenthal, 1976).
- Nature of reality—Reichardt and Rallis (1994) contend that most researchers (QUANs and QUALs) understand that social realities are constructed. Festinger's (1957) formulation of social reality in his cognitive dissonance theory and Thibaut and Kelley's (1959) concepts of comparison level and comparison level of alternative relationships in their social exchange theory exemplify social construction.

Reichardt and Rallis (1994, pp. 86–89) summarized these five points. Many QUALs and QUANs share these beliefs because they reflect shared viewpoints about the nature of reality and the conduct of human research in the second half of the 20th century.

Although many QUAN methodologists promoted postpositivism during the 1950–1970 era and beyond, they also worked within a tradition that emphasized methodological correctness (Smith, 1994). When choices came down to specific methodologies, most QUANs in psychology and the health sciences preferred the experimental or quasi-experimental research designs. Cook and Campbell (1979) made the following assertion:

> We assume that readers believe that causal inference is important and that experimentation is one of the most useful, if not *the* most useful, way of gaining knowledge about cause. (p. 91, italics in original)

On the other hand, a large number of QUAN researchers (e.g., Professor Numerico) continued to use nonexperimental methods to identify QUAN relationships between variables and explain these relationships quantitatively.[9] They did so in part because some topics (e.g., effects of television on violence) do not lend themselves to experimental research designs.

Also during this period Donald Campbell (1916–1996) and colleagues (e.g., Campbell, 1957; Campbell & Stanley, 1963) presented their validity concepts. Campbell and Lee Cronbach (1916–2001) had an ongoing discussion regarding the importance of *internal validity* (the degree to which we can be sure that the independent variable of interest has an effect on the dependent variable) versus *external validity* (the generalizability of results). Campbell argued for the preeminence of internal validity, whereas Cronbach (1982) argued for the importance of external validity. Cronbach also argued that the basic statistical models used during the 1970s and 1980s were far too blunt to accurately explain real-world complexity. For example, Cronbach suggested the use of models that examine multiple causal variables rather than the simpler causal models advocated by Campbell and colleagues. Two excellent statistical developments appeared during this period: hierarchical linear modeling and structural equation modeling. Both techniques led to significant advances in QUAN research.

Grounded Theory and Qualitative Research

The most important QUAL methodological advance during this period was the "discovery" of grounded theory by Barney Glaser (1930–) and Anselm Strauss (1916–1996) in the mid-1960s. *Grounded theory* is a methodology for theory development that is "grounded" in narrative data that are systematically gathered and inductively analyzed (e.g., Strauss & Corbin, 1998).

Charmaz (2000) described the impact of the introduction of grounded theory:

> [Glaser and Strauss] countered the dominant view that quantitative studies provide the only form of systematic social scientific inquiry. Essentially, grounded theory methods consist of systematic inductive guidelines for collecting and analyzing data to build middle-range theoretical frameworks that explain collected data. . . . Since Glaser and Strauss developed grounded theory methods, qualitative researchers have claimed the use of these methods to legitimate their work. (p. 509)

The emergence of grounded theory has two implications for our analysis in this chapter:

1. Grounded theory is inductive in nature; therefore, QUAL researchers could lay claim to the inductive end of the inductive-deductive continuum shortly after the H-DM led QUANs to embrace the deductive end.

2. Although QUAL research already had a well-defined fieldwork methodology, grounded theory provided QUAL researchers with a more systematic procedure for inductively generating theories and analyzing narrative data.[10]

Multimethod and Mixed Methods Research During the Postpositivist Era

The first explicitly defined multimethod designs emerged during the mid-1990s, when Campbell and Fiske (1959) proposed their **multitrait-multimethod matrix**, which employs alternative (concurrent or combined) QUAN methods to study the same phenomenon. Campbell and Fiske developed the matrix to ensure that the variance in their data was accounted for by the psychological trait under study, not by the particular QUAN method that was employed (e.g., Brewer & Hunter, 2006; Tashakkori & Teddlie, 1998).

Brewer and Hunter (2006) concluded that the multitrait-multimethod matrix "warned of overreliance upon, and overconfidence in, any single type of research method" (p. xiii). This matrix eventually led to the concept of triangulation, which led to a proliferation of MM designs in the ensuing years.

Though a distinct field of MM had not yet emerged, eminent scholars (e.g., Leon Festinger, Paul Lazarsfield, Kurt Lewin[11]) advocated the use of both QUAL and QUAN methods in social research (see Merton, Coleman, & Rossi, 1979). Numerous studies using those methods occurred, especially in psychology and sociology (see summaries in Fine & Elsbach, 2000; Maxwell & Loomis, 2003; Waszak & Sines, 2003):

- Festinger, Riecken, and Schacter's (1956) research on end-of-the-world cults
- The Robber's Cave study (Sherif, Harvey, White, Hood, and Sherif, 1961) of intergroup conflict and superordinate goals, involving a series of field experiments and extensive QUAL data
- Zimbardo's (1969) simulated "prison" studies of deindividuation conducted at Stanford University

- Research concerning motives for childbearing (e.g., Hoffman & Hoffman, 1973), in which the value of children was identified through QUAL methods (e.g., interviews) and then examined statistically in terms of its relationship with other variables

Stage 7: Diversification of and Advances in Methodologies in the Human Sciences (1970 to 1990)

The period from 1970 to 1990 was a time of much activity in human sciences methodology, which resulted in advances in all research communities, including increased popularity and sophistication of QUAL methods and the continued emergence of MM research.

With regard to the inductive-deductive continuum (or iterative cycle), the previous stage (Stage 6) witnessed a pendulum change. Many QUANs embraced the deductive end (H-DM) or the causal explanation position, in which deduction was taken to mean an emphasis on rigorous theory testing. Many QUALs embraced the inductive end, in which induction was taken to mean an emphasis on the discovery and generation of meaningful research findings. (Many QUALs rejected the part of induction that suggested searching for generalizations because of their emphasis on particularistic conclusions.)

Stage 7 witnessed an accommodation of both ends of the continuum by MM researchers, though some QUANs and QUALs (especially) continued to advocate for dichotomies.

The Causal Model of Explanation in Quantitative Research

Many problems surrounding causality in the human sciences have not been fully resolved and may prove to be irresolvable. Despite this, methodological progress occurred with the emergence of the *causal model of explanation*, which eclipsed the H-DM as the prototype for conducting QUAN research. The two viewpoints associated with this causal model (i.e., the *regularity theory of causation* and the *counterfactual approach*) are described in Box 4.3.

An MM solution regarding causality might recommend that a researcher use multiple sources of evidence for "justifying" his or her claim about a theory or explanation. An example of this kind of solution can be found in Johnson and Christensen (2008). These authors offer nine specific questions for consideration when evaluating the quality of a theory or explanation (e.g., Does the theory or explanation fit the available data? Has it survived numerous attempts by researchers to identify problems with it or to falsify it? Does it work better than rival theories or explanations?). We

Box 4.3
Emergence of the Causal Model of Explanation

One last historical change we want to describe is a shift in how QUAN researchers came to view the idea of explanation. As mentioned earlier, there was a general shift to the idea that "explanation" was a deductive phenomenon (i.e., one had "explained" an outcome when it deductively followed from a scientific law). During the 1960s and 1970s, however, a new twist on the idea of explanation occurred. The strict covering law version of the H-DM of explanation (see Box 4.1) was replaced with a **causal model of explanation** (e.g.,

(Continued)

(Continued)

Blalock, 1964, 1985; Mackie, 1974). Additionally, a fuller recognition that social scientific conclusions were probabilistic was integrated into this view of explanation (Cook & Campbell, 1979; Salmon, 1998).

This means that in QUAN research explanation and demonstration of causation were equated. One now had "explained" a phenomenon when one demonstrated its cause(s). Explanation became less of a deductive logical exercise based on general laws, and started focusing more on specifying particular causal factors. There are at least two viewpoints within this new causal model. First is the *regularity theory of causation*. This approach typically is based on nonexperimental, observational data and involves identifying and measuring statistical associations among causal factors and their outcomes. If associations between variables are observed repeatedly and one has controlled for alternative explanations, then one has evidence of causation. This approach is sometimes called the econometric approach because economists often use it.

Second is the *counterfactual approach*, which relies on experimental research designs and counterfactual logic. According to counterfactual logic, one should look at what happened to a group in an experiment that received a causal factor (treatment) and compare the effect to what that same group *would have been* like if it had *not* received the treatment. The hypothetical comparison (i.e., what the group would have been like) is the *counterfactual*. The value of the counterfactual typically is estimated by using a control group in an experiment or a pretest measure of the experimental group on the outcome variable. (A control group is similar to the experimental group except that it does not receive the treatment.) This counterfactual logic is comparative, which suggests that it is not enough to look at statistical associations. Experimental research using this counterfactual logic is explained in virtually every research methods book in the social and behavioral sciences today.

add to this list two specific questions based on our current discussion: Has strong experimental research evidence supported the causal claim? Moreover, have statistical modeling approaches supported the claim? By answering these kinds of questions, one is best able to draw conclusions about causality. Again, at this point, perhaps the best approach to evidence of causation is to use as many of the strongest types of evidence as are feasible.

Constructivism and the Paradigms Debate

Stages 4, 5, and 6 (with positivism, logical positivism, postpositivism) represented the apex of the received tradition in the human sciences. Criticisms of that tradition, which began gaining momentum in the 1950s and 1960s, blossomed in Stage 7. Whereas postpositivism sought to fix some of the obvious problems with positivism, newer paradigms sought to replace it with an alternative vision (e.g., Berger & Luckmann, 1966; Denzin, 1989a; Eisner, 1981; Geertz, 1973, 1983; Gergen, 1985; Lincoln & Guba, 1985).

These paradigms had several names, with constructivism being the most popular. Constructivists believe that "knowledge of the world is mediated by cognitive structures" that result "from the interaction of the mind and the environment" (Schwandt, 1997, p. 19). For constructivists, understandings of reality are constructed both individually and socially. Constructivists also emphasize that observations are value laden and that investigations must employ empathic understanding of those being studied, as advocated by Dilthey, Weber, and others. (See Chapter 3.)

Constructivism's emergence inevitably led to the *paradigms debate,* which was discussed in Chapter 1, so we will only briefly review it here. The *incompatibility thesis* stated that it was inappropriate to mix QUAL and QUAN methods due to fundamental differences in underlying paradigms. This thesis was reminiscent of Thomas Kuhn's (1922–1996) well-known argument that competing paradigms were **incommensurable paradigms,** meaning there is no way to directly compare one with another or to clearly communicate between paradigms (Kuhn, 1962, 1970, 1996). Many authors, including Davidson (1973), Phillips (1987), and Onwuegbuzie and Johnson (2006), have criticized the strong form of this concept.[12]

The philosophies of constructivism (associated with QUAL methods) and positivism/postpositivism (associated with QUAN methods) were depicted as incompatible on several basic dimensions (e.g., Lincoln & Guba, 1985). *Paradigm contrast tables* indicated that constructivism and postpositivism were either-or dualisms (e.g., value-free versus value-bound research). (Table 5.1 contains the original paradigm contrast table.)

The incompatibility thesis is, of course, contrary to our position presented in Chapter 2, which expands the QUAN/QUAL either-or dualism to a continuum with many points between the extremes (i.e., the *QUAL-MIXED-QUAN continuum*). We argue that most research projects fall somewhere along this continuum, rather than at either end.

As noted in Chapter 1, the *compatibility thesis* was posited by Howe (1988) and others to counter the incompatibility thesis. This compatibility thesis used *pragmatism* as its philosophical basis. Several authors traced the roots of pragmatism to such American scholars as Charles Sanders Peirce,[13] William James (1842–1910), and John Dewey. Pragmatism seeks to debunk

metaphysical concepts, such as Truth (with a capital *T*) (e.g., Nielsen, 1991; Rorty, 1990). Howe (1988) summarized pragmatism as follows:

> After all, much of pragmatic philosophy (e.g., Davidson, 1973; Rorty, 1982; Wittgenstein, 1958) is *deconstructive*—an attempt to get philosophers to stop taking concepts such as "truth," "reality," and "conceptual scheme," turning them into superconcepts such as "Truth," "Reality," and "Conceptual Scheme," and generating insoluble pseudoproblems in the process. (p. 15, italics in original)

Because pragmatism is such an important philosophy for MM research, we have included in Table 4.1 a summary of its tenets according to Peirce, James, and Dewey. We recommend that readers carefully consider the points listed in Table 4.1 to better understand pragmatism. Johnson, Onwuegbuzie, and Turner (2007) labeled the classical pragmatism described in Table 4.1 "pragmatism of the center." We suggest a further refinement, giving classical pragmatism as applied to MM research the following name: **dialectical pragmatism.** This title emphasizes that pragmatism for MM always takes QUAL and QUAN seriously but then develops a synthesis for each research study.[14]

A major reason that pragmatism is the philosophical partner for MM is that it rejects the either-or choices from the constructivism-positivism debate. Pragmatism offers a third choice that embraces superordinate ideas gleaned through consideration of perspectives from both sides of the paradigms debate in interaction with the research question and real-world circumstances.

The Growing Sophistication and Popularity of Qualitative Methods

Acceptance of the use of various QUAL methods grew during the second half of the 20th century. For instance, LeCompte and Preissle (1993)

Table 4.1   General Characteristics of Pragmatism

1. The project of pragmatism has been to find a middle ground between philosophical dogmatisms and skepticism and to find workable solutions to long-standing philosophical problems.

2. Pragmatism rejects binary (either-or) choices suggested in traditional dualisms (e.g. rationalism vs. empiricism, realism vs. antirealism, free will vs. determinism, appearance vs. reality, facts vs. values, subjectivism vs. objectivism).

3. Pragmatism replaces the historically popular epistemic distinction between subject and external object with the naturalistic and process-oriented organism-environment transaction.

4. Pragmatism views knowledge as being both constructed and based on the reality of the world one experiences and lives in.

5. Theories are viewed instrumentally (they are "true" to different degrees based on how well they currently work; workability is judged especially on the criteria of predictability and applicability).

6. Pragmatism endorses pluralism and carefully considered integrative eclecticism (e.g., different, even conflicting theories and perspectives can be useful; observations, experience, and experiments are all useful ways to gain an understanding of people and the world).

7. Pragmatism views inquiry as occurring similarly in research and day-to-day life. Researchers and people test their beliefs and theories through experience and experimenting, checking to see what works, what solves problems, what answers questions, what helps for survival.

8. Capital *T* Truth is what will be the final opinion, perhaps at the end of history. Lowercase *t* truths (i.e., the instrumental, partial, and provisional truths) are what one obtains and lives by in the meantime.

9. Pragmatism prefers action to philosophizing and endorses "practical theory."

10. Pragmatism takes an explicitly value-oriented approach to research that is derived from cultural values and specifically endorses shared values, such as democracy, freedom, equality, and progress.

11. According to Peirce, "reasoning should not form a chair which is no stronger than its weakest link, but a cable whose fibers may be ever so slender, provided they are sufficiently numerous and intimately connected" (1868, in Menand, 1997, p. 56).

12. Pragmatism offers the "pragmatic method" for solving traditional philosophical dualisms as well as for making methodological choices.

Note: Table is based on Johnson and Onwuegbuzie (2004).

catalogued QUAL data collection methods into more than 15 categories including the following:

- Observation—participant observation, nonparticipant observation
- Interviewing—key informant, career histories, surveys
- Content analysis of human artifacts—archival and demographic collection, physical trace data

QUAN researchers acknowledged the relevance and importance of QUAL methods with increasing frequency (e.g., Shadish, Cook, &

Campbell, 2002). Patton (2002) concluded: "When eminent measurement and methods scholars such as Donald Campbell and Lee J. Cronbach began publicly recognizing the contributions that qualitative methods could make, the acceptability of qualitative/naturalistic approaches was greatly enhanced" (p. 586).

This era also witnessed an expansion of QUAL analytical techniques including the following methods:

- The further expansion of grounded theory techniques, including explicit delineation of the constant comparative method (e.g., Lincoln & Guba, 1985) and different types of coding techniques (e.g., Strauss & Corbin, 1990)
- Geertz's (1973, 1983) delineation of how to make thick descriptions of events, rituals, and customs
- Spradley's (1979, 1980) presentation of a 12-step process for conducting ethnographic research (the developmental research sequence)
- Miles and Huberman's (1984, 1994) detailed procedures for analyzing QUAL data, including data displays
- Tesch's (1990) presentation and comparison of QUAL software programs for analyzing narrative data

A significant event for the QUAL tradition was the publication in 1994 of the first edition of the *Handbook of Qualitative Research*, edited by the prominent researchers Norman Denzin and Yvonna Lincoln. This popular volume, now in its third edition, provides state-of-the-art discourse on theory and practice in QUAL research.

Triangulation and the Continued Emergence of Mixed Methods

In their book on unobtrusive measures, first published in 1966, Webb, Campbell, Schwartz, and Sechrest (2000) made an early reference to triangulation: "Once a proposition has been confirmed by two or more independent measurement processes, the uncertainty of its interpretation is greatly reduced. The most persuasive evidence comes through a triangulation of measurement processes" (p. 3).

Denzin (1978) extended the discussion of triangulation to include four distinct types:

- **Data triangulation**—involving "the use of a variety of data sources in a study"
- *Methodological triangulation*—"the use of multiple methods to study a single problem" (see Chapter 2)
- **Investigator triangulation**—"involving several different researchers" in a single study
- **Theory triangulation**—"the use of multiple perspectives to interpret a single set of data" (Patton, 2002, p. 247)

The use of triangulation strategies eventually led to a wider range of MM techniques. Two influential books on multimethods and MM appeared around 1990: one by the sociologists Brewer and Hunter (1989) and the other by Morse (1991) from the field of nursing. Both books emphasized the use of QUAN and QUAL methods—but in research designs that kept the two methodological types separate. According to these authors, triangulation of *distinct methods* provides greater opportunities for accurate inferences.

Several scholars criticized the incompatibility thesis during the 1970–1990 era by pointedly noting that MM were already widely used (e.g., Brewer & Hunter, 1989; Greene, Caracelli, & Graham, 1989; Patton, 1990, 2002). For example, Greene et al. presented 57 studies that employed MM and described their characteristics and the purposes for their use.

Changes Occurring During Stage 7

Patton (2002) presented a history of the paradigms debate and its aftermath with regard to evaluation research:

- "The earliest evaluations focused largely on quantitative measurement of clear, specific goals and objectives . . .

- By the middle 1970s, the paradigms debate had become a major focus of evaluation discussions and writings.
- By the late 1970s, the alternative qualitative/naturalistic paradigm had been fully articulated. . . .
- A period of pragmatism and dialogue followed, during which calls for and experiences with multiple methods and a synthesis of paradigms became more common." (p. 585)

Patton's analysis of the changes in evaluation research agrees with our analysis of the changes that occurred in Stage 7 in our history of the human sciences. It is interesting that so many important methodological changes in the social and behavioral sciences occurred in such a relatively short time period.

Stage 8: The Institutionalization of Mixed Methods as a Distinct Methodological Orientation (1990 to the Present)

In the past 15 years, at least three significant events for MM research have occurred:

- Dialogues began between QUAL and QUAN researchers.
- Several seminal works appeared that helped establish MM as a separate methodological field.
- The number of MM research studies increased dramatically, especially in applied fields.

Beginning of Dialogues Between the Qualitative and Quantitative Communities

As the MM community continues to emerge as the third methodological movement, it will inevitably engage in dialogues with members of the other two communities. Contemporary examples include the following dialogues:

- MM responses to those advocating "scientifically based research," which stresses the QUAN orientation
- MM responses to criticisms from QUALs' statements that "mixed method designs are direct descendants of classical experimentalism" (Denzin & Lincoln, 2005b, p. 9)
- MM dialogue with individuals advocating positions associated with orientational and *critical theory* (e.g., transformative perspective)
- MM responses to individuals advocating positions associated with postmodernism

We only briefly introduce these dialogues here because more details are found in Chapter 5.

Scientifically based research (SBR) emerged from a distinctly postpositivist QUAN orientation in the United States Department of Education during the G. W. Bush administration. This position emphasizes the use of randomized controlled experiments as the "gold standard" for the study of causality in educational policy research (e.g., Cook, 2002). The MM community needs to respond to this new kind of "scientism," which claims to value other orientations (i.e., the QUAL tradition) yet behaves differently. The issue of causation is very complex, multiple positions are articulated in the philosophical literature, and the QUANs do not "own" the rights as the only group of scholars able to discuss issues surrounding causation. Building on House (1991), Maxwell (2004) challenged the quantitatively oriented version of SBR by proposing an alternative realist approach that uses qualitatively oriented research in causal investigations. In addition to challenging the decidedly QUAN orientation of SBR, Maxwell advocated combining QUAL and QUAN methods.

Recent criticisms of MM from the QUAL community (e.g., Denzin & Lincoln, 2005b; Denzin, Lincoln, & Giardina, 2006; Howe, 2004) erroneously associated "mainstream" MM with what they call mixed methods experimentation.

Among the misconceptions in these criticisms is the presumption that MM subordinates QUAL methods to QUAN methods. Creswell, Shope, Plano Clark, and Green (2006) responded forcefully to this criticism, citing empirical MM research articles that gave priority to QUAL research. Chapter 5 contains more information on this dialogue, including arguments we made in a recent chapter (Teddlie, Tashakkori, & Johnson, 2008).

Although critical theory[15] is an important perspective within the QUAL tradition (e.g., Creswell, 1998; Kinecheloe & McLaren, 2005; Willis, 2007), it also has a long history within the QUAN tradition. For example, inequality has a strongly objective side that QUAN research has been effective in studying (e.g., the subfield of social stratification in sociology, the interdisciplinary study of poverty). We believe that critical theory and orientational research are highly compatible with the MM research perspective. We hope that critical theorists and researchers will feel comfortable using MM strategies and employing useful ideas, data, and approaches from the QUAL and QUAN orientations.

An examination of critical theory is beyond the scope of this chapter, but we include an extensive discussion of the transformative perspective (a popular variant of critical theory) in Chapter 5. Although pragmatism is the philosophy most commonly associated with MM, Mertens (2003, 2005, 2007) posited the transformative perspective as an alternative epistemology. We address this issue in Chapter 5 by discussing the transformative perspective as an alternative philosophy for MM, adding that perspective to the paradigm contrast tables for comparison purposes.

As noted in Chapter 3, the Enlightenment Project was the beginning of modernism. **Postmodernism** critiques some of the defining characteristics of the Enlightenment, including the importance of the rational approach in science, the epistemologies of empiricism/positivism, the notions of social/intellectual progress through the application of scientific

theories and methodologies, and the value of grand theories of human behavior (e.g., Denzin & Lincoln, 2000b, 2005b; Foucault, 1970; Hall, 1999; Schwandt, 1997). There are several different families of thought within postmodernism (e.g., Schwandt, 1997). Hall (1999) distinguished between modern and postmodern thought:

> In recent years, the gap between objectivism and relativism has been remapped onto a divide between modern and postmodern sensibilities. Among strong postmodernists, the collapse of objectivity and science is taken as beyond serious debate, and inquiry is judged by humanistic . . . standards of aesthetics, poetics, morals, and interpretive insight, rather than by objective standards of truth. (p. 169)

Researchers working within the MM tradition may find certain aspects of "strong" postmodernism difficult to reconcile with the very act of performing research. For instance, Gorard and Taylor (2004) concluded that "by denying the possibility that there is any means of judging knowledge claims to be more or less true, postmodernism makes research a completely pointless activity" (p. 161).

Publication of Noteworthy Books and Articles on Mixed Methods as a Separate Research Movement

A short list of influential MM works that appeared during the past 15 years in the United States includes Creswell (1994, 2003), Creswell and Plano Clark (2007), Greene (2007), Greene and Caracelli (1997a), Johnson and Onwuegbuzie (2004), Morgan (1998), Morse (1991), Newman and Benz (1998), Patton (1990, 2002), Reichardt and Rallis (1994), Rossman and Wilson (1994) and Tashakkori and Teddlie (1998). These works have resulted in the creation of a basic MM terminology, the development of several MM design typologies, the presentation of different paradigm formulations, and so on.

Progress in MM research led to the publication of the *Handbook of Mixed Methods in Social and Behavioral Research* (Tashakkori & Teddlie, 2003a). This handbook contains discussions of important issues in the field, including nomenclature and basic definitions, rationale, paradigmatic foundations, design issues, issues in drawing inferences, and research logistics.

In the late 1980s, emphasis on the explicit use of MM grew in both the United Kingdom and continental Europe. This was a welcome sign for U.S. scholars, who can look to their European colleagues for both similar and diverse points of view on MM issues. Some of the more influential European sources include Bergman (2008); Brannen (1992, 2005); Bryman (1988, 1992, 2006a, 2006b); Debats, Drost, and Hansen (1995); Erzberger and Kelle (2003); Erzberger and Prein (1997); Gorard (2004); Gorard and Taylor (2004); Hammersley (1992a, 1992b, 1995); and Niglas (2004).

Additionally, the World Bank recently conducted several MM studies, including Bamberger (2000); Barron, Diprose, Smith, Whiteside, and Woolcock (2008); Gacitúa-Marió and Wodon (2001); Rao and Woolcock (2003); and Rawlings (2000). Rao and Woolcock (2003) identified several premises underlying their use of MM, such as starting a project with some general hypotheses and questions but allowing for change in hypotheses and questions as the project evolves. Another premise requires the use of both QUAL and QUAN designs, data collection and analysis techniques, and integration of the results to "create an understanding of both measured impact and process" (p. 173).

An interesting feature of this MM research from the United States, Europe, and the World Bank is that their authors rarely referenced research generated by the other groups. It seems that distinct traditions of mixed research emerged concurrently, with little mutual influence or interaction. Perhaps MM research is the methodological climate or *zeitgeist* of our time.

Proliferation of Mixed Methods Studies Throughout the Human Sciences

There has been a large increase in the number of studies explicitly described as mixed throughout the human sciences in the past 15 years. The following examples of MM research are from the *Handbook of Mixed Methods in Social and Behavioral Research*:

- Evaluation research—Riccio and Ornstein's (1996) evaluation of a welfare-to-work program
- Management and organizational research—Currall, Hammer, Baggett, and Doninger's (1999) study of a corporate board of directors
- Health sciences—Bryant, Forthofer, McCormack Brown, Alfonso, and Quinn's (2000) study of the determinants of mammography use
- Nursing—Cohen, Tripp-Reimer, Smith, Sorofman, and Lively's (1994) study of patient and professional explanations of diabetes
- Psychology—Johnson and Price-Williams's (1996) study of the cross-cultural occurrence of the Oedipal complex
- Sociology—Dykema and Schaeffer's (2000) study of how the patterning of experiences in the lives of respondents leads to errors in understanding and recall
- Education—Teddlie and Stringfield's (1993) study of school and teacher effectiveness variables

MM is a popular method in certain fields. For instance, Twinn (2003) reported that a review of nursing literature published between 1982 and 2000 yielded 112 English-language articles that described MM studies. Niglas (2004) classified more than 1,100 journal articles from 15 education journals as having a QUAN, QUAL, or MM design. Nineteen percent (19%) of the empirical articles had an MM design, and the percentage of MM designs ranged across the journals from 0% to 38%. MM is also well represented in dissertation research in applied fields (e.g., Cakan, 1999; Carwile, 2005; Freeman, 1997; Gatta, 2003; Ivankova, 2004; Kochan, 1998; Niglas, 2004; Stevens, 2001; Wu, 2005; Yuan, 2003).

Methodological Mixing Inherent in the Logic of Social and Behavioral Research

Mixed methodologists believe that much if not most research is inherently mixed. They believe that the inductive-deductive cycle of research (Figure 2.2) is an accurate description of how research is conducted; that is, one moves between perspectives and logics in an iterative fashion. The use of a specific type of research logic depends on where the researcher is in the cycle.

The discussion from Chapters 3 and 4 includes several points that illustrate the value of using both inductive and deductive logic:

1. Aristotle discussed both types of logic in his descriptions of two philosophies: one that uses pure deduction aimed at understanding the "innate forms" (*Prior Analytics*) and one that involves detailed empirical investigations of nature employing induction (*Posterior Analytics*).

2. During the Middle Ages, Abelard took the conceptualist position, claiming that universals exist in the mind and that particulars exist in objects in the world. His method was similar to some contemporary MM researchers as he attempted to find a logical and workable solution to an intractable issue.

3. Newton is a good example of a scientist who used both inductive logic to obtain the axioms used in developing his theory of universal gravitation and deductive logic to prove his conclusions and other implications that were testable.

4. In Kant's theory, quantity *and* quality were essential concepts for all human experiences. Kant was a proto-mixed methodological thinker in that he reconciled different viewpoints and emphasized quantity and quality.

5. There are numerous examples of well-known social and behavioral research projects in the 20th century, which employed MM before mixed research was explicitly introduced in the 1980s.

6. Popper, Hempel, and others turned the inductive logic of positivism into the H-DM of postpositivism.[16] During the paradigms debate, QUALs appropriated inductive logic and contrasted it with the H-DM of the QUANs. Nevertheless, several philosophers of science (e.g., Achinstein, 2004; Hollis, 2002; Schwandt, 1997) argued persuasively that QUAN-oriented research has had a major inductive component, and this remains so. Thus, the lines between the idealists (constructivists) and the positivists (postpositivists) and their use of inductive and deductive logic have been blurred for some time.

7. Glaser and Strauss believed that each form of data (QUAN, QUAL) is useful for both the generation and verification of grounded theory. In many instances, they felt that both forms of data are necessary.

8. Table 3.2 indicates that the dominant type of scientific reasoning has shifted in a cyclical manner across time. The human sciences appear to make more progress during mixed periods in which neither type of logic is overly dominant.

Other scholars share our perspective regarding the interrelatedness of the inductive/deductive processes. For example, Hammersley (1992b) made the following conclusion: "Indeed, it seems to me that all research involves induction and deduction in the broad sense of those terms; in all research we move from ideas to data as well as from data to ideas" (p. 168).

Similarly, Gilbert (2006) made the following statement:

[The paradigms debate is an] oversimplification that ignores, on the one hand, the thought processes involved in sustained enquiry where deduction and induction advance in an iterative process; and, on the other hand the range of traditions within social science enquiry, many of which make use of both modes of analysis. (p. 207)

Summary

This chapter traced the history of scientific thought from 1900 to the present in four stages:

Stage 5: The traditional period (from 1900 to World War II)—Positivism was the undisputed paradigm throughout the human sciences.

Stage 6: The postpositivist era (from the end of World II to 1970)—Postpositivism was the dominant paradigm in the human sciences, with an emphasis on addressing the problems of positivism, a focus on QUAN methods, and an adherence to the H-DM.

Stage 7: Diversification of and advances in methodologies in the human sciences (from 1970 to 1990)—First constructivism and then pragmatism emerged as important paradigms, and QUAL and MM techniques gained wider acceptance.

Stage 8: The institutionalization of mixed methods as a distinct methodological orientation (from 1990 to the present)—MM became a distinct third methodological community, several noteworthy publications on MM appeared, and MM research spread to numerous fields of study.

Chapter 5 continues our discussion of philosophical issues in MM research, focusing on contemporary paradigm issues. The chapter includes details regarding five philosophical orientations toward research in the human sciences. Contemporary points of view with regard to the use of paradigms are discussed. A table describing methodological distinctions among the three communities is presented as an advance organizer for the remainder of the text.

Review Questions and Exercises

1. What were the major events in the development of the QUAL, QUAN, and MM methodologies during stages described in Chapter 4? Summarize these events in terms of the inductive-deductive dimension.

2. Describe the evolution of empiricism into positivism, logical positivism, and postpositivism during the 20th century.

3. What are the problems of induction and verification? How did the works of philosophers in the 20th century "solve" these problems?

4. Why is mixed methodology called the *third methodological movement*? What events led to its development as an alternative to the

QUAN and QUAL approaches in the 20th century?

5. How did the compatibility thesis and pragmatism offset the arguments posed by the incompatibility thesis and the paradigms debate?

6. Explain at least seven tenets of classical pragmatism (Table 4.1) to demonstrate your understanding of this philosophy.

7. Why is the logic of the social and behavioral sciences inherently mixed?

8. Conduct an Internet search to learn more about the philosophers/scientists introduced in this chapter. Select three or four of these individuals who were born

within a span of years not to exceed 100 (e.g., Boas, Dewey, Thorndike). Discuss the similarities and differences among these three individuals.

9. Select one of the philosophers/scientists from Chapter 4 who particularly interests you. Write a short essay describing how he or she changed the human sciences.

10. Write a short essay describing the reaction of postmodernism to the Enlightenment Project. What is your opinion regarding this controversy?

11. The paradigms debate has occurred in all of the human sciences. Locate two articles that discuss the paradigms debate. Describe the similarities and differences between these two articles.

Key Terms

Causal model of explanation

Constructs

Data triangulation

Dialectical pragmatism

Experimenter effect

Falsification principle

Incommensurable paradigms

Investigator triangulation

Logical positivism

Multitrait-multimethod matrix

Postmodernism

Problem of induction

Problem of verification

Theory triangulation

Theory-ladenness of facts

Underdetermination of theory by fact

Value-ladenness of facts

Verifiability principle of meaning (verification principle)

Notes

1. There were exceptions, as seen in ethnographic work in anthropology and community studies and symbolic interactionism in sociology (e.g., Lancy, 1993; LeCompte & Preissle, 1993).

2. These perspectives included the symbolic logical methods of Gottlob Frege (1848–1925), the antirealism of Ernst Mach (1838–1916), and the "picture view of language" of Ludwig Wittgenstein (1888–1951), where words have a one-to-one correspondence to external reality.

3. Cognitive behaviorists, social learning theorists, and social exchange theorists deviated from the early behaviorists' positions later in the century. Those deviations included disbelief in direct causal links between stimuli and responses, a greater role for

cognition and perception, and a more probabilistic model of human behavior.

4. A third problem is the idea that a single hypothesis is never tested in isolation (i.e., the Duhem-Quine thesis or holism). You have to make many assumptions when you test a hypothesis. Because of this, one cannot claim that lack of support for a hypothesis necessarily means the hypothesis is false.

5. **Constructs** are important to QUAN researchers because they are "abstractions that cannot be observed directly but are useful in interpreting empirical data and in theory building" (Ary, Jacobs, Razavieh, & Sorenson, 2007, p. 38). These abstract constructs are often important elements of research questions or hypotheses.

6. Lancy (1993) concluded that Malinowski "discovered anthropology's version of grounded theory nearly 50 years earlier when . . . he was forced to spend much longer doing field work in the small Pacific community of the Trobriand Islands . . . than he had intended" (p. 10).

7. One potential problem with Popper's solution was described in Note 4, earlier in this chapter. When one's hypothesis is not supported, one can claim that the real problem is that a background assumption was wrong, which could be the reason the hypothesis appeared to fail its empirical test.

8. Practicing researchers are not nearly as aggressive as Popper would have liked about claiming that their hypotheses and theories were falsified. One reason for this is that researchers rely on inferential statistics, which makes such a negative claim very difficult.

9. As noted frequently in this text, the viewpoint that QUANs use experimental designs solely is inaccurate, especially in sociology, demography, and economics, where nonexperimental studies using regression analyses are common. Similarly, the belief that QUAN research typically involves hypotheses deduced from "theories" is also inaccurate. Many (if not the majority) of QUAN studies reported in journals in the past few decades were rooted in *conceptual frameworks* based on an integration of literature, theories, and other pertinent information.

10. *Content analysis* is another term used by some authors (e.g., Bazeley, 2003; Berg, 2004; Boyatzis, 1998; Flick, 1998; Patton, 2002) to describe systematic QUAL data analysis. This technique has a long history (e.g., Berelson, 1952; Holsti, 1968) but has been linked primarily with the QUAN tradition (*manifest content analysis*). It can also be a QUAL technique (*latent content analysis*).

11. Kurt Lewin (1890–1947) was known as one of the founders of social psychology and coined the term *action research.*

12. Onwuegbuzie and Johnson (2006, Table 12.7) described a form of validity for mixed research called *commensurability validity,* in which a highly trained researcher or team of researchers dialectically examines both points of view to construct an integrated superordinate viewpoint. (See Table 12.7.)

13. Peirce, the founder of pragmatism, also wrote extensively about a third type of logic that he called *abduction.* Abduction involves the gaining of explanatory insights and making inferences to the best explanation. Details regarding abduction are contained in Box 5.2.

14. This new title was inspired by the arguments of Greene (2007) and Greene and Caracelli (1997b, 2003) about the importance of a QUAL-QUAN dialectic as well as our observations of a dialectical logic present in Western philosophy since Plato's dialogues.

15. As noted in Chapter 2, critical theory from the QUAL perspective involves the examination of human phenomena through an ideological "lens" to seek social justice for oppressed groups.

16. Phillips and Burbules (2000) summarized postpositivism well in *Postpositivism and Educational Research.*

CHAPTER 5

Paradigm Issues in Mixed Methods Research

Objectives

Upon finishing this chapter, you should be able to:

- Describe the evolution of the paradigm contrast tables

- Distinguish between five points of view (constructivism, the transformative perspective, pragmatism, postpositivism, positivism) on basic dimensions of contrast, such as epistemology, axiology, ontology, and preferred methods

- Give examples of what is meant by the pragmatists' rejection of the either-or dichotomy
- Distinguish between the positions of pragmatists and transformative scholars
- Describe the QUAL-MM-QUAN methodological continua and compare the three communities as they relate to the continua
- Describe six contemporary points of view regarding the use of paradigms and select the one that, in your opinion, is most valid
- Discuss ongoing debates among the three methodology communities

Chapter 5 focuses on the philosophical issues related to the ongoing relationships among the three research communities. The *paradigms debate*, discussed in Chapters 1 and 4 as part of our historical analysis, helped set the stage for the emergence of mixed methods (MM) through the articulation of the *compatibility thesis*. In Chapter 5, this debate is discussed in terms of the philosophical differences that still exist among individuals who subscribe to five distinct paradigms (constructivism, the transformative perspective, pragmatism, postpositivism, and positivism) that are associated with the research communities. It is important that we review the philosophical differences that exist among those paradigms, and the individuals who prescribe to them, to further better communication among the three communities.

In Chapter 1, we concurred with several others in defining a *paradigm* as a worldview, together with the various philosophical assumptions associated with that point of view. The importance currently attributed to paradigms in the social and behavioral sciences derives to a large degree from Kuhn's (1962, 1970, 1996) influential book titled *The Structure of Scientific Revolutions*, which was also discussed in Chapters 1 and 4. In this book, Kuhn argues that paradigms are the philosophical models that are used within any given field and that competing paradigms may exist simultaneously within any given field (see Box 5.1 for further details).

As discussed in Chapters 1 and 4, the paradigms debate was resolved for many researchers during the 1990s and later with the emergence of the compatibility thesis. This pragmatist position stated that it was acceptable to mix qualitative (QUAL) and quantitative (QUAN) methods in research studies that called for different types of data to answer research questions.

Box 5.1
Thomas Kuhn and Paradigms

Several of Kuhn's (1962, 1970, 1996) insights are relevant to the issues discussed in this chapter:

1. Paradigms have high priority within any field of science (Kuhn, 1970, pp. 43–49). Paradigms underlie the "normal science" in any field of study. Kuhn's explicit declaration of their significance was an important element in the development of the paradigms debate.

2. Scientific revolutions (Kuhn, 1970, p. 92) are noncumulative (or nonevolutionary) developments in the history of science, in which an older paradigm is replaced in whole (or in part) by an incompatible younger one. These scientific revolutions are also known as *paradigm shifts*.

3. Competing paradigms may exist simultaneously, especially within immature sciences (e.g., Kneller, 1984; Kuhn, 1970, p. 17). Because many of the human sciences are relatively immature, having short histories, then it is likely that they will be characterized as having competing paradigms.

Unfortunately, some scholar-researchers in both the QUAL and QUAN communities behave as if the paradigms debate is still ongoing. Patton (2002) made this same point as follows:

> Though many have pronounced the war and even the debate over . . . not everyone has adopted a stance of methodological enlightenment and tolerance, namely, that methodological orthodoxy, superiority, and purity should yield to methodological appropriateness, pragmatism, and mutual respect. (p. 68)

For these individuals, "The past is never dead. It's not even past."[1]

This chapter uses some terms that were defined in Chapters 1–4. Readers who skipped Chapter 3 or 4, or both, should consult the glossary for definitions of those terms.

This chapter includes five sections:

1. A presentation of the philosophical and methodological differences among five distinct perspectives.

2. More detail regarding our use of the *QUAL-MM-QUAN continuum*, which was introduced in Chapter 2. We apply the continuum to methodological issues that are then detailed throughout the rest of the text.

3. A presentation of different contemporary positions regarding the use of paradigms in the social and behavioral sciences.

4. A discussion of ongoing dialogues related to the use of paradigms and theory in the human sciences.

5. A brief summary of the chapter.

A Review of Philosophical Issues Relevant to Paradigms

The Original Paradigm Contrast Table

A *paradigm contrast table* presents basic philosophical and methodological differences between paradigms. In their initial formulation of these tables, Lincoln and Guba (1985) presented two paradigms: *constructivism* (labeled naturalism) and *positivism*. Though they also discussed *postpositivism,* they did not include it in their table of contrasts.[2]

Lincoln and Guba (1985) presented five dimensions of contrast between constructivism and positivism.[3] They depicted the differences between the two positions in such distinct contrasts that the *incompatibility thesis* emerged based on these supposedly irreconcilable distinctions. Lancy (1993) noted that "Lincoln and Guba (1985) . . . have done a thorough job of building a rationale for the naturalistic paradigm by attacking positivism" and they "see qualitative research as utterly antithetical to quantitative research" (p. 10).

We present the original Lincoln and Guba (1985) paradigm contrast table in Table 5.1 as a reference point. We reorganized its contents to match the order in which we discuss the topics in this text. The right-hand column contains the positivists' beliefs, and the center column contains the constructivists' beliefs. Lincoln and Guba (1985) presented the following five dimensions of contrast:

Epistemology—Positivists believe that the knower and the known are independent, whereas constructivists believe that the knower and the known are inseparable.

Axiology—Positivists believe that inquiry is value free, whereas constructivists believe that inquiry is value bound.

Ontology—Positivists believe that there is a single reality, whereas constructivists believe that there are multiple, constructed realities.

The possibility of causal linkages—Positivists believe that there are real causes that are temporally precedent to or simultaneous with effects. Constructivists believe that it is impossible to distinguish causes from effects.

Generalizability—Positivists believe that **nomothetic statements** (time- and context-free generalizations) are possible. Constructivists

Table 5.1 The Original Paradigm Contrast Table

Dimensions of Contrast	Constructivist (Naturalist) Paradigm	Positivist Paradigm
Epistemology: the relationship of the knower to the known; the nature of knowledge and its justification	Knower and known are interactive, inseparable.	Knower and known are independent, a dualism.
Axiology: the role of values in inquiry	Inquiry is value bound.	Inquiry is value free.
Ontology: the nature of reality, being, and truth	Reality is multiple, constructed, and holistic.	Reality is single, tangible, and fragmentable.
The possibility of causal linkages	All entities are in a state of mutual, simultaneous shaping so that it is impossible to distinguish causes from effects.	There are real causes, temporally precedent to or simultaneous with their effects.
The possibility of generalization	Only time- and context-bound working hypotheses (ideographic statements) are possible.	Time- and context-free generalizations (nomothetic statements) are possible.

Note: From Lincoln and Guba (1985, p. 37). We reorganized the contents of this table to match the order in which we discuss the topics in the text.

believe that only **ideographic statements** (time- and context-bound working hypotheses) are possible.

The Evolution of the Paradigm Contrast Tables

The paradigm contrast tables evolved during the past 20 years. The initial two-column paradigm table (constructivism, positivism) became a four-column table in Guba and Lincoln (1994) and then a five-column table (Guba & Lincoln, 2005; Lincoln & Guba, 2000).

In a previous work, we compared four paradigms: positivism, postpositivism, pragmatism, and constructivism (Tashakkori & Teddlie, 1998). In the following discussion, we add a fifth paradigm, the transformative perspective (e.g., Mertens, 2003, 2005, 2007). We include both pragmatism and the transformative perspective

in our discussion because they have been linked to mixed research.[4]

Although both pragmatism and the transformative perspective advocate the use of MM, they have some characteristics that are quite divergent. Johnson and Onwuegbuzie (2004) characterized *pragmatism* as follows:

The project of pragmatism has been to find a middle ground between philosophical dogmatisms and skepticism and to find a workable solution . . . to many longstanding philosophical dualisms about which agreement has not been historically forthcoming. (p. 18)

Two major characteristics of pragmatism are the rejection of the dogmatic either-or choice between constructivism and postpositivism and the search for practical answers to questions that intrigue the investigator. (See Table 4.1 for more information about pragmatism.)

On the other hand, Mertens (2003) proposed the following definition of the **transformative perspective:**

The transformative paradigm is characterized as placing central importance on the lives and experiences of marginalized groups such as women, ethnic/racial minorities, members of the gay and lesbian communities, people with disabilities, and those who are poor. The researcher who works within this paradigm consciously analyzes asymmetric power relationships, seeks ways to link the results of social inquiry to action, and links the results of the inquiry to wider questions of social inequity and social justice. (pp. 139–140)

Paradigm Comparisons

Table 5.2 presents what we consider to be the primary distinctions among the five major paradigms across seven dimensions: methods, logic, and the five dimensions from Table 5.1.

Rejection of Either-Or in the Choice of Methods

In Table 5.2, we depict the two paradigms associated with MM (pragmatism, transformative perspective) as rejecting forced choices between positivism/postpositivism and constructivism with regard to methods, logic, and epistemology. In each of those cases, pragmatism and the transformative perspective embrace features associated with both points of view (positivism/postpositivism, constructivism).

We focus on the pragmatist orientation toward the use of both QUAL and QUAN methods throughout this text. Although Table 5.2 indicates that postpositivists may also use QUAL methods, the discussion of methodological "correctness" from Chapter 4 should be revisited. When researchers must choose between QUAL or QUAN methodology, postpositivists prefer using either quantitatively oriented experimental or survey research to assess relationships among variables and to explain those relationships statistically.

Similarly, constructivists have historically emphasized differences between the methodological orientations. For example, Denzin and Lincoln (2005b) presented the following typologies of what they consider to be nonoverlapping methodologies:

The five points of difference described above reflect qualitative and quantitative scholars' commitments to different styles of research, different epistemologies, and different forms of representation. Each work tradition is governed by a different set of genres. . . . Qualitative researchers use ethnographic prose, historical narratives, first-person accounts, still photographs, life histories, fictionalized "facts," and biographical and autobiographical materials, among others. Quantitative researchers use mathematical models, statistical tables, and graphs. (p. 12)

Pragmatists, on the other hand, believe that either method is useful, choosing to use the full array of both QUAL and QUAN methods. Pragmatists believe that decisions regarding the use of either (or both) methods depend on the current statement of the research questions and the ongoing phase of the *inductive-deductive research cycle.*

Transformative scholars also reject the either-or choice regarding methods, but they do so for different reasons. For these scholars, the creation of a more just society for oppressed groups dictates the research process (e.g., Mertens, 2005, 2007). Therefore, transformative scholars use any research method that produces results that promote greater social justice.

Use of Both Inductive and Deductive Logic

We presented an extended review of inductive and deductive logic in Chapters 3 and 4 and concluded that pragmatists do not perceive the use of logic as an either-or contrast. Instead, pragmatists believe that research on any given question at any point in time falls somewhere within the *inductive-deductive research cycle.*

Table 5.2 Expanded Paradigm Contrast Table Comparing Five Points of View

Dimensions of Contrast	Constructivism	Transformative	Pragmatism	Postpositivism	Positivism
Methods	QUAL	Both QUAL and QUAN; community of participants involved in methods decisions	Both QUAL and QUAN; researchers answer questions using best methods	Primarily QUAN	QUAN
Logic	Inductive	Both inductive and hypothetico-deductive	Both inductive and hypothetico-deductive	Hypothetico-deductive	Hypothetico-deductive (originally inductive)
Epistemology (researcher/ participant relationship)	Subjective point of view; reality co-constructed with participants	Both objectivity and interaction with participants valued by researchers	Both objective and subjective points of view, depending on stage of research cycle	Modified dualism	Objective point of view (dualism)
Axiology (role of values)	Value-bound inquiry	All aspects of research guided by social injustice	Values important in interpreting results	Values in inquiry, but their influence may be controlled	Value-free inquiry
Ontology (the nature of reality)	Ontological relativism— multiple, constructed realities	Diverse viewpoints regarding social realities; explanations that promote justice	Diverse viewpoints regarding social realities; best explanations within personal value systems	Critical realism (external reality that is understood imperfectly and probabilistically)	Naive realism (an objective, external reality that can be comprehended)
Possibility of causal linkages	Impossible to distinguish causes from effects; credibility of descriptions important	Causal relations that should be understood within the framework of social justice	Causal relations, but they are transitory and hard to identify; both internal validity and credibility important	Causes identifiable in a probabilistic sense that changes over time; internal validity important	Real causes temporally precedent to or simultaneous with effects
Possibility of generalization	Only ideographic statements possible; transferability issues important	Ideographic statements emphasized; results linked to issues of social inequality and justice	Ideographic statements emphasized; both external validity and transferability issues important	Modified nomothetic position; external validity important	Nomothetic statements possible

Note: We used numerous sources in the development of this table including Cherryholmes (1992); Cook and Campbell (1979); Denzin and Lincoln (2005a); Guba and Lincoln (1994, 2005); Howe (1988); Lincoln and Guba (1985, 2000); Mertens (2003); Miles and Huberman (1994); Shadish, Cook, and Campbell (2002); Tashakkori and Teddlie (1998); and Teddlie and Tashakkori (2003).

Research may start at any point in the cycle: Some researchers start from theories, minitheories, or conceptual frameworks, whereas others start from observations or facts. Regardless of where the researcher starts, a research project typically travels through the cycle at least once. In practice, instead of starting from a theory,[5] many researchers build a *conceptual framework* on the basis of current research literature, minitheories, and intuition. This process can be highly inductive.

At some point during the research process, researchers are likely to use both types of inferences and methods simultaneously. Pragmatists and transformative scholars recognize explicitly that they can choose to use both inductive and deductive logic to address their research questions, as indicated in Table 5.2.

A third type of logic, **abduction or abductive logic**, occurs when a researcher observes a surprising event and then tries to determine what might have caused it. It is the process whereby a hypothesis is generated so that the surprising event may be explained (e.g., Andreewsky & Bourcier, 2000). Abduction can be further defined as the process of working back from an observed consequence to a probable antecedent or cause (Denzin, 1978). The logic of abduction is explained in Box 5.2.

Epistemological Relativism: Subjectivity and Objectivity in Research

Epistemology concerns the relationship between the knower and the known (the researcher and the participant). Table 5.2 indicates that

---

Box 5.2

Abduction: The Third Type of Logic

Abduction refers to the logic associated with trying to explain a surprising, or unexpected, event. The American philosopher Charles S. Peirce wrote extensively about abduction. The following example demonstrates abductive logic (e.g., Erzberger & Kelle, 2003; Yu, 1994):

The surprising phenomenon, *X*, is observed.

Among potential hypotheses *A*, *B*, and *C*, *A* is capable of explaining *X*.

That is, if *A* were true, then *X* would be a matter of course.

Therefore, there is reason to believe that *A* is true.
    Several authors have discussed abduction with regard to its relationship to QUAL analysis (e.g., Denzin, 1978, Patton, 2002; Staat, 1993).
    Yu (1994) explained the three logics as follows:

For Peirce a reasoner should apply abduction, deduction and induction altogether in order to achieve a comprehensive inquiry. . . . At the stage of abduction, the goal is to explore the data, find out a pattern, and suggest a plausible hypothesis with the use of proper categories; deduction is to build a logical and testable hypothesis based upon other plausible premises; and induction is the approximation towards the truth in order to fix our beliefs for further inquiry. In short, abduction creates, deduction explicates, and induction verifies. (p. 19) positivists and postpositivists perceive this relationship as being "objective" with a dualism or separateness existing between the knower and the known. On the other hand, constructivists perceive research as "subjective," with researchers and participants working together to co-construct social realities. As explained in Chapters 3 and 4, the subjectivity of the constructivism is an intellectual product of Wilhem Dilthey (and others) and the *idealist* perspective from the 19th century.

Again, pragmatists challenge this distinct contrast between objectivity and subjectivity. They believe that epistemological issues exist on a continuum, rather than on two opposing poles. At some points during the research process, the researcher and the participants may require a highly interactive relationship to answer complex questions. At other points, the researcher may not need interaction with the participants, such as when testing a priori hypotheses using QUAN data that have already been collected or when making predictions on the basis of a large-scale survey.

Transformative scholars also value objectivity and subjectivity. Mertens (2003) contends that *objectivity* in transformative terms means providing a balanced view such that "bias is not interjected because of a lack of understanding of key viewpoints" (p. 141). Mertens also emphasizes the importance of researchers being present in communities so that they can obtain the understanding necessary to appreciate participants' subjective experiences.

Axiological Considerations

Positivists believe that inquiry is value free, whereas constructivists believe that inquiry is value bound. Postpositivists acknowledge both the value-ladenness and the theory-ladenness of facts (Reichardt & Rallis, 1994). Despite this recognition (and to a large degree because of it), postpositivists have devoted considerable effort to developing methods whereby the internal and external validity of their conclusions can be enhanced (e.g., Cook & Campbell, 1979; Shadish et al., 2002). (More details regarding internal and external validity are contained in Table 12.3.) These methods represent the postpositivists' attempt to reduce the influence of personal values, theoretical orientations, and so forth. Pragmatists believe that values play a large role in conducting research and in drawing conclusions from their studies, but they see no reason to be particularly concerned about it. Cherryholmes (1992) stated:

> For pragmatists, values and visions of human action and interaction precede a search for descriptions, theories, explanations, and narratives. Pragmatic research is driven by anticipated consequences. . . . . Beginning with what he or she thinks is known and looking to the consequences he or she desires, our pragmatist would pick and choose how and what to research and what to do. (pp. 13–14)

Pragmatists decide what they want to study based on what is important within their personal value systems. They then study that topic in a way that is congruent with their value system, including units of analysis and variables that they feel are most likely to yield interesting responses (e.g., Tashakkori & Teddlie, 1998). This description of pragmatists' behaviors is consistent with the way that many researchers actually conduct

---

Box 5.3

A Description of a Study Conducted Within the Pragmatist Tradition

Much of the research in school/teacher effectiveness has been conducted by self-proclaimed pragmatists (e.g., Teddlie, Reynolds, & Pol, 2000, pp. 42–49). An international study of school and teacher effectiveness (Reynolds, Creemers, Stringfield, Teddlie, & Schaffer, 2002) had both research hypotheses and questions that were answered using a combination of QUAN data (classroom observations employing numeric ratings, surveys, test scores) and QUAL data (interviews, observations, documentary evidence).

The International School Effectiveness Research Project (ISERP) was conducted in nine countries. Schools in each country were placed into more effective, typical, and less-effective categories based on achievement scores. Researchers then predicted that there would be greater evidence of effective teaching in the more effective schools than in the less effective schools. This hypothesis was statistically confirmed with regard to important classroom variables, such as the use of positive feedback, high-quality questioning, high expectations, and so forth.

Case studies allowed the researchers to answer three research questions: (1) Which school/teacher effectiveness factors are associated with schools/teachers being effective in different countries? (2) How many of these factors are *universals* and how many are *specific* to certain countries? (3) What might explain *why* some of the factors were universal and some specific, and what are the implications of these findings for policy and practice?

Each country team reported case studies of four schools (two more effective, two less effective). These case studies were primarily QUAL in nature, but some QUAN data were also reported. The research team then synthesized all the data and developed lists of universal characteristics of school/teacher effectiveness and lists of specific characteristics associated with effectiveness in one or more countries. The researchers used this information to explain how policymakers in any given country might fruitfully adapt effective educational practices from other countries.

ISERP was conducted within the pragmatist tradition: The researchers decided what they wanted to study based on their personal value systems and the existing literature, they conducted the study using a variety of QUAL and QUAN methods, and they reported the integrated QUAL/QUAN results in a manner consistent with their value systems.

their studies, especially research that has important societal consequences. (Box 5.3 presents an example of a research study conducted within the pragmatist tradition.)

A major contrast between pragmatists and transformative scholars concerns values. From the transformative perspective, the values that guide research function to enhance social justice

Box 5.4

A Description of a Study Conducted Within the Transformative Tradition

Donna Mertens (2005, p. 24) summarized results from a study by Oakes and Guiton (1995) as an example of research conducted within the transformative tradition. This study examined the effects of tracking on high school students, and the target group included low-income and minority students. The study's authors used the following research questions: What are the effects on students' course taking of educators' judgments about what courses are best for the students (plus other cultural/context variables)? What are the factors that contribute to the racial, ethnic, and social class patterns of curriculum participation?

The researchers generated MM case studies for three comprehensive high schools in adjacent communities in an urban center. Interviews were conducted with administrators, teachers, and students in various academic tracks. Transcripts, master schedules, and other documentary evidence were also collected and analyzed.

(Continued)

(Continued)

The study indicated that most administrators and teachers believed there was little hope for academic improvement once students reached high school. The most successful students were, therefore, placed in the better classes, and the least successful students were placed in the lower level classes. Teachers associated racial groups with specific tracks: Latinos were disproportionately placed in the lower tracks, and Asians were placed in higher tracks. The researchers concluded that curriculum opportunities were not made on the basis of an open, merit-based process but were largely determined by educators' perceptions about race and social-class differences in academic abilities and motivation.

This study was conducted within the transformative tradition because the researchers were interested in studying and delineating a social inequity (i.e., the disproportionate placement of low-income and minority students in lower academic tracks) and in enhancing social justice for those low-income and minority students.

rather than individual researcher interests. We elaborate on these differences later in this chapter. (Box 5.4 presents an example of a study conducted within the transformative tradition.)

Ontological Considerations

A defining distinction between positivism/postpositivism and constructivism concerns the nature of reality. Guba and Lincoln (2005) and Miles and Huberman (1994) defined the following types of realism:

- **Naïve realism**—Positivists believe there is a "real reality" that is "apprehendible" [*sic*] or understandable (Guba & Lincoln, 2005, p. 195).
- **Critical realism (transcendental realism)**—Postpositivists believe there is a "real reality," but it can be understood only "imperfectly and probabilistically" (Guba & Lincoln, 2005, p. 195). Another expression of the position is *transcendental realism,* or the belief that social phenomena exist in the objective world, and that there are some "lawful reasonably stable relationships" among them (Miles & Huberman, 1994, p. 429).
- Relativism—Constructivists believe there are "local and specific co-constructed realities" (Guba & Lincoln, 2005, p. 195); these realities are products of human intellects

and may change as their "constructors" change. (See Table 3.1.)

The pragmatist point of view regarding reality consists of two parts:

1. Pragmatists agree with the positivists/postpositivists on the existence of an external reality independent of our minds (Cherryholmes, 1992, p. 14).

2. On the other hand, pragmatists deny that Truth regarding reality can actually be determined. They are also unsure if one explanation of reality is better than any other. According to Cherryholmes (1992), the pragmatists' choice of a particular explanation indicates that it "is better than another at producing anticipated or desired outcomes" (p. 15).

Howe (1988) further explained the pragmatists' views regarding truth:

For pragmatists, "truth" is a normative concept, like "good," and "truth is what works" is best seen not as a theory or definition, but as the pragmatists' *attempt to say something interesting* about the nature of truth and to suggest, in particular, that knowledge claims cannot be totally abstracted from contingent beliefs, interests, and projects. (pp. 14–15, italics added)

Transformative scholars also believe that there are "diversities of viewpoints" regarding social realities (Mertens, 2003, p. 140). Consistent with their overall approach, these scholars choose alternative explanations that best promote social justice for oppressed groups.

Differences Regarding Causal Relations

Notions regarding causal relations follow from the ontological distinctions:

- Positivists believe that there are real causes that occur before or simultaneously with effects.
- Postpositivists believe that there are some reasonably stable relationships among social phenomena that may be known imperfectly (or probabilistically). For example, although prediction of a criterion variable from predictor variables is never possible with 100% accuracy (probability of 1.00), the accuracy of predictions can be improved over time as potent predictors are identified.
- Pragmatists believe that there may be causal relationships but that these relationships are transitory and hard to identify.
- Transformative scholars believe that there may be causal relationships that should be understood within the social justice framework.
- Constructivists believe that all entities are simultaneously shaping each other and that it is impossible to distinguish between causes and effects.

Postpositivists believe that we should strive for constantly better explanations of reality and causality, whereas pragmatists believe that we should employ those explanations of causality and reality that are closer to our own values because we will never understand causal relationships absolutely. Because the results of any research study contain multiple explanations, the choice often comes down to either the "better" explanation (postpositivist) or the explanation that is closer to the researchers' values (pragmatist). The options

for this choice of explanation are often the same because the researcher designed the study and gave the constructs their operational definitions.

The role of causality is related to the QUAN concept of internal validity and the QUAL concept of credibility. Postpositivists' concerns with causal relationships focus on the degree to which they can be sure that the independent variable (and not some other factor) caused the effect on the dependent variable. Constructivists want to be sure that their descriptions of social realities agree with those of the participants. Considerations of both internal validity and credibility are important to pragmatists and transformative scholars.

The Possibility of Generalizations

There are also differences with regard to the possibility of making generalizations:

- Positivists believe that time- and context-free generalizations are possible. Postpositivists subscribe to a modified nomothetic position that emphasizes the importance of techniques that increase the external validity of results.
- Constructivists believe that only time- and context-bound ideographic statements are possible. Constructivists emphasize the importance of the transferability of results from a specific sending context to a specific receiving context.
- Pragmatists emphasize ideographic statements and are concerned with issues of both the external validity and the transferability of results.
- Transformative scholars also emphasize ideographic statements. These researchers attempt to link results from a specific study to broader issues of social justice.

Methodological Distinctions Among the Three Communities: Continua, not Dichotomies

The paradigm contrast tables serve a valuable function from a didactic point of view: They can be used to introduce students to differences among certain researchers (e.g., methodological purists) who are still actively working in the human sciences. Reichardt and Cook (1979) noted the same benefit:

> Undoubtedly, there is some pedagogical advantage to the dialectic form of argument that polarizes qualitative and quantitative methods. For example, it is often easiest to state a case by dichotomizing a continuum into polar extremes *so that the dimension of interest is more clearly revealed.* (p. 27, italics added)

In the real world of research, however, continua of philosophical orientations, rather than dichotomous distinctions, more accurately represent the positions of most investigators. For example, it is more accurate to state that researcher opinions regarding the role of values in their work range from those who believe that inquiry is value free to those who believe that inquiry is value bound, with numerous intermediary positions.

Therefore, the information presented in Table 5.2 contrasting five distinct paradigms may be reconceptualized as continua, rather than dichotomies. In these continua, the positions of the pragmatists and the transformative scholars represent intermediate points of view between those of the constructivists on the left side of the table and the positivists/postpositivists on the right side. A theoretically infinite number of points on the QUAL/QUAN dimension, rather than the five points depicted in Table 5.2, would be present.

We also believe that it is possible to array components associated with research methods on continua. We introduced the concept of the *QUAL-MM-QUAN continuum* in Chapter 2, Figure 2.3, as a series of three overlapping circles. Figure 5.1 presents an alternative illustration: a rectangle with the pure QUAN orientation at one end and the pure QUAL orientation at the other, with a diagonal line crossing the rectangle to indicate the transformation from one orientation to the other. We should emphasize that this figure is for illustration purposes only because it reduces the continuum to only one dimension.

We believe that every component of a research project (e.g., purpose/questions, data, analysis, inference) may be placed along such a multidimensional continuum, as illustrated in Table 5.3.[6]

Most (but not necessarily all) components of a QUAN project are somewhere near the left end of the continuum in Table 5.3, whereas most (but not necessarily all) components of a QUAL project are close to the right end of the continuum. Despite this general tendency, it is possible to have QUAN projects that are exploratory, collect data via unstructured and open-ended procedures, and develop transformative inferences or explanations. Alternatively, it is possible to have QUAL projects that are explanatory or confirmatory, use probability sampling procedures, or include structured design (such as field experiments). Following this logic, all research projects may be considered mixed, at least to some degree. This is also supported by the difficulty (or impossibility) of placing *all* components of a research project on one absolute end of the continuum (e.g., it is hard to think of absolutely

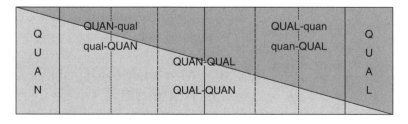

Figure 5.1   Mixed Methods as a Continuum of QUAL and QUAN Integration

Note: For the sake of diversity, we intentionally put QUAN on the left side of the figure, whereas most other tables and figures in this text have QUAN on the right side.

Table 5.3   Multidimensional Continuum of Research Projects

Sphere of Concepts: Purposes, Questions, Objectives		
Deductive questions	←——————————→	Inductive questions
Objective purpose	←——————————→	Subjective purpose
Value neutral	←——————————→	Value involved
Confirmation	←——————————→	Understanding
Explanatory	←——————————→	Exploratory
Sphere of Concrete Processes (Experiential Sphere)		
Numeric data	←——————————→	Narrative data
Structured/close-ended	←——————————→	Open-ended
Preplanned design	←——————————→	Emergent design
Statistical analysis	←——————————→	Thematic analysis
Probability sample	←——————————→	Purposive sample
Sphere of Inferences and Explanations		
Deductive inference	←——————————→	Inductive inference
"Objective" inferences	←——————————→	"Subjective" inferences
Value neutral	←——————————→	Value rich
Politically noncommittal	←——————————→	Transformative
Etic representation	←——————————→	Emic representation
Nomothetic	←——————————→	Ideographic

Note: Most QUAN research is closer to the left side of this table, whereas most QUAL research is closer to the right side. For the sake of diversity, we intentionally put QUAN on the left side, whereas most other tables and figures in this text have QUAN on the right side.

deductive or inductive questions or completely value-free investigators).

The continuum in Figure 5.1 and its multidimensional representation in Table 5.3 include several types of research projects:

- QUAN projects (e.g., those conducted by Professors Experimentalista and Numerico from Chapter 1) somewhere on the left side of Figure 5.1 or close to the left side of most or all dimensions of Table 5.3

- Projects that emphasize QUAN methods and also use QUAL information as supplemental data or have some components close to the right side of Table 5.3 (labeled QUAN-qual or qual-QUAN in Figure 5.1)
- Mixed methods projects that use both QUAN and QUAL approaches about equally (e.g., those conducted by Professor Eclectica) or have components that spread across the continuum in Table 5.3
- Projects that emphasize QUAL approaches but also use QUAN information as

supplemental data (QUAL-quan or quan-QUAL studies in Figure 5.1) or have some components located closer to the left side of continuum in Table 5.3

- QUAL projects (e.g., those conducted by Professor Holistico) close to the right side on most or all dimensions of Table 5.3

Studies that fall mainly on one side of the continuum with a few components on the opposite side (i.e., QUAN-qual, qual-QUAN, QUAL-quan, quan-QUAL) are referred to as *dominant-less dominant designs* (see Chapter 7 for more details).

Table 5.4 expands on this continuum by presenting other methodological dimensions (the *QUAL-MM-QUAN methodological continua*) that may be arrayed along a line from the purely QUAL to the purely QUAN orientation. These continua serve as an advance organizer for methodological issues to be discussed throughout the rest of the text, such as research questions/hypotheses, research designs, sampling, data collection strategies, data analysis, and inference quality (Chapters 6–12).

Contemporary Points of View Regarding the Use of Paradigms

Despite the compatibility thesis, paradigm issues remain an ongoing area of interest. Authors have generated lists of contemporary perspectives regarding the use of paradigms in MM research (e.g., Greene, 2007; Greene & Caracelli, 1997a). We (Teddlie & Tashakkori, 2003, pp. 17–24) delineated six contemporary points of view regarding paradigm use in MM research:

1. Some scholars believe that methods and paradigms are independent of one another; therefore, the epistemology-methods link is not an issue, and it is permissible to do MM research (**a-paradigmatic stance**).

2. Some researchers agree with the tenets of the incompatibility thesis and conclude that MM research is impossible (e.g., Guba, 1987; Sale, Lohfeld, & Brazil, 2002; Smith, 1983).

3. Some scholars believe that MM research is possible but that the QUAL and QUAN components must be kept separate so that the strengths of each underlying paradigmatic position can be realized (Brewer & Hunter, 1989, 2006; Morse, 1991, 2003). This point of view is known as the complementary strengths thesis.

4. Some researchers believe that a single paradigm (e.g., pragmatism, transformative perspective) should serve as the foundation for MM research.

5. Some scholars propose the dialectic stance, which does not advocate one paradigm above others but rather envisions MM research as intentionally engaging multiple sets of paradigms and their assumptions (e.g., Greene, 2007; Greene & Caracelli, 1997b, 2003). According to these theorists, all paradigms are valuable, but only partial, worldviews. To think dialectically means to examine the tensions that emerge from the juxtaposition of these multiple diverse perspectives.

6. Some scholars believe that multiple paradigms may serve as the foundation for research in the human sciences. This position has been applied to QUAL research explicitly (e.g., Denzin & Lincoln, 2000b, 2005b; Schwandt, 2000), but it is also applicable to MM research (e.g., Creswell, Plano-Clark, Gutmann, & Hanson, 2003). A difference between this position and the dialectic stance is that the multiple paradigm theorists believe that one type of paradigm is best used in a particular kind study and another paradigm is best used with another kind.

Details regarding these six perspectives are presented next.

Table 5.4   The QUAL-MIXED-QUAN Methodological Continua

General Issue (Chapter in Text)	QUAL Position	MIXED Position	QUAN Position
Statements of research purpose (Chapter 6)	Most (but not all) QUAL research is exploratory in nature; most QUAL research involves the statement of research questions.	MM may involve the statement of both research questions and hypotheses (both exploratory and confirmatory).	Most (but not all) QUAN research is confirmatory in nature; QUAN research may involve the statement of research hypotheses or research questions or both.
Design traditions (Chapter 7)	Ethnography; grounded theory; phenomenological research; biography; case study.	All design traditions are included in these studies including unique MM designs.	Research may be causal comparative, correlational, quasi-experimental, or experimental.
Sampling (Chapter 8)	Purposive sampling is emphasized in QUAL research; QUAL research may also involve probability sampling.	MM sampling includes both purposive and probability sampling	Probability sampling is emphasized in QUAN research, though purposive sampling may also be involved.
Data collection strategies (Chapters 9 & 10)	QUAL may include all types but typically involves unstructured observations, open-ended interviews, focus groups, and unobtrusive measures.	All data collection strategies are included.	QUAN may include all types but typically involves structured observations, closed-ended interviews, questionnaires, and tests.
Data analysis (Chapter 11)	QUAL includes qualitative (thematic) data analysis (categorical strategies, contextualizing strategies).	MM data analyses, both thematic and statistical analyses plus data conversion techniques, are used.	Statistical analysis (descriptive, inferential) is used.
Validity or inference quality issues (Chapter 12)	Trustworthiness, credibility, transferability, dependability, and various authenticity criteria are emphasized.	All inference and validity issues are subsumed under inference quality and inference transferability.	Statistical conclusion validity, internal validity, construct validity, and external validity are emphasized.

The A-Paradigmatic Stance

Some scholars see the epistemology-methods link as distracting or unnecessary and ignore it, continuing to work as they always have, using whatever methods seem appropriate for their research questions. Scholars working in applied fields, such as evaluation or nursing, often take this stance.

Patton (2002) made the following common-sense statement about the *a-paradigmatic thesis*:

> One might simply conduct interviews and gather observation data to answer concrete program and organizational questions without working explicitly with a particular theoretical, paradigmatic, or philosophical perspective. Well-trained and thoughtful interviewers can get meaningful answers to practical questions without making a paradigmatic or philosophical pledge of allegiance. (p. 145)

In a somewhat similar vein, Morgan (2007) critiqued what he called the metaphysical paradigm, which emphasizes philosophical (especially epistemological) issues. Morgan's (2007) "commitment to a Kuhnian view of paradigms as systems of shared beliefs among a community of scholars" (p. 65) led him to advocate for a pragmatic approach, which emphasizes shared meanings and joint action among researchers, rather than focusing on epistemological and other philosophical issues.

The Incompatibility Thesis

The *incompatibility thesis* states that the integration of QUAN and QUAL methods is impossible due to the incompatibility of the paradigms that underlie the methods. This thesis has already been discussed extensively in Chapters 1 and 4 of this text.

The incompatibility thesis has been largely discredited, partially because scholars have demonstrated that it is possible to successfully integrate MM in their research projects. Even though many researchers do not endorse the incompatibility thesis per se, it has influenced other contemporary positions (e.g., the complementary strengths thesis).

The Complementary Strengths Thesis

Some researchers (e.g., Brewer & Hunter, 1989, 2006; Morse, 2003; Stern, 1994) argue that MM research is possible but that the QUAN and QUAL components must be kept separate so that the strengths of each paradigmatic position can be realized (the **complementary strengths thesis**). For example, Morse (2003) viewed the ad hoc mixing of methods as a serious threat to the validity of MM research, arguing that each MM study must have a primary methodological thrust.

Similarly, Brewer and Hunter (2006) discussed disadvantages of what they labeled *composite* methods, which are composed of "elements borrowed from the basic styles" (p. 62). Though acknowledging the strengths of composite methods, these authors concluded that the basic methods lose some of their strengths when incorporated into competing methodologies. Additionally, they contended that this methodological eclecticism does not provide enough data for proper "cross-method comparisons" (Brewer & Hunter, 2006, p. 63).

On the other hand, Joe Maxwell and Diane Loomis (2003) do not believe that purely QUAL and purely QUAN research paradigms actually exist. Citing multiple sources, they convincingly argued that each of these two generic positions has a large number of separate and distinct components. They argued further that these QUAN and QUAL components can be put together in multiple, legitimate ways. Because the two research paradigms are not "pure" to begin with, researchers lose little when they creatively mix them.

The Single Paradigm Thesis

The paradigms debate involved scholars who had already identified a single paradigm that supported their methodological predilection. This has been called the **single paradigm thesis**, which Lincoln and Guba (1985) popularized with their postulation of single links between positivism and QUAN methods as well as constructivism (naturalism) and QUAL methods. Since QUAL and QUAN researchers had their own particular epistemologies, MM scholars inevitably began looking for a paradigm to support their methodological orientation.

As noted throughout this text, many scholars proposed that pragmatism is the best paradigm for justifying the use of MM research (e.g., Biesta & Burbules, 2003; Howe, 1988; Johnson & Onwuegbuzie, 2004; Maxcy, 2003; Morgan, 2007; Patton, 2002; Rallis & Rossman, 2003; Tashakkori & Teddlie, 1998, 2003c). On the other hand, Mertens (2003, 2005) posited the transformative perspective as a framework for the use of MM.

The major difference in the two positions concerns axiology. As noted earlier, we believe that research conducted in the tradition of pragmatism is carried out within the value system of the investigators involved and is based on answering research questions of interest to the investigators.

Some scholars have concerns about using pragmatism as the underlying value system for conducting MM research. Both House and Howe (1999) and Mertens (2003) are concerned that pragmatism is inadequate and unexamined because it does not specify "which values" or "whose values" are involved. Mertens (2005) concluded that the adoption of an explicit research agenda related to "the inclusion of values and viewpoints" of "marginalized groups" is a better axiological stance for those conducting MM research (p. 295).

We believe that some of the criticism of pragmatism is based on a fundamental misunderstanding of its basic premises (refer to Table 4.1), but that is a topic beyond the scope of this chapter. Instead, we conclude that both pragmatism and the transformative perspective can be used as alternative worldviews associated with the use of MM, depending on the type of research being conducted. Of course, other paradigms might also be appropriate, but these are the two most widely advocated within the MM field. This is, of course, an endorsement of the *multiple paradigms thesis*.

The Multiple Paradigms Thesis

Some scholars believe that multiple paradigms may serve as the foundation for MM research (the **multiple paradigms thesis**). For instance, John Creswell and colleagues (2003) presented six MM designs and argued that a single paradigm did not apply to all of them. Multiple paradigms may be applied to diverse MM designs, and researchers have to decide which paradigm is most appropriate given their choice of a particular MM design for a particular study. Creswell and colleagues gave several examples of the multiple paradigms thesis using the six designs they described (Creswell et al., 2003, p. 232).

This multiple paradigm perspective stems at least partially from writings that originated in QUAL research methodology. The editors of the *Handbook of Qualitative Research* came to the following conclusion:

A complex, interconnected family of terms, concepts and assumptions surround the term *qualitative research*. These include the traditions associated with foundationalism, positivism, postfoundationalism, postpositivism, poststructuralism, and the many qualitative research perspectives, and/or methods connected to cultural and interpretive studies. (Denzin & Lincoln, 2005b, p. 2, italics in original)

The multiple paradigms position (e.g., Guba & Lincoln, 2005; Schwandt, 2000) is an interesting change in position from a perspective that has historically tied particular methods (e.g., QUAL) to particular paradigms (e.g., constructivism) in a one-to-one correspondence.

The Dialectical Thesis

The **dialectical thesis** assumes that all paradigms have something to offer and that the use of multiple paradigms contributes to greater understanding of the phenomenon under study. Jennifer Greene and Valerie Caracelli (1997a, 1997b, 2003) are the foremost proponents of this position, which has also been adopted by other writers (e.g., Maxwell & Loomis, 2003).

Greene and Caracelli (2003) reject the continued search for the single best paradigm as a relic of the past and the paradigms debate. Instead, they believe that multiple, diverse perspectives are important because they are required to explain the complexity of an increasingly pluralistic society. In her latest book, Greene (2007) discussed a mixed methods way of thinking, which was defined as "the planned and intentional incorporation of multiple mental models . . . into the same inquiry space" to better understand the phenomenon under study (p. 30).

An important component of this position is the ability to think dialectically. This involves considering opposing viewpoints and interacting with the tensions caused by their juxtaposition. These tensions come from the differences in the assumptions of the different paradigms. There are several other points about conversations/dialogues in dialectic inquiry (Greene & Caracelli, 2003):

- These conversations/dialogues are not typically about philosophical issues but rather about the phenomena that are the subject of the research.
- Historical dualisms (e.g., those featured in Table 5.1) are not of particular importance in dialectical inquiry. There are no endless discussions of induction versus deduction, subjectivity versus objectivity, and so on.
- Greene and Caracelli (2003) listed some dichotomies that are important in dialectical inquiry: value-neutrality and value-commitment, *emic* and *etic*,[7] particularity and generality, social constructions and physical traces, and so on.

Ongoing Dialogues Among the Three Communities

Some ongoing dialogues among the three communities were introduced in Chapter 4, and details regarding two of those dialogues are presented next. It is worthwhile to note that QUAL theorists seem to be the most engaged participants in these dialogues, as has been the case historically concerning the paradigms debate. Bryman (2006b) summarized this tendency as follows:

Interestingly, the terms of this debate were, to a large extent, set by qualitative researchers; quantitative researchers tended not to get entangled in the philosophical distinctions that were being demarcated. To the extent that others, such as methodologists, became embroiled in the tussles, it was largely in terms of the battle lines drawn up by qualitative researchers. (p. 113)

The Neo-Paradigms Debate Between Qualitative and Quantitative Researchers

Many researchers, especially those working in the applied social and behavioral sciences, have accepted the compatibility thesis and go about their investigations mixing methods without concern for the paradigms debate or its aftermath. We would be disingenuous, however, to contend that the human sciences have entered a new era of methodological tolerance in which scholars no longer proclaim the superiority of their own orientation (e.g., Patton, 2002). Indeed, it seems that researchers will continue to go through cycles in which one or another of the three positions (QUAL, QUAN, MM) will claim predominance within particular fields or disciplines.

Despite the overall trend toward détente in the paradigms debate, the gap between the methodological "left" and "right" in educational research has widened recently in the United States. This, unfortunately, has resulted in a continued splintering of these methodological communities.

As noted in Chapters 1 and 4, the installation of the Bush-Cheney administration in 2001 resulted in a replay of some aspects of the paradigms debate due to the establishment of a distinctly postpositivist QUAN orientation in the U.S. Department of Education. Manifestations of that orientation included the passage of the No Child Left Behind Act (2002), which contained a detailed definition of *scientifically based research* (SBR) and required federal grantees to expend their research funds on "evidence-based strategies" (Feur, Towne, & Shavelson, 2002). The passage of the Education Sciences Reform Act of 2002 included the standard that causal relationships could be claimed "only in random assigned experiments or other designs (to the extent such designs substantially eliminate plausible competing explanations for the obtained results)" (Eisenhart & Towne, 2003, p. 36). There was also the publication of the National Research Council report (2002) titled *Scientific Research in Education,* which argues for "the preeminence of randomized experiments in causal investigation" (Maxwell, 2004, p. 3).

Thus, SBR in education emphasizes randomized controlled trials or experiments and QUAN methods in general[8] (e.g., Eisenhart & Towne, 2003; Slavin, 2003). QUAN purists and others in the federal education bureaucracy consider experimentation to be the gold standard for educational research (e.g., Cook, 2002; Fitz-Gibbon, 1996; Shadish et al., 2002; Slavin, 2003). For instance, Cook (2002) expressed his preference for using experiments in the evaluation of educational reforms:

> This article notes the paucity with which reform efforts in education have been evaluated experimentally, despite well nigh universal acknowledgment that experiments provide the best justification for causal conclusions. (p. 175)

The emergence of experimentation as the gold standard for educational research has led to predictable (and viable) charges of "scientism" from numerous critics who value QUAL methods (e.g., Berliner, 2002; Eisenhart & Towne, 2003; Howe, 2004; Lather, 2004; Maxwell, 2004; St. Pierre, 2002). Much of that criticism concerns the perceived narrowness of the definition of SBR proposed by the Institute of Educational Sciences and others.

The QUAL tradition in the human sciences has continued to gain in popularity and legitimacy. Despite this, many of its proponents continue to severely criticize the QUAN "received tradition" and argue for the preeminence of their philosophical position and methods (e.g., Denzin & Lincoln, 2000a, 2005a), perhaps because that posture has brought success to them in the past (e.g., Lancy, 1993).

This polarization between the "left" (QUALs) and "right" (QUANs) has also been influenced by some individuals on the left who continue to blur distinctions between the social sciences and the arts/humanities by expanding what constitutes QUAL methodology. For instance, the four-volume set titled *The American Tradition in Qualitative Research* concluded with the poetry of two anthropologists. Denzin and Lincoln (2001), the series editors, explained their inclusion of poetry in a series on research methods.

> In the literary, poetic form ethnographers enact a moral aesthetic that allows them to say things they could not otherwise say. In so doing, they push the boundaries of artful ethnographic discourse. Thus are the boundaries between the humanities and the human sciences blurred. In this blurring our moral sensibilities are enlivened. (p. xli)

The positions taken in some of these dialogues by the methodological left and right have left much of the middle ground in social and behavioral methodology to the MM community. An important point is that salient players on both sides of the QUAL-QUAN divide continue to find it advantageous to keep some vestiges of the paradigms debate alive.

A Contemporary Dialogue Between Qualitative and Mixed Methods Researchers

A new twist to these methodological commentaries involves criticisms of the MM orientation from some scholars working within the QUAL tradition (e.g., Denzin & Lincoln, 2005b; Denzin, Lincoln, & Giardina, 2006; Howe, 2004). The criticisms have been noted by others, such as Gorard and Taylor (2004):

> This chapter . . . devotes much of its space to a critique of the way that avowedly "qualitative" researchers use the notions of theory and paradigm to protect themselves

from having to deal with a larger range of evidence. This focus is necessary because they, more than any other group, are the ones suggesting that the combination of data from different "paradigms" is impossible. (pp. 143–144)

There is a tendency among some QUALs to doubt the viability of MM research, perhaps because they think mixed methodologists are attempting to appropriate QUAL methods in some manner. Recently there have been more specific criticisms from QUALs (e.g., Denzin & Lincoln, 2005b; Denzin et al., 2006; Howe, 2004) based on a limited view of MM research taken from the No Child Left Behind Act (2002) and the National Research Council (2002) report. As noted earlier, that act and that report placed much greater emphasis on QUAN experimentalism than on the QUAL orientation, resulting in something resembling the QUAN-qual orientation illustrated in Figure 5.1.

The criticism of experimental mixed methods by Denzin, Lincoln, Howe, and others centers on the secondary status afforded QUAL research in the SBR promoted by the Bush-Cheney administration. "Mainstream" mixed research, as presented in this text and discussed elsewhere for 20 years (e.g., Creswell, 2003; Creswell & Plano-Clark, 2007; Greene, Caracelli, & Graham, 1989; Johnson & Onwuegbuzie, 2004; Newman & Benz, 1998; Patton, 2002; Reichardt & Rallis, 1994; Tashakkori & Teddlie, 1998, 2003a), does *not* correspond to the SBR described earlier in this chapter.

These criticisms have been addressed by researchers writing from within the MM community (e.g., Creswell, Shope, Plano-Clark, & Green, 2006; Gorard & Taylor, 2004; Teddlie, Tashakkori, & Johnson, 2008). Creswell et al.'s (2006) response to these criticisms focused on three issues:

that mixed methods pushes qualitative research to secondary or auxiliary status, that this secondary status is expressed as an

adjunct to a more privileged experimental trial, and that mixed methods research does not employ critical, interpretive approaches to qualitative research. (p. 1)

In our opinion, Creswell et al.'s (2006) responses successfully refuted these three allegations by providing numerous specific examples of qualitatively driven MM research (e.g., Mason, 2006); nonexperimental MM research (e.g., Bryman, 2006a; Creswell et al., 2003; Morgan, 1998); and the use of interpretive frameworks in MM research (e.g., Brannen, 1992; Mertens, 2003; Oakley, 1998).

With a colleague (i.e., Teddlie et al., 2008), we developed a synopsis of the assertions made by Denzin and Lincoln (2005b) and the responses from the MM community. Though we repeat these assertions and rebuttals in this chapter, we hope that this minidebate will be reconciled soon because it echoes some of the nonproductive aspects of the paradigm debate.

In the following list, Denzin and Lincoln's (2005b, pp. 9–10) assertions regarding MM research are presented first, followed by the responses from the MM community:

- Denzin and Lincoln assertion—MM are "direct descendants of classical experimentalism."

- MM community response—On the contrary, MM grew out of both the QUAL and QUAN traditions from applied research fields, such as evaluation and education (e.g., Greene et al., 1989; Patton, 1990; Reichardt & Cook, 1979), which preceded the SBR era by 15 to 20 years. Most MM studies currently published integrate the findings of nonexperimental QUAN and thematically analyzed QUAL findings.

- Denzin and Lincoln assertion—MM presumes a "methodological hierarchy," with QUAN methods at the top and QUAL methods relegated to a largely auxiliary role.

- MM community response—On the contrary, QUAL and QUAN methods have been given equal priority in MM since the earliest writing in the field (e.g., Brewer & Hunter, 1989; Greene et al., 1989; Morse, 1991) up to the current time (e.g., Creswell & Plano-Clark, 2007; Johnson & Onwuegbuzie, 2004; Onwuegbuzie & Teddlie, 2003). For example, we (Tashakkori & Teddlie, 1998, 2003a, 2003b) have repeatedly cautioned against classifying QUAL projects as exploratory and QUAN methods as experimental or confirmatory.

- Denzin and Lincoln assertion—MM "divides inquiry into dichotomous categories" (e.g., exploration vs. confirmation), with QUAL work assigned to one category and QUAN research to the other.

- MM community response—On the contrary, many MM scholars refer to continua between different dimensions of QUAL and QUAN work (e.g., Johnson & Onwuegbuzie, 2004; Newman & Benz, 1998; Niglas, 2004; Tashakkori & Teddlie, 2003a; Teddlie, 2005). We reproduced the original contrast tables in this chapter as a didactic tool, but we emphasized the QUAL-MM-QUAN continuum as presented in Figures 2.3 and 5.1 and Table 5.3. Table 5.3 is a revised version of our previous (Tashakkori & Teddlie, 2003c) attempt to demonstrate this continuity.

- Denzin and Lincoln assertion—MM "excludes stakeholders from dialogue and active participation in the research process."

- MM community response—On the contrary, MM researchers welcome the participation of stakeholders in the research process as discussed in numerous MM studies (e.g., see Bamberger, 2000; Mertens, 2005; Rao & Woolcock, 2003; Teddlie et al., 2008). Mertens (2007) provided several examples of participatory and transformative mixed studies.

- Denzin and Lincoln assertion—The MM movement takes QUAL "methods out of their natural home, which is within the critical, interpretive framework."

- MM community response—It is difficult for us to understand what a "natural home" for any research method or project is. Instead, the MM perspective is that multiple frameworks or paradigms can be associated with any given method, so to claim that a method has a "natural home" is illogical. Ironically, Denzin and Lincoln argued (2005b) elsewhere that QUAL methods are associated with a variety of different philosophical orientations.

Summary

This chapter began with a review of the paradigms debate, including two contrast tables that differentiated the positions of different theorists in the human sciences. We argued that both the pragmatist and the transformative perspectives may be employed as underlying paradigms for the use of MM. The pragmatist position is particularly appealing because it specifically rejects the either-or argument of the incompatibility thesis.

We then discussed differences among the three research communities, arguing that these variations should be conceived pragmatically as positions along a continuum (the QUAL-MM-QUAN continuum). We presented a table consisting of methodological continua including research questions/hypotheses, research designs, and so forth. Contemporary points of view regarding the use of paradigms were then presented, followed by a discussion of recent debates among QUALs, QUANs, and mixed methodologists over a variety of topics, including the role of the QUAL component in MM research.

Chapter 6 starts the section titled "Methods and Strategies of Mixed Methods Research," which contains Chapters 6–12. This section describes the MM research process from initial planning to selection of a design to sampling to data collection to data analysis and finally to inference. Chapter 6 explains the very important step of generating research questions in MM research.

Review Questions and Exercises

1. What are the five contrasts between the constructivists and the positivists that were included on the original paradigm contrast table?

2. Describe how pragmatists deny the either-or distinctions of the paradigms debate. Give some specific examples.

3. What are the differences between pragmatists and transformative scholars on the one hand and constructivists and positivists on the other?

4. What are the differences between pragmatism and the transformative stance as alternative paradigms associated with the use of MM? Which one is the most valid from your point of view? Justify your position.

5. What is the QUAL-MM-QUAN continuum and how does it differ from the paradigm contrast tables?

6. What are six contemporary points of view regarding the use of paradigms in the social and behavioral sciences? Which one is the most valid from your perspective? Justify your choice.

7. What are the cultural differences (e.g., educational, socialization experiences, academic disciplines) among QUALs, QUANs, and mixed methodologists? How have these differences contributed to the continued splintering of the methodological community in the human sciences? (Also refer to Chapters 1 and 2.)

8. Envision a hypothetical research study. Describe how pragmatists and transformative scholars would differentially develop research questions for the study. State specific research questions derived from the pragmatist and the transformative points of view. Explain how these different research questions exemplify axiological differences between the two perspectives.

9. Howe (1988) discussed "the pragmatists' *attempt to say something interesting* about the nature of truth" (p. 14). What does this mean for researchers in terms of how they conduct and report their studies?

10. There has been some debate among scholars with regard to the type of logic that the famous fictional detective Sherlock Holmes used in solving his cases. Which of the three types of logic (abduction, deduction, induction) do you think Sherlock Holmes employed as his primary tool of investigation? Defend your answer. (Read Patton, 2002, pp. 470–471, for a discussion of Sherlock Holmes and the type of logic he used plus a reference to and description of William Sanders's 1974 publication titled *The Sociologist as Detective*.)

Key Terms*

Abduction or abductive logic

A-paradigmatic stance

Axiology

Complementary strengths thesis

Critical realism (transcendental realism)

Dialectical thesis

Emic perspective

Epistemology

---

*Several terms used in Chapter 5 were defined in Chapters 1–4. The reader should refer to those chapters or to the glossary for more information about them.

Etic perspective

Ideographic statements

Multiple paradigms thesis

Naïve realism

Nomothetic statements

Ontology

Single paradigm thesis

Transformative perspective

Notes

1. This quote is from William Faulkner's *Requiem for a Nun* (1951) and presented in *The Oxford Dictionary of Quotations* (1999, p. 307, quote 25).

2. Very few researchers in the social and behavioral sciences currently refer to themselves as positivists. We leave the positivist paradigm in the contrast tables as a historical reference.

3. Howe (1988) commented on the failure to include pragmatism as a third point of view as a "serious omission, for pragmatists were largely responsible for bringing down positivism and would clearly reject the forced choice between the interpretivist and positivist paradigms" (p. 13).

4. Critical theory and the transformative perspective are very similar. We discuss the transformative perspective in this text because it has been directly linked to MM.

5. Please note that there are very few widely accepted formal "theories" and some "minitheories" in the social and behavioral sciences.

6. Please note that for the sake of diversity, we intentionally put QUAN on the left side of Figure 5.1 and Table 5.3, though most other tables and figures in this text place QUAN on the right.

7. The *emic/etic* dimension is particularly important in dialectical inquiry. The **emic perspective** refers to the point of view of a cultural insider, such as a person who has lived in a specific village for 30 or 40 years. The **etic perspective** refers to the point of view of a cultural outsider, such as a scholar visiting the aforementioned village.

8. Though there is a persistent perception that QUAN research dominates SBR in the United States, the Committee on Scientific Principles for Education Research (National Research Council, 2002) specifically stated that "our vision of scientific quality and rigor applies to the two forms of education research that have traditionally been labeled 'quantitative' and 'qualitative'" (p. 19).

Methods and Strategies of Mixed Methods Research

CHAPTER 6

Generating Questions in Mixed Methods Research

Objectives

Upon finishing this chapter, you should be able to:

- List and describe the steps in a four-step model for generating research questions in the social and behavioral sciences
- Identify eight reasons for conducting research in the social and behavioral sciences
- List and describe four sources related to the identification of content areas of interest
- Define and provide an example of a line of research
- Describe the 12 steps in conducting a literature review
- Describe and identify preliminary, secondary, and primary sources
- Distinguish between causal effects and causal mechanisms
- Explain why a research question may be a dual focal point
- Generate integrated quantitative and qualitative research questions that are related to at least one common research objective
- Describe the current debate about mixed methods questions

Introduction: The Conceptualization Phase of Research

We have argued that there are three phases of the research process: conceptualization, methods, and inference (Tashakkori & Teddlie, 2003b). The conceptualization phase involves all of the planning that occurs from the time of the researcher's decision to conduct a study until the implementation of actual research. This chapter describes the first part of the conceptualization phase of a mixed methods (MM) study: the generation of the research questions. These research questions dictate the remaining components of the planning process, including the selection of a

specific MM research design, a sampling strategy, data collection protocols, and so on.

Figure 6.1 illustrates a four-step model for the generation of research questions in human science studies:

- The emergence of a reason or reasons for conducting research
- The identification of a researchable idea in a content area of interest
- The generation of research objectives (optional)
- The generation of research questions

Details regarding these four steps are presented in sequential order throughout the chapter. This model assumes that investigators start, either implicitly or explicitly, with at least one reason for conducting research based on their personal characteristics, experiences, and educational background. In this chapter, we present a *typology of reasons for conducting research* and demonstrate how these reasons affect the decisions that MM researchers make as they plan their studies.

We then discuss how investigators identify researchable ideas in *content areas of interest*. Content areas of interest are often highly interrelated with the investigator's initial reasons for conducting research. Four sources of content areas of interest are discussed: intuitions based on previous experiences, reactions to practical problems, results from previous research, and theory.

We then briefly describe the development of the **research objectives** for an MM study, which are the specific purposes or aims that guide a particular study. They are especially important in MM research because they provide a platform on which qualitative (QUAL) and quantitative (QUAN) questions may be synthesized into integrated themes.

We then discuss the generation of both *qualitative* and *quantitative research questions* (including hypotheses) for MM studies. We briefly introduced these types of questions in Chapter 1; this chapter provides details regarding how these questions are generated in MM research.

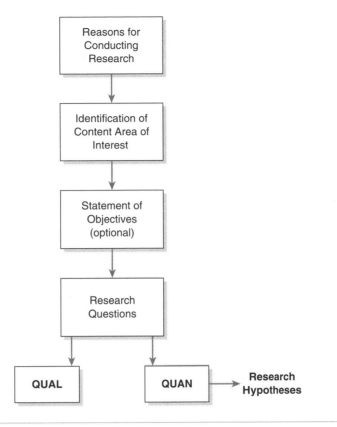

Figure 6.1   Flowchart Describing the Process of Generating Research Questions (and hypotheses) in MM Research

Reasons for Conducting Research in the Social and Behavioral Sciences

A Typology of Reasons for Conducting Research

We argue in this chapter that the investigator's reasons for performing research are the authentic starting point for research in the social and behavioral sciences. Any investigator inevitably has some underlying reason (or motivation) for conducting research *before* he or she actually identifies a specific content area in which to

work. The motivation (or reason) to conduct research precedes the conceptualization or the planning of an actual research project.

Isadore Newman and colleagues (i.e., Newman, Ridenour, Newman, & DeMarco, 2003) argued convincingly that, during the past four decades, the research purpose (or *reason* for conducting research in our terms)[1] has gained in importance relative to the research question. This has occurred because the role for research in the human sciences has expanded beyond the well-established postpositivist purpose of "knowledge generation" during that time. For example, the transformative scholars' focus on enhancing social justice for oppressed groups represents an expanded reason for conducting research beyond knowledge generation.

Before introducing our typology of reasons for conducting research, we need to make some general comments:

- Our typology is not exhaustive; other reasons for doing research could (and do) exist.
- The elements in our typology are not mutually exclusive; in fact, they overlap considerably.
- Typically, investigators have multiple reasons for conducting a research study.
- Investigators' reasons for conducting research may change over time as their careers evolve.

Despite these flaws and caveats, however, this typology serves as a good starting point for discussing how investigators conceptualize and conduct research. Our presentation of this typology serves three functions:

- It establishes a logical sequence of activities involved in performing a research project: determination of the reasons for the study to the generation of objectives[2] to the generation of questions to the development of methods to the implementation of methods and beyond.
- It enunciates several of the most important contemporary reasons for conducting research, thus illuminating the overall process.
- It may lead individual investigators to rethink or express differently their reasons for conducting research.

Box 6.1 lists the elements in our *typology of reasons for conducting research* in the social and behavioral sciences. This typology, which was informed by others (e.g., Maxwell, 1997; Newman et al., 2003), includes three general categories: personal reasons, reasons associated with advancing knowledge, and societal reasons.

QUAN and QUAL researchers have traditionally emphasized different subsets of the reasons in Box 6.1. Traditional QUALs tend to emphasize understanding complex phenomena as a reason for conducting research. On the other hand, traditional QUANs tend to emphasize the specification of relationships among variables, which might eventually lead to causal explanations.

Mixed methodologists embrace all of these reasons as valid ones for conducting research in

---

Box 6.1

A Typology of Reasons for Conducting Research in the Social and Behavioral Sciences

A. Personal Reasons
   1. To advance your career
   2. To satisfy your own curiosity about a phenomenon of interest

B. Reasons Associated With Advancing Knowledge
   3. To generate and test new ideas or innovations
   4. To develop causal explanations
   5. To understand complex phenomena
   6. To make predictions

C. Societal Reasons
   7. To improve society and its institutions
   8. To empower disadvantaged groups or constituencies

different discipline areas and in different settings or contexts. Following are details about each of these reasons.

Personal Reasons

These reasons may be more important at the beginning of an investigator's career when he or she is involved in the credentialing process (e.g., attaining required advanced degrees) and first begins research projects. At this phase, research ideas may more easily germinate from personal curiosity about meaningful phenomena in the researcher's life or the lives of others.

To Advance Your Career

Because of the dictates of the educational/credentialing processes necessary to obtain a position at a university, research institution, or government agency, almost all social and behavioral scientists understand "advancing your career" as a reason for conducting research. Beyond the credentialing phase, researchers often write grants and conduct research in areas in which they have little or no interest except to advance their careers or to satisfy employer requirements. These personal, practical reasons for conducting research should not be criticized, however, because the research enterprise in the social and behavioral sciences is a business not unlike others in society.

To Satisfy Your Own Curiosity About a Phenomenon of Interest

From an intellectual point of view, this is the "purest" reason to conduct research. It is often connected to another reason, such as understanding complex phenomena, yet the initial curiosity or spark that drives some fortunate researchers allows them the pleasure of truly enjoying their work. King, Keohane, and Verba (1994) described this reason as follows:

The specific topic that a social scientist studies may have a personal or idiosyncratic

origin. . . . These personal experiences and values often provide the motivation to become a social scientist and, later, to choose a particular research question. As such, they may constitute the "real" reasons for engaging in a particular research project—and appropriately so. (pp. 14–15)

Reasons Associated With Advancing Knowledge

To Generate and Test New Ideas or Innovations

The development and testing of innovations occur in the social and behavioral sciences, as well as in the biological and physical sciences. This work is often done in research laboratories or in governmental agencies with an emphasis on evaluation or research and development, or both.

For example, recently, considerable research has been conducted to determine the impact of systematic schoolwide reform programs—known as comprehensive school reform (CSR)—on student achievement. Research into the success of CSR efforts (e.g., Accelerated Schools, Success for All program) has fueled a new field of study in educational research (e.g., Datnow, Hubbard, & Mehan, 2002; Stringfield et al., 1997).

To Develop Causal Explanations

This is, of course, the *raison d'etre* for post-positivists of all genres. From a QUAN perspective, studies related to causal explanations involve the use of experimental, quasi-experimental, and sophisticated correlational methods. The importance of causal explanations and the unique ability of experiments to produce them have been trumpeted by many QUAN-oriented methodologists (e.g., Cook, 2002; Cook & Campbell, 1979; Shadish, Cook, & Campbell, 2002).

We increasingly recognize that QUAL researchers are also interested in studying causality (e.g., Maxwell, 1997, 2004; Miles & Huberman, 1994; Teddlie, 2005). This process in QUAL research may involve matching patterns or ruling out alternative explanations (e.g., Yin, 2003). Maxwell (1997) summarized this process as follows:

> Deriving causal explanations from a qualitative study is not an easy or straightforward task, but qualitative research is no different from quantitative research in this respect. Both approaches need to identify and deal with the plausible validity threats to any proposed causal explanation. (p. 75)

To Understand Complex Phenomena

Understanding complex phenomena involves considerations of context, process, meaning, and so on. QUALs have often been more comfortable with this reason for conducting research than causal explanations because *causality* often connotes *nomothetic statements* (time- and context-free), which QUALs avoid. Understanding a complex phenomenon may imply only a fleeting ideographic knowledge that disappears as the phenomenon changes. This process was described by Richardson and St. Pierre (2005) as follows:

> Crystals are prisms that reflect externalities and refract within themselves, creating different colors, patterns, and arrays, casting off in different directions. What we see depends on our angle of repose . . . not triangulation but rather crystallization. (p. 963)

There is a historical parallel to this reason for conducting research: *to understand complex events or phenomena that occurred in the past.* Most research in the human sciences involves the study of ongoing phenomena. Research into historical phenomena reflects an understanding that one can learn about contemporary events by studying past events. Researchers in political science, sociology, education, and other fields often use the methods of *historiography*, which employs the techniques of historical research, analysis, and writing. For instance, political scientists Allison and Zelikow (1999) explained the

Cuban missile crisis in a manner that made results from that historical case study directly applicable to many other situations involving government actions in foreign or domestic crises (Yin, 2003, p. 4).

To Make Predictions

Researchers, both QUAN and QUAL, often want to predict future events. **Prediction studies** are typically QUAN in nature and involve the prediction of an important *criterion variable* (or variables) on the basis of several *predictor variables.*[3] For example, researchers at a university might be interested in predicting the chances of students being successful at their institution based on several factors such as high school grade point average, standardized tests, and so on.

Some strategies for making predictions involve QUAL techniques. For instance, the *Delphi method* was developed in the 1960s as a technique for forecasting future events using interviews conducted with expert panels (e.g., Gordon & Helmer, 1964). This method has been applied to various areas, including educational policymaking, teacher effectiveness, and economic development (e.g., Covino & Iwanicki, 1996; Teddlie, Creemers, Kyriakides, Muijs, & Yu, 2006).

Societal Reasons

To Improve Society and Its Institutions

Improving society has not always been a clearly enunciated reason for conducting research in the human sciences, particularly in disciplines where postpositivism has dominated. Nevertheless, there is a growing understanding that improving society and its institutions is a valid, probably even essential, part of the work of social and behavioral scientists. Many influential writers have linked research to improving society or resolving societal problems, including the educational philosopher John Dewey (Stone, 1994).

This reason has been criticized for introducing bias into research, but the work of social psychologists and others in the 1960s and 1970s largely discredited the notion of value-free research, as explained in Chapter 4. This reason for conducting research is frequently linked with an earlier one: to satisfy curiosity about a phenomenon of interest.

Action research is a type of research in which investigators aim to improve society and its institutions and which sometimes involves the investigators' curiosity about their own place of work. Schmuck (1997) concluded that action research in educational settings "helps educators to reflect on their practice, collect data about their practice, and create alternative ways to improve their practice" (p. 20).

Evaluation research is another type of research aimed at improving society and its institutions, but this research is typically aimed at assessing the adequacy or effectiveness of existing societal and educational programs. In *program evaluation*, the research questions are as follows: Has the program met its overall goals (*outcome-based evaluation*)? How was the program implemented and how is it currently functioning (*process-based evaluation*)? Both outcome- and process-based evaluations were illustrated in Chapter 1 using the Trend (1979) evaluation of a federal housing subsidy program.

To Empower Disadvantaged Groups or Constituencies

The difference between this reason and the previous one can be simplified to an issue of sampling. Researchers aiming to improve society and its institutions in general are characteristically interested in a representative or typical sample of the population (e.g., public school students), whereas researchers interested in empowering specific groups or constituencies are interested in sampling members of groups that the researchers consider disadvantaged (e.g., African American male students in public schools). In Chapter 5, we noted that Mertens

(2003, 2005, 2007) and others (e.g., feminist scholars, disability scholars) place central importance on seeking social justice for and empowering marginalized groups, such as people with disabilities, ethnic/racial minorities, members of the gay and lesbian communities, women, and those living in poverty conditions.

The Emergence of Researchable Ideas in Content Areas of Interest

Content Areas of Interest and Researchable Ideas

Once investigators are committed to conducting research for any of the reasons cited earlier, they then need to identify a *researchable idea in a content area of interest*. Research areas range from the very general to the very specific, narrowing as an individual hones in on a specific, researchable idea. For individuals following academic tracks in traditional disciplines through undergraduate and graduate careers, research areas of interest move from the general to the specific as follows:

- Whole disciplines (e.g., psychology, education, political science, anthropology)—This broad level usually is important as a potential researcher begins to consider career options, typically as an undergraduate.
- Major subdisciplines within disciplines (e.g., social psychology, clinical psychology, developmental psychology, experimental psychology, school psychology, psychometrics)—This level becomes important as an undergraduate begins to take advanced courses and applies to graduate school.
- Broad research topics within major subdisciplines (e.g., attitude change, attribution theory, interpersonal attraction, whole-group behavior)—This level emerges for some as advanced undergraduates and for others in graduate school.
- Content areas of interest within broad research topics (e.g., the relationship between

proximity and interpersonal attraction)—At this level, the researcher is beginning to *locate himself or herself in the field.*

- Researchable idea in a content area of interest—At this level, the researcher has specified an area of interest and is ready to develop research objectives and questions.

To *locate oneself in the field* means to find a researchable idea in a content area of interest. A *content area of interest* is a specific problem area (e.g., the relationship between proximity and interpersonal attraction) within a general field of study (e.g., psychology) that a given researcher identifies as valuable to investigate. A **researchable idea** is a specific topic within a content area of interest that can be empirically examined using QUAL, QUAN, or MM research methods.

Researchers have at least four sources for locating researchable ideas (e.g., Johnson & Christensen, 2004, 2008):

- Intuitions based on previous experiences
- Reactions to practical problems
- Results from previous research
- Theory or conceptual frameworks

The following sections describe how researchers use these sources when planning their studies. The terms *content area of interest* and *researchable idea* are used somewhat interchangeably, with *researchable idea* connoting a narrower topic.

Intuitions Based on Previous Experiences

Many researchers, especially in applied fields, identify their initial content area of interest on the basis of insights they had in their workplaces, personal lives, or a combination of the two. For instance, a health service provider who works in a facility with a friendly-access approach to clients might become interested in the effect that such an approach has on the health outcomes of low-income mothers and their children (e.g., Albrecht, Eaton, & Rivera, 1999; Forthofer, 2003). Similarly, an elementary school teacher might become interested in the academic and social issues female students encounter that lead to feelings of inadequacy (Lock & Minarik, 1997).

Personal experiences can also lead to an interest in, and intuitions regarding, a particular content area. Box 6.2 contains a description of research on stigma and the experiences of families of children with disabilities, which was conducted by a sociologist (Green, 2002, 2003) whose daughter has cerebral palsy.

Box 6.2
What Do You Mean "What's Wrong With Her?"

In this MM study, Sara Green integrated a QUAN analysis of survey data collected from 81 mothers of children with disabilities with a QUAL analysis of interviews with 7 mothers and her own personal narrative. Green's experiences as the mother of a teenage daughter with cerebral palsy enabled her to "contextualize, humanize and help interpret the quantitative findings" (Green, 2003, p. 1361).

Though her interest in the families of children with disabilities was initiated through her own experiences, her formal training as a sociologist exposed her to the concept of the courtesy stigma. Goffman (1963) says this occurs when a caregiver is stigmatized along with the individual who has the stigmatizing trait. Green (2003) concluded that "as the mother of a teenager with cerebral palsy, my life has become a case study in the lived experience of courtesy stigma" (p. 1361).

Results from this MM study indicated that the courtesy stigma is not inevitable and that it can be diminished through a "pattern of frequent, positive, ordinary interactions between individuals with and without the stigmatizing trait" (Green, 2003, p. 1372).

Of course, a researcher's initial intuitions are only the starting point for her research, the results of which should lead to a deeper understanding of the phenomenon of interest. For example, Green's work (2003) required a blending of her intuitive insights regarding her daughter and her training as a sociologist, plus a skillful integration of QUAN and QUAL data sources and analyses. Her sociological training and research skills enabled Green to explore her initial intuitions regarding the experiences of the families of disabled individuals at a much more reflective and insightful level.

Reactions to Practical Problems

Human science research in the content areas often emerges from practical problems that need solutions. John Dewey believed that research should resolve practical problems in a manner that results in positive consequences for the individual's and the community members' quality of life (Stone, 1994). His writings, and those of the social psychologist Kurt Lewin, were influential in the establishment of action research, which was briefly described earlier in this chapter. Action research has been used in many fields and countries (e.g., Hollingsworth, 1997).

Titchen (1997) presented an example of an action research project that emerged as a reaction to a practical problem: the lack of personalized, individualized nursing care in the United Kingdom in the late 1980s. Titchen described traditional nursing in the United Kingdom at that time as highly task focused. Negative consequences of this task-oriented, top-down leadership style included centralized decision making, discontinuous care for patients, and distant nurse-patient relationships.

When nurses began to recognize that these traditional practices did not meet individual needs, patient-centered nursing emerged as a style of care based on close nurse-patient relationships. Titchen's (1997) particular research project involved cultural change among nurses in a hospital ward in Oxford, where a new ward culture was introduced that required more autonomy on the part of the nurses, more patient-centered care, and a new organizational goal of professional learning at work. *Ward culture* was defined as a unique pattern of cultural norms and shared values that exist among nurses and other staff members.

Titchen (1997) followed the change in ward culture and the movement toward patient-centered nursing for 3 years. Her research findings indicated that it took that long to see any significant cultural change. Titchen concluded that her research provided details about the "nature of the learning opportunities" and the creation of a "learning environment" necessary to change ingrained "ward culture" (p. 256).

Results From Previous Research

Research projects not only address the questions they were intended to answer, but they also result in new unanswered questions. This happens when investigators conducting research become aware of other aspects of the studied phenomenon that they had not previously considered. When research studies generate better, more focused questions for follow-up studies, the result is a line of research.

A **line (or program) of research** is a connected series of studies within a particular problem area that results in progressively more complex research findings regarding the phenomenon under study. These lines of research can cross over into other disciplines and generate new lines of research that diverge from the original line of research. When a researcher is searching for a content area of interest, identifying an ongoing, active line of research may prove beneficial. Active lines of research can be fertile areas for new research projects.

One of the more innovative lines of research in psychology and education in the past 40 years began in a psychology laboratory and ended up informing a generation of school-improvement efforts. The concepts of teacher and student academic expectation levels started in laboratory studies in psychology in the 1960s and extended into school-improvement efforts, evidenced still today.

As indicated in Chapter 4, an *experimenter effect* refers to an investigator's behaviors or expectations (or both) unintentionally affecting the results of a study. Rosenthal (1976) named this effect more broadly the *interpersonal expectancy effect* and expanded its application to a wide variety of settings (e.g., classrooms, jury rooms). Rosenthal's early work documented the experimenter effect on research conducted with lab animals (Rosenthal & Fode, 1963; Rosenthal & Lawson, 1964). In this research, Rosenthal and his colleagues told some of their experimenters that their albino rats had been bred for "good" maze learning performance; they told other experimenters that their rats had been bred for "bad" performance. Experimenters expecting better learning obtained significantly better outcomes from their rats than did experimenters expecting poorer learning. Actually, the albino rats were randomly assigned to the experimental condition.

Rosenthal and Jacobsen (1968) extended the experimenter effect results to the classroom in their formulation of the *self-fulfilling prophecy*, described in their book *Pygmalion in the Classroom*. In this research, randomly chosen students were identified as "bloomers" to school faculty. Later retesting showed that the IQ of these "bloomers" went up significantly more than that of the remainder of the class. This research is controversial, with replications of the effect occurring in some studies but not others (e.g., Spitz, 1999).

The self-fulfilling prophecy research in turn led Brookover and others (e.g. Cooper & Good, 1982) to study how teacher expectations account for between-school variations in student achievement. The research of Brookover and his colleagues (Brookover, Beady, Flood, Schweitzer, & Wisenbaker, 1979) occurred in school settings and did not involve any manipulation of teacher expectations; rather the study assessed the expectations that teachers (and principals) currently held for their students.

The results from school effectiveness research using scales measuring expectation levels led to the inclusion of high expectations for student achievement as one of the original correlates of effective schooling (e.g. Brookover & Lezotte, 1979; Edmonds, 1979; Levine & Lezotte, 1990). Numerous school-improvement projects have been launched based on these correlates or characteristics of effective schooling (e.g., Marzano, 2003; Reynolds & Teddlie, 2000; Taylor, 1990).

Thus, the *experimenter effect* literature in psychology led to study of the *self-fulfilling prophecy* effect in education, which then led to literature on the value of *high expectations* in school effectiveness research, which then led to school improvement projects in which reformers attempted *to alter teachers' expectations* of their students' academic achievement. This line of research continues to morph in the 21st century and is an excellent example of an active line of research that remains a fertile area for new research projects.

The Heuristic Value of Theory (or Conceptual Frameworks)[4]

Another source for identifying a researchable idea is theory (or *conceptual framework*). A critical consideration in assessing the status of any theory is its heuristic value in generating new research. A theory (or conceptual framework) has high **heuristic value** if it is capable of generating ideas or questions that can lead to interesting, valuable, and informative research studies. For example, contingency theory has had high heuristic value for the past 30–40 years, starting with the work of Fiedler (1967, 1973) in psychology and Mintzberg (1979) in management studies. Fiedler's contingency theory emphasized situational leadership, which states that no single leadership style is best but rather that leadership effectiveness depends on the interaction between the leader's style and the environmental characteristics of the workplace. Leadership effectiveness is contingent on local contextual factors.

The heuristic value of contingency theory can be ascertained by conducting a literature search using the term as a descriptor. A *Social Sciences Citation Index* (1956–) search using contingency theory as the subject and including the years

1982–2007 (25 years) yielded 765 articles across a wide variety of disciplines.[5]

The following five citations, selected from those that emerged from the search, come from business administration, communication sciences, health care, psychiatry, and sociology:

Hogarth, L., Dickinson, A., Hutton, S. B., et al. (2006). Contingency knowledge is necessary for learned motivated behavior in humans: Relevance for addictive disorder. *Addiction, 101,* 1153–1166.

Pickering, A. (1997). Contingency theory: Rethinking the boundaries of social thought. *American Journal of Sociology, 103,* 774–775.

Roll, J. M., Petry, N. M., Stiltzer, M. L., Brecht, M. L., Peirce, J. M., et al. (2006). Contingency management for the treatment of methamphetamine use disorders. *American Journal of Psychiatry, 163,* 1993–1999.

Torkzadeh, G., Chang, J. C. J., & Demirhan, D. (2006). A contingency model of computer and Internet self-efficacy. *Information and Management, 43,* 541–550.

Wallgrave, S., & Van Aelst, P. (2006). The contingency of the mass media's political agenda: Toward a preliminary theory. *Journal of Communication, 56*(1), 88–109.

When using a theory (or conceptual framework) to identify a researchable idea, the investigator plays out mental scenarios (*what ifs*) in which theoretical propositions are applied to a content area of interest. For instance, contingency theory states that leadership effectiveness depends on context factors. Let's assume that an investigator is interested in determining what makes an effective high school principal. Contingency theory contends that leadership effectiveness varies by situation, which in this case would be high school contexts. The investigator might then start playing out a variety of mental scenarios in which important high school context variables would differ. For instance, would the characteristics of effective leadership differ if the high school had a large number of low-socioeconomic-status students or a large number of upper-middle-class students? What leadership style might be more effective for high schools from each of these two conditions? Why?

The Three Research Communities and Their Use of Theory

The three research communities differ with regard to the importance they place on theory and when they use theory in their research projects, as noted in Chapter 2, Table 2.1.

The traditional QUAN hypothetico-deductive model starts with the a priori deduction of hypotheses from a theory or conceptual framework and the testing of those hypotheses through confirmatory research using numerical data and statistical analyses. This traditional QUAN model values theory (or conceptual models) preceding data collection.

Exploratory QUAN studies also rely on theory and conceptual frameworks derived from literature reviews. This theoretical/conceptual framework is used to identify possible elements that might be related to each other and to the focal variable under study. Instead of making predictions (i.e., hypotheses) about the presence or direction of relationship between variables, however, these studies use descriptive statistics to identify trends (e.g., data mining), or they use complex correlational techniques to identify relationships between variables. Christ (2007) provides numerous examples of such QUAN exploratory studies.

The QUAL orientation toward theory or conceptual frameworks is highly varied. John Creswell (2003) discusses four stances of QUAL researchers toward theory:

- Some QUAL researchers use their research projects to develop theory in an inductive manner (e.g., grounded theorists) and produce their theory as an endpoint of the research process.
- Some QUAL researchers use a **theoretical lens** (e.g., critical theorists) to guide their research and to raise issues of social justice related to ethnicity, gender, and so on.
- Some QUAL researchers use theory to explain behavior and attitudes, starting their research projects with an explicit statement of a theory or a conceptual

framework derived from a literature review in the same manner as QUANs.

- Some QUAL researchers claim to use no theory at all, instead constructing complex, detailed descriptions of the phenomenon of interest (e.g., researchers working in the tradition of *phenomenology*[6]) (pp. 131–133).

The MM orientation toward theory depends on the particular research design employed. We need to discuss two basic designs (previously defined in Chapter 2) here to illustrate the MM researchers' use of theory:

- *Parallel mixed designs*—These designs are MM projects in which the phases of the study (QUAN, QUAL) occur in a parallel manner, either simultaneously (starting and ending at approximately the same time) or with a time lapse. Refer to Figure 7.4 in Chapter 7 for a graphic illustration of a parallel MM design.

- *Sequential mixed designs*—In these projects, the QUAN and QUAL phases of the study occur in chronological order. Questions or procedures (e.g., the sample or data collection techniques) of one strand emerge from or depend on the previous strand. Refer to Figure 7.5 for a graphic illustration of a sequential MM design.

In parallel mixed designs, MM researchers might use theory in a different manner for the two strands of the study. For the QUAN component, the theory might be used deductively to generate hypotheses before the study begins or to identify the variables that might be related to the issue under study. Alternatively, the inductively constructed conceptual framework might be used to identify the variables that are related to the issue under study. On the other hand, for the QUAL component, the data might be collected first and then grounded theory might emerge from the analysis of those data. At the end of the study, inferences gleaned from both strands are combined to answer the research questions.

In sequential designs, theory is first used in a manner consistent with the component (QUAL or QUAN) that comes first. When the second strand starts, theory is used in a manner consistent with that phase. For instance, in a QUAN-QUAL sequential design, construction of a conceptual framework starts the first phase, and a theoretical generalization or explanation ends the second phase. It is likely that these two theoretical positions will differ from one another and that their differences will reflect what is learned during the study. On the other hand, in a QUAL-QUAN sequential design, the first phase ends with a theoretical perspective that might inform the generation of the research questions or hypotheses (or both) for the second phase.

Sometimes researchers study phenomena for which there is very little formal literature and even fewer theories or conceptual frameworks. For instance, individuals working in evaluation research frequently study educational or social programs for which there are few published articles, chapters, or books. The Trend (1979) evaluation study presented in Chapter 1 is a good example of this kind of research. In these cases, evaluators have to make many conceptual and methodological decisions independently, without the guidance of previous research or theory. This type of research environment forces evaluators to use all of the available methodological tools, which often leads to MM research.

Conducting Literature Reviews

This section contains three subsections that describe the literature review process:

The first section describes a 12-step process for conducting literature reviews, including an example using *SocINDEX with Full Text*.

The second section describes computerized databases from throughout the social and behavioral sciences that serve as preliminary sources of information for literature reviews.

The third section demonstrates how to use the *Social Sciences Citation Index*. Several terms are used throughout this section:

- **Preliminary information source**—index or abstract that assists investigators in locating relevant research articles; the most comprehensive of these sources are in easily accessible computerized databases
- **Secondary information source**—publication containing information on research studies, written by someone who was not a direct participant in conducting those studies
- **Primary information source**—the description of a research study by the individual(s) who conducted it
- **Keyword (descriptor)**—A search term that describes an important aspect of a research study that can be used to locate information in a computerized database

Twelve Steps in Conducting a Literature Review

We describe the literature review in this chapter as an integral part of the research process whereby an investigator develops research questions for a study. An investigator can conduct literature reviews at different points in the process, but these reviews are most efficient and productive when the investigator has identified keywords associated with a content area or with a researchable idea.

In some cases, the investigator uses a literature review to identify a researchable idea. In other cases, the investigator uses keywords associated with a content area, or researchable idea, to guide the literature review. Most researchers start their literature review after identifying a content area of interest.

A step-by-step process for conducting a literature review is presented later, but we first describe some general characteristics of reviews:

- Literature reviews typically employ a funnel approach, starting with a lot of extraneous material and gradually refining the information to the most relevant articles and sources.

- The typical order of review materials goes from preliminary to secondary to primary sources.
- The more narrowly specified the content area or researchable idea, the more efficient and productive the search.
- Literature reviews involve identifying themes related to the research topic in the narrative material being searched. Themes are recurrent patterns in narrative data; therefore, a literature review is a kind of QUAL analysis.
- Literature reviews are iterative; that is, certain steps are repeated until a desired outcome is obtained.
- Literature reviews are increasingly driven by computerized databases, which allow investigators to finish a maximum amount of work on a personal computer at an office or at home before working in a library.

Most research textbooks in the social and behavioral sciences contain sections on conducting literature reviews. The 12-step process summarized in this chapter was informed by several sources (e.g., Creswell, 2002; Gall, Gall, & Borg, 2006; Johnson & Christensen, 2004; Krathwohl, 2004; Mertens, 2005).

The remainder of this section details each of the 12 steps using a hypothetical search scenario in which a sociology graduate student is interested in the ongoing impact of the 1996 U.S. welfare reform bill. This is a very broad area, so the investigator used a literature review to more narrowly define a researchable idea, with the ultimate goal of developing some defensible research questions.

Step 1. Identify a research topic. As noted earlier, the more precisely specified the content area or researchable idea, the more efficient and productive the literature search. In our hypothetical scenario, a sociology graduate student identified welfare reform as her content area of interest but needed to look for a more refined researchable idea within that broad area. Welfare (or welfare reform) is a common topic in most introductory sociology texts, falling within broader topics such as class/social stratification and inequality (e.g., Giddens, Duneier, & Applebaum, 2003; Thio, 2005).

Step 2. Identify keywords or descriptors that are useful in locating materials. The graduate student identified *welfare reform* as a keyword or descriptor, but she was aware that a search based on this descriptor was too broad and would generate too many references. She began to think about other descriptors she might use. She was interested in the impact of the bill on the well-being of families, especially mothers and children. She was not interested in the effect of welfare reform on the number of caseloads, which has already been extensively researched.

Step 3. Develop an overall search strategy for the literature review. In conducting a literature review, it is good to have an overall plan that keeps one focused and thinking about the next step (e.g., Mertens, 2005). This is especially important in cases where one expects to be initially overwhelmed by the magnitude of existing research. An overall search strategy involves the identification of the most relevant preliminary sources, the most valuable secondary sources (journals that publish reviews, books that publish reviews, handbooks on specific topics), and the most relevant journals (for both primary and secondary sources). Though the typical materials-review process progresses from preliminary to secondary to primary sources, the process is iterative, and the order may be reversed at certain points in the search.

Step 4. Search preliminary sources. One of the two most comprehensive and valuable preliminary sources in sociology[7] is *SocINDEX,* which is available online through many libraries' online catalogs. For instance, Louisiana State University provides the LSU Libraries Online catalog. Once on the Web site, researchers can click on Research Tools, then click on Databases and Indexes, then select Social Sciences, and then select *SocINDEX with Full Text.*

The sociology graduate student selected *SocINDEX* as her computerized preliminary source. She then entered *welfare reform* as the keyword, and

the search yielded 2,748 matches![8] She knew she had to narrow the search, so she specified publication dates between 2000 and 2007. This narrower search still yielded 1,445 hits.

As the student scanned the first few pages of the results, she began to think more specifically about what she wanted to study. Several of the titles included names of family members (e.g., mothers, children). She checked the abstracts for a few of these articles and determined that studying the impact of welfare reform on those individuals might be interesting. She then entered the keywords *welfare reform* and *mothers.* This search yielded 195 hits—a number closer to her ideal number of references.

She decided to limit the search again. During her last search, she had noted a review article that seemed very relevant:

Lichter, D. T., & Jayakody, R. (2002). Welfare reform: How do we measure success? *Annual Review of Sociology, 28,* 117–141.

She knew this was a secondary source because the *Annual Review of Sociology* prints only review articles. The abstract indicated that the article contained 155 references, so it appeared to be a comprehensive review of the literature. The graduate student then looked at the list of descriptors associated with this article and noted that both the subject terms and the author-supplied keywords included the term *poverty.* This was a particular area of interest to her, so she entered the keywords *welfare reform, mothers,* and *poverty.* This search yielded 67 hits, which she printed for closer inspection.

Step 5. Select relevant primary and secondary sources. After the preliminary sources search, one needs to select 25–50 secondary and primary sources that seem most relevant. The graduate student in our example examined the list of sources and selected 31 that appeared to be most relevant to her study. She retained the entire list of 67 articles because the remainder might become relevant later.

The student researcher decided to read the secondary sources first because they would help her get a better perspective on the entire content area. She also selected some primary sources that had very interesting titles:

Jennings, P. K. (2004). What mothers want: Welfare reform and maternal desire. *Journal of Sociology and Social Welfare, 31*(3), 113–130.

Korteweg, A. C. (2003). Welfare reform and the subject of the working mother: "Get a job, a better job, then a career." *Theory and Society, 32,* 445–480.

Step 6. Search the library for the secondary and primary sources that have been identified. The student noticed that about half of the 67 articles were available in full text through *SocINDEX;* that is, she could download them directly from the system and read or print them. If an article was not available directly through *SocINDEX,* then further directions for locating it were given. In some cases, the library subscribed to the journal that published the article, and the student was able to find it in the stacks. In other cases, she ordered unavailable articles through interlibrary loan.

Step 7. Establish a computer and paper trail, including research summaries in your own words that will be used in the literature review. Documentation is very important when conducting a literature review. Researchers should make copies of the articles most relevant to their literature review for their private library. Some of these sources will be read and referenced repeatedly, so it is valuable to have easy access to them. Alternatively, articles may be stored electronically or in a bibliographic organizing program.

Researchers should develop a bibliographical listing for each of the sources they will use. Each listing should include the author's name, the year of publication, the article's title, the journal's (or other source's) title, the volume and page numbers, and so on. Researchers should build the reference list as they conduct their search and write the literature review. This compilation later serves as the reference list for the literature review.

Reference-management software can help researchers organize references and summaries. *EndNote, ProCite,* and similar programs allow researchers to download references from the Internet or retrieve the references that have been saved from other searches. Researchers can then construct a personal reference library using the software. This library allows references to be merged, sorted alphabetically, and converted to American Psychological Association (APA) publication style[9] or another style. As researchers add references or abstracts to the personal reference library, the software formats the references and summaries and places them in proper order. The advantages of learning to use one of these reference-management computer programs are evident.

Another advantage of a program such as *EndNote* is that it makes it much easier and faster to add citations to text as one types ideas in the word-processing program (e.g., Microsoft Word or WordPerfect). If researchers refer to a source that exists in the personal reference library, the program finds the full reference and places it at the end of the document, in the proper order and format (e.g., APA). Researchers may also save copies of the abstract or the entire article and their own notes and summary along with each reference. In addition to these advantages, learning to use these tools also helps researchers with future writing projects.

Researchers should summarize the most relevant reviews and studies as they are read. These research summaries, *written in one's own words,* are the building blocks for the literature review. Also important are direct quotations from reviews and articles. Particularly relevant quotes can sometimes make a point better and more succinctly as stated originally than as interpreted by a second author. Particularly relevant quotes should be placed, with accurate page numbers, on the bibliographical listing or summary for that source.

Step 8. Repeat Steps 4–7 as needed. Each time the search is more refined. This is the iterative part of the literature review process. The hypothetical sociology graduate student might go through these steps a few more times as her topic becomes more refined and as other sources are identified.

Step 9. Develop themes or concepts that synthesize the literature. The ultimate goal of the literature review is a synthesis of the existing work regarding a researchable idea in a given content area of interest. This synthesis involves the determination of themes in the literature, which are recurrent patterns of information across several different sources. Thematic analysis is the essence of QUAL research, which is discussed in Chapter 11. In the case of a literature review, the "data" are the narratives located in the existing literature.

It could be that the graduate student will seek to identify all those themes related to the impact of welfare reform on mothers in poverty. This would happen if a number of interesting themes (some of which may be contradictory) emerged regarding this topic.

Step 10. Relate the themes/concepts to one another through an outline of the literature review, or a literature map. The themes must be related to one another in a coherent manner that leads to the positioning of the research study within the literature. In this step, the researcher locates her study (and herself) within the field. Creswell (2003) suggested the use of literature maps to help with this process. Literature maps are visual summaries of the existing research about a topic that demonstrate how the proposed study fits within the larger literature.

Step 11. Produce a final literature review that structures or organizes the literature thematically or by important concepts. The overall argument throughout the literature should convince the reader that the proposed study is the next logical step in this particular line of research.

Step 12. Use the literature review to develop or refine the research questions (and hypotheses). Many researchers use the literature review to either develop or refine their research questions. In our example, the student might use the literature review to develop her initial research questions, which can then be refined through more review of the literature or through some pilot research. Her starting research questions might

include the following: What are the effects of welfare reform on mothers in poverty? Does the effect of welfare reform on mothers differ if there is a second parent in the household?

Preliminary Sources Used in the Social and Behavioral Sciences

As noted earlier, the typical order of reviewing materials starts with preliminary sources; therefore, we now present some additional information about the most popular preliminary sources that are available as electronic indexes. In recent years, libraries have begun leasing Internet versions of these indexes, making them available to their students and faculty members both on and off campus. Table 6.1 lists nine of the most popular electronic indexes from the social and behavioral sciences that are available through universities' online library services. The *Web of Knowledge* is a popular index that contains different databases from all areas of research including *SSCI*.

Social Sciences Citation Index (SSCI): Example of a Preliminary Source

The *SSCI* is an excellent place to start because it lists articles from 50 disciplines in the social and behavioral sciences. This index can be used to identify lines of research and to follow the work of particular authors of interest. An earlier search example employed *SSCI* to examine references to contingency theory, resulting in 765 articles across a wide range of disciplines.

Box 6.3 contains a simplified description of the use of *SSCI* involving the same hypothetical sociology graduate student described previously. This researcher located an important source for her literature search, a 2002 review article by Lichter and Jayakody on measuring the success of welfare reform. The student decided that it would be useful to find other researchers who had referenced this article because their lines of research might inform her own. Her *SSCI* search, described in Box 6.3, identified 20 articles that had referenced the Lichter and Jayakody (2002)

Table 6.1   Popular Electronic Indexes in the Social and Behavioral Sciences Located in Library-Leased Internet Versions

Subject	Electronic Index
All social and behavioral sciences	Social Sciences Citation Index (SSCI)
Education	ERIC Abstracts (Educational Resources Information Center)
Library science	Library Literature and Information Sciences
Medicine and related fields	MEDLINE
Nursing and related fields	CINAHL (Cumulative Index to Nursing and Allied Health Literature)
Psychology	PsycINFO
Sociology	SocINDEX Sociological Abstracts
Dissertations from the social and behavioral sciences	Dissertation Abstracts International
Information regarding instruments used in social and behavioral science research	Mental Measurement Handbook

article as of January 27, 2007, about 5 years after publication. The student could then locate these articles, read them, and use them to help formulate her research questions because these articles represent the most recent research directly related to her area of interest.

Box 6.3

Steps in Using the *SSCI*

The example used here involves the same sociology graduate student who was interested in welfare reform and conducted the *SocINDEX* search described earlier in this chapter. In this continued example, we assume that she is working at a university that allows her access to the *Web of Knowledge*. She uses the following steps to conduct a SSCI search using this electronic resource:

1. She accesses the *Web of Knowledge* from the list of licensed electronic indexes at her university.

2. She selects the database in which she is interested (*SSCI*), the range of years to search (the index starts in 1956 and searches to the present), and the type of search. For the purposes of this introductory *SSCI* example, we limit the choices she has to a general search (by topic, author, journal, etc.) or to a cited reference search for articles that cite a specific author or work.

(Continued)

(Continued)

3. The researcher is interested in specific authors (D. T. Lichter & R. Jayakody). Therefore, she selects cited reference search.

4. The next screen asks for cited author, cited work, or cited year. The student completes the cited author prompt, entering LICHTER DT. (She could have also entered the specific article here but decided to access all of the cited references out of curiosity.)

5. After clicking the Search option for LICHTER DT, a large number of cited references is displayed in alphabetical order by journal or book name. The student decides to save the results from this general author search and concentrate on finding citations for the specific 2002 *Annual Review of Sociology* article in which she is interested. D. T. Lichter is an often-cited author, with more than 150 works listed (some are duplicates) across four *SSCI* screens.

6. The student locates the entry *ANNU REV SOCL* and year *2002* on the first D. T. Lichter screen and checks the appropriate box. She then clicks the Finish Search option, and 20 individual records are displayed, each citing the Lichter 2002 article.

7. The student then has the option of locating these articles, reading them, and using them to formulate her research questions because they represent the most recent articles directly related to her area of interest.

Note: This search was conducted using *SSCI* on January 28, 2007.

Another example of the use of *SSCI* for MM research involves our analysis of *SSCI* citations for a book published in the late 1990s titled *Mixed Methodology: Combining the Qualitative and Quantitative Approaches* (Tashakkori & Teddlie, 1998). This book was among the first to treat MM as a distinct methodological orientation, and we were interested in determining which disciplines had researchers citing the book. We first ran a *SSCI* Cited Author Search using TASHAKKORI A as the author's name, and then we examined the resulting Cited Reference Index for all related references. This *SSCI* search yielded 152 citations[10] across a variety of disciplines, as illustrated in Figure 6.2.

Not only did this *SSCI* search allow us to determine which disciplines were citing our book, but it also allowed us to locate specific scholars who were interested in conducting MM research and to identify specific lines of MM research within disciplines. For instance, we were able to identify an active area of MM research in information and library sciences, which we had been unaware of until we conducted the *SSCI* search.

Generating Objectives for Mixed Methods Research

The next step in the process of generating MM research questions for many, but not all, studies involves the generation of research objectives. Research objectives are important in MM research because they help blend the two approaches (QUAL, QUAN) from the *onset of the research*. Research objectives can help specify how the QUAL and QUAN data sources and

Figure 6.2 Disciplines Associated With References to *Mixed Methodology: Combining the Qualitative and Quantitative Approaches* (Tashakkori & Teddlie, 1998)

analyses can be integrated to address questions that supersede what either set could answer independently. Research objectives provide a platform on which QUAL and QUAN questions may be synthesized into coherent and integrated themes.

In Chapter 2, we discussed the use of MM research, indicating that it can enable researchers to simultaneously ask confirmatory and exploratory questions and therefore verify and generate theory in the same study. Many of the research projects that we supervise are doctoral

dissertations, in which students want to simultaneously accomplish two goals: (1) demonstrate that a particular variable will have a predicted relationship with another variable (confirmatory research) and (2) answer questions about how that predicted (or other related) relationship actually occurs (exploratory research). Box 6.4 summarizes a recent dissertation by Lasserre-Cortez (2006) that generated a set of research hypotheses and questions from overall research objectives.

An interesting example of a research objective comes from Collins and Long's (2003) study of

---

Box 6.4

Summary of a Dissertation With Research Objectives

Shannon Lasserre-Cortez's (2006) dissertation investigated the impact of professional action research collaboratives (PARCs), which are faculty-driven professional development programs. The overall research objectives of this dissertation were to (1) investigate the empirical relationships between the presence of PARCs on the one hand and indices of school and teacher effectiveness on the other and (2) describe the mechanisms whereby that relationship works in actual schools.

Research hypotheses included the following:

1. Schools participating in PARCs will demonstrate greater effectiveness (larger increase in student achievement over time) than comparison schools.

2. Teachers in schools participating in PARCs will demonstrate higher levels of teacher effectiveness than teachers in comparison schools.

Research questions included the following: Do the QUAL interview data substantiate the hypothesized relationships? Does school climate affect teacher effectiveness in PARC schools?

Note: Lasserre-Cortez's dissertation was more complex than described here. The description presented here was simplified to fit the needs of this text.

---

the psychological effects of working in traumatic settings. This research was conducted after the August 15, 1998, car bomb explosion in the small market town of Omagh, Northern Ireland, in which 29 people and 2 unborn children died and more than 60 others were seriously injured. The trauma in this particular setting was complicated by the close relationships among many individuals living in this small community.

The overall objective of this research project was "to investigate the effects on caregivers across time, working with people traumatized as a result of the Omagh bombing, using both quantitative and qualitative methods" (Collins & Long, 2003, p. 20). The research participants were 13 health care workers on a trauma and recovery team sent to Omagh, and data were gathered from them during a 2.5-year period.

The project's objective was met through the gathering of (1) QUAN data, which measured the participants' levels of compassion fatigue, burnout, compassion satisfaction,[11] and satisfaction

with life at four points in time, and (2) QUAL data from interviews gathered from the participants toward the end of the study. The QUAN data demonstrated the degree to which compassion fatigue and burnout increased over time, whereas compassion satisfaction and satisfaction with life decreased over time for the participants. The QUAL interview data helped explain these QUAN results by generating themes associated with the most positive and most negative aspects of working on the trauma and recovery team. Thus, this study confirmed beliefs regarding the long-term psychological effects of working with trauma, while exploring participants' perceptions of and insights into the experience, thereby leading to implications for practice.

Though both QUAL and QUAN researchers are interested in studying causal relations, the two types of research have different strengths in terms of specifying those relationships (e.g., Maxwell, 2004; Shadish et al., 2002). Many QUAN-oriented researchers believe that QUAN experiments are better positioned to examine **causal effects** (i.e., *whether* X caused Y) because these research designs can better control for the impact of extraneous variables. On the other hand, many QUAL-oriented researchers believe that QUAL methods are better positioned to answer questions related to **causal mechanisms** or processes (i.e., *how* did X cause Y). Through a skillful mixture of both QUAL and QUAN methods, MM researchers can address both causal effects and causal mechanisms questions simultaneously, as in the case of the Omagh bombing study.

Generating Research Questions for Mixed Methods Research

Once the objectives of a research study are enunciated, researchers can derive specific questions and hypotheses. As noted in Chapter 1, *mixed methods research questions* are concerned with unknown aspects of a phenomenon and are answered with information that is presented in *both narrative and numerical* forms. A unique aspect of any given MM study is that it requires at least two research questions (one QUAL, one QUAN), whereas traditional QUAL or QUAN studies could be initiated with only one question.

In our first book on mixed research, we discussed the "dictatorship" of the research question (Tashakkori & Teddlie, 1998, p. 20). We argued that, for pragmatically oriented researchers, methodological considerations are of secondary importance "to the research question itself, and the underlying paradigm or worldview hardly enters the picture" (p. 21). We argued for the importance of the research question to emphasize the relative value of real-world research questions, as opposed to paradigmatic considerations. The research question also drives the selection of the research methods, which are often MM in nature due to the complexity of those research questions.[12]

Bryman (2006b) commented on the centrality of the research question:

> One of the chief manifestations of the pragmatic approach to the matter of mixing quantitative and qualitative research is the significance that is frequently given to the research question . . . This position with regard to the debate about quantitative and qualitative research prioritizes the research question and relegates epistemological and ontological debates to the sidelines. In doing so, it clears the path for research that combines quantitative and qualitative research. (p. 118)

The Research Question as a Dual Focal Point

The research process may be graphically represented as two triangles, one pointing down and the other pointing up, that meet at a center point. This center point represents the research question (or questions), the upper triangle represents the activities that precede the emergence of the question, and the lower triangle represents the activities that follow from the formulation of the question. Figure 6.3 illustrates the research question as a dual focal point.

The upper triangle symbolizes the funneling of a lot of diffuse information into a narrowly focused research question (or questions). The lower triangle symbolizes the expansion of information that occurs as evidence regarding the research question emerges. The research question serves as a dual focal point that liaises between what was known about the topic before the study and what is learned about the topic during the study. Everything flows through and from the research questions.

Examples of Integrated Quantitative and Qualitative Research Questions

Perhaps the most difficult intellectual (or creative) exercise that individuals undergo in

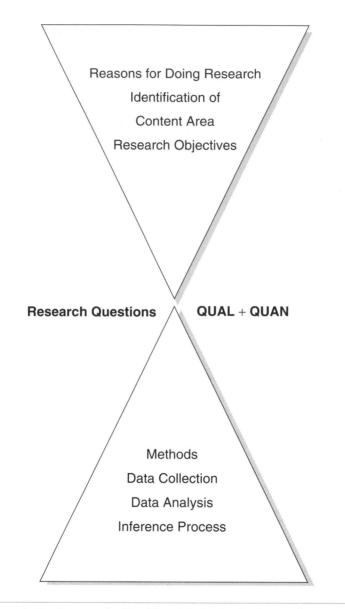

Figure 6.3 Research Qestions as the Dual Focal Point in the Research Process

conducting their own research is the generation of researchable questions in a content area of interest. Often, their initial questions are rather vague and overgeneralized. Whittling those initial questions into researchable ones is difficult, partially because many of the constructs that researchers work with in the human sciences are themselves rather vague and overgeneralized.

The process is even more complicated in MM research because these researchers typically want to integrate the QUAL research questions with the QUAN research questions. As noted in Chapter 1, we consider a *research hypothesis* to be a special form of a QUAN research question in which the investigators can make predictions about the relationships among social phenomena in advance of the actual research study taking place. Thus, research hypotheses are specialized types of QUAN research questions, as illustrated in the bottom portion of Figure 6.1.

The remainder of this section contains some examples of integrated QUAN and QUAL research questions. A simple example of a study with one QUAN research question (a research hypothesis in this case) integrated with one QUAL research question comes from Adalbjarnardottir's (2002) study of adolescent psychosocial maturity and alcohol use. His hypothesis and question were as follows:

- *QUAN research hypothesis:* More psychologically mature adolescents will be less involved in the risky behavior of heavy drinking than will less psychologically mature adolescents, both concurrently and longitudinally. Adalbjarnardottir (2002) studied a group of adolescents over a 22-month period, assessing their psychosocial maturity (on an instrument designed for that purpose) and their alcohol substance use on a self-report questionnaire.

- *QUAL research question:* What can we learn from adolescents' reflections on drinking by exploring their perspectives through thematic and developmental lenses both concurrently and longitudinally (Adalbjarnardottir, 2002, p. 27)? Interview data were gathered from adolescents regarding their concerns, experiences, and reflections regarding alcohol use to answer this research question.

A more complex example of the integration of QUAN and QUAL research questions involves the work of Teddlie and Stringfield (1993). These researchers conducted a longitudinal MM study in which they examined school and classroom processes in eight matched pairs of differentially effective elementary schools (one more effective school matched with one less effective school). Following are some of the research hypotheses for this study:

Research Hypothesis 1: Classrooms in more effective schools will have higher time-on-task than will classrooms in less effective schools.

Research Hypothesis 2: Classrooms in more effective schools will have better discipline than classrooms in less effective schools.

Research Hypothesis 3: Classrooms in more effective schools will have a friendlier ambience than classrooms in less effective schools.

These and other hypotheses were tested using data gathered in the classrooms by trained observers. These results were interesting to the researchers, but they were equally interested in how the relationship between effective schooling and teaching occurred. Consequently, they set out to study the relationship between school and teacher effectiveness processes using the following research questions:

QUAL Research Question 1: How are teachers selected at more effective schools as opposed to less effective schools?

QUAL Research Question 2: How are teachers socialized at more effective schools as opposed to less effective schools?

QUAL Research Question 3: What are the differences in school-level academic leadership in more effective schools as opposed to less effective schools?

QUAL Research Question 4: What are the differences in school-level faculty cohesiveness in more effective schools as opposed to less effective schools?

During a 10-year span, Teddlie and Stringfield (1993) examined these processes of effective schooling and teaching through hundreds of hours of QUAL interviews and observations in differentially effective schools in a longitudinal design that was guided by specific QUAL research questions.

Another complex and evolving MM research example involves a relatively new area of research: adolescent girls' experiences of sexual desire. Tolman and Szalacha (1999) presented a QUAL-QUAN-QUAL sequential series of three analyses that involved an initial QUAL research question, followed by two QUAN research questions, which were then followed by one more QUAL research question in an emerging MM design.

Tolman and Szalacha (1999) described the study:

> We begin with a qualitative analysis of their voiced experiences of sexual desire; follow with a quantitative analysis of the differences in how urban and suburban girls describe these experiences, assessing the role of reported sexual violation; and conclude with a second qualitative analysis exploring the interaction between social location and reported violation. (p. 7)

The authors referred to their study as feminist research that began with the voices of girls and resulted in an identification of the complexities of adolescent girls' experiences of sexual desire. Their initial QUAL research question was disarmingly simple:

Research Question 1 (QUAL): How do girls describe their experiences of sexual desire?

Though the question was simple, the responses were quite complex. For example, differences emerged between urban and suburban girls in their descriptions of their responses to sexual desire. The identification of general patterns in the narrative data led to two additional questions:

Research Question 2a (QUAN): What are the size and significance of the difference between urban and suburban girls' experience of their own sexual desire?

Research Question 2b (QUAN): Is there an interaction between social location and reported experience of sexual abuse or violence in whether urban and suburban girls associate their own desire with pleasure, vulnerability, or both?

A series of statistical tests confirmed the existence of an interaction among social location, experience of sexual violation, and the theme of pleasure. This led to a third research question:

Research Question 3 (QUAL): How do descriptions and narratives of sexual desire offered by suburban girls who have not reported sexual violence or abuse compare with the descriptions and narratives offered by the other three

groups (i.e., urban girls who have and have not reported sexual violence and abuse; suburban girls who have reported sexual violence and abuse)?

Tolman and Szalacha (1999) concluded that MM was very important in their research:

> Grounded in a method of data collection that gave girls an opportunity to interrupt the usual silence about their sexuality and using qualitative and quantitative methods to analyze these data, we learned far more about this aspect of female adolescent development than forcing a choice between qualitative and quantitative methods would have afforded. (p. 32)

Another example of integrated research questions and hypotheses may be found in a research report titled "Applying Mixed Methods Research to Community Driven Development Projects and Local Conflict Mediation: A Case Study From Indonesia (Barron, Diprose, Smith, Whiteside, & Woolcock, 2008). For your convenience, we have placed it on the companion Web site for this book (www.sagepub.com/foundations, see Appendix B).

Barron and colleagues (2008) applied MM in an evaluation project associated with a large World Bank–financed, community-driven development project (Kecamatan Development Project or KDP) in Indonesia. This project concerned the ability of communities to manage conflict, and the basic research question asked "how and under what conditions KDP *impacts* local conflict management capacity" (p. 4, italics in original). Several more detailed questions focused on localized factors that influence levels of violent conflict. We also use examples from this study in the Review Questions and Exercises sections of several chapters in this text.

The Current Debate About Mixed Methods Research Questions

By now, it should be obvious that a successful MM study must begin with a strong MM research question or objective, clearly justifying the need for using and integrating both QUAN and QUAL components. Answering questions that have interconnected QUAL and QUAN features (e.g., questions including *what* and *how* or *what* and *why*) should lead to final conclusions or explanations that then lead to interrelated QUAN and QUAL inferences. As we suggested before, the nature and form of research questions are usually different in sequential and parallel MM studies. In sequential studies, the questions of a second (or later) strand usually (but not always) emerge as a result of the findings from the first strand. In parallel designs, the questions are generated from the start of the study. (See Chapter 7 for details regarding design differences.) Despite this distinction, you should allow for a dynamic process in which the component questions are reexamined and reframed as your MM study progresses.

We summarized some of the attributes of MM research questions in earlier sections. A relatively unexplored issue remains to be investigated: How should we frame research questions in an MM study? Two general approaches are found in the current literature: (1) a single question that is overarching in nature and incorporates both the QUAL and QUAN subquestions or (2) separate QUAN and QUAL questions, followed by a question regarding the nature of integration (Creswell & Plano Clark, 2007).

The first approach entails first proposing an overarching mixed research question and then expanding it into separate QUAN and QUAL subquestions. We believe that in most MM studies (emerging sequential designs being an exception) an overarching question is necessary for justifying the choice of an MM design for the study and paving the way for alignment of the purpose and question. For example, an investigator might ask the following question: What are the effects of treatment X on the behaviors and perceptions of groups A and B? You can easily understand why this question necessitates an MM design. Such a question might be followed by three subquestions: Are groups A and B different on variables Y and Z? What are the perceptions and constructions of participants in groups A and B regarding

treatment X? Why does treatment X work differently in the two groups? The subquestions are answered in separate strands of the study.

Kaeding's (2007) comprehensive study of the transnational directives on transportation issues in the European Union (EU) is an excellent example of this hierarchical structure of MM research questions. According to Kaeding, "transposition of EU legislation entails that member states transpose legislation on time" and that "directives are not directly applicable at the national level, but have to be incorporated into national law first" (p. 14). Situated in such a context, the overarching question of Kaeding's comprehensive study was as follows: Why do member states miss deadlines when transposing EU internal market directives? The subquestions following this MM question were as follows: What factors determine delay when transposing EU directives? How do these factors influence the timeliness of the national transposition process? Under what conditions are transpositions of directives delayed? A combination of relationship (correlational) and case-study designs were used to answer these questions, largely in a sequential manner (i.e., case selection was based on the QUAN results of the first strand that was focused on the first subquestion).

Another example comes from a study by Parmelee, Perkins, and Sayre (2007), who asked the following question: "How and why the political ads of the 2004 presidential candidates failed to engage young adults," which was followed by three subquestions: "How does the interaction between audience-level and media-based framing contribute to college students' interpretations of the messages found in political advertising?" "To what extent do those interpretations match the framing found in the ads from the 2004 U.S. presidential election?" and "How can political ads be framed to better engage college students?" (pp. 184–186).

A second approach to stating MM research questions was suggested by John Creswell and Vicki Plano Clark (2007) and includes separate QUAN and QUAL questions followed by an explicit question about the nature of integration. For example, an investigator might ask: "Do the quantitative results and the qualitative findings converge?" or

"How do the follow-up qualitative findings help explain the initial quantitative results?" (p. 107). (Also see Tashakkori & Creswell, 2007b.)

Summary

This chapter began with a description of a four-step model for generating research questions in the social and behavioral sciences: reasons for conducting research, identification of content area of interest, statement of objectives, and generation of integrated QUAL and QUAN research questions. These four steps were described in sequential order.

Three general reasons (personal reasons, reasons associated with advancing knowledge, societal reasons), together with eight specific reasons, for conducting research in the social and behavioral sciences were identified. Sources related to the identification of content areas of interest were then described and examples of each were presented.

A 12-step sequence for conducting a literature review was also described, together with details regarding each step. The last part of the chapter discussed the generation of research objectives, QUAL and QUAN research questions, and the more complex (and hierarchical) nature of MM research questions.

Chapter 7 presents information on the next step of the research process: selecting an appropriate MM research design. A comprehensive typology of research designs, the Methods-Strands Matrix, is described, along with various decisions researchers encounter when using it.

Review Questions and Exercises

1. Write a short essay in which you compare and contrast the following three reasons for conducting research in the human sciences: to develop causal explanations, to understand complex phenomena, and to empower disadvantaged groups or constituencies.

2. Consider the reasons why you might want to do research on a topic of interest to you. Pick two of those reasons. Write a short essay in which you compare and contrast those reasons for conducting this research.

3. Consider the four sources described in Chapter 6 related to the identification of a content area of interest: intuitions based on previous experiences, reactions to practical problems, results from previous research, and theory. Of those four sources, which is the most important in your own research (actual or hypothetical)? Why?

4. Define a current line of research within your own discipline. Then list at least four studies in that line of research and note how they relate to one another.

5. Conduct a literature review on the relationship between proximity and interpersonal attraction (i.e., love the one you're near). Use one of the preliminary sources identified in Table 6.1. Briefly describe the process whereby you conducted this literature search, referring to as many of the 12 steps described in this chapter as possible. Identify at least two secondary sources and eight primary sources.

6. Distinguish between causal effects and causal mechanisms. Give an example of each with regard to the same phenomenon.

7. Describe a content area that is of interest to you. Develop and integrate two QUAL research questions and two QUAN research questions in your chosen content area. Briefly describe the QUAL and QUAN data sources you will use to answer these questions. (Use overall research objectives to provide the foundation for these integrated questions, if they are helpful.)

8. Conduct a literature search in which you locate six articles that use the MM approach. Write a half-page abstract for each of these articles in which you clearly identify the QUAL research questions and the QUAN research questions.

9. Appendix B contains the Barron et al. (2008) study briefly described in the section titled "Examples of Integrated Quantitative and Qualitative Research Questions" in this chapter. The research questions that drive this study are found on pages 4 and 5 of Appendix B. Describe those research questions and how they are integrated with one another in this MM study. You can find Appendix B on the companion Web site for this book (www .sagepub.com/foundations).

Key Terms

Action research	Phenomenology
Causal effects	Prediction studies
Causal mechanisms	Preliminary information source
Criterion variable	Primary information source
Evaluation research	Research objectives
Heuristic value	Researchable idea
Keyword (descriptor)	Secondary information source
Line (or program) of research	*Social Sciences Citation Index (SSCI)*
	Theoretical lens

Notes

1. We use the term *reason* for conducting research (rather than *purpose*) because *purpose* has multiple connotations (e.g., purpose statement of a study) in the human sciences.

2. Some studies do not require a statement of both research objectives and questions because the distinction between the two is trivial. For instance, if your research objective were to determine why children prefer certain types of humor more than other types, and your research question asked, "Why do children prefer certain types of humor more than other types?", then there is no reason to state both.

3. In much prediction research, one cannot assume a causal relationship between variables (i.e., *independent variables* having an effect on the *dependent variable*). Therefore, it is more appropriate to use the terms **criterion variable** (for the variable being predicted) and *predictor variable* (for variables used to predict the value of another variable). Furthermore, although prediction of future events is often the goal of this type of research, it is not a *requirement* of prediction studies because current or even past events can be (and are) statistically predicted.

4. Many research studies reported in professional journals in the past few decades were rooted in conceptual frameworks rather than theories. *Conceptual framework* was defined in Chapter 2, Note 2.

5. The ***Social Sciences Citation Index*** (***SSCI***) is a computerized database containing information on articles representing most of the disciplines in the behavioral and social sciences. The index may be accessed through university libraries (and other outlets) via the *Web of Knowledge*, which is an integrated database that allows access to a number of Institutes for Scientific Information (ISI) databases. The *SSCI* search on contingency theory described here was conducted on January 25, 2007.

6. **Phenomenology** is a research orientation stressing researchers' subjective experiences, social perceptions, and "naïve" analysis of events and phenomena (Heider, 1958). According to Creswell (1998), phenomenology "describes the meaning of lived experiences for several individuals about a concept or . . . phenomenon." This involves exploration of the "structures of consciousness in human experiences" (p. 51).

7. The two databases are *SocINDEX* and *Sociological Abstracts* (1953–). *Sociological Abstracts* is a well-known source that has been a favorite in university libraries for many years, whereas *SocINDEX* was introduced recently (Todd, 2006).

8. This search was conducted using *SocINDEX* on January 27, 2007.

9. The *Publication Manual of the American Psychological Association,* now in its 5th edition, is the style used in journals published by the APA, the American Educational Research Association, and "at least a thousand other journals" (APA, 2001, p. xxi).

10. This search was conducted using *SSCI* on January 27, 2007.

11. *Compassion fatigue* occurs when workers fall victim to secondary traumatic stress as a result of helping others. *Compassion satisfaction* refers to the satisfaction that workers derive from helping others.

12. Bryman (2006b) discussed the concern that some researchers might use MM in their studies because of its growing popularity, without considering the methodological direction specified by the research questions. We believe that many research questions are answered more appropriately and efficiently by using either QUAN techniques or QUAL techniques alone. MM should only be used in research situations where the research questions specifically require it.

CHAPTER 7

Mixed Methods Research Designs[1]

Objectives

Upon finishing this chapter, you should be able to:

- Explain the meaning of "families" of mixed methods research designs

- Define and describe quasi-mixed design and provide an example
- Recognize the basic terminology used to describe mixed methods research designs
- Describe the Methods-Strands Matrix and its associated decision points

- Identify the four implementation methods for mixed methods research design: parallel, sequential, conversion, and multilevel
- Distinguish between the methods employed in a study, the strands (or phases) of a study, and the stages that occur within a strand or phase
- Identify and define the five major types of multistrand mixed methods designs
- Describe the "ideal" types of research design in the Methods-Strands Matrix
- Describe other alternative typologies of mixed methods designs
- Identify and define the components of Maxwell and Loomis's (2003) interactive model
- Describe the seven-step process for selecting a particular MM design

Several points of view regarding mixed methods (MM) research designs are presented in this chapter. MM research designs are different from both quantitative (QUAN) and qualitative (QUAL) research designs in the following ways:

1. QUAN designs are well established, with the best-known typologies describing experimental, quasi-experimental, and survey research, which have evolved over the past 40 years.

2. Standardized QUAL research designs are virtually nonexistent, except in a generic sense (e.g., ethnographic research designs, case study research designs). The major reasons for this appear to be the emergent nature of much of QUAL research, which precludes the a priori specification of distinct typologies of QUAL research designs, and the lack of interest of most QUAL theoreticians in developing design typologies.

3. MM research designs combine elements of both the QUAN and QUAL orientations and require creativity and flexibility in their construction. Burke Johnson and

Anthony Onwuegbuzie (2004) recently described this characteristic of MM research:

A tenet of mixed methods research is that researchers should mindfully create designs that effectively answer their research questions; this stands in contrast to the common approach in traditional quantitative research where students are given a menu of designs from which to select. It also stands in stark contrast to the approach where one completely follows either the qualitative paradigm or the quantitative paradigm. (p. 20)

In the first section of this chapter, we explain why MM design typologies are valuable. We then briefly discuss the criteria that have been used by various authors to create MM design typologies.

We next present a comprehensive typology of research designs, the *Methods-Strands Matrix,* together with decision points that researchers encounter when using it. Special attention is paid to the MM designs, which include five distinct families: sequential, parallel, conversion, multilevel, and fully integrated. Quasi-mixed designs are also described; in these designs, QUAL and QUAN data are collected, but no true integration of findings and inferences for the overall study are made.

Other typologies of MM research design are then briefly described, and an alternative to the MM typologies is presented: Maxwell and Loomis's (2003) interactive model, which has five components (purposes, conceptual model, research questions, methods, validity). These authors present design maps, which enable investigators to analyze a study's MM design ex post facto.

The chapter ends with a seven-step process for selecting an MM design for a particular research study, with the caveat that many MM researchers will have to create their final design.

Issues Regarding Typologies of Mixed Methods Designs

Are Typologies of Mixed Methods Designs Necessary?

Scholars writing in the field of MM research have been developing typologies of mixed designs from the time the field emerged. For instance, Greene, Caracelli, and Graham (1989) examined a large number of MM studies and developed a typology for the designs used in those studies based on their design characteristics and functions.

Why have so many of their colleagues followed the lead of Greene et al. (1989) in developing MM typologies?

1. Typologies help researchers decide how to proceed when designing their MM studies. They provide a variety of paths, or ideal design types, that may be chosen to accomplish the goals of the study.

2. Typologies of MM research designs are useful in establishing a common language (e.g. notations, abbreviations) for the field.

3. Typologies of MM designs help to provide the field with an organizational structure. Currently, given the number of existing MM typologies, it is more accurate to say that typologies provide the field with multiple alternative organizational structures.

4. Typologies of MM designs help to legitimize the field because they provide examples of research designs that are clearly distinct from either QUAN or QUAL designs.

5. Typologies are useful as a pedagogical tool. A particularly effective teaching technique is to present alternative design typologies and then have students compare them.

Can a Typology of Mixed Methods Designs Be Exhaustive?

Although typologies of MM designs are valuable, researchers should not expect them to be *exhaustive*. This is an important point, especially because many researchers from the QUAN tradition expect a complete menu of designs from which they can select the "correct" one (e.g., Shadish, Cook, & Campbell, 2002).

We argue throughout this chapter that methodologists cannot create a complete taxonomy[2] of MM designs due to the designs' capacity to mutate into other forms. Similarly, Maxwell and Loomis (2003) concluded that "the actual diversity in mixed methods studies is far greater than any typology can adequately encompass" (p. 244).

This diversity in MM designs is produced by two factors:

1. *The QUAL component of MM research studies.* MM research uses an emergent strategy in at least the QUAL component of the design. **Emergent designs** may evolve into other forms as QUAL data collection and analysis occur.

2. *The opportunistic nature of MM design.* In many cases, an MM research study may have a predetermined research design, but new components of the design may evolve as researchers follow up on leads that develop as data are collected and analyzed. These "opportunistic" designs may be slightly different from those contained in previously published MM typologies.

What's more, even if we could list all of the MM research designs in this chapter, those designs will continue to evolve, thereby making the typology no longer exhaustive. Therefore, all MM researchers can do is to establish a set of ideal types or "families" of MM research designs, which researchers can then creatively manipulate in specific research settings. The purpose of this chapter is to introduce readers to a family of MM research designs, from which they can select the "best" one and then creatively adjust it to meet the needs of their particular research study.

Criteria Used in Mixed Methods Research Typologies

Table 7.1 presents seven criteria that authors have used to create their MM typologies (e.g., Creswell, Plano Clark, Gutmann, & Hanson, 2003; Greene & Caracelli, 1989; Greene et al., 1997b; Johnson & Onwuegbuzie, 2004; Morgan, 1998; Morse, 1991, 2003):

- Number of methodological approaches used*
- Number of strands or phases*
- Type of implementation process*
- Stage of integration of approaches*
- Priority of methodological approach
- Functions of the research study
- Theoretical or ideological perspective

Our typology uses the first four criteria[3] (designated with an*) to generate what we call the Methods-Strands Matrix. We do not use the other three criteria in our typology, which focuses on *methodological components* of research designs. We did not include these criteria for the following reasons:

- *The priority of methodological approach.* Though an important consideration, the relative importance of the QUAL or QUAN components of a research study cannot be completely determined before the study occurs. In the real world, a QUAN + qual study may become a QUAL + quan study if the QUAN data become more important in understanding the phenomenon under study and vice versa. Because the actual priority of approach is often determined after the study is complete, it is not part of our design typology.

- *The functions of the research study.* In our opinion, the intended function of a research study (e.g., triangulation, complementarity) is

not a design issue; rather, the function is related to the role that the outcomes from the study eventually serve (e.g., to corroborate findings). Bryman (2006a) analyzed a sample of MM studies and concluded that "practice does not always tally with the reasons given for using the approach" (p. 109). That is, the stated purpose for performing an MM study often does not agree with what the researchers actually do in practice. Because the outcomes of an MM study come *after* its design and may differ from the stated purpose, we do not include this criterion (i.e., function of the research study) in our design typology.

- *The theoretical or ideological perspective.* Some analysts include theoretical or ideological perspective (e.g., transformative orientation) as a design component. Although this is an important axiological consideration for conducting research, it is not a design component. For researchers working within the transformative orientation, the pursuit of social justice is not a design choice; rather, it is *the reason* for doing the research (see Chapter 5), which supersedes design choices. Therefore, we do not include theoretical perspective (or agenda) as a criterion in our design typology. With regard to this point concerning ideological perspectives, Gorard and Taylor (2004) state a similar position:

> Perhaps we therefore need to reconfigure our methods classifications in some way to make it clearer that the use of qualitative and quantitative methods is a *choice*, driven largely by the situation and the research questions, not the personality, skills or **ideology** of the researcher. (p. 2, italics in original, bold added)

We limit the number of dimensions in our typology because it could become overly *complex* otherwise (see Earley, 2007). As observed by Donna Mertens (2005), additional subtypes can easily be constructed or modified within the general types, depending on the purpose of the research and the research questions.

Table 7.1   Criteria Used in MM Research Typologies and the Design Questions They Answer

Criterion Used	What Design Questions Does This Criterion Answer?	What Possible Values for the Criterion Exist?	Is This Criterion Used in Our Typology?
1. Number of methodological approaches	Will the study involve one method (QUAN or QUAL) or both (QUAL and QUAN)?	• Monomethods study • Mixed methods study	Yes
2. Number of strands or phases	Will the study involve one phase or multiple phases?	• Monostrand • Multistrand	Yes
3. Type of implementation process	Will the QUAN and QUAL data collection occur sequentially or in a parallel manner? Will data conversion occur? Will QUAL and QUAN data be gathered at different levels of analysis?	• Parallel • Sequential • Conversion • Multilevel • Combination	Yes
4. Stage of integration of approaches	Will the study be mixed (QUAL, QUAN) in the experiential stage only, or across stages, or other combinations?	• Across all stages • Within experiential stage only • Other variants	Yes, but only to allow the inclusion of quasi-mixed designs
5. Priority of methodological approach	Does the QUAL or QUAN component have priority, or are they equal in importance, at the onset of the study?	• QUAL + quan • QUAN + qual • QUAN → qual • QUAL → quan	No
6. Functions of the research study	Which functions does the research design serve?	• Triangulation • Complementarity • Development • Initiation • Expansion • Other functions	No
7. Theoretical or ideological perspective	Will the design be driven by a particular theoretical or ideological perspective?	• Some variant of the transformative perspective or other perspectives • No theoretical or ideological perspective	No

Quasi-Mixed Designs

Recent conceptualizations of MM research recognize that a study is truly mixed only if there is an *integration* of approaches across the stages of the study. For example, a definition of MM presented in Chapter 1 referred to the integration of findings and inferences "using both qualitative and quantitative approaches or methods in a single study or program of inquiry" (Tashakkori & Creswell, 2007b, p. 4). This focus on integration allows us to distinguish between true MM research designs and those designs that we have labeled quasi-mixed designs (Teddlie & Tashakkori, 2006).

Quasi-mixed designs are ones in which two types of data are collected (QUAN, QUAL), with little or no integration of the two types of findings or inferences from the study. For example, a social psychologist might design a study to test a theory with specific hypotheses, using QUAN-oriented questionnaires completed by the study participants. The researcher might also ask each participant a few open-ended, QUAL-oriented questions in an interview following the completion of the study (e.g., What was the experience like?). (These debriefings usually function to determine if the participants were psychologically harmed by the experience or to assess the fidelity of the interventions, but they might also yield some interesting anecdotal evidence.) Despite the existence of both types of data, this study is not mixed because the QUAN component was the focus of the study and the QUAN and QUAL results and inferences were not integrated in answering the research questions.

Similarly, an educational researcher might study the experiences of students who speak English as a second language (ESL). This researcher might spend considerable time with the ESL students during 2 school years trying to reconstruct their experiences and determine how ESL students differ from other students. The educational researcher might also gather some basic QUAN data on the students (e.g., age, parental education level) but only present this information in sidebar descriptive tables. Even though both QUAL and QUAN data are gathered in the study, there is no true integration of the information in a meaningful way because the study focuses on the QUAL reconstructions of the students' life experiences. This study, therefore, also employs a quasi-mixed design because there is no true integration of QUAN and QUAL results.

The concept of quasi-mixed designs is important because it allows researchers to distinguish studies that are technically mixed because they have both QUAN and QUAL data from studies that are truly mixed because they meaningfully integrate QUAN and QUAL components. A requirement for truly mixed designs is the presence of two or more clearly identifiable (sets of) inferences, each gleaned from the findings of a strand of the study, followed by a deliberate attempt to integrate these inferences (see Chapter 12). We continue to use "stage of integration" as a fourth criterion in our typology (see Table 7.1) to allow for the inclusion of these quasi-mixed designs, as described later in this chapter.[4]

Basic Terminology for Mixed Methods Research Designs

Janice Morse (1991, 2003) developed the basic notational system (see Box 7.1) that is still used in MM research. This system consists of three important distinctions:

1. Whether a project is QUAL oriented or QUAN oriented

2. Which aspect of the design is *dominant* (designated with uppercase letters, such as QUAL) and which aspect of the design is *less dominant* (designated with lowercase letters, such as qual)[5]

3. Whether projects are conducted simultaneously (*simultaneous or concurrent designs*, designated by a plus [+] sign), or sequentially (sequential designs, designated by the arrow [→] symbol)

In Morse's system, the priority of one method over the other is an important dimension predetermined before data collection starts. *Dominant/less dominant designs* feature one

> **Box 7.1**
>
> **Morse's (2003) Notations and Designs for MM Research**
>
> The *plus* sign + indicates that projects are conducted simultaneously, with the uppercase indicating the dominant project.
>
> The *arrow* → indicates that projects are conducted sequentially, again with the uppercase indicating dominance.
>
> QUAL indicates a qualitatively driven project.
>
> QUAN indicates a quantitatively driven project.
>
> Therefore, we have eight combinations of triangulated designs:
>
> *Simultaneous designs:*
>
> QUAL + qual, indicates a qualitatively driven, qualitative simultaneous design.
>
> QUAN + quan, indicates a quantitatively driven, quantitative simultaneous design.
>
> QUAL + quan, indicates a qualitatively driven, qualitative and quantitative simultaneous design.
>
> QUAN + qual, indicates a quantitatively driven, quantitative and qualitative simultaneous design.
>
> *Sequential designs:*
>
> QUAL → qual, indicates a qualitatively driven project, followed by a second qualitative project.
>
> QUAN → quan, indicates a quantitatively driven project, followed by a second quantitative project.
>
> QUAL → quan, indicates a qualitatively driven project, followed by a quantitative project.
>
> QUAN → qual, indicates a quantitatively driven project, followed by a qualitative project.
>
> Projects may have complex designs containing combinations of the designs, depending on the scope and complexity of the research program.
>
> *Note:* This is based on a box in Morse (2003, p. 198).

major methodological focus, with the other methodological approach playing a secondary role (e.g., QUAL + quan or QUAN → qual). The **priority of methodological approach** is an important design component for many MM typologies, as noted in Table 7.1.

Whether research projects are conducted in a concurrent/parallel manner or in a sequential manner is a key design component included in many MM typologies. In Chapters 2 and 5, we distinguished between parallel and sequential mixed designs:

- *Parallel mixed designs* refer to MM projects where the phases of the study (QUAN, QUAL) occur in a parallel manner, either simultaneously or with some time lapse. These phases address related aspects of the same basic research question(s).

- *Sequential mixed designs* refer to MM projects where the phases of the study occur in chronological order, with one strand emerging from or following the other (QUAN followed by QUAL, or vice versa). The research questions and procedures for one strand depend on the previous strand. QUAL and QUAN phases are related to one another but may evolve as the study unfolds.

In Table 7.1, the distinction between parallel and sequential mixed designs is part of the criterion known as "type of implementation process."

An important distinction in terminology exists between Morse's (1991, 2003) *simultaneous* designs, some scholars' (e.g. Creswell & Plano Clark, 2007) *concurrent* designs, and what we call *parallel* designs. The terms *simultaneous* and *concurrent* imply that the QUAL and QUAN phases of a study occur at exactly the same time. Though that is often the case when the same researchers conduct both strands of an MM study simultaneously, there are also numerous cases in which the two data types are collected at different times due to practical considerations (e.g., the research team cannot collect all of the data at the same time). Therefore, we use the more inclusive term *parallel mixed designs*, rather than *simultaneous* or *concurrent mixed designs*, in our typology.

Though researchers have built on and deviated from the Morse system, they have maintained the basic notational structure, thereby resulting in considerable uniformity across different typologies in terms of key symbols (QUAN, QUAL, quan, qual, +, →), thus making it easier to compare the different approaches.

The Methods-Strands Matrix

Generation of the Methods-Strands Matrix

The approach to classifying MM research designs presented in this chapter has evolved over time (e.g., Tashakkori & Teddlie, 1998, 2003c; Teddlie & Tashakkori, 2005, 2006). The latest incarnation of this typology was developed for two reasons:

- To more specifically locate MM designs within the larger framework of a general typology of research designs in the social and behavioral sciences
- To present a perspective on MM research designs that features methodological components, rather than theoretical or ideological perspectives and research purposes or functions

A simplified version of our typology is presented in Table 7.2, which is a matrix created by crossing two dimensions:

- Type of approach or methods employed in the study (monomethod or mixed methods)
- Number of strands (or phases) of the study (monostrand or multistrand)

Each of the four cells in the matrix includes numerous designs.

Four Decision Points in the Methods-Strands Matrix

Investigators make four basic methodological decisions when selecting a design for their study from the matrix. (See Table 7.1, Criteria 1–4.) The first two decision points (number of methodological approaches, number of strands) create the matrix.

Number of Methodological Approaches. The Methods-Strands Matrix conceptually encompasses all three research approaches (QUAL, QUAN, MM) because it includes "pure" QUAN and QUAL designs. The emphasis in this chapter is on the MM designs, but it is also useful to consider how they are related to monomethod QUAL and QUAN designs.

We define monomethod and MM designs as follows:

- **Monomethod designs**—a type of research design in which only the QUAL approach, or only the QUAN approach, is used across all stages of the study
- **Mixed methods designs**—a type of research design in which QUAL and QUAN approaches are mixed across the stages of a study

Number of Strands or Phases in the Research Design. The second dimension of the Methods-Strands Matrix (Table 7.2) refers to whether the research study has only one strand or more than one strand. The terminology related to this dimension follows:

- **Strand of a research design**—phase of a study that includes three stages—the

Table 7.2   The Methods-Strands Matrix: A Typology of Research Designs Featuring Mixed Methods

Design Type	Monostrand Designs	Multistrand Designs

Monomethod designs	**Cell 1**
	
	Monomethod monostrand designs
	
	  1. Traditional QUAN designs
	  2. Traditional QUAL designs
		Cell 2
		
		Monomethod multistrand designs
		
		  1. Parallel monomethod
		     a. QUAN + QUAN
		     b. QUAL + QUAL
		
		  2. Sequential monomethod
		     a. QUAN → QUAN
		     b. QUAL → QUAL

Mixed methods designs	**Cell 3**
	
	Quasi-mixed monostrand designs
	
	  1. Monostrand conversion design
		Cell 4
		
		Mixed methods multistrand designs
		
		  1. Parallel mixed designs
		  2. Sequential mixed designs
		  3. Conversion mixed designs
		  4. Multilevel mixed designs
		  5. Fully integrated mixed designs
		
		Quasi-mixed multistrand designs (designs mixed at the experiential stage only, including the parallel quasi-mixed design)

Note: See Tashakkori and Teddlie (2003c, pp. 685–689) for more details regarding the quasi-mixed designs.

conceptualization stage, the experiential stage (methodological/analytical), and the inferential stage—often in an iterative or interactive manner (see Ridenour & Newman, 2008)

- **Monostrand designs**   employ only a single phase that encompasses all of the stages from conceptualization through inference
- **Multistrand designs**—employ more than one phase;[6] often multiple phases, with each encompassing all of the stages from conceptualization through inference

Following are definitions regarding stages:

- **Stage of a research strand**—a step or component of a strand/phase of a study

- **Conceptualization stage**—the sphere of concepts (abstract operations), which includes the formulation of research purposes, questions, and so forth
- **Experiential (methodological/analytical) stage**—the experiential sphere (concrete observations and operations), which includes methodological operations, data generation, analysis, and so on
- **Inferential stage**—the sphere of inferences (abstract explanations and understandings), which includes emerging theories, explanations, inferences, and so on (Tashakkori & Teddlie, 2003c, p. 681)

A simplified outline of the strand-stage terminology is presented in Figure 7.1, in which there

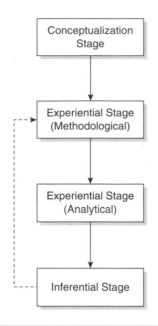

Figure 7.1   Graphic Illustration of Traditional QUAN or QUAL Designs (monomethod monostrand designs)

is one strand (QUAL or QUAN) in a monomethod design with three stages:

1. Conceptualization stage

2. Experiential stage
   a. Methodological
   b. Analytical

3. Inferential stage

Dividing a strand into distinct stages allows for the transformation of one methodological approach to another within a strand; that is, a strand might start out as QUAL but then become QUAN, or vice versa.

Type of Implementation Process (Parallel, Sequential, Conversion, Multilevel). The implementation process involves the mixing of QUAN and QUAL approaches. This process answers three questions: Will QUAN and QUAL data collection occur sequentially or in a parallel manner? Will data conversion occur? Will QUAL and QUAN data be gathered at different levels of

analysis? The first two implementation processes (involving parallel and sequential mixed designs) were discussed earlier in this chapter.

The third implementation method uses conversion designs, which are unique to MM research. This method involves the following terms:

- *Data conversion (transformation)*—Collected QUAN data types are converted into narratives that can be analyzed qualitatively or QUAL data types are converted into numerical codes that can be statistically analyzed or both data types are converted.
- *Quantitizing*—This method involves converting QUAL data into numerical codes that can be statistically analyzed (e.g., Miles & Huberman, 1994).
- *Qualitizing*—This process transforms QUAN data into data that can be analyzed qualitatively (e.g., Tashakkori & Teddlie, 1998).

The fourth MM implementation method involves collecting QUAL and QUAN data from multiple levels within an organization or other type of social institution, thereby generating multilevel research designs. These multilevel designs are possible only in hierarchically organized social institutions, such as schools and hospitals, in which one *level of analysis*[7] is nested within another (e.g., student within classroom within grade within school). Multilevel mixing occurs when one type of data (QUAL) is collected at one level (student) and another type of data (QUAN) is collected at another level (classroom) to answer interrelated research questions.

Stage of Integration of Approaches. The final decision point is the least important: Does the integration of approaches occur in the experiential (methodological/analytical) stage only, or does it occur across stages or other combinations? The most dynamic and innovative of the MM designs are mixed across stages, so why should we consider selecting a design that is mixed in only the experiential stage?

The answer to this question is simple: because these designs have been described in the literature and because one of them (the parallel quasi-mixed design in Cell 4 of Table 7.2) is a popular one. In these designs, researchers working primarily within one approach (e.g., the QUAN approach, with uppercase letters) might elect to gather and analyze data associated with the other approach (e.g., the qual approach, in lowercase letters) to enhance the study. In our view, these *dominant-less dominant designs* are quasi-mixed in nature, rather than truly mixed. If the design is mixed only in terms of data collection, without deliberate integration of the QUAL and QUAN analyses and inferences, it is a *quasi-mixed design* in our typology.

Designs in the Methods-Strands Matrix

We now present some of the more important and widely used designs from the matrix, together with illustrative figures. The general features of these figures are presented in Box 7.2.

Monomethod Designs

There are two types of monomethod research designs, those with only one strand (Cell 1 in Table 7.2) and those with more than one strand (Cell 2 in Table 7.2). Cell 1 designs are monomethod monostrand designs, whereas Cell 2 designs are monomethod multistrand designs.

Monomethod Monostrand Designs

Cell 1 designs use a single research method or data collection technique (QUAN or QUAL) and corresponding data analysis procedures to answer research questions employing one strand. This strand may be either QUAN or QUAL, but not both. All stages within the strand (conceptualization, experiential, inferential) are consistently either QUAN or QUAL. Figure 7.1 is an example of the **monomethod monostrand design**.

These designs appear to be the simplest of those presented in Table 7.2, yet they can be quite complicated (e.g., multilevel QUAN designs, detailed ethnographic QUAL designs) and have been written about in numerous books on QUAN and QUAL design. For example, the complex methodology for ethnographic studies has been discussed in detail in several texts (e.g., Chambers, 2000; Fetterman, 1998; Hammersley & Atkinson, 1995; LeCompte & Preissle, 1993).

Box 7.2

The General Features of Figures 7.1–7.7

Rectangles and ovals represent either a QUAL or a QUAN stage of a research strand. If the stages are all rectangles, the figure represents a monomethod design. If some of the stages are rectangles and some are ovals, the figure represents an MM design.

Each strand found in the figures has three stages (conceptualization, experiential, inferential). The experiential stage is broken into two parts (methodological and analytical) to allow for conversion designs. We have divided the experiential stage into those two parts on all figures for the sake of consistency.

There is a broken-line arrow from the inferential stage to the methodological stage in each figure. This indicates that conclusions emerging from the inferential stage of a study may lead to further data gathering and analysis in the same study. The methodological-analytical-inferential loop of each diagram is iterative.

These figures were first presented in Tashakkori and Teddlie (2003c, pp. 684–690).

We present only two examples (one QUAN, one QUAL) here because our focus is on the MM designs. Among the most well known of the QUAN designs in the social and behavioral sciences are the quasi-experimental designs first presented by Campbell and Stanley (1963) and revised in later texts (Cook & Campbell, 1979; Shadish et al., 2002). These authors used a simple notational system in which experimental treatments were designated as X, observations were designated as O (e.g., O_1, O_2), R represented random assignment to treatment, and a dashed line (--------) indicated nonrandom assignment to treatment. The following quasi-experimental design was presented in Campbell and Stanley (1963) as the nonequivalent control group design:

O_1 X O_2

O_1 O_2

When quasi-experimental studies involve the collection of QUAN data only, they are examples of monomethod monostrand designs.

The second example of a monomethod monostrand design is of a complex ethnography conducted by Spradley (1970) involving the collection of QUAL data. A summary of his ethnography of urban nomads is presented in Box 7.3.

Monomethod Multistrand Designs

Cell 2 designs employ a single method or data collection technique (QUAN or QUAL) and corresponding data analysis procedures to answer research questions. These **monomethod multistrand designs** use two or more strands, which may be either QUAN or QUAL (but not both), and are conducted in a sequential or parallel manner.

The *multitrait-multimethod matrix* of Campbell and Fiske (1959) is an example of parallel monomethod multistrand designs. Their study presented one of the first explicit multimethod designs in the social and behavioral sciences and was described previously in Chapter 4. Specifically, it used more than one QUAN method (e.g., a structured interview that yielded QUAN data, a structured observation protocol that also yielded QUAN data) to measure a single psychological trait.[8] (Refer to Figure 7.2 for an illustration of parallel monomethod multistrand designs.)

Box 7.3

Example of a Complex Ethnography
You Owe Yourself a Drunk: An Ethnography of Urban Nomads

Spradley (1979, 1980) presented the Developmental Research Sequence (DRS) as a 12-step integrated approach to conducting ethnographic research. The core of the DRS observational component consists of three levels of progressively focused observations (descriptive, focused, selected) together with three levels of analysis (domain, taxonomic, componential).

Spradley (1970) presented an ethnography of homeless men in Seattle, using several sources, including letters that one man (Bill) sent him from jail and elsewhere. Other data sources included months of participant observation and extensive key informant interviews. Spradley analyzed all data sources and developed a set of themes related to an alcoholic's life, including confinement, restricted mobility, and freedom.

The complexity of Spradley's analysis is demonstrated in the discovery of 15 stages of making the "bucket" (jail) and 15 dimensions for how urban nomads "make a flop" (find a place to sleep), including examples of 35 specific types of flops (e.g., car flop, weed patch, all night show, apple bin).

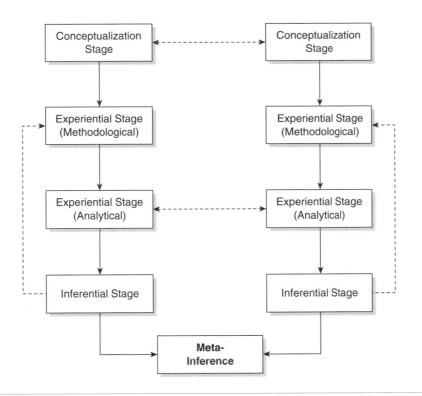

Figure 7.2   Graphic Illustration of Parallel Monomethod Multistrand Designs (two QUAN strands or two QUAL strands)

Mixed Methods Designs

There are two types of MM designs, those with only one strand (Cell 3 in Table 7.2) and those with more than one strand (Cell 4 in Table 7.2). Cell 3 designs are mixed methods monostrand designs, and Cell 4 designs are mixed methods multistrand designs.

Mixed Methods Monostrand Designs

The simplest of the MM designs, **mixed methods monostrand designs**, involve only one strand of a research study, yet they include both QUAL and QUAN components. Because only one type of data is analyzed and only one type of inference (QUAL or QUAN) is made, these are *quasi-mixed* designs. We discuss only one design from Cell 3 in this section: the monostrand conversion design. (Refer to Figure 7.3 for an illustration of monostrand conversion designs.)

Here are some characteristics of the monostrand conversion design:

- In general, conversion designs allow for data transformation where one data form is converted into another and then analyzed accordingly.

- **Monostrand conversion designs** (also known as **simple conversion designs**) are used in single strand studies in which research questions are answered through an analysis of transformed (quantitized or qualitized) data. These designs are mixed because they switch approach in the experiential phase of the study, when the data that were originally collected (narrative, numeric) are converted into the other form (numeric, narrative). Figure 7.3 depicts the monostrand conversion designs, with the transformation of data type occurring between the methodological and the analytical components of the experiential stage.

- Monostrand conversion designs may be planned before the study actually occurs, but

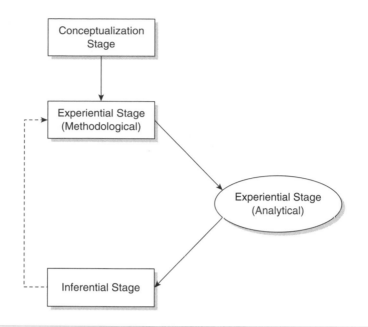

Figure 7.3   Graphic Illustration of Monostrand Conversion Designs (an example of quasi-mixed designs)

many applications occur serendipitously as a study unfolds. For instance, a researcher may determine that there are emerging patterns in the information gleaned from narrative interview data that can be converted into numerical form and then analyzed statistically, thereby allowing for a more thorough analysis of the data.

An interesting aspect of the monostrand conversion design is that it has been used frequently in both the QUAN and QUAL traditions, without being recognized as mixed (e.g., Hunter & Brewer, 2003; Maxwell & Loomis, 2003; Waszak & Sines, 2003). The following list includes some examples of quantitizing data:

• Morse's (1989) study of teenage mothers and the frequency of their use of the word *stuff*, converting that word into a frequency count that demonstrated the childish mode of speech used by young women with adult responsibilities

• Miles and Huberman's (1994) conversion of narrative data from their school improvement studies into frequency counts or rating scales; for

example, their conversion of the described "roughness" or "smoothness" of the implementation process into 3- to 5-point scales

• Sandelowski, Harris, and Holditch-Davis's (1991) transformation of interview data into a frequency distribution that compared the "numbers of couples having and not having an amniocentesis with the number of physicians encouraging or not encouraging them to have the procedure," which was then analyzed statistically to determine the "relationship between physician encouragement and couple decision to have an amniocentesis" (Sandelowski, 2003, p. 327)

Examples of qualitizing data are rarer than those of quantizing data, but they can be found. One example might be a qualitative analysis of personality profiles (e.g. Minnesota Multiphasic Personality Inventory or MMPI), each constructed to represent one participant's QUAN data. An illustration of qualitizing comes from an investigation of school restructuring effects by Taylor and Tashakkori (1997). In that study, all teachers in a district were asked to respond to a survey including items regarding their desire/motivation to participate and actual involvement in decision making at their schools. QUAL profiles of four extreme groups were generated on the basis of the teachers' QUAN scores on those two dimensions (desire for participation versus actual participation). The types were labeled "empowered," "disenfranchised," "involved," and "disengaged."

Another example of qualitizing data is found in Appendix A (see p. 16 at www.sagepub.com/foundations). In this study, Ivankova and her colleagues (2006) developed four qualitative profiles of typical doctoral students (beginning, matriculated, graduated, withdrawn/inactive) based on seven QUAN demographic variables. Further examples of quantitizing and qualitizing are found in Chapter 11, which presents data analysis issues in MM research.

Mixed Methods Multistrand Designs

Cell 4 of Table 7.2 contains the **mixed methods multistrand designs**, which are the most complex designs in the matrix. All of these designs include at least two research strands, and several examples of these designs in the literature include three or more strands. Mixing of QUAL and QUAN approaches may occur both within and across all three stages of the study. These designs include five "families," which are listed in Table 7.2, Cell 4:

- Parallel mixed designs
- Sequential mixed designs
- Conversion mixed designs
- Multilevel mixed designs
- Fully integrated mixed designs

There may be several permutations of each of these families of MM designs based on other specific criteria. Box 7.4 describes the basic characteristics of these five families of mixed designs.

Box 7.4
Five Families of MM Designs

Cell 4 of the Methods-Strands Matrix contains five families of MM designs based on implementation processes. *Families* means that there could be numerous permutations of each design based on other design characteristics. For example, the descriptions of these designs typically include only two strands, and the addition of more strands results in different "family members." Following are brief definitions of the five families of MM designs:

- *Parallel mixed designs*—In these designs, mixing occurs in a parallel manner, either simultaneously or with some time lapse; planned and implemented QUAL and QUAN phases answer related aspects of the same questions.
- *Sequential mixed designs*—In these designs, mixing occurs across chronological phases (QUAL, QUAN) of the study, questions or procedures of one strand emerge from or depend on the previous strand, and research questions are related to one another and may evolve as the study unfolds.
- *Conversion mixed designs*—In these parallel designs, mixing occurs when one type of data is transformed and analyzed both qualitatively and quantitatively; this design answers related aspects of the same questions.
- *Multilevel mixed designs*—In these parallel or sequential designs, mixing occurs across multiple levels of analysis, as QUAN and QUAL data from these different levels are analyzed and integrated to answer aspects of the same question or related questions.
- *Fully integrated mixed designs*—In these designs, mixing occurs in an interactive manner at all stages of the study. At each stage, one approach affects the formulation of the other, and multiple types of implementation processes occur.

Parallel mixed designs are designs with at least two parallel and relatively independent strands: one with QUAL questions, data collection, and analysis techniques and the other with QUAN questions, data collection, and analysis techniques. The QUAL and QUAN strands are planned and implemented to answer related aspects of the same overarching MM research question (see Chapter 6). Inferences based on the results from each strand are integrated to form meta-inferences at the end of the study (see Chapter 12). A **meta-inference** is a conclusion generated through an integration of the inferences that have been obtained from the results of the QUAL and QUAN strands of an MM study. (Refer to Figure 7.4 for an illustration of parallel mixed designs.)

A major advantage of MM research is that it enables researchers to simultaneously ask confirmatory and exploratory questions, thus verifying and generating theory in the same study. Parallel

mixed designs use QUAL and QUAN methods in independent strands to answer exploratory (typically, but not always, QUAL) and confirmatory (typically, but not always, QUAN) questions.

The parallel mixed design was used in the World Bank Guatemala Poverty Assessment (Rao & Woolcock, 2003).[9] The QUAN strand of the study included survey data. A purposive sample of five pairs of villages was selected for the QUAL study. The two strands of the study were kept independent (including the investigator teams) until after data analyses were finished. Mixing happened at the meta-inference stage. The integration provided "a more accurate map of the spatial and demographic diversity of the poor" (Rao & Woolcock, 2003, p. 173). (See Box 11.5 in Chapter 11 for a lengthier quote from this study.)

Lopez and Tashakkori (2006) provide another example of a parallel mixed study, examining the effects of two types of bilingual education programs on attitudes and academic achievement of

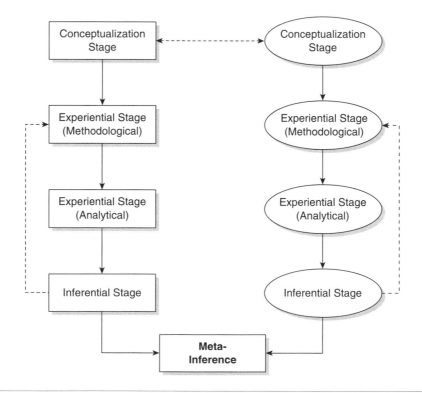

Figure 7.4   Graphic Illustration of Parallel Mixed Designs

fifth-grade students. The QUAN strand of the study included a Likert-type scale measuring self-perceptions and self-beliefs in relation to bilingualism, standardized achievement tests in various academic subjects, and linguistic competence in English and Spanish. The QUAL strand consisted of interviews with a random sample of 32 students. Each data set was analyzed independently, and conclusions were drawn. The findings of the two studies were integrated by comparing and contrasting the conclusions and trying to construct a more comprehensive understanding of how the programs differentially affected the children.

Although parallel mixed designs are very powerful, they are challenging to conduct due to the complexity of running multiple research strands often simultaneously. Different teams of researchers may be required to conduct these studies, as was the case in the World Bank Guatemala study described earlier and the evaluation study detailed in Chapter 1 (Trend, 1979). In the Trend study, a team of quantitatively oriented evaluators conducted the QUAN strand, while anthropologists independently conducted the QUAL strand. The QUAN data were expected to determine the success of the federal subsidy program, whereas the QUAL case studies were to provide a picture of program process. Meta-inferences across the two independent strands were employed to reconcile the divergent information gleaned from the two parallel strands.

Parallel mixed designs might prove difficult for novice researchers or researchers working alone for several reasons:

- In general, it requires considerable expertise to examine the same phenomenon using two different approaches in a parallel manner.
- Specifically, the parallel analysis of QUAN and QUAL data sources, and then the integration of those results into a coherent set of findings and inferences, can be difficult.
- Particular problems may develop when the results are discrepant, and the novice or

solo investigator may be unable to interpret or resolve these inconsistencies to make meta-inferences.

Hence, the powerful parallel mixed designs might be best accomplished using a collaborative team approach in which each member of the group can contribute to the complex, often evolving design (e.g., Shulha & Wilson, 2003). Nevertheless, there are numerous examples of such designs in dissertations completed by solo investigators.

Sequential mixed designs are designs in which at least two strands occur chronologically (QUAN → QUAL or QUAL → QUAN). The conclusions based on the results of the first strand lead to the formulation of design components for the next strand. The final inferences are based on the results of both strands of the study. The second strand of the study is conducted either to confirm or disconfirm inferences from the first strand or to provide further explanation for its findings (Tashakkori & Teddlie, 2003a, p. 715). (Refer to Figure 7.5 for an illustration of sequential mixed designs.)

Sequential mixed designs answer exploratory and confirmatory questions chronologically in a prespecified order. Though still challenging, these designs are less complicated to conduct by the solo investigator than are the parallel mixed designs, because it is easier to keep the strands separate and the studies typically unfold in a slower, more predictable manner.

One example of the use of the sequential mixed design is the Ivankova et al. (2006) study contained in Appendix A and described in Chapter 2. (See Appendix A at www.sagepub.com/foundations.) The purpose of this sequential QUAN → QUAL study was to understand why students persist in a doctoral program. The QUAN component first identified factors that significantly contributed to students' persistence; the QUAL component then focused on explaining how this occurred.

An example of a sequential QUAL → QUAN mixed design comes from the consumer marketing literature (Hausman, 2000). The first part of the

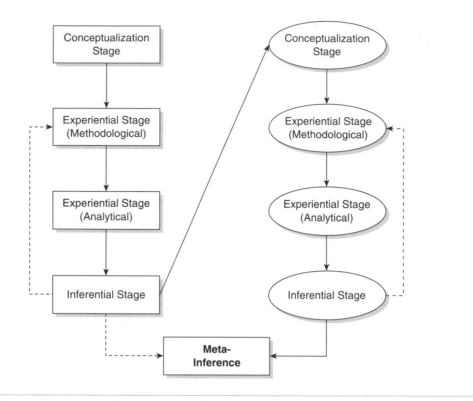

Figure 7.5   Graphic Illustration of Sequential Mixed Designs

study was exploratory in nature, using semistruc-tured interviews to examine several questions related to impulse buying:

- What are consumers' attitudes toward shopping?
- How do consumers make buying decisions?
- How do buying decisions result in impulse buying?

Interviewers conducted 60 interviews with consumers, and the resultant data were analyzed using grounded theory techniques. Based on these QUAL analyses, a series of QUAN hypothe-ses were developed and tested using a question-naire completed by 272 consumers. Hypothesis testing resulted in significant results for three of the hypotheses:

- Individual consumers' impulse buying is correlated with their desire to fulfill hedo-nic needs (e.g., fun, novelty, surprise).

- Individual consumer impulse buying behavior is correlated with desires to satisfy self-esteem considerations.
- Perceptions of decision-making accuracy mediate impulse buying.

Several of our graduate students conducted dissertation research using sequential mixed designs (e.g., Cakan, 1999; Carwile, 2005; Kochan, 1998; Lasserre-Cortez, 2006; Stevens, 2001; Wu, 2005). Some of the dissertations used more com-plex combinations of the two approaches rather than a simple sequential study. For example, Wu's (2005) dissertation consisted of a QUAL strand (administrator interviews) as well as a QUAN one (survey). Data were collected and analyzed independently, similar to a parallel mixed design. However, the strongest inferences were gleaned when a sequential data analysis was performed in which the themes obtained from the QUAL strand were used for comparison with the QUAN results. The inconsistency between the inferences of the two strands was the most striking conclusion from the study, in that it revealed a gap between the student applicants' and college administrators' perceptions of factors affecting college choice in Taiwan.

Iterative sequential mixed designs are more complex designs with more than two phases (e.g., QUAN → QUAL → QUAN). An example of one of these designs (Kumagai, Bliss, Daniels, & Carroll, 2004) is presented at the end of this chapter, and more examples are found in Chapter 11.

Conversion mixed designs are multistrand parallel designs in which mixing of QUAL and QUAN approaches occurs when one type of data is transformed (qualitized or quantitized) and then analyzed both qualitatively and quantitatively (Tashakkori & Teddlie, 2003a, p. 706). In these designs, data (e.g., QUAL) are gathered and analyzed using one method and then transformed and analyzed using the other method (e.g., QUAN). (Refer to Figure 7.6 for an illustration of conversion mixed designs.)

Witcher, Onwuegbuzie, Collins, Filer, and Wiedmaier (2003) conducted a conversion mixed design, which was subsequently described by Onwuegbuzie and Leech (2004). In this study, the researchers gathered QUAL data from 912 students regarding their perceptions of the characteristics of effective college teachers. A QUAL thematic analysis revealed nine characteristics, including student-centeredness and enthusiasm about teaching. The researchers then quantitized the data by assigning binary values for each of the students for each of the themes. Thus, if a female graduate student made responses that indicated that she thought student-centeredness was a characteristic of effective teaching, that student received a score of 1 for that theme. If another student did not make responses indicating that he or she thought student-centeredness was a characteristic of effective teaching, that student received a score of 0 for that theme. A series of binary codes (1, 0) were assigned to each student for each characteristic of effective teaching,

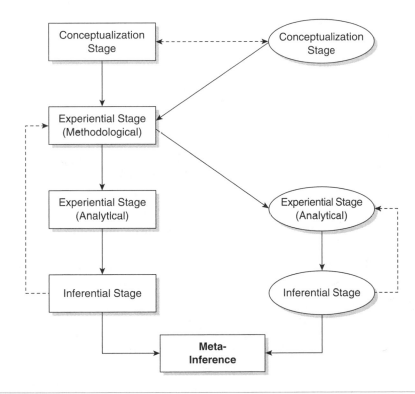

Figure 7.6   Graphic Illustration of Conversion Mixed Designs

resulting in what Witcher et al. (2003) called an inter-respondent matrix.

The analysts then subjected these quantitized data to a series of analyses that enabled them to statistically associate each of the nine themes of effective college teaching with four demographic variables. The researchers were able to connect students with certain demographic characteristics with preferences for certain effective teaching characteristics (e.g., female students were more likely to endorse student-centeredness than were male students).

Thus, one type of data (QUAL) was subjected to both thematic and statistical analysis and meta-inferences were possible using both sets of results simultaneously. Onwuegbuzie and Leech (2004) concluded that "subjecting quantitized data to statistical analysis aided Witcher et al. in the interpretation of the qualitative themes" (p. 784).

Multilevel mixed designs are multistrand designs in which QUAL data are collected at one *level of analysis* (e.g., child) and QUAN data are collected at another (e.g., family) in a parallel or sequential manner. Both types of data are analyzed accordingly, and the results are used to make multiple types of inferences, which then are integrated into meta-inferences. In these designs, the different strands of research are associated with the different levels of analysis.

We (Tashakkori & Teddlie, 1998) extended the concept of multilevel analysis to mixed methods research by noting that researchers working in schools used "different types of methods at different levels of data aggregation. For example, data can be analyzed quantitatively at the student level, qualitatively at the class level, quantitatively at the school level, and qualitatively at the district level" (p. 18). When the QUAN and QUAL data from the different levels are used to answer related questions about a topic of interest, then the resulting meta-inferences are necessarily mixed.

The unique characteristic of multilevel implementation concerns its use of naturally occurring nested, or hierarchical, structures within organizations to generate mixed designs. Consider the following multilevel or nested social structures:

- Students within schools within local educational agencies
- Patients within wards within hospitals
- Patients within general practitioners within clinics
- Mental health clients within counselors within mental health institutions
- Individuals within households within geographically defined communities

The diagrams that we use in this chapter to illustrate other types of mixed designs do not work for multilevel mixed designs because the diagrams in this chapter assume that data are gathered at the same level of analysis. A better depiction of multilevel mixed designs is located in Chapter 8, Figure 8.1, which illustrates five levels from the individual student level to the state school system level.

Multilevel mixed designs may be considered specialized designs because only certain types of data are structured in a nested manner with different levels of analysis. There are examples of multilevel mixed research in education (e.g., Teddlie & Stringfield, 1993), counseling (Elliott & Williams, 2002), and other fields, but these applications are not as numerous as the more common parallel and sequential designs. We discuss the multilevel mixed design in more detail in Chapter 8 because multilevel sampling issues—a topic of that chapter—are complex and provide good illustrations of the design.

The **fully integrated mixed design** is a multistrand parallel design in which mixing of QUAL and QUAN approaches occurs in an interactive (i.e., dynamic, reciprocal, interdependent, iterative) manner at all stages of the study. Multiple types of implementation processes may occur within these designs. At each stage, one approach (e.g., QUAL) affects the formulation of the other (e.g., QUAN) (Tashakkori & Teddlie, 2003a, p. 708). (Refer to Figure 7.7 for an illustration of fully integrated mixed design.)

The Louisiana School Effectiveness Study (LSES; Teddlie & Stringfield, 1993) included a longitudinal study of eight matched pairs of schools initially classified as either effective or ineffective

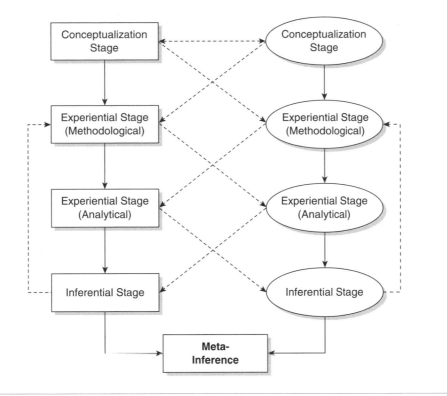

Figure 7.7   Graphic Illustration of Fully Integrated Mixed Designs

using baseline achievement data collected at time one (T$_1$, 1982–1984) and then compared across two phases of the study (T$_2$, 1984–1985 and T$_3$, 1989–1990). Two basic questions characterized the longitudinal phases of the study:

• Would the eight matched pairs of more effective and less effective schools remain differentially effective over time, or would some schools increase or decrease in effectiveness status over time? The major QUAN data used to answer this question were achievement scores and indices of student socioeconomic status.

• What are the processes whereby schools remain the same or change over time with regard to how well they educate their students? The major QUAL data used to answer this question were classroom and school level observations and interviews with participants.

The LSES employed a fully integrated mixed design as follows:

• At the conceptualization stage, the formulation of the QUAN-oriented questions informed the formulation of the QUAL-oriented questions, and vice versa.

• At the experiential (methodological/ analytical) stage, some of the QUAL data (classroom observations) were quantitized and analyzed statistically, and some of the QUAN data (socioeconomic and achievement data) were qualitized. Narrative profiles of schools were generated based on numeric data. The results of these statistical and profile analyses affected the formulation of additional QUAL and QUAN analyses.

• The two major QUAN and QUAL strands, and their crossover analyses, directly influenced the formulation of the meta-inferences, which resulted in a dozen or so major conclusions, each involving triangulated data.

• This complex design was accomplished by a research team that had a wide variety of methodological and experiential backgrounds, as recommended by Shulha and Wilson (2003).

Another example of a fully integrated mixed model design comes from the health sciences. Johnstone (2004) described a 20-step MM process that she used in her study of the organizational consequences of new artifact adoption in surgery. Her collective case study of five hospitals in Australia generated both QUAL and QUAN data that were analyzed inductively and deductively in a series of steps summarized in Box 7.5. Her QUAL data consisted of observations, interviews, and dialogues, and her QUAN information included organizational and staffing data, department of health documents,

preoperative work-time study data, and Likert-scale responses. The summary in Box 7.5 was derived from a complex figure presented by Johnstone (2004, p. 266).

The iterative nature of Johnstone's (2004) analyses illustrates the complexity of the fully integrated mixed model design. Familiarity with the subject matter of interest, with QUAL and QUAN analyses, and with inductive and deductive reasoning, is necessary to conduct these designs. It is rare that solo researchers successfully conduct these designs because they require epistemological and methodological diversity and expertise.

We include one final example of a fully integrated mixed model design (Schulenberg, 2007) in Box 7.6. This study, which comes from the field of criminology, examines the processes that occur in police decision making using a broad range of QUAN and QUAL analyses. We use it as an example in Chapter 11 also.

Box 7.5

A Fully Integrated Mixed Model Design From the Health Sciences

The series of iterative steps used in Johnstone's (2004) study may be summarized as follows:

Steps 1 and 2: The starting points were (1) Johnstone's health services work and (2) her academic study, which led to

Step 3: her earlier (3) "operating theater services" research, which led to

Steps 4 and 5: her (4) initial synthesis of the literature and (5) initial propositions and questions, which led to

Step 6: the (6) tentative study design, which led to

Steps 7 and 8: two initially separate research strands: (7) the collection and initial inductive analysis of QUAL data and (8) the collection of QUAN data. From this point, the QUAL data led to Steps 9 and 11, while the QUAN data concurrently led to Steps 10, 12, and 13.

Steps 9 and 11 (QUAL): Step 7 (the collection and initial analysis of QUAL data) led to (9) thematic analysis of the interviews and observations using inductive reasoning and (11) an analysis of all of the QUAL data, which together led to what Johnstone called Stage 1A triangulation.

Steps 10, 12, and 13: Step 8 (the collection of QUAN data) led to (10) the analysis of QUAN data using deductive reasoning, which (together with Step 7) led to (12) the analysis of relevant QUAN and QUAL data, which together led to what Johnstone called Stage 1B triangulation. Step 10 also separately led to (13) drawing secondary (positivist) paradigm conclusions.

Step 14: This step (14) resulted from Steps 11 and 12 and involved the synthesis of QUAL and QUAN analyses using inductive reasoning (which Johnstone called Stage 2 triangulation), which then led to

Step 15: Step (15), which involved evaluating the progress to date, which led to

Steps 16 and 17: asking more questions or refining existing questions and propositions (Step 16) and drawing some tentative conclusions (Step 17). These steps led to separate concurrent paths:

Steps 18 and 19 (from Step 16): further investigation of the literature on the same or emerging themes (Step 18) and then to modification of the study design or identification of additional data requirements, or both (Step 19) which then led back in an iterative loop to Step 7, the further collection and analysis of QUAL data.

Steps 18 (from Step 17): further investigation of the literature, which then led either indirectly back to Step 7 or directly back to Step 9, both in iterative loops.

Continued iterative loops: Johnstone indicated that the iterative loops continued until data analysis and inference were completed, which was indicated by Step 14, the final synthesis of all QUAL and QUAN analyses using inductive reasoning (Stage 2 triangulation), which then led to

Step 20: drawing primary (naturalistic) paradigm conclusions, which were compared with secondary (postpositivist) paradigm conclusions (Step 13).

Box 7.6
A Fully Integrated Mixed Model Design From Criminology

Another example of a fully integrated mixed model design comes from Schulenberg (2007), who examined the processes that occur in police decision making in a study conducted in Canada. This complex design involved 16 research questions and 29 hypotheses. Data sources included interviews with individual police officers, documents provided by the interviewees, qualitative data gathered from Web sites maintained by police departments, documents obtained from provincial governments, census data, and tabulations of statistical data on the proportion of apprehended youth actually charged with crimes (at the aggregate and individual levels). The interview data gathered from police officers were originally qualitative in nature (gathered from semistructured protocols) but were also quantitized.

The researcher used these diverse data sources to generate five databases that were employed to answer the research questions and hypotheses. In one of her tables, Schulenberg (2007, p. 110) cross-listed the five research databases with the 16 research questions and 29 hypotheses, so that the reader could see which data sources were used to address each of the research issues.

Another table from Schulenberg (p. 109) showed the eight types of qualitative thematic techniques and six types of quantitative statistical techniques that she used in her study. These techniques included *t* tests, chi-squares, multiple regression, analysis of variance, manifest content analysis, latent content analysis, the constant comparative method, and grounded theory techniques including open, axial, and selective coding. These techniques are discussed in Chapter 11.

As indicated in Cell 4 of Table 7.2, there are also *quasi-mixed multistrand designs*. In these designs, QUAL and QUAN data are collected, but there is no true integration of the findings and inferences. For example, in a parallel quasi-mixed study, QUAN survey data on marital satisfaction from 200 couples might be collected and analyzed in one strand, while a small number of couples (only 5) might be interviewed face-to-face in a QUAL strand. This study would be quasi-mixed if results from the QUAL interview data were treated as merely supplementary and were not meaningfully integrated with the results from the QUAN survey data.

The degree to which QUAL and QUAN analyses and inferences are truly integrated determines whether a study is mixed or quasi-mixed. Chapters 11 and 12 describe methods that make possible the true integration of analyses and inferences in MM research.

Other Typologies of Mixed Methods Research Designs

As noted earlier, scholars working in the field of MM research have presented typologies of mixed designs from the time the field emerged in the late 1980s. Currently, a handful of typologies in the MM "marketplace" are the most frequently cited in the methods sections of research studies. We believe that the most useful and adaptable of the typologies will be referenced more often over time and may ultimately become the standards for the field. In the meantime, researchers have an array of perspectives from which to select.

In this section, we briefly describe the more salient features of the following approaches:

- Greene and colleagues' (Greene & Caracelli, 1997b; Greene et al., 1989) typology of component and integrated designs based on design function
- Morse's (1991, 2003) typology of MM designs and similar schemes (e.g., Johnson & Onwuegbuzie, 2004; Morgan, 1998)

- Creswell and colleagues' (Creswell & Plano Clark, 2007; Creswell, Plano Clark, Gutmann, & Hanson, 2003) typologies of MM designs
- Maxwell and Loomis's (2003) alternative approach named the interactive model of research design

Greene et al. (1989) presented the first typology of MM designs in the literature. This typology was based on the functions, or purposes, of MM studies. Five designs were in Greene et al.'s initial typology: triangulation, complementarity, development, initiation, and expansion. A later revision (Greene & Caracelli, 1997b) included two broad classes of designs (component, integrated), with a total of seven distinct MM designs: component designs (triangulation, complementarity, expansion) and integrated designs (iterative, embedded or nested, holistic, transformative). Brief definitions of these designs are contained in Table 7.3.

In Jennifer Greene's (2007, pp. 123–125) latest writing, she again divided MM designs into component and integrated categories with two examples of the former (convergence, extension) and four examples of the latter (iteration, blending, nesting or embedding, mixing for reasons of substance or values). Again, her designs are "importantly anchored in mixed methods purpose" (p. 129), thereby maintaining a consistent and key perspective on how MM design typologies can be structured.

The priority of methodological approach is an important design component for several MM typologies, including those of Morse (1991, 2003), Morgan (1998), and Johnson and Onwuegbuzie (2004). Box 7.1 contains a summary of the designs in Morse's typology.

Morse used *predetermined designs*, which are established before the research occurs and which do not change during the course of the project's life. Morse further defined the theoretical drive as the overall thrust of the project, which is either deductive or inductive (QUAN or QUAL), and the imported component as the one with the lesser priority.

Table 7.3   A Typology of Mixed Methods Designs From Greene and Caracelli (1997b)

Design	Key Features
Component	Data gathering methods implemented as separate aspects of the evaluation and remain distinct throughout
Triangulation	Findings from one method used to corroborate findings generated through other methods
Complementarity	Findings from one dominant method are enhanced or elaborated through findings from another method
Expansion	Different methods are implemented to generate results for distinct components of the research study; results presented "side-by-side" (Greene & Caracelli, 1997b, p. 23)
Integrated	Methods integrated throughout the evaluation
Iterative	Dynamic interplay of findings generated through different methods throughout the evaluation
Embedded or nested	One method is located within another; framework of "creative tension" (Greene & Caracelli, 1997b, p. 24)
Holistic	Simultaneous integration of methods throughout the research study, building towards one integrated explanation of results
Transformative	Mixing methods to capture differing value commitments which can lead to "reconfiguring the dialog across ideological differences" (Greene & Caracelli, 1997b, p. 24)

Note: This table was reproduced from Rallis and Rossman (2003, p. 496).

Morgan's (1998) priority-sequence model consisted of a set of decision rules for combining QUAL and QUAN data collection. His model also placed importance on the distinction between dominant and less-dominant approaches. Decision rules in the priority-sequence model consist of (1) deciding the priority of either the QUAL or QUAN method and (2) deciding on the sequence of the two by identifying the time of occurrence of the less-dominant method (either preliminary or follow-up phase), therefore resulting in four basic designs.

Johnson and Onwuegbuzie (2004) presented their mixed methods design matrix, which they called a "parsimonious typology of mixed research designs" (p. 20). Their design typology emphasized two decisions: priority, which was either equal status or dominant status, and time order, which was either parallel or sequential. They further stated that researchers need to be creative in setting up their MM designs, rather than relying on a preset typology.

Creswell et al. (2003) identified four criteria for categorizing MM designs: type of implementation process, priority of methodological approach, stage of integration, and theoretical or ideological perspective. Using these dimensions as a framework, Creswell and his colleagues then proposed six types of MM designs: sequential explanatory, sequential exploratory, sequential transformative, concurrent triangulation, concurrent nested, and concurrent transformative.

John Creswell and Vicki Plano Clark (2007) recently updated their typology with the intent of creating a more "parsimonious and functional classification" because they believe that there are "more similarities than differences" among MM designs (p. 59). Their new typology includes four major types of MM designs (with variants in each): triangulation, embedded, explanatory, and exploratory. Table 7.4 summarizes the design types, variants (a total of 10), and notation used for each.

Some readers may tire of the different typological approaches to MM research designs and seek another point of view regarding how to conceptualize them. The interactive model of research design (Maxwell & Loomis, 2003) was proposed as an alternative to the typologies presented in this chapter.

Joseph Maxwell and Diane Loomis (2003) proposed what they called an interactive model, in which the components of research design are interrelated in a network, or web, rather than in a linear progression (e.g., from purpose to method to inference). Their model treats "the design of a study as consisting of the actual components of a study and the ways in which these components connect with and influence one another" (p. 245). The Maxwell and Loomis (2003) model has five components:

- Purposes—may be personal, practical, or intellectual
- Conceptual model—contains the theory that the researcher has developed or is developing
- Research questions—what questions guide the study
- Methods—how will the study be conducted
- Validity—how the researcher will address potential threats to the veracity of the conclusions from the study (pp. 245–246)

One can generate **design maps** of published studies to analyze those projects in terms of how they employed or integrated the five components. The interactive model of research design is visually depicted in Figure 7.8.

Table 7.4   Creswell and Plano Clark's (2007) Typology of MM Designs and Variants

Design Type	Variants	Notation
Triangulation	Convergence Data transformation Validating QUAN data Multilevel	QUAN + QUAL
Embedded	Embedded experimental Embedded correlational	QUAN (qual) or QUAL (quan)
Explanatory	Follow-up explanations Participant selection	QUAN → qual
Exploratory	Instrument development Taxonomy development	QUAL → quan

Note: This table is a simplified version of a table presented in Creswell and Plano-Clark (2007, p. 85). Please refer to their table for more details on the specific decisions associated with each of the design types.

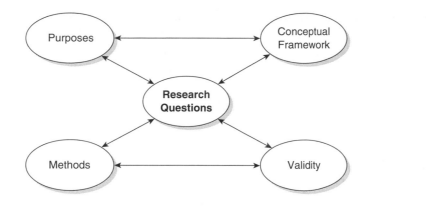

Figure 7.8   Maxwell and Loomis's (2003) Interactive Model of Research Design

Note: This figure was originally presented by Maxwell and Loomis (2003, p. 246).

Seven-Step Process for Selecting an Appropriate Mixed Methods Design

We argued that typologies of MM research designs are important for several reasons, including helping the researcher select a study design. The process of selecting the best MM research design is a complex one involving several steps, including both assumptions and actions. For a student working on a thesis or dissertation, this may be the first time that this individual has used such a procedure; therefore, we now explain the steps in selecting an MM design that best fits the requirements of the investigator's research questions. Details for much of this procedure were informed by Morgan (1998) and Creswell and colleagues (2003).

The following steps take the researcher from the determination of the appropriateness of an MM design to the selection/development of the best MM research design for a study.

1. *You must first determine if your research questions require a monomethod or MM design.* This decision is made primarily on the nature of the research questions and whether both QUAL and QUAN data are required to answer those questions. If all of the research questions can be answered by either QUAN data or QUAL data, then a monomethod design is more appropriate. (See Cells 1 and 2 in Table 7.2.)

On the other hand, if both QUAL and QUAN data are required to answer the research questions, then an MM design (most valuable ones in Cell 4 from Table 7.2) is warranted. The remaining steps in this procedure assume that your research study requires an MM design.

2. *You should be aware that a number of typologies of MM research design exist, and you should know how to access details regarding them.* Other design typologies have been introduced in this chapter. You should access the original presentations of these MM designs to locate sufficient detail concerning their characteristics.

3. *You want to select the best available MM research design for your study, but you realize that you may have to eventually generate your own.* It is important to recognize that it is impossible to enumerate all possible MM designs. Therefore, you should look for the most appropriate or single best available research design, rather than the "perfect fit." You may have to combine existing designs, or create new designs, for your study.

4. *You need to be aware of the criteria emphasized by each of the MM design typologies and of*

their implications for your study. We summarized the important criteria for several of the typologies described in this section. For example Creswell et al. (2003) used four criteria: implementation, priority, stage of integration, and theoretical or ideological perspective. These criteria identify the important components of the typology.

5. *You should list the general criteria before you select the specific criteria that are most important to your study.* We presented seven general criteria in Table 7.1 that have been used in MM research design typologies. Use these criteria to select the most important ones for your study.

6. *Apply the selected criteria to potential designs, ultimately selecting the best research design for your study.* You must determine which research design is most in accordance with the desired qualities on the selected criteria. For example, if you believe that QUAL research will play the dominant role in your study, then you should select a design that emphasizes it. Also, if theoretical or ideological perspective is important to you, then you may want to use one of Creswell and colleagues' (2003) transformative designs.

7. *In some cases, you may have to develop a new MM design, using flexibility and creativity, because no one best design exists for your research project, either when it starts or as it evolves.* Some MM studies change over the course of the research, resulting in designs with more strands than originally planned or with strands that change in relative importance.

As an example of this change process and of iterative sequential designs, Kumagai et al. (2004) reported on the causal attribution of fire. Their original research project (Phase I study) employed a QUAN-oriented design testing three hypotheses derived from causal attribution theory and using a survey sent to 1,000 randomly selected residents from the west slope of the Sierra Nevada Mountains, an area with a history of high fire frequency.

As the Phase I study was nearing completion, lightning ignited a series of wildfires (the Butte Complex Fires) near Chico, California. Kumagai and his colleagues (2004) quickly decided to conduct field interviews and another round of surveys (the Phase II surveys) with individuals affected by the Butte Complex Fires.

The time sequence of the research strands was as follows (with some overlap across phases): Phase I QUAN survey with a population of 1,000 participants → QUAL interviews with 33 participants directly affected by the Butte Complex Fires and chosen using purposive sampling → Phase II QUAN survey with a population of 400 residents from two communities from the Butte Complex Fires. Thus, the original monomethod QUAN survey study was converted into a three-strand time-sequenced MM research design (QUAN → QUAL → QUAN) featuring rich QUAL data and groups of survey respondents with different experiences.

The Kumagai et al. (2004) study is a good example of an MM research design that evolved when important, but unexpected, events occurred. The research team had sufficient epistemological and methodological flexibility to change their original research design and gather data to better understand "real-time reaction to wildfire and the causal attribution of wildfire damage by the residents who were experiencing wildfire" (p. 123). The researchers concluded that without the multiple data sets, and particularly the participant interviews, they would not have had enough information to comprehensively answer their original research questions.

Summary

In this chapter, we provided readers with the information necessary to select or adapt an MM design for their research project. We first discussed the usefulness of MM research design typologies, the dimensions that have been used by various authors to create MM design typologies, and the basic terminology and notational system employed in MM research.

We devoted much of the chapter to a discussion of our typology of research designs: the Methods-Strands Matrix. This matrix conceptually includes all designs (but emphasizes the MM designs). Five families of MM designs were featured in the matrix: parallel, sequential, conversion, multilevel, and fully integrated. Examples were presented for each of the families of designs in the matrix. We then briefly examined the MM design typologies of other scholars.

The final section presented probably the most practical information for novice researchers: how to select (and then adapt) an appropriate design. We proposed a seven-step process, including assumptions and actions, for selecting a design.

The final step in the process, flexibility and creativity in designing MM research studies, was emphasized throughout the chapter.

Chapter 8 presents information on the next step of the research process: selecting an appropriate MM sampling technique. The basic probability (QUAN) and purposive (QUAL) sampling techniques are presented first. Then characteristics of MM sampling are discussed. Four distinct families of MM sampling techniques are defined and illustrations of each are given. Finally, a set of guidelines for conducting MM sampling is listed.

Review Questions and Exercises

1. Why are typologies of MM research designs important? What do we mean when we discuss "families" of MM research designs?

2. What do the following abbreviations and symbols mean in describing an MM research design?

   QUAN
   QUAL
   quan
   qual
   +
   →

3. Seven criteria were discussed in this chapter for selecting an MM research design (summarized in Table 7.1). In your opinion, which are the two most important criteria? Which are the two least important criteria? Why?

4. What is a quasi-mixed design? How is it different from a mixed design? Give an example of a quasi-mixed design.

5. Distinguish between the methods employed in a study, the strands (or phases) of a study, and the stages that occur within a strand or phase.

6. Explain the four implementation processes in MM research: parallel, sequential, conversion, and multilevel. Give an example of an MM research study for each.

7. Two mixed methods analysis techniques are quantitizing and qualitizing data. Define and give an example of each. Provide a further example whereby QUAL data are transformed into QUAN data, which are then converted into QUAL data (you may use a real study or create one). Why is the *flexibility* inherent in MM data analytical techniques so important to the overall utility of those designs?

8. Consider the Methods-Strands Matrix depicted in Table 7.2. Then complete the following items:

   a. Contrast monostrand and multi-strand designs.
   b. Contrast monomethod and MM designs.
   c. Identify or describe a design that is an example from Cell 1.
   d. Identify or describe a design that is an example from Cell 2.
   e. Identify or describe a design that is an example from Cell 3.
   f. Identify or describe five designs that are examples from Cell 4.
   g. Why are the designs in Cell 4 so important in MM research?

9. In addition to the Methods-Strands Matrix typology of MM designs, we discussed other typologies or approaches

for describing MM designs (e.g., Creswell et al., 2003; Greene & colleagues, 1989; Maxwell & Loomis, 2003; Morse, 2003). Select two of these MM typologies or approaches, describe them, and then contrast them.

a. Describe components of the first typology or approach you selected or its associated designs, or both.

b. Describe components of the second typology or approach you selected or its associated designs, or both.

c. Contrast the two typologies or approaches you selected.

10. Describe a content area of interest to you. Write a short essay in which you apply the seven-step process for selecting an MM design for a hypothetical study in that content area.

11. Consider the Barron, Diprose, Smith, Whiteside, and Woolcock (2008) report in Appendix B located at www.sagepub .com/foundations. The design of the study is presented in a section entitled "Integration of Methods" (see pp. 8–9,

Appendix B). The researchers do not name their design, but it is one of the multistrand mixed designs presented in Table 7.2. Determine which of the mixed methods designs the researchers used: parallel mixed design, sequential mixed design, conversion mixed design, or multilevel mixed design. Justify your choice.

12. Jang, McDougall, Pollon, Herbert, and Russell (2008) recently published an MM article that may be found in Appendix C, located at www.sagepub.com/foundations. In the article, the authors describe their design as a concurrent MM research design (Appendix C, p. 6). (We refer to this design as a *parallel mixed design* in this chapter.) Briefly describe the authors' parallel mixed design and why it was appropriate for their study. Suppose you were interested in gathering the data sequentially, rather than in a parallel manner. Describe a *sequential mixed design* that would allow you to do this. Compare the differences between the parallel mixed design of Jang et al. and your sequential mixed design with regard to the research questions each might address.

Key Terms

Conceptualization stage

Conversion mixed designs

Design maps

Emergent designs

Experiential (methodological/analytical) stage

Fully integrated mixed designs

Inferential stage

Iterative sequential mixed designs

Level of analysis

Meta-inference

Mixed methods designs

Mixed methods monostrand designs

Mixed methods multistrand designs

Monomethod designs

Monomethod monostrand designs

Monomethod multistrand designs

Monostrand conversion designs (simple conversion designs)

Monostrand designs

Multilevel mixed designs

Multistrand designs

Priority of methodological approach

Quasi-mixed designs

Stage of a research strand

Strand of a research design

Notes

1. This chapter is based principally on an article published in *Research in the Schools* (Teddlie & Tashakkori, 2006), which was based on a presentation given at the 2005 annual meeting of the American Educational Research Association (Teddlie & Tashakkori, 2005).

2. We use the word *typology* rather than *taxonomy*. The typologies presented in this chapter are systematic classifications of "ideal types" of MM research designs. Taxonomies, on the other hand, "completely classify a phenomenon through mutually exclusive and exhaustive categories" (Patton, 2002, p. 457).

3. Our typology actually focuses on the first three criteria. The fourth criterion, stage of implementation, is retained because it allows for the inclusion of quasi-mixed designs, which are defined later in this chapter.

4. We previously (e.g., Tashakkori & Teddlie, 2003c) used the term *mixed model designs* to distinguish between studies in which true mixing occurs across all stages of the study and studies in which mixing occurs only in data collection. The term *quasi-mixed design* makes that distinction more clearly and succinctly. Therefore, we changed our classification accordingly, dropping the term *mixed model designs* in our Methods-Strands Matrix to avoid confusion (Teddlie & Tashakkori, 2006).

5. Although Morse (2003) uses the term *dominance* to describe the method that directs inquiry (QUAL or QUAN, inductive or deductive), she prefers the term *drive*. We use the terms *dominant/less dominant* to be consistent with previous work (e.g., Creswell, 1994; Tashakkori & Teddlie, 1998).

6. Throughout this chapter, multistrand designs are illustrated as having only two strands (with the exception of a brief reference to *iterative sequential mixed designs*) for the sake of simplicity. Multistrand designs can be more complex, involving three or more strands (e.g., QUAL → QUAN → QUAL) as described in Chapter 11.

7. **Level of analysis** refers to level of aggregation in a multilevel organizational or societal structure. For instance, data collected in hospitals could be analyzed at the patient level, the ward level, the hospital level, and so forth.

8. What Campbell and Fiske (1959) called multimethod is what we call multistrand in Cell 2, with two exceptions: They referred only to QUAN methods, whereas we also refer to QUAL methods, and their model emphasized the experiential stage alone, whereas we have added the conceptualization and inferential stages.

9. Throughout this chapter, we refer to particular studies as being examples of designs from our matrix. Our designation of these studies as particular types of MM designs is based on our ex post facto analysis of their characteristics.

CHAPTER 8

Sampling Strategies for Mixed Methods Research[1]

Objectives

Upon finishing this chapter, you should be able to:

- Identify and distinguish among four general types of sampling procedures
- Identify and distinguish among three general types of probability sampling techniques
- Identify and distinguish among three general types of purposive sampling techniques
- Distinguish between case sampling, material sampling, and sampling units of other elements in the social situation
- Discuss the issue of sample size in probability, purposive, and mixed methods sampling
- Define and discuss basic mixed methods sampling techniques
- Define and discuss parallel mixed methods sampling
- Define and discuss sequential mixed methods sampling
- Define and discuss multilevel mixed methods sampling
- Discuss how combinations of mixed methods sampling are used
- Discuss eight guidelines for conducting mixed methods sampling

This chapter presents a discussion of mixed methods (MM) sampling techniques. MM sampling involves combining well-established qualitative (QUAL) and quantitative (QUAN) techniques in creative ways to answer the research questions posed by the MM research design. The first parts of the chapter contain an overview of probability (QUAN) and purposive (QUAL) sampling techniques to set the stage for the discussion of MM sampling.

Sampling involves selecting units of analysis (e.g., people, groups, artifacts, settings) in a manner that maximizes the researcher's ability to answer research questions set forth in a study (Tashakkori & Teddlie, 2003a, p. 715). The **unit of analysis** refers to the individual case or group of cases that the researcher wants to express something about when the study is completed and is, therefore, the focus of all data collection efforts.

This chapter starts with the presentation of four basic types of sampling procedures: probability, purposive, convenience, and MM sampling. We discuss the characteristics of specific types of probability and purposive sampling to prepare readers for issues related to mixing them.

Several issues germane to MM sampling are then presented, including the differences between probability and purposive sampling. MM sampling often combines both purposive and probability sampling to meet the requirements specified by the research questions. Other topics in this section include determination of sampling units and appropriate sample sizes for MM studies.

Four types of MM sampling are then introduced: basic, parallel, sequential, and multilevel. Examples of each of these sampling techniques are provided to show readers how researchers put together MM samples. Finally, we provide some guidelines for drawing MM samples.

Typology[2] of Sampling Strategies in the Social and Behavioral Sciences

Although sampling procedures in the human sciences are often divided into two groups (probability and purposive), four broad categories actually exist, as illustrated in Box 8.1. Probability, purposive, and convenience sampling are discussed briefly in the following sections to provide a background for the later discussion of MM sampling.

Box 8.1

Typology of Sampling Techniques for the Social and Behavioral Sciences

I. Probability Sampling (4 techniques)
   A. Random sampling
   B. Stratified sampling
   C. Cluster sampling
   D. Sampling using multiple probability techniques

II. Purposive Sampling (15 techniques; see details in Box 8.3, 8.4, and throughout the text)
   A. Sampling to achieve representativeness or comparability
   B. Sampling special or unique cases
   C. Sequential sampling
   D. Sampling using multiple purposive techniques

III. Convenience Sampling (2 techniques)
   A. Captive sample
   B. Volunteer sample

IV. Mixed Methods Sampling (5 techniques)
   A. Basic mixed methods sampling
   B. Parallel mixed methods sampling
   C. Sequential mixed methods sampling
   D. Multilevel mixed methods sampling
   E. Combination of mixed methods sampling techniques

Our division of sampling techniques into probability, purposive, and MM sampling is consistent with the partition of the three communities exemplified throughout this text. Convenience sampling is added as a fourth category because it involves less than optimal sampling techniques that can occur in QUAN, QUAL, or MM sampling.[3]

Probability sampling techniques are primarily used in QUAN-oriented studies and involve "selecting a relatively large number of units from a population, or from specific subgroups (strata) of a population, in a random manner where the probability of inclusion for every member of the population is determinable" (Tashakkori & Teddlie, 2003a, p. 713). Probability samples aim to achieve **representativeness**, which is the degree to which the sample accurately represents the entire population. A **population** in probability sampling refers to "the totality of all elements, subjects, or members that possess a specified set of characteristics that define it" (Wiersma & Jurs,

2005, p. 490). An *accessible population* is the total number of elements, subjects, or members for which it is possible for a researcher to collect data.

Purposive sampling techniques are primarily used in QUAL studies and may be defined as selecting units based on specific purposes associated with answering a research study's questions (e.g., Tashakkori & Teddlie, 2003a, p. 713). Maxwell (1997) further defined purposive sampling as a type of sampling in which "particular settings, persons, or events are deliberately selected for the important information they can provide that cannot be gotten as well from other choices" (p. 87).

Convenience sampling involves drawing samples that are both easily accessible and willing to participate in a study yet may not be the most appropriate to answer the research questions. Convenience sampling is often erroneously classified as a purposive sampling technique because it can involve the use of faulty probability or purposive sampling procedures. For example, improper participant recruitment and participant attrition can turn an intended probability sample into a convenience sample.

Following are two types of convenience samples:

- Captive sample—A convenience sample taken from a particular environment where individuals may find it difficult not to participate (e.g., students in a classroom)
- Volunteer sample—A convenience sample in which individuals willingly agree to participate in a study

We do not cover convenience samples in detail in this chapter because they often result in biased data. Even a well-designed sample can become a volunteer sample if significant numbers of participants elect not to participate or later withdraw from the study. For example, consider a biomedical weight loss study in which 200 participants were initially selected but only 98 completed the research regimen. The remaining sample would be considered a volunteer sample that is composed of individuals who had the tenacity to complete the program. The final sample's average weight loss probably would be higher than the average weight loss of the entire group; therefore, volunteer sampling introduced biased results.

Mixed methods sampling techniques involve the selection of units or cases for a research study using both probability sampling and purposive sampling strategies. This fourth general sampling category is discussed infrequently (e.g., Collins, Onwuegbuzie, & Jiao, 2007; Kemper, Stringfield, & Teddlie, 2003; Teddlie & Yu, 2007), although numerous examples of it exist throughout the literature.

It should be noted that many of the research topics under examination in the human sciences are quite complex. To study these issues comprehensively, MM sampling techniques (not just purposive or probability techniques) are required.

The specific techniques that are included in our and others' sampling typologies are very similar. For instance, our typology includes 26 specific techniques (Box 8.1, with elaboration in the text and Box 8.3). This list is highly similar to the 24 techniques noted and defined by Collins et al. (2007).

Traditional Probability Sampling Techniques

An Introduction to Probability Sampling

As noted earlier, probability sampling techniques involve randomly selecting specific units or cases so that the probability of inclusion for every member of the population is "determinable." Following are three basic types of probability sampling, plus a category that involves multiple probability techniques:

- **Random sampling**—Each sampling unit in a clearly defined population has an equal chance of being included in the sample.
- **Stratified sampling**—The researcher identifies the subgroups (or strata) in a population, such that each unit belongs to a single stratum (e.g., male or female social workers), and then selects units from those known strata.
- **Cluster sampling**—The sampling unit is not an individual but a group (cluster) that occurs naturally in the population, such as neighborhoods, hospitals, schools, or classrooms.
- Multiple probability techniques—This involves a combination at least two of the probability techniques described in this list.

Probability sampling is based on underlying theoretical distributions of observations, or *sampling distributions*, the best known of which is the normal curve. Many human characteristics are normally distributed, especially when there are a large number of observations in the sample: height, weight, scores on standardized tests, and so forth. Box 8.2 presents the characteristics of the *normal curve distribution*. If a variable of interest is normally distributed in the population, then the distribution of those observations begins to more closely resemble the normal curve as the number of observations in the sample increases.

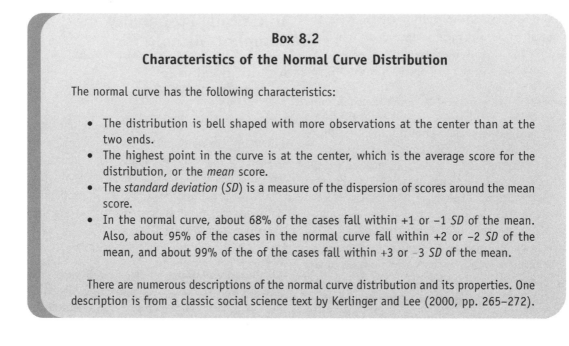

Random Sampling

Random sampling[4] is perhaps the most well known of all sampling strategies. A *simple random sample* is one in which each unit (e.g., persons, cases) in the accessible population has an equal chance of being included in the sample, and the probability of a unit being selected is not affected by the selection of other units from the accessible population (i.e., the selections are made independently of one another). Simple random sample selection may be accomplished in several ways, including drawing names or numbers out of a box, selecting numbers from a random number table in a statistics text, or using a computer program to generate the sample.

The major advantage of simple random sampling is that results can be generalized from the sample to the population within a computable *margin of error*. Thus, if a campaign manager wanted to know the percentage of registered voters who would vote for a gubernatorial candidate, a sufficiently large random sample of all registered voters would produce an estimate of that percentage with a margin of error.

A disadvantage of this method is that the selected units might be spread over a large geographic area, making the units costly to access. An example would be selecting 30 high-performing middle schools (from a population of California schools) for classroom observations. If 300 such middle schools were spread throughout the state, then it is likely that the researchers would have to travel extensively, making the sampling scheme inefficient and costly.

Stratified Sampling

If a researcher draws a random sample, then he or she typically wants the sample to be representative of the population on some characteristic, such as scores on achievement tests. The situation becomes more complicated when the researcher wants various subgroups of a population to be represented. In such cases, the researcher uses *stratified random sampling*, which combines stratified sampling with random sampling.

Assume that a researcher wanted a stratified random sample of men and women in a junior-level business class at a university. The researcher would first separate the entire population of the business class into two strata: one all male and one all female. The researcher would then independently select a random sample from each stratum. A further differentiation of stratified random sampling follows:

- In *proportional stratified random sampling*, the proportion of the units randomly selected from each stratum is the same as the proportion in the population. Thus, if 27% of the population of the business class was women, then 27% of the sample would be female.
- In *disproportional stratified sampling*, random samples of different sizes are taken from each stratum, with the sample sizes being selected on the size of the subpopulations. In this type of sampling, strata with smaller numbers of units are often oversampled, and strata with larger numbers of units are often undersampled. Thus, the sample in the business class example could be 50% female and 50% male by oversampling women and undersampling men.

Cluster Sampling

Cluster sampling occurs when the researcher wants to generate a more efficient probability sample in terms of monetary or time resources, or both. Instead of sampling individual units, which might be geographically spread out, the researcher samples groups (clusters) that occur naturally in the population (e.g., neighborhoods, schools).

There are also two basic types of cluster samples:

- In *simple cluster samples*, one stage of sampling occurs in which the clusters are randomly selected and then *all* of the units of interest are sampled within the clusters. For example, schools (the clusters) are selected, and then all of the teachers (the units of interest) in those schools are selected.
- In *multistage cluster samples*, clusters are randomly selected in the first stage of sampling. The units of interest are then sampled within clusters in the second stage of

sampling. For example, schools (the clusters) are randomly selected, and then teachers (the units of interest) in those schools are randomly sampled.

Sampling Using Multiple Probability Techniques

Often researchers use more than one probability sampling technique when selecting units for their QUAN studies. For instance, if a researcher were interested in studying the effect of a new training program on older and younger nurses, the researcher might first select sample hospitals, which include clusters of nurses. Then within the hospitals, nurses can be stratified into two strata (e.g., 20 to 39 years old, 40 to 59 years old). Then nurses within strata could be randomly assigned to the experimental or control conditions. In this example, the sample was drawn using multiple probability techniques in a sequential order: cluster first, stratified second, and random third.

Traditional Purposive Sampling Techniques

An Introduction to Purposive Sampling

As noted earlier, purposive sampling techniques involve selecting certain units or cases "based on a specific purpose rather than randomly" (Tashakkori & Teddlie, 2003a, p. 713). Researchers using purposive sampling want to generate a wealth of detail from a few cases; therefore, sampling decisions are crucial. Purposive sampling includes the following characteristics:

- Purposive sampling addresses specific purposes related to research questions; therefore, the researcher selects cases that are information rich in regard to those questions.
- Purposive samples are often selected using the *expert judgment* of researchers and informants.

- Purposive sampling procedures focus on the "depth" of information that can be generated by individual cases.
- Purposive samples are typically small (usually 30 or fewer cases), but the specific sample size depends on the type of QUAL research being conducted and the research questions.

Included in the following list are three basic families of purposive sampling techniques (Teddlie & Yu, 2007), plus a category that involves multiple purposive techniques:

- Sampling to achieve representativeness or comparability—The researcher wants to achieve one of two purposes: (1) select a purposive sample that represents, as closely as possible, a broader group of cases or (2) set up comparisons among different types of cases.
- Sampling special or unique cases—The individual case, or a specific group of cases, is a major focus of the investigation.
- Sequential sampling—The gradual selection principle is used when the goal of the research project is the generation of theory (or themes) or the sample evolves of its own accord as data are being collected. **Gradual selection** may be defined as the sequential selection of units or cases based on their relevance to the research questions of interest (e.g., Flick, 1998).
- Multiple purposive techniques—This involves a combination of at least two of the purposive techniques described in this list.

Box 8.3 presents our typology of purposive sampling techniques.

Box 8.3
A Typology of Purposive Sampling Strategies

A. Sampling to Achieve Representativeness or Comparability
   1. Typical case sampling (discussed in text)
   2. Extreme or deviant case sampling (discussed in text)
   3. Intensity sampling (defined in Box 8.4)
   4. Maximum variation sampling (discussed in text)
   5. Homogeneous sampling (discussed in text)
   6. Reputational case sampling (defined in Box 8.4)

B. Sampling Special or Unique Cases
   7. Revelatory case sampling (discussed in text)
   8. Critical case sampling (defined in Box 8.4)
   9. Sampling politically important cases (defined in Box 8.4)
   10. Complete collection (discussed in text)

C. Sequential Sampling
   11. Theoretical sampling (discussed in text)
   12. Confirming and disconfirming cases (defined in Box 8.4)
   13. Opportunistic sampling (defined in Box 8.4)
   14. Snowball sampling (defined in Box 8.4)

D. Sampling Using Combinations of Purposive Techniques (discussed in text)

In the following section, each of these broad families of purposive sampling techniques is briefly introduced, together with the specific techniques that each employs. Brief examples of some of these techniques are also given, but a full description of all techniques is beyond the scope of this text. Those purposive sampling techniques that are not described in the text are defined in Box 8.4.

Sampling to Achieve Representativeness or Comparability

The first broad category of purposive sampling techniques involves two general goals:

- Sampling to find instances that are *representative or typical* of a particular type of case on a dimension of interest
- Sampling to achieve *comparability across different types of cases* on a dimension of interest

There are six types of purposive sampling procedures that are based on achieving representativeness or comparability: typical case sampling, extreme or deviant case sampling, intensity sampling, maximum variation sampling, homogeneous sampling, and reputational sampling. Though some of these sampling techniques are aimed at generating representative cases, most are

---

Box 8.4

Definitions of Purposive Sampling Techniques Not Discussed in Text

Intensity sampling involves selecting very informative cases that represent a phenomenon of interest intensively (but not extremely), such as good teachers/poor teachers, above-average pianists/below-average pianists, and so forth (e.g., Patton, 2002).

Reputational case sampling involves selecting cases on the recommendation of an expert or key informant (e.g., LeCompte & Preissle, 1993; Miles & Huberman, 1994). Reputational case sampling occurs when the researchers do not have the information necessary to select a sample and must depend on the opinions of experts.

Critical case sampling involves selecting a single case that is particularly important to the understanding of a phenomenon because it permits maximum application of information to other cases.

Sampling of politically important cases is a special or unique case sampling procedure that involves selecting (or in some cases *not* selecting) politically significant or sensitive cases for study (e.g., Miles & Huberman, 1994; Patton, 2002).

Confirming and disconfirming cases involves selecting units of analysis that either verify or refute patterns in the data that have emerged (or were defined a priori) in order to further understand the phenomenon under study.

Opportunistic sampling (emergent sampling) involves adding new cases to a sample based on changes in the research design that occur as data are being collected (e.g., Kemper et al., 2003; Patton, 2002).

Snowball sampling (chain sampling) is a well-known purposive sampling technique that involves using informants or participants to identify additional cases who may be included in the study (e.g., Kemper et al., 2003; Patton, 2002).

aimed at producing contrasting cases. Comparisons or contrasts, such as those generated by the *contrast principle* and the *constant comparative technique*, are at the core of QUAL data analysis strategies (e.g., Glaser & Strauss, 1967; Mason, 2002; Spradley, 1979, 1980).

An example from this broad category is **typical case sampling**, which involves selecting those cases that are the most typical, normal, or representative of the group of cases under consideration. Representativeness is most often associated with probability sampling, but there are also situations where the QUAL researcher is interested in the most typical or representative instances of a phenomenon of interest.

For example, Wolcott (1994) described an ethnographic study in which he intensively studied an "average" elementary school principal. He began with a demographic profile of such a principal generated by a survey conducted by the National Education Association in 1968. This profile yielded the following information: "a male, married, between the ages of 35 and 49, has had 10–19 years total experience in schools, and was an elementary classroom teacher just prior to assuming his administrative post" (Wolcott, 1994, p. 117). Wolcott then looked for an actual principal with those characteristics to participate in his study.

Another example of this broad category of purposive sampling is **extreme or deviant case sampling,** which is also known as *outlier* sampling (e.g., Stringfield, 1994) because it involves selecting cases near the ends of the distribution of cases of interest. It involves selecting those cases that are the most outstanding successes or failures related to some topic of interest (e.g., scholastic performance, wealth accumulation). Such extreme successes or failures are expected to yield especially valuable information about the topic of interest.

Extreme/deviant cases also provide interesting contrasts with other cases, thereby allowing for comparability across those cases, such as extreme successes contrasted with extreme failures, extreme successes contrasted with typical cases, and extreme failures contrasted with typical

cases. These comparisons require that the investigator first determine a dimension of interest, then generate a distribution of cases on that dimension, and then locate extreme/deviant and other relevant cases on that distribution.

Sampling Special or Unique Cases

These sampling techniques include special or unique cases, which have long been a focus of QUAL research, especially those studies conducted in anthropology and sociology. Stake (1995) described an *intrinsic case study* as one in which the case, rather than an issue, is of primary importance.

Purposive sampling techniques that feature special or unique cases include four types: revelatory case sampling, critical case sampling, sampling of politically important cases, and complete collection.

Revelatory case sampling involves identifying and gaining access to a single case representing a phenomenon that previously was "inaccessible to scientific investigation" (Yin, 2003, p. 42). Such cases are rare and difficult to study yet yield valuable, original information.

The human sciences include several examples of revelatory cases:

• *God's Choice: The Total World of a Fundamentalist Christian School* (Peshkin, 1986). This is a revelatory case study because it was the first fundamental Christian school to be studied and described in detail. One of the interesting aspects of the study is the description by Peshkin of his earlier failed attempts to gain access to fundamentalist schools and how he finally was able to study "Bethany Christian School" and its "God-centered" environment.

• *Them Children: A Study in Language Learning* (Ward, 1986). This case study derives its revelatory nature from its depiction of a unique environment, the "Rosepoint" community, which was a former sugar plantation that is now a poor, rural African American community near New Orleans. Ward described how the Rosepoint community provided a "total environment" for the families she studied (especially the children) that is quite different from mainstream communities in the United States.

- *Buddha Is Hiding: Refugees, Citizenship, the New America* (Ong, 2003). This insightful commentary on Cambodian refugees in the Oakland and San Francisco area is described later in this chapter as a study using *multiple purposive sampling techniques*. At a general level, it is a revelatory case study of a previously unstudied Asian American refugee group.

Sequential Sampling

These techniques involve the principle of gradual selection. Four types of purposive sampling techniques involve sequential sampling:

- Theoretical sampling
- Confirming and disconfirming cases
- Opportunistic sampling
- Snowball sampling

Charmaz (2000) presented a definition of **theoretical sampling** (*theory-based sampling*) from the point of view of a "grounded theorist":

We use theoretical sampling to develop our emerging categories and to make them more definitive and useful. Thus the aim of this sampling is to refine *ideas,* not to increase the size of the original sample. Theoretical sampling helps us to identify conceptual boundaries and pinpoint the fit and relevance of our categories. (p. 519)

With theoretical sampling, the researcher examines particular instances of the phenomenon of interest so that he or she can define and elaborate on its various manifestations. The investigator samples people, institutions, scenes,

events, documents, or *wherever the theory leads the investigation.*

Research on the awareness of dying provides an excellent example of theoretical sampling used by the originators of grounded theory (Glaser & Strauss, 1965, 1967). Their research took them to various sites relevant to their emerging theory regarding awareness of dying. Each site in the following list provided unique information that previous sites had not:

- Premature baby services
- Neurological services where patients were comatose
- Intensive care units
- Cancer wards
- Emergency services

Theoretical sampling follows the principle of gradual selection, with each site or case providing information that leads to the next logical site or case. Investigators follow the dictates of gradual selection to the site or case that will yield the most valuable information for further theory refinement.

Sampling Using Multiple Purposive Techniques

Sampling using multiple purposive techniques involves using two or more sampling techniques in a study due to the complexities of the issues being examined. For instance, Poorman (2002) presented an interesting example of multiple purposive sampling techniques from the literature regarding the abuse and oppression of women. In this study, Poorman used four different purposive sampling techniques (theory-based, maximum variation, snowball, and homogeneous) in combination with one another in selecting the participants for a series of focus groups.

For another example, see the description of Ong's (2003) research in Box 8.5 as an illustration of a complex ethnography that used multiple purposive sampling techniques.

Box 8.5

An Example of Multiple Purposive Sampling Techniques—
Buddha Is Hiding: Refugees, Citizenship, the New America

Ong (2003) wrote an insightful commentary on Cambodian refugees and the stark contrasts between their Buddhist past and the secularism/bureaucracy of their life in the United States. Ong used extensive interviewing techniques and at least three types of purposive sampling:

- *Revelatory case study*—The entire case population included the approximately 15,000 members of the Cambodian community residing in the Bay Area (Oakland, San Francisco) in the mid- to late 1980s. Many of these individuals had lived through the genocidal Pol Pot regime before resettling in California. This study is particularly *revelatory* because "Southeast Asian refugees are among the most invisible groups in the North American consciousness" (Ong, 2003, p. xvi).
- Ong used the services of three Khmer-speaking assistants who put her in contact with most of her interviewees and later translated the interviews. This is an example of *snowball sampling* (see Box 8.4), in which the three Khmer-speaking informants identified additional cases to be included as the study progressed.
- Ong's (2003) specific study sample of 60 households (together with life histories of 20 women) came from a population that she described as having three parts: "Cambodian families in two low-income housing projects in Oakland, a self-help group in a poor neighborhood in San Francisco, and other informants who had moved out of the inner city and were engaged in middle-class occupations" (p. xv). If each of the three groups constitutes a stratum, then this is an example of *stratified purposive sampling,* which we classify in this text as an MM sampling technique but is often identified as a purposive sampling technique.

Complex ethnographic studies such as Ong (2003) often use an eclectic mixture of various purposive sampling techniques, plus occasional probability and mixed sampling procedures, where appropriate.

General Considerations Concerning Mixed Methods Sampling

Differences Between Probability and Purposive Sampling

Table 8.1 presents comparisons between probability and purposive sampling. These basic sampling types share two characteristics: Both are designed to provide a sample that will answer the research questions under investigation, and both are concerned with issues of generalizability (i.e., transferability or external validity).

On the other hand, the remainder of Table 8.1 presents a series of dichotomous differences between these two types of sampling. A purposive sample is typically designed to pick a small number of cases that will yield the most information about a particular phenomenon, whereas a probability sample is planned to select a large number of cases that are collectively representative

Table 8.1   Comparisons Between Purposive and Probability Sampling Techniques

Dimension of Contrast	Purposive Sampling	Probability Sampling
Other names	Purposeful sampling Nonrandom sampling QUAL sampling	Scientific sampling Random sampling QUAN sampling
Overall purpose of sampling	To generate a sample that will address research questions	To generate a sample that will address research questions
Issue of generalizability	Seeks a form of generalizability (transferability)	Seeks a form of generalizability (external validity)
Number of techniques	At least 15 specific techniques (nominally grouped under three general types)	Three basic techniques with modifications
Rationale for selecting cases/units	To address specific purposes related to the research questions; selection of cases deemed most informative in regard to the research questions	Selection of cases that are collectively representative of the population
Sample size	Typically small (usually 30 or fewer cases)	Large enough to establish representativeness (usually at least 50 units)
Depth/breadth of information per case/unit	Focuses on depth of information generated by the cases	Focuses on breadth of information generated by the sampling units
Time of sample selection	Before the study begins, during the study, or both	Before the study begins
Selection method	Uses expert judgment	Often applies mathematical formulas
Sampling frame	Informal sampling frame somewhat larger than sample	Formal sampling frame typically much larger than sample
Form of data generated	Focuses on narrative data, though numeric data can also be generated	Focuses on numeric data, though narrative data can also be generated

of the population of interest. There is a classic methodological trade-off related to the sample size difference between the two techniques: Purposive sampling leads to greater depth of information from a smaller number of carefully selected cases, whereas probability sampling leads to greater breadth of information from a larger number of units selected to be representative of the population of interest.

Purposive sampling can occur before or during data collection and often occurs during *both* time periods. Probability sampling is preplanned and does not change during data collection, unless serious methodological problems arise. Whereas probability sampling is often based on preestablished mathematical formulas, purposive sampling relies heavily on expert opinion.

The **sampling frame** for a study is a formal or informal list of units or cases from which the sample is drawn. As Miles and Huberman (1994) noted, "Just thinking in sampling-frame terms is good for your study's health" (p. 33). Probability sampling frames are usually formally laid out and represent a distribution with a large number of observations. Purposive sampling frames, on the other hand, are informal and based on the expert judgment of the researcher or some available resource identified by the researcher. In purposive sampling, a sampling frame is "a resource from which you can select your smaller sample" (Mason, 2002, p. 140).

The dichotomy between probability and purposive sampling becomes a continuum when MM sampling is added as a third sampling strategy. Many of the dichotomies presented in Table 8.1 are better understood as continua, with purposive sampling techniques at one end, MM sampling techniques in the middle, and probability sampling techniques at the other end.[5]

Characteristics of Mixed Methods Sampling

Table 8.2 presents the characteristics of MM sampling techniques, which are combinations of (or intermediate points between) the QUAN and QUAL traits. The information from Table 8.2 could be inserted into Table 8.1 between the columns describing purposive and probability sampling, but we present it separately here so that we can focus on the particular characteristics of MM sampling.

MM sampling strategies employ all of the probability and purposive techniques discussed in this chapter. Indeed, the researcher's ability to creatively combine these sampling techniques is one of the defining characteristics of MM research.

The *strand of a research design* is an important term that is used when describing MM sampling procedures. It was defined in Chapter 7 as a phase of a study that includes three stages: conceptualization, experiential (methodological/analytical), and inferential. These strands are typically either QUAN or QUAL, although transformation from one type to another can occur during the course of a study.

The MM researcher sometimes chooses procedures that generate representative samples, especially when addressing a QUAN strand of a study. On the other hand, when addressing the QUAL strand of a study, the MM researcher typically uses sampling techniques that yield information-rich cases. Combining the two orientations allows the researcher to generate complementary databases that include information with both depth and breadth (Kaeding, 2007).

Typically, an MM study includes multiple samples that vary in size from a small number of cases to a large number of units of analysis. Using an educational example, one might purposively select four schools for a study, then give questionnaires to all 100 teachers in those schools, then conduct eight student focus groups, followed by interviewing 60 randomly selected students. Large variance in sample size across research strands in an MM study is common.

In MM research, most sampling decisions are made before the study starts, but QUAL-oriented questions may lead to the emergence of other sampling issues during the study. MM research places a premium on using expert judgment in making sampling decisions across research strands because these decisions interact in terms of producing the overall studywide sample.

Both numeric and narrative data are typically generated from MM samples, but occasionally MM sampling techniques may yield only one type of data. Hence, it is important to present a brief discussion of the relationship between sampling techniques and the generation of different types of data.

Table 8.3 presents a theoretical matrix that crosses type of sampling technique (probability, purposive, mixed) by type of data generated (QUAN only, QUAL only, mixed).[6] This 3 × 3 matrix illustrates that certain types of sampling

Table 8.2   Characteristics of Mixed Methods Sampling Strategies

Dimension of Contrast	Mixed Methods Sampling
Overall purpose of sampling	Designed to generate a sample that will address research questions
Issue of generalizability	Focus on external validity issues for some strands of a design; focus on transferability issues for other strands
Number of techniques	All those employed by both probability and purposive sampling
Rationale for selecting cases/units	Focus on representativeness for some strands of a design; focus on seeking out information-rich cases in other strands
Sample size	Multiple samples varying in size from a small number of cases to a large number of units of analysis; sample size dependent on the research questions
Depth/breadth of information per case/unit	Focus on both depth and breadth of information across the research strands
Time of sample selection	Mostly before a study starts, though QUAL-oriented questions may lead to the emergence of other samples during the study
Selection method	Focus on expert judgment across the sampling decisions, especially because they interrelate with one another; application of mathematical sampling formulae required for some QUAN-oriented strands
Sampling frame	Both formal and informal frames
Form of data generated	Both numeric and narrative data

techniques are theoretically more frequently associated with certain types of data: probability samples with QUAN data (Cell 1), purposive samples with QUAL data (Cell 5), and mixed samples with mixed data (Cell 9). Despite these general tendencies, there are other situations where sampling techniques occasionally (Cells 3, 6, 7, and 8) or rarely (Cells 2 and 4) are associated with studies that generate different types of data.

What Is Sampled in Mixed Methods Research?

The first decision required in developing an MM sampling strategy concerns *what* is to be selected. Three general types of units can be sampled: cases, materials, and other elements in the social situation. The MM methodologist should consider all three data sources and how they relate to the study's research questions.

Case sampling may be defined as the selection of the individual participant or groups of participants (e.g., employees of hospitals) under study. *Material sampling* (e.g., Flick, 1998) may be defined as selecting units of written information, artifacts, and other narrative matter from all available materials. *Sampling other elements in the social situation* involves the selection of other components relevant to the unit of analysis (e.g., settings or sites, units of time, events, processes).

Miles and Huberman (1994) presented an illustration of the variety of elements that could be sampled in a study of "police work":

Table 8.3   Theoretical Matrix Crossing Type of Sampling Technique By Type of Data Generated

Type of Sampling Technique	Generation of Quantitative Data Only	Generation of Qualitative Data Only	Generation of Both Qualitative and Quantitative Data
Probability sampling techniques	Happens often (Cell 1)	Happens rarely (Cell 2)	Happens occasionally (Cell 3)
Purposive sampling techniques	Happens rarely (Cell 4)	Happens often (Cell 5)	Happens occasionally (Cell 6)
Mixed method sampling strategies	Happens occasionally (Cell 7)	Happens occasionally (Cell 8)	Happens often (Cell 9)

Note: This table was originally presented in Kemper et al. (2003, p. 285).

- Actors—different types of police officers and suspects, police "beat" reporters
- Settings—crime scene, police station, squad car, suspect's residence
- Events—pursuits, arrests, bookings
- Processes—arresting suspects, booking suspects, interpreting laws (p. 30)

To this one could add artifacts—arrest reports, reports of bookings, logs of calls to the precinct, criminal records of those arrested. Each of these parameters could involve different types of sampling, thereby generating a rather complex, multifaceted overall MM sampling strategy.

How Do We Determine Sample Size in Mixed Methods Research?

MM research typically involves combining two different types of sample sizes: larger QUAN samples based on well-defined populations and carefully selected smaller QUAL samples based on informal sampling frames. Tables 8.4 and 8.5 illustrate the differences between probability and purposive samples with regard to sample sizes. Table 8.4 is an example of tables found in QUAN-oriented publications that estimate the

sample size required to generate a representative sample of a population (e.g., Bartlett, Kotrlik, & Higgins, 2001; Fitz-Gibbon & Morris, 1987; Wunsch, 1986). These probability samples are based on mathematically defined estimates of the number of cases required to estimate the characteristics of the population within a prescribed margin of error. The information in Table 8.4 indicates that if one has a population size of 1,000, then a sample size of 278 is required to estimate the characteristics of the population within +/− 5%.[7]

Though the precise estimates of sample size from Table 8.4 are valuable for QUAN researchers, the sample sizes used in QUAL research are typically so small that they are transferable to only a small sampling frame. Michael Quinn Patton (2002) emphatically stated, "**There are no rules for sample size in qualitative inquiry**" because the size depends on a number of factors such as "what you want to know" and "what will have credibility" (p. 244, bold in original). Though there are no universally accepted rules for sample size in QUAL research, there are some general guidelines.

Methodologists writing about QUAL research (e.g., Creswell, 1998; Mertens, 2005; Miles & Huberman, 1994; Morse, 1994) base their estimates

Table 8.4 Relationship Between Sample and Population Sizes Using Probability Sampling Techniques

Population Size	Confident That the Sample Estimates Population Within (+/– 1%)	Confident That the Sample Reflects Population Within (+/– 5%)
100	99	80
500	476	218
1,000	906	278
2,000	1,656	323
3,000	2,286	341
Infinity	9,604	384

Note: This table uses a confidence limit of .05, which means that there is a 95% chance (19 out of 20) that the sample statistic will be representative of the population parameter. This table was adapted from Bartlett, Kotrlik, and Higgins (2001), Wunsch (1986), and others.

of minimal required sample size on their own research experiences and on the sample sizes reported in journals and other research reports. Table 8.5 presents minimum sample size estimates for five common types of QUAL research designs.

These are general guidelines only. For example, a wide range of possible sample sizes for case study research depends on a variety of design factors. By definition, *revelatory case studies* are unique, but most case studies involve multiple cases. As a general rule, case studies of institutions vary from a minimum of approximately 4 to 12 organizations, whereas case studies involving individuals may be larger, often ranging from 6 to 24 participants. Sample size in case study research, as well as in other types of QUAL research, often depends on the availability of research funds and researcher time. For example, Norton's (1995) study of 6 beginning principals and their schools was a dissertation completed by 1 researcher, whereas an international study conducted by Reynolds, Creemers, Stringfield, Teddlie, and Schaffer (2002) involved 36 schools and more than 30 researchers.

Perhaps the most useful way to look at QUAL research sample size involves saturation of information[8] (e.g., Glaser & Strauss, 1967; Strauss & Corbin, 1998). For example, in focus group studies, new information gained from conducting additional sessions decreases as more sessions are held. Krueger and Casey (2000) expressed this guideline in practical terms:

> The rule of thumb is, plan three or four focus groups with any one type of participant. Once you have conducted these, determine if you have reached saturation. *Saturation* is a term used to describe the point when you have heard the range of ideas and aren't getting new information. If you were still getting new information after three or four groups, you would conduct more groups. (p. 26, italics and bold in original)

Saturation in purposive sampling occurs when the addition of more units does not result in new information that can be used in theme development. Saturation is the general rule

Table 8.5   Estimated Minimum Sample Size Required for Different Types of Qualitative Research Designs

Type of QUAL Research Design	Estimated Sample Size Required
Case studies	One can suffice, especially if it is a *revelatory case study* or has unique characteristics; an upper limit of 15 is suggested by some methodologists; case studies of institutions often vary from approximately 4 to 12 studies; case studies of individuals may be larger, often ranging from approximately 6 to 24 cases.
Ethnography	Typically one cultural group is sampled; about 30 to 50 interviews are conducted.
Focus groups	Three to four groups per demographic category are sampled (e.g., White Republican women, African American Democratic men), with 6 to 8 participants per group.
Grounded theory	Around 20 to 50 interviews are conducted.
Phenomenology	Sample size typically includes 6 to 10 participants but it can be larger.

Note: These estimates were taken from several sources, including Krueger and Casey (2000) for focus groups; Miles and Huberman (1994) for some of the case studies estimates; Morse (1994), Mertens (2005), and Creswell (1998) for phenomenology, ethnography, and grounded theory; Collins et al. (2007); and Teddlie and Yu (2006).

used for purposive sampling, whereas representativeness is the general rule for probability sampling.

MM sampling decisions must be counterbalanced across the entirety of the research study and involve trade-offs between the requirements of purposive and probability sampling. Sample size specific for MM research studies depends on several factors:

- The design and evolution of the study in terms of the dominance of the QUAL and QUAN components

- The trade-off between the breadth and depth of the required information
- The trade-off between the requirements of external validity and transferability
- What is practical

There is a simple rule for MM sampling, which we call the representativeness/saturation trade-off: As more emphasis is placed on the representativeness of the QUAN sample, less emphasis can be placed on the saturation of the QUAL sample, and vice versa. Box 8.6 presents an example of the representativeness/saturation rule.

Box 8.6

Example of the Representativeness/Saturation Rule

Carwile (2005) studied the leadership characteristics of program directors in radiologic technology. She had both QUAN- and QUAL-oriented research questions. The QUAN questions were answered using an online survey administered to all radiologic program directors. The QUAL questions were answered using a telephone interview with a small sample of directors whose responses to the online survey indicated that they differed on two important dimensions (type of program administered, such as baccalaureate, associate, or certificate, and type of leadership style, such as transformational transactional), resulting in six cells. Carwile wanted the survey study to have a representative sample and the interview study to result in "saturated" QUAL data.

Of the 590 program directors surveyed, 284 responded for a 48% response rate. Extrapolating from the samples and population sizes noted in Table 8.4, it appears that Carwile could be confident that her sample reflected the population within +/- 5%.

There were no clearly established standards for how large the interview sample should be to generate trustworthy results. Based on her intuition and the expert advice of her dissertation committee, Carwile selected 12 program directors. This number also allowed her to select a stratified purposive sample in which program type and leadership style were the strata. She selected two interviewees for each of the six cells, resulting in 12 program directors and then (undeterred by superstition) selected a 13th interviewee whom she felt was a particularly information-rich case (extreme or deviant case sampling).

If Carwile had attempted to increase the sample size of her survey data to reflect the population within +/- 1%, she would have had to send out at least one more round of surveys to all who had not already participated, thereby decreasing the time she had left to select and interact with the participants in the interview study. On the other hand, if she had increased the sample size of the interview study to 24, she would have had to reduce the amount of time and resources that she invested in the survey study. Her sampling choices appeared to meet the requirements for representativeness of QUAN sources and saturation of QUAL sources.

Types of Mixed Methods Sampling Strategies

We now turn our attention to descriptions of different types of MM sampling strategies, together with examples. Not much literature has been published about MM sampling strategies per se (e.g., Collins et al., 2007; Kemper et al., 2003; Teddlie & Yu, 2007), so we searched for additional examples throughout various literatures.

There is no widely accepted typology of MM sampling strategies. In generating the provisional typology used in this text, we faced the general issues of nomenclature in MM research, which are discussed in Chapter 2. Sampling in the social and behavioral sciences has so many well-defined QUAL/QUAN techniques with commonly understood names that it would be foolhardy to develop

a new terminology for them. On the other hand, our literature review indicates that mixed methodologists have combined probability and purposive sampling techniques in certain unique prescribed manners to meet the specification of popular MM designs (e.g., parallel, sequential designs). Therefore, it seems reasonable to overlay the probability and purposive sampling terms with MM meta-terms that encompass the totality of the sampling techniques used in research projects.

The following is our provisional typology of MM sampling strategies:

- Basic mixed methods sampling strategies
- Sequential mixed methods sampling
- Parallel mixed methods sampling
- Multilevel mixed methods sampling
- Sampling using multiple MM sampling strategies[9]

The "backgrounds" of the techniques presented in our typology are interesting. The basic MM sampling strategies (i.e., stratified purposive sampling, purposive random sampling) are typically discussed as types of purposive sampling techniques (e.g., Patton, 2002), yet by definition they also include a component of probability sampling (stratified, random). These basic MM techniques may be used to generate narrative data only in QUAL-oriented research (Cell 8 in Table 8.3) or to generate MM data (Cell 9 in Table 8.3).

Parallel and sequential MM sampling follow from the design types described in Chapters 2 and 7. **Parallel mixed methods sampling** involves the selection of units of analysis for an MM study through the parallel use (simultaneously or with some time lapse) of both probability and purposive sampling strategies. One type of sampling procedure does not set the stage for the other in parallel MM sampling studies; instead, both probability and purposive sampling procedures are used simultaneously.

Sequential mixed methods sampling involves the selection of units of analysis for an MM study through the sequential use of probability and purposive sampling strategies (QUAN → QUAL), or vice versa (QUAL → QUAN). Sequential QUAN → QUAL sampling is a common technique, as described by Kemper et al. (2003): "In sequential mixed models studies, information from the first sample (typically derived from a probability sampling procedure) is often required to draw the second sample (typically derived from a purposive sampling procedure)" (p. 284).

Multilevel mixed methods sampling is a general sampling strategy in which probability and purposive sampling techniques are used at different levels of analysis (Tashakkori & Teddlie, 2003a, p. 712). This sampling strategy is common in settings where different units of analysis are nested within one another, such as schools, hospitals, and various types of bureaucracies.

Sampling using multiple MM sampling strategies involves a combination of the MM sampling techniques defined earlier. For instance, a study using multilevel MM sampling could also employ parallel MM sampling at one level and sequential MM sampling at another. Further discussion of these complex sampling strategies is beyond the scope of this text.

Basic Mixed Methods Sampling Techniques

One well-known basic MM sampling technique is **stratified purposive sampling**. The stratified nature of this sampling procedure is similar to probability sampling, and the small number of cases it generates is characteristic of purposive sampling. In this technique, the researcher first identifies the subgroups of the population of interest and then selects cases from each subgroup in a purposive manner. This allows the researcher to discover and describe in detail characteristics that are similar or different across the strata or subgroups. Patton (2002) described this technique as selecting samples within samples.

One example of stratified purposive sampling was presented in Box 8.6, in which Carwile (2005) interviewed a small sample of directors (two each) from six strata (produced by crossing three levels of program type by two levels of leadership style). Another example comes from Kemper and Teddlie (2000), who generated six strata based on two dimensions (three levels of community type crossed by two levels of implementation of innovation). Their final sample had six schools altogether (one purposively selected school per stratum): one "typical" urban, one "typical" suburban, one "typical" rural, one "better" urban, one "better" suburban, and one "better" rural. This sampling scheme allowed the researchers to discuss the differences between "typical" and "better" schools at program implementation across a variety of community types. Study results indicated that what differentiated a pair of schools in one context (e.g., urban) was quite different from what differentiated a pair of schools in another context (e.g., rural).

Purposive random sampling (also known as **purposeful random sampling**) involves taking a random sample of a small number of units from a much larger target population (Kemper et al., 2003). The random nature of this sampling procedure is characteristic of probability sampling, and the small number of cases it generates is characteristic of purposive sampling. This sampling strategy is typically used to add credibility to the results of a larger study.

Kalafat and Illback (1999) presented an example of purposive random sampling in their evaluation of a large statewide program that used a school-based family support system to enhance the educational experiences of at-risk students. There were almost 600 statewide sites, and a statistically valid sample would have required in-depth descriptions of more than 200 cases (see Table 8.4), which was beyond the resources allocated to the evaluation. Before the intervention began, Kalafat and Illback (1999) used a purposive random sampling approach to select twelve cases from the overall target population. The researchers then closely followed these cases throughout the life of the project. This purposive random sample of a small number of cases from a much larger target population added credibility to the evaluation by generating QUAL, process-oriented results to complement the large-scale, QUAN-oriented research that also took place.

Parallel Mixed Methods Sampling

Parallel MM designs permit researchers to triangulate results from the separate QUAN and QUAL components of their research, thereby allowing them to "confirm, cross-validate, or corroborate findings within a single study" (Creswell, Plano Clark, Gutmann, & Hanson, 2003, p. 229). We located several articles that enhanced our understanding of how researchers actually combine probability and purposive sampling in their parallel MM studies. We delineated two basic, overall parallel MM sampling procedures, but we are certain that there are others:

1. Parallel MM sampling in which probability sampling techniques are used to generate data for the QUAN strand and purposive sampling techniques are used to generate data for the QUAL strand. These sampling procedures occur independently.

2. Parallel MM sampling using a single sample generated through the joint use of probability and purposive techniques to generate data for both the QUAN and QUAL strands. This occurs, for example, when a sample of participants, selected through the joint application of probability and purposive techniques, responds to an MM survey that contains both closed-ended and open-ended questions.

Lasserre-Cortez (2006) completed a dissertation (see Box 6.4 from Chapter 6) that is an example of the first type of parallel MM sampling procedure (independent probability and purposive sampling strands). The goals of the study were twofold:

- The researcher wanted to test QUAN hypotheses regarding the differences in the characteristics of teachers and schools participating in professional action research collaboratives (PARCs) as opposed to matched control schools.
- The researcher wanted to answer QUAL questions about how school climate affects teacher effectiveness in PARC schools.

Lasserre-Cortez (2006) drew two different samples, a probability sample to answer the QUAN research hypotheses and a purposive sample to answer the QUAL research questions. The probability sample involved a multistage cluster sample of schools participating in PARC programs and a set of control schools matched to the PARC schools. A total of 165 schools (about half PARC and half control schools) were selected. Three teachers were then randomly selected within each school to complete climate surveys.

The purposive sample involved 8 schools (4 PARC schools, 4 control schools) from the larger 165-school sample. These schools were chosen using **maximum variation sampling**, which involves purposively selecting a wide range of cases or units to get full variation on dimensions of interest and to generate a broad diversity of comparisons (e.g., Flick, 1998; Patton, 2002). This purposive sampling process resulted in four types of schools: urban high achievement, urban low achievement, rural high achievement, and rural low achievement.

Lasserre-Cortez (2006) used two different sampling procedures to separately answer her QUAN hypotheses and QUAL questions. The only point of commonality between the two samples was that the purposively drawn sample was a subset of the probability drawn sample. The data were collected in a parallel manner and were compared in the meta-inferential phase of the data analysis.

Parasnis, Samar, and Fischer (2005) presented an example of the second type of parallel MM sampling procedure: those using a single sample generated through the joint use of probability and purposive techniques. Their study was conducted on a college campus that included a large number of deaf students (about 1,200). Selected students were sent surveys that included both closed-ended and open-ended items; therefore, data for the QUAN and QUAL strands were gathered simultaneously.

The MM sampling procedure included both purposive and probability sampling techniques. All of the individuals in the sample were deaf college students. This is an example of **homogeneous sampling**, which involves the selection of participants from a particular subgroup for in-depth study (e.g., Kemper et al., 2003; Patton, 2002). The research team used different sampling procedures for selecting minority deaf students (purposive procedures) versus White deaf students (probability procedures). A large number of White deaf students attended this college, and a randomly selected number of them were sent surveys through postal mail and e-mail. Because the number of racial/ethnic minority deaf students was much smaller, the purposive sampling technique known as **complete collection (criterion sampling)** was used (e.g., Patton, 2002). In this technique, all members of a population of interest who meet a special criterion are selected.

The research team distributed 500 surveys altogether and received a total of 189 responses, 32 of which were eliminated because they were from foreign students. Of the remaining 157 respondents, 81 were from racial/ethnic minority groups (African Americans, Asians, Hispanics), and 76 were White. The combination of purposive and probability sampling techniques in this parallel MM study yielded a sample that allowed interesting comparisons between the two racial subgroups on a variety of issues, such as their perception of the social psychological climate on campus and the availability of role models.

Another example of parallel MM sampling from the medical literature is provided in Box 8.7.

Box 8.7

An Example of Parallel Mixed Methods Sampling

Telishevka, Chenett, and McKeet (2001) presented an example of parallel MM sampling from the medical literature. This study investigated the incidence and causes of high death rate among young people with diabetes. The study was conducted in the city of Lviv and its surrounding area in western Ukraine. The region had a population of 2.75 million and had witnessed a sharp increase in diabetes-related deaths between 1987 and 1998 among people younger than 50 years.

The sample of this study was obtained through the parallel use of QUAN simple random sampling and QUAL maximum variation and complete collection sampling. In the city of Lviv, people who died between 1998 and 1999 because of diabetes were identified through a hand search of death certificates at the region's statistical office. The hand search produced 35 such cases, from which 20 were randomly selected. For the area surrounding the city of Lviv, 13 out of 20 districts were purposefully selected to ensure coverage of more and less remote areas. All qualified cases in the 13 selected districts were included in the study.

The parallel mixed methods sampling produced 85 qualified cases (i.e., persons with diabetes listed on their death certificate and younger than age 50 at death). Twenty-one cases were excluded due to unclear or incomplete death records, travel constraints, and other practical reasons, leaving a final sample of 64 deceased persons. Their surviving family members and neighbors were traced, and interviews were conducted regarding the circumstances leading to the death of the individual. Numerous descriptive statistics were reported on the final sample based on documents and interviews (e.g., percent who drank alcohol heavily). Results of the interviews indicated that unstable treatment caused by limited access to insulin after the collapse of the Soviet Union in 1991 was one of the major reasons for the early death of these diabetes patients.

Sequential Mixed Methods Sampling

Examples of QUAN → QUAL and QUAL → QUAN mixed methods sampling procedures can be found throughout the human sciences. Typically, the results from the first strand inform the methodology (e.g., sample, instrumentation) employed in the second strand. In our examination of the literature, we found more examples of QUAN → QUAL studies in which the results from the QUAN strand influenced the methodology subsequently employed in the QUAL strand. In many of these cases, the final sample used in the QUAN strand was then used as the sampling frame for the subsequent QUAL strand.

An example of QUAN → QUAL mixed methods sampling comes from the work of Hancock, Calnan, and Manley (1999) in a study of perceptions and experiences of residents concerning dental service in the United Kingdom. In the QUAN portion of the study, the researchers conducted a postal survey that involved both cluster and random sampling: First, the researchers selected 13 wards out of 365 in a county in southern England using cluster sampling, and then they randomly selected 1 out of every 28 residents in those wards,

resulting in an accessible population of 2,747 individuals, from which they received 1,506 responses (55%). As indicated in Table 8.4, the researchers could be confident that their sample reflected the accessible population within +/− 5%.

The questionnaires included items measuring satisfaction with dental care (DentSat scores). The researchers next selected their sample for the QUAL strand of the study using intensity and homogeneous sampling:

1. Using intensity sampling, researchers selected 20 individuals with high DentSat scores (upper 10% of the scores).

2. Next, using intensity sampling, researchers selected 20 individuals with low DentSat scores (lower 10 percent of the scores).

3. Finally, using homogeneous sampling, 10 individuals were selected who had not received dental care in the past 5 years and who did not have full dentures.

In this study, the information generated through the QUAN strand was necessary to select participants with particular characteristics for the QUAL strand.

An example of a QUAL → QUAN sampling procedure comes from Nieto, Mendez, and Carrasquilla (1999), who studied knowledge, beliefs, and practices related to malaria control in an area of Colombia where the incidence of the disease was the highest. In the QUAL strand of the study, Nieto et al. asked leaders from five urban districts to select individuals to participate in focus groups that would meet three times during the study. The focus groups were formed using four criteria designed to facilitate both diversity of the groups and discussion in the sessions.

The five focus groups discussed a wide range of issues related to health problems in general and malaria in particular. The researchers used the focus group results to design the QUAN interview protocol, which was subsequently given to a large sample of households in the community under study. The research team used stratified random sampling, with three geographical zones constituting the strata. The total sample for the QUAN strand was 1,380 households, each of which was visited by a researcher team member.

The QUAL and QUAN data gathered through the overall MM sampling strategy were highly comparable in terms of the participants' knowledge of symptoms, perceptions of the causes of malaria transmission, and prevention practices. The QUAN strand of this study could not have been conducted without the information initially gleaned from the QUAL strand.

Multilevel Mixed Methods Sampling

Multilevel MM sampling techniques are very common in educational systems and other organizations in which different units of analysis are nested within one another. In studies of these nested organizations, researchers are often interested in answering questions related to two or more levels or units of analysis.

Multilevel MM sampling from K–12 educational settings often involves the following five levels: state school systems, school districts, schools, teachers or classrooms, and students. Figure 8.1 illustrates the structure of the sampling decisions required in studies conducted in K-12 settings. The resultant overall sampling strategy quite often requires multiple sampling techniques, each of which is employed to address one of more of the research questions.

Many educational research studies focus on the school and teacher levels because those are the levels that most directly affect students' learning. Box 8.8 contains an example of a school/teacher effectiveness study that involved a multilevel MM sampling strategy, with purposive sampling at the school level and probability sampling at the classroom level. Altogether, this example involves eight sampling techniques at five levels.

Another example of a multilevel MM sampling strategy is the Prospects study of Title I (Puma et al., 1997), which is a federally funded program for high-poverty schools that targets children with low achievement. The complex multilevel sampling strategy for this congressionally mandated study involved sampling at six levels, ranging from region of country (four regions) to the individual student level (approximately 25,000 students). The researchers in this study gathered QUAN data at all six levels of sampling, involving three cohorts of students, during a 5-year period.

The sampling strategies employed across the six levels of the Prospects study included complete collection, stratified sampling, stratified purposive sampling, intensity sampling, homogeneous sampling, and sampling of politically important cases. Stratified sampling and intensity sampling occurred at more than one level. Details on the complex sampling strategy used in Prospects can be found in the original research syntheses (e.g., Puma et al., 1997) and later syntheses (e.g., Kemper et al., 2003).

Because the sampling strategy was MM and the data generated were strictly QUAN, the Prospects study belongs in Cell 7 of Table 8.3. The study is a good example of how a complex MM sampling scheme can be used to gather only one type of data.

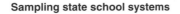

Sampling state school systems

- *Purposive or convenience* sampling
- Sampling scheme depends on practical issues

Sampling school districts

- Often involves *probability* sampling of districts, which are clusters of schools
- Also involves stratified or stratified *purposive* selection of districts

Sampling schools within districts

- *Purposive* sampling of schools often includes deviant/extreme, intensity, or typical case sampling

Sampling teachers or classrooms within schools

- *Probability* sampling of teachers or classroom often involves random sampling or stratified random sampling, or
- *Purposive* sampling, such as intensity, or typical case sampling

Sampling students within classrooms

- May involve *probability* sampling of students such as random sampling, or
- *Purposive* sampling, such as typical case or complete collection (criterion) sampling

Figure 8.1   Illustration of Multilevel MM Sampling in K–12 Educational Settings

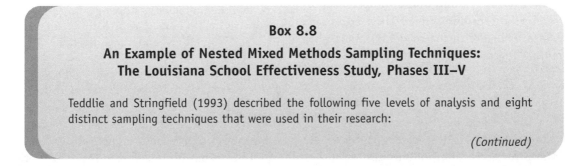

Box 8.8

An Example of Nested Mixed Methods Sampling Techniques: The Louisiana School Effectiveness Study, Phases III–V

Teddlie and Stringfield (1993) described the following five levels of analysis and eight distinct sampling techniques that were used in their research:

(Continued)

1. Twelve school systems were selected based on *maximum variation sampling* so that a wide range of district conditions were included. An additional school district (for a total of 13) was included because of pressures from a stakeholder group, thereby introducing *sampling politically important cases*. A district is a cluster of schools, and *cluster sampling* is a probability technique.

2. Pairs of school were selected within districts. Each pair of schools included one school that was more effective and one that was less effective, based on their students' scores on standardized tests. *Intensity sampling* was used in selecting these pairs of more effective or less effective schools, such that the schools were above average or below average, but not extremely so. The schools in each pair were matched on other important dimensions. Among the potential pairs of schools, three pairs were selected to be from rural areas, three from suburban areas, and three from urban areas. This is an example of *stratified purposive sampling*. One pair was dropped when it was discovered that the schools were not well matched at the third-grade level, leaving eight pairs of schools in the study.

3. The third grade at each school was selected for closer examination. The selection procedure for grade level was *homogeneous sampling*, used to reduce variation across schools and to simplify data analyses. Other grade levels were also used to gather the classroom observation data, but the student- and parental-level data were gathered at the third-grade level.

4. Classrooms for observation were selected using *stratified random sampling* such that all grades were selected and classes were randomly selected within grade levels.

5. Student test and attitudinal data and parent attitudinal data were collected at the third grade only and involved *complete collection* or *criterion sampling* of information on all third graders and their parents. Of course, some data were missing, but this was kept to a minimum by administering the student tests and questionnaires during regularly scheduled class periods.

Guidelines for Mixed Methods Sampling

The following section borrows from guidelines presented by others (e.g., Curtis, Gesler, Smith, & Washburn, 2000; Kemper et al., 2003; Miles & Huberman, 1994), plus consideration of important issues from this chapter. These are general guidelines that researchers should consider when putting together a sampling procedure for an MM study.

1. *Your sampling strategy should stem logically from the research questions and hypotheses being addressed by the study.* In most MM studies, this involves both probability and purposive techniques,

but in some cases either probability sampling (see Cell 3 in Table 8.3) or purposive sampling (see Cell 6 in Table 8.3) alone is appropriate.

a. Will the purposive sampling strategy lead to the collection of data focused on the QUAL questions under investigation?

b. Will the probability sampling strategy lead to the collection of data focused on the QUAN questions under investigation?

2. *You should be sure to follow the assumptions of the probability and purposive sampling techniques that you are using.* In several of the MM studies that we analyzed, the researchers started with established probability and purposive techniques but violated the assumptions of one or

the other during the course of the study. This is particularly the case with the probability sampling component because failure to recruit properly and participant attrition can lead to a convenience sample.

3. *Your sampling strategy should generate thorough QUAL and QUAN databases on the research questions under study.* This guideline relates to the representativeness/saturation trade-off.

a. Is the overall sampling strategy sufficiently focused to allow researchers to gather the data necessary to answer the research questions?

b. Will the purposive sampling techniques used in the study generate "saturated" information on the QUAL research questions?

c. Will the probability sampling techniques used in the study generate a representative sample related to the QUAN research questions?

4. *Your sampling strategy should allow you to draw clear inferences from both the QUAL and the QUAN data.* This guideline refers to the researchers' ability to "get it right" with regard to explaining what happened in their study or what they learned from their study. Sampling decisions are important here because if you do not have a good sample of the phenomena of interest, then your inferences related to the research questions will be inadequate.

a. From the QUAL design perspective, this guideline refers to the credibility of the inferences.

b. From the QUAN design perspective, this guideline refers to the internal validity of the inferences.

5. *Your sampling strategy must be ethical.* There are very important ethical considerations in MM research, which are discussed in more detail in Chapter 9. Specific issues related to sampling include informed consent to participate in the study, the potential benefits and risks to the participants, the need for absolute assurance that any promised confidentiality be maintained, and the right to withdraw from the study at any time.

6. *Your sampling strategy should be feasible and efficient.* Kemper et al. (2003) noted that "sampling issues are inherently practical" (p. 273).

a. The feasibility or practicality of an MM sampling strategy involves several issues. Do the researchers have the time and money to complete the sampling strategy? Do the researchers have access to all of the data sources? Is the selected sampling strategy congruent with the abilities of the researchers?

b. The efficiency of an MM sampling strategy involves techniques for focusing the finite energies of the research team on the central research questions of the study.

7. *Your sampling strategy should allow the research team to transfer or generalize the conclusions of their study to other individuals, groups, contexts, and so forth.* This guideline refers to the external validity and transferability issues that were referred to earlier in this chapter.

a. From the QUAL design perspective, this guideline indicates that the researchers should know a lot of information about the characteristics of "*both* sending and receiving contexts" (Lincoln & Guba, 1985, p. 297, italics in original). The sending context is the study sample. Results based on the study sample are transferable to other receiving contexts with similar characteristics. Thus, when purposive sampling decisions are made, the researchers should know the characteristics of the study sample and the characteristics of other contexts to which they want to transfer their study results.

b. From the QUAN design perspective, this guideline indicates that the researchers would want to increase the representativeness of the study sample as much as possible. Techniques to accomplish this include increasing sample size, using methods to ensure that that all subjects have an equal probability of participating, and so forth (Kemper et al., 2003).

8. *You should describe your sampling strategy in enough detail so that other investigators can understand it and perhaps use it in future studies.* The literature related to MM sampling strategies

is in its infancy, and more detailed descriptions of those strategies in the literature will help guide other investigators in drawing complex samples.

Creativity and flexibility in the practical design of MM sampling schemes is extremely important to the success of the research study. The success of MM research in answering a variety of questions is a function, to a large degree, of the combination of sampling strategies that one employs.

Summary

The overall purpose of this chapter was to provide readers with the information necessary to develop MM sampling strategies for their research projects. To accomplish this, we presented basic information related to both probability sampling and purposive sampling strategies.

The underlying rationales for probability and purposive sampling were presented first. Then specific probability and purposive sampling strategies were described and examples of the most frequently used techniques were given.

The characteristics of MM sampling were then described, followed by a typology of MM sampling strategies: basic MM sampling, parallel MM sampling, sequential MM sampling, multi-level MM sampling, and sampling using multiple MM sampling strategies. Examples of these MM sampling techniques were presented from several fields including education, evaluation research, social services, dentistry, human resource management, and medicine.

The final section of the chapter presented several guidelines for putting together a sampling procedure for an MM study.

Chapters 9 and 10 present information on issues related to data collection in MM studies. Chapter 9 presents important considerations regarding what researchers need to do before collecting data. These concerns include ethical considerations, details regarding entry into the field, methods of conducting pilot studies (and what to expect from them), and various issues related to the quality of collected QUAN and QUAL data.

Review Questions and Exercises

1. Identify and compare three general types of probability sampling techniques. Describe the circumstances in which each of the three probability sampling techniques is optimally used.

2. Identify and compare three general types of purposive sampling techniques. Describe the circumstances in which each of the three purposive sampling techniques is optimally used.

3. Identify and distinguish four general types of mixed methods sampling techniques. Give brief hypothetical research examples (including research questions) of each of these sampling strategies.

4. Discuss the issue of sample size in MM sampling strategies. Describe the representativeness/saturation trade-off and

how it relates to sample size. Briefly describe a hypothetical or actual MM study and how the trade-off might work as you increase the size of either the probability or the purposive sample.

5. Conduct a literature search to locate a study in which researchers employed two types of probability sampling. Write a brief abstract of this article or chapter, identifying the research questions and describing why two probability sampling techniques were used.

6. Conduct a literature search to locate a study in which researchers employed two types of purposive sampling. Write a brief abstract of this article or chapter, identifying the research questions and describing why two purposive sampling techniques were used.

7. Conduct a literature search to locate a study in which researchers employed MM sampling with at least one probability sampling technique and one purposive sampling technique. Write a brief abstract of this article or chapter, identifying the research questions and describing why MM sampling techniques were used.

8. In this chapter, we explained eight criteria for putting together a sampling procedure for an MM study. In your opinion, which are the two most important criteria? Why? In your opinion, which are the two least important criteria? Why?

9. Describe a content area of interest to you and a hypothetical or an actual study in this area. Write a short essay in which you apply the eight guidelines for putting together an MM sampling procedure for the study.

10. Pages 10–12 of Appendix B at www.sagepub.com/foundations contain the sampling strategy for the Barron, Diprose, Smith, Whiteside, and Woolcock (2008) study that we first presented in Chapter 6. Write a short summary of the sampling scheme presented in that study and how it addresses the QUAN and QUAL research questions.

11. Box 8.8 presents a summary of a sampling procedure used in a school-based study (Teddlie & Stringfield, 1993). Altogether, five levels of analysis and eight sampling techniques were used, resulting in a complex, multilevel MM sampling scheme. Briefly present and define the sampling techniques used in the study and note how they were integrated into a coherent procedure.

12. Please answer the following two questions regarding the sampling techniques used in Jang McDougall, Pollon, Hebert, and Russell (2008) in Appendix C of at www.sagepub.com/foundations.
   a. Jang et al. (2008, pp. 6–8) discussed several types of sampling procedures used to select units of analysis in their study, which included 20 schools, 20 principal surveys and interviews, 420 teacher surveys, 60 teacher interviews, 20 student focus groups, and 20 parent focus groups. Describe the sampling techniques used by the researchers.
   b. Jang et al. (2008, pp. 18–19) discussed a complex procedure that they used to select six schools (Schools C, N, O, B, D, and P in Figure 4 on p. 19). Describe the procedure and why those schools were selected for further study.

Key Terms

Cluster sampling

Complete collection (criterion sampling)

Confirming and disconfirming cases

Critical case sampling

Extreme or deviant case sampling (outlier sampling)

Gradual selection

Homogeneous sampling

Intensity sampling

Maximum variation sampling

Mixed methods sampling techniques

Multilevel mixed methods sampling

Opportunistic sampling (emergent sampling)

Parallel mixed methods sampling

Population

Purposive random sampling (purposeful random sampling)

Random sampling

Representativeness

Reputational case sampling

Revelatory case sampling

Sampling

Sampling frame

Sampling of politically important cases

Saturation

Sequential mixed methods sampling

Snowball sampling (chain sampling)

Stratified purposive sampling

Stratified sampling

Theoretical sampling (theory-based sampling)

Typical case sampling

Unit of analysis

Notes

1. This chapter is based principally on an article published in the *Journal of Mixed Methods Research* (Teddlie & Yu, 2007), which was based on a presentation given at the 2006 annual meeting of the American Educational Research Association (Teddlie & Yu, 2006).

2. Consistent with the logic presented in Chapter 7 (Note 2) regarding design typologies, it is impossible to construct an exhaustive list of sampling strategies because new ones emerge and old ones continue to evolve.

3. The traditional typology for classifying sampling techniques includes only two categories: probability (random) and purposive (nonrandom). We believe that it is advisable to distinguish MM sampling from either traditional purposive or probability categories, just as it is beneficial to consider MM research to be different from strict QUAL or QUAN research. Sampling is an integral part of the overall MM research process, and it is distinctive from either traditional approach.

4. *Systematic random sampling* is a special technique that involves selecting every *x*th member of an accessible population (e.g., selecting Cases 5, 10, 15, 20, and 25 out of a population of 25 cases).

5. A set of methodological continua was presented in Table 5.4 (see Chapter 5). One component of these continua was sampling, which was presented as the purposive-mixed-probability sampling continuum.

6. The matrix is theoretical because it is *not* based on empirical research examining the frequency of sampling techniques by type of data generated. Common sense dictates that the diagonal cells (1, 5, and 9) represent the most frequently occurring combinations of sampling techniques and types of data generated. The information contained in the other cells is based on informed speculation.

7. Collins et al. (2007, p. 273) presented some useful estimates of the minimum number of participants required for certain QUAN designs: correlational designs (64 for one-tailed hypotheses; 82 for two-tailed test hypotheses); causal-comparative designs (51 for a one-tailed hypotheses; 64 for a two-tailed test hypotheses); and experimental (21 participants per group for one-tailed hypotheses). These estimates were based on previous work by Anthony Onwuegbuzie and colleagues (Onwuegbuzie, Jiao, & Bostick, 2004).

8. Other important factors in determining QUAL sample size include the generation of a variation of ranges, the creation of comparisons among relevant groups, and representativeness.

9. Collins et al. (2007) presented a two-dimensional MM sampling typology that crosses time orientation (concurrent, sequential) by relationship of samples (identical, parallel, nested, multilevel).

CHAPTER 9

Considerations Before Collecting Your Data

Objectives

Upon finishing this chapter, you should be able to:

- Identify the ethical issues involved in data collection, including the role of internal review boards and participants' rights of anonymity and confidentiality

- Describe issues related to gaining entry to data collection contexts
- Discuss the importance of pilot studies
- Describe the Matrix of Data Collection Strategies for Mixed Methods Research
- Identify six basic data collection strategies
- Describe general issues pertaining to the quality of data in mixed methods studies
- Compare the concepts of (1) data/measurement validity and (2) credibility of data
- Compare the concepts of (1) data/measurement reliability and (2) dependability of data
- Describe the procedures for ensuring data quality in the quantitative and qualitative strands of a study
- Explain why a diverse, collaborative research team may be required to deal with data quality issues in mixed methods studies

This chapter presents a discussion of general considerations to think about before collecting data in a mixed methods (MM) research study. It also serves as a prelude to Chapter 10, where issues of data collection in the human sciences are discussed in detail.

First, we review ethical issues in human research and the particulars of the institutional review board process. The preparation required for gaining entry into the field, working with gatekeepers, and ensuring cooperation is presented next. We then discuss how pilot studies help you to identify potential conceptual and operational problems in your design, thereby allowing you to take appropriate steps to alleviate those problems.

We then introduce the characteristics of traditional typologies of quantitative (QUAN) and qualitative (QUAL) data collection strategies and explain the reasons why these strategies should *not* be labeled either QUAL or QUAN. This leads to a discussion of the QUAL-MM-QUAN data collection continuum, which we introduced in Chapter 5. The Matrix of Data Collection Strategies for Mixed Methods Research is then introduced. It serves as the organizational structure for the numerous data collection strategies we present in Chapter 10.

The last section of the chapter is devoted to data quality issues in QUAN, QUAL, and MM studies. This section includes recommendations for evaluating and maximizing the quality of your data.

Setting the Stage: Before You Start

You have planned every step of your study, and you think that you are ready to start. Before you start collecting data, however, you need to take a number of actions to increase your chances of success. These actions involve certain legal and ethical requirements that you should understand and adhere to, including the steps that you must take to protect the identity and well-being of your participants.

Ethical Consideration and Internal Review Boards[1]

Although the main goal of your study is to find credible answers to your research questions, such answers are only acceptable if they also ensure the well-being of the participants in your study. *Ethical standards for research* are well documented by many professional organizations, such as the American Educational Research Association, the American Evaluation Association, the American Medical Association, the American Psychological Association, the American Sociological Association, and others. In the United States, all of these ethical guidelines are closely aligned with the federal government's procedures for conducting human research, especially the standards of the National Institutes of Health (NIH). In other countries, comparable governing agencies regulate and monitor the protection of research participants.

The NIH established a Human Research Protection Program to help researchers better understand their ethical responsibilities when conducting research with human participants (refer to the Office for Human Research Protections 2008 *Policy Guidelines* at http:/www .hhs.gov/ohp/policy/).

Federal government guidelines regarding human research require the establishment of **institutional review boards** (IRBs) that monitor research projects in all disciplines. IRBs are responsible for evaluating and approving or disapproving research proposals, offering suggestions for proposal revisions as deemed necessary for protecting the research participants, conducting periodic reviews of approved projects, and mandating modifications (or even termination) of projects if indications of possible harm are shown.

Before you start your research project, you must apply for IRB approval from the appropriate bureaucratic entity at your institution. The NIH provides a decision tree to help you identify the necessity for, and level of, approval. Be sure to consult your university or research organization for information regarding the level and type of approval needed.

Most U.S. universities and research organization have their own process and guidelines for incorporating the NIH procedures. Also, most universities and research organizations require you to pass an online course and obtain a certificate number before you apply for IRB approval. When conducting research in other countries, you should refer to your affiliated university or research organization for appropriate procedures.

Usually, the first step in planning for IRB approval is to determine what level of risk your study might pose to your participants' psychological, physical, or social well-being. In *minimal risk* projects, participants will experience no stress beyond what they might experience in their everyday lives. Projects involving more than minimal risk pose stresses beyond what might be experienced in participants' typical daily life. After determining the level of participant risk involved in a project, you must determine the IRB review level.

There are three IRB review levels: *exempt*, *expedited*, and *full-board*. *IRB-exempt research* includes questionnaires and interviews involving nonsensitive topics in projects that are not supported by funding agencies. Exempt projects may not include participants from vulnerable populations, such as children, the elderly, and people with disabilities. Many institutions do not require an IRB application for exempt projects, although you should consult with your IRB representative regarding this issue. Research projects qualify for *IRB-expedited review* when they involve minimal risk to nonvulnerable populations. Projects that require *IRB full-board review* are those that place participants at more than minimal risk and include most research projects involving vulnerable populations (see www.unl .edu/research for more details). Once you determine the required level of review, you should start the application process. Usually, if the researcher is a student, a faculty adviser must also sign on as the *secondary investigator.*

The next step in the application process is to generate an informed consent form. **Informed consent** refers to a participant's agreement to participate in a research study, with explicit understanding of the risks involved. Consent forms are generated and distributed to potential participants to ensure that the voluntary nature of participation in the research project is explained and the details of the study have been directly and clearly explained to the participants. Obtaining informed consent is necessary if the study poses a potential risk to participants, if minors are involved, if the potential for privacy invasion exists, or if there is "potentially distasteful self-knowledge which may result from participation" (Krathwohl, 2004, p. 208).

Consent forms may also include provisions related to the participants' right to *privacy*, which include the related issues of *anonymity* and **confidentiality**. Box 9.1 describes these privacy rights.

We recommend that consent forms be printed on the letterhead of the institution under which the research will take place. Consent forms should

---

Box 9.1

Participants' Rights to Confidentiality and Anonymity

Ary, Jacobs, Razavieh, and Sorenson (2007, p. 592) distinguished between participants' rights to privacy as follows:

> Two aspects of the privacy issue are: *anonymity* and *confidentiality*. *Anonymity* refers to the process of protecting the identity of specific individuals. No identification is attached to the data obtained; not even the researcher knows who contributed the data. *Confidentiality* refers to the process of keeping the information obtained from an individual during a study secret and private. . . . If the researcher does not need to collect the individual's name and other identifying information, it is recommended that the information not be collected. If it is necessary to collect the data for follow-up or other purposes, then it is the researcher's responsibility to provide secure storage for that information and to control access to it. (Ary et al., 2007, p. 592, italics in original)

Ary et al. (2007) further warned that anonymity may be compromised under certain circumstances. For example, Teddlie and Stringfield (1993, pp. 231–233) presented a cautionary tale in which the *public's right to know* was deemed more important by a state court system than the individual's (principal's) right to privacy in a research study in which the disputed data were partially gathered using taxpayers' money. Identifying information was required to merge databases. Once sued by the local newspaper to reveal the identity of the schools (and therefore principals) involved in the study, the researchers could not guarantee the anonymity of the adult participants in the study because the names of their schools were included in the merged databases.

---

be written to best target the populations from which the consent is being obtained. It is necessary that participants completely understand the purpose and possible outcomes of their participation. Therefore, it would be inappropriate to send the same written consent form to vulnerable populations and to nonvulnerable populations. The vocabulary level must be adjusted to best serve the participants' needs. Further, it may be necessary to translate written consent forms for individuals who do not speak English (see http://fiu.edu/~dsrt/human/consent_docs.htm).

If a research participant is younger than 19 years of age, written consent must be obtained from the participant's parent (or legal guardian) prior to the participant's involvement in the research project. It is both illegal and unethical to conduct research on minors without obtaining written consent from their legal caretakers. With regard to other vulnerable populations, researchers must also obtain informed consent from a legal guardian. An alternative to obtaining third party consent in these instances would be to appoint an individual specially trained to work with members of that specific population to assist participants with the consent process. In addition, this individual may serve as a witness to the consent process and verify that participants were treated ethically (Krathwohl, 2004).

In some instances, an explicit disclosure of the purpose of the study jeopardizes the research intent. In these cases, the IRB might allow a waiver of the informed consent process. These instances are rare and often require that the investigator *debrief* participants soon after their participation.

Debriefing is a personal communication, typically verbal, in which the investigators provide detailed information to the participants regarding the study's purpose, any instances of withholding information, and any instances of *deception* (and the reasons for that deception). Debriefing is the process of making things right by the participants. Debriefing provides participants an educational opportunity in return for their contribution to the research study and allows them the opportunity to provide feedback about the study.

Ethical issues for MM researchers are not different from other researchers, except that they must consider the context and demands of both QUAL and QUAN research settings. Sometimes, IRBs allow flexibility for the emergence of the particulars of QUAL research during certain aspects of the project. Also, they acknowledge that many QUAL studies do not involve questionnaires, observation/interview protocols, or other detailed data collection instruments. You need to be aware of these variations in expectations and plan your IRB application accordingly.

The QUAL component of an MM study often requires greater sensitivity to the feelings of the participants because the nature of the research sometimes involves highly personal information:

> Because qualitative methods are highly personal and interpersonal, because naturalistic inquiry takes the researcher into the real world where people live and work, and because in-depth interviewing opens up what is inside people—qualitative inquiry may be more intrusive and involve greater reactivity than surveys, tests, and other quantitative approaches. (Patton, 2002, p. 407)

MM researchers must understand the potential for intrusiveness and behave in an ethically appropriate manner. For instance, how far should an interviewer push an interviewee for information if the participant is demonstrating discomfort with the line of questioning? This is an issue that each investigator must handle individually, and the answer requires professional judgment based on prior experiences.

Whether the data collected are QUAL or QUAN, researchers must explicitly communicate the strategy they have followed to address complex ethical issues. Box 9.2 summarizes how Canadian researchers in a study handled ethical issues related to the participation of orphans and other children from families affected by HIV. This example concerns potential discrimination against the participants, including their identification and stigmatization.

Box 9.2
Procedure for Obtaining Student Consent in an HIV Research Study

Canadian researchers (Maticka-Tyndale, Wildish, & Gichuru, 2007) working on a research study in Kenya were faced with ethical issues related to the participation of orphans and other children from HIV-affected families. The researchers followed a complex series of steps to be sure that the rights of their "vulnerable population" were taken into consideration:

1. Research protocols were reviewed by two ethics boards (one in Canada, one in Kenya) before the study started.

(Continued)

(Continued)

2. The process of obtaining parental consent could have potentially discriminated against children's participation either because parental consent was not possible or not likely (due to potential stigmatization). Therefore, schools (with parental representation) exercised their authority to grant researchers access to students, who would make their own decision about participation.

3. AIDS orphans were not invited to take part in in-depth focus group sessions, where unintended disclosure of their status was possible.

4. Before each data collection activity, information related to informed consent was given to students in both oral and written format.

Gaining Entry in the Field

The quality of your data is highly dependent on how participants and others in your research context view you and the legitimacy of your project. Research contexts are often complex social systems with their own norms, expectations, interpersonal dynamics, and insider-outsider boundaries. As a researcher, you might be fortunate to have some role in the site under study (i.e., you might be an insider). More often, however, researchers are outsiders who need permission (officially or informally) to conduct a research project at a particular site.

How you are perceived by the participants and gatekeepers undoubtedly affects how you conduct your study and the quality of your data. Before you start your study, you need to become acquainted with your gatekeepers and educate them about the importance of the study (without stating your specific objectives if it is important that they be kept undisclosed at the time). Sometimes, graduate students provide too much information, or even create unnecessary expectations, by telling gatekeepers and participants that they are doing thesis or dissertation research. We believe it is better not to be too detailed in your explanations for why you want to conduct a study.

Bogdan and Biklen (2003) listed five common questions that gatekeepers and participants might have about your study (especially the QUAL component):

1. *What are you going to do?* Bogdan and Biklen suggest that you be honest, of course, but also avoid being too specific or lengthy in your description.

2. *Will you be disruptive?* You need to assure gatekeepers and participants that your study will be unobtrusive and nondisruptive. In educational environments, you need to indicate that you will fit your research schedule into that of the schools under study.

3. *What are you going to do with your findings?* You need to assure gatekeepers and participants that your research reports will not lead to negative publicity or be used for political purposes.

4. *Why us?* People are often interested in why they were selected for your research study. In most cases, it is best to tell them that they were *not* selected for any specific reason but rather they were selected because their participation (e.g., as an emergency room nurse) will inform your research topic.

5. *What will we get out of this?* Participants often ask for reciprocity: What do I get in return for taking part in your study? Bogdan and Biklen warn, "Try not to promise too much." Typically, researchers can offer a research paper for public consumption that describes what was learned during the research. Bogdan and Biklen distinguish between this research paper and your field

notes, which are private and typically should not be shared. (pp. 78–79)

Pilot Studies

A pilot or feasibility study is either a small-scale implementation of your design or a set of steps taken to ensure quality of future data collection procedures. A **pilot study** is a stage of your project in which you collect a small amount of data to "test drive" your procedures, identify possible problems in your data collection protocols, and set the stage for your actual study. (If this reminds you of a dress rehearsal, you are getting the point!)

Van Teijlingen and Hundley (2001) identified 16 reasons (several are presented in Box 9.3) why pilot studies can be crucial. These reasons vary from developing research questions in an emergent design to demonstrating the feasibility of the study to others to validating research instruments and procedures in highly planned studies. How you conduct your pilot study (and who participates in it) depends on your design, sampling frame, and your study's context.

Often a pilot study involves collecting data on a limited number of participants who will not be included in the actual study. For example, in a

dissertation study by Chebbi (2005), the sample consisted of three specific groups of stakeholders: principals, media specialists, and teachers. Each of these groups had a different role in the facilitation, support, and use of technology. An initial pool of items was constructed, consisting of performance indicators for six identified technology standards, and was independently reviewed by four evaluation and research experts from the local district's Office of Research and Evaluation. The revised questionnaire was then reviewed by three faculty members with relevant expertise. Several items were deleted, a few items were modified, and a few additional items were added as a result of this phase of the pilot study.

The revised instrument was then reviewed by three recently retired principals, who made suggestions for further clarification. Two district evaluation experts and two College of Education faculty members made a final review, leading to no further suggestions for changes. Participants in the last stage of the pilot study were five recently retired principals who worked part-time at the district. They were asked to answer the questions as if they were still principals at their respective schools. An analysis of these results and also the participants' personal feedback revealed that the questionnaire was clear and comprehensive. The only concern was that in

---

Box 9.3

Reasons for Conducting Pilot Studies

- Developing and testing adequacy of research instruments
- Assessing the feasibility of a (full-scale) study/survey
- Designing a research protocol
- Assessing whether the research protocol is realistic and workable
- Establishing whether the sampling frame and technique are effective
- Assessing the likely success of proposed recruitment approaches
- Identifying logistical problems that might occur using proposed methods
- Estimating variability in outcomes to help determine sample size
- Collecting preliminary data
- Determining which resources (finance, staff) are needed for a planned study (Van Teijlingen & Hundley, 2001, Table 1)

some questions, the principal might not know the answer and might need the assistance of the technology coordinator. To address this concern, the letter accompanying the questionnaire was updated to inform principals that they might request the assistance of their technology coordinators in answering some of the technical questions.

We discuss Chebbi's (2005) dissertation procedures to demonstrate that a pilot study does not need to be overly extensive to be useful. Although larger pilot studies are preferable, they create new problems when the pool of potential participants is small and becomes even smaller with each new participant in the pilot. Also, pilot studies may contaminate the context of research by creating participant expectancy, reactivity, and awareness of the purposes and procedures.

Introduction to Data Collection Issues in Mixed Methods Research

This section introduces three data collection issues in MM research, as outlined in the following questions:

- What are the traditional typologies of QUAN and QUAL data collection strategies in the social and behavioral sciences? Are these typologies still useful?
- Are data collection methods a dichotomy (QUAL-QUAN) or a continuum (QUAL-MM-QUAN)?
- What would a typology of MM data collection techniques look like?

Traditional Typologies of QUAN and QUAL Data Collection Strategies

Numerous typologies of QUAL data collection strategies exist, but they almost always include three elements: observations, interviews, and documents (or variants thereof) (e.g., LeCompte &

Preissle, 1993; Mason, 2002; Patton, 2002; Stake, 1995). On the other hand, QUAN data collection strategies almost always include questionnaires, tests, and some form of structured interview (e.g., Gall, Gall, & Borg, 2006; Johnson & Christensen, 2008; Kerlinger & Lee, 2000).

The basic distinction between these QUAN and QUAL data collection strategies is rather mechanical: The QUAL strategies generate narrative data that are analyzed using thematic analysis, whereas the QUAN strategies generate numeric data that are analyzed statistically. Specific data collection techniques also differ in the degree to which they are predesigned and structured (with QUAN techniques more likely to be predesigned and more structured).

The more detailed and specific the research questions, the more likely the instruments or protocols used in the study will be predesigned and structured. The less detailed and specific the research questions, the more likely the instruments or protocols will be unstructured and designed as the study evolves. MM studies are often situated between the two extremes. Arguments for and against predesigned instruments/protocols are presented in Box 9.4.

The QUAL-MM-QUAN Data Collection Continuum

There are several reasons *not* to label data collection strategies as either QUAL or QUAN, as they are often depicted in introductory research texts:

- All of the major data collection strategies can generate both QUAL and QUAN data and can do so even in a single research setting. For example, observational protocols used in classrooms can simultaneously generate both summative QUAN data reflecting group or subgroup differences on indices of teacher effectiveness and narrative QUAL data detailing the behaviors of individual teachers. Orihuela's (2007) study discussed in Chapters 11 and 12 exemplifies this.

Box 9.4
Arguments for Few or Many Predesigned Instruments/Protocols

Arguments for Few Predesigned Instruments

- Predesigned and structured instruments blind the researcher to the site. If the most important phenomena or underlying constructs . . . are not in the instruments, they will be overlooked or misrepresented.
- Prior instrumentation is usually context-stripped. . . . But qualitative research lives and breathes through seeing the context; it is the particularities that produce the generalities, not the reverse.
- Many qualitative studies involve single cases, with few people involved. Who needs questionnaires, observation schedules, or tests—whose usual function is to yield economical, comparable, and parametric distributions for large samples?
- The lion's share of fieldwork consists of taking notes, recording events . . . , and picking up things. . . . *Instrumentation* is a misnomer. Some orienting questions, some headings for observations, and a rough and ready document analysis form are all you need at the start—perhaps all you will need in the course of the study.

Arguments for Many Predesigned Instruments

- If you know what you are after, there is no reason not to plan in advance how to collect the information.
- If interview schedules or observation schedules are not focused, too much superfluous information will be collected. An overload of data will compromise the efficiency and power of the analysis.
- Using the same instruments as in prior studies is the only way we can converse across studies.
- A biased or uninformed researcher will ask partial questions, take selective notes, make unreliable observations, and skew information. The data will be invalid and unreliable. Using validated instruments well is the best guarantee of dependable and meaningful findings. (Miles & Huberman, 1994, p. 35)

- Many research studies benefit from a mixed approach that includes different data collection strategies. The emergence of *data triangulation* techniques highlighted the practicality and power of combining multiple data sources, which blur the boundaries between traditional QUAL and QUAN data collection strategies.

- The conversion of data from one form to the other (through *quantitizing* and *qualitizing*) further blurs the distinctions between the traditional QUAL and QUAN data collection strategies.

- Specific techniques within each traditional data collection strategy can be placed on a continuum from the highly structured (QUAN end of the continuum) to the highly unstructured (QUAL end of the continuum). We introduced several QUAL-MM-QUAN methodological continua in Table 5.4 in Chapter 5, including one directly related to data collection strategies. Compared with a simple dichotomy, continua of data collection strategies better describe the actual range of specific techniques within a given data collection strategy.

Instead of discussing different data collection strategies within the context of the two traditional approaches in Chapter 10, we discuss each of these strategies separately and then present information about collecting MM data within each strategy.[2]

Other Typologies of Mixed Methods Data Collection Strategies

Until recently, typologies of MM data collection strategies were seldom found in research texts in the social and behavioral sciences. We introduced one such typology based on the activities associated with data gathering (Tashakkori & Teddlie, 1998). This typology, presented in Box 9.5, included the following features:

- Asking individuals for information or experiences (self-report techniques), or both
- Seeing what people do (observational methods)
- Asking individuals about their relationships with others (sociometry or network analysis)

- Using data collected or documented by others
- Using multiple modes of data collection

An excellent typology of MM data collection strategies was presented by Burke Johnson and Lisa Turner (2003). The logic of this approach is appealing and the typology is as exhaustive as any can be, so we adapted it for use in this text. The Johnson and Turner (2003) matrix is presented in the next section and provides the organizational structure for much of Chapter 10.

A Matrix of Data Collection Strategies for Mixed Methods Research

The Johnson and Turner (2003) data collection matrix consists of 18 cells produced by crossing two dimensions:

1. Six major strategies[3] for data collection, including questionnaires, interviews, focus groups, tests, observation, and secondary data

---

Box 9.5

Activity Typology of Mixed Methods Data Collection Strategies

I. Asking Individuals for Information or Experiences: Self-Report Techniques
   A. Interviews
   B. Questionnaires
   C. Attitude scales
   D. Personality questionnaires, inventories, and checklists
   E. Indirect self-reports: Projective techniques

II. Seeing What People Do: Observational Methods
   A. Participant observation
   B. Nonparticipant observation

III. Asking Individuals About Their Relationships With Others: Sociometry (Network Analysis)

IV. Using Data Collected or Documented by Others
   A. Archival analysis
   B. Meta-analysis

V. Using Multiple Modes of Data Collection (Tashakkori & Teddlie, 1998)

2. Three levels of methodological approaches—the familiar QUAN, MM, and QUAL approaches.

We reproduced the resultant 3 × 6 matrix as the **Matrix of Data Collection Strategies for Mixed Methods Research**, as shown in Table 9.1.[4]

The matrix makes the essential point that data collection strategies are not within the specific dominion of any one of the methodological approaches. Thus, though many introductory texts consider tests to be a QUAN data collection strategy, one needs to understand that there are also QUAL tests and MM tests. Likewise, though many introductory texts consider observation to be a QUAL data collection strategy, there are also QUAN observational techniques and MM observational techniques.

Table 9.2 presents six MM data collection strategies crossed by two dimensions:

1. Types of activities associated with each strategy, which were partially based on the activity typology presented in Box 9.5

2. Combinations of different techniques that result in MM data collection, which was adapted from Johnson and Turner (2003)

For example, the QUEST-MM strategy involves participants completing self-report instruments that measure their attitudes, beliefs, and so forth regarding the phenomenon of interest. These questionnaires can include both closed-ended items (generating QUAN data) and open-ended items (generating QUAL data). Often mixed questionnaires of this type are designed to answer simultaneously both confirmatory and exploratory research questions.

All of the data collection combinations described in Table 9.2 involve a single data collection strategy. *Within-strategy MM data collection* involves the gathering of both QUAL and QUAN data using the same data collection strategy. *Between-strategies MM data collection* involves the gathering of both QUAL and QUAN data using more than one data collection strategy (e.g., QUAL observational techniques with QUAN interview techniques).[5]

Table 9.1   A Matrix of Data Collection Strategies for MM Research

Data Collection Strategy	QUAL Research	MM Research	QUAN Research
Observation (OBS)	OBS-QUAL	OBS-MM	OBS-QUAN
Unobtrusive measures (UNOB)	UNOB-QUAL	UNOB-MM	UNOB-QUAN
Focus groups (FG)	FG-QUAL	FG-MM	FG-QUAN
Interviews (INT)	INT-QUAL	INT-MM	INT-QUAN
Questionnaires (QUEST)	QUEST-QUAL	QUEST-MM	QUEST-QUAN
Tests (TEST)	TEST-QUAL	TEST-MM	TEST-QUAN

Note: This table was adapted from Johnson and Turner (2003, p. 298). See Note 4 in this chapter for a description of the adaptations.

Table 9.2   Activities and Data Collection Techniques Associated With MM Strategies

MM Data Collection Strategy	Activities Associated With Data Collection Strategy	Combinations of Data Collection Techniques
Observation (OBS-MM)	Researchers observe participants. Researchers play a variety of roles.	Mixture of observation protocols that include both free response open-ended prompts and precoded closed-ended items.
Unobtrusive measures (UNOB-MM)	Researchers gather documents, physical trace evidence, and so on.	Mixture of documents and other data sources that include both nonnumeric and numeric information.
Focus Groups (FG-MM)	Researchers interview groups of participants.	Focus group protocols that include predetermined open-ended questions (with probes) and questions that generate numeric data.
Interviews (INT-MM)	Researchers interview individual participants.	Mixture of open-ended interview questions (with probes) that generate rich narrative data and closed-ended items that have predetermined response categories.
Questionnaires (QUEST-MM)	Participants complete instruments measuring attitudes, behaviors, and so forth.	Mixture of closed-ended questionnaire items with predetermined response categories and open-ended questionnaire items that require narrative responses.
Tests (TEST-MM)	Participants complete examinations measuring knowledge, skills, and so on.	Mixture of standardized or researcher-developed closed-ended test items and open-ended essay questions.

Note: Columns 1 and 3 of this table were adapted from Johnson and Turner (2003, p. 298).

Data Quality in the Quantitative and Qualitative Strands of Mixed Research

General Data Quality Issues

QUAN research is often planned in detail and frequently employs highly structured, closed-ended data collection procedures. QUAL researchers often allow their procedures to evolve as they use grounded theory (and other) techniques to capture the essence of the phenomenon under study. In spite of these (somewhat arbitrarily dichotomized) differences, both groups take precautions to ensure high data quality, often by repeating their observations or measurements, using multiple modes of data collection, and obtaining as much information as possible about the phenomenon under investigation.

High-quality data are necessary (but not sufficient) requirements for high-quality answers to research questions. The famous *GIGO principle* in research (garbage in, garbage out) is a simple expression of the need to generate high-quality data. **Data quality** in mixed research (with one exception) is determined by the separate standards of quality in the QUAL and QUAN strands: If the QUAL and QUAN data are valid and credible, then the mixed study will have high overall data quality. The exception to this general rule (i.e., the aspect that is unique to MM) involves the qualitizing or quantitizing processes in a conversion mixed design (see Chapter 7), where transformed data are analyzed again, using an alternative approach. We discuss this in a later section of this chapter.

A challenge facing MM researchers is that they use two different sets of standards for assessing their data quality: one for QUAL methods and one for QUAN methods. QUAN researchers evaluate (or often fail to evaluate) their data quality in terms of **data/measurement validity** (whether the data represent the constructs they were assumed to capture) and **data/measurement reliability** (whether the data consistently and accurately represent the constructs under examination).

QUAL research, on the other hand, "is rooted in phenomenology," the intent of which is "to understand the social reality experienced by the participants" in a research study (Ary et al, 2007, p. 25). As noted in Chapter 2, *credibility* is defined as whether or not the researcher's writings "are *credible to the constructors of the original multiple realities*" (Lincoln & Guba, 1985, p. 296, italics in original). In other words, is the QUAL research report credible to the participants whom the researchers were studying? **Dependability** is a QUAL analogue for the QUAN concept of *data measurement/reliability* and is concerned with the extent to which variation in a phenomenon can be tracked or explained consistently using the "human instrument" across different contexts (e.g., Ary et al., 2007; Lincoln & Guba, 1985).

Regardless of the data collection procedures, the researcher must answer two basic questions pertaining to data quality. The first question concerns *measurement validity/credibility*: Am I truly measuring/recording/capturing what I intend to, rather than something else? For example, assume that your research question involves principal leadership style. If you administer a QUAN questionnaire to teachers regarding the leadership style of their principals, then the validity question is as follows: To what extent are the obtained scores for each principal true indicators of their leadership style rather than other constructs, such as sociability and/or extroversion? If you qualitatively interview teachers, then the credibility question changes: Have I truly captured the teachers' constructions of the role of the principal as an instructional leader, rather than my own comprehension of the phenomenon, or something else entirely? If the study is mixed, then both sides of the measurement validity/credibility criterion are relevant. With multiple mixed measures, you are afforded a much better opportunity to assess the overall "goodness" of the data.

The second question involves the *measurement reliability/dependability* of the data: Assuming that I am measuring/capturing what I intend to, is my measurement/recording consistent and accurate (i.e., yields little error)? If procedures yield reliable/dependable results, then they should consistently record QUAN-oriented information (data reliability) and consistently track variation across different QUAL contexts (data dependability). Again with multiple mixed measures, you are afforded a much better opportunity to assess the overall consistency of the data quality across a variety of settings.

Much of the controversy regarding research findings is rooted in researchers' ability to answer these two questions efficiently and unambiguously. This is especially true regarding measurement validity/credibility because most attributes in social and behavioral research are not directly observable. Thus, it is impossible to directly observe the degree of correspondence between a QUAN construct (e.g., creativity) and obtained data. How do you know if you are measuring "creativity" if you can't directly see a person's creativity? Or, from the QUAL perspective, how do you know if you are truly capturing the way your participants perceive "creativity," rather than your own understanding of the phenomenon, or something else entirely (e.g., the participants' perception of intelligence)?

To make judgments regarding the measurement validity of your QUAN data you have to define the constructs in an observable and recordable manner. An instrument that "looks like" it measures political conservatism (or a QUAL open-ended interview designed to describe such an attribute) might be capturing a range of additional attributes from the need for approval to religiosity. Hence, what the data collection procedure looks like it measures (*face validity*) is not really a good index of what it *truly* measures (**construct validity**). Face validity is *not* a true indicator of the validity of an instrument. In fact, the less a research instrument reveals what it is intended to capture (i.e., the less *obtrusive* it is), the less respondents will react to their awareness of the researcher's objectives (i.e., *subject reactivity*). (See Chapter 10 for examples of *unobtrusive measures*.)

Because face validity is not a good index of measurement validity, you need other strategies to determine the quality of your data. There are two general strategies (i.e., use of experts, audits) that you might follow. One is to ask "experts" to help you judge the degree to which a particular data collection procedure measures what it is supposed to measure. Because experts often disagree with one another, this type of validation is useful only for clearly defined attributes or phenomena. In QUAN research, this is referred to as judgmental validation. A similar concept in QUAL research is *peer debriefing*.

Another method for determining the validity of your data is to conduct an empirical audit/study. In QUAN research, this is known as empirical validation. Similar concepts in QUAL research are *audit trail* and *reflexivity*. We discuss these in more detail later in this chapter and in Chapter 12.

Data Quality Issues in the Quantitative Strand of Mixed Methods Studies

Determining measurement validity. Sometimes, you may ask others (e.g., peers, experts) to judge if your data collection instrument actually measures what you intend it to assess. This type of

judgmental validation is typically useful only if your instrument intends to measure *a specific and well-defined attribute* (e.g., academic ability, mastery of a skill). Evaluating the degree to which a math test measures mastery of course objectives is an example of this type of validation, which is called **content validity**. This type of validation is not suitable if the content of an attribute is ill-defined. For example, what exactly is the content of one's attitude toward abortion or toward a specific politician? Although some authors refer to content validity of attitude scales, or other similar measures, this type of validity is mostly applicable to measurements of academic ability.

For most attributes in human research, measurement validity may be assessed by comparing and contrasting the components of the obtained results. Usually, two types of information are *simultaneously* needed for this type of validation: data related to the similarity/convergence of measurement outcomes and data related to the contrast/divergence of measurement outcomes.

Convergent validity refers to the degree to which the measurement outcomes representing a construct agree (are consistent) with other indicators of the same construct. An indicator of a construct is often called a **criterion**. These criteria are usually external to (or outside of) the test itself, although sometimes a total score of an instrument (e. g., overall score on a Likert-type attitude scale; see Chapter 10) is also used as a criterion for validating test items. For example, when developing a new attitude scale, you may use the total test score as a criterion for evaluating the degree of validity of each individual item if there is no suitable external criterion representing the construct. If an obtained item score is highly consistent with the total test score (e.g., high item-total correlation), that item is considered a valid measure of the construct. This type of item validation alone is risky and should be combined with at least one other method.

A specific example of convergent validity is **concurrent validity**, which occurs when measurement outcomes are highly correlated with the results of *other* measures of the *same* construct. To determine the concurrent validity of a new data collection procedure/instrument, one administers the instrument to a group of individuals, along with an already validated measure of the same construct. The new instrument is considered valid if the obtained score on the new test has a high correlation with scores on the established test.

Another specific example of convergent validity is **predictive validity**, which occurs when an instrument correlates highly with the outcomes it is intended to predict. For example, the American College Test (ACT) scores of entering college students must be highly correlated with their freshman college grade point averages, or other indicators of success in college, to have high predictive validity.

Discriminant validity (or **divergent validity**) refers to the degree to which measurement outcomes differentiate groups of individuals who are expected to be different on a particular attribute. **Known group validity** is an example of this type of validity in which the data obtained from groups that are theoretically (or culturally) expected to be different are compared. If the groups show a difference in the obtained results, the results are considered valid. For example, assume that you have constructed a test/procedure for assessing the "creativity" of a group of young adults. For this test/procedure to be deemed valid, artists (who by definition are expected to have high creativity) should have a higher average score than other groups who might be expected to score lower on this construct. Measures of divergent validity are often combined with measures of convergent validity to determine if differences and similarities in the database mirror the expected theoretical patterns.

Determining measurement reliability. Data/measurement reliability is the degree to which the results of a measurement consistently and accurately represent the true magnitude or "quality" of a construct. Because we can't directly see the construct, determining the degree of accuracy of the measurement outcome is not an easy task. Nevertheless, there are indirect, and usually efficient, ways of determining the degree of accuracy

(amount of error) in the measurement of attributes. Two assumptions underlie most methods of evaluating reliability. One is that if a measurement is accurate, it should be repeatable over time, or obtainable with an identical method of measurement (e.g., a parallel test, a second observer). This is a type of measurement triangulation that uses two or more identical methods with the *same* group (or situation) or the *same* method on two or more occasions.

The second assumption is that if measurement has random error, these errors in representing the true magnitude or quality of the attribute will cancel each other out over repeated measurements. For example, if one observer has a tendency to rate an attribute more positively than it should be rated, another observer might have a slightly negative tendency when rating the same attribute. As the number of observations (or number of test items) increases, the errors in measurement of the true attribute approach zero.

The rest of this section summarizes different methods of evaluating the reliability of measurements/observations. Please note that although these reliability techniques are usually discussed in relation to the QUAN approach, the basic principles can also be applied to QUAL observations.

Test-retest reliability is based on the assumption that a test is reliable if the results of its repeated administration differentiate the members of a group in a consistent manner. This is evaluated through calculating the correlation coefficient between two administrations of the test for the *same* group of individuals. If the two tests accurately measure the same attribute, the correlation between the two administrations should be strong (close to 1.00). If the results of a measurement are reliable, then the rankings of group members on one test administration should be close to the rankings on a second administration.

Split half reliability is determined by calculating the correlation between two halves of a test. The degree to which the results obtained from the two halves are correlated (consistent) is an indication of the reliability of each of the two half tests. This correlation is, in truth, an underestimate of the reliability of the full test. To obtain an estimate of the reliability of the full test, this obtained correlation is adjusted via a formula known as the Spearman-Brown correction.

Parallel forms reliability is assessed by calculating the correlation between two alternate forms of the same test, administered concurrently to a group of individuals. In comparison, *internal consistency reliability* is based on the average correlation between *all* items of a test and is an indication of the degree to which items measure the attribute consistently. Cronbach's coefficient alpha and Kuder-Richardson Formulas 20 and 21 are examples of internal consistency reliability.

Interrater reliability (also called interjudge or interobserver reliability) provides information about the degree to which ratings of two or more raters are consistent. Interrater reliability is determined by calculating the correlation between two sets of ratings produced by two individuals who rated an attribute in a group of individuals. For categorical (or even unstructured QUAL) observations, interrater reliability is determined by evaluating the degree of agreement of two observers observing the same phenomenon in the same setting. The definition and method of determining agreement depends on the attribute under investigation.

Data Quality Issues in the Qualitative Strand of Mixed Methods Studies

There are fundamental differences between the data quality issues discussed in this chapter and inference quality issues discussed in Chapter 12. Data quality concerns all of the issues discussed in this section (e.g., measurement validity, credibility, reliability, dependability) but are limited to the "goodness" of the collected QUAL and QUAN data. On the other hand, *inference quality*, introduced in Chapter 2, is an umbrella term for evaluating the overall quality of conclusions made on the basis of the findings from research studies.

Given the emergent nature of QUAL research design and data, QUAL scholars have not been particularly concerned with distinguishing the issues of data quality and inference quality. For this and other reasons, it is difficult to distinguish the issues of data quality presented in this section from the issues of inference quality presented in Chapter 12. The difficulty may be best explained by the following quote from Freeman, de Marrais, Preissle, Roulston, and St. Pierre (2007) regarding the quality of QUAL data:

> Data are produced from social interactions and are therefore constructions or interpretations. There are no "pure," "raw" data, uncontaminated by human thoughts and action, and the significance of data depends on how material fits into the architecture of corroborating data . . . In other words, qualitative data and information are always already interpretations made by participants as they answer questions or by researchers as they write up their observations. Neither research participants nor researchers can be neutral, because . . . they are always positioned culturally, historically, and theoretically. (p. 27)

Expanding on this logic, we emphasize that participants' interpretations in QUAL studies are considered data and are similar to self-report information (see Chapter 10) from QUAN research. Thus, researchers must capture these interpretations accurately and without distortion. QUAL researchers' interpretations of these data must be minimized and subjected to quality control techniques discussed in Chapter 12. In this section, we focus on strategies relevant to increasing the quality of data from a QUAL inquiry.

Trustworthiness (defined in Chapter 2) is a global QUAL concept introduced by Lincoln and Guba (1985) as a substitute, or analogue, for many of the design and measurement quality issues in QUAL research. Lincoln and Guba introduced four criteria (*credibility*, transferability, *dependability*, confirmability)[6] that collectively indicate the quality of the data from a QUAL inquiry.

The following strategies are important in determining the trustworthiness of QUAL data:

- *Prolonged engagement.*[7] It is important that investigators spend an adequate amount of time in the field to build trust, learn the "culture," and test for misinformation either from informants or their own biases. The purpose of prolonged engagement is to provide scope for researchers by making them aware of the multiple contextual factors and multiple perspectives of participants in any given social scene.

- *Persistent observation.* The purpose of persistent observation is to provide depth for researchers by helping them to identify the characteristics or aspects of the social scene that are most relevant to the research questions.

- *Use of triangulation techniques.* These include triangulation of sources (e.g., interviews, observations), methods (QUAN, QUAL), and investigators. Of course, many QUAL researchers do *not* believe that there is a single reality that can be triangulated. They interpret differences in representation of events and phenomena as the alternative realities of the participants in their studies.

- *Member checks.* As a strategy for ensuring data quality, member checks involve asking members of the social scene to verify the investigator's representations of events, behaviors, or phenomena. This is perhaps the most important strategy for determining the credibility of the researcher's interpretation of the participants' perceptions.

- *Thick descriptions.* This technique provides evidence for the *transferability* of interpretations and conclusions from QUAL investigations. As noted in Chapter 2, QUALs are interested in the transferring of inferences from a specific sending context to a specific receiving context, and this necessarily involves the detailed description of all information concerning the sending context. Thick descriptions are often referred to in the QUAL literature (e.g., Geertz, 1973). Lincoln and Guba (1985) argued that it "is the responsibility

of the inquirer to provide a sufficient base to permit a person contemplating application in another receiving setting to make the needed comparisons of similarity" (pp. 359–360).

- *Reflexive journal.* This technique provides information for all four trustworthiness criteria. Lincoln and Guba (1985) describe the technique as follows:

> [The reflexive journal is] a kind of diary in which the investigator on a daily basis, or as needed, records a variety of information about *self* . . . and *method*. With respect to the self, the reflexive journal might be thought of as providing the same kind of data about the *human* instrument that is often provided about the paper-and pencil or brass instruments used in conventional studies. With respect to method, the journal provides information about methodological decisions made and the reasons for making them—information also of great import for the auditor. (p. 327, italics in original)

Overall Data Quality in Mixed Methods Studies

We hope that this overview of data quality issues in QUAL and QUAN strands has demonstrated their close similarity. Although, out of necessity, we had to discuss the two approaches separately, in practice there are common denominators for most judgments/standards of data quality across QUAL and QUAN research.

Data triangulation has been widely suggested as a strategy for assessing the overall quality of data, especially in mixed research. Such triangulation might be much more difficult in MM research than in monomethod studies. An example of such difficulty is provided by Shaffer (2002):

> It would be extremely difficult, if not impossible, to determine the validity of results of a fixed response household survey and a focus group discussion in exactly the same way. . . . the former relies on the

notion of an idealized subject and attempts to approximate that ideal in practice by removing, or standardizing, the "investigator effect" from the inquiry. It is much more difficult to do this in focus groups where interaction between facilitators and other participants is much less structured and the scope for interpreting results is much greater. As a consequence, it seems likely that an idealized dialogue or speech situation should constitute the relevant referent to determine validity of results, rather than an idealized subject. (p. 18)

As an MM researcher, you will face the difficult task of comparing these types of data for consistency, or trying to understand why they are different.

As noted earlier, data quality in mixed research is determined by standards of quality in the QUAL and QUAN strands. Thus, if the QUAL and QUAN data are credible and valid, then the MM study has high-data quality. The only exception to this principle pertains to the quality of qualitizing or quantitizing efforts in a conversion mixed design (see Chapter 7). In such designs, the converted data are analyzed again, using an alternative approach. For example, already content-analyzed QUAL data are quantitized and then analyzed again using statistical procedures. MM researchers face the following question: Do the converted data accurately represent the meaning inherent in the original data? The *quality of conversions* adds an additional condition beyond the quality of data coming from the initial strands of the MM study. Because data conversion often occurs during data analysis, this might be considered an attribute of data analytic techniques. (See the discussion of analytic efficacy in Chapter 12.)

One final note on pre-data-collection processes concerns the makeup of the MM research team. As noted in Chapter 7, complex MM designs are often best accomplished with the services of a research team with a wide variety of methodological, experiential, and epistemological backgrounds (Shulha & Wilson, 2003).

This is especially important when one considers data quality issues, where expertise is required to ensure that the various technical considerations for both the QUAN component (e.g., concerns related to various validities, such as concurrent, construct, convergent, predictive) and the QUAL component (e.g., strategies such as prolonged engagement, the use of triangulation techniques, member checks, thick descriptions, reflexive journaling) are met. Though there are *renaissance researchers* competent in all areas of QUAL and QUAN methods, the collaborative MM team approach allows for dialectical conversation among the researchers that greatly enhances the quality of the collected and analyzed data.

Summary

The overall purpose of this chapter was to describe preparatory steps that should be taken before data collection in (valid and credible) MM research studies. Among these steps were careful consideration of ethical issues, preparation for IRB approval, conceptualization of the different types of data collection procedures, completion of pilot studies, and engagement in various activities meant to enhance the quality of the collected data.

Issues related to participants' rights to privacy (anonymity, confidentiality) were introduced. The role of the MM researcher in addressing ethical issues related to both QUAL and QUAN research was emphasized. The Matrix of Data Collection Strategies for Mixed Methods Research was then introduced as a prelude to the numerous data collection strategies presented in Chapter 10.

Particular attention was paid to data quality issues in QUAL and QUAN research and how researchers should be aware of various strategies to enhance that quality. The importance of the collaborative MM team approach was highlighted at the end of the chapter.

Chapter 10 follows up on Chapter 9 by presenting details and examples of MM data collection.

Chapter 10 centers on the Matrix of Data Collection Strategies for Mixed Methods Research, which includes 18 data collection strategies, 6 of which are MM. An important distinction is made between within-strategy and between-strategies MM data collection.

Review Questions and Exercises

1. Locate the NIH online course that includes training on federal policies and guidance concerning research with human subjects (including vulnerable populations) at http://cme.cancer.gov/clinicaltrials/learning/humanparticipant-protections.asp. Browse the Web site and note information that is of interest to you. Write a short synopsis of your site visit.

2. Think about a research question that interests you professionally or theoretically. Define the persons whom you have to study to get answers to your questions. What ethical issues do you see in asking for (or otherwise collecting) information from them? How can you minimize any possible negative effects on your participants?

3. You have probably participated in one or more research studies. Reflect on your experiences. Can you remember any personal concerns that were (or were not) addressed or alleviated by the investigator? Would you have conducted the study differently?

4. Describe the IRB procedure at your university. In your description, include all of the steps in the process, emphasizing the major requirements.

5. In Box 9.1, we discussed a situation where researchers (Teddlie & Stringfield, 1993) could not guarantee the anonymity of the participants (school principals) in their study. What could the researchers have done differently to avoid this situation?

6. Distinguish between anonymity and confidentiality as aspects of a participant's right to privacy.

7. Think about a psychological, a cultural, or an educational *construct*. How can you measure or record it in a group of individuals? How can you be certain that you are capturing that specific attribute and not another? How would you know if you are accurate in your attempt, as far as the quality or magnitude of the *construct* is concerned?

8. What are the most critical issues of data quality in MM research? Does the inconsistency/disagreement between two indicators/sources pose a problem?

9. Describe and give examples of the procedures for ensuring data quality in the QUAN strand of MM studies.

10. Describe and give examples of the procedures for ensuring data quality in the QUAL strand of MM studies.

11. Explain why a collaborative research team with a wide variety of backgrounds may be required to deal with data quality issues in MM research studies.

Key Terms

Concurrent validity

Confidentiality

Construct validity

Content validity

Convergent validity

Criterion

Data quality

Data/measurement reliability

Data/measurement validity

Debriefing

Dependability

Discriminant validity
  (divergent validity)

Informed consent

Institutional review boards

Known group validity

Matrix of Data Collection Strategies for Mixed
  Methods Research

Pilot study

Predictive validity

Notes

1. We would like to thank Tiffany Vastardis for her assistance in preparing this section on the ethics of human research.

2. For example, in the presentation of interviews as a data collection strategy in Chapter 10, we discuss both open-ended (QUAL) instruments and structured or closed-ended (QUAN) protocols. Then we discuss how the open-ended and the closed-ended formats can generate complementary data and provide a better understanding of a phenomenon of interest.

3. Johnson and Turner (2003) referred to these data collection strategies as "methods of data collection" (p. 298). We use the term *strategy* instead because we have already used the term *method* for the QUAL/MM/QUAN research design distinctions.

4. We made minor modifications to the Johnson and Turner (2003) matrix: We changed the order of presentation of the data collection strategies, we gave the cells names that are acronyms rather than numbers, and we changed the name *secondary data* to the more inclusive term *unobtrusive measures*.

5. Johnson and Turner (2003) referred to these combinations of data collection procedures as *intramethod* (within-strategy MM data collection) and *intermethod* (between-strategies MM data collection) *mixing*. We changed the terminology here because of the distinction between methods (QUAN/MM/QUAL) and strategies (e.g., interviews, observations, tests) that is detailed in the overview of Chapter 10.

6. We defined credibility and transferability in Chapter 2 and discussed credibility and dependability in this chapter. All criteria are discussed in more detail in Chapter 12.

7. We noted in Chapter 2 (Note 5) that Guba and Lincoln (1989) later developed authenticity criteria for assessing the quality of QUAL research. Nevertheless, they continue to believe that their earlier "methodological criteria are still useful for a variety of reasons, not the least of which is that they ensure that such issues as prolonged engagement and persistent observation are attended to with some seriousness" (Guba & Lincoln, 2005, p. 205).

Data Collection Strategies for Mixed Methods Research

Objectives

Upon finishing this chapter, you should be able to:

- Distinguish between methodological orientations, data collection strategies, data collection techniques, and data sources
- Distinguish between within-strategy and between-strategies mixed methods data collection
- Describe a mixed methods study for each of the six data collection strategies
- Describe the participant-observer dimension of observational research
- Define unobtrusive measures and distinguish between archival data and physical trace evidence
- Explain why focus groups is a separate data collection strategy
- Discuss different formats used in closed-ended questionnaires
- Describe performance assessment and the role of rubrics within that type of assessment
- Define between-strategies mixed methods data collection

- Discuss the strengths and weaknesses of the six data collection strategies
- Identify at least three popular between-strategies mixed methods data collection combinations
- Cite an example of a study that employed between-strategies mixed methods data collection with several data sources

This chapter presents a variety of specific data collection techniques that are used in the social and behavioral sciences, with an emphasis on mixed methods (MM) techniques. These techniques are organized around the Matrix of Data Collection Strategies for Mixed Methods Research, which is summarized in Table 9.1 (see Chapter 9).

Our data collection typology employs a somewhat arbitrary nomenclature with four levels:

Level 1 refers to *methodological orientation:* qualitative (QUAL), quantitative (QUAN), or MM.

Level 2 refers to *data collection strategies,* of which there are six major types: observations, unobtrusive measures, focus groups, interviews, questionnaires, tests.

Level 3 refers to specific *data collection techniques* that are included under one of the data collection strategies (e.g., unstructured and structured observations).

Level 4 refers to *data sources,* which are specific data sets within a research study that are generated by one of the data collection strategies or techniques.

Mixed methods data collection refers to the gathering of both QUAN and QUAL data in a single study. There are two basic MM data collection strategies:

- **Within-strategy MM data collection** involves the gathering of both QUAL and QUAN data using the same data collection strategy. Most of Chapter 10 contains presentations of these within-strategy MM data collection techniques. We want readers to understand that different data collection techniques can be used in all types of research (QUAL, QUAN, or MM), so we present numerous examples demonstrating their flexibility.
- **Between-strategies MM data collection** involves the gathering of both QUAL and QUAN data using more than one data collection strategy (e.g., observation, interviews).

Two major types of data collection using between-strategies are introduced: those that use two strategies and those that use three or more. Several examples of between-strategies MM data collection are then presented.

Major Data Collection Strategies and Mixed Methods Research

The following subsections describe the 18 cells contained in Table 9.1. Emphasis is placed on the within-strategy MM data collection cells associated with each of the six strategies (e.g., the OBS-MM cell).

Observations and Mixed Methods Research

Figure 10.1 presents a typology of different types of observations and unobtrusive measures that are used in the human sciences; thereby, Figure 10.1 serves as the organizer for the next two subsections of this chapter. Figure 10.1 indicates that the observational data collection strategy includes several techniques.

The **observational data collection strategy** may be defined as the recording of units of interaction occurring in a defined social situation based on visual examination or inspection of that situation (e.g., Denzin, 1989b; Flick, 1998). The

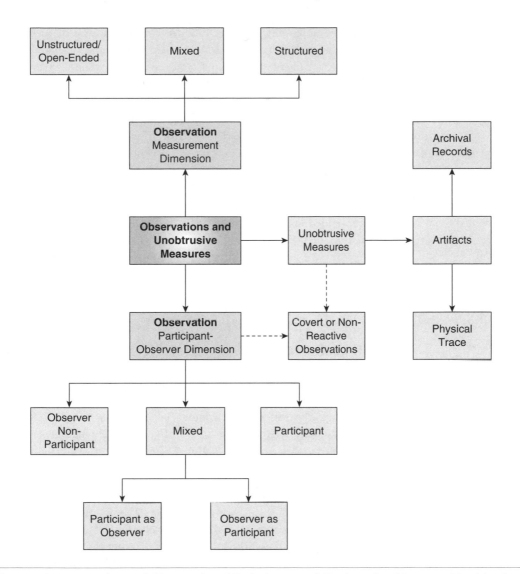

Figure 10.1   Typology of Observational Techniques and Unobtrusive Measures Used in the Social and Behavioral Sciences

three cells in Table 9.1 that represent this strategy are OBS-QUAL, OBS-MM, and OBS-QUAN.

Two important dimensions of observational research are presented in Figure 10.1:

- The *structured-unstructured dimension*, which varies depending on whether the observation protocol yields primarily structured or primarily unstructured data

- The *participant-observer dimension*, which varies depending on how much the observer is actually part of the social situation

The unstructured-structured dimension is a measurement continuum depicted in the upper left-hand corner of Figure 10.1. Observations may be recorded in two basic manners: They may be recorded as a running narrative, which means that the observer takes extensive field notes and records as many interactions as possible, or observations may be recorded using instruments or protocols with a prespecified, structured format including numeric scales.

The first type of observation protocol is known as an *unstructured (open-ended) observation instrument* and may simply involve the use of blank sheets of paper (scripting forms) or a series of prompts that guide the observer in terms of what to record. Narrative (QUAL) data result from the use of these open-ended instruments, which are situated in the OBS-QUAL cell in Table 9.1.

Box 10.1 presents an example of an unstructured (open-ended) observation instrument, the Revised Classroom Observation Instrument or RCOI (Teddlie & Stringfield, 1999). Researchers using this instrument are presented with a series of 14 teaching effectiveness attributes and are asked to record all behaviors related to each of them. The RCOI is not *completely* unstructured. It divides teacher behaviors into predetermined areas, but the responses are completely narrative. The prompts help researchers organize their written field notes while gathering them. The resultant data are totally QUAL, fitting into the OBS-QUAL cell of Table 9.1.

Box 10.1
RCOI Qualitative Observation Field Notes

The RCOI (Teddlie & Stringfield, 1999) provides the following instructions to observers: The 14 attributes on the RCOI include prompts that ask questions (Does the class start promptly?) or that are positive examples of the attribute (Teacher adjusts lesson when appropriate). These prompts are only illustrative examples of the attributes. Teachers may display these behaviors, other positive behaviors related to the attributes, or negative behaviors associated with the attribute (e.g., not being aware of classroom disruptions). It is your task as an observer to "script" (record) all behaviors related to each of the attributes. Use direct quotes and verbatim accounts of interactions where possible. "M" stands for Management attributes, and there are four of them (M1-M4). "I" stands for Instruction attributes, and there are six of them (I5-I10). "C" stands for Classroom Climate attributes, and there are four of them (C11-C14). Item 15 concerns "other comments," and observers should record all information there relevant to the effectiveness of the teacher that is not related to the other 14 attributes.

The text below presents the first two attributes and prompts from the RCOI. The protocol contains several lines for responses to the prompts.

M1. Overall Time-on-Task (Get, and keep, the show on the road.)

Does the class start promptly? What percent of time spent on academics versus social/managerial?

Teacher uses time during transitions effectively.

Teacher maximizes amount of time for instruction.

SEVERAL BLANK LINES OF SPACE WERE LEFT FOR RESPONSE

M2. Number of interruptions minimal during the observation

Number of times students and adults enter and leave classroom

Number of times intercom comes on

Number of times other events occur that disrupt classroom

SEVERAL BLANK LINES OF SPACE WERE LEFT FOR RESPONSE

The second type of observation protocol is known as a *structured (closed-ended) observation instrument* and consists of items accompanied by different precoded responses. These standardized coding instruments present the observer with a series of behavioral indicators, and the observer is supposed to select the most appropriate response for each behavior. Numeric (QUAN) data result from coding these instruments, which are situated in the OBS-QUAN cell in Table 9.1.

Box 10.2 presents an example of a structured observation instrument, the Virgilio Teacher Behavior Inventory (VTBI). This instrument has established *psychometric properties* (Teddlie, Virgilio, & Oescher, 1990), based on pilot testing of the protocol.

Box 10.2
The Virgilio Teacher Behavior Inventory (VTBI)

The VTBI (Teddlie et al., 1990) provides the following instructions to observers: The VTBI was designed as an observational tool to consistently measure specific teacher behaviors described in teacher effectiveness research. The observation should be conducted in a regular classroom setting and last for an entire class period (50 to 60 min.). The observer should rate each behavior according to the following rating scale.

    1—Poor
    2—Below average
    3—Average
    4—Good/Above average
    5—Excellent
    NA—Not applicable/Unable to observe

The following are the first 2 items on the 38-item scale:

Section A. Teacher Demonstrates Routine Classroom Management Techniques
    Item #1 The teacher clearly states rules and consequences.
    1—Poor
    2—Below average
    3—Average
    4—Good/Above average
    5—Excellent
    NA—Not applicable/Unable to observe
    Item #2 The teacher uses time during class transitions effectively.
    1—Poor
    2—Below average
    3—Average
    4—Good/Above average
    5—Excellent
    NA—Not applicable/Unable to observe

Note: These directions and items were reformatted to fit this text box.

The 38-item VTBI is much more structured than the RCOI. Each item is accompanied by a 5-point scale, ranging from 1 (*poor*) to 2 (*below average*) to 3 (*average*) to 4 (*good/above average*) to 5 (*excellent*), plus a not available (NA) category. The resultant data are totally QUAN, fitting into the OBS-QUAN cell of Table 9.1.

Many research studies employ both structured and unstructured observational instruments, either sequentially or in a parallel manner. Researchers conducting teacher effectiveness research have generated numerous QUAN and QUAL instruments designed to assess how effective teachers are in elementary and secondary classrooms (e.g., Brophy & Good, 1986; Teddlie & Meza, 1999). More sophisticated applications of teacher effectiveness research often employ both structured and unstructured protocols. Mixed data result from the coding of these instruments, which are situated in the OBS-MM cell in Table 9.1.

An example of OBS-MM data collection comes from a pilot study of a state educational accountability system (Teddlie, 1998). In this study, teachers were assessed using a new teacher evaluation system that included the following subparts:

- A manual with definitions of each of the components of effective teaching
- A scripting form consisting of a series of sheets of paper with numbered lines, which generates narrative data
- A summary form that lists each of the components together with 4-point scales, which generates numeric data

Observers in the study first completed the scripting forms while observing in classrooms. They then used information from the scripted QUAL narrative data to complete the QUAN numeric ratings for each teacher. The resultant mixed data were then used to generate case studies. The QUAN data were used to compare the effectiveness of teaching across schools and between subgroups within schools, and the QUAL data were used to describe the complex differences between the schools and between subgroups that led to those QUAN results.

The other dimension of observational data collection depicted in Figure 10.1, the **participant-observer continuum**, varies depending on how much the observer is actually part of the social situation. Authors have differentiated four roles on this continuum: complete participant, participant as observer, observer as participant, and complete observer (e.g., Denzin, 1989b; Gold, 1958; Patton, 2002). The participant-observer continuum is depicted in the lower left-hand corner of Figure 10.1.

In the complete participant role, observers become full-fledged members of the group they are studying. In the complete observer role, the researcher is removed entirely from interaction with the participants. Several factors contribute to the researcher's position on this continuum, including the purpose, length, and setting of the study. In most cases, researchers will be at a "mixed" position somewhere between the two extremes. Box 10.3 describes research roles along this continuum in elementary and secondary school settings.

Box 10.3

The Participant-Observer Continuum in K–12 Educational Settings

Educational research carried out in schools and classrooms has a wide range of participant-observer roles:

1. At the extreme observer level, researchers can install and activate cameras throughout a school (never entering the school or its classrooms when people are there) retrieve the videotapes, and analyze them.

2. Researchers can announce their intentions to study a school and its classrooms, enter the school dressed as outsiders (e.g., wearing "dressy" apparel), act like outsiders, gather information in a very prescribed, "by the book" manner, and so forth.

3. Researchers can announce their intentions to study a school and its classrooms, enter the school dressed as insiders (e.g., dress informally, if appropriate), act like insiders as much as possible (e.g., attempt to get to know the staff and teachers informally by asking nonresearch questions), and gather information in a more casual manner as the opportunities present themselves.

4. Researchers can announce their intentions to study a school and its classrooms, behave as indicated in the previous scenario, and (with the permission of the principal and staff) find activities to do around the school (e.g., copying papers), such that the researchers begin to blend in with the staff.

5. Researchers might pose as new staff members, conduct their research activities covertly, and behave as if they were actual staff members. There are ethical issues here that would have to be addressed by the appropriate internal review boards (IRBs).

6. Some staff members at the school can be solicited to covertly carry on research activities at the school without the knowledge of the other staff members. Again, this type of covert research would have to be approved by the appropriate IRBs.

Unobtrusive Measures and Mixed Methods Research

We have changed the name *secondary data* from the Johnson and Turner typology (2003) to the more inclusive term *unobtrusive measures*. Unobtrusive measures were first discussed by Webb and his colleagues in the 1960s (Webb, Campbell, Schwartz, & Sechrest, 1966, 2000; Webb, Campbell, Schwartz, Sechrest, & Grove, 1981) and were more recently described by Lee (2000). They are illustrated in the right-hand side of Figure 10.1.

Unobtrusive measures (nonreactive measures) allow investigators to examine aspects of a social phenomenon without interfering with or changing it. The individuals being studied do not realize that they are being observed. These unobtrusive measures are considered to be *nonreactive* because they are hidden within the context of the social situation; therefore, individuals under observation will not react to being observed. They will, instead, "act naturally."

Webb and his colleagues (1966, 1981, 2000) concluded that unobtrusive measures are particularly valuable due to the methodological weaknesses of self-report measures. Participants often react to interviews and questionnaires in a suspicious or distrustful manner, thereby skewing the accuracy of their responses.

A major theme emerging from the work of Webb and his colleagues (1966, 1981, 2000) was the value of using unobtrusive measures as one of the multiple sources of information in research studies. A typology of unobtrusive measures is presented in Box 10.4 and defines several components of the measures, including *artifacts* (*archival records, physical trace evidence*), *covert observations, and nonreactive observations.*

Box 10.4

Typology of Unobtrusive Measures

I. **Unobtrusive or nonreactive measures.** These research techniques allow investigators to examine aspects of a social phenomenon without interfering with or changing that phenomenon.

   A. **Artifacts.** These objects result from some human activity and may or may not have a symbolic meaning (e.g., LeCompte & Preissle, 1993).

      1. **Archival records.** These are artifacts that have symbolic meanings; they include various types of written materials (e.g., letters, newspapers) or information stored in various other formats (e.g., photographs).

      2. **Physical trace evidence.** These nonsymbolic materials are a result of some human activity and are generally categorized into two types (erosion measures, accretion measures).

   B. **Covert or Nonreactive Observations.** These observations allow for the examination of a social phenomenon without the knowledge of the individuals being observed.

      1. Covert observations. In these types of observations, the observer conceals his or her identity as a researcher in the social situation.

      2. Nonreactive observations. These "simple observations" were defined by Webb et al. (2000) as follows: "situations in which the observer has no control over the behavior . . . in question, and plays an unobserved, passive, and nonintrusive role in the research setting" (p. 113).

Archival records can be valuable as either a standalone source for studying a phenomenon of interest or a complementary data source related to a topic on which the researcher has gathered other data. Different categories of archival records have been identified (e.g., Berg, 2004; Denzin, 1989b; Johnson & Turner, 2003; Webb et al., 1966, 2000):

- Written public records
- Written private records
- Archived databases from research studies conducted previously
- Information stored in various nonwritten formats (e.g., audiotapes, photographs, videotapes), which were initially produced for public audiences, private use, or as part of a research project

Written public records are what many researchers define as archival material and include both governmental and commercial archives produced for general consumption. The most important government archives include actuarial records (e.g., birth, marriage, death), judicial and political records, and other records produced for limited audiences (e.g., police reports).

One of the most famous, and oldest, examples of research based on archival data was the sociologist Emile Durkheim's study of suicide. This is an excellent example of how a UNOB-QUAN study can generate an important theory based solely on archived databases. Refer to Box 10.5 for more details on Durkheim's work.

Box 10.5

Durkheim's Study of Suicide Based on Statistical Analysis of Archived Data

In this research, which was first published in 1897, the French sociologist Emile Durkheim explained suicide rates by relating them to a variety of other variables collected from archived documents from several European countries. These variables included religion, marital status, country of residence, number of children, education, race, and seasonal variation. Durkheim reported that the suicide rate was lower for Catholics, lower for married people, lower for people with children, lower during periods of national unification, and higher in the winter.

Durkheim concluded that suicide is often related to the lack of integration into a social group, which formed the basis for his concept of *anomic suicide* (Durkheim, 1951). Much of the information for his theory came from archival material that he could not have generated alone.

Lee (2000) described the potential of the Internet to greatly expand access to several types of archival materials. As an example, he referenced a Web site that contains a database of major constitutional cases heard by the United States Supreme Court since 1791, plus other materials (www.oyez.org).

Written private records include various types of autobiographies, diaries, personal journals, letters, and, more recently, Internet-based Weblogs (or blogs). Autobiographies and other types of written private records are often used as major data sources for the generation of case studies and life histories.

Archived databases from research studies conducted previously have increasingly become a source of archival data for researchers. For example, data from the National Education Longitudinal Study have been reanalyzed by a variety of researchers studying topics such as dropout and attainment rates.

Information stored in various nonwritten formats provides some of the more interesting sources of archival data. For instance, videotaped coverage of famous legislative hearings and court trials (e.g., the Watergate congressional hearings, the O. J. Simpson trial) has generated data for

research studies (e.g., Molotch & Boden, 1985; Schmalleger, 1996).

Photography has often been used to provide valuable information on topics of interest throughout the human sciences. Photographic archival data are a good example of the UNOB-QUAL cell from Table 9.1 because no numeric information is included, unless the data are somehow quantitized.

Following are examples of UNOB-QUAL photographic data:

- Van Maanen, Dabbs, and Faulkner's (1982) use of photographs to illustrate aspects of police department fieldwork, including "cityscape as viewed from the patrol unit" and "swarming . . . the squad turns up on the scene of a domestic violence" (pp. 124, 131)
- Edge's (1999) use of family photographs that were reprinted in the national press in Northern Ireland to provide a "humanistic" component to what she called "Loyalist murders"
- Harper's (2000) presentation of 15 photographs that were taken from his "study of the cultural phenomenon of bicycling down the same street at the same time over several days" (p. 724)

Another reason that Webb and his colleagues (1966, 2000) wrote about unobtrusive measures was to describe unusual techniques for collecting data. *Physical trace evidence* (defined in Box 10.4) is used in a variety of disciplines and provides interesting examples of unorthodox data.

Accretion and erosion measures provide the physical evidence for various types of investigations (e.g., crime scene investigations) within the behavioral and social sciences. Indeed, Webb and his colleagues (2000) introduced their chapter on physical trace evidence with an example involving Sherlock Holmes and Dr. Watson and the relative wear on the steps of two sides of a duplex.

Accretion measures are concerned with the deposit of materials, whereas *erosion measures* consider selective wear on materials. Following are accretion measures:

- The estimation of liquor sales in a city without package stores by counting the number of empty liquor bottles in household trash (Webb et al., 2000, p. 41)
- The number and types of inscriptions and graffiti left in bathrooms as indicators of gender and ethnic differences (e.g., Blake, 1981; Webb et al., 1966, 2000)
- The use of omnipresent, multicolored student drawings of their principal as an example of the principal's "cult of personality" (Teddlie & Stringfield, 1993, p. 147)
- The work of Rathje and Murphy (1992) in their Garbage Project, which involved the collection and analysis of condom wrappers, beer cans, plastic items, toys, ring-pull tabs, and so forth (labeled *garbology* by Lee, 2000)
- Information left at crime scenes (e.g., ballistic records, body recovery location, fingerprints) that was in a variety of investigative psychology studies (e.g., Canter & Alison, 2003)

The following erosion measures are described in the literature:

- Dirty edges of pages and wear on library books as signs of their popularity (e.g., Webb et al., 2000, p. 38)

- "Wear spots," such as worn rugs or tiles, as indicators of popular exhibits at museums (e.g., Wolf & Tymitz, 1978)
- Consumption of coffee as a measure of the interest of paper sessions at a staff training (Patton, 2002)

Covert or nonreactive observations are depicted in Figure 10.1 at the intersection of unobtrusive measures and participant-observation, thereby illustrating their joint roles. While conducting *covert observations* (defined in Box 10.4), a researcher might be asked his or her true identity, and the researcher must conceal it to preserve the integrity of his or her role. The last two roles of the participant-observer in K–12 educational settings, as presented in Box 10.3, involve covert observations. Ethical issues associated with covert roles must be addressed by the appropriate IRBs.

Nonreactive observations (defined in Box 10.4) involve simple observations where the researcher has no control over the behavior being examined and plays a nonintrusive role in the setting where the behavior occurs. The first role of the participant-observer in K–12 educational settings, as presented in Box 10.3, involves nonreactive observations—the observer acts as a camera. Other examples of nonreactive observations include observing shoppers at a mall and observing children at a public park. In these simple social situations, researchers do not have to conceal their roles because they are passively observing behavior in a public place.

More complex applications of unobtrusive measures, which are situated in the UNOB-MM cell in Table 9.1, result in the gathering of both QUAN and QUAL data. Johnson and Turner (2003) describe these applications generically as "mixtures of non-numerical and numerical documents; archived data based on open- and closed-ended items" (p. 299).

Specific examples of research studies from the UNOB-MM cell come from the school effectiveness literature and involve the parallel or sequential gathering of the following information:

- Archived QUAN data (e.g., attendance rates, dropout rates)
- Physical trace QUAL data (e.g., student artwork, academic and athletic trophies, academic honor rolls)

A recent example of a study situated in the UNOB-MM cell in Table 9.1 comes from a study of the effect of Hurricane Katrina on future housing patterns in New Orleans (Logan, 2006). Preliminary results (to be updated periodically) from this study are presented in Box 10.6. This research example demonstrates the power of unobtrusive measures to generate socially meaningful research.

Focus Groups and Mixed Methods Research

Johnson and Turner (2003) designate focus groups as a separate data collection strategy, and we concur with their recognition of the unique role of this approach. **Focus groups** are both an interview and an observational technique, as described by Morgan and Spanish (1984):

In essence, the strengths of focus groups come from a compromise between the strengths found in other qualitative methods. Like participant observation, they allow access to a process that qualitative researchers are often centrally interested in:

Box 10.6

The Impact of Hurricane Katrina: Unobtrusive Measures Using Multiple Data Sources

John Logan, a sociologist at Brown University, conducted one of the first detailed studies of the impact of Hurricane Katrina on storm-damaged neighborhoods in New Orleans. Logan used the following unobtrusive data sources, both QUAN and QUAL, in his study:

- A wide variety of population characteristics derived from the Federal Emergency Management Agency (FEMA) Census 2000 disaster classifications for each geographical area
- A Web-based map system denoting the specific areas that were classified as flooded or moderately to catastrophically damaged by FEMA
- Photos of individual houses to demonstrate categories of damage from FEMA's classification system

Though the data were unobtrusive, requiring no interviews or structured observations, the results of this preliminary study has far-ranging implications for New Orleans, as demonstrated in the following excerpt:

In January 2006, the full-time population of the city has been estimated at only 150,000. The analysis in this report suggests that if the future city were limited to the population previously living in zones undamaged by Katrina it would lose risking about 50% of its white residents but more than 80% of its black population. This is why the continuing question about the hurricane is this: whose city will be rebuilt? (Logan, 2006, p. 16) interaction. Like in-depth interviewing, they allow access to content that we are often interested in: the attitudes and experiences of our informants. (p. 260)

Although primarily a group interviewing technique, observations of interactions among group members are considered a major part of focus group data collection.

Krueger and Casey (2000) defined a focus group as "a carefully planned series of discussions designed to obtain perceptions on a defined area of interest in a permissive, non-threatening environment" (p. 5). Krueger and Casey ascribed the following characteristics to focus groups:

- A size of 5 to 10 participants is best.[1]
- The group composition should be homogeneous.
- Procedures should involve a group interview conducted by a moderator who is often accompanied by an assistant.
- Group sessions typically last no longer than 2 hours.
- Sessions involve a focused discussion of a topic of interest.

Most researchers writing about focus groups describe them as a QUAL technique because they are considered to be a combination of interviewing and observation, both of which are presented as QUAL techniques in many texts, and focus group questions are (typically) open-ended, thereby generating narrative data.

Therefore, a large majority of studies using focus groups fall within the FG-QUAL cell in Table 9.1. For example, the Nieto, Mendez, and Carrasquilla (1999) study of attitudes and practices toward malaria control described in Chapter 8 included a FG-QUAL component. Focus groups were formed to discuss a wide range of issues related to health problems and malaria. The initial questions were very broad, concerning such topics as the definition of *health* and the identification of the most serious health problems. The questions became more focused over the course of the sessions based on participants' previous responses. The QUAL focus group results were

then used to design a QUAN questionnaire for a separate component of the study.

The typical focus group protocol is a semistructured questionnaire designed to elicit narrative responses. Johnson and Turner (2003) described FG-QUAN research in which "the protocol items would be closed-ended, allowing little in-depth discussion" (p. 309). FG-QUAN studies are rare because they defeat the purpose of focus groups, which are to elicit the in-depth perceptions and attitudes of participants in a permissive, non-threatening environment.

Focus groups yielding MM data (cell FG-MM in Table 9.1) are more common than described in the traditional focus group literature, which tends to emphasize purely QUAL applications. There are several practical reasons for including QUAN data in focus groups:

- Researchers may want to know the percentage of participants who support opposing viewpoints.
- Researchers may want to know the order of the importance of options that emerge regarding an issue.
- Researchers may want to count the frequency with which certain themes emerge.
- If differences emerge among participants with different characteristics, researchers may want to know the proportions of subgroups who responded differently.

Thus, focus groups with MM data are primarily QUAL in nature but may use some simple QUAN data collection strategies to supplement the major findings (QUAL + quan). An example of a study employing FG-MM techniques was reported by Henwood and Pidgeon (2001) in the environmental literature. In this study, researchers conducted "community" focus groups in Wales in which the topic was the importance and value of trees to people. The focus group had a seven-step protocol that involved open discussions, exercises, and individual rankings of eight value issues, both for the participants individually and for the country of Wales. Although the data were primarily QUAL, the rankings provided interesting QUAN information on participants' attitudes about the importance of trees from wildlife habitat (*most important*) to commercial-economic value (*least important*).

Interviews and Mixed Methods Research

An **interview** is a research strategy that involves one person (the interviewer) asking questions of another person (the interviewee). The questions may be open-ended, closed-ended, or both. Interviews are a powerful data collection strategy because they use one-to-one interaction between researchers and interviewees. Interviews provide ample opportunity for interviewers to ask for explanations of vague answers or to provide clarification if a question is not clear.

Open-ended QUAL interviews (INT-QUAL) are featured more frequently than are closed-ended QUAN interviews (INT-QUAN). QUAL interviews are usually nondirective and very general ("tell me about your school"). QUAN interviews are more structured and usually closed-ended ("which of the following describes the food in the school cafeteria—*very good, good, bad, very bad*").

Open-ended interviews generate considerable information, which may lead to reconceptualization of the issues under study. They are often used in initial studies on topics unfamiliar to researchers, which is very important in cross-cultural and multicultural research, when the psychological repertoire of a population is not readily known.

Michael Quinn Patton (2002) defined three types of open-ended interviews, ranging from the least structured (*informal conversational interview*) to more structured (*general interview guide approach*) to the most structured (*standardized open-ended interview*). He also described the *closed fixed-response interview* but did not advocate using it. Patton (2002) distinguished between interviews with open-ended items that "allow respondents to express their own understanding in their own terms" as opposed to interviews with closed-ended items "that force respondents to fit their knowledge, experiences, and feelings into the researchers' categories" (p. 348). Box 10.7 summarizes Patton's four types of interviews.

Box 10.7
Four Types of Interviews

Following are the characteristics of four types of interviews presented by Patton (2002):

1. *Informal conversational interview*—Questions emerge from the immediate context and are asked in the natural course of things; there is no predetermination of question topics or wording.

2. *General interview guide approach*—Topics and issues are specified in advance, in outline form; interviewer decides sequence and wording of questions in the course of the interview.

3. *Standardized open-ended interview*—The exact wording and sequence of questions are determined in advance. All interviewees are asked the same basic questions in the same order. Questions are worded in a completely open-ended format.

4. *Closed fixed-response interview*—Questions and response categories are determined in advance. Responses are fixed; respondent chooses from among those fixed responses. (p. 349)

Researchers employing the INT-QUAL strategy may use one of the open-ended interview approaches described in Box 10.7, or they may combine them. Following is a common sequence of interview techniques used in QUAL studies:

- Start with the unstructured informal conversational interview approach, which can be used to build rapport and elicit spontaneous responses
- Move to the interview guide approach that provides a more comprehensive outline of topics yet maintains a conversational tone
- Finish with the highly structured, standardized open-ended interview approach, which greatly increases response comparability

Interviews using the open-ended question format have traditionally occurred face-to-face, but they may also take place over the telephone and via the Internet (e.g., Crichton & Kinash, 2003). Following are examples of QUAL interviews (INT-QUA):

- A study of beliefs and concerns regarding tuberculosis among newly arrived Vietnamese refugees (Carey, Morgan, & Oxtoby, 1996)
- An *oral history* of individuals who had personal knowledge of an important political figure from the 1920s and 1930s (Williams, 1969)
- A study of how low-income single mothers find and keep affordable housing (Clampet-Lundquist, 2003)
- A study involving lengthy interviews with newlyweds that were then used to predict marital stability (Carrere, Buehlman, Gottman, Coan, & Ruckstuhl, 2000)

An example from the medical field is the study of Kern and Mainous (2001), which examined disease management strategies for diabetes patients. The researchers conducted interviews with 12 physicians to gather data on strategies the physicians employed to manage patients with Type 1 and Type 2 diabetes. The researchers'

semistructured interview protocol included the following questions:

- How do you manage patients with diabetes to ensure that they are receiving appropriate monitoring tests?
- Are there things related to diabetes that you try to work into a visit and others that you do not?
- How does your strategy for diabetes management differ according to different patient characteristics (e.g., Type 1 vs. Type 2)?

Interesting aspects of this study include the development of the interview protocol, which was a team effort that included physicians and social scientists. The open-ended items were written such that *probes* could be introduced to prompt the interviewees to reflect more deeply on topics of interest. For instance, the question on differences in strategies for different types of patients included a probe regarding variations in approaches used with compliant/noncompliant patients.

Studies using INT-QUAN techniques are conducted less frequently because interviewing lends itself more readily to a format allowing interviewees the freedom to express themselves explicitly and candidly. QUAN interviews force participants to fit their responses into predetermined categories, thereby generating data that are constrained by the researchers' points of view. Studies using the INT-QUAN strategy occur when questionnaires are not feasible (e.g., the interviewees are illiterate). They are sometimes large scale in nature because interviews are replacing the typically used questionnaires.

For example, the Nieto et al. (1999) study of malaria control referred to in Chapter 8 and earlier in this chapter included an INT-QUAN component. The researchers described this component as a "prevalence" study aimed at determining a baseline regarding the knowledge and practices of the general population. The sample of 1,380 households was visited by research team members, and one individual per household was designated to be interviewed. A mail survey was not used due to the low literacy of many of the respondents.

Interviews featuring closed fixed-responses are often criticized for the lack of participant freedom in responding, yet there are some circumstances where this constraint is necessary. A well-known example of QUAN interviews is conducted by the U.S. Census Bureau every decade in conjunction with the Decennial Census. Though most individuals complete a survey and mail it back to the Census Bureau, some individuals (e.g., homeless people without addresses) are interviewed by *enumerators*, who collect census data by visiting places where people live. These enumerators must first locate the respondent assigned to them, read the census form to that individual, and then record the closed-ended responses.

The INT-QUAN data gathered by census enumerators are very valuable. The ethnic information generated through the closed-ended items located in Box 10.8 is particularly important for a number of reasons, such as the drawing of state legislative lines to properly represent minority groups.

Box 10.8

Sample Demographic Items From the Short Form of the 2000 Decennial Census (U.S. Census Bureau)

Sample Item 1.

Is this person Spanish/Hispanic/Latino? Mark X the "No" box if not Spanish/Hispanic/Latino.

_____ No, not Spanish/Hispanic/Latino
_____ Yes, Mexican, Mexican Am, Chicano
_____ Yes, Puerto Rican
_____ Yes, Cuban
_____ Yes, Other Spanish/Hispanic/Latino   Print group ↓

Sample Item 2.

What is this person's race? Mark one or more races to indicate what this person considers himself/herself to be.

_____ White
_____ Black, African Am, Negro
_____ American Indian or Alaska Native—Print name of principal tribe ↓
_____ Asian Indian
_____ Chinese
_____ Filipino
_____ Japanese
_____ Korean
_____ Vietnamese
_____ Native Hawaiian
_____ Guamanian or Chamorro
_____ Samoan
_____ Other Pacific Islander—Print race ↓
_____ Some other race—Print race ↓

Note: The Short Form from the 2000 Decennial Census can be accessed through the United States Census Bureau Web site (www.census.gov).

The census example demonstrates how closed-ended and open-ended items (the "other" categories) may be included on the same interview form, thereby generating mixed data, although in the census enumerator case the interview was definitely QUAN-qual. When research studies combine the open- and closed-ended interview formats, they generate INT-MM data.

Julia Brannen (2005) presented an informative example of INT-MM interviews, including an explicit rationale for including both QUAN and QUAL items. Her research was longitudinal in design and was conducted during a 6-year period in the 1980s (Brannen & Moss, 1991). The study topic was mothers and their return to work after maternity leave. The study was initially purely QUAN in nature focusing on the participants' behavior and health.

As the study evolved, the researchers became more interested in the QUAL nature of the mothers' experiences and perspectives. The interview protocol changed accordingly as described by Brannen (2005):

> The result was an interview schedule which combined structured questions (the responses to which were categorized according to predefined codes) with open-ended questions giving scope for probing (responses were transcribed and analyzed qualitatively). We remained committed to collecting the structured data originally promised but required the interviewers to collect such data while seeming to adopt a flexible, in-depth mode of interviewing. (p. 179)

The resulting data generated by the open-ended and closed-ended items reflected the totality of the experience for the working mothers. When inconsistencies or discrepancies appeared in the analyses of the mixed data set, the overall conclusions were illuminated by the QUAL items that had been added to the interview protocol (Brannen, 2005). If the researchers had kept only the closed-ended items with predefined codes, they would have generated a skewed account of the experiences of mothers returning to work.

Questionnaires and Mixed Methods Research

When **questionnaires**[2] are used in a study, the researcher is employing a strategy in which participants use self-report to express their attitudes, beliefs, and feelings toward a topic of interest. Questionnaires have traditionally involved paper-and-pencil methods for data collection, but the proliferation of personal computers has led to the Internet as a popular data collection venue. Depending on the complexity of issues under study, questionnaires require a level of reading ability that might not be present in the population under study. However, when literacy is not an issue, questionnaires are a very efficient data collection strategy.

Questionnaire items may be closed-ended, open-ended, or both. Closed-ended QUAN questionnaires (QUEST-QUAN) are employed more frequently in research studies than are open-ended QUAL questionnaires (QUEST-QUAL) because items with closed-ended responses are more efficient to collect and analyze.

A major advantage of questionnaires is that researchers can mail or e-mail them to their respondents. Mail surveys are less expensive to conduct than in-person interviews or questionnaires. However, the researcher must use an extensive follow-up method consisting of reminders and remailings to nonrespondents (e.g., Ary, Jacobs, Razavieh, & Sorenson, 2007; Gall, Gall, & Borg, 2006). Despite repeated efforts, some individuals in a selected sample will never participate in a study (or will stop participating), resulting in **attrition**. This attrition might pose a threat to the *external validity* (or generalizability) of the findings, especially if the nonrespondents are systematically different from the respondents.

There are several similarities, and a number of interesting differences, between interviews and questionnaires, which are summarized in Box 10.9.

Box 10.9

Similarities and Differences Between Interviews and Questionnaires

Interviews and questionnaires share several similarities but also differ in many interesting ways. Following are similarities:

- They both seek to determine the attitudes, feelings, and beliefs of respondents toward the topic of interest.
- They both involve self-reports on the part of the participants.
- They both may be used to generate QUAN, QUAL, and MM data.
- They both use a variety of somewhat overlapping formats.
- Used together, they generate complex mixed data.

Interviews and questionnaires differ in the following ways:

- Interviews involve face-to-face interactions, or some variant thereof; questionnaires involve respondent self-report that does not require contact with researchers.
- Traditionally, interviews have used open-ended formats more often, whereas questionnaires have used closed-ended formats more often.
- Studies using interviews typically involve fewer participants than studies using questionnaires, but attrition can be a problem for questionnaires.
- Interviews are typically more expensive to conduct than studies using questionnaires, primarily due to the cost of the interviewers.

Types of Quantitative Questionnaires and Formats

There are several types of QUEST-QUAN questionnaires. The following two types are frequently used:

- **Attitude scales** include measures of attitudes, beliefs, self-perceptions, intentions, aspirations, and a variety of related constructs toward some topic of interest.
- **Personality inventories,** questionnaires, and checklists are used for the measurement of the personality attributes of respondents, which are theoretically expected to be somewhat stable and to differentiate individuals from each other.

Attitude scales are questionnaires commonly used in survey research. Construction of a formal attitude scale is difficult and time consuming;

however, numerous scales in the literature have already been developed and validated.

For example, there are a number of scales used to measure the climate for learning in schools. School climate is reflected in the attitudes of individuals toward the social psychological conditions that exist at their school. A set of school climate scales was developed by Brookover and his colleagues (Brookover, Beady, Flood, Schweitzer, & Wisenbaker, 1979), including subscales such as safe and orderly environment, future educational expectations, and academic futility. The scales that Brookover developed have been augmented by other researchers (e.g., Teddlie & Stringfield, 1993) to measure different components of the school environment (e.g., quality of instruction, staff development), and they have been successfully translated and used in other countries, such as China (e.g., Liu, 2006).

Personality inventories are used for the measurement of the *personality attributes* of respondents. For example, the Beck's Depression Inventory (BDI) is a personality inventory that measures attitudes and symptoms that are characteristic of depression (Beck, Ward, Mendelson, Mock, & Erbaugh, 1961). The BDI is a 21-item self-report scale that includes inventory items measuring sadness, social withdrawal, indecisiveness, and sense of failure. Numerical values of 0, 1, 2, or 3 are assigned each item, resulting in a range of scores from 0 to 63, with higher total scores indicating more severe depressive symptoms.

Other commonly used personality inventories include measures of self-perceptions, locus of control,[3] and self-efficacy. Researchers in education, psychology, and other behavioral sciences use these scales to collect data regarding personal attributes that might be related to behaviors. An example is the measurement of "teachers' sense of efficacy" and its relationship to participation in decision making (e.g., Taylor & Tashakkori, 1995, 1997).

Response formats associated with closed-ended questionnaires include Likert scales, semantic differentials, checklists, and rank orders. **Likert scales** were introduced several decades ago (Likert, 1932) and measure respondents' level of agreement or disagreement to multiple items related to a topic of interest. The traditional Likert scales are 5-point scales with a variant of *Neither agree nor disagree* as the midpoint of the scale, as shown in the following example:

Summer is the best season of the year.

1 = *Strongly agree*

2 = *Agree*

3 = *Neither agree nor disagree*

4 = *Disagree*

5 = *Strongly disagree*

Some researchers prefer 4- or 6-point scales because there is no neutral option.

In educational applications, Likert-type questionnaires are often given to several types of participants (e.g., students, teachers, principals, parents). Likert scales for each group can be *parallel worded* so that the scores of participant groups can be compared.

Another common attitude scale is the *semantic differential* (Osgood, Suci, & Tannenbaum, 1957). In this scale, respondents are asked to express their opinions about an object or a concept (e.g., site-based management) by rating it on a series of *bipolar scales*, which traditionally have 7 points. Bipolar scales have contrasting adjectives at their endpoints. The following example illustrates semantic differentials:

Your school established a school improvement team recently. Please rate that team on each of the following scales. Place a check above the space that best describes your feelings.

Successful __ __ __ __ __ __ __ *Unsuccessful*
Democratic __ __ __ __ __ __ __ *Authoritarian*
Active __ __ __ __ __ __ __ *Passive*
Temporary __ __ __ __ __ __ __ *Permanent*

Checklists are simple instruments that allow respondents to check all appropriate (or correct) response categories for an object or concept that is the focus of the study. These responses are then coded 0 (*not checked*) or 1 (*checked*) and statistical analyses are conducted. The following example illustrates a checklist:

Consider Candidate X who is running for president. Please check all the following categories that apply to Candidate X.

_____ Honest
_____ Liberal
_____ Ambitious
_____ Even-tempered
_____ Intelligent
_____ Risk taker

Another format for closed-ended questionnaires is the rank order scale. When using *rank order scales*, respondents are presented with several characteristics or objects simultaneously and asked to rank them, typically in terms of priority or importance. For example, job applicants for entry level management positions could be asked the following question:

Consider the following job attributes. Please rank order them from 1 (*most important*) to 5 (*least important*) in terms of your decision to take a job.

_____ Working conditions
_____ Coworkers
_____ Benefits
_____ Pay
_____ Flexible scheduling of hours

An Example of a Qualitative Questionnaire (QUEST-QUAL). Though questionnaires with closed-ended items are used more frequently, questionnaires with open-ended items also feature in many studies, either alone or in conjunction with closed-ended items. QUAL questionnaires allow respondents to generate their own categories of meaning.

Huston (2001) reported research from a study of child care subsidies, which also included teachers' perceptions of factors related to children's school achievement. Researchers did not know what the teachers thought about student achievement, so they used the open-ended format. The teacher questionnaire was sent out early in the study and contained "open-ended questions asking why the teacher thought the child did or did not achieve at a level commensurate with ability" (p. 8). The researchers coded teachers' responses into several categories, including the child's motivation and personal characteristics, the child's classroom behavior, the child's home environment, and the child's intellectual ability. Huston noted that, interestingly, the "teacher almost never mentioned factors in the school environment as possible positive or negative causes of children's achievement" (p. 9).

Information from the open-ended teacher responses was then used to generate a closed-ended questionnaire, which asked teachers to rate the "causes" generated from the open-ended questionnaire as obstacles to or supports for children's achievement. Though they are valuable, open-ended questionnaire items are harder to administer and analyze than are closed-ended items.

Examples of Mixed Methods Questionnaires (QUEST-MM). An MM questionnaire includes both open-ended and closed-ended items. For example, the researcher might ask broad, open-ended questions to elicit candid, unrestricted information from respondents and then follow up with a number of closed-ended questions that have a preplanned response format. Or the researcher might include predetermined response options for several questions, followed by a set of open-ended questions written to illuminate some aspect of the phenomenon under study.

A good example of the use of QUEST-MM comes from the Parasnis, Samar, and Fischer (2005) study of deaf students, which we introduced in Chapter 8. Students were sent surveys that included 32 closed-ended and 3 open-ended items. Data for the QUAN and QUAL strands were gathered and analyzed simultaneously, and the analysis of data from each strand informed the analysis of the other.

The closed-ended items addressed a variety of issues, including comparisons between the two campuses where the information was gathered, the institutional commitment to diversity, friendship patterns, and racial conflict on campus. The open-ended items asked the following questions:

- Has anything happened to make you feel *comfortable* on this campus (related to race relations and diversity)? Please describe.
- Has anything happened to make you feel *uncomfortable* on this campus (related to race relations and diversity)? Please describe.
- Do you have any comments about the experiences of deaf ethnic minority students on this campus? Please describe. (Parasnis et al., 2005, p. 54)

Some of the most interesting information from this QUEST-MM study came from the direct quotes generated by the open-ended questions.

Tests and Mixed Methods Research

We define **tests** as a data collection strategy somewhat narrowly: Tests are various techniques designed to assess knowledge, intelligence, or ability. Each reader of this text has taken literally hundreds of tests, some of which have a large impact on future options, such as in the following examples:

- High school exit examinations, the American College Test (ACT), or SAT Reasoning Test can affect admission to undergraduate school.
- The Graduate Record Examination (GRE), Medical College Admission Test (MCAT), or Law School Admission Test (LSAT) can affect admission to postgraduate programs.

When researchers use tests as a data collection strategy, they often employ it as a *dependent variable*, which we defined in Chapter 2 as a variable that is presumed to be affected or influenced by *independent variables*. Educational researchers predict the scores of students on an achievement test (the dependent variable) based on the socioeconomic status of their parents, various measures of school environment (e.g., academic expectations), and other relevant factors (all of which are independent variables).

Tests have formats similar to those presented throughout this chapter. For instance, closed-ended items on tests (e.g., multiple-choice items, true/false items) generate TEST-QUAN data, whereas open-ended items (e.g., essay questions) produce TEST-QUAL data. Qualitative test data are often quantitized because researchers interested in test data typically want numeric information.

Of course, the tests noted previously as being important for one's future (e.g., ACT, GRE) fall into the TEST-QUAN category. These are labeled *standardized tests*, which are tests that are uniformly developed, administered, and scored usually by a commercial publishing house. The developmental process involves determining the psychometric properties of the tests (i.e., their reliability and validity[4]). This process is one of the differences between standardized tests and teacher-made tests—teachers typically do not have the resources or expertise to establish their instruments' psychometric properties.

Standardized tests may be divided into several different types, but in this text we limit it to the following two types:

- *Aptitude tests* measure innate abilities to acquire knowledge or develop skills. Additionally, aptitude tests (e.g., ACT, GRE) are developed to predict how well someone will perform later on some specific behavior or skill. Several authors consider intelligence tests to be an aptitude test (e.g., Johnson & Christensen, 2004; Wiersma & Jurs, 2005), although others put them into a separate category (e.g., Gall et al., 2006).

- *Achievement tests* measure acquired knowledge or facts that are already known. There are two basic types of achievement tests: norm-referenced and criterion-referenced tests. A *norm-referenced test* (NRT) compares an individual's score with that of the performance of the members of a normative group. The distribution of test scores produced by the normative group generates a *normal curve* (Popham, 2002), the properties of which are described in Box 8.2. A *criterion-referenced test* (CRT) compares an individual's score to a set standard. These CRTs typically measure mastery of an academic topic such as reading comprehension (e.g., Woolfolk, 2004).

When investigators use QUAN tests in their research, they should be aware of the differences between standardized and teacher-made tests, between aptitude and achievement tests, and between NRTs and CRTs to avoid misinterpretations of their data. Researchers should also be aware of *cultural bias* in standardized tests and how it affects the test scores of minority groups, leading some scholars to develop what they call culture-fair tests (e.g., Cattell, 1960).

Researchers wanting to use a particular test in their studies have two important resources: the

Mental Measurement Yearbook (MMY) and *Tests in Print*, both of which are published by the Buros Institute of Mental Measurements. The *Sixteenth Mental Measurement Yearbook* (Spies, Plake, & Murphy, 2005) contains reviews of about 300 tests, and *Tests in Print VI* (Murphy, Plake, Impara, & Spies, 2002) contains descriptive listings of tests in about 20 major categories.

Though the emphasis in this section has been on standardized tests, researchers also create their own closed-ended tests when they cannot find a test that measures the specific content that their study requires. In these cases, investigators often generate basic psychometric data on their newly developed test as they use it.

The TEST-QUAL data collection strategy is less formal, not requiring the extensive psychometric work associated with TEST-QUAN procedures. QUAL test data are almost always collected with instruments that researchers develop. Essays are probably the most frequently used QUAL test data collection technique. Participants taking an essay test are given a writing prompt that requires a free, written response. The prompt can be more or less structured, ranging from, for example, "write what you know about ships" to a scenario in which a particular type of ship is described in a particular setting.

Rubrics are used to determine if participants presented the correct information in their written responses to open-ended test items. Rubrics are rating scales with systematic guidelines for assessing responses to open-ended questions, performances on tasks, and products related to the topic of interest (e.g., Mertens, 2005; Mertler, 2001). Rubrics typically include a set of criteria for assessing a written response, performance, or product plus a series of corresponding points on a numeric scale. In most cases, researchers use the numeric scales to summarize results across participants, thereby quantitizing the original information.

Alternative assessment, *performance assessment*, and portfolio assessment have been advocated as optional techniques to traditional TEST-QUAN instruments. As a data source, we consider them to be TEST-QUAL because they are based on observation of individual performance on some task related to the objectives of a curriculum. Mertens (2005) explained the distinctions among the terms associated with alternatives for traditional tests as follows:

> Performance assessment is a process for collecting information through systematic observation in order to make decisions about an individual. . . . Performance assessment is an essential element of alternative assessment and the portfolio is the vehicle through which performance assessment information is stored. (p. 369)

TEST-MM data collection techniques involve researchers' gathering of information about participants' knowledge and skills using both QUAN and QUAL methods. The simplest application of TEST-MM is a test that contains both closed-ended and open-ended items. This test would be MM if the closed-ended items were used to assess knowledge of facts across a variety of curriculum topics and the open-ended items were used to assess depth of understanding about key concepts within the curriculum. If investigators were using multiple-choice and essay items, then an MM report based on those data would integrate the two forms of information to give a holistic picture of the breadth and depth of the participants' knowledge.

Between-Strategies Mixed Methods Data Collection

Between-strategies MM data collection refers to research in which QUAL and QUAN data are gathered using more than one data collection strategy. For example, combining QUEST-QUAN techniques with FG-QUAL techniques is an example of between-strategies MM data collection. The use of different data collection strategies using QUAN and QUAL sources in the same study has also been called methodological triangulation (see Chapter 2) or intermethod mixing (Johnson & Turner, 2003).

Table 10.1 presents 30 between-strategies MM data collection combinations.[5] The cells in this table were generated by crossing the six types of QUAN strategies by the six types of QUAL strategies introduced in Table 9.1 and then eliminating the within-strategy MM data collection combinations.

We first describe MM data collection combinations that use two strategies and then those that use three or more. Between-strategies MM data collection combines the same QUAN and QUAL techniques that we have already discussed in this chapter. Therefore, we focus on describing some of the more popular between-strategies MM data collection combinations in this section, rather than discussing all 30 of them.

Between-strategies MM data collection may be associated with any of the sequential or parallel designs presented in Chapter 7. In these studies, one data collection strategy is used to produce one type of data in one strand, and another data collection strategy is used to produce another type of data in the other strand. For instance, consider Cell 21 in Table 10.1, which combines OBS-QUAL and QUEST-QUAN data collection. In a study of this type, a researcher might use both an open-ended observation instrument (e.g., the RCOI described in Box 10.1) and a closed-ended questionnaire (e.g., the school climate scales described earlier in this chapter).

Burke Johnson and Lisa Turner (2003) refer to the **fundamental principle of mixed methods research**, which is that "*methods should be mixed in a way that has complementary strengths and nonoverlapping weaknesses*" (p. 299, italics in original). Thus, when researchers are putting together between-strategies MM data collection combinations, they should be aware of the strengths and weaknesses of each of the data collection strategies. Table 10.2 summarizes some of those strengths and weaknesses, which were initially presented in Johnson and Turner (2003).

Table 10.1   Thirty Between-Strategies MM Data Collection Combinations

Data Collection Strategy	OBS-QUAL	UNOB-QUAL	FG-QUAL	INT-QUAL	QUEST-QUAL	TEST-QUAL
OBS-QUAN	31	1	2	3	4	5
UNOB-QUAN	6	32	7	8	9	10
FG-QUAN	11	12	33	13	14	15
INT-QUAN	16	17	18	34	19	20
QUEST-QUAN	21	22	23	24	35	25
TEST-QUAN	26	27	28	29	30	36

Note: Cells 1–30 represent different types of between-strategies MM data collection. The shaded diagonal cells numbered 31–36 represent different types of within-strategy MM data collection.

Table 10.2   Salient Strengths and Weaknesses of Six Data Collection Strategies

Strategy	Strengths	Weaknesses
Observation	(1) Allows one to directly see what people do without having to rely on what they say they do. (2) Can be used with participants with weak verbal skills. (3) Good for description.	(1) Reasons for behavior may be unclear. (2) More expensive to conduct than questionnaires and tests. (3) Data analysis sometimes time consuming.
Unobtrusive Measures	(1) Unobtrusive, making reactive and investigator effects very unlikely. (2) Can be collected for time periods occurring in the past (e.g., historical data). (3) Archived research data are available on a wide variety of topics.	(1) May be incomplete because of selective reporting or recording. (2) Data possibly dated. (3) Access to some types of content may be difficult.
Focus groups	(1) Useful for exploring ideas. (2) Allows study of how participants react to each other. (3) Allows probing.	(1) Sometimes expensive. (2) May be dominated by one or two participants. (3) Focus group moderator possibly biased.
Interviews	(1) Good for measuring attitudes and most other content of interest. (2) Allows probing by the interviewer. (3) Can provide in-depth information.	(1) In-person interviews are expensive and time consuming. (2) Reactive and investigator effects may occur. (3) Data analysis sometimes time consuming for open-ended items.
Questionnaires	(1) Good for measuring attitudes and eliciting other content from research participants. (2) Inexpensive. (3) Quick turnaround.	(1) Must be kept short. (2) Might have missing data. (3) Response rate may be low for mail questionnaires.
Tests	(1) Can provide good measures of many characteristics of people. (2) Instruments usually already developed. (3) Wide range of tests is available.	(1) Can be expensive. (2) Possibly reactive effects may occur. (3) Sometimes biased against certain groups of people.

Note: These strengths and weaknesses were reproduced from tables located in Johnson and Turner (2003, pp. 306, 308, 310, 312, 315, 319). Additional strengths and weaknesses were listed in the Johnson and Turner tables.

Between-Strategies Data Collection Using Two Strategies

We discuss only some of the more commonly used between-strategies MM data collection combinations from Table 10.1 because to describe them all is beyond the scope of this text. Also, the most commonly used of these combinations constitute the majority of the MM studies found in the literature.

Quantitative Questionnaires With Qualitative Interviews

Probably the most commonly occurring MM combination in the literature is closed-ended questionnaires and QUAL interviews (Cell 24 from Table 10.1). This combination allows for the strengths of each strategy to be combined in a complementary manner with the strengths of the other. QUAN questionnaires can be used to inexpensively generate large numbers of responses that produce information across a broad range of survey topics. Data gathered using QUAL interviews, on the other hand, are based on a relatively small number of participants, who generate in-depth information in response to queries from the interview protocol.

QUAN questionnaire and QUAL interview studies can be generated using sequential or parallel designs, together with other variants discussed in Chapter 7. Combining all of those permutations can result in a large number of data collection strategies for researchers.

For example, the Carwile (2005) dissertation (see Box 8.6) used a QUEST-QUAN → INT-QUAL sequence to study the leadership characteristics and job satisfaction of program directors in radiologic technology. In the initial QUAN strand, Carwile used two questionnaires, including one that assessed the directors' leadership styles. A relatively large number of directors (284) completed the questionnaire, which included a statistical test of the hypothesis that their level of job satisfaction was related to their leadership style.

The subsequent QUAL strand involved several research questions, including one that looked at the relationship between type of program and directors' leadership style. The QUAL strand followed the QUAN strand because the directors' leadership style was assessed from responses to the questionnaire administered in the first strand. Carwile (2005) drew a purposeful sample of 13 program directors based on leadership style and program type. She then interviewed the program directors regarding their perception of their leadership style and why they thought it worked in their type of degree program.

Another example of the QUEST-QUAN → INT-QUAL sequence comes from a study of child welfare administrators' responses to increased demands on their agencies' services (Regehr, Chau, Leslie, & Howe, 2001). These researchers first administered a set of questionnaires (including a depression scale and the Impact of Events Scale) to a sample of agency administrators and then conducted semistructured interviews focusing on job stress. Data included 47 completed questionnaires and 8 interviews.

Results from the study's QUAN component indicated that about one half of the administrators "fell in the high or severe range of post-traumatic symptoms on the Impact of Event Scale" (Regehr et al., 2001, p. 17). The purpose of the follow-up QUAL interviews with the eight administrators was to better understand the nature of the stressors.

A thematic summary of the data gathered from the QUAL interviews indicated that new child welfare reform regulations resulted in increased workload, increased accountability, and the introduction of new staff. These factors led to stress on the administrators, which then led either to resilience or to "giving up." The sequential QUAN and QUAL data from this study were highly complementary—one component quantitatively confirmed the high levels of job stress and the other qualitatively interpreted the effects of that stress.

A final example of the popular QUAN questionnaires with QUAL interviews data collection combination involves a sequential INT-QUAL → QUEST-QUAN study. This consumer marketing study was previously described in Chapter 7. Hausman (2000) employed a sequential design with the following components:

- The first part of the study included 60 QUAL interviews that asked questions related to impulse buying (e.g., How do buying decisions result in impulse buying?).
- The results from the interviews were then used to generate a series of five QUAN hypotheses concerning impulse buying. These hypotheses were empirically grounded in the QUAL data.
- A final sample of 272 consumers completed questionnaires in the QUAN strand of the study. Several significant results were identified, including the finding that individual consumers' impulse buying is correlated with their desires to fulfill hedonic needs.

Quantitative Observation With Qualitative Interviews

Another commonly occurring MM combination in the educational literature is OBS-QUAN with INT-QUAL (Cell 3 from Table 10.1). In these studies, researchers observe teachers using closed-ended protocols, such as the VTBI (see Box 10.2), which presents observers with a series of behavioral indicators that quantitatively describe teacher classroom behavior at the school and classroom levels.

Researchers then interview the teachers who were observed, asking questions about topics of interest, which may change depending on the QUAN results from the first strand. For instance, if the average teacher scores were low on classroom management measures, then researchers might ask open-ended questions regarding the teachers' perceptions of orderliness in their classrooms—why disorder was occurring and what could be done to improve classroom management. The combination of QUAN and QUAL data resulting from this MM research strategy is

very powerful, especially for educators who want to improve classroom teaching practices.

Qualitative Focus Groups With Quantitative Interviews

The combination of FG-QUAL and INT-QUAN data collection strategies results in Cell 18 of Table 10.1. The Nieto et al. (1999) study of attitudes and practices toward malaria control in Colombia is an example of this combination:

- The FG-QUAL component included focus groups that were formed to discuss a wide range of health-related issues.
- Focus group results were subsequently employed by the investigators to construct an interview protocol with closed-ended items (INT-QUAN).
- QUAN interviews were conducted to determine a baseline regarding the knowledge and practices of the population based on a large household sample.

The study employed a sequential FG-QUAL → INT-QUAN design, and results from the QUAL and QUAN components were congruent, as the authors noted: "The information obtained by the two methods was comparable on knowledge of symptoms, causes and ways of malaria transmission, and prevention practices like the use of bednets or provision of health services" (Nieto et al., 1999, p. 601).

Quantitative Unobtrusive Measures With Qualitative Interviews

Another MM combination is UNOB-QUAN with INT-QUAL (Cell 8 from Table 10.1). In these studies, researchers mix QUAN information gathered from unobtrusive data sources (e.g., archival records) with QUAL interview data.

An interesting example of this combination of strategies comes from Detlor (2003), who contributed to the information systems (IS) literature. Detlor's research questions concerned how individuals working in organizations search for and use information from Internet-based information systems. Two primary data sources were in this study: Web tracking of participants' use of the Internet followed by one-on-one interviews with participants. The unobtrusive QUAN information from this study was described as follows:

> *Web tracking* consisted of the use of history files and custom-developed software installed on participants' computers that ran transparently whenever a participant's web browser was used. . . . Most participants commented that they forgot they were being tracked during the data collection period and used the internet-based IS as they would normally. (p. 123, italics in original)

The tracking software recorded a large amount of unobtrusive data on the participants' activities, including identification of Web sites visited and frequency of participants' Web page visits. Log tables indicating extended or frequent visits to particular Web sites were used to pinpoint "significant episodes" of information seeking.

One-on-one QUAL interviews were used to discuss the "significant episodes" in detail so that the researcher could understand why the particular Web sites were accessed and the degree to which participants successfully resolved their information needs. The MM data allowed the researcher to describe and then explain an iterative cycle of "information needs–seeking use activities" (Detlor, 2003, p. 113) that the participants employed in their Internet environment.

A Further Comment on Unobtrusive Measures

In evaluation research, investigators are asked to determine whether a particular social/educational program is successful. In most cases, interviews and surveys of participants and program managers are the primary sources, but unobtrusive measures are also important. For example, if one were evaluating a program intended to increase the early identification and treatment of dyslexic students, the archival

"paper trail" could include the original legislation that funded the program, memos of program managers from the state bureau administering the program, annual reports of the program, records of the number and types of students identified as dyslexic, records of the number and types of students treated through the program, archived test scores for those students who completed the program, and so forth.

In this scenario, the archived material could be either UNOB-QUAL or UNOB-QUAN, whereas the information gathered directly from participants could consist of QUAN or QUAL interviews or questionnaires. Four of the cells in Table 10.1 (Cells 8, 9, 17, and 22) fit these possible data collection patterns.

Between-Strategies Data Collection Using Three or More Strategies

Each of the between-strategies MM data collection combinations presented in Table 10.1 involve only two data collection strategies. The number of possible combinations expands exponentially when three or more data collection strategies are used (e.g., OBS-QUAL with INT-QUAL with TEST-QUAN). There are too many possible data collection combinations to enumerate or describe them all.

Therefore, we only present a few examples of these combinations. We start by presenting a few combinations that use three data collection strategies because these are the simplest permutations. Then, we present more complicated prototypes of between-strategies MM data collection combinations using sources from the education and evaluation fields, which are described as *data source rich environments*.

Between-Strategies Data Collection Using Three Strategies

Box 10.10 presents an MM study (Lockyer, 2006) that examined ethical issues in humor, based on information gleaned from a British satirical serial named *Private Eye*. The three data collection strategies in this study were UNOB-QUAL—narrative data taken from the serial and subjected to QUAL analysis; UNOB-QUAN—narrative data that was content analyzed using a predetermined coding scheme, thereby resulting in QUAN data; and INT-QUAL—interviews with individuals associated with *Private Eye*. See Box 10.10 for more details.

Another example of between-strategies data collection using three strategies comes from Papadakis and Barwise (2002) in the field of management. These researchers were interested in how important chief executive officers (CEOs) and top managers were in making strategic business decisions. They

constructed a database centering on 70 strategic decisions and then used three data collection strategies:

- QUAL interview with CEOs and other participants
- Two QUAN questionnaires, one for CEOs and the other for key participants
- Unobtrusive QUAL information gleaned from internal documents, reports, and minutes of meetings

This combination of interview, questionnaire, and unobtrusive measures is a frequently occurring data collection pattern. Often the QUAN data are in the form of a widely distributed questionnaire, and the QUAL data come from a smaller sample of selected interviews,

---

Box 10.10

An Example of the Use of Three Data Collection Strategies in MM Research

Lockyer (2006) demonstrated how MM research could be used to study "ethics" in humor, which was explored by examining instances of offense caused by the British satirical serial *Private Eye*. There were three major sources of data:

1. Complaint letters to the *Private Eye* editor, indicating various levels of offense at something printed in the serial, such as a cartoon that made a joke about rape.

2. The editors' management and treatment of readers' letters of complaint, which indicated a dismissive and mocking orientation. This information came from the letters pages of the serial and included techniques intended to ridicule the letter writers. (*Private Eye* editors rarely apologize for anything written in the serial.)

3. Interviews with past and present *Private Eye* journalists and libel lawyers.

There were three types of data collection strategies used in this research: unobtrusive measures generating qualitative data, unobtrusive measures generating quantitative data, and interviews generating qualitative data. The UNOB-QUAL data were generated from the narratives of 479 readers' letters and the responses of the editors to those letters. The UNOB-QUAN data were generated by a (QUAN) content analysis of the readers' letters using predetermined categories and codes (e.g., author type, with codes such as reader, spokesperson, official) that resulted in frequency counts on eight numerically defined variables. The INT-QUAL data came from interviews with *Private Eye* staffers.

Lockyer (2006) concluded that "combining different modes of data collection and analysis facilitated a description of the research phenomenon which is altogether much more complex and more precise than would be achieved from mono-method approaches" (p. 54).

plus archival sources that establish the study context.

A final example of between-strategies data collection using three strategies has been published in economics and anthropology (e.g., Katz, Kling, & Liebman, 2001; Kling, Liebman, & Katz, 2005). This project examined the impact of randomly assigning housing vouchers to applicants who lived in high-poverty housing. The initial focus of the research was on the QUAN economics data, but the QUAL data became more crucial as the study evolved.

Three data collection strategies were employed:

- QUAN questionnaires administered to household heads before and after enrollment
- Informal QUAL observations conducted over the course of the project
- QUAL interviews conducted with household heads

QUAL data led to a refocusing of the QUAN component of the study as the researchers became aware that the project was having an impact on outcomes not included in the original plan, such as safety and health. Kling et al. (2005) reported that interviews with program participants were dominated by their fear that their children would become victims of violence if they did not move to safer neighborhoods.

Between-Strategies Data Collection Using Numerous Strategies

Some studies employ numerous data collection strategies and, consequently, have several data sources. At least four factors lead to research studies with numerous data sources:

- Some researchers work in *data source rich environments* (e.g., educational research and some program evaluation settings).
- Studies that have numerous research questions are more likely to require multiple data sources.

- Longitudinal research studies are more likely to have multiple data sources, some of which emerge as the research evolves.
- Studies using the complex MM designs described in Chapter 7 (e.g., sequential, multilevel, fully integrated) often generate multiple data sources.

These factors can result in complex, multifaceted databases. For example, the Trend (1979) evaluation described in Chapter 1 employed a parallel MM design, had several QUAN and QUAL evaluation questions, was longitudinal, and was conducted in a *data source rich environment* with housing units and program offices. Eventually, the QUAN database comprised more than 55 million characters, and the anthropologists' field notes and logs totaled more than 25,000 pages.

Luo and Dappen (2005) recently presented an even more complex MM evaluation that included 10 data collection strategies and 19 data sources. The study employed all of the QUAN/QUAL data collection types presented in Table 10.1, except for QUAN interviews and QUAN focus groups. The study had four objectives that were evaluated longitudinally and is an excellent example of the complexity that can be generated when studying programs across time using MM. Table 10.3 summarizes the four objectives and 10 types of data collection strategies used in the Luo and Dappen study.

Educational researchers working in K–12 settings are operating in a *data source rich environment*. Teddlie, Kochan, and Taylor (2002) devised the ABC+ Data Collection Matrix, presented in Table 10.4, for gathering data in these environments.

The matrix has four levels of data analysis (parent, student, classroom/teacher, and school/principal) and four types of variables, which are defined as follows:

1. *Attitude variables*—the emotions or feelings of individuals associated with a school

2. *Behavioral variables*—representing the overt actions of individuals associated with a school, including classroom behaviors

Table 10.3   Evaluation Objectives Crossed by Data Collection Strategies

Evaluation Objective	Data Collection Strategy and Specific Data Source
Objective 1 To increase the number of nonminority students in each of the magnet schools (p. 111)	(1) UNOB-QUAN—Enrollment data (2) UNOB-QUAL—Examination of recruitment plan, school portfolio, meeting minutes (3) OBS-QUAL—Observation of recruitment activities (4) OBS-QUAN—Checklist for Objective 1
Objective 2 To use state-approved content standards in instruction and to use reliable assessments for assessing and rating students (p. 112)	(5) UNOB-QUAL—Records of staff development activities (6) QUEST-QUAN—Surveys of staff, parents, community members (7) OBS-QUAN—Classroom observations using checklists (8) INT-QUAL—Interviews with observed teachers (9) TEST-QUAL—Student portfolios (10) QUEST-QUAN—Teacher survey of professional development (11) QUEST-QUAL—Participant survey of general impressions (12) FG-QUAL—Focus group with selected parents (13) OBS-QUAN—Checklist for Objective 2
Objective 3 To offer a challenging curriculum (p. 113)	(14) TEST-QUAL—Examination of school portfolios (15) OBS-QUAL—Classroom observations (16) UNOB-QUAL—Minutes of advisory committee meetings (17) QUEST-QUAN—Surveys of staff, parents, and so forth (18) OBS-QUAN—Checklist for Objective 3
Objective 4 To help students achieve equal to or better than control group (p. 114)	(19) TEST-QUAN—Achievement tests, both criterion referenced and norm referenced

Note: Page numbers refer to pages in Luo and Dappen (2005) where the objective is listed. Objective 4 was truncated due to lengthiness.

3. *Cognitive variables*—in the school context, the level of cognitive functioning or knowledge that individuals exhibit

4. *Context variables*—included because effective schooling practices are context sensitive (e.g., Hallinger & Murphy, 1986; Teddlie & Stringfield, 1993; school context factors include socioeconomic status of student body, community type, grade phase of schooling, and governance structure)

Examples of data collection strategies and data sources are also presented in Table 10.4.

Summary

The overall purpose of this chapter was to provide readers with information on the variety of available

Table 10.4   The ABC+ Matrix: A Model for Data Collection in Educational Settings, Including Sample Data Collection Instruments

Level of Analysis	Attitudinal Indicators	Behavioral Indicators	Cognitive Performance Indicators	Context Variables
Student	Attitudinal questionnaires using closed-ended format **QUEST-QUAN**	Observations of a student during a whole school day **OBS-QUAL**	Achievement tests **TEST-QUAN**	Demographic characteristics of students **UNOB-QUAN**
Classroom (or teacher)	Focus group interview with teachers from one grade level **FG-QUAL**	Observations in classrooms using protocols with closed-ended responses **OBS-QUAN**	Portfolio assessing awareness of best practices **TEST-QUAL**	Records on selection and retention of teachers **UNOB-QUAN**
School (or principal)	Interview with principal using open-ended format **INT-QUAL**	Self-report of principal's activities **UNOB-QUAL**	Portfolio demonstrating school change efforts **TEST-QUAL**	Questionnaire asking principal to describe history of school **QUEST-QUAL**
Parent	Individual interviews with parents using open-ended format **INT-QUAL**	Inventory of parental activities at the school **OBS-QUAN**	Test assessing awareness of direct parental involvement **TEST-QUAN**	Photographs of community where parents live **UNOB-QUAL**

Note: This table was adapted and expanded from Teddlie et al. (2002). Each cell of the matrix can contain QUAN, QUAL, or MM data collection strategies. The examples in this table are QUAN or QUAL for simplicity of presentation.

MM data-gathering strategies. We used the Matrix of Data Collection Strategies for Mixed Methods Research, which consists of 18 cells produced by crossing Level 1 (the three major methods) and Level 2 (the six types of data collection strategies).

MM data collection refers to the gathering of both QUAN and QUAL data in a single study. There are two basic MM data collection strategies:

within-strategy MM data collection, which entails the gathering of QUAL and QUAN data using the same data collection strategy, and between-strategies MM data collection, which entails the gathering of QUAL and QUAN data using more than one data collection strategy.

Each of the 18 cells in the matrix was briefly discussed and examples for each were presented. We emphasized that each of the data collection strategies could be used to generate both QUAL and QUAN data.

This chapter presents numerous examples of MM data collection strategies, starting with the simplest combination of data sources (e.g., the within-strategy MM data collection combinations) and concluding with highly complex applications (e.g., the between-strategies MM data collection combinations using numerous sources).

Chapter 11 presents information on the next step of the research process: selecting an appropriate MM data analysis strategy. The chapter starts with a review of QUAL data analysis techniques, followed by a discussion of QUAN data analysis procedures. Most of Chapter 11 is devoted to a discussion of the five MM data analysis strategies that correspond to the five MM design types described in Chapter 7.

Review Questions and Exercises

1. Write a short essay in which you distinguish between methodological orientations, data collection strategies, data collection techniques, and data sources. Provide an example of a specific qualitative data source and the data collection strategy and technique that it represents. Then give an example of a specific quantitative data source and the data collection strategy and technique that it represents.

2. Identify the six basic data collection strategies. Describe a hypothetical research study. Give an example of how each of the six data collection strategies could be used in that study.

3. Distinguish between within-strategy MM data collection and between-strategies MM data collection. Give an example of each.

4. Consider the six data collection strategies. Conduct a literature search to locate a source in which the researchers employed at least three of the strategies. Describe the study, including whether it is a qualitative, quantitative, or mixed study.

5. Describe a hypothetical study in which you would conduct observational research. Describe the roles that you might play when participating as a complete participant as opposed to a complete observer and when participating in a mixed role.

6. Conduct a literature search to locate a source that employs at least one unobtrusive measure plus another data collection technique. Describe the study, including whether it is a qualitative, quantitative, or mixed study.

7. Explain why the focus group strategy is considered a separate data collection strategy. Present a hypothetical study involving focus groups to generate both qualitative and quantitative data. Give examples of the kinds of questions you might ask in this focus group study.

8. Conduct a literature search to find an article or chapter about a study that employed between-strategies MM data collection. Describe the qualitative and quantitative data sources and how they are used to answer the study's research questions.

9. Describe one strength and one weakness of each of the six data collection strategies.

10. Identify three or four of the most popular between-strategies MM data collection combinations. Conduct a literature review and find an example of at least one of these strategies.

11. Provide a hypothetical example of a research study of interest to you that theoretically employs between-strategies MM data collection using several data sources. Describe the data sources and

the data collection strategies that they represent.

12. The Barron et al. (2008) study included on the companion Web site (www.sage pub.com/foundations) required several QUAN and QUAL data sources to answer its research questions. Look at the description of those data sources on pages 5–9 of Appendix B located at www .sagepub.com/foundations. Describe the different types of data collection strategies used in this study and the databases they generated.

Key Terms

Archival records

Artifacts

Attitude scales

Attrition

Between-strategies MM data collection

Covert or nonreactive observations

Focus groups

Fundamental principle of mixed methods research

Interviews

Likert scales

Observational data collection strategy

Participant-observer continuum

Personality inventories

Physical trace evidence

Questionnaires

Rubrics

Tests

Unobtrusive measures (nonreactive measures)

Within-strategy MM data collection

Notes

1. Focus groups of 6–8 participants are considered optimal by many researchers (e.g., Tashakkori & Teddlie, 2003a).

2. The words *questionnaire* and *survey* are used interchangeably in the literature. Nevertheless, we prefer to use the word *questionnaire* to connote a particular data collection strategy that can be combined with other strategies because *survey* is often used to describe a more general orientation known as survey research.

3. Locus of control was popularized by Rotter (1966) and is an often-researched dimension in personality theory (e.g., Lefcourt, 1982). Individuals with an *internal locus of control* believe that their own actions can have an efficacious impact on their environment and the rewards they receive from it. Individuals with an *external locus of control* believe that their own actions do not have much of an impact on their environment and what they receive from it.

4. *Reliability* refers to the consistency of the test in measuring whatever it measures, whereas *validity* refers to the extent to which a test measures whatever it is supposed to measure (e.g., Wiersma & Jurs, 2005). Issues of data/measurement reliability and validity are discussed in more detail in Chapter 9.

5. Between-strategies MM data collection is found more frequently in the MM literature than is within-strategy MM data collection, partially because there are so many more possible combinations with the former.

CHAPTER 11

The Analysis of Mixed Methods Data

Objectives

Upon finishing this chapter, you should be able to:

- Distinguish among and give examples of three types of qualitative data analysis strategies
- Discuss why themes are so important in qualitative data analysis
- Describe the constant comparative method
- Describe phenomenological analyses
- Distinguish between descriptive and inferential statistics
- Distinguish between univariate and multivariate statistical techniques
- Distinguish between parametric and nonparametric statistics
- Describe a study that employed a parallel mixed data analysis strategy
- Describe a study that employed a conversion mixed data analysis strategy
- Describe a study that employed a sequential mixed data analysis strategy
- Explain what fused data analysis and morphed data mean
- Describe a study that employed a multilevel mixed data analysis strategy
- Describe a study that employed fully integrated mixed data analysis strategies
- Describe a technique that uses traditional quantitative analysis to analyze qualitative data

This chapter emphasizes the analysis of data generated in mixed methods (MM) studies, but we begin the chapter with two sections on the analysis of qualitative (QUAL) and quantitative (QUAN) data. The reason for this is simple: Readers need to be acquainted (or reacquainted) with the basic strategies for analyzing QUAL and QUAN data before they can understand how these analysis techniques are combined in MM studies.

Therefore, we first present an overview of data analysis strategies in the QUAL research tradition, including descriptions of the major characteristics of this orientation. Three general types of QUAL analysis, along with examples of each type, are presented.

We then present an overview of data analysis strategies in the QUAN research tradition. Emphasis is placed on three distinctions among these strategies: descriptive versus inferential, univariate versus multivariate, and parametric versus nonparametric.

Then we discuss different types of MM data analysis strategies, which combine the other two types of analysis in one study, and we provide examples of these strategies from the literature. The section on MM data analysis highlights the implementation processes for MM research designs as discussed in Chapter 7 (parallel, conversion, sequential, multilevel, fully integrated), plus application of analytical techniques from one tradition to application in the other.

There are two general issues regarding the similarity of QUAL and QUAN analyses to keep in mind as you read this chapter: The first has to do with the nature of inductive and deductive logic, and the second concerns the continuing evolution of computer programs to analyze QUAL and QUAN data. First, QUAL data analysis is often (but not always) inductive because it is typically used to discover *emergent themes*. Nevertheless, QUAL analytical techniques, such as *analytic induction*, can also have a deductive component, as described later in this chapter.

Similarly, QUAN data analysis is often (but not always) deductive because it is often used to test predictions or hypotheses. Nevertheless, QUAN analysis might also be inductive, especially when used in exploratory studies. Looking for patterns in large archival data sets by examining summary tables and visual displays is an example of this analysis.

Therefore, readers should be aware that no one-to-one correspondence exists between induction and QUAL data analysis or between deduction and QUAN data analysis. Both QUAL and QUAN data analyses can use both inductive and deductive logics.

The second issue to keep in mind is that the most recent versions of QUAL data analysis programs (e.g., NVivo and AtlasTi) are also used for some (often descriptive) statistical analysis. The emergence of these programs is leading to further erosion of the assumed divide between QUAL and QUAN data analyses.

Analysis Strategies for Qualitative Data

Qualitative data analysis is the analysis of various forms of narrative data, including data stored in audio, video, and other formats. These narrative data are usually prepared for analysis by converting raw material into partially processed data, which are then subjected to a particular analysis scheme. There are many ways of analyzing QUAL data and few absolute rules for selecting the most appropriate techniques for any given database. In the following section, we first discuss the general characteristics of the analysis of narrative data and then present information about and examples of three distinct types of QUAL data analyses. (Also, see QUAL analytic terms previously defined in Chapter 2.)

Qualitative Data Analysis Is Inductive, Iterative, and Eclectic

Qualitative data analysis is predominantly inductive in nature. Patton (2002) listed "inductive data analysis and creative synthesis" (p. 41) as one of the 12 major principles of QUAL research. Inductive data analysis involves arguing from particular facts or data to a general theme or conclusion. (Refer to Table 3.1 for a more detailed and complete definition of inductive reasoning.) Therefore, inductive data analysis leads to themes or theoretical criteria that are "grounded in the data, and are not given a priori" (Lincoln & Guba, 1985, p. 344). *Grounded theory* is the most well-known methodology for inductively analyzing QUAL data (e.g., Charmaz, 2000, 2005; Strauss & Corbin, 1998).

As noted in the introduction to this chapter, QUAL data analysis can also involve deductive logic. For instance, some QUAL researchers use a process known as **analytic induction** (e.g., Berg,

2004; Denzin, 1989b; Patton, 2002; Taylor & Bogdan, 1998), which may be defined as follows:

> This strategy involves scanning the data for categories of phenomena and for relationships among such categories, developing working typologies and hypotheses on an examination of initial cases, and then modifying and refining them on the basis of subsequent cases. (LeCompte & Preissle, 1993, p. 254)

A key feature of analytic induction is **negative case analysis**, which involves searching for cases that do *not* fit the expected or established pattern in the QUAL data so one can expand or adapt the emerging hypothesized relationships or theory (e.g., Berg, 2004).

Qualitative data analysis is iterative, involving a back-and-forth process between data collection and data analysis. QUAL data analysis is an iterative process (e.g., Dey, 1993; Patton, 2002) that starts in the field during data collection and continues even as research reports are being written. Taylor and Bogdan (1998) described this concept as follows: "Unlike quantitative research, qualitative research usually lacks a division of labor between data collectors and coders. . . . In qualitative research, data collection and analysis go hand in hand" (p. 141). Repeated combing of the various data sources during and after data collection eventually yields themes.

The iterative nature of QUAL data collection and analysis is different from most QUAN data analysis. In QUAN research, data collection typically concludes before data analysis begins, whereas in QUAL research the data collection often continues while the analysis is ongoing. In both cases, however, the analysis process may be iterative. For example, QUAN researchers might examine and reexamine previously collected data and use different analytic strategies until they are confident that a stable pattern has been found or the hypotheses have been adequately tested.

The differences in the iterative nature of QUAL as opposed to QUAN research follow from distinctions between the deductive and inductive reasoning processes. During the deductive process, a hypothesis might be generated predicting specific results, data are gathered, and then the hypothesis is tested. During the inductive QUAL process, on the other hand, the data are used to build the theory, themes, or conclusions. This process is more iterative than in QUAN research because the researcher-analyst gradually interprets the meaning of each piece of information, and those interpretations change as other data are gathered.

Dey (1993) described the iterative nature of QUAL data analysis as follows:

> It is more realistic to imagine qualitative data analysis as a series of spirals as we loop back and forth through various phases within the broader progress of the analysis. . . . In reading and annotating data, for example, we anticipate the tasks of categorizing and linking the data. While making connections between categories, we review our initial links and categories. At any particular phase in our analysis, we may return to re-reading the data or look forward to producing our account. (pp. 264–265)

Qualitative data analysis is eclectic. It is difficult to "prescribe" a single, particular data analysis scheme for a particular QUAL database (e.g., Coffey & Atkinson, 1996). Typically, each researcher analyzing QUAL data employs an eclectic mix of the available analytical tools that best fit the data set under consideration.

A major reason for this mix is that QUAL databases often require a variety of different analytic techniques to be thoroughly analyzed. When constructing QUAL databases, researchers frequently gather information from a variety of sources. When analyzing observational, interview, and secondary information from the same research study, analysts often have to employ more than one type of analysis to accommodate the differences among the sources.

Denzin and Lincoln (2005b, p. 4) refer to QUAL researchers as *bricoleurs*, who employ a wide range of available data collection methodologies and analysis strategies. According to these authors, the choice of which analytical tools to use is not set in advance but depends on what is available within a particular research context.

The Search for Themes in Qualitative Data Analysis

There is a search for **themes**, which are the dominant features or characteristics of a phenomenon under study, across all types of QUAL data analysis. Most QUAL analytic techniques involve generating **emergent themes** that evolve from the study of specific pieces of information that the investigator has collected. Some QUAL data analyses, on the other hand, use deductive data analysis and **a priori themes** based on theory or extensive research findings (e.g., Miles & Huberman, 1994), but these are not as common.

Although called a variety of different names, **thematic analysis** has been used in virtually all human sciences. Boyatzis (1998) described the process of thematic analysis as a way of "seeing": "Observation precedes understanding. Recognizing an important moment (seeing) precedes encoding it (seeing it as something), which in turn precedes interpretation. Thematic analysis moves you through these three phases of inquiry" (p. 1).

Similarly, Eisner (1998) described thematic analysis with regard to holistic strategy as follows:

> The formulation of themes *within* an educational criticism means identifying the recurring messages that pervade the situation about which the critic writes. Themes are the dominant features of the situation or person, those qualities of place, person, or object that define or describe identity. In a sense, a theme is a pervasive quality. Pervasive qualities tend to permeate and unify situations and objects. (p. 104)

For example, James Spradley (1970) summarized analyses related to the lives of urban nomads (homeless men), as described earlier in Box 7.3 of Chapter 7. Several of his dimensions of contrast concerned a theme he eventually called mobility. One of the analytic domains related to that theme was "stages in making the bucket," which gave an overview of the steps involved in the jailing and later release of urban nomads (the "bucket" being jail).

Three General Types of Qualitative Data Analysis

Several taxonomies of QUAL data analyses have been proposed (e.g., Coffey & Atkinson, 1996; Creswell, 1998; Dey, 1993; Flick, 1998; Maxwell, 1997). In this chapter, we refer to the following three QUAL data analysis strategies:

1. *Categorical strategies* break down narrative data and rearrange those data to produce categories that facilitate comparisons, thus leading to a better understanding of the research questions.

2. *Contextualizing (holistic) strategies* interpret the narrative data in the context of a coherent, whole "text" that includes interconnections among statements, events, and so forth. These techniques involve looking for patterns across the interconnecting narratives. Moustakas (1994) characterized these methods as "focusing on the wholeness of experience rather than solely on its objects or parts" (p. 21).

This distinction between "fracturing" (categorical) strategies and "contextualizing" strategies is a fundamental one (e.g., Mason, 2002; Maxwell, 1997). The "fractured" data are put back together based on similarities, whereas the "contextualized" data are understood based on contiguous information. Atkinson (1992) described this contrast as working with a "patchwork quilt" as opposed to the "whole cloth" (p. 460). Mason (2002) described reasons for using contextualizing strategies: The interrelated elements in the data set are too complicated to be analyzed using categorical strategies; there is an emphasis on

context in the study, such as how phenomena are different in different settings; or the researcher rejects the idea that everything should be indexed into a common set of categories.

3. **Qualitative data displays** are visual presentations of the themes that emerge from QUAL data analysis. Displays may be used to summarize information from either categorical or contextualizing strategies or as a separate data analysis scheme.

Table 11.1 presents a summary of some of the types of techniques associated with the three QUAL data analysis strategies.

The Similarity and Contrast Principles

Two major principles in thematic analysis are the similarity and contrast principles, which Spradley (1979) defined as follows:

1. The **similarity principle** states that the meaning of a symbol can be discovered by finding out how it is similar to other symbols.

2. The **contrast principle** states that the meaning of a symbol can be discovered by finding out how it is different from other symbols. (pp. 157–158)

The similarity principle is used in virtually all of the analytical systems listed in Table 11.1. For example, categories are determined by looking for units of information with similar content (e.g., the constant comparative method) or by looking for terms that can be included under a "cover term" (e.g., Spradley, 1979, 1980). The similarity principle guides the thematic process by facilitating the analyst's search for commonalities in the data.

The contrast principle is explicitly used during the final stage of Spradley's analysis system (1979, 1980). It is also a part of the constant comparative

Table 11.1   Examples of Three Types of Qualitative Data Analyses

General Type	Examples
Categorical	Latent and manifest content analysis
	Constant comparative analysis
	Grounded theory techniques
	Developmental Research Sequence (Spradley, 1979, 1980)
Contextualizing (holistic)	Phenomenological analysis
	Narrative analysis
	Individual case studies
	Ethnographic analysis
	Artistic approaches
	Metaphorical analyses
	Critical theory approaches to QUAL data analysis
Data displays	Effects matrices
	Sociograms
	Concept or mental maps
	Figures and tables associated with Spradley's (1979, 1980) Developmental Research Sequence
	Taxonomic structures (box diagrams, line diagrams, outline forms)

method through the search for mutual exclusivity (i.e., distinctiveness) between the emerging categories. Yin (2003) also used the contrast principle in his comparative case studies when he examined the differences that exist between cases.

Example of a Categorical Strategy: The Constant Comparative Method

The **constant comparative method** for QUAL data analysis, formulated by Glaser and Strauss (1967) and later refined by Lincoln and Guba (1985), among others, is one of the most frequently used categorical strategies. This technique allows analysts to compare different pieces of data, refine or tighten up categories, and move on to higher conceptual levels. Taylor and Bogdan

(1998) asserted that the QUAL researcher using the constant comparative method "simultaneously codes and analyzes data in order to develop concepts. By continually comparing specific incidents in the data, the researcher refines these concepts, identifies their properties, explores their relationships to one another, and integrates them into a coherent theory" (p. 137).

The constant comparative method was described by Glaser and Strauss (1967) as having four stages:

1. Comparing incidents applicable to each category—each "incident" is compared to a category to which it might (or might not) belong

2. Integrating categories and their properties—comparing "incidents" to tentative

versions of rules that will describe the category

3. Delimiting the theory—reducing the original larger list of categories to a parsimonious set of more inclusive, saturated categories

4. Writing the theory (p. 105)

Lincoln and Guba (1985) presented some operational refinements for the constant comparative method, focusing on the initial stages of the Glaser and Strauss (1967) method: unitizing and categorizing. The **unitizing process** involves dividing the narrative data into what we call units of information (UOIs), which are the smallest pieces of meaningful information. UOIs are usually phrases that may be associated with themes, but they may also be words, paragraphs, characters, items, concepts, and so forth (Berg, 2004). Each UOI should be associated with its source, the site where data were gathered, the data collection episode, and so forth.

The **categorizing process** involves bringing together into provisional categories those UOIs that relate to the same content, devising rules that describe category properties, and rendering each category set internally consistent and the entire set mutually exclusive. Reviewing each category for *internal consistency* means that all UOIs included within a category adhere to the same rule that defines that category. Internal consistency is based on the similarity principle. Reviewing across the categories for *mutual exclusivity* means that all categorical definitions are distinct from one another. Mutual exclusivity is based on the contrast principle. The article by Schulenberg (2007), described previously in Box 7.6, contains an interesting example of unitizing and categorizing.

Example of a Contextualizing Strategy: Phenomenological Analysis

Moustakas (1994) expressed the importance of context in QUAL analysis as follows: "The understanding of meaningful concrete relations implicit in the original description of experience *in the context of a particular situation* is the primary target of phenomenological knowledge" (p. 14, italics in original).

We now present an example of a study that used *phenomenology* (previously defined in Chapter 6, Note 6). This exemplar of contextualizing strategies comes from Clark Moustakas's (1994) book on phenomenological research methods. Moustakas (1994) listed several principles of what he called transcendental phenomenology, five of which may be paraphrased as follows:

1. Transcendental phenomenology is concerned with wholeness, which involves examining entities from many perspectives until the "essence" of the phenomenon is revealed.

2. It seeks meaning from "appearances" and arrives at "essences" through "intuition and reflection on conscious acts of experience."

3. It is committed to "descriptions of experiences," not analyses or explanations.

4. The investigator has a "personal interest" in the entity under investigation; therefore, the process is necessarily "autobiographical."

5. The primary evidence of scientific investigation is the investigator's "thinking, intuiting, reflecting, and judging." (pp. 58–60)

Intentionality is an important concept in phenomenology, and Moustakas uses it as a synonym for *consciousness*. As researchers examine any phenomenon, they become intentionally conscious of it by focusing all of their experiences on the essence of that phenomenon. Moustakas (1994) presented an extended example of how one of his students (Cathy) studied the phenomenon of power by examining her own interpersonal relations with family members. See Box 11.1 for a description of Cathy's phenomenological analysis of power.

Box 11.1

Cathy's Phenomenological Understanding of Power

Moustakas (1994) described the understanding of power that his student Cathy developed through a phenomenological exploration:

Power, as developed by Cathy, is the power of the role, the oldest child, consciously and deliberately creating dependencies in order to feel strength, in order to teach others, take care of them, and help them feel secure. Through these ways she evokes in other family members the need for her opinions and approval. Cathy views these qualities as forms of negative power and would prefer to move toward a personal power that focuses on fulfillment of self-interests, yet there remains in her the need to retain her power over others and to some degree over their lives. (p. 64)

Example of Qualitative Displays: Social Network Analysis

QUAL data displays allow analysts to reduce the volume of their data and present those data in a form that permits the reader to visualize the information as a coherent whole. For example, sociometric data can be presented in the form of sociograms (network diagrams), which summarize the complex relationships in a group of people. The field of research associated with the analysis of sociometric data was originally called *sociometry* and is now called *social network analysis*, which involves "the identification and the analysis of the structure of relationships within groups" (Fredericks & Durland, 2005, p. 15).

Sociometric questions are typically very simple; for example, they may ask students to list everyone they talked to in their classroom last week, or they may ask faculty members to indicate the three teachers with whom they talked the most in the past month. Data generated from these simple questions can generate both of the following products:

- *Sociograms* (network diagrams), which are two-dimensional QUAL drawings of relationships among individuals, which provide a visual representation of the social structure that is being studied
- *Sociomatrices*, which are QUAN indices of relationships among social units

Social network analysis is necessarily an MM technique because it generates both QUAL and QUAN results.

Figure 11.1 presents a sociogram of clique formation at an ineffective high school (Kochan & Teddlie, 2005). In this faculty of only 20 teachers, there were several *cliques* and *isolates*. This visual representation of the interpersonal relations among the teachers is highly convincing in demonstrating the dysfunctional dynamics that existed within this ineffective faculty.

Analysis Strategies for Quantitative Data

Quantitative data analysis is the analysis of numeric data using a variety of statistical techniques. There are several different ways of categorizing QUAN data analysis strategies (e.g., Gravetter & Wallnau, 2007; Hinkle, Wiersma, & Jurs, 1998; Jaccard & Becker, 2002; Shavelson, 1996). In this summary, we discuss three distinctions among the numerous QUAN data analysis techniques:

1. Descriptive versus inferential statistics

2. Univariate versus multivariate statistics

3. Parametric versus nonparametric statistics

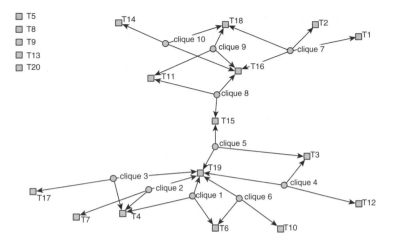

Figure 11.1   Network Analysis (sociogram) of Clique Formation at an Ineffective High School. Boxes represent individual teachers, circles indicate cliques of teachers, and boxes in upper left-hand corner indicate isolated teachers.

Source: Kochan and Teddlie (2005, p. 48).

We first provide an overview of these three distinctions, and then we provide more information about each one. (Also, see QUAN analytic terms previously defined in Chapter 2.)

Most traditional QUAN methods of data analysis may be categorized as either descriptive or inferential methods/statistics. *Descriptive methods* are procedures for summarizing data, with the intention of discovering trends and patterns, and summarizing results for ease of understanding and communication. The outcome of these strategies is usually called *descriptive statistics* and includes results such as frequency tables, means, and correlations.

Inferential techniques are typically generated after descriptive results have been examined. They are normally used for testing hypotheses or for confirming or disconfirming the results obtained from the descriptive results. An example of inferential statistics is the use of *t* tests to determine whether students learning Spanish by one method score better than students taught by a different method. Confirmatory factor analysis is another inferential technique that can be used to confirm or disconfirm the pattern of QUAN

descriptive results that emerged previously from the study. (More information on terms such as *t* tests and factor analysis are presented later in the chapter.)

A second major differentiation for QUAN data analysts is between univariate and multivariate procedures. **Univariate statistics** involve linking *one variable* that is the focal point of the analysis (e.g., a predicted event, a single dependent variable in an experiment) with one or more other variables (e.g., a few predictors in a prediction study, a few independent variables in an experiment). **Multivariate statistics** link *two or more sets of variables to each other*, such as the simultaneous relationship between multiple dependent (predicted) and independent (predictor) variables (e.g., *canonical correlation*). These multivariate analyses are typically followed by simpler univariate ones to determine the more important (a) relationships between variables or (b) differences between groups. For example, if a strong multivariate correlation is found between two sets of variables (e.g., various measures or indicators of mental health and various indicators of socioeconomic status), then the correlation between each single dependent or predicted variable (e.g., depression scores) and the collection of independent variables (or predictors, such as education and income) is explored.

A third important differentiation for QUAN data analysts is between what are called *parametric* and *nonparametric* statistics. This differentiation illustrates that QUAN data analysis techniques greatly depend on the type of data being analyzed. Parametric statistics are very powerful techniques, but they require that the analyzed data meet certain assumptions (i.e., independence, normality, homogeneity of variance), which are described later in this chapter. Such data are gathered using either interval (or ratio)[1] measurement scales. *Interval scales* are scales that measure with order (e.g., a score of 5 is greater than a score of 4, which is greater than a score of 3) and generate numerically equal distances between points on the scale. Many attitude scales and personality inventories, such as the *Likert-type scales* introduced in Chapter 10, are assumed to be interval scales. To summarize, interval scales are analyzed using parametric statistics and generate data sets that can meet the assumptions of those parametric statistics.

Nonparametric statistics "require few if any assumptions about the population under study. They can be used with ordinal and nominal scale data" (Wiersma & Jurs, 2005, p. 391). *Nominal scales* measure variables without order (e.g., open-ended QUAL scales such as the following: What type of school do you attend?). *Ordinal scales* measure with order (i.e., can be used to generate rank order data), but there is no assumption of equal intervals between points on those scales. Nonparametric statistics are generally considered less powerful than parametric statistics, but they can be used to analyze data that are far less structured than data used for interval scales.

Descriptive Statistical Methods

Descriptive statistical methods include techniques for summarizing numeric data in easily interpretable tables, graphs, or single representations of a group of scores. The goal is to be able

to understand the data, detect patterns and relationships, and better communicate the results. These goals are achieved through images, graphs, and summaries that can help the reader understand the nature of the variables and their relationships. The most commonly used methods of descriptive data analysis are summarized in Table 11.2. Please review this table before going on to the next section of the chapter, making sure that you recall these basic terms.

Inferential Statistical Methods

Descriptive statistics are not sufficient for most research purposes, including estimation (i.e., making inferences about a population based on information from a sample) and hypotheses testing. Data analysis methods for testing hypotheses are based on estimations of how much error is involved in obtaining a difference between groups or a relationship between variables.

These data analysis methods are usually classified as *inferential statistical methods*, as defined in Chapter 2. Examples of these methods are the *t* test, which is used to test for significance of differences between two group means, and multiple regression analysis, which is used to determine the degree of relationship between variables. Box 11.2 contains details regarding inferential statistics, including definitions of null and alternative hypotheses, alpha level, and statistical significance. A more detailed discussion of these inferential methods is beyond the scope of this book.

The following brief outline lists some of the most frequently used statistical techniques divided into two categories: determining whether relationships between variables are truly different from zero or comparing means to test for differences between groups:

1. Determining if relationships between variables (correlation coefficients or regression slopes) are truly different from zero:
   A. *t* test for the significance of Pearson *r* from zero
   B. *F* test for the significance of multiple correlation

Table 11.2   Summary of Descriptive Statistics

Descriptive Statistic	Definition	Examples
Frequency tables and graphs	Summary displays of variables and their frequency (or proportion) of occurrence, which may involve one variable or more than one variable at a time	Tables Graphs Contingency tables containing different variables on their rows and columns
Measures of central tendency	Single-score summary of a group of observations/scores	Mode, which is the most frequent score in a group Mean, which is the average of scores (sum divided by number of scores) Median, which is the score at or below which 50% of the scores fall
Measures of variability	Indicate dispersion of scores within a data set; deviation scores, which indicate each score's distance from the mean	Deviation scores, such as average deviation and variance Standard deviation, which is the most widely used indicator of the average difference between the mean and individual scores
Measures of relative standing	Single indicators of the relative position of a score in relation to others	Percentile rank, which is the percent of scores that fall at or below a specific score z score Standard score
Measures of association/ relationship	Single indicators of the degree of relationship between two or more variables	Correlation coefficients, which indicate the strength of the relationships between variables (e.g., Pearson's correlation coefficient)

    C. t test for the significance of slopes in multiple regression analysis

2. Testing differences between group means:
    A. z test to compare the mean of a sample with the mean of a population
    B. t tests to compare the means of two samples:
        i. Independent sets of observations: t test for independent groups
        ii. Nonindependent sets of observations (matched groups, repeated observations, etc.): t test for nonindependent groups

    C. Analysis of variance (ANOVA) to compare the means of two or more samples or to compare means in factorial designs (those with more than one independent variable)

Box 11.2

Basics of Inferential Statistical Analysis: The Null Hypothesis, Alpha Levels, and Statistical Significance

In inferential statistical analysis, tests of statistical significance provide information regarding the possibility that the results are due to chance and random error, versus a true relationship between variables. If the results are statistically significant, then the researchers conclude that the results did not occur by chance alone.

Inferential statistics are methods of estimating the degree of such chance variation. Additionally, they provide information regarding the magnitude of the relationship or effect. Here are some definitions related to inferential statistical analysis:

- **Null hypothesis** states that there is no difference between group means or no relationship between variables.
- *Alternative hypothesis* states that there is a true difference between groups or relationship among variables.
- *Alpha level* is the maximum probability at which the null hypothesis is rejected. By convention, this is typically set at .05.
- **Statistical significance** is the determination that the null hypothesis can be rejected based on obtained differences between group means or relationships between variables. The obtained probability of occurrence by chance (p) is compared to the alpha level to decide if a finding is *statistically significant*. For example, if alpha is set at .05 before the study starts, and if the obtained probability is less than that alpha (i.e., if $p < .05$), then the results are considered statistically significant (i.e., the null hypothesis is rejected).

D. Analysis of covariance (ANCOVA) to compare the means of two or more samples while controlling for the variation due to an extraneous variable

Wood and Williams (2007) conducted a study that is an example of statistical analyses (Pearson correlation coefficients) used to determine *whether the relationships between variables are truly different from zero.* They collected 12 retrospective self-reports of gambling behavior plus a diary estimate of daily gambling. They wanted to determine which of the retrospective self-report items was more highly correlated with the diary rating, which (based on previous research) is an accurate measure of actual gambling. Correlations of .50 or higher indicate large effect sizes (e.g., Cohen, 1988). Only one self-report item had a *positive correlation* with the diary

entries of that size: an estimate of how much time was spent on specific gambling activities each day. The .72 correlation coefficient was significant: $p < .001$. The authors concluded that the self-report item estimating the amount of time spent on specific gambling activities was the best single item to use on retrospective surveys because it was the most highly correlated with a measure known to accurately assess actual gambling (the diary ratings).

The Lasserre-Cortez (2006) research described in Chapter 6, Box 6.4, is an example of a study with statistical analyses *testing the differences between group means.* Hypothesis 1 tested the difference between the means of two different groups of schools (professional action research collaboratives, or PARCs, vs. comparison schools). Hypothesis 2 tested the difference between the means of two different groups of teachers

(teachers in PARC schools vs. teachers in comparison schools). The *t* test analyses of the two hypotheses indicated that results supported Hypothesis 1 at the $p < .01$ level but failed to support Hypothesis 2.

Univariate Versus Multivariate Methods

The previous section was concerned with *univariate statistics*, which are based on one (dependent) variable, or, in the case of correlations, they represent the relationship between one variable and one or more other variables. Though these univariate applications are important, much research in the human sciences addresses the simultaneous relationships among sets of variables. The "real world" is rarely univariate with one variable at a time being related to or shaped by others, and the same applies to most research in human sciences.

For example, assume that you are interested in finding the relationship between success in college and a combination of contextual and personal variables. Success in college is often defined by more than one indicator. A correlation between multiple indicators of success (e.g., grade point average, length of time to graduation) and a *combination* of other variables (e.g., high school grade point average, parental education, parental income) is a multivariate correlation (i.e., *canonical correlation*). On the other hand, the correlation between grade point average (alone) and the combination of other variables is a univariate correlation (known as a *multiple correlation*).

In multiple regression analysis, researchers predict one variable (such as college grade point average) from a set of predictors. Multiple correlation summarizes the adequacy of the prediction.

On the other hand, if researchers predict a combination of indicators of success from a combination of other variables, they have a multivariate regression/prediction. In such a case, the adequacy of the prediction is summarized by canonical correlation coefficients. For example,

researchers might be interested in determining the canonical correlation between self-efficacy, academic self-concept, and previous year's grade point average with the combination of three indicators of achievement (math, science, and reading test scores) of high school students.

Examples of other multivariate methods are multivariate analysis of variance (MANOVA) and factor analysis. MANOVA and its variations (see Stevens, 2002; Tabachnick & Fidell, 2007) are used to compare the differences between a combination of variables between groups. In exploratory factor analysis, the objective is to determine the underlying dimensions (constructs) of a set of measures/variables. In confirmatory factor analysis and its variants, such as structural equation modeling, the objective is to ascertain whether the predicted structure of the construct occurs in the data and to test hypotheses about such occurrences.

It can be argued that almost all topics studied in QUAN research are in truth multivariate. Even in simple experiments, a good researcher collects data on multiple indicators of the dependent variable. Therefore, it is probable that as an MM researcher, your QUAN strand will include relationships between sets of variables, with each set representing multiple indicators of a construct. As a result, you should always start with multivariate analysis before you engage in a larger number of disparate univariate analyses. For example, if you are comparing three groups of participants, and you have a set of "dependent" variables, you would start with MANOVA or multivariate analysis of covariance (MANCOVA). If you find that the multivariate differences between the groups are statistically significant, then you compare the groups on one dependent variable at a time, using ANOVA or ANCOVA. Each univariate test is tested at a reduced alpha (e.g., a Bonferroni-adjusted alpha; see Tabachnick & Fidell, 2007), rather than the overall alpha (e.g., the overall alpha of .05, referred to in Box 11.2).

For example, Orihuela (2007), in a recent dissertation, compared two groups of teachers: one whose members had taken a course in instructional strategies, the other whose members had not taken the course. The two groups were compared on two sets of variables, each consisting of six instructional components. A MANOVA conducted on each set showed that the two groups were significantly different on the combination of variables (tested at alpha = .05). Orihuela followed up each of these two multivariate differences with a set of univariate analysis of variances, each tested at an adjusted alpha of .008 (.05 divided by 6). Box 11.3 presents Orihuela's dissertation in more detail.

Table 11.3 provides a brief list of important QUAN inferential data analytic techniques.

Parametric Versus Nonparametric Statistical Methods

As noted earlier, the difference between parametric and nonparametric statistics depends on the measurement scales used: Parametric statistics use data obtained from interval (and ratio) scales, whereas nonparametric scales use data obtained from nominal and ordinal scales.

Box 11.3
Example of MANOVA for Testing Differences Between Groups

Orihuela's (2007) main purpose for conducting the study was to explore the degree to which theoretically effective teaching strategies taught in a course during initial teacher training in college were implemented by teachers in their actual classroom teaching practices. Orihuela used a multivariate ex post facto design, including classroom observations of 72 teachers: One group (n = 36) consisted of teachers who had taken a general instructional strategies course in their previous college training, and the other group consisted of those who had not (n = 36). Orihuela developed and used an observation protocol to quantitize the degree of use of effective instructional strategies in the classroom. His observers also took open-ended field notes during classroom observations.

He used MANOVA to compare the teaching strategies (set, effective explanation, hands-on activity, cooperative learning activity, higher order questioning, and closure) of the groups. Results showed a statistically significant multivariate difference between the groups, in favor of the group that had taken the course. He then followed with univariate tests of the dependent variables. Univariate ANOVAs indicated significant differences between the two groups in five of the six areas.

He also conducted a second MANOVA to compare the groups on the effective use of attending behaviors (e.g., teacher movement, eye contact, body language, physical space, verbal acknowledgments, use of visuals, and voice inflection, modulation, and pitch). Once again, he found a multivariate difference between them. Subsequent univariate ANOVAs on the related dependent variables showed significant differences between the two groups in five of the six variables in this category. The group that had taken the course implemented the strategies more effectively.

Orihuela concluded that specific skills often taught in preservice teaching-methods courses are transferred to actual practices in classroom. Qualitative analysis of the field notes revealed pervasive differences in the behaviors and practices of teachers, beyond the specific quantitized indicators discussed earlier. Combination of the two sets of inferences provided a more general and meaningful meta-inference than would have been possible on the basis of either sets of findings.

Table 11.3   Illustrative List of Inferential Quantitative Data Analysis Techniques Used in the Social and Behavioral Sciences

Techniques That Function to Summarize or Find Patterns/Relationships Among Variables	Techniques That Function to Test Hypotheses
Canonical correlation/regression	t test for independent samples
Multiple correlation/regression	MANOVA → ANOVA
Bivariate correlation (r, phi, rho)/regression	MANCOVA → ANCOVA
Exploratory Factor Analysis	Discriminant analysis
Confirmatory factor analysis	Sign test
Path analysis	Wilcoxon matched pairs
Structural equation modeling	
Hierarchical linear models	
Logistic regression	
Chi-square test of independence/association	
Cluster analysis	

Individuals using parametric statistics must be aware of four assumptions associated with their use (e.g., Wiersma & Jurs, 2005):

- The dependent variable(s) must be measured with an interval (or ratio) scale.
- The observations or scores of one individual are not influenced by those of another (i.e., assumption of independence).
- The dependent variables are selected from a population that is normally distributed (i.e., assumption of normality; refer to Box 8.2).
- When two or more populations are being studied, they should have about the same variance within their distribution of scores (i.e., homogeneity of variance).

We introduce these assumptions of parametric statistics to underscore the point that MM researchers must be aware of the assumptions associated with both statistical (QUAN) and thematic (QUAL) analyses when conducting their research.

Strategies for Analyzing Mixed Methods Data

Overview of Mixed Methods Data Analysis

MM data analysis involves the processes whereby QUAN and QUAL data analysis strategies are combined, connected, or integrated in research studies. Several authors have classified different MM data analysis strategies (e.g., Caracelli & Greene, 1993; Creswell & Plano Clark, 2007; Onwuegbuzie & Teddlie, 2003; Rao & Woolcock, 2003; Tashakkori & Teddlie, 1998). An excellent set of examples of MM data analysis in international development research may be found in Nastasi et al. (2007).

Jennifer Greene (2007) recently presented an insightful summary of MM data analysis strategies that included phases of analysis and analysis strategies that correspond with those phases. Following are her four phases of analysis:

- Data transformation
- Data correlation and comparison

- Analysis for inquiry conclusions and inferences
- Using aspects of the analytic framework of one methodological tradition within the analysis of data from another tradition (this is referred to as a "broad idea"). (p. 155)

We provide details on some of Greene's insightful MM analysis strategies later in this chapter.

Our typology of MM data analysis strategies in this chapter differs somewhat from one we presented a decade ago (Tashakkori & Teddlie, 1998). This time, we organized the typology of MM data analysis strategies around the five types of MM design implementation processes presented in Box 7.4, plus applications of analytical techniques from one tradition to the other. Thus, Chapters 7 and 11 are linked by common MM typologies, one based on designs and the other on analyses. Box 11.4 contains an overview of our MM data analysis typology:

- Parallel mixed data analysis
- Conversion mixed data analysis
- Sequential mixed data analysis
- Multilevel mixed data analysis

- Fully integrated mixed data analysis
- Application of analytic frameworks of one tradition to data analysis within another tradition

As with the MM design typology (Chapter 7), we caution that the list of MM data analysis strategies in Box 11.4 is not exhaustive because of their capacity to mutate into other forms. For example, the subcategory *iterative sequential mixed data analysis strategies* (described later) has an ever-expanding set of members depending on how many strands it takes to answer the research questions (both a priori and emerging) under study.

Before discussing these alternative data analysis techniques, we first present some issues to consider before initiating MM analyses.

Preanalysis Considerations

Onwuegbuzie and Teddlie (2003) presented 12 preanalysis considerations for researchers to contemplate. We discuss some of the important considerations in the following paragraphs.

Box 11.4
Typology of Mixed Methods Data Analysis Techniques

1. *Parallel Mixed Data Analysis* (parallel analysis of QUAL and QUAN data from different data sources)

2. *Conversion Mixed Data Analysis*
   A. Quantitizing narrative data
   B. Qualitizing numeric data, including profile formation
   C. Inherently mixed data analysis techniques

3. *Sequential Mixed Data Analysis*
   A. Sequential QUAL→QUAN analyses, including typology development
   B. Sequential QUAN→QUAL analyses, including typology development
   C. Iterative sequential mixed analysis

4. *Multilevel Mixed Data Analysis*

5. *Fully Integrated Mixed Data Analysis*

6. *Application of Analytical Techniques From One Tradition to the Other*

The first preanalysis consideration concerns the purpose of the MM research study. Greene, Caracelli, and Graham (1989) presented a list of purposes for MM research (e.g., complementarity, expansion), which has been augmented by others. (See Table 7.3 for a revised list of these purposes.) Researchers can match the purpose of their studies with particular mixed data analysis strategies during the preanalysis phase. For example, if the purpose of the MM research study is complementarity, then the QUAN and QUAL analyses should seek to determine the degree to which the research strands yield complementary results regarding the same phenomenon. Complementarity is assessed most often using parallel mixed designs and analyses.

If the purpose of the MM research study is expansion, then it is likely that a sequential mixed design will be used and the QUAL analysis will expand on the initial understanding gained from the QUAN analysis, or vice versa. We should also note that the purpose for using MM often emerges during or shortly after the first strand of a study; therefore, appropriate mixed data analysis strategies cannot always be developed beforehand.

A second preanalysis consideration concerns whether the MM research study is more variable oriented or case oriented (e.g., Greene, 2007; Miles & Huberman, 1994; Ragin, 1987; Ragin & Zaret, 1983). Case-oriented research looks at the complexity of a phenomenon within its context, whereas variable-oriented research examines a phenomenon from the perspective of identifying important variables. The former is more characteristic of QUAL research, and the latter is more typical of QUAN research. This preanalysis consideration affects the emphasis that researchers give to QUAL or QUAN analytic strategies and to their assumptions.

A third preanalysis consideration is whether the MM research study is primarily exploratory or confirmatory. We have emphasized that both QUAL and QUAN research can be used for both exploratory and confirmatory purposes. Therefore, your MM project might be exploratory, confirmatory, or both (an advantage of MM research). Being aware of the confirmatory or exploratory nature of your MM study and each of its strands helps you plan more effective analytic strategies.

A fourth preanalysis consideration concerns the extent to which researchers anticipate that the QUAL and QUAN data analyses will inform each other during the overall analytical process. If the two sets of data analyses occur separately and neither follows up on the other during the process, then it is likely that the researcher will be undertaking a parallel mixed analysis. On the other hand, if there is a definite order to the QUAL and QUAN analyses, with one informing or shaping the other, then the overall strategy is likely to be one of the sequential mixed data analyses.

A fifth preanalysis consideration specifies that MM researchers should be aware of the assumptions that underlie both QUAN and QUAL data analysis techniques. These assumptions are straightforward for QUAN parametric analyses, which were described earlier (e.g., assumption of normality). Assumptions associated with QUAL data collection and analyses are not spelled out as clearly, but many researchers understand that issues related to trustworthiness and credibility are very important in QUAL studies.[2] Onwuegbuzie and Teddlie (2003) emphasized the importance associated with persistent observations, prolonged engagement, and triangulation as techniques that underlie the trustworthiness of QUAL data collection and analysis. (These techniques are discussed in Chapters 9 and 12.)

A sixth preanalysis consideration concerns the use of data analysis tools, especially computer software. Whereas the use of software for QUAN analysis is expected in most studies, the use of QUAL-oriented computer software requires a bit more consideration. Computer-assisted QUAL data analysis has been discussed often in the past 15–20 years (e.g., Bazeley, 2003; Creswell, 1998; Miles & Huberman, 1994; Richards, 1999; Tesch, 1990). Several software programs for QUAL data analysis (e.g., NVivo, ATLAS.ti) are particularly suitable for categorizing strategies and data display. The applicability of QUAL software programs to contextualizing analysis is more problematic.

Patricia Bazeley (2003, 2006, 2007) has made important contributions to the area of the computerized analysis of MM data. Bazeley discussed transferring QUAN data to a QUAL program, transferring QUAL data to a QUAN program, integrating text (including audio, pictorial, video material) and statistical analysis in the same project, fusing QUAL and QUAN data analysis, and so forth. Whether to use QUAL software and to create computerized, mixed databases are important, practical issues to deliberate before beginning MM data analysis.

See Onwuegbuzie and Teddlie (2003) for a discussion of other MM preanalysis considerations. The remainder of this chapter presents details regarding the mixed data analyses introduced in Box 11.4.

Parallel Mixed Data Analysis

The first analysis strategy that we discuss is related to the parallel mixed designs illustrated in Chapter 7, Figure 7.4. Parallel mixed analysis is probably the most widely used MM data analysis strategy in the human sciences, and it has been associated with other design concepts, such as triangulation and convergence. This analysis strategy has been discussed from the earliest writings on MM data analysis (e.g., Caracelli & Greene, 1993) and continues to be a topic in the literature (e.g., Creswell & Plano Clark, 2007; Greene, 2007).

Parallel mixed data analysis involves two *separate* processes: QUAN analysis of data, using descriptive/inferential statistics for the appropriate variables, and QUAL analysis of data, using thematic analysis related to the relevant narrative data.[3] Although the two sets of analyses are independent, each provides an understanding of the phenomenon under investigation. These understandings are linked, combined, or integrated into meta-inferences.

Also, although the two sets of analyses are by design independent, in practice the investigators might allow their knowledge of one to shape their analysis of the other. The best analogy is that researchers allow the two sets of analyses to "talk to each other" in at least a semi-iterative

manner. These analyses can lead to convergent or divergent results.

The following process occurs in these parallel designs with their attendant parallel mixed analyses:

- QUAN and QUAL research strands are planned and implemented to answer related aspects of research questions regarding the same phenomenon. There are at least two parallel and relatively independent research strands, one with QUAN questions and the other with QUAL questions.
- QUAN and QUAL data collection procedures occur in a parallel and separate manner.
- QUAN and QUAL data analysis procedures then follow in a parallel and separate manner. The QUAN data analyses generate inferences regarding the QUAN-oriented questions, while the QUAL data analyses are used to generate inferences regarding the QUAL-oriented questions. Some informal "cross-talk" between strands may occur during analysis.
- Inferences made on the basis of the results from each strand are then integrated or synthesized to form *meta-inferences* at the end of the study. These meta-inferences are conclusions generated through an integration of the inferences that were obtained from both strands of the study.

The relative separateness of the QUAN and QUAL analyses is very important in certain research settings. For instance, Box 11.5 presents the use of a parallel design with separate analyses in a complex international research setting (Rao and Woolcock, 2003).

The parallel analysis of QUAL and QUAN data from different data sources also occurs in much simpler research settings, such as that described by Parasnis, Samar, and Fischer (2005). This study (previously discussed in Chapters 8 and 10) used the same protocol (with both closed-ended and open-ended items) to answer interlocking research questions. Selected deaf students from two higher education institutions

---

Box 11.5

An Example of Parallel MM Data Analysis and Inference Processes: Guatemala Poverty Assessment Project

Two separate teams were responsible for collecting the qualitative and quantitative data. Previous survey material was used to help identify the appropriate sites for the qualitative work (five pairs of villages representing the five major ethnic groups in Guatemala), but the findings themselves were treated as an independent source of data and were integrated with the quantitative material only in the write-up phase of both the various background papers and the final report—that is, while useful in their own right, the qualitative data did not inform the design or construction of the quantitative survey, which was done separately. These different data sources were especially helpful in providing a more accurate map of the spatial and demographic diversity of the poor, as well as, crucially, a sense of the immediate context within which poverty was experienced by different ethnic groups, details of the local mechanisms that excluded them from participation in mainstream economic and civic activities, and the nature of the barriers they encountered in their efforts to advance their interests and aspirations. The final report also benefited from a concerted effort to place both the qualitative and quantitative findings in their broader historical and political context, a first for a World Bank poverty study. (Rao & Woolcock, 2003, p. 173)

---

were sent questionnaires that included 32 closed-ended and 3 open-ended items. Data from the two strands were gathered and analyzed separately, and the results of both strands were integrated in the meta-analysis phase.

The 32 closed-ended items were analyzed using a series of ANOVAs that compared responses of different groups of deaf students on issues such as diversity and their perceptions of their college environment. Thematic analysis was used to analyze the narrative responses to the three open-ended items. Parasnis et al. (2005) concluded that the "qualitative data analyses supported quantitative data analyses and provided rich detail that facilitated interpretation of deaf students' experiences related to racial/ethnic identity" (p. 47).

Another example of parallel mixed analysis from Lopez and Tashakkori (2006) (previously discussed in Chapter 7) is located in Box 11.6.

The parallel analysis of QUAL and QUAN data from different sources can lead to either convergent or divergent meta-inferences. Greene (2007) perceptively emphasized the importance of divergent

results in mixed research: "Convergence, consistency, and corroboration are overrated in social inquiry. The interactive mixed methods analyst looks just as keenly for instances of divergence and dissonance, as these may represent important nodes for further and highly generative analytic work" (p. 144). Other writers have reiterated the value of discrepant results in MM research (e.g., Deacon, Bryman, & Fenton, 1998; Erzberger & Kelle, 2003; Erzberger & Prein, 1997; Johnson & Turner, 2003; Schulenberg, 2007). In Chapter 2, we argued that the ability to provide a greater assortment of divergent views was one of the major advantages of MM.

Trend's (1979) evaluation study presented in Chapter 1 is an excellent example of how a parallel mixed study can generate divergent results that may then be creatively resolved. The basic steps in that study follow:

• While the study became mixed as it evolved, it began with two distinct QUAL and QUAL components.

Box 11.6

Example of Parallel Mixed Analysis

A study by Lopez and Tashakkori (2006) compared the effects of two types of bilingual education programs (two-way, transitional) on the attitudes and academic achievement of fifth-grade students. The two-way program emphasized a dual language model (English, Spanish), whereas the transitional program emphasized English only. In the QUAN strand, several MANOVAs and ANOVAs were run to determine the effect of the two programs on standardized achievement tests in academic subjects, linguistic competence in English and Spanish, and measures of self-perceptions and self-beliefs. QUAN results indicated no significant differences between the two groups on standardized tests of academic achievement, but there were significant differences on the other measures of achievement and the affective indicators.

The QUAL component of the Lopez and Tashakkori study consisted of interviews with a random sample of 32 students in the two programs. The narrative data from these interviews were analyzed and yielded four themes that indicated that students in the two-way program were more likely to express positive attitudes toward bilingualism than were students in the transitional program. The results were then integrated in the meta-inference phase of the study. The authors concluded that the mixed data demonstrated that two-way and transitional programs have differential effects, with the two-way programs having a more positive effect on the pace at which oral language is acquired, proficiency in Spanish, and attitudes toward bilingualism. The additional QUAN measures (beyond standardized achievement tests) and the QUAL interviews yielded a more detailed analysis of the effect of two-way programs than had previous monomethod studies (QUAN only) of the same phenomenon.

- The QUAN component had its own research questions and data collection and analysis procedures. QUAN analyses included numeric counts of households enrolled in the program, analysis of customer satisfaction, and cost analysis for the different sites. The QUAN results indicated that certain preestablished program goals had been met.

- The QUAL component had its own (emerging) research questions, data collection procedures, and data analysis procedures. Themes emerged that indicated that there were serious problems (e.g., office strife, managerial incompetence) at one of the sites that had not been captured by the QUAN analysis.

- Trend and an observer reanalyzed the mixed data several times (through the *meta-inference*

process), looking for information that might help them reconcile the results. They discovered that different processes were working at rural and urban sites and thus were able to write a report that resolved many of the discrepancies between the QUAL and QUAN results: The program was working in *certain contexts* but not others.

Parallel mixed designs and data analysis techniques remain popular alternatives for mixed research, as indicated by recent examples (e.g., Bernardi, Keim, & Lippe, 2007; Driscoll, Appiah-Yeboah, Salib, & Rupert, 2007). The type of separate parallel mixed analysis described thus far has been referred to as *parallel tracks* analysis (e.g., Greene, 2007; Li, Marquart, & Zercher, 2000). Datta (2001) noted that in parallel tracks analyses "the analyses are conducted independently, according to the standards of quality and excellence for each method. The findings are brought together after each strand has been taken to the point of reaching conclusions" (p. 34).

On the other hand, some researchers allow the two sets of parallel analyses to "talk to each other" during the analysis phase. This has been called the *crossover tracks* analysis (e.g., Greene, 2007; Li et al., 2000). Datta (2001) noted that in crossover tracks analysis "findings from the various methodological strands intertwine and inform each other throughout the study" (p. 34). Therefore, the findings from the QUAL analysis inform the analysis of the QUAN data, and vice versa.

Thus, the simple parallel mixed analyses can be made more complex by the following actions:

- Having more than two strands in the design
- Allowing the analysis of the strands to inform one another by mixing those analyses in earlier phases of the study, rather than waiting for the meta-inference stage (i.e., cross-tracks analysis)
- Consolidating the QUAL and QUAN data sets early in the study and analyzing them together (i.e., the *single-track* analysis; Li et al., 2000)
- Combining the parallel mixed analysis with other types of mixed analysis strategies (e.g., conversion, sequential) in studies involving more complex designs

Conversion Mixed Data Analysis

The conversion mixed data analysis strategies are related to designs illustrated in Chapter 7, Figures 7.3 and 7.6. Following are three of these strategies:

1. Quantitizing narrative data

2. Qualitizing numeric data, including profile formation

3. Inherently mixed data analysis techniques

Conversion mixed data analysis occurs when collected QUAL data are converted into numbers (*quantitizing*) or QUAN data are converted into narratives or other types of QUAL data (*qualitizing*). Data conversion (or transformation) is one of the unique characteristics of MM design and data analysis.

In conversion mixed data analysis, data are gathered at the same time because there is only one data source. Then two types of data are generated, first in the form of the original source, which is then converted into the other form. Conversion mixed data analysis is distinguished from concurrent and sequential mixed data analyses in that there is only one original data source in the former case, while there are at least two original data sources in the latter cases.

Quantitizing narrative data is the process whereby QUAL data are transformed into numerical data that can be analyzed statistically (e.g., Miles & Huberman, 1994; Tashakkori & Teddlie, 1998). In most cases, QUAL data are converted into narrative categories, which are then converted into numeric codes (e.g., 0, 1 or 1, 2, 3), which can then be analyzed statistically. As noted by Elliott (2005), "Categorical approaches resemble traditional content analysis and are more amenable to quantitative or statistical methods of analysis" (p. 38) than are contextualizing approaches. Box 11.7 presents an illustration of quantitizing.

Quantitizing might involve a simple frequency count of certain themes or responses. Conversely, it may consist of more complex ratings of the strength or intensity of those themes or responses. Simple descriptive statistics might be used to summarize frequency counts. More complex inferential statistics might be performed on the transformed data that include ratings of strength or intensity.

We discussed several examples of quantitizing data in Chapter 7 (e.g., Miles & Huberman, 1994; Morse, 1989; Sandelowski, Harris, & Holditch-Davis, 1991). These examples included converting the following QUAL data into numeric codes: teenage mothers' use of childish modes of speech, descriptions of the "roughness" or "smoothness" of school improvement processes, and deliberations of couples regarding amniocentesis.

Box 11.7

Example of Quantitizing Narrative Data

Teddlie and Stringfield (1993) analyzed a large QUAL database consisting of classroom observations gathered by researchers in a longitudinal study of school/teacher effectiveness. There were eight matched pairs of schools in the study and each pair included a more effective school and a less effective school based on prior achievement. More than 700 classroom observations were conducted using an open-ended instrument with 15 prompts representing indicators of teaching effectiveness.

The researchers analyzed more than 10,000 open-ended responses. The investigators wanted to make some overall conclusions concerning whether or not better teaching was ongoing in the more effective schools compared to the less effective ones. To expedite this analysis, the researchers quantitized 10 of the 15 open-ended responses using a process in which raters first coded each narrative response into one of three categories:

1. This response contained evidence of effective teaching behavior regarding the particular teaching component.
2. This response contained evidence of contradictory teaching behavior regarding the particular teaching component.
3. This response indicated an absence of effective teaching behavior regarding the particular teaching component.

These codes were converted into numeric ratings, with 1 indicating evidence of effective teaching, 2 indicating contradictory evidence, and 3 indicating absence of effective teaching. MANOVAs and univariate ANOVAs were conducted, and statistically significant results were found overall and for 9 of the 10 individual indicators. This study demonstrated that teachers in more effective schools display better teaching skills than those from less effective ones.

A recent example of quantitizing data demonstrates how researchers can make effective use of software programs to transform and analyze narrative data. Driscoll et al. (2007) undertook a mixed study in which they had both narrative (i.e., QUAL open-ended survey data and interview data) and numeric data (i.e., QUAN closed-ended survey data). The study examined the perceptions of federal agency officials regarding vaccine-safety guidelines and reports. The researchers wanted to quantitize the QUAL data and then perform statistical analyses on the combined database. They undertook five steps to do this:

1. The survey data were entered into an Access database. . . . This process was fairly straightforward and similar to that used to manage any structured database.

2. The qualitative data were analyzed for codes or themes using NVivo. These codes were then developed into qualitative response categories that were entered into a second Access database.

3. These two databases were linked by key informant identification numbers to ensure that each record contained both the survey and in-depth interview data.

4. The coded qualitative data were then quantified into dichotomous variables (0 or 1) based on absence or presence of each coded response.

5. Associations were analyzed using SAS. (p. 22)

The combined QUAN and quantitized database was analyzed using chi square analysis. Discrepancies in the QUAN analysis were explained using the quantitized variables, which had *not* initially been gathered for that purpose. This study is a good example of how QUAL data can be quantitized and then analyzed statistically using a series of easily accessible computer programs (Access, NVivo, and SAS in this particular case).

Qualitizing Numeric Data, Including Profile Formation

Qualitizing narrative data is the process whereby QUAN data are transformed into QUAL categories or some other narrative form (e.g., Onwuegbuzie & Teddlie, 2003; Tashakkori & Teddlie, 1998). John Creswell and Vicki Plano Clark (2007) wrote about the opportunities that the qualitizing (and quantitizing) processes currently provide:

> More work needs to be done to expand the techniques for quantifying qualitative data and to develop the analysis options for such transformed data. Writers have written even less about transforming quantitative data into qualitative data. This area is ripe for researcher innovation and future research. (p. 188)

The simplest of the qualitizing techniques takes a distribution of numeric data on a single variable and then generates separate narrative categories based on subranges of values within that distribution. This is such a common procedure that we often do not see it as an MM technique. A simple example involves taking the range of hours completed in an undergraduate degree program (requiring 128 hours for completion) and classifying students into groups: freshman (0–32 hours), sophomores (33–64 hours), juniors (65–96 hours), and seniors (97–128 hours). Ivankova, Creswell, and Stick (2006) performed a more complicated version of this process when they formed four categories of graduate students in their study, as explained in Appendix A (pp. 7, 16) on the companion Web site (www.sagepub.com/foundations).

More complex examples of qualitizing are found throughout the human sciences:

- We described a study by Taylor and Tashakkori (1997) in Chapter 7 that generated four profiles of teachers (empowered, disenfranchised, involved, disengaged) based on their responses to questionnaire items asking about their desire to participate in decision making and their reports of actual involvement in decisions. QUAN scores on those two dimensions were converted into the four QUAL profiles.

- Sandelowski (2003) described a general process for qualitizing in which the researcher uses QUAN cluster analysis[4] to generate groups of individuals who are different from one another based on their responses to questionnaires or other data collection tools. These groups are then assigned categorical names based on their characteristics.

- Ben Jaafar (2006) used the process described by Sandelowski (2003) to identify three administrator groups (consequence-inclined, consequence-disinclined, and moderate) based on a cluster analysis of their responses to a secondary school administrator survey.

- Onwuegbuzie and Teddlie (2003) described an evaluation study in which the researchers used frequency distributions of numeric responses to 12 activities associated with aquatic resource education to generate two distinct categories of wildlife agents.

A common element in these examples of qualitizing data is the generation of QUAL categories (profiles), which then can be used in further analyses. These qualitizing techniques have been called *narrative profile formation*[5] (e.g., Tashakkori & Teddlie, 1998). We identified five narrative profile prototypes based on how they are generated: average, comparative, holistic, modal, and normative. Box 11.8 defines these different narrative profile prototypes.

We now present a few more details regarding some of the narrative profiles prototypes presented in Box 11.8. An example of *comparative profiles* comes from a study by Fals-Stewart, Birchler, Schafer, and Lucente (1994). In this study of more than 100 couples seeking marital therapy, five distinct "types" of couples were identified through a cluster analysis of their scores on the Minnesota Multiphasic Personality Inventory (MMPI), a clinical/personality test. The five obtained groups were labeled: conflicted, depressed, dissatisfied wives, domestic calm, and dysphoric. A verbal profile of the depressed type indicated that it "consisted of partners who were generally anxious, worried, and pessimistic in their general outlook at the time of the testing. These individuals show a narrowing of interests, low frustration tolerance,

poor morale, and generally are lacking in self-confidence" (p. 235).

Normative profiles are based on the comparison of an individual or a group with a standard (e.g., a test norm, a specific population) and are common in clinical psychology and psychiatry. An example of a normative profile is found in a study by Wetzler, Marlowe, and Sanderson (1994) in which a number of clinical/personality inventories were administered to a group of depressed patients. Each patient was identified with code types resulting from comparison of their scores with the test norms for each test. Narrative profiles of these types were then constructed. For example, the "incapacitated depressive type" was described as "confused, ineffective, and unable to see solutions to problems. They have impaired memory and concentration" (p. 762).

As noted in Box 11.8, some narrative profiles might be mixed (i.e., some combination of the five prototypes). For example, a profile might be based on most frequent attributes, some averages,

---

Box 11.8

Five Prototypes of Narrative Profiles Based on Qualitizing Techniques

Tashakkori and Teddlie (1998) identified five types of narrative profiles that can be constructed using qualitizing techniques. These profile prototypes are not mutually exclusive: Their results may be overlapping in some applications.

An *average profile* is a narrative profile based on the average (e.g., mean) of a number of attributes of the individuals or situations. The profile consists of a detailed narrative description of the group on the basis of these averages.

A *comparative profile* is the result of comparison of one unit of analysis with another, including possible differences or similarities between them.

A *holistic profile* consists of the overall impressions of the investigator regarding the unit of investigation. Unlike the average profile, the specific information that provides the basis for such holistic impressions may not be presented or available.

A *modal profile* is a narrative description of a group based on the most frequently occurring attributes in the group. For example, if the majority of men in the group are at least 80 years old, the group may be identified as elderly.

A *normative profile* is similar to the comparative profile but instead is based on the comparison of an individual or group with a standard. The "standard" might be a standardization sample or a specific population.

and a final overall (holistic) inference. A study by Tashakkori, Boyd, and Sines (1996) is an example of this type of mixed profile analysis. The data for the study came from the National Education Longitudinal Study of Eighth Graders (NELS-88). Hispanic students who dropped out of school between the 8th and 10th grades were identified in this national sample. A variety of family background, achievement, and attitudinal data were available about each member of this group. Based on these data, profiles were constructed separately for Hispanic male and female dropouts. These profiles were based on the most frequent type of characteristics in each of the two groups, average scores for some variables, and overall inferences on the basis of data and the literature.

Though profiles are relatively easy to understand and communicate, they should be used cautiously because they might present an oversimplified view of the groups under study. Also, most profiles assume group homogeneity by taking modal or average responses, even though there are large individual differences within each profile.

Inherently Mixed Data Analysis Techniques

Quantitizing and qualitizing involve one data source and its conversion to the other form. This process often occurs serendipitously, with researchers discovering unexpected patterns in the original data that then lead to its conversion to the other form. There is often a time lag in these conversion analyses, with the original data being analyzed in the traditional manner first, followed by the conversion analysis.

There is another type of conversion analysis, which we call **inherently mixed data analysis**. In these techniques, researchers plan in advance to generate both QUAL and QUAN information using the same data source to answer interlinked questions.

An exemplar of inherently mixed data analysis techniques is *social network analysis* (SNA), which was discussed earlier in this chapter (e.g.,

Fredericks & Durland, 2005). SNA includes two types of data: QUAN sociomatrices and QUAL *sociograms* (network diagrams), which were also defined earlier in this chapter.

The raw data for SNA are based on responses to simple questions such as the following: Who are the three faculty members you interacted with the most last week? These raw data are numeric, such as 1 = *interacted with*, 0 = *did not interact with*. These data generate numeric indices, such as measures of receptiveness (how many times each individual is selected) or measures of centrality (the degree to which an individual is in a central role in a network).

Technically, SNA uses a qualitizing conversion technique because the original raw data and the sociomatrices are QUAN and are then used as input to generate the QUAL visualizations of the data (sociograms or network diagrams). We prefer to call SNA an *inherently mixed data analysis technique* because researchers who use it intend to generate both QUAN and QUAL results using the same data source *before* they start data collection.

For example, the SNA study illustrated in Figure 11.1 (Kochan & Teddlie, 2005) asked the faculty and administrators at a highly ineffective high school to select individuals they would prefer to associate with in four different situations. Based on participant responses to this instrument, researchers generated both QUAN sociomatrices and QUAL sociograms (network diagrams) using UCINET6 (Borgatti, Everett, & Freeman, 2002) and NetDraw (Borgatti, 2002), respectively. The researchers intended to generate MM results as they planned the study. In fact, they were more interested in the QUAL visual network that would emerge from the NetDraw program because the cliques and isolates display the data in a manner that QUAN sociomatrices cannot.

SNA was introduced more than 70 years ago (Moreno, 1934), and advances during the past 15 years (e.g., Durland & Fredericks, 2005; Wasserman & Faust, 1994) allow the generation of integrated QUAN/QUAL analyses that were not previously possible. The joint use of UCINET6 and NetDraw in generating numeric and visual representations of the same data reminds us of what Patricia Bazeley (2003) called *fused data analysis*:

> Software programs for statistical analysis and for qualitative data analysis can be used side-by-side for parallel or sequential analyses of mixed form data. In doing so, they offer... the capacity of qualitative data analysis (QDA) software to incorporate quantitative data into a qualitative analysis, and to transform qualitative coding and matrices developed from qualitative coding into a format which allows statistical analysis.... The "fusing" of analysis then takes the researcher beyond blending of different sources to the place where the same sources are used in different but interdependent ways in order to more fully understand the topic at hand. (p. 385)

Fused data analysis involves the use of QUAL and QUAN software programs for the analysis of the same data sources in distinct, but mutually dependent, ways. Fused data analysis may result in new kinds of inherently mixed data analysis techniques in the future.

Sequential Mixed Data Analysis

Three sequential mixed data analysis strategies are related to designs illustrated in Chapter 7, Figure 7.5:

1. *Sequential QUAL → QUAN analysis, including typology development*

2. *Sequential QUAN → QUAL analysis, including typology development*

3. *Iterative sequential mixed analysis*

Sequential mixed data analysis occurs when the QUAL and QUAN strands of a study occur in chronological order, such that the analysis in one strand emerges from or depends on the previous strand. Analysis strategies for the QUAL and QUAN phases may evolve as the study unfolds.

If a study has two chronological strands, yet the analysis strategy from the second is *independent* from that of the first, then this is *not* an instance of sequential mixed data analysis. For example, Parmelee, Perkins, and Sayre (2007) described a study that examined why political advertising fails to engage college students. A QUAL focus group of college students was conducted, which was then followed by a QUAN manifest content analysis (e.g., Holsti, 1968) of 2004 political ads. The two strands were designed before the study began, and the analyses from the first strand did *not* affect how the analyses from the second strand were conducted. The second strand analyses were planned to confirm and elaborate on the analyses from the first, but they were not otherwise dependent on one another.

The distinction between sequential QUAL → QUAN and sequential QUAN → QUAL designs was defined in Chapter 7 and is based on which strand (QUAL or QUAN) comes first. John Creswell and Vicki Plano Clark (2007) referred to these designs as *exploratory* (QUAL → quan as the primary design type with other variants) and *explanatory* (QUAN → qual as the primary design type with other variants). (See Table 7.4.)

The third type of sequential mixed data analysis is **iterative sequential mixed analysis**, which occurs in any sequential design with more than two phases. Examples of such designs vary from more simple ones (QUAN → QUAL → QUAN) to increasingly more complex ones (QUAL → QUAN → QUAL → QUAN → QUAN → QUAL).

In more complex designs, *one particular data source* can change from QUAL to QUAN then back to QUAL and so forth. We refer to data that are changed from one form to another in an iterative manner as **morphed data**. We present an example of morphed data later in this section.

Sequential QUAL → QUAN Analysis, Including Typology Development

In these studies a QUAL phase occurs first, followed by a QUAN phase, and the analyses from the two phases are interlinked. The

Hausman (2000) study (discussed in Chapter 7) provides a good example of the sequential QUAL → QUAN mixed design. Hausman used semi-structured interviews in the QUAL phase to examine several questions, such as "How do buying decisions result in impulse buying?"

The responses gathered during the initial QUAL phase of the study led Hausman (2000) to formulate five hypotheses that were tested during the subsequent QUAN phase. One of the hypotheses was "individual consumer impulse buying behavior is correlated with desires to satisfy esteem, as measured by style consciousness" (p. 408). These hypotheses were tested using closed-ended response questionnaires administered to more than 250 consumers. The statistical analyses used in the QUAN phase (correlational analyses and ANOVA) were related to the results from the previous QUAL phase because the QUAL results generated the hypotheses that were tested in the QUAN phase.

Caracelli and Greene (1993) discussed a type of MM data analysis strategy related to sequential designs, which they called **typology development**: "The analysis of one data type yields a typology (or set of substantive categories) that is then used as a framework applied in analyzing the contrasting data type" (p. 197). Greene (2007) recently relabeled this strategy *data importation*, which she defined as "the importation of mid-stream results from the analysis of one data type into the analysis of a different data type" (p. 148).

In an earlier text (Tashakkori & Teddlie, 1998), we further subdivided sequential QUAL → QUAN typology development into:

1. Groups of *people* on the basis of QUAL data/observations, then comparing the groups using QUAN analysis (e.g., MANOVA, cluster analysis, discriminant analysis)

2. Groups of *attributes/themes* through QUAL (e.g., content) analysis, followed by confirmatory QUAN analysis (e.g., factor analysis, structural equation modeling), using the processes of *construct identification* and *validation*

In the first type of QUAL → QUAN typology development study, researchers generate distinct groups of people, whom researchers then import into the QUAN phase of the study for further analysis. For example, teachers might be categorized into groups labeled "more effective" and "less effective" on the basis of extensive field notes taken during classroom observations of their teaching abilities. These two groups of teachers might then be compared on QUAN variables, such as their students' performance on tests or their responses to survey instruments measuring self-efficacy. Comparisons might be performed through univariate or multivariate analysis of variance or covariance, discriminant analysis, or other statistical techniques noted in Table 11.3. The result of a discriminant analysis, for example, is the identification of variables that "discriminate" between the groups (e.g., more effective and less effective teachers) along with some statistical indicators that show which of these variables best discriminates the groups. These data might have implications for the teacher effectiveness literature and teacher improvement programs.

The second type of QUAL → QUAN typology development study involves forming groups of attributes/themes through QUAL analysis followed by confirmatory statistical analysis using QUAN data that are collected (or are available). An example is the QUAL analysis of principals' statements (obtained from focus groups) resulting in themes (*construct identification*) that represent different aspects of a "good teacher." The emergent themes or categories are indicators of subconstructs related to the general construct of "teacher effectiveness." These themes are formed on the basis of similarities (or differences, or both similarities and differences) between principals' perceptions and beliefs obtained from the focus groups. Closed-ended survey instruments that include these groups of themes (or categories) might then be constructed and administered to another group of principals. The obtained QUAN data might then be factor analyzed to determine the degree of agreement with the initial QUAL categories (*construct validation*).

Iwanicki and Tashakkori (1994) presented an example of this strategy in a study in which the proficiencies of effective principals that had been obtained through content analysis of QUAL data were assessed again through a survey instrument sent to school principals. The data were then subjected to confirmatory factor analysis, and much of the initial QUAL typology of proficiencies was confirmed in the QUAN study.

Sequential QUAN → QUAL Analysis, Including Typology Development

In these studies, a QUAN phase occurs first, followed by a QUAL phase, and the analyses from the two phases are related to one another. The Ivankova et al. (2006) study presented in Appendix A (see the companion Web site: www.sagepub .com/foundations) is a good example of the sequential QUAN → QUAL mixed design. The study's purpose was to explain why students persist (or do not persist) in a doctoral program. In this study, Ivankova and her colleagues used discriminant analysis in the QUAN phase to identify factors that significantly contributed to students' persistence. They then used multiple case analysis and thematic analysis in the QUAL phase to explain the processes whereby this occurred. The analyses were linked because the five factors that were significant predictors of student persistence from the QUAN phase were represented as open-ended questions on the QUAL interview protocol.

Another illustration of this design is presented in Figure 11.2, which was previously described in Box 8.6.

Studies using sequential QUAN → QUAL typology development procedures also do this differently for forming groups of *people* and forming groups of *attributes/themes*. An example of *forming groups of people* on the initial basis of QUAN data and then comparing the groups on QUAL data is a study in which an initial QUAN analysis is conducted on data derived from the administration of a questionnaire measuring principals' perceived efficacy and locus of causality for school improvement. Principals might then be divided into four groups based on the QUAN analysis of their survey responses (i.e., high vs. low efficacy crossed by internal vs. external locus of causality). The four groups of principals could then be compared using a variety of different types of QUAL data (e.g., responses to interview items asking about different ways to improve schools).

A widely used example of sequential QUAN → QUAL analysis is the QUAL follow-up of groups of individuals who are initially identified on the basis of their *residual scores* (actual scores minus expected scores) from multiple regression or a similar statistical technique. Detailed QUAL data are then collected on these individuals in a search for possible factors that led to their initial high (or low) QUAN scores. The QUAL data might then be analyzed through content analysis, or they may be converted to QUAN data for further statistical analysis.

An example of this sequence of analyses is the Wall, Devine-Wright, and Mill (2008) study in which residual scores from a logistic regression analysis were calculated on a sample of 392 drivers, predicting intentions to use cars for various purposes. In a second strand of the study, the researchers selected 24 participants using a purposive sampling strategy based on the residual scores. These participants were then interviewed in a semistructured format about their commuting behaviors and beliefs, expanding or confirming the findings of the first strand of the study.

Another example is the initial classification of schools into effective and ineffective categories on the basis of standardized tests using regression residuals (e.g., Kochan, Tashakkori, & Teddlie, 1996). These two types of schools were then observed and compared with each other to explore possible differences between them on other dimensions, such as school climate.

Forming categories of attributes/themes through QUAN analysis, and then confirming these categories with the QUAL analysis of other data, involves the same processes as the *construct identification* and *construct validation* procedures described previously for QUAL → QUAN studies. In this strategy, the objective is to identify the subcomponents of a construct through factor analysis of QUAN data and then to collect QUAL data to validate the categories or to expand on

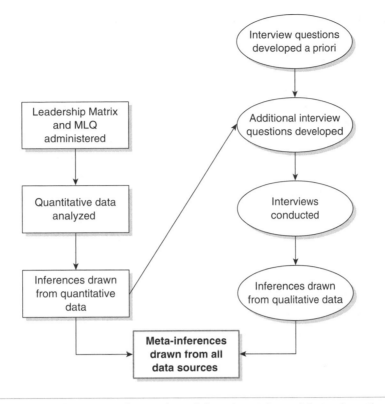

Figure 11.2   Example of Sequential Mixed Model Design Adapted From Carwile (2005, p. 63). During the QUAN phase of the study, the Leadership Matrix and MLQ (Multifactor Leadership Questionnaire) were administered to almost 300 administrators. The QUAL phase involved interviews with 13 purposively selected administrators. Some of the questions in the interview protocol were developed a priori, and some emerged as a result of the QUAN analyses.

the available information about these subcomponents. An example of this type of mixed data analysis might involve the initial classification of dimensions of teachers' perceptions of school climate through factor analysis of survey data completed by a sample of faculties. Focus group interviews, observations, and other types of data might then be used to confirm or disconfirm the existence of the initial dimensions or to explore the degree to which these different dimensions are present in everyday interactions.

Iterative Sequential Mixed Analysis

The third type of sequential mixed analysis is *iterative sequential mixed analysis*, which is defined as the analysis of data from a sequential study that has more than two phases. This flexibility in the number of strands available to researchers allows for a wide variety of iterative sequential analyses, which is one of the reasons why theoreticians cannot develop an exhaustive typology of MM research designs.

Examples of such iterative sequential designs vary from simple to increasingly complex. The more complex iterative sequential designs are often examples of MM research studies that have evolved as new salient events occurred in the research setting. In these situations, some research teams have sufficient epistemological and methodological flexibility to change the original research design and gather more data to better understand the phenomenon under study.

We have discussed several iterative sequential designs in this text already, including Tolman and Szalacha (1999) in Chapter 6 and Kumangai, Bliss, Daniels, and Carroll (2004) in Chapter 7. These studies and others are briefly reviewed here within the context of iterative sequential mixed analysis.

Tolman and Szalacha (1999) presented a QUAL → QUAN → QUAL series of three phases/analyses that involved an initial QUAL research question, followed by QUAN research questions in an emerging MM design, which were then followed by one more QUAL research question. This study is a good example of how an initial research question (How do girls describe their experiences of sexual desire?) can yield results that naturally lead to another phase of the study, the results of which then can lead to a third phase of the study. The authors noted that "this study as a whole has three iterations that are organized by three separate and synergistically related questions, which emerged sequentially in response to the findings generated by pursuing the previous research question" (p. 13).

The causal attribution of fire study described by Kumagai et al. (2004) is a good example of how unexpected events in a research setting can result in an iterative sequential mixed design (and analyses). The original research project employed a QUAN-oriented design that tested hypotheses using a survey of residents in an area with a history of high fire frequency. As this initial QUAN phase was nearing completion, a series of wildfires erupted at a second site. Kumagai and his colleagues immediately decided to conduct field interviews and another round of surveys of individuals affected by the Butte Complex Fires. These two additional phases (field interviews, additional surveys) constituted the study's second and third phases (QUAL → QUAN).

The original QUAN-only survey study was, therefore, converted into a three-strand research design (QUAN → QUAL → QUAN) featuring rich QUAL data and questionnaires from two comparative groups of respondents. The researchers later concluded that the multiple MM data sets provided them with the necessary information to comprehensively answer their research questions, which could not have been answered with the original one-phase monomethod design.

Teddlie, Creemers, Kyriakides, Muijs, and Yu, (2006) conducted a six-stage sequential MM study (QUAL → QUAN → QUAL → QUAN → QUAN → MM) that resulted in the development of an internationally validated teacher observation and feedback protocol. This study is interesting in the current context for two reasons:

- The six-stage sequential iterative research design illustrates that these designs can have multiple phases (beyond two or three).
- The design was planned before data collection began and did not change over time, thereby demonstrating that sequential iterative designs do not always emerge as a response to results or historical events.

Earlier in this chapter, we defined *morphed data* as consisting of data from a single source that is changed from one form to another in an iterative manner. Onwuegbuzie and Teddlie (2003) described a sequential mixed study in which the same data source was morphed from QUAL → QUAN → QUAL. This study was an evaluation of 10 aquatic resource education programs funded by the United States Fish and Wildlife Service. One phase of the study required the program coordinators to list all of the activities that they had undertaken during their last funding cycle. These lists provided the raw data that were then morphed as follows:

- The coordinators described more than 1,000 activities that they had undertaken during the designated time period. This information was simplified in a two-step process using the QUAL constant comparative method: First the list of total activities was reduced to 108 descriptor codes that were further reduced to 12 generic categories. For example, the generic category Fishing Events was composed of nine descriptor codes (e.g., Fishing Clinics, Fishing Rodeos, Fish Identification).

- In the QUAN phase, the 12 generic categories were quantitized; that is, the QUAL data were converted into a frequency distribution, which was then used to rank-order the generic categories from most to least frequently occurring. The category with the highest frequency was General/Training Activities with 14.9% of the total number of coded units. Conservation/Education Issues was second with 14.4% of the coded units, and Fishing Events was third with 11.7% of the coded units.

- In the final QUAL phase, the aquatic education coordinators were classified into one of two profiles based on the frequency distribution of their coded units from the QUAN phase. These two profiles described two types of professionals involved in the programs: educators, who had been well trained in aquatic resource and environmental issues, and marine biologists, who emphasized fishing activities and had a minimum of educational training.

Thus the same data source (written lists of activities for aquatic education programs) was morphed first into a set of generic QUAL codes, then into a quantitized frequency distribution based on the overall occurrence of the coded units, and then into two QUAL profiles based on most frequently occurring QUAL codes for each separate state program. The morphing process demonstrates the flexibility of data to change from one form to another and then back to the original form in an iterative fashion.

Multilevel Mixed Data Analysis

Multilevel mixed designs were presented in Chapters 7 and 8 of this text and are discussed in several sources (e.g., Creswell & Plano Clark, 2007; Creswell, Plano Clark, Gutmann, & Hanson, 2003; Tashakkori & Teddlie, 1998; Teddlie & Tashakkori, 2006). Multilevel designs are possible only in hierarchically organized social institutions, such as hospitals and schools, in which one *level of analysis* (defined in Chapter 7, Note 7) is nested within another (e.g., patient within ward within hospital).

Multilevel mixed data analysis is a general analytic strategy in which QUAL and QUAN techniques are used at different levels of aggregation within a study to answer interrelated research questions. Multilevel mixed data analysis occurs when one type of analysis (QUAL) is used at one level (e.g., student) and another type of analysis (QUAN) is used in at least one other level (e.g., classroom). Multilevel mixed data analysis is theoretically possible in several disciplines and has been reported in a few:

- Probably the most commonly reported examples of multilevel mixed data analysis (e.g., Reynolds, Creemers, Stringfield, Teddlie, & Schaffer, 2002; Teddlie & Stringfield, 1993) come from studies conducted in education, where organizational units are deeply nested. For example, Figure 8.1 illustrates the multilevel structure found in K–12 education in the United States.

- In the field of counseling psychology, Elliott and Williams (2002) studied an employee counseling service that had four nested levels: client, counselor, director, overall organization. These researchers employed QUAL analyses at the client, counselor, and director levels and QUAN analyses at the organizational level.

- In a study of postsecondary disability support services, Christ (2007) conducted what he called the "concurrent collection of data at multiple levels" (p. 232). The levels that he used were student, support staff, supervisor, and coordinator. Although all of Christ's analyses were QUAL in nature, his study demonstrated the possibility of conducting multilevel mixed data analysis in postsecondary disability settings by adding a QUAN analysis at one of the levels.

- Disciplines such as medicine, nursing, and health care can use the structure of hospitals/clinics to conduct studies using multilevel mixed data analysis. Some of the possible nested structures include patients within wards within hospitals, patients within general practitioners within clinics, mental health clients within counselors within mental health institutions, and so forth.

- Disciplines such as demography, geography, sociology, and economics can use the multilevel structure of individuals within households within geographically defined communities within cities.

Fully Integrated Mixed Data Analysis

The *fully integrated mixed design* was described in Chapter 7 as a multistrand parallel design in which mixing of QUAL and QUAN approaches occurs in an interactive manner at all stages of the study. Figure 7.7 illustrates these designs.

Fully integrated mixed data analysis occurs when there is an interactive mixing of QUAL and QUAN analyses that may be characterized as iterative, reciprocal, and interdependent. We have discussed other analyses in this chapter that aim to break down the barriers between the traditional QUAN statistical and QUAL thematic dichotomy (e.g., cross-tracks analysis, crossover tracks analysis, fused data, and morphed data). All of these analyses can be part of *fully integrated mixed data analysis.*

One of the examples of the fully integrated mixed designs from Chapter 7 was the Louisiana School Effectiveness Study (Teddlie & Stringfield, 1993). This study had two major parallel strands (one QUAL, one QUAN), but some of the QUAL data (classroom observations) were quantitized and analyzed statistically, and some of the QUAN data (e.g., socioeconomic indicators, achievement data, student absenteeism, stability of faculty) were qualitized, thereby generating school profiles.

The conversion of the QUAL observation data to QUAN data and the subsequent statistical analysis of that quantitized data yielded results that indicated that much more effective teaching was ongoing at schools designated as effective than was ongoing in schools designated as ineffective (see Box 11.7). The results from these quantitized data then affected further QUAL analyses, which initially aimed to answer the following question: What are the processes whereby schools remain the same or change over time with regard to how well they educate their students? After considering the results from the quantitized data, researchers asked the additional QUAL question: What are the processes whereby schools are able to maintain

a high level of teacher effectiveness even as staff leave and are replaced by new teachers?

Eight numeric indices were qualitized as the longitudinal study continued, and the qualitized information was then used to reclassify the original "effective" and "ineffective" schools into four new profiles: stable effective, improving, declining, and stable ineffective. This new QUAL classification scheme was then used to generate QUAN analyses that made statistical comparisons among the new groups of schools on various numeric indicators. The study started with two major QUAN and QUAL analytic strategies, but as it evolved data conversion strategies led to some interesting findings, which then led to further changes in the directions that the QUAN and QUAL analyses took.

The Schulenberg (2007) article previously described in Box 7.6 provides an excellent example of the use of eclectic QUAN analyses (six different types) and QUAL analyses (eight different types) in a single study designed to answer a complex set of research questions and hypotheses. Also, Appendix C on the companion Web site (www.sagepub.com/foundations) contains a recent example of a study that used integrative data analytic procedures (Jang, McDougall, Pollon, Herbert, & Russell, 2008). This study did not employ a fully integrated MM design, but it used integrative analysis strategies in a manner consistent with fully mixed analyses.

The Jang et al. (2008) study of successful schools in "challenging circumstances" employed a parallel MM design in which the QUAL and QUAN strands were analyzed independently using thematic and factor analyses, respectively. After these traditional analyses were completed, the authors used four additional integrative strategies:

1. *Parallel integration for member checking*— The sets of 11 QUAL themes and 9 QUAN factors were presented to participants for feedback.

2. *Data transformation for comparison*—The nine QUAN factors were qualitized into narrative descriptions, which were then compared with the QUAL themes; overlapping and nonoverlapping aspects of school improvement were ascertained.

3. *Data consolidation for emergent themes*—Eight consolidated themes emerged from comparisons of original and reorganized QUAL and QUAN data.

4. *Case analysis for the generation of refined school profiles*—Narrative profiles were generated for case study schools using the consolidated themes from Strategy 3; an iterative analytic process then examined the different ways schools coped with the consolidated themes (e.g., high vs. low parental involvement in successful schools).

Applying Aspects of Analytic Frameworks of One Tradition to Data Analysis Within Another Tradition

In Jennifer Greene's (2007) summary of MM data analysis, she included the "broad idea" of "using aspects of the analytic framework of one methodological tradition within the analysis of data from another tradition" (p. 155). We believe that this is one of the more fruitful areas for the further development of MM analytical techniques.

One of Greene's (2007) examples was the application of the traditional QUAN use of matrices and graphs to QUAL research. Though we included data displays as one of the three general types of QUAL data analysis, their inclusion as a distinct QUAL data analytic technique in the general literature is still rare (e.g., Maxwell, 1997).

As noted by Greene (2007), Matthew Miles and Michael Huberman (1984, 1994) first demonstrated the potential of effects matrices and network displays as an integral part of QUAL data analysis more than 20 years ago. Matrices in the QUAN tradition (e.g., contingency tables, sociomatrices) typically consist of the crossing of two dimensions with a resultant table of cells, each containing numeric data. Miles and Huberman applied that framework to the QUAL tradition by crossing two dimensions and then completing the cells with narrative information. In one example, they illustrated a longitudinal school improvement project by using columns that represented years (1976–1980) and rows that represented intervention levels (state, macro, district, local schools). The narrative information in the matrix cells described what was happening in each combination of year and intervention level.

Another example from Greene (2007) was the application of effect sizes to QUAL data. Effect sizes in QUAN research refer to the strength of the relationship between two numeric variables calculated by statistical indices[6] (e.g., Ary, Jacobs, Razavieh, & Sorenson, 2007). Thus, if there is a large effect size between two numeric variables, they have a strong relationship.

Onwuegbuzie and Teddlie (2003), following up on work by Onwuegbuzie (2003), identified a typology of effect sizes in QUAL research, including three broad categories: manifest effect size, adjusted effect size, and latent effect size. One example that Onwuegbuzie and Teddlie (2003) used for effect sizes was the aquatic education program evaluation described in the earlier discussion of morphed data. They calculated *manifest intensity effect sizes* by looking at the percentage of total units for each theme out of the total number of units. In this example, the category with the highest percentage of total units was General/Training Activities, which translated into a manifest intensity effect size of 14.9%. Conservation/Education Issues had the second highest percentage of total units, which equated to a manifest intensity effect size of 14.4%. This is an example of what some have called *quasi-statistics*, in which descriptive statistics (e.g., frequencies, percentages) are used to quantitize thematic data generated from QUAL analyses (e.g., Becker, 1970; Maxwell, 1997; Onwuegbuzie & Daniels, 2003).

As these examples demonstrate, there are a number of analytical processes in QUAL and QUAN research that are analogous to one another. Table 11.4 presents a partial list of these analogous processes.

In the future, we believe that MM researchers will examine more closely the analytical frameworks used in either the QUAL or QUAN tradition and then develop analogous techniques for the other tradition.

Summary

Chapter 11 first presented a brief summary of QUAL data analysis strategies, which were described as inductive, iterative, and eclectic. The search for themes was described as a universal characteristic of QUAL data analysis.

QUAN data analysis was then presented using three basic distinctions: descriptive versus inferential, univariate versus multivariate, and

parametric versus nonparametric. Examples of each type of statistic were presented.

Most of Chapter 11 concerned MM data analysis, which was tied directly to the five MM research designs presented in Chapter 7: parallel, conversion, sequential, multilevel, and fully integrated. Conversion mixed data analysis was further divided into quantitizing, qualitizing, and inherently mixed data analysis techniques. Sequential mixed data analysis was further divided into sequential

Table 11.4 A Partial List of Analogous Analytical Processes in QUAN and QUAL Research

Analytical Process	Application in QUAN Research	Application in QUAL Research
Data displays	QUAN data displays (e.g., numeric contingency tables)	QUAL data displays or matrices (e.g., Miles & Huberman, 1994)
Effect sizes	Statistical indices, such as Cohen's (1988) *d* and Smith and Glass's (1977) delta	QUAL effect sizes, such as manifest intensity effect size (Onwuegbuzie, 2003)
Generation of themes	Exploratory factor analysis, quantitative data mining	Thematic analysis in general, including grounded theory; text mining
Maximizing between-group variation and minimizing within-group variations	Cluster analysis to identify a set of groups that both maximize between-group variation and minimize within-group variations	The categorizing component of the constant comparative method to maximize between-theme variations and minimize within-theme variations
Comparing analysis from one part of a sample with analysis from another part of the sample	In prediction studies, splitting the sample randomly into two, running exploratory regression analysis on the first subsample, then conducting confirmatory regression analysis on the second subsample	Archival storage of some of the QUAL data, using the concept of referential adequacy, for later reanalysis; comparing original interpretations made on the basis of the first sample of data with new interpretations based on the second sample (e.g. Eisner, 1998; Lincoln & Guba, 1985)
Comparison of actual results with expected results	Pattern matching studies using QUAN data; in regression analysis, examining residual values, which compare expected versus predicted scores	Pattern matching studies using QUAL data—for example, the use of replication logic in multiple case designs that compares empirical results with predicted results based on previous cases (Yin, 2003); negative case analysis
Contrasting components of research design or elements to find differences	Focused contrast analysis to look for specific differences in particular parts of an analysis of variance design	Asking contrast questions (e.g., What is the difference between X and Y?) to determine the meaning of a phenomenon of interest (Spradley, 1979, 1980)

QUAL→QUAN analysis, sequential QUAN→QUAL data analysis, and iterative sequential mixed analysis. Examples of each analysis type were presented.

New types of analytical techniques were presented in which the boundaries between the QUAL/QUAN dichotomy disappeared and data appeared to be transferable or interchangeable between the two forms. These types of analyses included fused data analysis, inherently mixed data analysis, iterative sequential analysis, morphed data analysis, and analysis of fully integrated designs.

There is a new consideration of a datum as a unit of information with the capacity to transition between the two traditional forms. As mixed data analysis evolves, researchers will think of data less in terms of words or numbers and more in terms of transferable units of information that happen to be initially generated in one form or the other.

Chapter 12 presents information on the next (and final) step in the research process: drawing inferences from the data gathered during an MM study. The first part of the chapter is concerned with general issues regarding the inference process. Then we discuss what constitutes good QUAN and QUAL inferences. An integrative framework for making inferences in MM research is then presented along with two major components (design quality, interpretive rigor). Finally, we address the issue of transferability in MM research.

Review Questions and Exercises

1. Give an example of a research study that would generate narrative data best analyzed by a *categorical strategy*. Note how you would analyze the data.

2. Give an example of a research study that would generate qualitative data best analyzed by a *contextualizing strategy*. Note how you would analyze the data.

3. Conduct a literature search to locate a QUAL-oriented study. Describe the type of qualitative analysis that was used and the themes that were generated through the analysis.

4. Conduct a literature search to locate a QUAN-oriented study that compared two or more groups. Describe the type of quantitative analytical techniques that were used and the results that were generated.

5. Conduct a literature search to locate a QUAN-oriented study that analyzed the relationships between two or more variables. Describe the types of quantitative analytical techniques that were used and the results that were generated.

6. Conduct a literature search in which you locate an article or chapter describing an MM study. Describe both the QUAN and QUAL results that were generated and the

type of analyses that were used (i.e., at least one QUAL and one QUAN technique).

7. Identify and distinguish between parallel, conversion, and sequential mixed data analysis. Describe studies in which it would be appropriate to use parallel mixed data analysis, conversion mixed data analysis, and sequential mixed data analysis.

8. Describe a hypothetical study in which researchers use quantitizing techniques. Why would they use quantitizing techniques in this study?

9. Describe a hypothetical study in which you use qualitizing techniques. Why would you use qualitizing techniques in this study?

10. Explain fused and morphed data analyses. Why are they important in MM research?

11. Describe a hypothetical MM study with multiple levels of analysis. Indicate which type of analysis you would use at each level.

12. Define fully integrated mixed data analysis. Describe a hypothetical study that would use such an analysis procedure.

13. Consider the information in Table 11.4. Select one pair of analyses and find examples of the QUAN and QUAL applications.

Describe the similarities in the QUAN and QUAL analyses.

14. The Jang et al. (2008) study in Appendix C on the companion Web site (www.sagepub.com/foundations) used four different types of integrative strategies: parallel integration for member checking, data transformation for comparison, data consolidation for emergent themes, and case analysis for the generation of refined school profiles. Describe each of these techniques and how they can be used in MM research in general.

15. Locate the Schulenberg (2007) article and (a) briefly describe the different types of analyses used in this study and (b) describe how they are interrelated in the overall study. (See the References at the end of this book to find information to locate the article.)

Key Terms

A priori themes

Analytic induction

Categorizing process

Constant comparative method

Contrast principle

Conversion mixed data analysis

Effect sizes in QUAL research

Emergent themes

Fully integrated mixed data analysis

Fused data analysis

Inherently mixed data analysis

Iterative sequential mixed analysis

Morphed data

Multilevel mixed data analysis

Multivariate statistics

Negative case analysis

Null hypothesis

Parallel mixed data analysis

Qualitative data displays

Sequential mixed data analysis

Similarity principle

Statistical significance

Thematic analysis

Themes

Typology development

Unitizing process

Univariate statistics

Notes

1. Ratio scales require a true zero point (as in zero weight), which is rare in research conducted in the human sciences. Therefore, for most practical purposes, interval and ratio scales are treated the same in statistical applications (e.g., Wiersma & Jurs, 2005).

2. As noted in Chapter 2, Note 5, Guba and Lincoln (e.g., 1989, 2005) generated alternative, nonfoundational criteria for assessing the quality of QUAL research (e.g., fairness, ontological authenticity, catalytic authenticity).

3. We limit our discussion of parallel mixed designs in this chapter to those with two strands for the sake of simplicity. There could, of course, be more than two strands (e.g., two QUAN strands and one QUAL strand).

4. Cluster analysis is an exploratory QUAN method that sorts respondents into homogeneous subgroups of cases in a population. It seeks to identify a set of groups that both maximizes between-group variation and minimizes within-group variations.

5. Narrative profiles and typology development (discussed later in the chapter) are similar to one another, but they are also different in that narrative profiles are a component of conversion analysis, whereas typology development is a step in sequential analysis.

6. These indices include Cohen's (1988) *d* or Smith and Glass's (1977) delta.

CHAPTER 12

The Inference Process in Mixed Methods Research[1]

Objectives

Upon finishing this chapter, you should be able to:

- Identify and distinguish between quality of data and quality of inferences made on the basis of study results
- Differentiate between inference as a process and inference as an outcome of research
- Identify and distinguish between quality of inferences and transferability of inferences

- Discuss the issues/audits of inference quality for qualitative and quantitative approaches to research
- Define and discuss various audits or quality criteria in multimethod and mixed methods research
- Discuss issues of importance in the integration of conclusions from the qualitative and quantitative strands of a mixed methods study
- Differentiate between triangulation and integration of inferences in mixed methods research

- Define and discuss inference transferability and different aspects of transferability

This chapter presents a discussion of issues related to quality of **inferences** (conclusions, interpretations) in research. In previous chapters, we suggested that although data, results of data analysis, and the inferences that are gleaned from the findings are interdependent, the criteria or standards for evaluating quality at each stage are not the same. In this chapter, we elaborate on this issue and discuss considerations about inference quality and steps for quality assessment in mixed methods (MM) research. First, we define and discuss the basic concepts relevant to making inferences: inference quality (internal validity, credibility) and inference transferability (external validity, transferability). We summarize the standards/audits for evaluation of inference quality and transferability as has been discussed by scholars in the qualitative (QUAL) and quantitative (QUAN) traditions. We then point to similarities in these standards/audits before we present our **integrative framework for inference quality and transferability**.

The integrative framework differentiates between two interactive and iterative components of meaning making. One component consists of the quality of the inputs to the interpretive process (i.e., quality of the data, design, data analysis procedures). The second component consists of the process of making meaning through systematic linking and interpreting of findings. The quality of inferences depends on the quality of inputs to the process (i.e., **design quality**) and the integrity of the process of making meaning (i.e., **interpretive rigor**). We believe that the process of making research inferences is a more systematic and formal extension of our everyday social perceptions, problem solving, and meaning making (Heider, 1958). Therefore, as a general guide in our construction of quality audits, we use a social-perception (or attribution; see Heider, 1958; Kelley, 1967) model for assessing the quality and integrity of research inferences. Finally, the integrative framework suggests that inference transferability

is relative—that is, every inference has a degree of transferability to a context, to a group of people or entities, or to the alternative ways of conceptualizing the behaviors and phenomena under investigation.

Mixed Methods Research and Inferences

In our view, the most important step in any MM study is when the results (i.e., findings, conclusions) from the study's QUAL and QUAN strands are incorporated into a coherent conceptual framework that provides an effective answer to the research question. The main reason for using an MM approach is to provide a better understanding of the phenomenon under investigation. In sequential MM studies, the addition of QUAL or QUAL strands improves one's understanding of the phenomenon and answers the research questions by suggesting modifications in questions or design, by providing new hypotheses, or by exploring the reasons and meanings behind the findings of a previous strand. Sequential studies might occur in a planned or emergent manner. Parallel designs, on the other hand, involve planning the strands in advance, in hopes of obtaining a fuller understanding of the phenomenon.

In all MM studies (sequential, parallel, conversion, multilevel, or fully integrated designs; see Chapter 7), an enhanced understanding is possible only if the outcomes of research strands are effectively linked or integrated, if possible areas of agreement or disagreement are identified through comparisons of results and inferences, and if the possibility of a higher order conceptual framework of the phenomenon is actively explored.

From the start, it should be emphasized that integration of the inferences drawn from multiple strands of an MM study does not require an implied or actual agreement (consistency) of the inferences. We discuss this in more detail later in this chapter. For now, suffice to say that inconsistency between two (or more) sets of findings provides information that would otherwise be lost (i.e., not uncovered) if only a QUAN or QUAL study were used. Although we often see a fear of inconsistency in graduate students and other researchers, we believe that more seasoned scholars appreciate the opportunities to confront multiple meanings and constructions that MM research provides.

In earlier efforts (Tashakkori & Teddlie, 1998) to find nomenclature to represent the complexity and inclusiveness of integrated methods, we proposed the term *inference* to denote the last and most important stage of research. This term is currently used by both QUAL and QUAN scholars. We agree with these scholars (e.g., Greene, 2007) that the most important aspect of a research project is answering the research questions by actively interpreting the results. Both during and after a research project, researchers return to why they conducted the investigation to try to answer questions. At the end of the process, the findings (i.e., results or outcomes of data analysis) must be interpreted to provide answers and to develop a solid understanding of the phenomenon under investigation. We use the term *inference* for three related concepts:

- **Inference process** is the process of making sense out of the results of data analysis. Although it might seem that this process starts when the data are summarized and analyzed, it actually starts much earlier (e.g., during data collection). In other words, the inference process consists of a dynamic journey from ideas to data to results in an effort to make sense of data by connecting the dots.

- *Inference quality* is an umbrella term denoting the standards for evaluating the quality of conclusions that are made on the basis of research findings. Inference quality includes the QUAN terms *internal validity* and *statistical conclusion validity* and the QUAL terms related to credibility and trustworthiness.

- *Inference transferability* is the degree to which these conclusions may be applied to other similar settings, people, time periods, contexts, and theoretical representations of the constructs.

It corresponds to *generalizability* and *external validity* in QUAN research and *transferability* in QUAL research.

Although these terms are proposed to assist MM researchers in conceptualizing and discussing their studies, we believe that they might also be employed in the presentation of the research results from traditional QUAL or QUAN research projects.

What Is a Research Inference?

Inferences are conclusions and interpretations that are made on the basis of collected data in a study. As such, they must be distinguished from the data from which they were derived. Unfortunately, few scholars have made this distinction. An implicit distinction may be found in Lancy's (1993) discussion of publishing QUAL research results:

> One can write up a mostly descriptive piece devoid of analysis and conclusions; these are extremely hard to get published. One can write a piece that is long on conclusions and short on description. This is most commonly done but it is a practice that throws away what is most valuable about qualitative research—the "believability" that comes from thorough familiarity with the phenomenon. Or, and I think this is the preferred route, one can, like a gem cutter, fracture one's study along natural division lines and provide several complete accounts of these separate pieces. (p. 23)

We tried to clarify this distinction in Chapter 7 by placing data in the *experiential sphere* and placing the interpretations and conclusions in the *sphere of inferences*. Regardless of this distinction, we believe that in a dynamic research project the investigator might continuously make inferences on the basis of every newly acquired datum or finding. These inferences might in turn influence the data-gathering process, leading to a continuous feedback loop between the data, data analysis results, and the conclusions, until a satisfactory level of certainty is attained about these conclusions (similar to the concept of saturation in sampling discussed in Chapter 8).

Following Miller's (2003) discussion, we use the term *inference* to denote both a process and an outcome. As a process, making inferences consists of a set of steps (i.e., cognitive processes) that a researcher follows to create meaning out of a relatively large amount of collected information. We used the term *inference process* to denote this aspect of meaning making. As an outcome, an inference is a conclusion (i.e., a meaning, an understanding) made on the basis of obtained results.

Although for the sake of simplicity (and pedagogy) we distinguish these two aspects of the term *inference* (as process, as outcome), in actuality, the two proceed hand-in-hand, in a dynamic and interactive manner. It is impossible to draw a line to denote the end of the process and the start of the outcome. We also believe that an effective presentation of research findings emulates the think-aloud process. In such a process, the researcher communicates how he or she reaches an inference by following a question-and-answer style: examining the results, making a conclusion, evaluating the conclusion, and proceeding to the next level of inferences.

Obviously, a researcher's inferences may or may not be acceptable to other scholars and are subject to evaluation by the community of scholars and consumers of research. In academia, this is known as peer review. Peer reviewed publications are often valued both by evaluators of faculty and by policy makers who need credible evidence to guide planning decisions. During the peer review process, research inferences may be evaluated in terms of their consistency with the findings of the study (i.e., the results) and the theories and state of knowledge in a specific field or discipline. Or inferences might be evaluated in terms of their relevance and usefulness to policy makers (Collins, Onwuegbuzie, & Jiao, 2007). Scholars have also discussed the benefits of inference-quality evaluation

(or research-process evaluation) in terms of the extent to which the inferences lead to improvements for disadvantaged populations (e.g., Mertens, 2007).

Inferences are not limited to answers to research questions; they also develop new understandings and explanations for events, phenomena, and relationships. They create an understanding (e.g., "gestalt" or whole) on the basis of all results, a whole that is bigger than a simple set of isolated conclusions made on the basis of different findings of a study.

Inferences are a researcher's etic construction of the relationships among people, events, and variables; efforts to represent respondents' emic expressions, perceptions, behaviors, feelings, and interpretations; and construction of how these (*emic* and *etic* constructions) relate to each other in a coherent and systematic manner. In an earlier section, we noted that we are now more inclined to consider respondents' interpretations and constructions as data, regardless of how we capture them in research (i.e., either QUAL or QUAN methods). The researcher's interpretations and constructions of what their participants have expressed is what we and others call inference. An issue of debate has been strategies (audits/ standards) for determining "the trustworthiness of inferences drawn from data" (Eisenhart & Howe, 1992, p. 644), especially in QUAL studies. In integrated research, these two perspectives (emic, etic) are skillfully represented and linked, preventing an overreliance on either one. As we noted in Chapter 5, Table 5.3 (and elsewhere), we do not subscribe to the validity of the etic-emic dichotomy. Instead, we believe that any research inference may be placed on a continuum, with each inference representing different shades of participants' and investigators' interpretations of events and phenomena. Figure 12.1 presents a humorous look at the overreliance on the emic perspective.

Examining inferences as research outcomes, King, Keohane, and Verba (1994) distinguished between descriptive and explanatory inferences. A descriptive inference "is the process of understanding an observed phenomenon on the basis of

"The solution to global warming is very simple —
just take me to the vet and have me shaved!"

Figure 12.1

a set of observations" (p. 55). Explanatory inferences build on descriptive inferences, and they go beyond them by "connecting causes and effects" (p. 34). Closely similar to this distinction, Krathwohl (2004) differentiated between descriptive-exploratory, explanatory, and validation "roles and outcomes of research" (p. 32). He suggested that validation (i.e., confirming or disconfirming inferences) is based on explanation and helps researchers "determine whether predictions based on an explanation will prove accurate" (p. 34).

The Process of Making Inferences

Making inferences is both an art and a science. It involves elements of creativity, intuition, and meaning making as well as the ability to compartmentalize components or aspects of a phenomenon, understand each, and then reconstruct them for a full understanding. QUAL researchers explicitly acknowledge that the ultimate goal and final product of their research is to make meaning. For example, Rossman and Rallis (2003) stated that the "researcher makes meaning of (interprets) what he learns as he goes along. Data are filtered through the researcher's unique ways of seeing the world" (pp. 35–36).

Although they might not attach primary importance to these artistic aspects of research, most seasoned QUAN researchers would also agree that making conclusions involves elements of creativity and intuition. In our own experience with research/evaluation projects, we are keenly aware that some QUAN researchers are much more skillful in making meaningful conclusions based on their seemingly "objective" results than are other scholars.

A golden rule of making inferences in human research is *know thy participants*! Having a solid understanding of the cultures of the participants and the research context is a valuable asset in the process of making inferences. Elsewhere (Tashakkori & Teddlie, 1998), we discussed cultural knowledge as a source or type of data in most research projects. Even if researchers do not analyze this type of data separately (i.e., if one does not analyze field notes separately during the course of a study), they can use these notes to interpret the results. Even in highly structured QUAN studies, making meaningful inferences on the basis of the obtained results will be enhanced by your knowledge of the respondents and how they perceived the research process (and its purposes) as well as the meaning of behaviors in the cultural context of the participants.

To demonstrate the importance of understanding the context and culture of your research participants, consider Figure 12.2, a photograph that was taken by one of the text authors (Tashakkori) in 2006. Pretend that you are a researcher studying the structure and function of public spaces in everyday functioning of citizens across cultures. Regardless of your research design or data collection strategy (e.g., survey, field observations,

Figure 12.2

ethnography, case study), it is almost impossible to make credible and meaningful inferences about such a research objective without a deep cultural knowledge of your research participants. Such understanding involves knowing the importance of rituals, social habits, interaction patterns, norms, values, and other cultural elements.

Figure 12.2 captures a corner of a public park in Isfahan, Iran, on a lazy, hot weekend afternoon. Take a moment to write your interpretation of what you see. How do you interpret this scene? What is the importance of what you see, in terms of the components and the meaning of public space for the individuals in the photo?

Would it help your understanding (interpretation) if we told you that the watermelons belong to families who are picnicking in the park? Would it help if we told you that each space under a water stream is reserved by a family and has an invisible privacy wall around it? We can tell you much more about the meaning and the function of this public space by analyzing the role of these melons in each family's interaction patterns (i.e., as a habit, a shared experience, a focus for interaction and laughter).

We can also tell you more about the possible functions of the physical space on the sideline, in the social functioning of the individuals who are engaged in interaction. But we are sure that you get the point! Regardless of the type of research, credible inferences require a solid understanding of the culture of the investigation and the participants. Regardless of your methodological approach, a deep and thorough knowledge of the social and cultural contexts of behaviors and events will strengthen the credibility of your inferences.

How do we make MM research inferences that are culturally rooted, credible, and comprehensive? The answer depends on your research question, the type of design you used, and the findings of your study. The type of question you ask affects your inferences. Understanding and exploratory questions lead to answers that are tentative. Inferences researchers make are often inductive and lead to initial grounded theories about the phenomenon under investigation. Explanatory and confirmatory questions are more rooted in the literature and previous studies than are exploratory questions. Inferences that are made to provide answers to these questions are more integrative of the available literature.

Understanding and mastery of the current literature and previous studies related to the phenomenon under study is the first step in making inferences. Regardless of your methodological approach, you must have a deep understanding of the literature related to your research questions. Some scholars (e.g., Creswell, 2002, p. 53) have suggested that initial literature reviews are not as essential in QUAL research as they are in QUAN research. The main logic for this is the need to be open to new answers and understandings in QUAL research.

We agree with this necessity of being open to new discoveries in *both* QUAL and QUAN research. On the other hand, we do not think that it benefits investigators to start searching for answers and understanding without an awareness of other possible answers in the current literature. We distinguish between being open to new ideas and starting off unaware of others' insights into the issues under investigation. Therefore, we strongly advocate for a thorough understanding of attempts by other researchers to find answers to similar (or related) research questions. You should acquire this understanding before, during, and at the end of your study. For example, we believe that, regardless of the methodological orientation, a dissertation should include a serious attempt to explore others' responses to similar questions about the same, or similar, phenomenon proposed for the investigation. A convincing rationale for a new study must be presented after this thorough review.

During data analysis, you have taken your preliminary notes concerning initial answers (hunches) to research questions. Some of these notes link what you observed or gleaned from the literature you reviewed. Now is the time to return to your preliminary notes to determine whether they help you interpret your final results. Hopefully some of these notes are about the cultural context of your study (e.g., what you saw when entering the hospital or school, patterns of interaction in groups, participant comments following a treatment). These field notes are invaluable assets in making sense of results at this stage.

Here are some general guidelines for making credible inferences during the course of data analysis (or even data collection, such as in ethnographies) or at the final stage of your study:

- In making inferences, you must keep the research purposes and research questions in the foreground of all of your analyses and interpretations.

- State each question (or subquestion) separately and examine or summarize all of the results that are relevant to that question. Obviously, you have analyzed your data with the explicit objective of answering each question. Various parts of your analysis might include tentative answers to each question or subquestion. Examine your results, your field notes, and your summary notes from the literature reviews. Think aloud (yes, talk to yourself!) about the meaning of the findings. Talk to your peers about the findings. Ask yourself: What does this mean, from my participants' point of view?

- Make tentative interpretations about each part of your results, in the form of an answer to a research question or a component of it.

- After going through this exercise for each question, examine your answers to the questions, or your interpretations, to see if you can combine them. Compare, contrast, combine, or try to explain differences.

- The quality of the inferences you make in an MM study also depends on the strength of inferences that emerge from the QUAL and QUAN strands of your study. High-quality QUAL and QUAN strands are necessary (but not sufficient) for a high-quality MM study. In other words, you might make very credible inferences on the basis of your QUAL and QUAN results but fail to integrate them well at the end of the study.

- You should be cognizant that the strength of a good MM study depends on the extent that it fulfills the purpose for using those methods. Why did you initially decide to use MM? What was the need, purpose, or rationale? Now is the time to go back and try to see if each has been achieved. Unfortunately, the reasons for using MM are not always explicitly delineated or recognized by authors (e.g., Bryman, 2007; Niglas, 2004). Table 7.3 presented some of these *reasons for conducting MM research*, such as complementarity and expansion (Greene & Caracelli, 1997b). (See Greene, 2007, for an excellent summary and further elaboration.) The inferences that you make at the end of your MM study must directly address the initial and intended purpose for using such methods. For example, if the purpose for using MM is to gain a fuller understanding of a phenomenon, your final conclusions must provide such an understanding. Quality issues in mixed research must be discussed in the context of the correspondence between the meta-inferences and the stated purposes for using an MM design. Borrowing a concept from O'Cathain, Murphy, and Nicholl (2007) and Bryman (2006a, 2006b), we tentatively call this the interpretive correspondence of inferences (for MM, this might also be called integrative correspondence). Bryman and O'Cathain et al. demonstrated that many MM studies do not attain their stated purpose for using MM designs.

- How you make inferences also depends on your MM study design (which in turn is affected by your purpose or question). For parallel MM designs, the purpose for mixing must be known from the start, although it might be modified during the course of the project. For sequential and conversion MM, the purpose might be known from the start, or it might emerge from the inferences of the first strand (i.e., the questions of the second strand emerge at the end of the first strand).

Obviously, the quality of the entire research project depends on the degree to which integration, blending, or linking of QUAL and QUAN inferences is achieved. Although the integration of QUAL and QUAN approaches is possible throughout a study, few studies actually accomplish this. For example, in an examination of the published studies in health sciences, O'Cathain et al. (2007) concluded that integration of QUAL and QUAN approaches "occurred mainly at the interpretation stage of a study" (p. 160).

A study by Sargeant, Wymer, and Hilton (2006) illustrated how inferences are made, modified, and finalized during the course of a study. They employed a sequential mixed design for finding answers to their main research question: Among individuals who have a history of donating to (three specific) charities, what factors differentiate those who make bequests (i.e., charitable bequests in a will) from those who do not (i.e., nonpledgers)? In the first strand of the study, the authors identified possible motives for charitable giving through eight 90-minute focus groups of individuals who had previously pledged bequests to nonprofit organizations. Conducting an emergent themes analysis of the recorded narrative data, the authors identified nine themes, calling each a motive. Making inferences from these findings, the authors categorized these themes into three categories of motives: organizational, individual, and bequest specific. On the basis of each of these obtained themes, they formed a hypothesis, to be tested in the next strand of the study.

The data for the second strand were collected using a questionnaire that was developed on the basis of statements made by focus group participants. The questionnaire was mailed to a sample of 624 donors. The nine hypotheses were tested individually to compare the responses of the pledgers and nonpledgers. Inferences were made from each test of a hypothesis, followed by linking of the two sets of findings on each theme. Then, the authors examined all findings regarding all themes and made inferences about the three categories of motives noted earlier. In making inferences and policy recommendations, they incorporated all other available information and insights, including their own experiences as evaluators, participant and organizational information in the databases, and their personal knowledge and observations of the organizations participating in the study.

Judging (Auditing) the Quality of Research Inferences

How does one know if inferences that are made are good or bad? Highly consistent with our (Tashakkori & Teddlie, 2003c) previous call for distinguishing the standards of data quality from inference quality, Greene (2007) suggested two general approaches to thinking about quality: making judgments about the quality of the method and data obtained and making judgments about the quality of inferences, interpretations, and conclusions.

Responding to the question, "What constitutes 'good' science," Paul (2005, pp. 11–16) summarized three recent "markers" in research that demonstrate the complexity of answers. The first is the publication of *Scientific Research in Education* (2002), sponsored by the National Academy of Sciences in the United States. Although the report intended to span both scientifically based QUAL and QUAN approaches, it has been considered to be more applicable to QUAN research (Maxwell, 2004). Among the concerns expressed in the report was the "lack of standards for evaluating educational research" (Paul, 2005, p. 12). The report presents six criteria for good research:

- Pose significant questions that can be investigated empirically;
- Link research to relevant theory;
- Use methods that permit direct investigation of the question;
- Provide a coherent and explicit chain of reasoning;
- Replicate and generalize across studies; and
- Disclose research to encourage professional scrutiny and critique. (Paul, 2005, p. 13)

The second marker identified by Paul (2005) is the No Child Left Behind Act of 2001, which provides another view of quality as "research that applies rigorous, systematic, and objective procedures to obtain valid knowledge" (p. 13):

- Employs systematic, empirical methods that draw on observation or experiment;
- Involves rigorous data analyses that are adequate to test the stated hypotheses and justify the general conclusions drawn;
- Relies on measurement or observation methods that provide valid data across evaluators and observers and across multiple measurement and observations; and
- Has been accepted by a peer-reviewed journal or approved by a panel of independent experts through a comparably rigorous, objective, and scientific review. (Paul, 2005, pp. 13–14)

The third marker identified by Paul (2005) for demonstrating quality in research is the intense political and academic discourse in 2002 over the 1998 publication of a paper in *Psychological Bulletin*. The paper was based on a meta-analysis of data collected from college students. Of main controversy were the conclusions made by the authors indicating that child sexual abuse did not cause pervasive harm to the victims. Despite seemingly solid methodology, the inferences were clearly objectionable to the public, the policy makers, and even some members of the research community. Paul (2005) summarized the controversy by raising a general question: "Does a finding that something is true trump a social value that declares that finding to be harmful?" (p. 16).

Paul's (2005) three markers of quality demonstrate the complexities involved in answers to simple questions that ask "what constitutes a good inference?" These answers sometimes go beyond the quality of the method and design of a study. Regarding the question posed before (i.e., how one knows whether inferences are good or bad), Krathwohl (2004) characterized good inferences ("credible results," p. 148) in terms of four sets of standards: plausibility (explanation credibility), quality of implementation (translation fidelity), congruence of evidence and explanations (demonstrated results), and lack of other plausible conclusions from the results (rival explanations eliminated). Each of these standards is applicable to any QUAL or QUAN research finding, to some degree. Expanding on an earlier framework proposed by Krathwohl (1993), Tashakkori and Teddlie (1998) proposed six types of audits for assessing the credibility of inferences in research. A brief description of these six **credibility audits** is presented in Table 12.1.

Building on these ideas, we are expanding the integrative framework we previously presented (Tashakkori & Teddlie, 2003c, 2008) for assessing the quality (and transferability) of inferences in MM studies. To facilitate your understanding of this integrative framework, we first review the characteristics of quality inferences in QUAL and QUAN research.

As we show in the following sections, much of the discussion of inference quality in QUAN research has focused on internal validity (and variants, including statistical conclusion validity). QUAL researchers, on the other hand, have evaluated inference quality mostly in terms of credibility. We examine details regarding internal validity and credibility in the following sections. A major difference between QUAL and QUAN conceptualization of inference quality concerns the evaluator of the credibility of the inferences. QUAN researchers assess quality in terms of the degree of credibility of the inferences to others (e.g., to other experts). Most QUAL researchers, however, determine credibility by how well they, as human, data-gathering instruments, represent the multiple constructions of reality given to them by their informants (e.g., Lincoln & Guba, 1985; Spradley, 1979). This, however, does not preclude the role of other experts (e.g., peers, journal editors) in assessing the credibility of conclusions in QUAL studies.

Table 12.1   General Credibility Audits for Inferences in Research

Type of Audit	General Question Asked
Explanation credibility	Are the explanations for the relationship between variables theoretically and conceptually sound and acceptable?
Translation fidelity	Are the conceptual frameworks of the study (questions, hypotheses) translated into elements of the design (e.g., appropriate sampling, measurement/observation, other procedures)?
Demonstrated results	Did some result occur, and was this the one that was expected?
Credible results	Were the results consistent with previous findings in the literature?
Rival explanations eliminated	Were there other plausible conclusions on the basis of the results, or were there other explanations for the relationships?
Inferential consistency	Were the inferences and interpretations consistent with the analysis of obtained data/information? Were the inferences from parts of the same study consistent with each other?

Note: Based on Tashakkori and Teddlie (1998, pp. 69–70) and Krathwohl (1993, pp. 271–280).

Characteristics of Good Inferences in Qualitative Research

In QUAL research, a good inference should capture the meaning of the phenomenon under consideration for study participants. Druckman (2005) uses "authenticity" to characterize this:

> Issues of internal and external validity framed in a positivistic tradition are supplemented by the concerns of authenticity in the constructivist tradition. . . . Validity is evaluated from the standpoint of the participants in the research process or in terms of the joint vantage points of researcher and participant. This kind of subjective validity reflects an attempt to capture the meanings of experiences or interactions. (pp. 331, 341–342)

Guba and Lincoln (1989) consider an inference good if it is *credible*. An inference is credible if "there is a correspondence between the way the respondents actually perceive social constructs and the way the researcher portrays their viewpoints" (Mertens, 2005, p. 254). Bryman (2004, p. 284) uses *transparency* as one of the indicators of quality, both for QUAN and QUAL studies. Transparency refers to researchers' clarity of explanation regarding all stages of the study (who the participants were, how they were selected, how the data were analyzed, how the conclusions were derived).

Tobin and Begley (2004) echo the recommendation of Arminio and Hultgren (2002) to use *goodness* as an indicator of quality in QUAL research. As summarized by Tobin and Begley (2004), the aspects of goodness are as follows:

- Foundation (epistemology and theory)— this provides the philosophical stance and gives context to and informs the study
- Approach (methodology)—specific grounding of the study's logic and criteria
- Collection of data (method)—explicitness about data collection and management

- Representation of voice (researcher and participant as multicultural subjects)— researchers reflect on their relationship with participants and the phenomena under exploration
- The art of meaning making (interpretation and presentation)—the process of presenting new insights through the data and chosen methodology
- Implication for professional practice (recommendations) (p. 391)

Lincoln and Guba (1985, pp. 300–331) presented a variety of techniques for evaluating and enhancing the quality of inferences in QUAL research. Of particular interest here are dependability audit, confirmability audit, member checks, peer debriefing, negative case analysis, referential adequacy, and thick description. (See Table 12.2 for more details.)

Dependability audit concerns the *process* of the inquiry, including the appropriateness of inquiry decisions and methodological shifts.

Confirmability audit is an examination of the *product* of the inquiry to gain confidence that the interpretations are supported by the results and are internally coherent.

Member checking (discussed in Chapter 9) is a particularly powerful technique for determining the trustworthiness of interpretations and involves asking participants and other members of the social scene to check on the accuracy of the themes, interpretations, and conclusions. If participants agree with the investigators' interpretations, then evidence for the trustworthiness of the results is provided.

Peer debriefing introduces another individual into the QUAL data-gathering and analysis procedure: the "disinterested" peer. Having a dialogue with a disinterested peer (e.g., a professionally trained researcher working on other topics) about QUAL data as they are gathered and analyzed allows the researcher to clarify interpretations and identify possible sources of bias.

Negative case analysis (discussed in Chapter 11) consists of an examination of instances and cases

Table 12.2 Types of Criteria for Trustworthiness in Qualitative Research

Criterion and Definition	QUAN Analogue	Technique for Enhancement
Credibility—whether or not the reconstructions of the inquirer are "credible to the constructors of the original multiple realities" (Lincoln & Guba, 1985, p. 296)	Internal validity	1. Prolonged engagement 2. Persistent observation 3. Triangulation techniques 4. Peer debriefing 5. Negative case analysis 6. Referential adequacy 7. Member checks
Transferability—transferring of inferences from a specific sending context to a specific receiving context	External validity	8. Thick Description
Dependability—the extent to which the process of the inquiry is dependable; the ability of the human instrument to yield consistent results	Reliability	9. Dependability Audit
Confirmability—the extent to which the product of the inquiry is confirmable, including whether results are grounded in data, whether inferences are logical, whether there is inquirer bias, and so forth	Objectivity	10. Confirmability audit 11. Reflexive journal, which is relevant to credibility, transferability, dependability, and confirmability

Note: These criteria come from Lincoln and Guba (1985). Trustworthiness encompasses all four criteria and is defined as the extent to which an inquirer can persuade audiences that his or her findings are "worth paying attention to" (Lincoln & Guba, 1985, p. 290).

that do not fit within the overall pattern of results that have emerged from the QUAL analysis. It is used to revise, modify, and refine working typologies and theories. Both referential adequacy and negative case analysis are among the analogous analytical processes in QUAN and QUAL research listed in Table 11.4.

Referential adequacy (e.g., Eisner, 1975, 1998; Lincoln & Guba, 1985), another strategy for assessing and improving the quality of inferences, consists of setting aside a part of the raw data and reanalyzing it to assess the quality of inferences. A direct analogy can also be drawn between referential adequacy and QUAN statistical analyses. Researchers using certain types of statistical analysis sometimes split their sample, running the

analysis on the first half for exploratory purposes and then on the second half for confirmatory purposes. Similarly, researchers gathering QUAL data can split their data and then compare the themes that emerge from the analysis of the first part of the data with those that emerge from the second part.

Thick description (discussed in Chapter 9) involves making detailed descriptions of the context and other aspects of the research setting so that other researchers can make comparisons with other contexts in which they are working.

Reflexive journal (discussed in Chapter 9) is a diary (daily or as needed) of information about the investigator, such as the investigator's possible biases and the methodological decisions that the researcher makes. It can be used later in conducting dependability and confirmability audits and in writing reports with thick descriptions.

Finally, the *triangulation techniques* (discussed in Chapters 2, 4, and 9) are among the most important techniques for assessing and improving the quality of (data and) inferences. As we discuss later, triangulation of investigators (comparing the interpretations of more than one researcher) is controversial in QUAL research because lack of agreement might indicate that there is more than one interpretation of the same evidence.

These strategies strengthen *credibility* (comparable to *internal validity* in QUAN research), which is based on the degree of fit between the participant's realities and the investigator's constructions and representation of those realities.

Characteristics of Good Inferences in Quantitative Research

Much discussion about inference quality in QUAN research has centered on the issue of internal validity. The initial (and some of the revised) conceptualization of internal validity was solely focused on causal relationships in experimental designs. However, because much of today's QUAN social and behavioral research is nonexperimental, internal validity has been used in a less restrictive manner by scholars to denote an inference that rules out alternative plausible explanations of obtained results (see Krathwohl, 2004, p. 139). Figure 12.3 illustrates the importance of plausible alternative conclusions on the basis of the results.

Table 12.3 details current criteria and definitions of four well-known types of validity in QUAN research (e.g., Shadish, Cook, & Campbell, 2002). Table 12.4 defines eight common threats to the internal validity of QUAN research.

In the QUAN research literature, a good inference has the following characteristics:

• A good inference establishes relations between variables while providing reasonable certainty that such relationships did not happen by chance. This is often achieved by using tests of statistical significance.

"Let's run some tests before we blame it on global warming."

Figure 12.3

Table 12.3   Types of Validity in Quantitative Research

Criterion and Definition	Indicators or Threats
Statistical conclusion validity—the degree to which the statistical procedures are appropriate and adequate to detect differences or relationships; the degree to which dependable inferences about relationships between variables may be made on the basis of the results of statistical analyses	1. Low statistical power 2. Violated assumptions of statistical tests 3. Fishing and the error rate problem 4. Unreliability of measures 5. Restriction of range 6. Unreliability of treatment implementation 7. Extraneous variance in the experimental setting 8. Heterogeneity of units 9. Inaccurate effect size estimation
Internal validity—the degree to which alternative explanations for the obtained results can be ruled out; validity of the inferences about whether observed covariation between A (presumed treatment) and B (presumed outcome) reflects a causal relationship from A to B as those variables were manipulated or measured (Shadish, et al., 2002, p. 53)	1. Ambiguous temporal precedence 2. Selection 3. History 4. Maturation 5. Regression 6. Attrition 7. Testing 8. Instrumentation 9. Additive and interactive threats to internal validity
Construct validity—the degree to which the constructs under investigation are captured/measured; the degree to which inferences may be made about specific theoretical constructs, on the basis of the measured outcomes	1. Inadequate explication of constructs 2. Construct confounding 3. Mono-operation bias 4. Monomethod bias 5. Confounding constructs with levels of constructs 6. Treatment-sensitive factorial structure 7. Reactive self-report changes 8. Reactivity to the experimental situation 9. Experimenter expectancies 10. Novelty and disruption effects 11. Compensatory equalization 12. Compensatory rivalry 13. Resentful demoralization 14. Treatment diffusion
External validity—the degree to which the inferences made on the basis of the results are consistent across variation in persons, settings, treatment variables, and measurement variables	1. Interaction of the causal relationship with units 2. Interaction of the causal relationship over treatment variations 3. Interaction of causal relationship with outcomes 4. Interaction of causal relationship with settings 5. Context-dependent mediation

Note: The criteria and definitions were compiled from various sources, including Shadish et al. (2002). The indicators or threats were taken from Shadish et al. (2002, pp. 45, 55, 73, and 87), where each is defined.

Table 12.4   Threats to Inference Quality, Especially in Experimental Studies

Threat	Description
Selection	Certain attributes of one group are different from another before the study starts. Hence, differences after treatment (or a specific event in nonexperimental or qualitative research) are not solely attributable to the independent/criterion variable.
History	Events during a study might affect one group but not another, leading to differences between groups that are not solely the result of the independent variables. In nonexperimental or qualitative studies, history might refer to events happening (to a group of individuals) beyond the event that the researcher is studying.
Statistical regression	When individuals are selected on the basis of an extreme attribute (e.g., high or low performance), any difference between the pretest and the posttest might be a result of the tendency toward less extreme scores. (If there is random variation, where can the scores of students with extreme low score go?) The same threat applies to nonexperimental or qualitative studies of already established extreme cases/groups.
Maturation	Difference between the pre- and posttest might be the result of physical or psychological maturation of the participants rather than differences in the independent variable. Also, differences between two groups might be a result of one group changing at a different pace than another (selection-maturation interaction).
Pretesting	Difference (or lack of difference) between pre- and posttest might be a result of familiarity with the test (carry-over effect) rather than differences in the independent variable.
Instrumentation	Differences between pre- and posttests might be the result of random variation (unreliability) of the measures rather than the independent/criterion variable. Applications include experimental and nonexperimental or qualitative research.
Implementation	The obtained relationship between variables might be a result of experimenter/researcher/observer expectancy or participant reactivity to being studied.
Attrition/mortality	Differences between the pre- and posttest (or between the scores of two groups) might result from different individuals leaving the two groups.

Note: Sources include Ary, Jacobs, Razavieh, and Sorenson (2007), Shadish et al. (2002), and Tashakkori and Teddlie (1998, p. 87).

- Its intensity matches the demonstrated magnitude of the relationship between variables, supported by the results of data analysis. For example, there are clear problems in the literature when strong inferences and policy recommendation are made on the basis of small correlations or small effect sizes.

- It is free of systematic bias in interpretation of the results. As discussed in Chapters 4 and 5, much of today's QUAN research is postpositivist. This position acknowledges the impact of the researcher in interpretation but also recognizes the necessity of providing enough evidence for the reader to make inferences that are (it is hoped) similar to the investigator's. A good research report is one in which the researcher both reports and evaluates the inferences. The evaluator role allows the researcher to be an expert reader and reduces the possibility of systematic bias in the inferences. QUAL researchers deal with bias differently. By critically reflecting on how one's own possible biases might have shaped the inferences, and sharing these reflections with the reader, the researcher informs the reader of the possible impact of researcher bias on the inferences.

Characteristics of Good Inferences in Mixed Methods Research (Integrative Framework)

Despite the increasing use of MM in human research, there is a dearth of systematic literature on the quality (and transferability) of inferences in such research. From one point of view, scholars have considered MM as a vehicle for improving the quality of inferences that are potentially obtainable from either the QUAL or QUAN stands of a study. From another point of view, some scholars have expressed concern that MM research is potentially susceptible to weak inferences, given the difficulty of implementing two diverse types of designs/procedures for answering the same research question (or closely related aspects of a single question). A third view is that, given the assumed inconsistency between the standards for assessing the quality of inferences derived from QUAN and QUAL designs, assessing inference quality in mixed research is impossible.

An ostensible obstacle for MM researchers is that they must employ three sets of standards for assessing the quality of their inferences:

- Evaluating the inferences derived from the analysis of QUAN data using QUAN standards
- Evaluating the inferences made on the basis of QUAL data using QUAL "standards"
- Assessing the degree to which the meta-inferences made on the basis of these two sets of inferences are credible, which is

especially difficult when the two sets of inferences are inconsistent

One strategy for reducing the gap between the two sets of standards is to create an integrative framework of inference quality that incorporates both. We agree with Maxwell (2004) in his discussion of the need for greater understanding between individuals in the QUAL and QUAN camps: "Practitioners of both approaches will need to develop a better understanding of the logic and practice of the other's approach, and a greater respect for the value of the other perspective" (p. 9).

For an MM researcher, a crucial stage of the study is to integrate (e.g., compare and contrast, infuse, link, modify one on the basis of another) the two sets of inferences generated by the two strands of the study. The quality of the meta-inferences from such an integration is assessed through the process described next in this chapter. We call the process and the outcome of this evaluation an integrative framework for inference quality (Tashakkori & Teddlie, 2006, 2008). Because the integrative framework incorporates many of the standards of quality from the QUAL and QUAN approaches, it is also applicable to each of the strands and assists the MM researcher by providing at least partially common sets of standards.

A strong inference is only possible if there is an appropriate design that is implemented with quality. In such a study, research questions dictate the research design and procedures. If the procedures are not implemented with quality and rigor, the quality of obtained inferences will be uncertain. On the other hand, even with strong and well-implemented procedures, one might fail to make defensible and credible inferences. Based on these two considerations (quality of design and of interpretations), two broad families of criteria for evaluating the quality of inferences may be generated: *design quality* and *interpretive rigor*.

Table 12.5 presents various attributes and components of these two criteria. Table 12.6 provides an overview of the processes whereby the quality of MM studies is broken down by stages of the research process.

Table 12.5   Integrative Framework for Inference Quality

Aspects of Quality	Research Criterion	Indicator or Audit
Design quality	1. Design suitability (appropriateness)	1a. Are the methods of study appropriate for answering the research questions? Does the design match the research questions? 1b. Does the mixed methods design match the stated purpose for conducting an integrated study? 1c. Do the strands of the mixed methods study address the same research questions (or closely related aspects of questions)?
	2. Design fidelity (adequacy)	2. Are the QUAL, QUAN, and MM procedures or design components (e.g., sampling, data collection procedures, data analysis procedures) implemented with the quality and rigor necessary for (and capable of) capturing the meanings, effects, or relationships?
	3. Within-design consistency	3a. Do the components of the design fit together in a seamless manner? Is there within-design consistency across all aspects of the study? 3b. Do the strands of the MM study follow each other (or are they linked) in a logical and seamless manner?
	4. Analytic adequacy	4a. Are the data analysis procedures/strategies appropriate and adequate to provide possible answers to research questions? 4b. Are the MM analytic strategies implemented effectively (see Chapter 11)?
Interpretive rigor	5. Interpretive consistency	5a. Do the inferences closely follow the relevant findings in terms of type, scope, and intensity? 5b. Are multiple inferences made on the basis of the same findings consistent with each other?
	6. Theoretical consistency	6. Are the inferences consistent with theory and state of knowledge in the field?
	7. Interpretive agreement	7a. Are other scholars likely to reach the same conclusions on the basis of the same results? 7b. Do the inferences match participants' constructions?
	8. Interpretive distinctiveness	8. Is each inference distinctively more credible/plausible than other possible conclusions that might be made on the basis of the same results?

(Continued)

Table 12.5 (Continued)

Aspects Quality	Research Criterion	Indicator or Audit
	9. Integrative efficacy (mixed and multiple methods)	9a. Do the meta-inferences adequately incorporate the inferences that are made in each strand of the study?
		9b. If there are credible inconsistencies between the inferences made within/across strands, are the theoretical explanations for these inconsistencies explored, and possible explanations offered?
	10. Interpretive correspondence	10a. Do the inferences correspond to the stated purposes/questions of the study? Do the inferences made in each strand address the purposes of the study in that strand?
		10b. Do the meta-inferences meet the stated need for using an MM design? (i.e., is the stated purpose for using MM met?)

Design quality. Design quality refers to the degree to which the investigator has selected and implemented the most appropriate procedures for answering the research questions. Design quality is equally applicable to both QUAL and QUAN research. Table 12.5 presents questions you need to ask about the quality of your research design and its implementation including questions related to the following criteria:

1. **Design suitability/appropriateness** (also known as translation fidelity; Krathwohl, 2004): Was the method of study appropriate for answering the research questions? Were the study's research questions adequately and appropriately translated into design elements (e.g., sampling, data collection) that could potentially answer those questions? Depending on the type of question and research purpose (see Newman, Ridenour, Newman, & DeMarco, 2003), a different research design is needed. To explain this, Johnson and Christensen (2008) used a metaphor of needing a hammer to draw a nail. An example of a suitability problem is deciding on a design (or theoretical/methodological orientation) before one's question is framed.

2. **Design fidelity/adequacy**: Were the components of the design (e.g., sampling, data collection) implemented adequately? In experimental designs, implementation fidelity refers to the degree to which experimental procedures were strong enough (and were credible to participants) to create the expected effect. In ethnography, prolonged engagement with the group/culture under investigation is a necessary condition for credible understanding of that group/culture.

3. **Within-design consistency**: Did the design components fit together in a seamless and cohesive manner? There is a problem with design consistency if the data collection procedures (e.g., interview or focus group questions) are inconsistent with the sampling (e.g., do not match respondents' level of education or language ability). This problem has been reported in cross-cultural studies in which instruments or instructions are translated from one language or dialect to another, losing their appropriateness for the new group or context (e.g., see Van de Vijver & Poortinga, 2005).

4. **Analytic adequacy**: Are the data analysis techniques appropriate and adequate for answering

Table 12.6   Quality Issues in Mixed Methods Studies Broken Down by Stage of Study

Stage of Study	Approach	Quality Issues	Indicators of Quality	Integrative Framework
Data collection	QUAL	QUAL data quality	Credibility; dependability	Data quality
	QUAN	QUAN data quality	Reliability; validity	Data quality
Data analysis	QUAL	Within QUAL strand: issues related to appropriate and adequate analytic strategies		Analytic adequacy
	QUAN	Within QUAN strand: issues related to appropriate and adequate analytic strategies	Statistical conclusion validity	Analytic adequacy
Inference	QUAL	Within QUAL strand: issues related to making conclusions on the basis of QUAL data analysis results	Some aspects of credibility and confirmability	Interpretive rigor
			Transferability	Inference transferability
	QUAN	Within QUAN strand: issues related to making conclusions on the basis of QUAN data analysis results	Internal validity; statistical conclusion validity; some aspects of construct validity	Interpretive rigor
			External validity	Inference transferability
Integration	Mixed methods	Across strands: meta-inferential issues related to integration of QUAL and QUAN findings and inferences	Design quality; interpretive rigor	Design quality; interpretive rigor
			Inference transferability	Inference transferability

Note: This table does not include quality issues pertinent to the conceptualization stage of the QUAL and QUAN strands or the overall mixed methods design.

the research questions? Examples of problems in this respect are using parametric statistical analysis for few observations or using a priori themes analysis when a study is designed to discover new aspects of a phenomenon.

Interpretive rigor. The degree to which credible interpretations have been made on the basis of obtained results (Lincoln & Guba, 2000; Tashakkori & Teddlie, 2003c) is identified as

interpretive rigor. To assess such rigor, and improve the quality of inferences, one has to meet certain criteria:

5. **Interpretive consistency:** Does each conclusion closely follow the findings? Also, do multiple conclusions based on the same results agree with each other? There are at least two indications of interpretive consistency. First is

the consistency of the type of inference with the type of evidence. For example, causal inferences made on the basis of correlational data are clearly problematic. So are blanket policy recommendations on the basis of a few case studies or very few observations. Figure 12.4 provides an illustration of interpretive inconsistency.

Second is the inference of intensity, when the magnitude of events or effects is relatively small. In QUAN research, a multiple correlation of .50 (*r* square = .25) indicates that 75% of the variation in the predicted variable remains unaccounted. In QUAL research, a comparable problem might be found when a researcher makes strong conclusions and recommendations on the basis of limited and lukewarm evidence. Lancy (1993) addressed this problem:

> Then there is the "soapbox" problem which occurs when the data are not commensurate with the analysis, that is, either there simply isn't enough data presented to carry the elaborate analyses and conclusions or the data seem to have been selectively

arranged to support what appears to be a preexisting thesis. (p. 28)

6. **Theoretical consistency:** Is each inference (explanation for the results or for the relationships) consistent with current theories and empirical findings of other researchers? (This has also been called explanation credibility; Krathwohl, 2004.)

7. **Interpretive agreement:** Will other scholars reach the same conclusions on the basis of this particular result? If the research approach or purpose necessitates or values participants' interpretations, do the conclusions agree with their interpretations? Both in QUAN and QUAL research, a standard of quality has been the degree to which peers (i.e., other scholars or the scientific community) agree with the manner in which conclusions are drawn. A formal demonstration of this is reflected in the peer-reviewed process of journals and the evaluation of doctoral research projects by dissertation committees. In QUAL research, peer debriefing is considered an important mechanism for assessing *credibility* of the inferences.

"Stocks plummeted today on forecasts that the sun will rise again and tomorrow will be another day."

Figure 12.4

In most QUAL and QUAN research, disagreement between scholars (i.e., peers) is usually an indication of the existence of other plausible interpretations of the same results: "What qualitative researchers attempt to do, however, is to objectively study the subjective states of their subjects" (Bogdan and Biklen, 2003, p. 33).

Bogdan and Biklen (2003, p. 36) consider inconsistency a problem *only if* researchers make incompatible or contradictory conclusions. Other QUAL researchers (e.g., Richardson, 2000; Richardson & St. Pierre, 2005; Rossman & Rallis, 2003) feel comfortable about multiple explanations or interpretations (i.e., multiple realities). Other scholars have expressed concern about such inconsistencies, especially when the inferences are offered to support policy and intervention.

8. **Interpretive distinctiveness:** Is each conclusion distinctively different from other plausible conclusions based on the same results? In other words, is a conclusion clearly different and more defensible than other plausible conclusions that are ignored or refuted by the investigator? To meet this condition, the investigator must be clearly able to refute (eliminate, discount) other possible interpretations of the results. Some of the strategies for attaining this in QUAL research are the audit trail, peer debriefing, and negative case analysis. In QUAN research, much of the literature on the control of extraneous variables in experimental and quasi-experimental research has centered on interpretive distinctiveness. In such research, one must be able to show that extraneous variables are adequately accounted for and do not provide alternative plausible interpretations of the results. For example, is a change in the reading scores of third-grade children a consequence of their normal maturation and progress in school or a result of a specific after-school intervention program?

Although QUAL researchers are expected to emphasize an emic perspective in their interpretations, one of the criticisms of QUAL research focuses on the gap between the investigator's construction of the events or actions as opposed to that of their participants. In ethnography, reflective analysis is used as a process of identifying and analyzing one's biases to make sure the interpretations reflect the "truth" rather than one's personal biases (e.g., Creswell, 2003).

9. **Integrative efficacy:** This is the degree to which inferences made in each strand of an MM study are effectively integrated into a theoretically consistent meta-inference. Previously in this chapter, we indicated that all criteria/standards of quality are applicable both to each strand *and* to the meta-inferences that emerge when the inferences of two or more strands are integrated. Integrative efficacy, in contrast, is unique to meta-inferences in mixed research (i.e., it does not apply to QUAL/QUAN strands separately). It addresses the degree to which an MM researcher adequately integrates the findings, conclusions, and policy recommendations gleaned from each of the study's strands. Creswell and Tashakkori (2007a) summarized this concept as follows:

> Mixed methods research is simply more than reporting two distinct "strands" of quantitative and qualitative research; these studies must also integrate, link, or connect these "strands" in some way . . . Conclusions gleaned from the two strands are integrated to provide fuller understanding of the phenomenon under study. Integration might be in the form of comparing, contrasting, building on, or embedding one type of conclusion with the other. (p. 108)

Integration does not necessarily mean creating a single understanding on the basis of the results. We are using the term *integration* as an MM term that denotes making meaningful conclusions on the basis of consistent or inconsistent results. The term incorporates linking, elaboration, completeness, contrast, comparison, and the like.

In both QUAL and in QUAN traditions, between-methods consistency has been interpreted as an indicator of confidence, credibility, or inferential validity (e.g., Creswell, 2002; Webb, Campbell, Schwartz, & Sechrest, 1966). For MM research, consistency between two sets of inferences derived from QUAL and QUAN strands has been widely considered an indicator of quality. However, some scholars have cautioned against a simple interpretation of such consistency.[2] A major value of MM research lies in specific instances in which the two sets of inferences do not agree with each other, forcing investigators to examine their findings more closely or to create a more advanced theoretical explanation to account for multiple explanations.

Rao and Woolcock (2003) suggested that inconsistent findings might be an indication of methodological or data quality problems in one or the other strand of the study using the Delhi slums project (Jha, Rao, & Woolcock, 2005) as an example. In that study, the focus groups suggested that individuals were leaving the slums. Conversely, QUAN results did not indicate any such mobility (i.e., that there were households living outside the slums). According to Rao and Woolcock, this inconsistency in the findings might indicate problems in the QUAN sampling procedures.

Another source of inconsistency between the two sets of inferences in this study concerned the role of religious institutions in helping the urban poor. The QUAL findings gave the impression that religious institutions were important sources of credit and social support. Because the QUAN findings did not show such a role for religious institutions, Rao and Woolcock (2003) concluded that the inferences might not be transferable to the residents of Delhi slums in general but were probably unique to the participants in the focus group discussions and in-depth interviews.

If a reexamination does not reveal problems in the design of the different strands, then the next step would be to evaluate the degree to which inconsistency might indicate that the two sets are revealing two different aspects of the same phenomenon (complementarity). Also, lack of a plausible explanation for the inconsistency might indicate that one set of inferences provides the conditions for the applicability of the other (elaboration, conditionality).

Figure 12.5 summarizes the general steps or decision points in this process. Regardless of the final explanation for the inconsistency, we agree with Freshwater's (2007) suggestion that MM researchers should present the inconsistent inferences to their readers, as two possible pictures of reality.

Erzberger and Kelle (2003) argued that agreement between two or more sets of inferences increases the investigator's confidence in the conclusions. On the other hand, if the two sets of inferences are dissimilar, they might provide insight into different aspects of the same phenomenon. In such a case, when combined, the two provide a more complete meaning, a Gestalt that is bigger than the sum of its parts. This is specifically crucial in cross-cultural studies in which investigators must situate all their findings in the cultural context, habits, norms, and political realities of the participants. Chapter 11 (Box 11.5) provides an example of the attainment of this type of completeness from a World Bank study conducted in Guatemala (Rao & Woolcock, 2003).

This notion of completeness has been discussed both by QUAL and QUAN scholars. Tobin and Begley (2004) provide one example of such discussion:

> Completeness is important to qualitative inquirers, as it allows for recognition of multiple realities. Inquiries are thus not using triangulation as a means of *confirming* existing data, but as a means of enlarging the landscape of inquiry, offering a deeper and more comprehensive picture. (p. 393)

Greene, Caracelli, and Graham (1989) considered these outcomes of MM research complementary inferences. Lancy (1993) offered an example in which case studies used QUAL and QUAN evidence in a complementary manner ("qualitative and quantitative research has the potential to contribute vital information bearing on a question or a problem") or encapsulated one within the other ("embedded in a large-scale quantitative study,

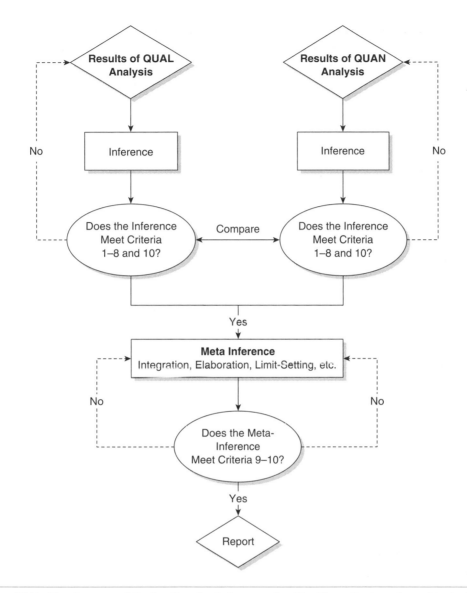

Figure 12.5 The Process of Evaluation for Inference Quality. The criteria referred to in this figure were presented in Table 12.5.

a few in-depth case studies are done to provide added context for and checks on the validity of the quantitative procedures)" (p. 11).

Sometimes, the two sets of inferences are not the same, but one reveals the conditions under which the other might or might not apply (elaboration; see Brannen, 2005, p. 176). Once again, by virtue of setting the expected limits of applicability, the meta-inference is stronger than either of

the two component inferences. Erzberger and Kelle (2003) discussed a similar instance in which multiple inferences gleaned from strands of a mixed research study are contradictory (dissonant). According to them, such inconsistency might lead to the identification of alternative theoretical explanations for the phenomenon under study. Inconsistency between two types of inferences is less problematic than is inconsistency between those inferences and the associated theoretical framework. The inconsistency might be an indicator that there are two plausible but different answers to the question (i.e., two different but equally plausible realities exist).

Divergent inferences in an MM study might be a result of two different definitions of reality that can be linked theoretically. This leads to a better understanding of the phenomenon under study. An example is Shaffer's (2002) description of two outcomes of a poverty analysis:

> In Guinea . . . household survey data suggest that women are not more likely than men to be consumption poor or to suffer greater consumption poverty. The incidence, intensity and severity of poverty is higher in male-headed households than female-headed households. . . . Further, almost no indicators of intra-household distribution of food or health care (nutritional outcome and mortality indicators, aggregate female-male ratio) reveal that girls or women are worse off than men or boys. . . . Data from the village of Kamatiguia however, suggest that women as a group are worse off than men as a group. In focus group discussions, two dimensions of deprivation were singled out by men and women which disproportionately affect women: excessive work load and restricted decision-making authority. In group discussions, a substantial majority of men and women maintained that women were "worse off" than men, and a larger majority held that in a second life they would prefer to be born male than female. Further, in well-being ranking exercises, groups of both men and women separately ranked *all but two* married village women below *all* male household heads in terms of their own criteria of well-being/ill-being. (p. 19)

Shaffer concluded that the main reason for the inconsistency was "different underlying conceptions of ill-being," rather than a result of sampling errors.

10. **Interpretive (integrative) correspondence:** Closely related to integrative efficacy, interpretive correspondence is the extent to which meta-inferences satisfy the initial purpose for using an MM design. This is the final "audit" of your study and its inferences. Earlier in this chapter (and in Chapter 7, Table 7.3), we discussed various reasons for using MM designs. The purpose of using a particular MM design might be to integrate the answers that are gleaned from multiple strands of the study (e.g., to expand, identify the limiting conditions, complement, support). On the other hand, the purpose might be to identify alternative answers to the research questions, alternative aspects of a phenomenon, or alternative constructions of reality (Freshwater, 2007). The expectation is that the meta-inferences will meet your stated purpose for mixing.

Integrative efficacy must be assessed in the context of such diversity of purposes. Unfortunately, Bryman (2006a, 2006b) and O'Cathain et al. (2007) indicated that many published MM articles fail on this criterion of quality.

As you have surely noticed, interpretive correspondence is not limited to the meta-inferences. In each strand (QUAL or QUAN), the conclusions that are made on the basis of the results must correspond to the initial research questions asked in that strand.

Elaborations and Alternatives to the Integrative Framework

Since the presentation of the integrative framework (Tashakkori & Teddlie, 2003c, 2006, 2008), other scholars have put forth either alternatives to or elaborated models of the framework. We now briefly review two of these alternatives: the *legitimation model* (Onwuegbuzie & Johnson, 2006) and the *validation framework* (Dellinger & Leech, 2007).

Anthony Onwuegbuzie and Burke Johnson (2006) used the term **legitimation** to denote all aspects of quality in MM research. Their approach is consistent with our conclusion (Teddlie & Tashakkori, 2003) that the term *validity* is so overused that it has no meaning. Onwuegbuzie and Johnson presented nine types of legitimation, each of which might be considered an audit or standard for assessing quality, although the authors refrain from proposing this. Most of these criteria are rooted in the idea of consistency between purpose and inference, research questions and research design, and inferences within the (sociopolitical) context. Others address the adequacy of paradigmatic assumptions, as well as methodological rigor/quality. Their nine types of legitimation are summarized in Table 12.7.

Onwuegbuzie and Johnson (2006) situated their discussions of quality in the context of three interrelated problems in mixed research (representation, integration, and legitimation):

The *problem of representation* refers to the difficulty in capturing (i.e., representing) lived experiences using text in general and

Table 12.7   Onwuegbuzie and Johnson's Legitimation Typology

Legitimation type	Description
Sample integration	The extent to which the relationship between the quantitative and qualitative sampling designs yields quality meta-inferences.
Inside-outside	The extent to which the researcher accurately presents and appropriately utilizes the insider's view and the observer's views for purposes such as description and explanation.
Weakness minimization	The extent to which the weakness from one approach is compensated by the strengths from the other approach.
Sequential	The extent to which one has minimized the potential problem wherein the meta-inferences could be affected by reversing the sequence of the quantitative and qualitative phases.
Conversion	The extent to which the quantitizing or qualitizing yields quality meta-inferences.
Paradigmatic mixing	The extent to which the researcher's epistemological, ontological, axiological, methodological, and rhetorical beliefs that underlie the quantitative and qualitative approaches are successfully (1) combined or (2) blended into a usable package.
Commensurability	The extent to which the meta-inferences made reflect a mixed worldview based on the cognitive process of Gestalt switching and integration.
Multiple validities	The extent to which addressing legitimation of the quantitative and qualitative components of the study result from the use of quantitative, qualitative, *and* mixed validity types, yielding high quality meta-inferences.
Political	The extent to which the consumers of mixed methods research value the meta-inferences stemming from *both* the quantitative and qualitative components of a study.

Note: Italics in original.

Source: From Onwuegbuzie and Johnson (2006), with permission.

words and numbers in particular. The *problem of legitimation* refers to the difficulty in obtaining findings and/or making inferences that are credible, trustworthy, dependable, transferable, and/or confirmable. Indeed, in many instances, these problems are exacerbated in mixed research because both the quantitative and qualitative components of studies bring into the setting their own problems of representation and legitimation, likely yielding either an additive or a multiplicative threat—hence the *problem of integration.* (p. 52, italics in the original)

Legitimation is conceptualized as a process of continuous evaluation (audit) throughout a mixed research project:

> While, clearly, making inferences is a vital part of the research process, giving inference quality primary emphasis could give the false impression that one does not have to scrutinize as carefully some of the other steps of the research process. Also, it is not clear yet what role the validity types presented in this paper . . . will play in the evaluation process. Moreover, legitimation in mixed research should be seen as a continuous process rather than as a fixed attribute of a specific research study. Mixed research tends to be iterative and interactive . . . such that, in a sense, *inference closure* (i.e., being able to make definitive statements about the quality of inferences made) might never be fully reached within a particular study or even over a series of systematically linked studies. (Onwuegbuzie & Johnson, p. 56, italics in the original)

We refer our readers to this excellent article for more details.

Amy Dellinger and Nancy Leech (2007) provide another perspective on the issue of quality: the **validation framework** (VF). Their VF is heavily rooted in the idea of construct validity, which they perceive as "encompassing all validity evidence" (p. 316):

The VF takes us beyond the idea that validity is equated with "goodness," quality, or credibility. While these are all critically important ideals and are desirable characteristics of research, we would ask, "Goodness to what purpose?" Validity as goodness ignores the purpose of research; quality serves a purpose: to make us pay attention to or value the meanings set forth by the study. Quality is important only in that it supports construct validation or the meaning of our data. It is researchers' desire to produce meaningful data and inferences through negotiation that makes it natural, practical and useful, or pragmatic, to use mixed methods approaches. (p. 329)

Dellinger and Leech's (2007) VF has four components: foundational element, inferential consistency, utilization element, and consequential element. *The foundational element* "reflects researchers' prior understanding of a construct and/or phenomenon under study" (p. 323). Such prior knowledge is important because it influences the researcher's initial attitudes, perceptions, and preferences about the research questions, methods of study, and inference-making tasks. They included "reflections on personal understanding and experiences, theoretical understanding, and understanding gained through analysis and evaluation of research related to the construct or phenomenon" (p. 323). Their discussion indicated that quality audits must include explicit examination and understanding of the researcher's assumptions, possible biases, and knowledge of current literature.

Inferential consistency is somewhat similar to what we presented in our *integrative framework* and examines the degree to which inferences are consistent with the current body of knowledge and theory, with the study's design and findings, and with each other (including examination of the consistency of the meta-inferences with the component inferences from different strands of an MM study). The *utilization/historical element* refers to the degree to which the inferences in a study contribute to the meaning of a construct as judged by others: "Utilization or historical validity evidence accrues to a study's inferences, measures, or findings because of use (appropriate or not) in extant literature or in other applications, such as decision making or policy development." Finally, the *consequential element* is based on judging the "social acceptability of consequences that occur as a result of using a study's findings, measures, or inferences" (Dellinger & Leech, 2007, p. 325).

We find both the Onweugbuzie and Johnson (2006) and Dellinger and Leech (2007) frameworks creative and thought provoking. Both have common elements with our *integrative framework*, which we presented earlier. However, neither is able to provide a cohesive and comprehensive alternative for evaluating and improving the quality of inferences in MM research. It is highly probable that a future set of standards for MM research will emerge, combining both models with our *integrative framework* (or others).

Transferability of Inferences in Mixed Methods Research

Although we mentioned inference transferability earlier, we postponed a detailed discussion of it until now for a reason: Until you are confident that your inferences are well conceived and credible, transferability issues (to whom, in what context, under what circumstances) are irrelevant. We must also reiterate that social/behavioral research is done to solve a problem or answer a question of importance to society and its organizations. (Refer to Chapter 6.) As such, the outcome of most research must be useful to those who make policy or produce social changes. We believe that any type of research should be relevant to someone, somewhere, under some conditions.

For most published research, findings and inferences that do not have *any relevance* to settings and people outside of the context studied are of little value. Even in action research, projects in which the investigator might be searching for solutions to a specific problem in a specific setting, the setting and the individuals who are studied change over time. Transferability of the findings to a future time in the lives of the individuals or units under investigation is always an important consideration. Also, findings from such action research projects might be useful to others who are working or solving problems in comparable settings.

Thus, your inferences and the resulting recommendations are always transferable (in varying degrees) to other settings, people, organizations, time periods, or ways of defining your constructs. Transferability is a matter of degree and depends highly on the extent of the similarity between the context and people in your study and the "receiving" context. It is always a good idea to specify the possible boundaries of transferability in the conclusion of your study report.

The reader should understand that MM studies enjoy a dual advantage in terms of inference transferability. From one point of view, larger and more representative samples in your QUAN strand might provide greater confidence in generalizing your findings to other samples, settings, or populations. From another point of view, the rich and inclusive understandings that you obtain from your QUAL strand may provide the details necessary for a comprehensive assessment of the conditions from which the inferences were made and to which the recommendations may be transferred. Depending on the goals and circumstances of your research, your inferences might have different types and degrees of transferability, which are not mutually exclusive.

Ecological transferability is the degree to which your inference and your policy and practice recommendations might be applicable to other settings similar to yours. Though it is hard to imagine any two contexts or social settings that are completely similar, it is also difficult to imagine that there are no other settings similar to the one you have studied.

For these reasons, your inferences and recommendations are always at least partly applicable to other related settings. In the Orihuela (2007) study presented in Chapter 11 (Box 11.3), the inferences are almost certainly transferable to similar schools in the district and probably to similar schools and classrooms in other geographical areas. The inferences made regarding the teaching-strategy training might also be transferable to colleges of education that teach the specific teacher preparation course. Obviously, the more similar these settings are to the one studied by Orihuela, the more transferable the inferences and recommendations. Ecological transferability issues overlap with those for population transferability.

Population transferability is the degree to which your inferences and recommendations are applicable to other people (individuals/groups) or other entities (texts, artifacts). In some types of studies (e.g., survey designs), transferability to a population is of utmost importance. In others (e.g., ethnographies), although the possibility of transferability is desirable, it is not crucial. Regardless, in both examples, you should use whatever precautions and strategies you can (e.g., thick description, audit trail) to maximize the transferability of your inferences.

Temporal transferability is the degree to which your inferences and recommendations may be applicable in the future. This also may be considered ecological transferability because social and cultural contexts change continuously. Once again, it is desirable to adopt all possible strategies to make sure your findings are not unique to only the specific time period (e.g., the specific week or month of studying a school district or a social organization). Would Orihuela's (2007) inferences hold if the study were conducted next quarter? Next year?

Theoretical/conceptual transferability is the degree to which the findings and inferences of a study can be replicated if the main theoretical constructs are defined and observed differently. For example, in the Orihuela (2007) study described in Box 11.3, if teaching effectiveness were defined in the form of student performance on standardized high-stakes tests, would the differences between the two groups of teachers show the same pattern of results?

Summary

We presented a detailed discussion pertaining to the quality of inferences in MM research, starting with an examination of previous views about such quality in QUAL and QUAN traditions. Deliberately avoiding the term *validity* due to the controversies and disagreements over its definition, we focused on the concepts of *inference quality* and *inference transferability*. We summarized the standards/audits for evaluation of inference quality and transferability in QUAL and QUAN traditions and pointed to their similarities and differences. We then presented our integrative framework of inference quality and transferability, which consists of design quality and interpretive rigor. The first component addresses the quality of the data, design, and data analysis procedures. The second component addresses the process of making inferences on the basis of the findings from a study.

Review Questions and Exercises

1. Explain why we need separate standards for evaluating the quality of inferences and the quality of data and results on which those inferences are based.

2. Explain why the standards for evaluating the quality of inferences might not be the same in QUAL and QUAN approaches. What are some of the possible differences?

3. Describe some of the possible conceptual similarities between the QUAL and QUAN approaches to evaluating research inferences.

4. What similarities and differences do you see between the QUAN concept of external validity and the QUAL concept of transferability? Can the two be bridged? Explain how.

5. Provide some examples of different types of inference transferability in research.

6. An advantage of MM might be in providing an opportunity to maximize the inference quality and transferability of the inferences in a single study. Explain how this might happen. Find a research example that demonstrates this (e.g., a study that provides credible answers to research questions while also providing inference transferability to other settings or populations).

7. Examine the Barron et al. (2008) study in Appendix B on the companion Web site (www.sagepub.com/foundations). Did the use of QUAL and QUAN methods/ approaches enhance both transferability and inference quality? Explain your answer.

8. What is the main difference between design quality and interpretive rigor? How can you, as an investigator, maximize both?

9. Do a search to locate an MM study in the literature. Evaluate each strand of the study in terms of design quality criteria and interpretive rigor. Identify how the authors integrated the data, results, and inferences of multiple strands of the study. Evaluate the quality of their integration by linking the final meta-inferences to original research questions and stated purposes for using an MM design.

10. Explain how a parallel MM study might be different from a sequential MM study in the way the inferences are made and integrated.

11. Examine the Barron et al. study (2008) in Appendix B on the companion Web site (www.sagepub.com/foundations). The authors report that the "quantitative instruments were designed and developed while the qualitative work was being conducted; as such, their design reflected the ongoing findings of—and methodological lessons learned from—the qualitative fieldwork." Given this and other information about the study, how would you classify their MM design? After you examine all of the reported steps and possible inferences made in each, identify the strategies that the authors used to increase or audit the quality of their inferences. What other strategies can you recommend to them?

Key Terms

Analytic adequacy

Credibility audits

Design fidelity (adequacy)

Design quality

Design suitability (appropriateness)

Ecological transferability

Inferences

Inference process

Integrative efficacy

Integrative framework for inference quality and transferability

Interpretive agreement

Interpretive consistency

Interpretive (integrative) correspondence

Interpretive distinctiveness

Interpretive rigor

Legitimation

Population transferability

Temporal transferability

Theoretical consistency

Theoretical/conceptual transferability

Validation framework

Within-design consistency

Notes

1. An earlier version of this chapter was published in Max M. Bergman (2008). The chapter by Tashakkori and Teddlie (2008) was titled "Quality of Inferences in Mixed Methods Research: Calling for an Integrative Framework."

2. An issue for future development is the determination of inconsistency. Is it possible to have some differences between the two sets, without calling them inconsistent (i.e., different but not meaningfully)? How much difference is acceptable?

Epilogue

Politics, Challenges, and Prospects

In this chapter we first examine some of the current issues and controversies in mixed methods (MM) research, which has experienced progress and growth during the past two decades. This rapid growth has created an excellent opportunity for discourse, development, and creativity plus fertile ground for divergence of thought (and, at times, disagreement). In this chapter, against the backdrop of such fast development, we discuss some of the political and theoretical issues that require attention.

Controversies relating to the role of worldview in MM are revisited (also see Chapter 5), followed by a review of issues pertaining to researching, writing, and publishing papers and dissertations. We then present a brief overview of pedagogical challenges. The chapter ends with a reexamination of the challenges facing research methodology in general and integrated methodology specifically. We call for the acceleration of the process of creating bridges between diverse viewpoints in MM.

Politics, Challenges, and Prospects Facing Mixed Methods

We reviewed many concepts and processes concerning MM research in this text because, like a traveler on a journey, we need to identify exactly where we are before the next stage of the journey begins. The developmental trajectory of MM has been very steep, resulting in an exciting, volatile, and occasionally contentious discourse.

Like many other "movements," MM has faced philosophical, methodological, and political challenges. Probably the political challenges are the least evident but the most contentious. Criticism of MM research comes from purists who see it as a threat to their traditional qualitative (QUAL) or quantitative (QUAN) domains. They are concerned that MM might somehow dilute the purity and legitimacy of the traditional methodologies. Support for MM comes from scholars and practitioners who seek additional tools for answering their research questions and do not support the traditional QUAL-QUAN dichotomy. Unfortunately, graduate students who are engaged in thesis and dissertation research are often caught in political and academic disputes about the type of approach or method their committees sanction.

As demonstrated by the historical review in Chapters 3 and 4, MM research is not new; its intellectual roots date to antiquity. It is not old because an active attempt to systematically define, refine, and use MM is only a couple of decades old.

Throughout this book, we presented examples of MM research projects in the social and behavioral sciences from the past five decades. Some forms of integrated research projects in anthropology and sociology were even conducted early in the 20th century (e.g., the Hawthorne Studies and the Mariental project conducted in the 1920s and 1930s and reviewed in Chapter 4). What is new is a systematic way of looking at integrated research in the context of the paradigm wars between proponents of QUAL and QUAN approaches. As an alternative to the dichotomy of QUAL and QUAN approaches, MM categorizes research endeavors on multiple dimensions, each consisting of a continuum, as described in Chapter 5 and elsewhere (e.g., Teddlie, Tashakkori, & Johnson, 2008).

Throughout this book, we argued that the three methodological orientations (QUAL, QUAN, and MM) are each a "proxy" for many different (but related) ideas, perspectives, methods, and sociopolitical orientations. Russell Bernard (2007), a prominent anthropologist speaking at the American Educational Research Association in Chicago, strongly advocated against a simplistic and exclusive acceptance of the terms *qualitative* and *quantitative* as two sides of a dichotomy. We echo his wisdom and remind our readers that these terms do not mean the same thing to all scholars. For example, qualitative research invokes broad reactions to a myriad of concepts, philosophical orientations, research questions, research methods/designs, methods of analyzing data, preferences in making certain types of inferences as compared to others, and variations in how the findings of qualitative studies may be used for policy, as demonstrated by the three editions of the *Handbook of Qualitative Research* (e.g., Denzin & Lincoln, 2005a). A similar diversity of representations is also present regarding quantitative research.

To at least partially demonstrate this, early in this book we introduced a multidimensional view of integrated methodology. Dimensions included various components or aspects of the process of inquiry (see Chapters 2 and 5). Among them were the worldviews (e.g., from postpositivist to constructivist), the types of questions (e.g., from inductive to deductive), the types of data collection strategies (e.g., from fully unstructured interview to rigidly structured questionnaires), the types of data analysis strategies (e.g., from highly preplanned structural equation modeling to emergent themes analysis), and the role of the investigator in the process (e.g., from a predominantly emic to a highly etic perspective).

One consequence of these considerations is the recognition that there is no single mixed/integrated approach to research. When discussing the issue of integration (of QUAL and QUAN approaches) in MM, one must be keenly aware of the dimensions or levels in which integration might occur. For example, integration might happen at the level of research questions, via numeric and narrative data collection, multiple modes of data analysis (e.g. reanalysis of quantitized or qualitized data), and inference making on the basis of findings of the QUAL and QUAN strands of a study. Box E.1 presents the observations and personal reflections of a mixed methods researcher regarding some of these issues.

Box E.1

Reflections of an International Development Researcher on Avoiding False Divides

The question of whether quantitative research is preferable to qualitative research creates a false divide for researchers. It is particularly important to avoid subscribing to the notion that quantitative research is "scientific," "hard," "masculine," and "objective," while qualitative research is "interpretive," "soft," "feminine," and "subjective." This perception leads to the unfortunate conclusion that research done by women is by definition qualitative, and that only qualitative research can understand and give voice to women. Qualitative research should not be equated with gender analysis, and quantitative research should not be equated with universalistic analysis. All research, regardless of method or technique, must deal with constant tradeoffs between cost, time, validity, generalizability, completeness, and resonance with both those who are the subjects of the research and those who will read the research. Issues such as power relations between researchers and subjects, empowerment of subjects, links between studies and practice, and involvement and detachment of researchers in practice are critical for all researchers, regardless of the methods used. It is important that all researchers use two types of indicators when they investigate broad social issues such as poverty; race, ethnic, and gender discrimination; and social and economic restructuring. These are, first, indicators of the standpoints and actions of the actors in the situation, especially the often left-out voice of poor women (agency), and, second, indicators of change or lack of change in relations of persistent inequalities such as those between employers and workers, landlords and tenants, or husbands and wives (structure). My own experience in conducting research to bring about social change and influence social policy indicates that the most persuasive policy research includes both of these elements: *numbers* that define the scope and patterns of the problem, and a *story* that shows how the problem works in daily life and provides for empathetic understanding. These two elements stem from quantitative and qualitative research. Integrated approaches are as effective for the analysis of victims' stories of exploitation and oppression as they are for the analysis of "success stories" of programs, policies, or actions that helped to overcome persistent inequalities. (Spalter-Roth, 2000, p. 48)

Top-Down Versus Bottom-Up View of Mixed Methods

Recently, Creswell and Tashakkori (2007b) introduced their thoughts on the multiple perspectives that MM scholars and researchers have taken or advocated in their publications and presentations. They identified four perspectives: methods, methodology, paradigm, and practice, which are delineated in the rest of this section. Some scholars consider MM at the technical level, including data collection and analysis strategies to answer questions.

Such questions could be rooted in the QUAL or QUAN orientation of the investigator. The most important concept about MM for these scholars is the technical efficacy of procedures for using both QUAL and QUAN methods of data collection and analysis.

A second group of scholars views MM in a slightly more general manner. They consider MM as more than a new set of techniques for collecting and analyzing data. They are interested in MM as a distinct methodology of integration that can lead to an enhanced worldview, more comprehensive research questions, more dependable/reliable data, greater options for data analysis, and stronger opportunities for making credible and meaningful inferences.

A third group of scholars is interested in philosophical foundations for MM. They write to elaborate on or to introduce new philosophical and theoretical foundations for mixed methods or to convince other scholars of the reasons why MM is not possible. These scholars write about a paradigm or worldview and how it might affect the outcome of MM studies. David Morgan (2007) has called this a top-down perspective on MM (and research methods in general).

Finally, a fourth group of scholars has used multiple and mixed methods in their own research efforts, borrowing whatever idea, method, or perspective needed from QUAL and QUAN approaches. They have a bottom-up view of MM (to differentiate it from the top-down approach described earlier). To these scholars, the QUAL-QUAN dichotomy is largely irrelevant because they tend to modify their practice as necessary to answer their research/evaluation questions. Creswell and Tashakkori (2007b) called this a practice perspective to MM. This is probably the oldest perspective in MM because it has been practiced by numerous researchers and program evaluators for 50 or more years.

This last category of scholars possesses attributes that tilt in favor of MM and will probably help to maintain its developmental trajectory. They are rooted in all disciplines of human sciences and constitute the largest group of MM scholars. To skeptics' criticism that one can't do MM research due to incompatibility of worldviews, these scholars simply respond that they have done it already! Few of these researchers and evaluators explicitly acknowledge a paradigm stance in their work or reports (see Bryman, 2007, for examples). This, however, should not be interpreted as a lack of worldview. As Greene (2007) suggested, these scholars' mental models have undoubtedly been integral to their process of research.

We hope that this brief discussion demonstrates an area of agreement among MM scholars: The integration of approaches might occur in different forms, in multiple stages, and with different intensities. As discussed in Chapter 7, MM projects are often creatively dynamic, changing their designs as needed to maximize the opportunity for finding credible answers to questions.

General Guidelines for Conducting and Publishing Mixed Methods Studies

In Chapters 9 and 12, we discussed various issues in assessing the quality of data and inferences in MM research. We would like to expand on these discussions by describing the attributes of a strong MM manuscript, grant proposal, or dissertation and then make some tentative suggestions about them. (See Figure E.1.)

Figure E.1

Rao and Woolcock (2003) suggested several guidelines for conducting a strong MM evaluation project. Although they discussed the guidelines in terms of international development projects, we think they are appropriate for research in other disciplines as well. Parts of their guidelines are quoted here:

• Use . . . an iterative approach where qualitative work informs the construction of a quantitative questionnaire. Allow for findings from the field to broaden your set of outcome or explanatory variables.

• Unlike quantitative questionnaires, qualitative questions should be open-ended to allow respondents to give relatively unconstrained responses. The question should be an opportunity to have an extended discussion.

• Qualitative work should follow principles of evaluation design similar to those for quantitative work.

• The qualitative sample should be large enough to reflect the major elements of heterogeneity in the population.

• Spend enough time in the community to allow an in-depth examination. This may sometimes mean anything from a week to several weeks depending upon the size and heterogeneity of the community.

• Hypotheses derived from the qualitative work should be tested for their generalizability with the more representative quantitative data.

- Use the qualitative information to interpret and contextualize quantitative findings.

- A poor and inexperienced qualitative team can have a much larger adverse impact on the collection of good quality qualitative information than on quantitative data.

- *Qualitative methods should be thought of not as an inexpensive alternative to large surveys, but as tools to collect information that is difficult to gather and analyze quantitatively.* (p. 185, italics in the original)

In an editorial in the second issue of the *Journal of Mixed Methods Research,* Creswell and Tashakkori (2007a) provided three broad attributes of a publishable MM manuscript:

First, the manuscripts need to be well-developed in both quantitative and qualitative components. The article is expected to have two distinct strands, one qualitative and one quantitative, each complete with its own questions, data, analysis, and inferences. The databases for both components need to be sizable, to be obtained through accepted and rigorous data collection (or conversion) methods, and to be analyzed using sophisticated analytic procedures. Meaningful inferences must be made from the results of each strand, and validation procedures reported. . . . Second, mixed methods research is simply more than reporting two distinct "strands" of quantitative and qualitative research; these studies must also integrate, link, or connect these "strands" in some way. . . . The expectation is that by the end of the manuscript, conclusions gleaned from the two strands are integrated in order to provide a fuller understanding of the phenomenon under study. Integration might be in the form of comparing, contrasting, building on, or embedding one type of conclusion with the other. . . . A third attribute of a strong empirical mixed methods manuscript is that it includes mixed methods components that add to the literature about mixed methods research. Granted, this literature-base is emerging and may not be well known to individuals in specific discipline fields, but it might be located in several places. (pp. 108–109)

Similar guidelines may be applicable to grant proposals and dissertation projects.

Based on these guidelines, we make the following suggestions:

1. State your research questions clearly and explain why MM is necessary. Vague statements such as "mixed methods was used to gain better understanding" are not sufficient. Explain how such understanding was needed and how it was gained. Explain how the use of both approaches made it possible to make inferences that would have been different if only one approach or strand had been used.

2. Make sure your manuscript has a structure similar to other manuscripts in the mainstream journals that publish MM. For example, a paper by Thomas W. Christ (2007) had the following sections and headings:
   - Title
   - Abstract
   - Introduction (no heading)
   - Mixed Method Study Overview
   - Phase I: National Survey Analysis
   - Phase II: Cross-Case Analysis

- Phase III: Longitudinal Analysis
- Synopses of the Results
  - Phase I Results
  - Phase II Results
  - Phase III Results
- Mixed Methods and Longitudinal Design Implications
- Limitations
- Discussion
- References

You can find other styles of presentation by searching for MM articles in your area of study or by reviewing the *Journal of Mixed Methods Research.*

One possible model for a mixed methods dissertation has the following structure, plus tentative components:

- Title pages.
- Abstract—Make sure you include a brief summary of every section, especially your purpose, questions, sample or data sources, design, results, and inferences.
- Chapter 1: Introduction—State the importance of the problem, purpose of doing your study, questions, sociocultural context of study, and so on. Also include a section regarding the advantages of using an MM design.
- Chapter 2: Related Literature—State your research questions up front and then present an extensive discussion of tentative answers to these questions in the literature. Critically review previous attempts to answer related questions by other researchers (make sure you present the methods, findings, and inferences of the main studies in the field) and demonstrate a need for a new study with enhanced methods (especially the advantage of doing MM research).
- Chapter 3: Methods—State your research questions again (it is OK to repeat them!) and describe all the steps you will take to answer them, including sampling procedures and rationale, data collection procedures, research design, and brief data analysis plan. You might have to divide each section into subsections to present information about your strands. Alternatively, it might be easier (especially in sequential MM designs) to present one strand fully and then present the other.
- Chapter 4: Analysis of Qualitative Data—Present a summary of the research questions that needed a QUAL strand. Clearly explain your QUAL analysis strategies and present the results that answer relevant questions/objectives. Make tentative conclusions, on the basis of your findings, as answers to the research questions. Audit every conclusion for inference quality (see Figure 12.5). Provide evidence to help readers reach the conclusions you made with certainty.
- Chapter 5: Analysis of Quantitative Data—This is similar to your QUAL analysis in Chapter 4. (If your QUAL or QUAN strand is relatively small, you might want to combine Chapters 4 and 5 into one chapter, with two sections.)
- Chapter 6: Discussion and Conclusions—Present your research questions again, and answer them by making inferences based on the tentative answers from Chapters 4 and 5. Integrate your QUAL and QUAN inferences and expand your conclusions to a higher (more comprehensive, abstract) level by comparing, contrasting, expanding, or limiting each answer based on the others. Theories may be generated here; therefore,

link your findings to the current literature and offer a more comprehensive and cohesive understanding of the phenomenon you are studying.

- References—Follow relevant formats and requirements.
- Appendixes—Add instruments and protocols and supporting documents as needed to help your readers understand your process.

3. If your manuscript is based on your dissertation, restructure using the format of the journal to which you are submitting. In general, avoid dissertation title headings, such as Problem Statement, Research Question, and so on.

4. Rejection of a manuscript typically does not happen for only one reason (unless your method is inappropriate for your questions or your design is obviously flawed). In our experiences as journal editors and reviewers, we have found that a number of small problems can easily lead to rejection of a manuscript, whereas the presence of one or two major problems that can be fixed might result in an author receiving instructions to "revise and resubmit." Small, easily preventable problems that might lead to rejection include typos, grammatical errors, missing references, a mismatch between the text and reference list (e.g., listing references not referred to in the text), violations of required style (e.g., American Psychological Association [APA], American Sociological Association [ASA], or other required professional formats), tables that are directly copied from statistical programs (i.e., have unnecessary or redundant columns or information), too many small tables, and extensive quotes.

5. Make sure that at the end of your manuscript you link the conclusions of various strands of your study and explain how the use of only one approach (QUAL or QUAN) could have led to different or limited conclusions and recommendations; emphasize that you were able to make your conclusions because you used both approaches. It is not enough to say a better understanding was gained. How? Why? Compare and contrast the findings and inferences and link the final conclusions to theory and previous literature to show that using both approaches did, indeed, provide a different picture.

6. Most journals require that you add your tables and figures at the end of the manuscript but include placeholders in the text. For example, immediately following the paragraph in which you mention a table in your text (e.g., Table 1), add a placeholder, like this:

Insert Table 1 about here

The publisher will format your tables and graphs and put them close to where they are mentioned in the text.

7. Documents have a nasty habit of changing format as they go from one computer to another. To prevent this, save your manuscript (including tables, graphs, etc.) in PDF format. A manuscript saved in this format does not change its editing structure (e.g., spaces, headings, lines, paragraphs, table format).

8. Most journals require that you upload your manuscript into their system online. When given an option, upload PDF files rather than regular word processing files.

Teaching of (Integrated) Research Methodology

We are often asked by our colleagues about the best way to train graduate students in MM. We consider this to be more a question of how to teach research methodology in general, rather than MM, because we believe that all research methodology courses, regardless of their level, should be taught in an integrated manner. Examination of research textbooks published in the last 30 years reveals a clear trend toward this integrated orientation (Tashakkori, Newman, & Bliss, 2008). Before the 1990s, almost all textbooks lacked a QUAL methods section, or at most had a section on historical research. In the 1990s, a two-part division appeared in an increasing number of textbooks, with little effort to link the QUAL and QUAN sections of the texts. In the 21st century, this strict dichotomy of QUAL and QUAN approaches seems to be deemphasized or diminishing. Furthermore, textbooks are increasingly adding sections or chapters on integrated methods. Despite this gradual shift in textbook content, we do not have any data regarding changes in actual classroom teaching practices. Based on shifts in textbook content, we expect that at least some instructors are teaching research methods courses in a relatively integrated manner, but this issue needs further study.

In 1998, concurrent with Isadore Newman and Carolyn Benz (Ridenour), we wrote about the need to reform how faculty members teach research methodology in the social and behavioral sciences. We complained pointedly about our colleagues encouraging (or coercing) students to choose a QUAL or QUAN track early in their graduate studies. We also expressed our frustration with the wall between the two approaches that is implied in research methods books. A decade later, even though we can report a sharp reduction in both practices, there are still indications of tracking of graduate students and a dichotomy of methods in most general research methodology textbooks. (For more details, see Tashakkori & Teddlie, 2003b.) We challenge the research methodology community (not just MM scholars) to explore the similarities and bridges between the QUAL and QUAN approaches, rather than focus on their differences.

A similar concern regarding dissertations has emerged from our interactions with graduate students across disciplines and geographic locations (e.g., universities in the United States, Europe, Japan, Australia, New Zealand, Taiwan). Many of these students complain that they are being strongly advised against using both QUAL and QUAN approaches in their dissertations, when they themselves clearly see advantages in doing so. We hear stories about dissertation committee members threatening to quit ("only over my dead body," one student quoted a member!) or actually refusing to serve on committees if the two approaches were used in the same project. Certainly, the escalating number of publications advocating the use of both approaches is providing persuasive tools for graduate students to use, but discouraging statements by visible figures in the QUAL (and to some extent the QUAN) research communities are not making life any easier for some of the students.

Additionally, an Internet search for texts reveals many "cookbooks" about how to do a qualitative dissertation or a quantitative dissertation. In many academic programs, professors are explicitly "cloning" themselves by training a cadre of new QUAL or QUAN researchers, who will remain one-dimensional in their future research endeavors, regardless of the topics of their research projects. Undoubtedly, there are social, political, and monetary incentives for some scholars to keep QUAL and QUAN methods separate. This is a sensitive subject for some, but researchers must remain open to discussing it. We are often told by faculty in various universities that "I am a QUAL researcher and I do not understand QUAN methods and results," or vice versa. Many of our colleagues choose research questions that fit their methodological training and impose a rigid framework of research on any other question that they encounter. We believe that applying a single approach, with a limited set of methods, to all research problems seriously limits the quality of the answers to researchers' questions.

Following this line of reasoning, we believe even more so than before that research methods courses should be taught with a focus on the integration of, and commonality between, QUAL and QUAN approaches/methods. Therefore, we challenge our colleagues and students to set the stage for competency in both approaches, as well as in possible ways of combining, integrating, or linking them.

Assuming and advocating a single worldview (research paradigm) is arbitrary because it does not match our authentic human problem-solving and decision-making process. In everyday life, we do not understand the world through a single lens. Pretending that a researcher transforms into something less denies the authenticity of the research process and the skills of the individuals who are engaged in research. Teaching research in such a one-dimensional manner is unfair to our students.

More Details About the Teaching of Mixed Methodology

In a recent paper (2007), Mark Earley presented an eloquent account of his attempt to develop an effective syllabus for teaching MM. Using a 12-step process (adopted from Fink, 2003), he dynamically involved his students in the development of this syllabus. A set of class activities was planned to reach four primary learning goals of the course (Earley, 2007, p. 149, Table 2):

- Highlighting of terminology used in various texts read for class
- Tracking of verbiage used in published studies about methods and design
- Peer discussion of drafts
- Reading of published studies
- Instructor's presentation of examples throughout the course
- Class discussions about the research process
- Reflections
- Class discussions about locating mixed methods resources

For each activity, specific assessment strategies were planned. We strongly urge our readers to examine Earley's description of this developmental process.

What types of competencies are needed in an MM course? Natalya Ivankova's course syllabus[1] provides an excellent answer. She summarized these competencies in the form of 12 expected course outcomes:

1. Understand the philosophical assumptions underlying the use of mixed methods research.

2. Articulate the key characteristics of a mixed methods research study.

3. Use appropriate search terms for locating mixed methods research studies using computerized databases.

4. Understand and explain the rationale for using a mixed methods research approach in a study.

5. Understand and explain the major types of mixed methods research designs; their strengths and weaknesses.

6. Develop a purpose statement and research questions for a mixed methods research study.

7. Summarize the types of data that are often collected in mixed methods research and be able to distinguish between quantitative and qualitative types.

8. Summarize the data analysis strategies within mixed methods research designs.

9. Integrate or mix quantitative and qualitative data within mixed methods research designs.

10. Report and evaluate mixed methods research studies.

11. Draw a visual model of the mixed methods procedures used in the study.

12. Apply the steps in designing a mixed methods research study and develop a mixed methods study proposal.

We are confident that you will find other examples by searching the Internet. If you are planning to teach a course in MM, you can use these examples as models to create your own. If you are a student, we hope these models will sharpen your focus on learning specific competencies.

Challenges and Future Directions

Like many events and trends in our world, the evolution of MM research methodology is difficult to predict. In our previous work (Teddlie & Tashakkori, 2003), we detailed a number of challenges facing mixed methods.

1. The nomenclature, definitions, and conceptualization of MM research

2. The use of, and rationale for, MM research (why do we do it)

3. The paradigm issues in MM research

4. Design issues and classification in MM research

5. Issues in drawing inferences and assessing their quality in MM research

6. The logistics of teaching, learning, and conducting MM research

An impressive number of books and journal articles have appeared in the last few years that have responded to several of these challenges. The list includes excellent books by Bergman (2008), Creswell and Plano Clark (2007), Greene (2007), Ridenour and Newman

(2008), and others. A new journal (*Journal of Mixed Methods Research*) was proposed in 2004 and the first issue was published in 2007. Hundreds of articles about integrated methods have appeared in journals in the past few years. There are also visible changes in the publication policies of many journals in social and behavioral sciences; these journals are now increasingly embracing and accepting MM manuscripts for publication. A few journals (e.g., *Research in the Schools*,[2] *Quality and Quantity*, *Journal of Educational Research*, *International Journal of Social Research Methodology*) have recently devoted special issues to MM. In July 2008, the MM community celebrated its fourth international conference in Cambridge, England. (Many of these advances were also described in the final section of Chapter 4.)

Despite considerable progress in reaching common ground among MM scholars, some issues mentioned earlier are still present today. For example, there is a need for discourse on the nature of research questions in MM, there are multiple design classifications, and there are multiple frameworks for evaluating the quality of inferences. We discussed these issues and dilemmas throughout this text, and we make final observations about them now.

Issues regarding the conceptualization of MM research questions are in need of further discussion. We need to answer the following simple questions: How does one frame a research question in an MM study? Should it be stated as a combination of separate QUAL and QUAN questions, or as a single question that is general and incorporates both? Exploring possible responses to these questions, Tashakkori and Creswell (2007a) presented three different models:

1. Separate QUAL and QUAN questions followed by an explicit question regarding the nature of integration (e.g., "Do the quantitative and qualitative findings converge?", Creswell & Plano Clark, 2007, p. 107)

2. Overarching, mixed (hybrid, integrated) questions (similar to what we discussed in Chapter 6)

3. Separate research questions as each phase of the study evolves

The implications of each option require further discussion by the MM community.

Other issues mentioned earlier have changed over time but still need discussion and development. For example, there has been progress in developing a nomenclature for MM. However, the issue of nomenclature has taken a new shape, due to the mushrooming of taxonomies, terminologies, and concept maps. There is a need for examining of multiple frameworks, taxonomies, and terminologies, with the goal of reaching common ground.

Closely related to the old issues and dilemmas, mentioned earlier, three questions have recently dominated the discourse in the MM scholarly community. We frame them here exactly as we hear them being asked by conference and workshop participants and by our students and colleagues:

1. "Why do we do MM, given that it adds cost, complexity, and the possibility of headaches if inconsistent inferences emerge from the QUAL and QUAN components?" The last part of this question is more salient for graduate students and beginning researchers who are concerned that they will be stuck at the end with divergent results.

2. "How do we integrate QUAL and QUAN components, findings, inferences?" Alan Bryman's (2006a) article titled "Integrating Quantitative and Qualitative Research:

How Is It Done?" contains a recent example. He reports the results of content analysis of 232 social science articles, which revealed more than 16 different ways of integration. Although he found examples of integration at all stages of the research process (e.g., instrument development, sampling), many of the studies seemed to be integrating at the inference stage (e.g., triangulation, completeness, explanation, confirmation, discovery). Another interesting finding was that the rationale given for MM did not necessarily match the actual practice at the end, suggesting that "there is quite often a mismatch between the rationale for the combined use of quantitative and qualitative research and how it is used in practice" (p. 110).

3. "How do we know what is a good MM project or article?" In Chapter 12, we offered detailed discussions of the quality issue in MM research, which seems to be one of the most salient for scholars today. In addition to our own integrative framework, several other scholars have put forth models of quality, including Onwuegbuzie and Johnson's (2006) *legitimation model* and Dellinger and Leech's (2007) *validity framework*. We discussed these alternative frameworks in Chapter 12. Each has similarities and differences with others and conceptualizes quality in a slightly different manner. It is conceivable that in the near future, MM researchers will be able to create a more comprehensive system that incorporates components of these (and other) ideas to create a more unified set of audits or standards for integrated research (and for QUAL and QUAN components).

It is often said that MM is in its adolescence. Diversity of definitions, conceptualizations, and nomenclature is a healthy step in the development of this still developing field. We believe that we are now at a stage to incorporate these rich and creative ideas into more cohesive frameworks for MM. As an example of such need, we would like to quote Mark Earley's (2007) account of students' experiences in his MM course:

> After discussing designs by Greene, Caracelli, and Graham (1989), Creswell, Plano Clark, Gutmann, and Hanson (2003), and Tashakkori and Teddlie (1998, 2003c), students counted a total of 52 different design possibilities. . . . This was a very overwhelming set of classes because of this variety of designs offered. (p. 155)

A number of salient issues emerged from the discussions and presentations at the Third Annual Mixed Methods Conference in Cambridge, England (2007), as nearly 200 researchers and scholars engaged in discourse regarding the current status of MM. We summarize some of these issues in this section because they are shared by scholars from across the globe and across multiple disciplines, and they need to be addressed by MM practitioners in the very short term:

- MM is considered the "hip" trend that facilitates publications and getting grants! This might create a problem in that scholars report using MM simply to improve the probability of publishing their manuscripts, while in truth, such an approach/design is not necessary for answering their research questions.

- The rationale for using MM is not explicitly presented in some published articles.

- Ways of integration is probably the most uncharted area of MM. When is integration done? How are the understandings from QUAL and QUAN strands integrated?

- MM studies are often more complex than the current texts and methodological articles discuss. It is often impossible to find distinct QUAL and QUAN strands in studies because investigators use both approaches in each stage of their studies (this is specifically true of some parallel MM designs).

- A single study might include multiple typologies in various stages. At times, it is not clear what the typologies are referring to. For example, a study might start with a single MM question, select a probability sample, select a subsample purposively, collect and analyze data in both samples concurrently, and make inferences on the basis of all results. Does the sequential selection of the samples make this a sequential design, even though the data collection and analyses are parallel (or even concurrent)?

As a final note, we would like to point to a recent suggestion about the feasibility of integrating the inferences based on multiple paradigmatic stances. Reacting to Greene's (2007) statement that "when one mixes methods, one may also mix paradigmatic and mental model assumptions as well as broad features of inquiry methodology" (p. 114), Leonard Bliss (2008) suggested that such mixing or integration is only possible if multiple researchers with different paradigmatic perspectives (e.g., QUAL and QUAN approaches) collaborate on a single project:

> Since this would require the inquirer to shift back and forth between incommensurable paradigmatic stances, such a mixing is simply not possible. However, this does not preclude studies that mix at the paradigmatic level. It is important to consider that paradigmatic mixing primarily occurs at the point at which questions are asked and at the point where inferences are made; the beginning and the end of any inquiry. Methods, the middle, more or less follow from the questions. Since the world view (the paradigmatic beliefs) of the inquirer delimits the questions and inferences that he or she can conceive of, mixing paradigms will often require the inquirer to hold mutually exclusive beliefs; that is to have multiple minds. Having multiple minds is not all that difficult. All we have to have is multiple people involved in a dialog at least at the points of question generation and inference making; a truly integrated design. (pp. 190–192)

Though we do not agree with Bliss (2008) about the "incommensurability" of paradigms, he makes a good point regarding the value of the team approach that has been stated elsewhere (e.g., Shulha & Wilson, 2003). MM studies may be conducted by teams or individuals, but the team approach undoubtedly has many advantages. On the other hand, if single researchers were incapable of conducting MM research, there would be no MM dissertations.

We are especially interested in the ability of single researchers to examine issues and research problems from multiple perspectives. Toward this goal, we would like to reiterate our call for more integrated training of our young researchers and graduate students.

Notes

1. This syllabus is posted on the Bridges Web site (retrieved January 20, 2008, from http://www.fiu.edu/~bridges).

2. The special issue of *Research in the Schools* (2006, Vol. 13, Issue 1), edited by Burke Johnson and Tony Onwuegbuzie, included a particularly strong set of articles that has been frequently referenced.

Glossary

Glossary terms are italicized when they appear in the definition of another term, except for frequently occurring words, such as methods and sampling.

Abduction or abductive logic is the third type of logic and involves the process of working back from an observed consequence (or effect) to a probable antecedent (or cause). Abduction entails creatively generating insights and making *inferences* to the best possible explanation.

Absolutism is the doctrine that there are many natural laws and unchanging "Truths" concerning the world. (Competing doctrine is *relativism*.)

Action research involves the direct application of results to social issues and often engages investigators in their own workplace (e.g., educators in schools, classrooms).

Analytic adequacy is the extent to which the data analysis techniques are appropriate and adequate for answering the *research questions*.

Analytic induction is a QUAL analysis strategy that "involves scanning the data for categories of phenomena and for relationships among such categories, developing working typologies and hypotheses on an examination of initial cases, and then modifying and refining them on the basis of subsequent cases" (LeCompte & Preissle, 1993, p. 254). A key feature of the process is *negative case analysis*.

A-paradigmatic stance is the belief of some scholars that *paradigm* issues (particularly *epistemological* ones) and methods are independent of one another.

A priori themes (predetermined themes) are developed before data collection begins based on *theory*, *conceptual frameworks*, previous research findings, and other sources.

Archival records are *artifacts* that have symbolic meanings, including various types of written materials (e.g., letters) or information stored in various other formats (e.g., audiotapes).

Artifacts are objects (*archival records*, *physical trace evidence*) that are a result of some human activity, which may have a symbolic meaning or may be nonsymbolic (e.g., LeCompte & Preissle, 1993).

Attitude scales measure attitudes, beliefs, self-perceptions, and a variety of related *constructs* toward some object (including self) or topic of interest.

Attrition refers to a loss in the number of participants in a research study.

Axiology refers to the role of values in inquiry.

Between-strategies MM data collection involves the gathering of both QUAL and QUAN data using more than one data collection strategy (e.g., *observations, interviews*).

Case study research entails developing an in-depth analysis of a single case or of multiple cases. *Cases* are empirical studies of a "contemporary phenomenon within its real-life context, especially when the boundaries between the phenomenon and context are not clearly evident" (Yin, 2003, p. 13).

Categorical strategies refer to QUAL data analysis strategies that break down narrative data and rearrange them to produce categories that facilitate comparisons and understanding of the phenomenon under study.

Categorizing process is a QUAL analysis process involving bringing together into provisional categories those units of information related to the same content, devising rules that describe category properties, and rendering each category set internally consistent and the entire set mutually exclusive.

Causal effects are the determination of whether variable X (an *independent variable*) caused some change in variable Y (a *dependent variable*).

Causal mechanisms are the determination of the processes whereby variable X (an *independent variable*) caused some change in variable Y (a *dependent variable*).

Causal model of explanation is a QUAN research model that is more focused on identifying specific causal factors for a particular effect and less focused on deductive processes associated with general laws.

Cluster sampling occurs when the sampling unit is not an individual but a group (cluster) that occurs naturally in the *population*, such as neighborhoods, hospitals, or schools.

Compatibility thesis states that combining QUAL and QUAN methods is a good research strategy and denies the contention that these two orientations are "epistemologically incoherent" (Howe, 1988, p. 10).

Complementary strengths thesis is the argument that, though MM research is possible, investigators should keep the QUAN and QUAL components as separate as possible so that the strengths of each paradigmatic position can be realized.

Complete collection (criterion sampling) is a QUAL sampling strategy in which all members of a *population* of interest who meet some special criteria are selected (e.g., all hearing impaired, female students at a certain college).

Conceptual framework refers to a "consistent and comprehensive theoretical framework emerging from an inductive integration of previous literature, theories, and other pertinent information" (Tashakkori & Teddlie, 2003a, p. 704).

Conceptualization stage is the first *stage* of an MM research design. Theoretically, it is placed in the sphere of concepts (abstract operations), which includes the formulation of research purposes, questions, and so forth.

Concurrent validity is a specific example of *convergent validity*, which occurs when measurement outcomes are highly correlated with the results of other measures of the same construct.

Confidentiality is a component of a participant's right to privacy, which entails "the process of keeping the information obtained from an individual during a study secret and private" (Ary, Jacobs, Razavieh, & Sorenson, 2007, p. 592).

Confirmatory research refers to investigations aimed at testing propositions typically based on a *theory* or *conceptual framework*. QUAN research is characteristically, but not always, confirmatory in nature.

Confirming and disconfirming cases is a sampling strategy that involves selecting units of analysis that either verify or refute patterns in the data (emerging or defined a priori) to further understand the phenomenon under study.

Constant comparative method is a basic QUAL categorical analysis technique that employs two general processes (*unitizing* and *categorizing*) to develop categories and *themes* (e.g., Lincoln & Guba, 1985; Tashakkori & Teddlie, 1998).

Constant conjunction is one of David Hume's three conditions for causal *inferences*: The cause had to be present whenever the effect was obtained. This criterion has led some researchers to rely on high statistical correlations as evidence for causal relationships.

Constructivism is the view that researchers individually and collectively construct the meaning of the phenomena under investigation; observation cannot be pure in the sense of excluding altogether the interests and values of individuals; and investigations must employ empathic understanding of study participants. This *paradigm* supports QUAL methods (e.g., Howe, 1988; Lincoln & Guba, 1985; Maxcy, 2003).

Constructs are "abstractions that cannot be observed directly but are useful in interpreting empirical data and in theory building" (Ary, Jacobs, Razavieh, & Sorenson, 2007, p. 38).

Construct validity is the degree to which a data collection procedure (e.g., instrument, *interview* procedure, *observational strategy*) truly captures the intended *construct* that is being studied.

Content validity is the degree to which a data collection procedure (e.g., *instrument*, observation protocol) truly measures specific and well-defined skills or objectives that are taught in a course or text (e.g., academic ability).

Context or logic of discovery is the process associated with coming up with *theories* and *hypotheses*.

Context or logic of justification is the process associated with the testing of *theories* and *hypotheses*.

Contextualizing (holistic) strategies refer to QUAL data analysis strategies that interpret narrative data in the context of a coherent whole "text" that includes interconnections among narrative elements. These strategies search for *themes* across the interconnecting narrative elements.

Contrast principle is a principle in *thematic analysis* that states that "the meaning of a symbol can be discovered by finding out how it is different from other symbols" (Spradol, 1979, p. 157). In content analysis, the ideas in each theme must be different from those in another theme. *See also* Themes.

Convergent validity refers to the degree to which the measurement outcomes representing a *construct* or phenomenon are consistent with other indicators of the same *construct* or phenomenon.

Conversion mixed data analysis is an MM analysis that occurs when collected QUAL data are converted into numbers (*quantitizing*) or QUAN data are converted into narratives or other types of QUAL data (*qualitizing*).

Conversion mixed designs are a family of MM multistrand designs in which mixing occurs when one type of data is transformed and then analyzed both qualitatively and quantitatively.

Correlational research refers to research that looks at the strength of the relationships between variables, events, or phenomena.

Covert or nonreactive observations allow for the examination of a social phenomenon without the knowledge of the individuals being observed. In covert observations, the observer conceals his or her identity as a researcher. Nonreactive observations are "situations in which the observer has no control over the behavior . . . in question, and plays an unobserved, passive, and nonintrusive role in the research setting" (Webb, Campbell, Schwartz, & Sechrest, 2000, p. 113).

Credibility has been used as a QUAL analogue to *internal validity* (Lincoln & Guba, 1985, p. 300). It may be defined as whether or not a research report is "credible" to the participants in the study. Credibility may be attained through a series of techniques including member checks, prolonged engagement, persistent observation, and *triangulation*. In MM, this is *inference quality*.

Credibility audit is a self-evaluation of the acceptability, goodness, and validity of the *inferences* made by the researcher. In MM, this is known as inference quality audit.

Criterion is an indicator of a construct. It is used as a basis of comparison to determine the validity of a data collection procedure (e.g., observation protocol) for capturing or measuring a *construct* of interest.

Criterion variable is the variable that is being predicted in prediction studies.

Critical case sampling is a sampling strategy that involves selecting a single case which is particularly important to the understanding of a phenomenon because it permits maximum application of information to other cases.

Critical realism (transcendental realism) refers to the postpositivists' belief that there is "a real" reality, but it can be understood only "imperfectly and probabilistically" (Lincoln & Guba, 2000, p. 168). An alternative expression of the position is transcendental realism, or the belief that social phenomena exist in the objective world and that there are some "lawful reasonably stable relationships" among them (Miles & Huberman, 1994, p. 429).

Critical theory is an orientation that involves studying human phenomena through an ideological perspective (e.g., feminism) and seeking social justice for oppressed groups.

Cultural relativist is an individual who believes that each culture or group must be studied and accepted as having its own way of doing things.

Data conversion (transformation) refers to a process in which QUAN data types are converted into narratives that can be analyzed qualitatively (i.e., *qualitized*), or QUAL data types are converted into numerical codes that can be statistically analyzed (i.e., *quantitized*).

Data quality is the degree to which the data collection procedures provide trustworthy, valid, and reliable outcomes.

Data triangulation refers to using a variety of data sources or multiple indicators of an attribute, *construct*, or phenomenon in a study.

Data/measurement reliability indicates whether or not the data consistently and accurately represent the *constructs* under examination.

Data/measurement validity indicates whether or not the data represent the *constructs* they were assumed to capture.

Debriefing is a personal communication in which investigators provide information to participants regarding the study's purpose, any instances of withholding information, and any deception (and the reasons for that deception). This occurs at the end of the study.

Deductive logic or reasoning may be defined as either arguing from the general (e.g., theory) to the particular (e.g., data points) or the process of drawing a conclusion that is necessarily true if the premises are true.

Dependability is a QUAL analogue for the QUAN concept of *reliability* and is concerned with the extent to which variation in a phenomenon of interest can be explained consistently using the "human instrument" across different contexts (e.g., Ary, Jacobs, Razavieh, & Sorenson, 2007; Lincoln & Guba, 1985).

Dependent variable is a variable (often designated *y*) that is presumed to be affected or influenced by an *independent variable*.

Descriptive research is concerned with exploring the attributes of a phenomenon or possible relationships between variables. This term is often used to represent nonexperimental research. *See also* Exploratory research.

Descriptive statistical analysis refers to the analysis of numeric data for the purpose of obtaining summary indicators that describe a sample, a *population*, or the relationships among the variables in each.

Design fidelity (adequacy) refers to adequate implementation of the components of the research design (e.g., sampling, data collection, intervention) to provide opportunities for obtaining potential answers to *research questions*.

Design maps involve analyzing a mixed study using five components suggested by Maxwell and Loomis (2003): purposes, conceptual model, *research questions*, methods, and validity.

Design quality is the degree to which the investigator used and effectively implemented the most appropriate procedures for answering the *research questions*. Design quality consists of *design suitability, design fidelity, within-design consistency*, and *analytic adequacy*.

Design suitability (appropriateness) is the appropriateness of the research design for answering the *research question*.

Dialectical pragmatism is *pragmatism* for MM. The base word *pragmatism* refers to the applicability of philosophical pragmatism. The adjective *dialectical* emphasizes that MM researchers should carefully consider and dialogue with the QUAL and QUAN perspectives and the natural tensions between these perspectives when developing a workable synthesis for a research study.

Dialectical thesis assumes that all *paradigms* have something to offer and that the use of multiple paradigms contributes to greater understanding of the phenomenon under study. To think "dialectically" involves consideration of opposing viewpoints and inter-action with the "tensions" caused by their juxtaposition (e.g., Greene, 2007; Greene & Caracelli, 1997, 2003).

Discriminant validity (divergent validity) is the degree to which the outcomes of the data collection procedure (e.g., observational protocol) have a weak relationship with theoretically unrelated indicators of the *construct* under study or are different in the groups that are theoretically expected to be different on that construct.

Ecological transferability is the degree to which inference and policy or practice rec-ommendations are applicable to other similar settings.

Effect size in QUAL research is an analytical process (e.g., Onwuegbuzie, 2003) in which the strength of the relationship between narrative variables is calculated after these vari-ables have been quantitized. This is an example of applying an analytic framework from one tradition (QUAN) to another (QUAL) (e.g., Greene, 2007).

Emergent designs evolve when new aspects of a phenomenon are uncovered during data collection and analysis.

Emergent themes are QUAL *themes* that evolve from the study of specific pieces of information that investigators have collected during an ongoing study.

Emic perspective refers to the point of view of a cultural insider, or the individual par-ticipant in a study. *See also* Ideographic methods.

Empiricism is the doctrine that knowledge comes from experience. This orientation relies on "active" *observation strategies* and personal experiences. (Competing doctrine is *rationalism.*)

Enlightenment Project was an 18th century European philosophical movement that emphasized the use of reason, empirical methods in science (e.g., *empiricism*), human progress, and humanitarian political goals (e.g., Hollis, 2002).

Epistemology may be defined either as the branch of philosophy concerned with the "nature of knowledge and justification" (Schwandt, 1997, p. 39) and involving questions about whether and how valid knowledge can be achieved or, second, as the relationship of the knower to the known (Lincoln & Guba, 1985, p. 37).

Ethnography is research that has the goal of gaining an in-depth understanding of the culture of a group, organization, or society using different procedures, such as partici-pant observation, *interviews*, and examination of *artifacts*.

Etic perspective refers to the point of view of a cultural outsider or the investigator of a study. *See also* Nomothetic methods.

Evaluation research is research that is typically aimed at assessing the effectiveness of societal and educational programs by looking at program outcomes and processes.

Experiential (methodological/analytical) stage is the second *stage* of an MM research design. Theoretically, it is placed in the sphere of concrete processes, which includes methodological operations, data generation, analysis, and so forth.

Experimental research is research in which the investigator manipulates one or more *independent variables* (treatments, interventions) to ascertain their effects on one or more *dependent variables.*

Experimenter effect refers to the fact that an investigator's behaviors or expectations (or both) may unintentionally affect the results or the process of a study. The interpersonal expectation effect expands the experimenter effect to other settings, such as classrooms, nursing homes, and so forth (Rosenthal, 1976).

Exploratory research refers to investigations concerned with generating information about unknown aspects of a phenomenon. QUAL research is typically, but not always, exploratory in nature. *See also* Descriptive research.

External validity was defined by Shadish, Cook, and Campbell (2002) as follows: "The validity of inferences about whether the causal relationship holds over variations in persons, settings, treatment variables, and measurement variables" (p. 507).

Extreme or deviant case sampling (outlier sampling) is a sampling strategy that involves selecting cases near the "ends" of the distribution of cases of interest (e.g., scholastic performance) from the group of cases under consideration. Such extreme successes or failures are expected to yield especially valuable information.

Falsification principle asserts that a *research hypothesis* must be "falsifiable"—that is, it must be possible to determine a priori the pattern of data that would demonstrate that the hypothesis was false. This principle supposedly addressed the *problem of verification* because *observations* are not used to confirm (verify) a *research hypothesis* anymore but rather to disconfirm (falsify) it.

Focus groups is a data collection strategy that occurs in "an interactive interview setting in which a small number of respondents (preferably six to eight) engage in discussion in response to a moderator's questions" (Tashakkori & Teddlie, 2003a, p. 708).

Fully integrated mixed data analysis occurs in *fully integrated designs* and uses an interactive mix of QUAL and QUAN analyses that may be characterized as iterative, reciprocal, and interdependent.

Fully integrated mixed designs are a family of MM designs in which mixing occurs in an interactive manner at all *stages* of the study; at each stage, one approach affects the formulation of the other.

Fundamental principle of mixed methods research states that "*methods should be mixed in a way that has complementary strengths and nonoverlapping weaknesses*" (Johnson & Turner, 2003, p. 299, italics in original).

Fused data analysis involves the use of QUAL and QUAN software programs for the analysis of the same data sources in distinct, but mutually dependent, ways (Bazeley, 2003).

Gradual selection is a sampling strategy that involves the sequential selection of cases based on their relevance to the *research questions* of interest, not their *representativeness* (e.g., Flick, 1998).

Grounded theory is a well-known QUAL methodology for theory development that is "grounded" in narrative data that are systematically gathered and *inductively* analyzed (e.g., Glaser & Strauss, 1967; Strauss & Corbin, 1998).

Heuristic value of a *theory* (or *conceptual framework*) refers to its capacity to generate ideas or questions that can lead to interesting and informative research studies.

Homogeneous sampling is a sampling strategy that involves the selection of members of a sample who are highly similar on certain characteristics.

Humanism is the doctrine that researchers should focus on the more human characteristics of people, including their free will and autonomy, their creativity, emotionality, rationality, morality, love for beauty, and their uniqueness. (Competing doctrine is *naturalism*.)

Hypothetico-deductive model (H-DM) is a QUAN model involving the a priori deduction of a *research hypothesis* (or hypotheses) from a *theory* or *conceptual framework* and the testing of those hypotheses using numerical data and statistical analyses.

Idealism is the doctrine that it is ideas and "the mental" (including the social and cultural) that are most fundamentally real. (Competing doctrine is *materialism*.)

Ideographic methods are methods that are concerned with individual, specific, particular, and oftentimes unique facts. The humanities tend to employ methods that are more ideographic in approach and focus. *See also* Emic perspective.

Ideographic statements are time- and context-bound working hypotheses.

Incommensurable paradigms is a term that Kuhn (1962, 1970, 1996) used in his argument that competing *paradigms* are incommensurable, meaning there is no way to directly compare one with another or for clear interparadigmatic communication. This argument is consistent with the *incompatibility thesis*.

Incompatibility thesis stated that it was inappropriate to mix QUAL and QUAN methods due to fundamental differences in the *paradigm*s (i.e., *positivism*, *constructivism*) underlying those methods.

Independent variable refers to a variable (often designated x) that is presumed to influence or affect a *dependent variable*.

Inductive logic or reasoning may be defined either as arguing from the particular (e.g., data points) to the general (e.g., theory) or as the process of drawing a conclusion that is probably true.

Inductive-deductive research cycle (chain of reasoning, cycle of scientific methodology) is a model that indicates that research on any given question at any point in time falls somewhere within a cycle of inference processes (e.g., Krathwohl, 1993). The cycle may be seen as moving from grounded results through *inductive inference* to general *inferences*, then from those general inferences (or *theory*, *conceptual framework*, model) through *deductive inference* to predictions to the particular (a priori *research hypotheses*).

Inferences are either an outcome or a process of an investigation. As an outcome, inference is a conclusion or interpretation in response to a research question, made on the basis of the results of the data analysis. As a process, *see also* Inference process.

Inference process involves making sense out of the results of data analysis, which consists of a dynamic journey from ideas to data to results of data analysis, in an effort to make sense of the findings. *See also* Inferences.

Inference quality is proposed as an MM term to incorporate the QUAN terms *internal validity* and statistical conclusion validity and the QUAL terms *trustworthiness* and *credibility*. Inference quality is the extent to which the interpretations and conclusions made on the basis of the results meet the professional standards of validity, rigor, credibility, and acceptability. In the *integrative framework*, it consists of *design quality* and *interpretive rigor*.

Inference transferability refers to the generalizability or applicability of *inferences* obtained in a study to other individuals, settings, times, and ways of collecting data.

It consists of *population transferability, temporal transferability, ecological transferability,* and *theoretical/conceptual transferability* (Tashakkori & Teddlie, 2003a, p. 710). This term subsumes the QUAN terms *external validity* and generalizability, as well as the QUAL term *transferability.*

Inferential stage is the third *stage* of an MM research design. Theoretically, it is placed in the sphere of *inferences* (abstract explanations and understandings), which includes emerging theories, explanations, inferences, and so forth.

Inferential statistical analysis refers to the analysis of numeric data to test hypotheses regarding group differences or relationships between variables.

Informed consent refers to agreement to participate in a research study in which the participant has explicit understanding of the risks involved.

Inherently mixed data analysis entails planning in advance to generate both QUAL and QUAN information using the same data source in an effort to answer interlinked questions.

Institutional review board (IRB) is an entity responsible for evaluating and overseeing the researchers' adherence to ethical standards.

Integrative efficacy is the degree to which *inferences* made in each *strand* of a mixed (or multi-) methods study are effectively integrated into a theoretically consistent *meta-inference.*

Integrative framework for inference quality and transferability is a framework for assessing and improving the quality and transferability of inferences in research and incorporating quality indicators/audits from qualitative and quantitative research traditions.

Intensity sampling is a sampling strategy that involves selecting highly informative cases that represent a phenomenon of interest intensively (but not extremely), such as good teachers/poor teachers, above average pianists/below average pianists and so forth (e.g., Patton, 2002).

Internal validity was defined by Shadish, Cook, and Campbell (2002) as "the validity of inferences about whether the relationship between two variables is causal" (p. 508). This term has been used more broadly in research to represent the degree to which alternative conclusions or interpretations based on the same results may be convincingly ruled out.

Interpretive agreement is the extent to which other scholars (peers) reach the same conclusions that the investigator made on the basis of specific findings of the study.

Interpretive consistency is the consistency of each conclusion made in a study with other conclusions made in the same study.

Interpretive (integrative) correspondence is the fit of the *inferences* (as answers) to the initial *research question* or purpose of the study. It is the extent to which *meta-inferences* satisfy the initial purpose for using an MM design.

Interpretive distinctiveness is the extent to which each conclusion is distinctively different from and judged by other scholars or study participants (or both) to be more credible than other conclusions that could potentially be made on the basis of the same results.

Interpretive rigor is the determination of the degree to which credible interpretations have been made on the basis of obtained results. It consists of *interpretive consistency,* *theoretical consistency, interpretive agreement, interpretive distinctiveness, integrative effi-cacy,* and *interpretive correspondence.*

Interview is a method of data collection that involves one person (the interviewer) asking questions of another person (the interviewee).

Investigator triangulation refers to "involving several different researchers" in a single study (Patton (2002, p. 247).

Iterative sequential mixed analysis is a type of mixed analysis that occurs in any *sequential design* with more than two *strands* or phases.

Iterative sequential mixed designs are *sequential designs* that have more than two *strands* or phases. Examples vary from simple (QUAN → QUAL → QUAN) to increasingly more complex (QUAL → QUAN → QUAL → QUAN).

Keyword (descriptor) is a search term that describes an important aspect of a research study and can be used to locate information in a computerized database.

Known group validity is a type of *discriminant validity* in which data are gathered and compared from groups that are theoretically (or culturally) expected to be different from one another.

Legitimation is a dynamic and iterative process of evaluation for demonstrating the quality of *inferences* in MM research. Legitimation was developed by Onwuegbuzie and Johnson (2006), who presented nine types of legitimation.

Level of analysis refers to levels at which aggregated data can be analyzed in a multilevel organizational or societal structure (e.g., student, class, school).

Likert scales measure respondents' level of agreement or disagreement to a series of items related to a given topic of interest.

Line (or program) of research refers to a connected series of studies within a particular problem area that results in progressively more in-depth research findings regarding the phenomenon under study.

Logical positivism is the name of a philosophy developed in the 1920s by members of the Vienna Circle that marked the beginning of the philosophy of science as a distinct field of study. One of its tenets was the *verifiability principle of meaning,* which stressed *empiricism* and logic.

Materialism is the doctrine, held by many natural scientists, that the world and reality are most essentially and fundamentally composed of matter. (Competing doctrine is *idealism.*)

Matrix of Data Collection Strategies for Mixed Methods Research was developed by Johnson and Turner (2003). It presents a comprehensive data collection matrix with 18 cells produced by crossing six strategies of data collection by the three methodological approaches (QUAN, MM, QUAL).

Maximum variation sampling is a sampling strategy that involves purposively selecting a wide range of cases to get full variation on dimensions of interest and to generate a diversity of comparisons.

Meta-inference is a conclusion generated by integrating the *inferences* obtained from the QUAL and QUAN *strands* of an MM study.

Methodological triangulation refers to "the use of multiple methods to study a single problem" (Patton (2002, p. 247).

Methodology (research) is a broad approach to scientific inquiry specifying how *research questions* should be asked and answered. This includes worldview considerations, general preferences for designs, sampling logic, data collection and analytical strategies, guidelines for making *inferences*, and the criteria for assessing and improving quality.

Methods (research) include specific strategies and procedures for implementing research design, including sampling, data collection, data analysis, and interpretation of the findings.

Mixed methodologists are researchers who work primarily within the *pragmatist paradigm* and are interested in using both QUAL and QUAN approaches and procedures for answering complex research questions.

Mixed methods (MM) refers to "research in which the investigator collects and analyzes data, integrates the findings, and draws inferences using both qualitative and quantitative approaches or methods in a single study or program of inquiry" (Tashakkori & Creswell, 2007b, p. 4).

Mixed methods data analysis are the processes whereby QUAN and QUAL data analysis strategies are combined, connected, or integrated in research studies. There are five types of MM data analysis that match the types of *mixed methods designs*, plus another type in which analytic frameworks from one tradition (QUAN or QUAL) are applied within the other (e.g., Greene, 2007).

Mixed methods design refers to a type of research design in which QUAL and QUAN approaches are mixed across the stages of the study. There are five families of mixed methods designs: *parallel, sequential, conversion, multilevel,* and *fully integrated.*

Mixed methods monostrand designs are the simplest of the MM designs, involving only one *strand* of a research study, yet including both QUAL and QUAN components.

Mixed methods multistrand designs are the most complex of the MM designs. All of these designs contain QUAL and QUAN components and at least two research *strands.*

Mixed methods sampling techniques involve the selection of units or cases for a research study using both *probability* and *purposive sampling strategies.*

Monomethod designs are designs in which a single approach (only QUAL or only QUAN) is used.

Monomethod monostrand designs are designs that use a single research approach (QUAN or QUAL) to answer *research questions* employing one *strand* only. This strand may be either QUAN or QUAL, but not both.

Monomethod multistrand designs are designs that use a single research approach (QUAN or QUAL) to answer *research questions* employing two or more *strands.* All of these strands may be either QUAN or QUAL, but not both.

Monostrand conversion designs (simple conversion designs) are used in single *strand* studies in which *research questions* are answered through an analysis of transformed data (i.e., *quantitized* or *qualitized* data).

Monostrand designs employ only a single phase encompassing all of the activities from *conceptualization* through *inference.*

Morphed data are data from a single source that change from one form to another (e.g., from QUAN to QUAL) in an iterative manner. Morphed data may change form several times in *iterative sequential designs.*

Multilevel mixed data analysis is a general analytic strategy in which QUAL and QUAN techniques (*thematic*, statistical) are used at different levels of aggregation within a research study to answer interrelated *research questions.*

Multilevel mixed designs are a family of MM designs in which mixing occurs across multiple levels of sampling. Mixing occurs as QUAN and QUAL data from different levels are analyzed and integrated to answer the same or related *research questions* (Tashakkori & Teddlie, 1998).

Multilevel mixed methods sampling is a general sampling strategy in which *probability* and *purposive* sampling techniques are used at different levels of the study (e.g., student, class, school, district) (Tashakkori & Teddlie, 2003a, p. 712).

Multiple paradigms thesis is the argument that multiple paradigms may serve as the foundation for MM research. Multiple paradigms may be applied to diverse MM designs, and researchers must decide which paradigm is appropriate given their choice of a particular design for a particular study.

Multistrand designs employ more than one phase; there are multiple parts to the study and each encompasses all of the activities from conceptualization through inference.

Multitrait-multimethod matrix is a data representation table for assessing data validity and reliability. It shows the correlation between different ways of assessing a set of attributes when these attributes are theoretically expected to have different degrees of relationship with each other. It was one of the first multimethod applications in the human sciences.

Multivariate statistics link two sets of variables to each other, such as the simultaneous relationship between multiple *dependent* (predicted) and *independent* (predictor) variables.

Naïve realism is the positivists' belief that there is an objective, external reality that can be comprehended (Lincoln & Guba, 2000, p. 168).

Naturalism is the doctrine that the focus of science should be on the natural or material world and that researchers should search for physical causes of phenomena. (Competing doctrine is *humanism.*)

Negative case analysis involves searching for cases that do not fit the expected or established pattern in the QUAL data in an effort to expand or adapt the emerging hypothetical relationships or *theory.*

Nomothetic methods are concerned with identifying laws and that which is predictable and general. The natural sciences tend to employ nomothetic methods, although natural scientists might study single cases in search of general laws. *See also* Etic perspectives.

Nomothetic statements are relatively time- and context-free generalizations.

Nonreactive observations. *See also* Covert or nonreactive observations.

Null hypothesis states that there is no difference between group means or no relationship between variables.

Observational data collection strategy is the recording of units of interaction occurring in a defined social situation based on visual examination of that situation.

Ontology refers to the nature of reality. For example, positivists believe that there is a single reality, whereas constructivists believe that there are multiple, constructed realities.

Opportunistic sampling (emergent sampling) is a sampling strategy that involves adding new cases to a sample based on design changes that occur as data are being collected.

Paradigm (e.g., *postpositivism, constructivism, pragmatism*) may be defined as a "worldview, complete with the assumptions that are associated with that view" (Mertens, 2003, p. 139).

Paradigm contrast tables compare the differences between philosophical orientations (e.g., *positivism, constructivism*) on issues such as *ontology, epistemology, axiology*, the possibility of generalizations, and so forth (e.g., Lincoln & Guba, 1985).

Paradigms debate refers to the conflict between the competing worldviews of *positivism* (and its variants) and *constructivism* (and its variants) on philosophical and methodological issues, such as the nature of reality and the use of QUAN or QUAL methods.

Parallel mixed data analysis involves the separate statistical analysis of QUAN data sources and *thematic analysis* of QUAL data sources within their respective *strands*. Although the strand analyses are independent, each provides an understanding of the phenomenon under investigation.

Parallel mixed designs (also known as concurrent, simultaneous designs) are a family of MM designs in which mixing occurs in an independent manner either simultaneously or with some time lapse. The QUAL and QUAN *strands* are planned and implemented to answer related aspects of the same questions.

Parallel mixed methods sampling involves the independent selection of units of analysis for an MM study through the use of both *probability* and *purposive sampling* strategies.

Participant-observer continuum is a dimension that varies depending on how much the observer is actually part of the social situation.

Personality inventories are self-report scales that measure relatively stable attributes that differentiate each individual from others (e.g., depression, locus of control, self-efficacy).

Phenomenology is a research orientation stressing the subjective experiences, social perceptions, and "naïve" analysis of events and phenomena by individuals (Heider, 1958). Also, it involves exploration of the "structures of consciousness in human experiences" (Creswell, 1998, p. 51).

Physical trace evidence includes nonsymbolic materials (accretion, erosion measures) that are a result of some human activity. Accretion measures are concerned with the deposit of materials, whereas erosion measures consider selective wear on materials.

Pilot study is a small-scale preliminary research project in which the investigator tests procedures to set the stage for the actual study.

Population refers to the totality of all elements, individuals, or entities with an identifiable boundary consisting of specific and well-defined characteristics (e.g., population of rural hospitals in India or population of autistic children in Oregon).

Population transferability is the degree to which *inferences* and policy or practice recommendations are applicable to other people (individuals, groups) or entities (texts, *artifacts*).

Positivism is the view that "social research should adopt scientific method . . . and that it consists of the rigorous testing of hypotheses by means of data that take the form of quantitative measurements" (Atkinson & Hammersley, 1994, p. 251).

Postmodernism is a philosophy that presents reactions to and critiques of the defining characteristics of modernism, including the importance of the rational approach in science and the epistemologies of *empiricism* or *positivism*. Modernism itself was a product of the *Enlightenment* (Schwandt, 1997).

Postpositivism generically refers to any *paradigm* posited as a replacement for *positivism* (Schwandt, 1997). In this text, we describe postpositivism as a replacement that is still bound to the QUAN orientation (e.g., Reichardt & Rallis, 1994). Postpositivism allows for the possibility of prediction at the group level and in probabilistic form; the culture-boundness of research questions, methods, and inferences; and differentiating social reality from physical reality (Festinger, 1957).

Pragmatism may be defined as "a deconstructive *paradigm* that debunks concepts such as 'truth' and 'reality' and focuses instead on 'what works' as the truth regarding the research questions under investigation. Pragmatism rejects the either/or choices associated with the *paradigm* wars, advocates for the use of mixed methods in research, and acknowledges that the values of the researcher play a large role in interpretation of results" (Tashakkori & Teddlie, 2003a, p. 713).

Prediction studies are typically QUAN in nature and involve the prediction of an important *criterion (predicted) variable* on the basis of one or more predictor variables.

Predictive validity occurs when an instrument correlates highly with the outcomes it is intended to predict. It is a specific example of *convergent validity*.

Preliminary information source is an index or abstract typically found in computerized databases, which assist investigators in locating relevant sources.

Primary information source is the description of a research study written by the individuals who conducted it.

Priority of methodological approach indicates which methodological orientation (QUAN, QUAL) is dominant in a mixed study.

Probability sampling involves "selecting a relatively large number of units from a population, or from specific subgroups (strata) of a population, in a random manner where the probability of inclusion for every member of the population is determinable" (Tashakkori & Teddlie, 2003a, p. 713).

Problem of induction may be defined as follows: No matter how many times researchers observe that *y* follows *x*, they can never be sure that their next observation of *x* will be followed by *y*. Researchers can never "prove" a theory using *inductive logic* alone because one cannot observe all cases (e.g., Hollis, 2002; Phillips, 1987).

Problem of verification refers to the fact that a wide range of observations can confirm more than one theory and that competing theories often appear to have abundant evidence confirming them (e.g., Phillips, 1987, pp. 11–12).

Purposive random sampling (purposeful random sampling) involves taking a *random sample* of a small number of units from a larger target *population*. The random nature of this sampling procedure is characteristic of *probability sampling*, whereas the small number of cases generated through it is characteristic of *purposive sampling*.

Purposive sampling is the process of selecting units (e.g., individuals, institutions) based on specific purposes associated with answering a study's research questions.

Qualiphobe is a researcher who has a fear or disliking for QUAL methods (Boyatzis, 1998).

Qualitative data displays are visual presentations of the *themes* that emerge from QUAL data analysis. Displays summarize information from either *categorical* or *contextualizing strategies* or as a separate data analysis scheme.

Qualitative (QUAL) methods may be most simply and parsimoniously defined as the techniques associated with the gathering, analysis, interpretation, and presentation of narrative information.

Qualitative (thematic) data analysis refers to the analysis of narrative data using a variety of inductive and iterative techniques, including *categorical* and *contextualizing strategies.*

Qualitizing refers to the process by which quantitative data are transformed into data that can be analyzed qualitatively (e.g., Tashakkori & Teddlie, 1998).

QUALs are qualitatively oriented human researchers working primarily within the *constructivist paradigm* and principally interested in narrative data and analyses.

QUANs are quantitatively oriented human researchers working primarily within the *postpositivist paradigm* and principally interested in numerical data and analyses.

Quantiphobes are researchers who have a fear or disliking for QUAN methods (Boyatzis, 1998).

Quantitative (QUAN) methods may be most simply and parsimoniously defined as the techniques associated with the gathering, analysis, interpretation, and presentation of numerical information.

Quantitative (statistical) data analysis is the analysis of numerical data using techniques that include (1) simply describing the phenomenon of interest or (2) looking for significant differences between groups or relationships among variables.

Quantitizing refers to the process of converting qualitative data to numerical codes that can be statistically analyzed (Miles & Huberman 1994).

Quasi-experimental research is similar to *experimental research* in terms of having treatments, outcome measures, and experimental units, but it does not employ random assignment of participants to treatment conditions.

Quasi-mixed designs are designs in which two types of data are collected (QUAN, QUAL), but there is little or no integration of findings and *inferences* (Teddlie & Tashakkori, 2006).

Questionnaires are a method of data collection in which participants complete a self-report instrument or protocol about their attitudes, beliefs, judgments, or other attributes.

Random sampling occurs when each sampling unit in a clearly defined *population* has an equal chance of being included in the sample.

Rationalism is a type of philosophy that emphasizes the idea that reason is the primary way to gain knowledge and that the human mind has a priori categories of understanding that organize our sense experiences (e.g., Schwandt, 1997). (Competing doctrine is *empiricism.*)

Relativism is a doctrine that rejects broad generalizations and holds that true or warranted knowledge can vary by person or group, place, and time. (Competing doctrine is *absolutism.*)

Representativeness refers to the degree to which the sample accurately represents the *population*.

Reputational case sampling is a sampling strategy that involves selecting cases on the recommendation of an "expert" or "key informant" (e.g., LeCompte & Preissle, 1993; Miles & Huberman, 1994). This sampling occurs when researchers do not have the information necessary to select a sample and must depend on experts' opinions.

Research hypothesis is a specialized form of a *research question* in which investigators make predictions about the relationships among social phenomena before the actual conduct of a study. These predictions are based on theory, previous research, or some other rationale.

Research objectives refer to specific aims or rationales for the study.

Research questions guide the research investigation and are concerned with unknown or ambiguous aspects of a phenomenon of interest.

Researchable idea refers to a specific topic within a content area of interest that can be empirically examined.

Revelatory case sampling is a sampling strategy that involves identifying and gaining access to a single case representing a phenomenon that was previously "inaccessible to scientific investigation" (Yin, 2003, p. 42). Such cases are rare and difficult to study but yield valuable information.

Rubrics are sets of guidelines for recording or categorizing observations, responses to open-ended questions, performance outcomes, or other products related to a topic of interest.

Sampling involves selecting units of analysis (e.g., people, *artifacts*) "in a manner that maximizes the researcher's ability to answer research questions that are set forth in a study" (Tashakkori & Teddlie, 2003a, p. 715).

Sampling frame refers to a formal or informal list of units or cases from which the sample is drawn.

Sampling politically important cases is a strategy that involves selecting of politically significant or sensitive cases for a research study.

Saturation occurs in *purposive sampling* when the addition of more units (e.g., more cases) does not result in new information for theme development.

Scholasticism was the dominant philosophy of the Middle Ages and was based on the Church's authority and selected Aristotelian principles.

Secondary information source is a publication containing information on research studies and written by someone who was not a direct participant in those studies.

Sequential mixed data analysis is used when the QUAL and QUAN *strands* of a study occur in chronological order, such that the analysis in one strand emerges from or depends on the previous strand. Analysis strategies may evolve as the study unfolds.

Sequential mixed designs are a family of MM designs in which mixing occurs across chronological phases (QUAL, QUAN) of the study; questions or procedures of one *strand* emerge from or depend on the results of the previous strand; *research questions* are built on one another and may evolve as the study unfolds.

Sequential mixed methods sampling involves the selection of units of analysis for an MM study through the sequential use of *probability* and *purposive sampling* strategies (QUAN → QUAL) or (QUAL → QUAN). In sequential MM studies, information from the first sample is often required to draw the second sample.

Similarity principle is a principle in *thematic analysis* that states that "the meaning of a symbol can be discovered by finding out how it is similar to other symbols" (Spradley, 1979, p. 157). *See also* Themes.

Single paradigm thesis is the belief that a single paradigm should serve as the foundation for a particular methodological orientation (e.g., *positivism* and QUAN methods, *constructivism* and QUAL methods).

Snowball sampling (chain sampling) is a sampling strategy that involves using informants or participants to identify additional cases for inclusion in the study.

Social Sciences Citation Index (SSCI) is a computerized database of searchable journal citations in the social and behavioral sciences, making it possible to find published articles either by author (author search) or through other specialized searches.

Stage of a research strand refers to a step or component of a *strand* of a research study. There are three stages in a research strand: *conceptualization stage, experiential (methodological/ analytical) stage,* and *inferential stage.*

Statistical significance is the obtained probability that the observed results happened by chance. It is the determination that the *null hypothesis* can be rejected based on obtained differences between group means or relationships between variables.

Strand of a research design is a phase of a study that includes three stages: *conceptualization stage, experiential stage (methodological/analytical),* and *inferential stage.*

Stratified purposive sampling is a technique in which the researcher first identifies existing subgroups in the population and then selects a small number of cases to study intensively within each subgroup based on *purposive sampling* techniques.

Stratified sampling occurs when the researcher identifies the subgroups (or strata) in a population such that each unit belongs to a single stratum (e.g., male, female) and then randomly selects units from those strata.

Survey research is a research design in which self-report data are collected via questionnaires or interviews (or both) with the goal of predicting the behaviors or attributes of the general population. Strong transferability (external validity, generalizability) to the population is the utmost consideration in conducting this type of research.

Tabula rasa is a phrase originating from John Locke, who described the human mind as a "blank tablet" before it receives experiences through the senses and reflection.

Temporal transferability is the potential stability of *inferences* over time in the same or other contexts. It is the degree to which inferences and recommendations may be applicable in the future.

Tests are a data collection strategy designed to assess knowledge, intelligence, or ability.

Thematic analysis refers to different types of strategies for the analysis of narrative data, whereby resultant *themes* are identified.

Themes are the dominant features or characteristics of a phenomenon under study in QUAL research. A theme is a set of concepts, ideas, or narrative segments that are similar to each other (*similarity principle*) and are also different from comparable elements in other themes (*contrast principle*).

Theoretical consistency is the consistency of each conclusion with the current state of theory, knowledge, and findings of other researchers.

Theoretical/conceptual transferability is the degree to which the findings or *inferences* of a study can be replicated if the main theoretical *constructs* are defined and observed differently.

Theoretical lens is used by some researchers (especially QUALs) to guide their research and to raise social justice issues related to ethnicity, gender, and so on.

Theoretical sampling (theory-based sampling) is a sampling procedure in which the researcher examines particular instances of the phenomenon of interest to define and elaborate on its various conceptual boundaries. The investigator samples people, institutions, scenes, events, documents, or wherever the *theory* leads the investigation.

Theory "is generally understood to refer to a unified, systematic explanation of a diverse range of social phenomena" (Schwandt, 1997, p. 154).

Theory-ladenness of facts refers to the influence of a researcher's theory or framework on the research that he or she conducts and on the results from that research.

Theory triangulation refers to "the use of multiple perspectives to interpret a single set of data" (Patton, 2002, p. 247).

Transferability is the generalization of *inferences* from a particular sending context to a particular receiving context.

Transformative perspective "is characterized as placing central importance on the lives and experiences of marginalized groups such as women, ethnic/racial minorities, members of the gay and lesbian communities, people with disabilities, and those who are poor." Researchers working within this *paradigm* link research results to "wider questions of social inequity and social justice" (Mertens, 2003, pp. 139–140).

Triangulation refers to the "combinations and comparisons of multiple data sources, data collection and analysis procedures, research methods, investigators, and/or inferences that occur at the end of a study" (Tashakkori & Teddlie, 2003a, p. 717). Denzin (1978) elaborated on the term by describing *data triangulation, theory triangulation, investigator triangulation,* and *methodological triangulation*.

Trustworthiness is a global term introduced as a substitute, or analogue, for many of the QUAN validity issues. Lincoln and Guba (1985) defined the term broadly: "How can an inquirer persuade his or her audiences (including self) that the findings of an inquiry are worth paying attention to, worth taking account of? What arguments can be mounted, what criteria invoked, what questions asked, that would be persuasive on this issue?" (p. 290).

Typical case sampling involves selecting those cases that are the most typical, normal, average, or representative of the group of cases under consideration.

Typology development (data importation) occurs when "the analysis of one data type yields a typology (or set of substantive categories) that is then used as a framework applied in analyzing the contrasting data type" (Caracelli & Greene, 1993, p. 197; Greene, 2007).

Underdetermination of theory by fact occurs when "a number of theories can equally (but perhaps differently) account for the same finite body of evidence" (Phillips, 1987, p. 206).

Unit of analysis refers to the individual case (or group of cases) that the researcher wants to express something about when the study is completed and is, therefore, the focus of all data collection efforts.

Unitizing process involves dividing narrative data into units of information, which typically are phrases that may be associated with themes, although they could also be words, paragraphs, characters, and so forth (Berg, 2004).

Univariate statistics link one variable that is the focal point of the analysis (e.g., a predicted event in a relationship study or a single *dependent variable* in an experiment) with one or more others (e.g., a few predictors in a prediction study or a few *independent variables* in an experiment).

Unobtrusive measures (nonreactive measures) are data collection strategies that allow investigators to examine a social phenomenon without changing it. They are nonreactive because they are hidden within the social context of the research study; therefore, observed individuals will not react to their being observed.

Validation framework was presented by Dellinger and Leech (2007) as a framework for defining the quality of *inferences* in terms of four elements (foundational element, inferential consistency, utilization element, and consequential element), all rooted in the ideas of construct and consequential validity.

Value-ladenness of facts refers to the influence of investigators' values on their research and/or the results of that research.

Verifiability principle of meaning (verification principle) refers to a *logical positivism* tenet that stated that something "is meaningful only if it is verifiable empirically (directly, or indirectly, via sense experience), or if it is a truth of logic or mathematics" (Phillips, 1987, p. 204).

Verstehen is a German term proposed by Wilhem Dilthey and Max Weber for understanding what distinguishes the human from the natural sciences.

Within-design consistency is the degree to which the components of the design (e.g., sampling, data collection, data analysis) fit together in a seamless and cohesive manner.

Within-strategy MM data collection involves the gathering of both QUAL and QUAN data using the same data collection strategy (e.g., *questionnaires* with open- and closed-ended items).

References

Achinstein, P. (Ed.). (2004). *Science rules: A historical introduction to scientific methods.* Baltimore: Johns Hopkins University Press.

Adalbjarnardottir, S. (2002). Adolescent psychosocial maturity and alcohol use: Quantitative and qualitative analysis of longitudinal data. *Adolescence, 37,* 19–54.

Albrecht, T. L., Eaton, D. K., & Rivera, L. (1999, February). *Portal to portal: Friendly access healthcare for low-income mothers and babies: A technical report prepared for the Lawton and Rhea Chiles Center for Healthy Mothers and Babies.* Paper presented at the Friendly Access Advisory Board Meeting, Orlando, FL.

Alioto, A. M. (1992). *A history of Western science.* Englewood Cliffs, NJ: Prentice Hall.

Allison, G. T., & Zelikow, P. (1999). *Essence of decision: Explaining the Cuban missile crisis.* Boston: Little, Brown.

American Psychological Association. (2001). *Publication manual of the American Psychological Association* (5th ed.). Washington, DC: Author.

Andreewsky, E., & Bourcier, D. (2000). Abduction in language interpretation and law making. *Kybernetes, 29,* 836–845.

Arminio, J. L., & Hultgren, F. H. (2002). Breaking out from the shadow: The question of criteria in qualitative research. *Journal of College Student Development, 43,* 446–456.

Arrington, R. (Ed.). (2001). *A companion to the philosophers.* Oxford, UK: Blackwell.

Ary, D., Jacobs, L. C., Razavieh, A., & Sorenson, C. (2007). *Introduction to research in education* (7th ed.). Belmont, CA: Wadsworth.

Atkinson, P. (1992). The ethnography of a medical setting: Reading, writing, and rhetoric. *Qualitative Health Research, 2,* 451–474.

Atkinson, P., & Hammersley, M. (1994). Ethnography and participant observation. In N. K. Denzin & Y. S. Lincoln (Eds.), *Handbook of qualitative research* (pp. 248–261). Thousand Oaks, CA: Sage.

Bakker, H. (1999). William Dilthey: Classical sociological theorist. *Quarterly Journal of Ideology, 22*(1&2), 43–82.

Bamberger, M. (Ed.). (2000). *Integrating quantitative and qualitative research in development projects.* Washington, DC: World Bank.

Barron, P., Diprose, R., Smith, C. Q., Whiteside, K., & Woolcock, M. (2008). *Applying mixed methods research to community driven development projects and local conflict mediation: A case study from Indonesia* (Report Number 34222). Washington, DC: World Bank.

Bartlett, J. E., Kotrlik, J. W., & Higgins, C. C. (2001). Organizational research: Determining sample size in survey research. *Information Technology, Learning, and Performance Journal, 19*(1), 43–50.

Bazeley, P. (2003). Computerized data analysis for mixed methods research. In A. Tashakkori & C. Teddlie (Eds.), *Handbook of mixed methods in social and behavioral research* (pp. 385–422). Thousand Oaks, CA: Sage.

Bazeley, P. (2006). The contribution of computer software to integrating qualitative and quantitative data analysis. *Research in the Schools, 13*(1), 64–74.

Bezeley, P. (2007). *Qualitative data analysis with NVivo.* London: Sage.

Beck, A. T., Ward, C. H., Mendelson, M., Mock, J., & Erbaugh, J. (1961). An inventory for measuring depression. *Archives of General Psychiatry, 4,* 561–571.

Becker, H. S. (1970). *Sociological work: Method and substance.* New Brunswick, NJ: Transaction Books.

Belozerov, S. (2002). *Inductive and deductive methods in cognition.* Retrieved December 1, 2005, from http://www.matrixreasoning.com/pdf/inductiondeduction.pdf

Ben Jaafar, S. (2006). *Relating performance-based accountability policy to the accountability practices of school leaders.* Unpublished doctoral dissertation, University of Toronto.

Berelson, B. (1952). *Content analysis in communication research.* New York: Free Press.

Berg, B. L. (2004). *Qualitative research methods for the social sciences* (5th ed.). Boston: Allyn & Bacon.

Berger, P., & Luckmann, T. (1966). *The social construction of reality.* New York: Doubleday.

Bergman, M. M. (2007). Multimethod research and mixed methods research: Old wine in new bottles? [Review of the book *Foundations of multimethod research: Synthesizing styles* (2nd ed.)]. *Journal of Mixed Methods Research, 1*(1), 101–102.

Bergman, M. M. (Ed.). (2008). *Advances in mixed methods research: Theories and applications.* London: Sage Ltd.

Berkenkotter, C. (1989). The legacy of positivism in empirical composition research. *Journal of Advanced Composition, 9,* 69–82.

Berliner, D. (2002). Educational research: The hardest science of all. *Educational Researcher, 31*(8), 18–20.

Bernard, R. (2007, April). *Publishing your mixed methods article: Journal editors' recommendations.* Paper presented at the annual meeting of the American Educational Research Association, Chicago.

Bernardi, L., Keim, S., & Lippe, H. (2007). Social influences on fertility: A comparative mixed methods study in Eastern and Western Germany. *Journal of Mixed Methods Research, 1*(1), 23–47.

Biesta, G., & Burbules, N. C. (2003). *Pragmatism and educational research.* Lanham, MD: Rowman and Littlefield.

Blake, C. F. (1981). Graffiti and racial insults: The archaeology of ethnic relations in Hawaii. In R. A. Gould & M. B. Shiffer (Eds.), *Modern material culture: The archaeology of us* (pp. 87–100). New York: Academic Publishers.

Blalock, H. M. (1964). *Causal inferences in non-experimental research.* Chapel Hill: University of North Carolina Press.

Blalock, H. M. (Ed.). (1985). *Causal models in the social sciences.* New York: Aldine de Gruyter.

Bliss, L. (2008). Review of Jennifer Greene's *Mixed Methods in Social Inquiry. Journal of Mixed Methods Research, 2*(2), 190–192.

Boas, F. (1911). *Handbook of American Indian language: Part 1.* Washington, DC: Smithsonian Institution, Bureau of American Ethnology.

Bogdan, R. C., & Biklen, S. K. (2003). *Qualitative research for education: An introduction to theory and methods* (4th ed.). Boston: Allyn & Bacon.

Borgatti, S. P. (2002). *NetDraw: Version 1.* Harvard, MA: Analytic Technologies.

Borgatti, S. P., Everett, M. G., & Freeman, L. C. (2002). *UCINET 6 reference manual.* Harvard, MA: Analytic Technologies.

Boyatzis, R. E. (1998). *Transforming qualitative information: Thematic analysis and code development.* Thousand Oaks, CA: Sage.

Bragg, M. (1998). *On giants' shoulders: Great scientists and their discoveries—From Archimedes to DNA.* New York: Wiley.

Brannen, J. (1992). *Mixing methods: Quantitative and qualitative research.* Aldershot, UK: Avebury.

Brannen, J. (2005). Mixed methods: The entry of qualitative and quantitative approaches into the research process. *International Journal of Social Research Methodology, 8*(3), 173–184.

Brannen, J., & Moss, P. (1991). *Managing mothers and earner households after maternity leave.* London: Unwin Hymen.

Brewer, J., & Hunter, A. (1989). *Multimethod research: A synthesis of styles.* Newbury Park, CA: Sage.

Brewer, J., & Hunter, A. (2006). *Foundations of multimethod research: Synthesizing styles* (2nd ed.). Thousand Oaks, CA: Sage.

Brookover, W. B., Beady, C., Flood, P., Schweitzer, J., & Wisenbaker, J. (1979). *Schools, social systems and student achievement: Schools can make a difference.* New York: Praeger.

Brookover, W. B., & Lezotte, L. W. (1979). *Changes in school characteristics coincident with changes in student achievement.* East Lansing: Institute for Research on Teaching College of Education, Michigan State University.

Brophy, J. E., & Good, T. L. (1986). Teacher behavior and student achievement. In M. Wittrock (Ed.), *Third handbook of research on teaching* (pp. 328–375). New York: Macmillan.

Brumbaugh, R. S. (1981). *The philosophers of Greece.* Albany: State University of New York Press.

Bryant, C. A., Forthofer, M. S., McCormack Brown, K., Alfonso, M., & Quinn, G. (2000). A social marketing approach to increasing breast cancer screening rates. *Journal of Health Education, 31,* 320–328.

Bryman, A. (1988). *Quantity and quality in social research.* London: Unwin Hyman.

Bryman, A. (1992). Quantitative and qualitative research: Further reflections on their integration. In J. Brannen (Ed.), *Mixing methods: Quantitative and qualitative research* (pp. 57–58). Aldershot, UK: Avebury.

Bryman, A. (2004). *Social research methods* (2nd ed.). Oxford, UK: Oxford University Press.

Bryman, A. (2006a). Integrating quantitative and qualitative research: How is it done? *Qualitative Research, 6*(1), 97–113.

Bryman, A. (2006b). Paradigm peace and the implications for quality. *International Journal of Social Research Methodology Theory and Practice, 9*(2), 111–126.

Bryman, A. (2007). Barriers to integrating quantitative and qualitative research. *Journal of Mixed Methods Research, 1*(1), 8–22.

Bunnin, N., & Tsui-James, E. (Eds.). (2003). *The Blackwell companion to philosophy* (2nd ed.). Oxford, UK: Blackwell.

Cakan, M. (1999). *Interaction of cognitive style and assessment approach in determining student performance on tests of second language proficiency.* Unpublished doctoral dissertation, Louisiana State University, Baton Rouge.

Campbell, D. T. (1957). Factors relevant to the validity of experiments in social settings. *Psychological Bulletin, 54,* 297–312.

Campbell, D. T. (1988). Definitional versus multiple operationism. In E. S. Overman (Ed.), *Methodology and epistemology for social science: Selected papers* (pp. 31–36). Chicago: University of Chicago Press.

Campbell, D. T., & Fiske, D. W. (1959). Convergent and discriminant validation by the multitrait-multimethod matrix. *Psychological Bulletin, 56,* 81–105.

Campbell, D. T., & Stanley, J. (1963). Experimental and quasi-experimental designs for research on teaching. In N. L. Gage (Ed.), *Handbook of research on teaching* (pp. 171–246). Chicago: Rand McNally.

Canter, D., & Alison, L. (2003). Converting evidence into data: The use of law enforcement archives as unobtrusive measurement. *The Qualitative Report, 8*(2), 151–176.

Capper, C. A. (1998). Critically oriented and postmodern perspectives: Sorting out the differences and applications for practice. *Educational Administration Quarterly, 34,* 354–379.

Caracelli, V. J., & Greene, J. C. (1993). Data analysis strategies for mixed-method evaluation designs. *Educational Evaluation and Policy Analysis, 15,* 195–207.

Carey, J. W., Morgan, M., & Oxtoby, M. J. (1996). Intercoder agreement in analysis of responses to open-ended interview questions: Examples from tuberculosis research. *Cultural Anthropology Methods Journal, 8*(3), 1–5.

Carrere, S., Buehlman, K. T., Gottman, J. M., Coan, J. A., & Ruckstuhl, L. (2000). Predicting marital stability and divorce in newlywed couples. *Journal of Family Psychology, 14*(1), 42–58.

Carwile, L. (2005). *Responsibilities and leadership styles of radiologic technology program directors: Implications for leadership development.* Unpublished doctoral dissertation, Louisiana State University, Baton Rouge.

Cattell, R. B. (1960). *Measuring intelligence with the Culture Fair Tests.* Savoy, IL: Institute for Personality and Ability Testing.

Chambers, E. (2000). Applied ethnography. In N. K. Denzin & Y. S. Lincoln (Eds.), *Handbook of qualitative research* (2nd ed., pp. 851–869). Thousand Oaks, CA: Sage.

Charmaz, K. (2000). Grounded theory: Objectivist and constructivist methods. In N. K. Denzin & Y. S. Lincoln (Eds.), *Handbook of qualitative research* (2nd ed., pp. 509–536). Thousand Oaks, CA: Sage.

Charmaz, K. (2005). Grounded theory in the 21st century: Applications for advancing social justice studies. In N. K. Denzin & Y. S. Lincoln (Eds.), *Handbook of qualitative research* (3rd ed., pp. 507–535). Thousand Oaks, CA: Sage.

Chebbi, T. (2005). *The impact of technology professional development of school principals on the effective integration of technology in elementary public schools.* Unpublished doctoral dissertation, Florida International University, Miami.

Cherryholmes, C. C. (1992). Notes on pragmatism and scientific realism. *Educational Researcher, 21,* 13–17.

Christ, T. W. (2007). A recursive approach to mixed methods research in a longitudinal study of postsecondary education disability support services. *Journal of Mixed Methods Research, 1*(3), 226–241.

Clampet-Lundquist, S. (2003). Finding and keeping affordable housing: Analyzing the experiences of single-mother families in North Philadelphia. *Journal of Sociology and Social Welfare, 30*(4), 123–140.

Clert, C., Gacitua-Mario, E., & Wodon, Q. (2001). Combining quantitative and qualitative methods for policy research on poverty within a social exclusion framework. In E. Gacitúa-Marió & Q. Wodon (Eds.), *Measurement and meaning: Combining quantitative and qualitative methods for the analysis of poverty and social exclusion in Latin America* (pp. 1–9). Washington, DC: The World Bank.

Coffey, A., & Atkinson, P. (1996). *Making sense of qualitative data: Complementary research strategies.* Thousand Oaks, CA: Sage.

Cohen, J. (1988). *Statistical power analysis for the behavioral sciences* (2nd ed.). Hillsdale, NJ: Lawrence Erlbaum.

Cohen, M. Z., Tripp-Reimer, T., Smith, C., Sorofman, B., & Lively, S. (1994). Explanatory models of diabetes: Patient practitioner variation. *Social Science and Medicine, 38,* 59–66.

Collins, J. (1967). *The British empiricists: Locke, Berkeley, Hume.* Milwaukee, WI: Bruce Publishing.

Collins, K. M. T., Onwuegbuzie, A. J., & Jiao, Q. C. (2007). A mixed methods investigation of mixed methods sampling designs in social and health science research. *Journal of Mixed Methods Research, 1,* 267–294.

Collins, S., & Long, A. (2003). Too tired to care? The psychological effects of working with trauma. *Journal of Psychiatric and Mental Health Nursing, 10,* 17–27.

Cook, T. D. (2002). Randomized experiments in educational policy research: A critical examination of the reasons the educational evaluation community has offered for not doing them. *Educational Evaluation and Policy Analysis, 24*(3), 175–199.

Cook, T. D., & Campbell, D. T. (1979). *Quasi-experimentation: Design and analysis issues for field settings.* Boston: Houghton Mifflin.

Cooper, H., & Good, T. (1982) *Pygmalion grows up: Studies in the expectation communication process.* New York: Longman.

Cottingham, J. (1988). *The rationalists.* Oxford, UK: Oxford University Press.

Covino, E. A., & Iwanicki, E. (1996). Experienced teachers: Their constructs of effective teaching. *Journal of Personnel Evaluation in Education, 10,* 325–363.

Creswell, J. W. (1994) *Research design: Qualitative and quantitative approaches.* Thousand Oaks, CA: Sage.

Creswell, J. W. (1998). *Qualitative inquiry and research design: Choosing among five traditions.* Thousand Oaks, CA: Sage.

Creswell, J. W. (2002). *Educational research: Planning, conducting, and evaluating quantitative and qualitative research.* Upper Saddle River, NJ: Prentice Hall.

Creswell, J. W. (2003). *Research design: Qualitative, quantitative, and mixed methods approaches set* (2nd ed.). Thousand Oaks, CA: Sage.

Creswell, J. W., & Plano Clark, V. (2007). *Designing and conducting mixed methods research.* Thousand Oaks, CA: Sage.

Creswell, J. W., Plano Clark, V., Gutmann, M., & Hanson, W. (2003). Advanced mixed methods research designs. In A. Tashakkori & C. Teddlie (Eds.), *Handbook of mixed methods in social and behavioral research* (pp. 209–240). Thousand Oaks, CA: Sage.

Creswell, J. W., Shope, R., Plano Clark, V., & Green, D. (2006). How interpretive qualitative research extends mixed methods research. *Research in the Schools, 13*(1), 1–11.

Creswell, J. W, & Tashakkori, A. (2007a). Developing publishable mixed methods manuscripts. *Journal of Mixed Methods Research, 1,* 107–111.

Creswell, J. W., & Tashakkori, A. (2007b). Differing perspectives on mixed methods research. *Journal of Mixed Methods Research, 1,* 303–308.

Crichton, S., & Kinash, S. (2003). Virtual ethnography: Interactive interviewing online as method. *Canadian Journal of Learning and Technology, 29*(2) 101–115.

Cronbach, L. J. (1982). *Designing evaluations of educational and social programs.* San Francisco: Jossey-Bass.

Cronbach, L. J. (1991). *Essentials of psychological testing* (4th ed.). New York: Harper & Row.

Currall, S. C., Hammer, T. H., Baggett, L. S., & Doninger, G. M. (1999). Combining qualitative and quantitative methodologies to study group processes: An illustrative study of a corporate board of directors. *Organizational Research Methods, 2,* 5–36.

Curtis, S., Gesler, W., Smith, G., & Washburn, S. (2000). Approaches to sampling and case selection in qualitative research: Examples in the geography of health. *Social Science and Medicine, 50,* 1001–1014.

Dancy, R. M. (2001). Aristotle. In R. Arrington (Ed.), *A companion to the philosophers* (pp. 132–141). Oxford, UK: Blackwell.

Datnow, A., Hubbard, L., & Mehan, H. (2002). *Extending educational reform: From one school to many.* London: RoutledgeFalmer Press.

Datta, L. (1994). Paradigm wars: A basis for peaceful coexistence and beyond. In C. S. Reichardt & S. F. Rallis (Eds.), *The qualitative-quantitative debate: New perspectives* (pp. 53–70). Thousand Oaks, CA: Sage.

Datta, L. (2001). The wheelbarrow, the mosaic, and the double helix: Challenges and strategies for successfully carrying out mixed methods evaluation. *Evaluation Journal of Australasia, 1*(2), 33–40.

Davidson, D. (1973). On the very idea of a conceptual scheme. *Proceedings of the American Philosophical Association, 68,* 5–20.

Deacon, D., Bryman, A., & Fenton, N. (1998). Collision or collusion? A discussion of the unplanned triangulation of quantitative and qualitative research methods. *International Journal of Social Research Methodology Theory and Practice, 1,* 47–64.

Debats, D., Drost, J., & Hansen, P. (1995). Experiences of meaning in life: A combined qualitative and quantitative approach. *British Journal of Psychology, 86*(3), 359–375.

Dellinger, A. B., & Leech, N. L. (2007). Toward a unified validation framework in mixed methods research. *Journal of Mixed Methods Research, 1,* 309–332.

Denzin, N. K. (1978). *The research act: A theoretical introduction to sociological method* (2nd ed.). New York: McGraw-Hill.

Denzin, N. K. (1989a). *Interpretive biography.* Thousand Oaks, CA: Sage.

Denzin, N. K. (1989b). *The research act: A theoretical introduction to sociological method* (3rd ed.). New York: McGraw-Hill.

Denzin, N. K., & Lincoln, Y. S. (Eds.). (1994). *Handbook of qualitative research.* Thousand Oaks, CA: Sage.

Denzin, N. K., & Lincoln, Y. S. (Eds.). (2000a). *Handbook of qualitative research* (2nd ed.). Thousand Oaks, CA: Sage.

Denzin, N. K., & Lincoln, Y. S. (2000b). Introduction: The discipline and practice of qualitative research. In N. K. Denzin & Y. S. Lincoln (Eds.), *Handbook of qualitative research* (2nd ed., pp. 1–28). Thousand Oaks, CA: Sage.

Denzin, N. K., & Lincoln, Y. S. (Eds.). (2001). *The American tradition in qualitative research* (Vol. 1). Thousand Oaks, CA: Sage.

Denzin, N. K., & Lincoln, Y. S. (Eds.). (2005a). *Handbook of qualitative research* (3rd ed.). Thousand Oaks, CA: Sage.

Denzin, N. K., & Lincoln, Y. S. (2005b). Introduction: The discipline and practice of qualitative research. In N. K. Denzin & Y. S. Lincoln (Eds.), *Handbook of qualitative research* (3rd ed., pp. 1–32). Thousand Oaks, CA: Sage.

Denzin, N. K., Lincoln, Y. S., & Giardina, M. D. (2006). Disciplining qualitative research. *International Journal of Qualitative Studies in Education, 19,* 769–782.

Detlor, B. (2003). Internet-based information systems: An information studies perspective. *Information Systems Journal, 13,* 113–132.

Dey, I. (1993). *Qualitative data analysis: A user-friendly guide for social scientists.* London: Routledge.

Driscoll, D. L., Appiah-Yeboah, A., Salib, P., & Rupert, D. J. (2007). Measuring qualitative and quantitative data in mixed methods research: How to and why not. *Ecological and Environmental Anthropology, 3*(1), 19–28.

Druckman, D. (2005). *Doing research: Methods of inquiry for conflict analysis.* Thousand Oaks, CA: Sage.

Durkheim, E. (1951). *Suicide: A study in sociology.* Glencoe, IL: Free Press. (Original work published 1897)

Durland, M., & Fredericks, K. (Eds.). (2005). *New directions for evaluation: Number 107. Social network analysis in program evaluation.* San Francisco: Jossey Bass.

Dykema, J., & Schaeffer, N. C. (2000). Events, instruments, and error reporting. *American Sociological Review, 65,* 619–629.

Earley, M. A. (2007). Developing a syllabus for a mixed methods research course. *International Journal of Social Research Methodology, 10*(2), 145–162.

Edge, S. J. (1999). Why did they kill Barney? Media, Northern Ireland and the riddle of loyalist terror. *European Journal of Communication, 14*(1), 91–116.

Edmonds, R. R. (1979). Effective schools for the urban poor. *Educational Leadership, 37*(10), 15–24.

Eisenhart, M., & Howe, K. (1992). Validity in educational research. In M. LeCompte, W. Millroy, & J. Preissle (Eds.), *The handbook of qualitative research in education* (pp. 642–680). San Diego, CA: Academic Press.

Eisenhart, M., & Towne, L. (2003). Contestation and change in national policy on "scientifically based" education research. *Educational Researcher, 32*(7), 31–38.

Eisner, E. W. (1975). The perceptive eye: Toward the reformulation of educational evaluation. In *Occasional Papers of the Stanford Evaluation Consortium* (mimeo). Stanford, CA: Stanford University.

Eisner, E. W. (1981). On the differences between scientific and artistic approaches to qualitative research. *Educational Researcher, 10*(3–4), 5–9.

Eisner, E. W. (1998). *The enlightened eye: Qualitative inquiry and the enhancement of educational practice.* Upper Saddle River, NJ: Merrill.

Elliott, J. (2005). *Using narrative in social research: Qualitative and quantitative approaches.* Thousand Oaks, CA: Sage.

Elliott, M. S., & Williams, D. I. (2002). A qualitative evaluation of an employee counselling service from the perspective of client, counsellor, and organization. *Counselling Psychology Quarterly, 15*(2), 201–208.

Erzberger, C., & Kelle, U. (2003). Making inferences in mixed methods: The rules of integration. In A. Tashakkori & C. Teddlie (Eds.), *Handbook of mixed methods in social and behavioral research* (pp. 457–490). Thousand Oaks, CA: Sage.

Erzberger, C., & Prein, G. (1997). Triangulation: Validity and empirically based hypothesis construction. *Quality and Quantity, 2,* 141–154.

Fals-Stewart, W., Birchler, G., Schafer, J., & Lucente, S. (1994). The personality of marital distress: An empirical typology. *Journal of Personality Assessment, 62,* 223–241.

Festinger, L. (1957). *A theory of cognitive dissonance.* Stanford, CA: Stanford University Press.

Festinger, L., Riecken, H. W., & Schacter, S. (1956). *When prophecy fails: A social and psychological study of a modern group that predicted the destruction of the world.* New York: Harper & Row.

Fetterman, D. M. (1998). *Ethnography: Step by step* (2nd ed.). Thousand Oaks, CA: Sage.

Feur, M. J., Towne, L., & Shavelson, R. J. (2002). Scientific culture and educational research. *Educational Researcher, 31*(8), 4–14.

Fiedler, F. E. (1967). A *theory of leadership effectiveness.* New York: McGraw-Hill.

Fiedler, F. E. (1973). The contingency model and the dynamics of the leadership process. *Advances in Experimental Social Psychology, 11,* 60–112.

Fine, G., & Elsbach, K. (2000). Ethnography and experiment in social psychological theory building: Tactics for integrating qualitative field data with quantitative lab data. *Journal of Experimental Social Psychology, 36,* 51–76.

Fink, L. D. (2003). *Creating significant learning experiences in college classrooms.* San Francisco: Jossey-Bass.

Fitz-Gibbon, C. T. (1996). *Monitoring education: Indicators, quality and effectiveness.* London: Cassell.

Fitz-Gibbon, C. T., & Morris, L. L. (1987). *How to design a program evaluation.* Thousand Oaks, CA: Sage.

Flick, U. (1998). *An introduction to qualitative research.* Thousand Oaks, CA: Sage.

Forthofer, M. (2003). Status of mixed methods in the health sciences. In A. Tashakkori & C. Teddlie (Eds.), *Handbook of mixed methods in social and behavioral research* (pp. 527–540). Thousand Oaks, CA: Sage.

Foucault, M. (1970). *The order of things: An archaeology of the human sciences.* New York: Pantheon.

Fredericks, K., & Durland, M. (2005). The historical evolution and basic concepts of social network analysis. In M. Durland & K. Fredericks (Eds.), *New directions for evaluation: Number 107. Social network analysis in program evaluation* (pp. 15–24). San Francisco: Jossey- Bass.

Freeman, J. (1997). *A methodological examination of naturally occurring school improvement in Louisiana schools.* Unpublished dissertation, Louisiana State University, Baton Rouge.

Freeman, M., de Marrais, K., Preissle, J., Roulston, K., & St. Pierre, E. A. (2007). Standards of evidence in qualitative research: An incitement to discourse. *Educational Researcher, 36*(1), 25–32.

Freshwater, D. (2007). Reading mixed methods research: Contexts for criticisms. *Journal of Mixed Methods Research, 2,* 134–146.

Gacitúa-Marió, E., & Wodon, Q. (2001) *Measurement and meaning: Combining quantitative and qualitative methods for the analysis of poverty and social exclusion in Latin America* (Technical paper 518). Washington, DC: The World Bank.

Gage, N. (1989). The paradigm wars and their aftermath: A "historical" sketch of research and teaching since 1989. *Educational Researcher, 18,* 4–10.

Gall, M. D., Gall, J. P., & Borg, W. R. (2006). *Educational research: An introduction* (8th ed.). Boston: Allyn & Bacon.

Gatta, J. (2003). *Mixed methodology survey research: A nested paradigm approach.* Unpublished dissertation, Loyola University, Chicago.

Gay, P. (1969). *The enlightenment: The science of freedom.* New York: W. W. Norton.

Geertz, C. (1973). *The interpretation of cultures: Selected essays.* New York: Basic Books.

Geertz, C. (1983). *Local knowledge: Further essays in interpretive anthropology.* New York: Basic Books.

Gergen, K. (1985). The social constructionist movement in modern psychology, *American Psychologist, 40,* 266–275.

Geymonat, L. (1965). *Galileo Galilei.* New York: McGraw-Hill.

Giddens, A., Duneier, M., & Applebaum. R. P. (2003). *Introduction to sociology* (4th ed.). New York: W. W. Norton.

Gilbert, T. (2006). Mixed methods and mixed methodologies: The practical, the technical and the political. *Journal of Research in Nursing, 11,* 205–217.

Gilgen, A. (1982). *American psychology since World War II: A profile of the discipline.* Westport, CT: Greenwood Press.

Gjertsen, D. (1986). *The Newton handbook.* Boston: Routledge & Kegan Paul.

Glaser, B. G., & Strauss, A. L. (1965). *Awareness of dying.* Chicago: Aldine.

Glaser, B. G., & Strauss, A. L. (1967). *The discovery of grounded theory: Strategies for qualitative research.* Chicago: Aldine.

Gleick, J. (2003). *Isaac Newton.* New York: Pantheon Books.

Glesne, C. (2006). *Becoming qualitative researchers: An introduction* (3rd ed.). Boston: Pearson.

Goffman, E. (1963). *Stigma: Notes on the management of spoiled identity.* Englewood Cliffs, NJ: Prentice Hall.

Gold, R. L. (1958). Roles in sociological field observations. *Social Forces, 36,* 217–223.

Gorard, S. (2004) Skeptical or clerical? Theory as a barrier to the combination of research methods. *Journal of Educational Enquiry, 5*(1), 1–21.

Gorard, S., & Taylor, C. (2004). *Combining methods in educational and social research.* Buckingham, UK: Open University Press.

Gower, B. (1997). *Scientific method: An historical and philosophical introduction.* London: Routledge.

Gracia, J. J. E. (2003). Medieval philosophy. In N. Bunnin & E. Tsui-James (Eds.), *The Blackwell companion to philosophy* (2nd ed., pp. 619–633). Oxford, UK: Blackwell.

Gravetter, F. J., & Wallnau, L. B. (2007). *Essentials of statistics for the behavioral sciences* (6th ed.). Belmont, CA: Wadsworth.

Green, S. (2002). Mothering Amanda: Musings on the experience of raising a child with cerebral palsy. *Journal of Loss and Trauma, 7,* 21–34.

Green, S. (2003). "What do you mean 'what's wrong with her?'": Stigma and the lives of families of children with disabilities. *School Science and Medicine, 57,* 1361–1374.

Greene, J. C. (2006). Toward a methodology of mixed methods social inquiry. *Research in the Schools, 13*(1), 93–99.

Greene, J. C. (2007). *Mixing methods in social inquiry.* San Francisco: Jossey-Bass.

Greene, J. C., & Caracelli, V. J. (Eds.). (1997a). *New directions for evaluation: Number 74. Advances in mixed-method evaluation: The challenges and benefits of integrating diverse paradigms.* San Francisco: Jossey-Bass.

Greene, J. C., & Caracelli, V. J. (1997b). Defining and describing the paradigm issue in mixed-method evaluation. In J. C. Greene & V. J. Caracelli (Eds.), *New directions for evaluation: Number 74: Advances in mixed-method evaluation: The challenges and benefits of integrating diverse paradigms.* San Francisco: Jossey-Bass.

Greene, J. C., & Caracelli, V. J. (2003). Making paradigmatic sense of mixed-method practice. In A. Tashakkori & C. Teddlie (Eds.), *Handbook of mixed methods in social and behavioral research* (pp. 91–110). Thousand Oaks, CA: Sage.

Greene, J. C., Caracelli, V. J., & Graham, W. F. (1989). Toward a conceptual framework for mixed-method evaluation designs. *Educational Evaluation and Policy Analysis, 11,* 255–274.

Guba, E. G. (1987). What have we learned about naturalistic evaluation? *Evaluation Practice, 8,* 23–43.

Guba, E. G., & Lincoln, Y. S. (1989). *Fourth generation evaluation.* Newbury Park, CA: Sage.

Guba, E. G., & Lincoln, Y. S. (1994). Competing paradigms in qualitative research. In N. K. Denzin & Y. S. Lincoln (Eds.), *Handbook of qualitative research* (pp. 105–117). Thousand Oaks, CA: Sage.

Guba, E. G., & Lincoln, Y. S. (2005). Paradigmatic controversies, contradictions, and emerging confluences. In N. K. Denzin & Y. S. Lincoln (Eds.), *Handbook of qualitative research* (3rd ed., pp. 191–215). Thousand Oaks, CA: Sage.

Hall, J. R. (1999). *Cultures of inquiry: From epistemology to discourse in sociocultural research.* Cambridge, UK: Cambridge University Press.

Hallinger, P., & Murphy, J. (1986). The social context of effective schools. *American Journal of Education, 94,* 328–355.

Hammersley, M. (1992a). The paradigm wars: Reports from the front. *British Journal of Sociology of Education, 13*(1), 131–143.

Hammersley, M. (1992b). *What's wrong with ethnography.* London: Routledge.

Hammersley, M. (1995). Opening up the quantitative-qualitative divide. *Education Section Review, 19*(1), 2–15.

Hammersley, M., & Atkinson, P. (1995). *Ethnography: Principles in practice* (2nd ed.). London: Routledge.

Hancock, M., Calnan, M., & Manley, G. (1999). Private or NHS dental service care in the United Kingdom? A study of public perceptions and experiences. *Journal of Public Health Medicine, 21*(4), 415–420.

Hanson, N. R. (1958). *Patterns of discovery: An inquiry into the conceptual foundations of science.* Cambridge, UK: Cambridge University Press.

Harper, D. (2000). Reimagining visual methods: Galileo to Neuromancer. In N. K. Denzin & Y. S. Lincoln (Eds.), *Handbook of qualitative research* (2nd ed., pp. 717–732). Thousand Oaks, CA: Sage.

Harrington, A. (2000). In defence of *verstehen* and *erklaren:* Wilhem Dilthey's ideas concerning a descriptive and analytical psychology. *Theory and Psychology, 10,* 435–451.

Hausman, A. (2000). A multi-method investigation of consumer motivations in impulse buying behavior. *Journal of Consumer Marketing, 17*(5), 403–419.

Heider, F. (1958). *The psychology of interpersonal relations.* New York: John Wiley & Sons.

Hempel, C. G. (1965). *Aspects of scientific explanation*. New York: Free Press.

Hempel, C. G., & Oppenheim, P. (1948). Studies in the logic of explanation. *Philosophy of Science, 15*, 135–175.

Henwood, K., & Pidgeon, N. (2001). Talk about woods and trees: Threat of urbanization, stability, and biodiversity. *Journal of Environmental Psychology, 21*, 125–147.

Hinkle, D. E., Wiersma, W., & Jurs, S. G. (1998). *Applied statistics for the behavioral sciences* (5th ed.). Boston: Houghton Mifflin.

Hoffman, L., & Hoffman, M. (1973). The value of children to parents. In J. Fawcett (Ed.), *Psychological perspectives on population* (pp. 19–76). New York: Basic Books.

Hollingsworth, S. (Ed.). (1997). *International action research: A casebook for educational reform*. London: Falmer Press.

Hollis, M. (2002). *The philosophy of science: An introduction* (Rev. ed.). Cambridge, UK: Cambridge University Press.

Holsti, O. R. (1968). *Content analysis for the social sciences and humanities*. Reading, MA: Addison-Wesley.

Hothersall, D. (1995). *History of psychology* (3rd ed.). Columbus, OH: McGraw-Hill.

House, E. R. (1991). Realism in research. *Educational Researcher, 20*(6), 2–9, 25.

House, E. R., & Howe, K. R. (1999). *Values in evaluation and social research*. Thousand Oaks, CA: Sage.

Howe, K. R. (1988). Against the quantitative-qualitative incompatibility thesis or dogmas die hard. *Educational Researcher, 17*, 10–16.

Howe, K. R. (2004). A critique of experimentalism. *Qualitative Inquiry, 10*(1), 42–61.

Hunter, A., & Brewer, J. (2003). Multimethod research in sociology. In A. Tashakkori & C. Teddlie (Eds.), *Handbook of mixed methods in social and behavioral research* (pp. 577–594). Thousand Oaks, CA: Sage.

Huston, A. C. (2001, January). *Mixed methods in studies of social experiments for parents in poverty: Commentary*. Paper presented at the Conference on Discovering Successful Pathways in Children's Development, Santa Monica, CA.

Ivankova, N. V. (2004). *Students' persistence in the University of Nebraska-Lincoln distributed doctoral program in educational leadership in higher education: A mixed methods study*. Unpublished dissertation, University of Nebraska–Lincoln.

Ivankova, N. V., Creswell, J. W., & Stick, S. (2006). Using mixed methods sequential explanatory design: From theory to practice. *Field Methods, 18*(1), 3–20.

Iwanicki, E., & Tashakkori, A. (1994). *The proficiencies of the effective principal: A validation study*. Baton Rouge: Louisiana Department of Education.

Jaccard, J., & Becker, M. A. (2002). *Statistics for the behavioral sciences* (4th ed.). Belmont, CA: Wadsworth.

Jahoda, M., Lazersfeld, P. F., & Zeisel, H. (1971). *Marienthal: The sociography of an unemployed community*. Chicago: Aldine.

Jang, E. E., McDougall, D. E., Pollon, D., Herbert, M., & Russell, P. (2008). Integrative mixed methods data analytic strategies in research on school success in challenging circumstances. *Journal of Mixed Methods Research, 2*(2), 221–247.

Jha, S., Rao, V., & Woolcock, M. (2005). *Governance in the gullies: Democratic responsiveness and leadership in Delhi's slums*. Washington, DC: The World Bank.

Jick, T. D. (1979). Mixing qualitative and quantitative methods: Triangulation in action. *Administrative Science Quarterly, 24*, 602–611.

Johnson, A. W., & Price-Williams, D. (1996). *Oedipus ubiquitous: The family complex in world folk literature*. Stanford, CA: Stanford University Press.

Johnson, R. B. (2008). *A classification scheme for unpacking methodological paradigm beliefs in the social and behavioral sciences*. Mobile: University of South Alabama.

Johnson, R. B., & Christensen, L. (2004). *Educational research: Quantitative, qualitative, and mixed methods* (2nd ed.). Boston: Pearson.

Johnson, R. B., & Christensen, L. B. (2008). *Educational research: Quantitative, qualitative, and mixed approaches* (3rd ed.). Thousand Oaks, CA: Sage.

Johnson, R. B., & Onwuegbuzie, A. (2004). Mixed methods research: A research paradigm whose time has come. *Educational Researcher, 33*(7), 14–26.

Johnson, R. B., Onwuegbuzie, A., & Turner, L. (2007). Toward a definition of mixed methods research. *Journal of Mixed Methods Research, 1,* 112–133.

Johnson, R. B., & Turner, L. (2003). Data collection strategies in mixed methods research. In A. Tashakkori & C. Teddlie (Eds.), *Handbook of mixed methods in social and behavioral research* (pp. 297–320). Thousand Oaks, CA: Sage.

Johnstone, P. L. (2004). Mixed methods, mixed methodology health services research in practice. *Qualitative Health Research, 14,* 259–271.

Kaeding, M. (2007). *Better regulation in the European Union: Lost in translation of full steam ahead? The transposition of EU transport directives across member states.* Leidene, Netherlands: Leidene University Press.

Kalafat, J., & Illback, R. J. (1999). *Evaluation of Kentucky's school-based family resource and youth services center, part 1: Program design, evaluation conceptualization, and implementation evaluation.* Louisville, KY: REACH of Louisville.

Katz, L. F., Kling, J. R., & Liebman, J. B. (2001). Moving to opportunity in Boston: Early results of a randomized mobility experiment. *The Quarterly Journal of Economics, 116,* 607–654.

Kelley, H. H. (1967). Attribution theory in social psychology. In D. Levine (Ed.), *Nebraska symposium in motivation* (pp. 192–198). Lincoln: University of Nebraska Press.

Kemper, E., Stringfield. S., & Teddlie, C. (2003). Mixed methods sampling strategies in social science research. In A. Tashakkori & C. Teddlie (Eds.), *Handbook of mixed methods in social and behavioral research* (pp. 273–296). Thousand Oaks, CA: Sage.

Kemper, E., & Teddlie, C. (2000). Mandated site-based management in Texas: Exploring implementation in urban high schools. *Teaching and Change, 7,* 172–200.

Kerlinger, F. N., & Lee, H. B. (2000). *Foundations of behavioral research* (4th ed.). Fort Worth, TX: Harcourt .

Kern, D. H., & Mainous, A. G., III (2001). Disease management for diabetes among family physicians and general internists: Opportunism or planned care? *Family Medicine, 33,* 621–625.

Kincheloe, J. L., & McLaren, P. (2005). Rethinking critical theory and qualitative research. In N. K. Denzin & Y. S. Lincoln (Eds.), *Handbook of qualitative research* (3rd ed., pp. 303–342). Thousand Oaks, CA: Sage.

King, G., Keohane, R. O., & Verba, S. (1994). *Designing social inquiry: Scientific inference in qualitative research.* Princeton, NJ: Princeton University Press.

Kling, J. R., Liebman, J. B., & Katz, L. F. (2005). Bullets don't got no name: Consequences of fear in the ghetto. In T. S. Weisner (Ed.), *Discovering successful pathways in children's development: Mixed methods in the study of childhood and family life* (pp. 243–281). Chicago: University of Chicago Press.

Kneller, G. F. (1984). *Movements of thought in modern education.* New York: John Wiley & Sons.

Kochan, S. (1998). *Considering outcomes beyond achievement: Participation as an indicator of high school performance.* Unpublished dissertation, Louisiana State University, Baton Rouge.

Kochan, S., Tashakkori, A., & Teddlie, C. (1996, April). *You can't judge a high school by achievement alone: Preliminary findings from the construction of behavioral indicators of school effectiveness.* Paper presented at the annual meeting of the American Educational Research Association, New York.

Kochan, S., & Teddlie, C. (2005). An evaluation of communication among high school faculty using network analysis. In M. Durland & K. Fredericks (Eds), *New directions for evaluation: Number 107. Social network analysis in program evaluation* (pp. 41–53). San Francisco: Jossey-Bass.

Kovach, F. (1987). *Scholastic challenges: To some mediaeval and modern ideas.* Stillwater, OK: Western Publications.

Krathwohl, D. R. (1993). *Methods of educational and social science research: An integrated approach.* White Plains, NY: Longman.

Krathwohl, D. R. (2004). *Methods of educational and social science research: An integrated approach* (2nd ed.). Long Grove, IL: Waveland Press.

Krüger, H. (2001). Social change in two generations: Employment patterns and their costs for family life. In V. W. Marshall, W. R. Heinz,

H. Krüger, & A. Verma (Eds.), *Restructuring work and the life course* (pp. 401–423). Toronto, Canada: University Press of Toronto.

Krueger, R. A., & Casey, M. A. (2000). *Focus groups: A practical guide for applied research* (3rd ed.). Thousand Oaks, CA: Sage.

Kuhn, T. S. (1962). *The structure of scientific revolutions.* Chicago: University of Chicago Press.

Kuhn, T. S. (1970). *The structure of scientific revolutions* (2nd ed.). Chicago: University of Chicago Press.

Kuhn, T. S. (1996). *The structure of scientific revolutions* (3rd ed.). Chicago: University of Chicago Press.

Kumagai, Y., Bliss, J. C., Daniels, S. E., & Carroll, M. S. (2004). Research on causal attribution of wildfire: An exploratory multiple-methods approach. *Society and Natural Resources, 17,* 113–127.

Lagemann, E. C. (2000). *An elusive science: The troubling history of education research.* Chicago: University of Chicago Press.

Lancy, D. F. (1993). *Qualitative research in education: An introduction to the major traditions.* New York: Longman.

Lasserre-Cortez, S. (2006). *A mixed methods examination of professional development through whole faculty study groups.* Unpublished doctoral dissertation, Louisiana State University, Baton Rouge.

Lather, P. (2004). This is your father's paradigm: Government intrusion and the case of qualitative research in education. *Qualitative Inquiry, 10*(1), 15–34.

Laudan, L. (1971). Towards a reassessment of Comte's "Methode Positive." *Philosophy of Science, 38*(1), 35–53.

LeCompte, M. D., & Preissle, J., with Tesch, R. (1993). *Ethnography and qualitative design in educational research* (2nd ed.). San Diego, CA: Academic Press.

Lee, R. M. (2000). *Unobtrusive methods in social research.* Buckingham, UK: Open University Press.

Lefcourt, H. M. (1982). *Locus of control: Current trends in theory and research.* Hillsdale, NJ: Lawrence Erlbaum.

Levine, D. U., & Lezotte, L. W. (1990). *Unusually effective schools: A review and analysis of research and practice.* Madison, WI: The National Center for Effective Schools Research and Development.

Li, S., Marquart, J. M., & Zercher, C. (2000). Conceptual issues and analytic strategies in mixed-method studies of preschool inclusion. *Journal of Early Intervention, 23,* 116–132.

Lichter, D. T., & Jayakody, R. (2002). Welfare reform: How do we measure success? *Annual Review of Sociology, 28,* 117–141.

Likert, R. (1932). A technique for the measurement of attitudes. *Archives of Psychology, 140,* 5–53.

Lincoln, Y. S. (1990). The making of a constructivist: A remembrance of transformations past. In E. G. Guba (Ed.), *The paradigm dialog* (pp. 67–87). Thousand Oaks, CA: Sage.

Lincoln, Y. S., & Guba, E. G. (1985). *Naturalistic inquiry.* Thousand Oaks, CA: Sage.

Lincoln, Y. S., & Guba, E. G. (2000). Paradigmatic controversies, contradictions, and emerging confluences. In N. K. Denzin & Y. S. Lincoln (Eds.), *Handbook of qualitative research* (2nd ed., pp. 163–188). Thousand Oaks, CA: Sage.

Liu, S. (2006). *School effectiveness research in the People's Republic of China.* Unpublished doctoral dissertation, Louisiana State University, Baton Rouge.

Lock, R. S., & Minarik, L. T. (1997). Gender equity in an elementary classroom: The power of praxis in action research. In S. Hollingsworth (Ed.), *International action research: A casebook for educational reform* (pp. 179–189). London: Falmer Press.

Lockyer, S. (2006). Heard the one about . . . applying mixed methods in humor research? *International Journal of Social Research Methodology, 9,* 41–59.

Logan, J. (2006). *The impact of Katrina: Race and class in storm-damaged neighborhoods.* Retrieved February 18, 2006, from http://www.s4.brown.edu/Katrina/report.pdf

Lopez, M., & Tashakkori, A. (2006). Differential outcomes of TWBE and TBE on ELLs at different entry levels. *Bilingual Research Journal, 30*(1), 81–103.

Losee, J. (2001). *A historical introduction to the philosophy of science.* Oxford, UK: Oxford University Press.

Lovejoy, A. O. (1976). *The great chain of being: A study of the history of an idea.* Cambridge, MA: Harvard University Press. (Original work published 1936)

Luo, M., & Dappen, L. (2005). Mixed-methods design for an objective-based evaluation of a magnet school assistance project. *Evaluation and Program Planning, 28,* 109–118.

Mackie, J. L. (1974). *The cement of the universe: A study of causation.* Oxford, UK: Clarendon.

Malinowski, B. (1922). *Argonauts of the western Pacific: An account of native enterprise and adventure in the archipelagos of Melanesian New Guinea.* New York: Dutton.

Marzano, R. J. (2003). *What works in schools: Translating research into action.* Alexandria, VA: Association for Supervision and Curriculum Development.

Mason, J. (2002). *Qualitative researching* (2nd ed.). Thousand Oaks, CA: Sage.

Mason, J. (2006). Mixing methods in a qualitatively driven way. *Qualitative Research, 6*(1), 9–25.

Maticka-Tyndale, E., Wildish, J., & Gichuru, M. (2007). Quasi-experimental evaluation of a national primary school HIV intervention in Kenya. *Evaluation and Program Planning, 30,* 172–186.

Maxcy, S. (2003). Pragmatic threads in mixed methods research in the social sciences: The search for multiple modes of inquiry and the end of the philosophy of formalism. In A. Tashakkori & C. Teddlie (Eds.), *Handbook of mixed methods in social and behavioral research* (pp. 51–90). Thousand Oaks, CA: Sage.

Maxwell, J. (1997). Designing a qualitative study. In L. Bickman & D. J. Rog (Eds.), *Handbook of applied social research methods* (pp. 69–100). Thousand Oaks, CA: Sage.

Maxwell, J. (2004). Causal explanation, qualitative research, and scientific inquiry in education. *Educational Researcher, 33*(2), 3–11.

Maxwell, J., & Loomis, D. (2003). Mixed methods design: An alternative approach. In A. Tashakkori & C. Teddlie (Eds.), *Handbook of mixed methods in social and behavioral research* (pp. 241–272). Thousand Oaks, CA: Sage.

Mead, M. (1928). *Coming of age in Samoa: A psychological study of primitive youth for Western civilization.* New York: W. Morrow.

Mcdawar, P. (1990). *The threat and the glory: Reflections on science and scientists.* Oxford, UK: Oxford University Press.

Menand, L. (1997). *Pragmatism: A reader.* New York: Vintage.

Mertens, D. M. (2003). Mixed models and the politics of human research: The transformative-emancipatory perspective. In A. Tashakkori & C. Teddlie (Eds.), *Handbook of mixed methods in social and behavioral research* (pp. 135–166). Thousand Oaks, CA: Sage.

Mertens, D. M. (2005). *Research and evaluation in education and psychology: Integrating diversity with quantitative, qualitative, and mixed methods* (2nd ed.). Thousand Oaks, CA: Sage.

Mertens, D. M. (2007). Transformative paradigm: Mixed methods and social justice. *Journal of Mixed Methods Research, 1,* 212–225.

Mertler, C. A. (2001). Designing scoring rubrics for your classroom. *Practical Assessment, Research and Evaluation, 7*(25). Retrieved July 19, 2006, from http://PAREonline.net/getvn.asp?v=7&n=25

Merton, R., Coleman, J., & Rossi, P. (Eds.). (1979) *Qualitative and quantitative social research: Papers in honor of Paul Lazersfield.* New York: Free Press.

Miles, M., & Huberman, M. (1984). *Qualitative data analysis: A sourcebook for new methods.* Thousand Oaks, CA: Sage.

Miles, M., & Huberman, M. (1994). *Qualitative data analysis: An expanded sourcebook* (2nd ed.). Thousand Oaks, CA: Sage.

Miller, S. (2003). Impact of mixed methods and design on inference quality. In A. Tashakkori & C. Teddlie (Eds.), *Handbook of mixed methods in social and behavioral research* (pp. 423–456). Thousand Oaks, CA: Sage.

Mintzberg, H. (1979). *The structuring of organizations.* Englewood Cliffs, NJ: Prentice Hall.

Moghaddam, F., Walker, B., & Harré, R. (2003). Cultural distance, levels of abstraction, and the advantages of mixed methods. In A. Tashakkori & C. Teddlie (Eds.), *Handbook of mixed methods in social and behavioral* research (pp. 111–134). Thousand Oaks, CA: Sage.

Molotch, H., & Boden, D. (1985). Talking social structure: Discourse, domination, and the Watergate hearing. *American Sociological Review, 50,* 273–287.

Moreno, J. L. (1934). *Who shall survive? Foundations of sociometry, group psychotherapy, and sociodrama.* Beacon, NY: Beacon House.

Morgan, D. (1998). Practical strategies for combining qualitative and quantitative methods: Applications to health research. *Qualitative Health Research, 8,* 362–376.

Morgan, D. (2007). Paradigms lost and pragmatism regained: Methodological implications of combining qualitative and quantitative methods. *Journal of Mixed Methods Research, 1,* 48–76.

Morgan, D., & Spanish, M. (1984). Focus groups: A new tool for qualitative research. *Qualitative Sociology, 7,* 253–270.

Morphet, C. (1977). *Galileo and Copernican astronomy.* London: Butterworth Group.

Morse, J. M. (1989). *Qualitative nursing research: A contemporary dialogue.* Thousand Oaks, CA: Sage.

Morse, J. M. (1991). Approaches to qualitative-quantitative methodological triangulation. *Nursing Research, 40*(2), 120–123.

Morse, J. M. (1994). Designing funded qualitative research. In N. K. Denzin & Y. S. Lincoln (Eds.), *Handbook of qualitative research* (pp. 220–235). Thousand Oaks, CA: Sage.

Morse, J. M. (2003). Principles of mixed methods and multimethod research design. In A. Tashakkori & C. Teddlie (Eds.), *Handbook of mixed methods in social and behavioral research* (pp. 189–208). Thousand Oaks, CA: Sage.

Moustakas, C. (1994). *Phenomenological research methods.* Thousand Oaks, CA: Sage.

Murphy, L. L., Plake, B. S., Impara, J. C., & Spies, R. A. (2002). *Tests in print VI.* Lincoln: University of Nebraska Press.

Nastasi, B. K., Hitchcock, J., Sarkar, S., Burkholder, G., Varjas, K., & Jayasena, A. (2007). Mixed methods in intervention research: Theory to adaptation. *Journal of Mixed Methods Research, 1,* 164–199.

National Education Association. (1968). *Estimates of school statistics, 1967–68.* Washington, DC: Author.

National Research Council. (2002). *Scientific research in education.* Washington, DC: National Academy Press.

Newman, I., & Benz, C. R. (1998). *Qualitative-quantitative research methodology: Exploring the interactive continuum.* Carbondale: University of Illinois Press.

Newman, I., Ridenour, C., Newman, C., & DeMarco, G. M. P., Jr. (2003). A typology of research purposes and its relationship to mixed methods research. In A. Tashakkori & C. Teddlie (Eds.), *Handbook of mixed methods in social and behavioral research* (pp. 167–188). Thousand Oaks, CA: Sage.

Nielsen, K. (1991). *After the demise of the tradition: Rorty, critical theory, and the fate of philosophy.* Boulder, CO: Westview Press.

Nieto, T., Mendez, F., & Carrasquilla, G. (1999). Knowledge, beliefs and practices relevant for malaria control in an endemic urban area of the Colombian Pacific. *Social Science and Medicine, 49,* 601–609.

Niglas, K. (2004). *The combined use of qualitative and quantitative methods in educational research.* Tallinn, Estonia: Tallinn Pedagogical University.

No Child Left Behind Act of 2001, PL. No. 107–110, 115 Stat. 1425 (2002).

Norton, S. (1995). *The socialization of beginning principals in Louisiana: Organizational constraints on innovation.* Unpublished dissertation, Louisiana State University, Baton Rouge.

Notturno, M. A. (2001). Popper. In R. Arrington (Ed.), *A companion to the philosophers* (pp. 447–451). Oxford, UK: Blackwell.

Oakes, J., & Guiton, G. (1995). Matchmaking: The dynamics of high school tracking decisions. *American Educational Research Journal, 32*(1), 3–33.

Oakley, A. (1998). Gender, methodology and people's way of knowing: Some problems with feminism and the paradigm debate in social science. *Sociology, 32,* 707–732.

O'Cathain, A., Murphy, E., & Nicholl, J. (2007). Integration and publication as indicators of "yield" from mixed methods studies. *Journal of Mixed Methods Research, 1,* 147–163.

Office for Human Research Protections. (2008). *Policy guidelines: Office for Human Research Protections.* Washington, DC: United States Department of Health and Human Services.

Ong, A. (2003). *Buddha is hiding: Refugees, citizenship, the new America.* Berkeley: University of California Press.

Onwuegbuzie, A. J. (2003). Effect sizes in qualitative research: A prolegomenon. *Quality and Quantity: International Journal of Methodology, 37,* 393–409.

Onwuegbuzie, A. J., & Daniels, L. G. (2003). Typology of analytical and interpretational errors in quantitative and qualitative educational research. *Current Issues in Education, 6*(2). Retrieved March 27, 2008, from http://cie.ed.asu.edu/volume6/number2

Onwuegbuzie, A. J., Jiao, Q. C., & Bostick, S. L. (2004). *Library anxiety: Theory, research, and applications.* Lanham, MD: Scarecrow Press.

Onwuegbuzie, A. J., & Johnson, R. B. (2006). The validity issue in mixed research. *Research in the Schools, 13*(1), 48–63.

Onwuegbuzie, A. J., & Leech, N. L. (2004). Enhancing the interpretation of "significant" findings: The role of mixed methods research. *The Qualitative Report, 9,* 770–792.

Onwuegbuzie, A. J., & Leech, N. L. (2005). Taking the "Q" out of research: Teaching research methodology courses without the divide between quantitative and qualitative paradigms. *Quality and Quantity: International Journal of Methodology, 39,* 267–296.

Onwuegbuzie, A., & Teddlie, C. (2003). A framework for analyzing data in mixed methods research. In A. Tashakkori & C. Teddlie (Eds.), *Handbook of mixed methods in social and behavioral research* (pp. 351–384). Thousand Oaks, CA: Sage.

Orihuela, L. (2007). *The effects of a general instructional strategies course on the utilization of effective instructional strategies by teachers.* Unpublished doctoral dissertation, Florida International University, Miami.

Osgood, C. E., Suci, G. J., & Tannenbaum, P. H. (1957). *The measurement of meaning.* Urbana: University of Illinois Press.

Oxford University Press. (1999). *Oxford Dictionary of Quotations* (5th ed., p. 307). Oxford, UK: Author.

Papadakis, V. M., & Barwise, P. (2002). How much do CEOs and top managers matter in strategic decision making? *British Journal of Management, 13,* 83–95.

Parasnis, I., Samar, V. J., & Fischer, S. D. (2005). Deaf college students' attitudes toward racial/ethnic diversity, campus climate, and role models. *American Annals of the Deaf, 150*(1), 47–58.

Parmelee, J. H., Perkins, S. C., & Sayre, J. J. (2007). "What about people our age?" Applying qualitative and quantitative methods to uncover how political ads alienate college students. *Journal of Mixed Methods Research, 1,* 183–199.

Patton, M. Q. (1990). *Qualitative research and evaluation methods* (2nd ed.). Thousand Oaks, CA: Sage.

Patton, M. Q. (2002). *Qualitative research and evaluation methods* (3rd ed.). Thousand Oaks, CA: Sage.

Paul, J. L. (2005). *Introduction to the philosophical foundations of research and criticism in education and the social sciences.* Upper Saddle River, NJ: Prentice Hall.

Peshkin, A. (1986). *God's choice: The total world of a fundamentalist Christian school.* Chicago: University of Chicago Press.

Phillips, D. C. (1987). *Philosophy, science and social inquiry: Contemporary methodological controversies in social science and related fields of research.* Oxford, UK: Pergamon Press.

Phillips, D. C. (1990). Postpositivistic science: Myths and realities. In E. Guba (Ed.), *The paradigm dialog* (pp. 31–45). Thousand Oaks, CA: Sage.

Phillips, D. C., & Burbules, N. C. (2000). *Postpositivism and educational research.* Lanham, MD: Rowman & Littlefield.

Ponterotto, J. G. (2005). Qualitative research in counseling psychology: A primer on research paradigms and philosophy of science. *Journal of Counseling Psychology, 2,* 126–136.

Poorman, P. B. (2002). Perceptions of thriving by women who have experienced abuse or status-related oppression. *Psychology of Women Quarterly, 26*(1), 51–62.

Popham, W. J. (2002). *Classroom assessment: What teachers need to know* (3rd ed.). Boston: Allyn & Bacon.

Popper, K. R. (1959). *The logic of scientific discovery.* New York: Basic Books. (Original work published 1934)

Popper, K. R. (1968). *Conjectures and refutations.* New York: Harper Torchbooks.

Popper, K. R. (1974). Autobiography of Karl Popper. In P. A. Schilpp (Ed.), *The philosophy of Karl Popper* (pp. 1–181). La Salle, IL: Open Court.

Prasad, A. (2002). The contest over meaning: Hermeneutics as an interpretative methodology for understanding texts. *Organizational Research Methods, 5*(1), 12–33.

Puma, M., Karweit, N., Price, C., Ricciuti, A., Thompson, W., & Vaden-Kiernan, M. (1997). *Prospects: Final report on student outcomes.* Washington, DC: U.S. Department of Education, Planning and Evaluation Services.

Punch, K. F. (1998). *Introduction to social research: Quantitative and qualitative approaches.* Thousand Oaks, CA: Sage.

Ragin, C. C. (1987). *The comparative method.* Berkeley: University of California Press.

Ragin, C. C., & Zaret, D. (1983). Theory and method in comparative research: Two strategies. *Social Forces, 61,* 731–754.

Rallis, S. F., & Rossman, G. B. (2003). Mixed methods in evaluation contexts. In A. Tashakkori & C. Teddlie (Eds.), *Handbook of mixed methods in social and behavioral research* (pp. 491–512). Thousand Oaks, CA: Sage.

Rao, V. & Woolcock, M. (2003). Integrating qualitative and quantitative approaches in program evaluation. In F. J. Bourguignon & L. Pereira de Silva (Eds.), *Evaluating the poverty and distribution impact of economic policies* (pp. 165–190). New York: The World Bank.

Rathje, W., & Murphy, C. (1992). *Rubbish! The archaeology of garbage.* New York: Harper-Collins.

Rawlings, L. B. (2000). Evaluating Nicaragua's school-based management reform. In M. Bamberger (Ed.), *Integrating quantitative and qualitative research in development projects* (pp. 85–97). Washington DC: The World Bank.

Regehr, C., Chau, S., Leslie, B., & Howe, P. (2001). An exploration of supervisor's and manager's responses to child welfare reform. *Administration in Social Work, 26*(3), 17–36.

Reichardt, C. S., & Cook, T. D. (1979). Beyond qualitative versus quantitative methods. In T. D. Cook & C. S. Reichardt (Eds.), *Qualitative and quantitative methods in program evaluation* (pp. 7–32). Thousand Oaks CA: Sage.

Reichardt, C. S., & Rallis, S. F. (1994). Qualitative and quantitative inquiries are not incompatible: A call for a new partnership. In C. S. Reichardt & S. F. Rallis (Eds.), *The qualitative-quantitative debate: New perspectives* (pp. 85–92). Thousand Oaks, CA: Sage.

Reynolds, D., Creemers, B., Stringfield, S., Teddlie, C., & Schaffer, E. (2002). *World class schools: International perspectives on school effectiveness.* London: Routledge/Falmer.

Reynolds, D., & Teddlie, C. (2000). The processes of school effectiveness. In C. Teddlie & D. Reynolds (Eds.), *The international handbook of school effectiveness research* (pp. 134–159). London: Falmer Press.

Riccio, J. A. (1997). MDRC's evaluation of GAIN: A summary. *Evaluation Practice, 18,* 241–242.

Riccio, J. A., & Orenstein, A. (1996). Understanding best practices for operating welfare-to-work programs. *Evaluation Review, 20*(3), 3–28.

Richards, L. (1999). *Using NVivo for qualitative data analysis.* Thousand Oaks, CA: Sage.

Richardson, L. (2000). Writing: A method of inquiry. In N. K. Denzin & Y. S. Lincoln (Eds.), *Handbook of qualitative research* (2nd ed., pp. 923–948). Thousand Oaks, CA: Sage.

Richardson, L., & St. Pierre, E. A. (2005). Writing: A method of inquiry. In N. K. Denzin & Y. S. Lincoln (Eds.), *Handbook of qualitative research* (3rd ed., pp. 959–978). Thousand Oaks, CA: Sage.

Ridenour, C. S., & Newman, I. (2008). *Mixed methods research: Exploring the interactive continuum.* Carbondale: Southern Illinois University Press.

Roethlisberger, F. J., & Dickson, W. J. (1939). *Management and the worker.* Cambridge MA: Harvard University Press.

Rorty, R. (1982). Pragmatism, relativism, and irrationalism. In R. Rorty (Ed.), *Consequences of pragmatism* (pp. 160–175). Minneapolis: University of Minnesota Press.

Rorty, R. (1990). Introduction. In J. P. Murphy (Ed.), *Pragmatism: From Peirce to Davidson.* Boulder, CO: Westview Press.

Rosenthal, R. (1976). *Experimenter effects in behavioral research.* New York: Irvington.

Rosenthal, R., & Fode, K. L. (1963). The effect of experimenter bias on the performance of the albino rat. *Behavioral Science, 8,* 183–189.

Rosenthal, R., & Jacobsen, L. (1968) *Pygmalion in the classroom.* New York: Holt, Rinehart, & Winston.

Rosenthal, R., & Lawson, R. (1964). A longitudinal study of the effects of experimenter bias on the operant learning of laboratory rats. *Journal of Psychiatric Research, 2,* 61–72.

Rossman, G. B., & Rallis, S. F. (2003). *Learning in the field: An introduction to qualitative research* (2nd ed.). Thousand Oaks, CA: Sage.

Rossman, G. B., & Wilson, B. (1985). Numbers and words: Combining quantitative and qualitative methods in a single large scale evaluation study. *Evaluation Review, 9,* 627–643.

Rossman, G. B., & Wilson, B. (1994). Numbers and words revisited: Being "shamelessly eclectic." *Quality and Quantity, 28,* 315–327.

Rotter, J. B. (1966). Generalized expectancies for internal versus external control of reinforcement. *Psychological Monographs, 80*(1, Serial No. 609).

St. Pierre, E. A. (2002). "Science" rejects postmodernism. *Educational Researcher, 31*(8), 25–27.

Sale, J., Lohfeld, L., & Brazil, K. (2002). Revisiting the qualitative-quantitative debate: Implications for mixed-methods research. *Quality and Quantity, 36,* 43–53.

Salmon, W. C. (1998). *Causality and explanation.* Oxford, UK: Oxford University Press.

Sandelowski, M. (2003). Tables or tableux? The challenges of writing and reading mixed methods studies. In A. Tashakkori & C. Teddlie (Eds.), *Handbook of mixed methods in social and behavioral research* (pp. 321–350). Thousand Oaks, CA: Sage.

Sandelowski, M., Harris, B. G., & Holditch-Davis, D. (1991). Amniocentesis in the context of infertility. *Health Care for Women International, 12,* 167–178.

Sanders, W. (1974). *The sociologist as detective.* New York: Praeger.

Sargeant, A., Wymer, W., & Hilton, T. (2006). Marketing bequest club membership: An exploratory study of legacy pledgers. *Nonprofit and Voluntary Sector Quarterly, 35,* 384–404.

Schmalleger, F. (1996). *The trial of the century: People of the State of California vs. Orenthal James Simpson.* Englewood Cliffs, NJ: Prentice Hall.

Schmuck, R. A. (1997). *Practical action research for change.* Arlington Heights, IL: IRI Skylight Training and Publishing.

Schulenberg, J. L. (2007). Analyzing police decision-making: Assessing the application of a mixed-method/mixed-model research design. *International Journal of Social Research Methodology, 10,* 99–119.

Schwandt, T. (1997). *Qualitative inquiry: A dictionary of terms.* Thousand Oaks, CA: Sage.

Schwandt, T. (2000). Three epistemological stances for qualitative inquiry: Interpretivism, hermeneutics, and social constructionism. In N. K. Denzin & Y. S. Lincoln (Eds.), *Handbook of qualitative research* (2nd ed., pp. 189–214). Thousand Oaks, CA: Sage.

Shadish, W., Cook, T. D., & Campbell, D. T. (2002). *Experimental and quasi-experimental designs for general causal inference.* Boston: Houghton Mifflin.

Shaffer, P. (2002, July). *Assumptions matter: Reflections on the Kanbur typology.* Paper presented at the Conference on Combining Quantitative and Quantitative Methods in Development Research, Wales, UK.

Shavelson, R. J. (1996). *Statistical reasoning for the behavioral sciences* (3rd ed.). Boston: Allyn & Bacon.

Sherif, M., Harvey, O. J., White, B. J., Hood, W. R. & Sherif, C. W. (1961). *Intergroup conflict and cooperation: The robber's cave experiment.* Norman: University of Oklahoma Institute of Intergroup Relations.

Sherratt, Y. (2006). *Continental philosophy of social science: Hermeneutics, genealogy, and critical theory from Greece to the twenty-first century.* Cambridge, UK: Cambridge University Press.

Shulha, L. M., & Wilson, R. J. (2003). Collaborative mixed methods research. In

A. Tashakkori & C. Teddlie (Eds.), *Handbook of mixed methods in social and behavioral research* (pp. 639–670). Thousand Oaks, CA: Sage.

Slavin, R. E. (2003). A reader's guide to scientifically based research. *Educational Leadership, 60,* 12–16.

Smith, J. K. (1983). Quantitative versus qualitative research: An attempt to clarify the issue. *Educational Researcher, 12,* 6–13.

Smith, J. K. (1996). An opportunity lost? In L. Heshusius & K. Ballard (Eds.), *From positivism to interpretivism and beyond: Tales of transformation in educational and social research* (pp. 161–168). New York: Teachers College Press.

Smith, J. K., & Heshusius, L. (1986). Closing down the conversation: The end of the quantitative-qualitative debate among educational researchers. *Educational Researcher, 15,* 4–12.

Smith, M. L. (1994). Qualitative plus/versus quantitative: The last word. In C. S. Reichardt & S. F. Rallis (Eds.), *New directions for program evaluation: Number 61. The qualitative-quantitative debate* (pp. 37–44). San Francisco: Jossey-Bass.

Smith, M. L., & Glass, G. V. (1977). Meta-analysis of psychotherapy outcome studies. *American Psychologist, 32,* 752–760.

Social sciences citation index (database). (n.d.). Philadelphia: Thomson Scientific.

Spalter-Roth, R. (2000). Gender issues in the use of integrated approaches. In M. Bamberger (Ed.), *Integrating quantitative and qualitative research in development projects* (pp. 47–53). Washington, DC: The World Bank.

Spies, R. A., Plake, B. S., & Murphy, L. L. (2005). *The sixteenth mental measurements yearbook.* Lincoln: University of Nebraska Press.

Spitz, H. H. (1999). Beleaguered Pygmalion: A history of the controversy over claims that teacher expectancy raises intelligence. *Intelligence, 27,* 199–234.

Spradley, J. P. (1970). *You owe yourself a drunk: An ethnography of urban nomads.* Boston: Little, Brown.

Spradley, J. P. (1979). *The ethnographic interview.* New York: Holt, Rinehart & Winston.

Spradley, J. P. (1980). *Participant observation.* New York: Holt, Rinehart & Winston.

Staat, W. (1993). On abduction, deduction, induction and the categories. *Transactions of the Charles S. Peirce Society, 29,* 225–237.

Stake, R. E. (1995). *The art of case study research.* Thousand Oaks, CA: Sage.

Stake, R. E. (2005). Qualitative case studies. In N. K. Denzin & Y. S. Lincoln (Eds.), *Handbook of qualitative research* (3rd ed., pp. 443–466). Thousand Oaks, CA: Sage.

Stern, P. N. (1994). Eroding grounded theory. In J. Morse (Ed.), *Critical issues in qualitative research methods* (pp. 214–215). Thousand Oaks, CA: Sage.

Stevens, J. (2001) *Differential modes of external change agent support in diffusion of innovation.* Unpublished doctoral dissertation, Louisiana State University, Baton Rouge.

Stevens, J. P. (2002). *Applied multivariate statistics for the social sciences* (4th ed.). Mahwah, NJ: Lawrence Erlbaum.

Stigler, S. (2002). *The history of statistics: The measurement of uncertainty before 1900.* Cambridge, MA: Harvard University Press.

Stocking, G. (1992). *The ethnographer's magic and other essays in the history of anthropology.* Madison: University of Wisconsin.

Stone, G. C. (1994). Dewey on causation in social science. *Educational Theory, 44,* 417–428.

Strauss, A., & Corbin, J. (1990). *Basics of qualitative research: Techniques and procedures for developing grounded theory.* Thousand Oaks, CA: Sage.

Strauss, A., & Corbin, J. (1998). *Basics of qualitative research: Techniques and procedures for developing grounded theory* (2nd ed.). Thousand Oaks, CA: Sage.

Stringfield, S. (1994) Outlier studies of school effectiveness. In D. Reynolds, B. P. M. Creemers, P. S. Nesselrodt, E. C. Schaffer, S. Stringfield, & C. Teddlie (Eds.), *Advances in school effectiveness research and practice* (pp. 73–84). London: Pergamon.

Stringfield, S., Millsap, M. A., Herman, R., Yoder, N., Brigham, N., Nesselrodt, P., et al. (1997). *Urban and suburban/rural special strategies for educating disadvantaged children: Final report.* Washington, DC: U.S. Department of Education.

Tabachnick, B. G., & Fidell, L. S. (2007). *Using multivariate statistics* (5th ed.). Boston: Allyn & Bacon.

Tashakkori, A., Boyd, R., & Sines, M. (1996, July). *Predictors of drop-out and persistence of 8th grade Hispanic youth in the U.S.* Paper presented at the 54th annual convention of the International Council of Psychologists, Banff, Alberta, Canada.

Tashakkori, A., & Creswell, J. W. (2007a). Exploring the nature of research questions in mixed methods research. *Journal of Mixed Methods Research, 1,* 207–211.

Tashakkori, A., & Creswell, J. W. (2007b). The new era of mixed methods. *Journal of Mixed Methods Research, 1,* 3–7.

Tashakkori, A., Newman, I., & Bliss, L. A. (2008). *Historical trends in teaching of social/behavioral research methodology across disciplines.* Unpublished manuscript, Florida International University, Miami.

Tashakkori, A., & Teddlie, C. (1998). *Mixed methodology: Combining the qualitative and quantitative approaches.* Thousand Oaks, CA: Sage.

Tashakkori, A., & Teddlie, C. (Eds.). (2003a). *Handbook of mixed methods in social and behavioral research.* Thousand Oaks, CA: Sage.

Tashakkori, A., & Teddlie, C. (2003b). Issues and dilemmas in teaching research methods courses in social and behavioral sciences: U.S. perspective. *International Journal of Social Research Methodology, 6,* 61–77.

Tashakkori, A., & Teddlie, C. (2003c). The past and future of mixed methods research: From data triangulation to mixed model designs. In A. Tashakkori & C. Teddlie (Eds.), *Handbook of mixed methods in social and behavioral research* (pp. 671–702). Thousand Oaks, CA: Sage.

Tashakkori, A., & Teddlie, C. (2006, April). *Validity issues in mixed methods research: Calling for an integrative framework.* Paper presented at the annual meeting of the American Educational Research Association, San Francisco.

Tashakkori, A., & Teddlie, C. (2008). Quality of inference in mixed methods research: Calling for an integrative framework. In M. M. Bergman (Ed.), *Advances in mixed methods research: Theories and applications* (pp. 101–119). Thousand Oaks, CA: Sage.

Taylor, B. O. (Ed). (1990). *Case studies in effective schools research.* Madison, WI: National Center for Effective Schools Research and Development.

Taylor, D., & Tashakkori, A. (1995). Participation in decision making and school climate as predictors of teachers' job satisfaction and sense of efficacy. *Journal of Experimental Education, 63,* 217–230.

Taylor, D., & Tashakkori, A. (1997). Toward an understanding of teachers' desire for participation in decision making. *Journal of School Leadership, 7,* 1–20.

Taylor, S. J., & Bogdan, R. (1998). *Introduction to qualitative research methods: A guidebook and resource* (3rd ed.). New York: John Wiley & Sons.

Teddlie, C. (1998, July). *Integrating school indicators, school effectiveness, and school improvement research: The Louisiana School Effectiveness and Assistance Pilot (SEAP).* Symposium presented at the annual meeting of the American Educational Research Association, San Diego, CA.

Teddlie, C. (2005). Methodological issues related to causal studies of leadership: A mixed methods perspective from the USA. *Educational Management and Administration, 33,* 211–217.

Teddlie, C., Creemers, B., Kyriakides, L., Muijs, D., & Yu, F. (2006). The International System for Teacher Observation and Feedback: Evolution of an international study of teacher effectiveness constructs. *Educational Research and Evaluation, 12,* 561–582.

Teddlie, C., Kochan, S., & Taylor, D. (2002). The ABC+ model for school diagnosis, feedback, and improvement. In A. J. Visscher & R. Coe (Eds.), *School improvement through performance feedback* (pp. 75–114). Lisse, Netherlands: Swets and Zeitlinger.

Teddlie, C., & Meza, J. (1999) Using informal and formal measures to create classroom profiles. In J. Freiberg (Ed.), *School climate: Measuring, improving and sustaining healthy learning environments* (pp. 48–64). London: Falmer Press.

Teddlie, C., Reynolds, D., & Pol, S. (2000). Current topics and approaches in school effectiveness research: The contemporary field. In C. Teddlie & D. Reynolds (Eds.), *The international handbook of school effectiveness research* (pp. 26–51). London: Falmer.

Teddlie, C., & Stringfield, S. (1993). *Schools make a difference: Lessons learned from a 10-year study of school effects.* New York: Teachers College Press.

Teddlie, C., & Stringfield, S. (1999). *The revised classroom observation instrument.* Baton Rouge: Louisiana State University.

Teddlie, C., & Tashakkori, A. (2003). Major issues and controversies in the use of mixed methods in the social and behavioral sciences. In A. Tashakkori & C. Teddlie (Eds.), *Handbook of mixed methods in social and behavioral research* (pp. 3–50). Thousand Oaks, CA: Sage.

Teddlie, C., & Tashakkori, A. (2005, April). *The methods-strands matrix: A general typology of research designs featuring mixed methods.* Paper presented at the annual meeting of the American Educational Research Association, Montreal.

Teddlie, C., & Tashakkori, A. (2006). A general typology of research designs featuring mixed methods. *Research in the Schools, 13*(1), 12–28.

Teddlie, C., Tashakkori, A., & Johnson, B. (2008). Emergent techniques in the gathering and analysis of mixed methods data. In S. Hesse-Biber & P. Leavy (Eds.), *Handbook of emergent methods in social research* (pp. 389–413). New York: Guilford Press.

Teddlie, C., Virgilio, I., & Oescher, J. (1990). Development and validation of the Virgilio Teacher Behavior Inventory. *Educational and Psychological Measurement, 50,* 421–430.

Teddlie, C., & Yu, F. (2006, April). *Mixed methods sampling procedures: Some prototypes with examples.* Paper presented at the annual meeting of the American Educational Research Association, San Francisco.

Teddlie, C., & Yu, F. (2007). Mixed methods sampling: A typology with examples. *Journal of Mixed Methods Research, 1,* 77–100.

Tedlock, B. (2000). Ethnography and ethnographic representation. In N. K. Denzin & Y. S. Lincoln (Eds.), *Handbook of qualitative research* (2nd ed., pp. 455–486). Thousand Oaks, CA: Sage.

Telishevka, M., Chenett, L., & McKeet, M. (2001). Towards an understanding of the high death rate among young people with diabetes in Ukraine. *Diabetic Medicine, 18,* 3–9.

Teo, T. (2001). Karl Marx and Wilhelm Dilthey on the socio-historical conceptualization of the mind. In C. Green, M. Shore, & T. Teo (Eds.), *The transformation of psychology: Influences of 19th-century philosophy, technology and natural science* (pp. 195–218). Washington, DC: American Psychological Association.

Tesch, R. (1990). *Qualitative research: Analysis types and software tools.* London: Falmer Press.

Thibaut, J., & Kelley, H. H. (1959). *The social psychology of groups.* New York: John Wiley & Sons.

Thio, A. (2005). *Sociology: A brief introduction* (5th ed.). Boston: Allyn & Bacon.

Thomas, W. I., & Znaniecki, F. (1920). *The Polish peasant in Europe and America.* Boston: Badger Press.

Thompson, W. N. (1975). *Aristotle's deduction and induction: Introductory analysis and synthesis.* Amsterdam: Rodopi N.V.

Titchen, A. (1997). Creating a learning culture: A story of change in hospital nursing. In S. Hollingsworth (Ed.), *International action research: A casebook for educational reform* (pp. 244–260). London: Falmer Press.

Tobin, G. A., & Begley, C. M. (2004). Methodological rigour within a qualitative framework. *Journal of Advanced Nursing, 48*(8), 388–396.

Todd, J. (2006). Choosing databases for sociology studies: SocINDEX or Sociological Abstracts? *ONLINE, 30*(4), 35–38.

Tolman, D., & Szalacha, L. (1999). Dimensions of desire: Bridging qualitative and quantitative methods in a study of female sexuality. *Psychology of Women Quarterly, 23,* 7–39.

Toulmin, S. (1960). *The philosophy of science: An introduction.* New York: Harper & Row.

Trend, M. G. (1979). On the reconciliation of qualitative and quantitative analyses: A case study. In T. D. Cook & C. S. Reichardt (Eds.), *Qualitative and quantitative methods in program evaluation* (pp. 68–85). Thousand Oaks, CA: Sage.

Twinn, S. (2003). Status of mixed methods in nursing. In A. Tashakkori & C. Teddlie (Eds.), *Handbook of mixed methods in social and behavioral research* (pp. 541–556). Thousand Oaks, CA: Sage.

Van Maanen, J., Dabbs, J. M., & Faulkner, R. (Eds.). (1982). *Varieties of qualitative research*. Thousand Oaks, CA: Sage.

Van Manen, M. (1990). *Researching lived experience: Human science for an action sensitive pedagogy*. Albany: State University of New York Press.

Van Teijlingen, E. R., & Hundley, V. (2001, Winter). The importance of pilot studies. *Social Research Update, 35*. Retrieved January 6, 2008, from http://sru.soc.surrey.ac.uk/SRU35.html

Van de Vijver, F. J. R., & Poortinga, Y. H. (2005). Conceptual and methodological issues in adapting tests. In R. K. Hambleton, P. F. Meranda, & C. D. Spielberger (Eds.), *Adapting educational and psychological tests for cross-cultural assessment* (pp. 39–63). Mahwah, NJ: Lawrence Erlbaum.

Vidich, A. J., & Lyman, S. M. (2000). Qualitative methods: Their history in sociology and anthropology. In N. K. Denzin & Y. S. Lincoln (Eds.), *Handbook of qualitative research* (2nd ed., pp. 37–84). Thousand Oaks, CA: Sage.

Viney, W., & King, D. B. (1998). *A history of psychology: Ideas in context*. Boston: Allyn & Bacon.

Wall, R., Devine-Wright, P., & Mill, G. A. (2008). Interactions between perceived behavioral control and personal normative-motives: Qualitative and quantitative evidence from a study of commuting-mode choice. *Journal of Mixed Methods Research, 2*(1), 63–86.

Ward, M. (1986). *Them children. A study in language learning*. Long Grove, IL: Waveland Press.

Warner, W. (1937). *A black civilization: A social study of an Australian tribe*. New York: Harper & Brothers.

Warner, W., & Lunt, P. S. (1941). *The social life of a modern community. Yankee city series: Volume 1*. New Haven, CT: Yale University Press.

Wasserman, S., & Faust, K. (1994). *Social network analysis: Methods and applications*. Cambridge, UK: Cambridge University Press.

Waszak, C., & Sines, M. (2003). Mixed methods in psychological research. In A. Tashakkori & C. Teddlie (Eds.), *Handbook of mixed methods in social and behavioral research* (pp. 557–576). Thousand Oaks, CA: Sage.

Webb, E. J., Campbell, D. T., Schwartz, R. D., & Sechrest, L. (1966). *Unobtrusive measures: Nonreactive research in the social sciences*. Chicago: Rand McNally.

Webb, E. J., Campbell, D. T., Schwartz, R. D., & Sechrest, L. (2000). *Unobtrusive measures* (Rev. ed.). Thousand Oaks, CA: Sage.

Webb, E. J., Campbell, D. T., Schwartz, R. D., Sechrest, L., & Grove, J. B. (1981). *Nonreactive measures in the social sciences*. Boston: Houghton Mifflin.

Welty, P. J. (2001). Dilthey. In R. Arrington (Ed.), *A companion to the philosophers* (pp. 222–226). Oxford, UK: Blackwell.

Wetzler, S., Marlowe, D. B., & Sanderson, W. C. (1994). Assessment of depression using the MMPI, MILLON, and MILLON-II. *Psychological Reports, 75*, 755–768.

Whyte, W. F. (1955). *Street corner society: The social structure of an Italian slum*. Chicago: University of Chicago Press. (Original work published 1943)

Wiersma, W., & Jurs, S. G. (2005). *Research methods in education* (8th ed.). Boston: Allyn & Bacon.

Williams, T. H. (1969). *Huey Long*. New York: Alfred A. Knopf.

Willig, C. (2001). *Introducing qualitative research in psychology: Adventures in theory and method*. Buckingham, UK: Open University Press.

Willis, J. W. (2007). *Foundations of qualitative research: Interpretive and critical approaches*. Thousand Oaks, CA: Sage.

Witcher, A. E., Onwuegbuzie, A. J., Collins, K. M. T., Filer, J., & Wiedmaier, C. (2003, November). *Students' perceptions of characteristics of effective college teachers*. Paper presented at the annual meeting of the Mid-South Educational Research Association, Biloxi, MS.

Wittgenstein, L. (1958). *The philosophical investigations* (2nd ed.). New York: Macmillan.

Wolcott, H. F. (1994). *Transforming qualitative data: Description, analysis, and interpretation.* Thousand Oaks, CA: Sage.

Wolcott, H. F. (1999). *Ethnography: A way of seeing.* Walnut Creek, CA: AltaMira.

Wolf, R. L., & Tymitz, B. L. (1978). *Whatever happened to the giant wombat: An investigation of the impact of ice age mammals and emergence of man exhibit.* Washington, DC: National Museum of Natural History and the Smithsonian Institute.

Wood, R. T., & Williams, R. J. (2007). "How much money do you spend on gambling?" The comparative validity of question wordings used to assess gambling expenditure. *International Journal of Social Research Methodology, 10*(1), 63–77.

Woolfolk, A. (2004). *Educational psychology* (9th ed.). Boston: Allyn & Bacon.

Woolhouse, R. S. (1988). *The empiricists.* Oxford, UK: Oxford University Press.

Wu, C. (2005). *Correlates of college choice among Taiwanese youth: Relative importance of personal, social, and institutional considerations.* Unpublished doctoral dissertation, Florida International University, Miami.

Wunsch, D. R. (1986). Survey research: Determining sample size and representative response. *Business Education Forum, 40*(5), 31–34.

Yin, R. K. (2003). *Case study research: Design and methods* (3rd ed.). Thousand Oaks, CA: Sage.

Yu, C. H. (1994, April). *Abduction? deduction? induction? Is there logic of exploratory analysis?* Paper presented at the annual meeting of the American Educational Research Association, New Orleans, LA.

Yuan, Y. (2003). *Perceptions regarding intercollegiate alliance among administrators of Taiwanese technical higher education institutions.* Unpublished doctoral dissertation, Florida International University, Miami.

Zimbardo, P. G. (1969). The human choice: Individuation, reason and order versus deindividuation, impulse and chaos. In W. Arnold & D. Levine (Eds.), *Nebraska Symposium on Motivation, 17,* 237–307.

Author Index

Subject Index

About the Authors

Charles Teddlie (PhD, Social Psychology, University of North Carolina at Chapel Hill) is the Jo Ellen Levy Yates Distinguished Professor (Emeritus) in the College of Education at Louisiana State University. He also taught at the University of New Orleans and has been a Visiting Professor at the University of Newcastle-upon-Tyne (UK) and the University of Exeter (UK). He also served as Assistant Superintendent for Research and Development at the Louisiana Department of Education. He has been an investigator on several mixed methods research studies, including the Louisiana School Effectiveness Study and the International School Effectiveness Research Project. His major writing interests are social science research methodology and school effectiveness research. Professor Teddlie has taught research methods courses for 25 years, including statistics, qualitative methods, and mixed methods. He has been awarded the Excellence in Teaching Award from the LSU College of Education. He is the author of numerous chapters and articles and of 12 books including: *Schools Make a Difference: Lessons Learned from a Ten-Year Study of School Effects* (1993, with Sam Stringfield), *The International Handbook of School Effectiveness Research* (2000, with David Reynolds), and the *Handbook of Mixed Methods in the Social and Behavioral Sciences* (2003, with Abbas Tashakkori).

Abbas Tashakkori (PhD, Social Psychology, University of North Carolina at Chapel Hill) is a distinguished Frost Professor of Research and Evaluation Methodology at Florida International University. His professional leadership in the past five years included serving as the Chair of the Department of Educational and Psychological Studies and as the Associate Dean of Research and Graduate Studies in the College of Education of Florida International University. He has been a Postdoctoral Fellow of the Carolina Population Center and the University of North Carolina at Chapel Hill and a visiting scholar at Texas A&M University. He has taught social psychology and research methodology for three decades in undergraduate and graduate programs at Shiraz University (Iran), Stetson University, Louisiana State University, and Florida International University. He has extensive experience as a program evaluator, and is the founding coeditor (with John Creswell) of the *Journal of Mixed Methods Research*. In addition to books, book chapters, and articles on integrated research methodology, his published work covers a wide spectrum of research and program evaluation in cross-cultural and multicultural contexts, including self-perceptions, attitudes, and gender/ethnicity. His work in progress includes *Research Methods for Education and Behavioral Sciences: An Integrated Approach* (with Charles Teddlie).